Now I Know Only So Far

Now
I Know
Only
So Far

Essays in Ethnopoetics

Dell Hymes

UNIVERSITY OF NEBRASKA PRESS : LINCOLN AND LONDON

Acknowledgments for the use of previously published
material appear on pages 495–96, which constitute an
extension of the copyright page.

Library of Congress Cataloging-in-Publication Data
Hymes, Dell H.
Now I know only so far : essays in ethnopoetics / Dell
Hymes.
p.   cm. Includes bibliographical references and index.
ISBN 0-8032-2407-9 (cloth : alkaline paper) –
ISBN 0-8032-7335-5 (paperback : alkaline paper)
1. Indian poetry – North America – History and criti-
cism. 2. Indians of North America – Folklore. I. Title.
PM170 .H96 897—dc21 2002075094

Contents

Introduction

This book grows out of my involvement for many years with Native American myths and tales, especially those of western North America. It also grows out of my own intellectual ancestry, a mingling of anthropology, folklore, linguistics, and literature. Its main focus, of course, is the narratives themselves, to understand them more accurately, to help others to recognize their worth more fully, and to encourage fuller recognition for those who thought them and told them.

Some years ago I published *"In Vain I Tried to Tell You"* (1981), a series of papers showing what I understood about this subject at the time. The Chinookan peoples that once lived along the Columbia River in what are now the states of Oregon and Washington were its focus. Most of my own first-hand experience of Native American narrative and language is rooted there. I first heard and wrote a Native American language at Warm Springs Reservation, Oregon, mostly while visiting and going around with Hiram Smith, a Wasco, but also while working with Philip Kahclamat, who had been the partner of Walter Dyk, in writing the first grammar of the language, and who had gone to New Haven to take part in a course taught by Edward Sapir. (Philip also lived at Warm Springs then but was from the Washington side, where the language was called Wishram.) And the dissertation I had to complete in a year (1954–55) to take a job at Harvard was a grammar of Kathlamet, a sister language that had been spoken near the mouth of the Columbia and is known now almost entirely through the work of Franz Boas in the last decade of the nineteenth century. And I am from that part of the world and go back there.

Since *"In Vain,"* I have come to grasp more fully the knowledge, the competence, one might say, that underlies and informs such narratives. Comparative perspective, awareness of transformations such as Claude Lévi-Strauss has discovered, knowledge of what the fish in the rivers are like, and when grizzly bears last were seen in Oregon, all contribute to this fuller understanding. It remains true that the narratives exist in languages and, like what we otherwise know as language, are organized coherently, from beginning to end, according to implicit principles of form.

Indeed, it has come to seem likely that narratives everywhere in the world involve such principles, although only a tiny fraction of the world's narratives have been approached in such a way. (Appendixes 2 and 3 list the languages for which I know at least one text to have been so analyzed.)

Pursuit of such knowledge will add to understanding of language itself and contribute to the many fields of inquiry for which the use of language in telling stories is a part. Such fields have many names—ethnopoetics, sociolinguistics, psycholinguistics, rhetoric, semiotics, pragmatics, narrative inquiry, English, literary criticism—but they share a common purpose: understanding.

Such understanding must realize that oral narratives are organized in terms of lines, of patterned sequences of lines. One way to get to the heart of the matter is to consider that until recently, every published oral narrative, Native American and other, has been presented as a series of paragraphs. Paragraphs, of course, are what our culture has expected. In my experience, however, paragraphs conceal or at best make it difficult to recognize what actually goes on in a narrative: how action is shaped, how emphasis is distributed, what is marked against a common background. If the nature of the work that is necessary can be summed up, it is: not paragraphs but lines.

To say this is not to discredit those who have not done such work. Only recently has anyone had an inkling of such organization. And if a text has been written down or recorded carefully, its implicit lineaments still can be discerned. The narratives taken up in the pages that follow are examples.[1]

There was a time when many thought unwritten languages to be more or less without form, without grammar. Thanks in important part to the work of anthropologists, the presence of pervasive form in all languages, unwritten as well as written, has come to be recognized. Differences in form, yes; lack of form, no.

In my experience this has proven true with oral narratives, such as those represented in this book. It took a number of years to discover such form. I began such interpretation merely by being puzzled by Louis Simpson's repeated use of the initial particle pair "Now then" in the stories he dictated to Sapir in Wishram Chinook. After I recognized that they and some other elements went together in relations of three and five, there still were surprises ahead—such as three or five pairs, couplets of such markers (in "The Deserted Boy"). Until recently I had no idea that gender could be related to choice of the two main kinds of relations: three and five, two and four (see chaps. 4 and 11). Surely there is more to be learned about their use.[2]

There is much still to learn, then, as individual traditions are addressed. It was only by the chance of coming to know a British scholar of epic, A. T. Hatto, that my attention became focused on Mohave narratives taken down early in the past century by A. L. Kroeber. It was by the good fortune of a friend, Leanne Hinton, being at Berkeley that I obtained microfilm of Kroeber's notebooks and was able to discover consistent pattern of a kind not seen pervasively before, relations of five and two (see Hymes 2000b). The published version here and there lacked a word in the notebook that formed a pair, instances that at the time must have seemed incidental. It is in revising this manuscript now that I came to understand better differences in prevalent form between two Tonkawa myths (see chap. 11) and the principle that may underlie them.

Of course, individual cases are not the only source of insight. Two kinds of comparative perspective are also important. One has to do with analogous cases. Stith Thompson's work on Native American materials is, of course, always worth consulting, as are the efforts of Boas and others to identify elements of the narratives. The structural comparisons of Lévi-Strauss should always be consulted.[3] Always there is the unavoidable task of just looking around.

My investigation of this type of narrative in other cultural traditions illuminated my understanding of the ending of the Winnebago trickster cycle. The trickster's positive deeds at the end have been considered suspect. But it turns out that Winnebago is not the only tradition in which a trickster figure emerges at the end with beneficent powers. The same holds true for an independent cycle among the Quinault of the Washington coast (Blue Jay is the trickster), and a myth among the Ute of the Southwest involving Coyote. And just as in the Winnebago cycle, so in the Quileute and Ute sequences: the beneficent ending follows an episode with benevolent and bungling hosts (cf. chap. 8). Such a sequence is evidently old in North America and perhaps more common than these three cases.

The host episode in the Winnebago cycle is particularly telling. The trickster (he has no animal identity) has abandoned his social role to travel about alone. At last he comes to settled people, and he starts to take part again in reciprocity. Four times, he receives from them but is unable to reciprocate (as a trickster always fails in such circumstances). But tacitly he gains. He gains resocialization. Now he has relatives again, a social place; he is four times part of social interaction. Following this he undertakes a series of transformations that benefit the people. That he can continue to undertake them, I think, is to be understood.

Another source of insight comes from the study of literature itself. I am one of those who hope and believe that Native American texts will come to be recognized generally as the first literature of the New World (cf. Bringhurst 1998). Certainly, my own work has been influenced by literary scholars. In reading this book, or in looking through the "Index of Narrators and Narratives," one can find discussion of Robert Alter, Michael Riffaterre, A. J. Greimas, and C. S. Lewis (in chap. 15). The chapter exists because I was invited by Ralph Cohen to contribute to an issue of *New Literary History.* And my work has always been informed by ideas from Kenneth Burke. I studied with him at a School of Letters one summer at Indiana University (1952), had an office next to him at the Center for Advanced Studies in the Behavioral Sciences (1957–58), and through him met Marianne Moore and William Carlos Williams. My sense of what I do probably owes more to KB than to anyone else.[4]

All this comes round to an essential point: such narratives may be taken to have been memorized, to have persisted unchanged, to have been for children (who were, indeed, a required audience in winter for myths). Close study, close comparison, shows them to be much more than that. It shows them, for many at least, to be ways of thinking, to be ways of making sense of the world. To this making of sense many narrators bring both their own experience and mastery of form, even in the last years of a tradition (chap. 1). Sometimes it is new wine in old bottles (Charles Cultee's Sun's Myth, Victoria Howard's "Coyote Made the Land Good" perhaps), at other times, one among several vintages offered by familiar grapes (Louis Simpson and Hiram Smith with the news about Coyote). None of the narrators would have considered himself or herself an author, nor would they have been so considered by other members of their community. But I hope that these chapters will make clear that such stories show minds at work.

Chapters 6 through 12 (part 3, "Stories Twice-Told and Complemented") may best serve this purpose. They offer comparison, often close comparison, of one and the same story, or related stories, realized in different ways. Such comparison makes especially clear the necessity of what I call "verse analysis." Narratives consist, not only of lines, but of lines in patterned relation to one another. Differences in emphasis and shape and interpretation can be specified in the texts themselves.

Part 2, "Overview," considers aspects of the history of such work, and of its prospects. Part 4, "Contexts and Perspectives," considers the sometimes overlooked role of editing in what becomes known to an audience (chaps. 13, 14) and the relation of such texts and principles to literature in general.

Let me say again how much there is still to be learned. It is for that reason that I adopt as the title a line with which Victoria Howard sometimes ended what she told in Clackamas: Now I know only this far.

I hope to have the privilege of continuing to learn more and of contributing more to this part of the interpretation of tongues. And that many others will join in this work.[5]

Let me close by mentioning recent work of interest and value by others: Bahr, Smith, Allison, Hayden 1994; Evers and Toelken 2001; Kroeber 1997, 1998; Ramsey 1999; Sammons and Sherzer 2000; Swann 1994, forthcoming; Tedlock 1983; and Zolbrod 1995.[6]

I urge anyone who wishes to use this book in a class to consider White 1998 on the evolving intellectual context of Native American studies and Moore 1998 on the various backgrounds students, especially Native Americans, may bring to such classes. Shanley 1998 and Valentine 1998 are valuable on the relation of the contents of such a book to Native American studies and the study of languages (for ethnopoetics, cf. Shanley, p. 132, and Valentine, pp. 162, 175–76).

Part 1. Prologue

I

Survivors and Renewers

I am honored that the editors of *Folklore Forum* found stimulation for an issue in my address as president of the American Folklore Society in 1974 (published as Hymes 1975b) and was glad to contribute to it.

The address was delivered more than a quarter-century ago, but I would not much change what I said then about a dialectic between tradition and situation, mediated by re-creation and spurred by a human need to traditionalize. Work such as that in Feintuch 1995 deepens such thoughts. I am struck particularly by the felicity of Glassie's opening dictum, "tradition is the creation of the future out of the past," or, as he rephrases it at the end, "tradition is the means for deriving the future from the past" (Glassie 1995: 393, 409).[1] I want to discuss an example of that, if one can rephrase yet further: "tradition offers means for facing the future, having faced the past."

Sun's Nature

I have in mind the myth with which my 1974 address ended, "Sun's Nature" (to be exact about the second word), told to Franz Boas more than a century ago by Charles Cultee, the only person, so far as is known, then capable of telling myths in Kathlamet Chinook or, indeed, in its sister language, Chinook proper.

What Cultee told Boas is original, strikingly so. There is nothing else like it known from the region. There is much that can no longer be known, of course. Still, from what is known, this myth stands apart.

Those who have read or heard the myth realize it is an account of the destruction of the towns pertaining to a chief, destruction brought on by his own hubris. Living near the coast, he cannot see the sun rise and decides to go east toward it, despite cautioning from his wife. After days of travel, beyond any people, he comes to a large house and a young girl. The house is filled with wealth on either side. The girl explains that when she is ready to marry (at menarche), her mother will give the wealth away. The chief stays, and there is a characteristic Chinookan scene for the union of a hero and a woman associated with spiritual power. Each morning the mother (the Sun) goes out early (to carry the sun across the sky); each evening she returns with various kinds of wealth. The scene ends, "Every day like this."

The chief becomes homesick (natural enough, in Native terms). The mother offers him every kind of human goods, but he refuses. He wants the shining thing she carries each day. When he looks at it, his eyes close, but he wants only that. His wife tells him she will never give it to anyone, but finally she does. One cannot forever refuse a relative. But she warns him and gives him an axe as well.

He comes to each town of his people in turn. Each time the shining thing he carries says, "We two shall strike your town," he loses consciousness. When he recovers, there is blood; he has destroyed his people. Each time he tries to rid himself of what he carries and cannot. When he reaches his own town, he tries to stop but cannot.[2] When he recovers, the old woman is there.

He looked back.
Now she is standing near him, that old woman.
"You"
        she told him,
                "You.
"In vain I try to love you.
        In vain I try to love your relatives.
"Why do you weep?
        It is you who choose.
                Now you carried that 'blanket' of mine."

Now she took it,
        she lifted off what he had taken.
Now she left him,
        she went home.
He stayed there,
        he went a little distance.
There he built a house,
        a small house.

If you know the history of the Pacific Northwest, you know no European ship crossed the bar of the Columbia River until 1792 and that at the time Chinookan-speaking people dominated either side of the river's mouth. They were wealthy through local resources and trade and socially stratified,

with slaves. A half-century later few were left. Most had died as a result of introduced diseases (see Boyd 1994; Rubin 1999, chap. 23, "Cole Sik Waum Sik" August 1830).

"Sun's Nature" is a way of thinking that experience. Of course, Cultee was quite aware of what we would consider history-steady encroachment of whites as traders and missionaries and settlers and eventually soldiers, new goods, new weapons, another language, forced removal from the river. None of this appears in the myth. The myth addresses the nature of a power understood to sustain the world, and which in the myth, still does.[3]

At the very end, indeed, the myth changes form in expressing this. After a brief introduction, everything has been told in terms of relations of three and five (and in catalogs, of ten). But after the old woman's final speech to the chief, each of the two has just a pair of verses, four in all. Four-part relations, in fact, have been discovered within several western Native American narratives as a foregrounding of a woman or women, as actors or as premise (see chap. 4, this volume).

Creativity of Survivors

Again and again, in coming to know better some of the tellings in the region by survivors, I come to a sense of a mind working within the framework of a tradition, still wrestling with the nature of figures in the myths and relations among them. Thereby in their tellings carrying tradition further. Exercising a kind of creativity inherent in the tradition, I would argue.

The traditions themselves, after all, were not closed but open. In principle the way things were was explained in stories. One might not have heard a story explaining this creature or that landscape or some kind of human conduct such as men marrying women and lying to them (see the Maidu myth in chap. 4, this volume), but someone else might have. And the stories one knew could be extended or linked in good faith. No one would have thought of himself or herself as an "author." One might think of oneself as coming to understand more deeply.

This is not to say that there is nothing at all from which the myth Cultee told may have come. There is a recurrent plot in the region in which a young man reaches a house, finds a young woman, and marries her, or wishes to marry her, but has to overcome a hostile father or father-in-law. And, in fact, such a story has come to light upriver among the Wishram, Chinookan speakers living across from The Dalles, Oregon, a source for transformation that Cultee could have known (Trafzer 1998:44–46; Hines 1998:183–85).[4] If

not this version, then some other along the river seems likely to have been a starting point for Cultee.[5]

Biblical Excursus

I am not suggesting that Cultee was the first Kathlamet speaker to revise a story or to imagine a story adequate to experience with a sense of continuing a tradition. I assume that communities are like that, that they always have members who are creative in that way. There is indeed a parallel close to hand, one whose refashionings of narratives in good faith are well known and continue to be studied. I am thinking, of course, of the re-creations over the centuries of the Jewish and Christian traditions. (I don't discuss Islamic and East and South Asian traditions because I barely know them.)

Some associate these traditions of our own society with pedantry and literalism, dogma and inquisition. And, of course, there is much in history to give them a bad name. As Native Americans well knew, religious power can be dangerous.

Yet both in Native American communities and for many members of Jewish and Christian communities, the point of having stories was for those who encounter them to make them their own. Therein, of course, is a continuing source of change. Let me quote a study of the Dutch theologian Edward Schillebeeckx: "[T]elling stories properly also involved being caught up in them . . . in the end what we are concerned with is the fusing of two stories, the story of the gospel tradition of faith and the story of our own personal and communal life. . . . Tradition and its interpretation can therefore be summed up in another of Schillebeeckx's formidable phrases, 'the tradition of faith which discloses meaning with liberating force'" (Bowden 1983: 134–35). No rote learning there.

Or compare a feminist scholar, concerned to avoid the faults of some feminist scholars: "[T]heir ahistorical examination of the Bible, and their homogenization of its diversity. My readings call for a consideration of the heterogeneticy of the Hebrew canon, for an appreciation of the variety of socio-ideological horizons evident in this composite text" (Pardes 1992:3).

The general truth is that these traditions have been questioned and reconfigured from as early as we know them. To give two examples:

1. There are two accounts of the origin of man and woman in Genesis, one simultaneous (1:27), one successive (2:21–24), accompanied outside the canon by a story of Adam's first wife, Lilith (see Graves and Patai 1966, chap. 10, "Adam's Helpmeets").

2. In Exodus 20:24 the Lord tells Moses "in *every* place where I cause my

name to be remembered I will come to you and bless you," but in Deuteronomy 12:1–4, Moses first says that the Lord told them to demolish all the places where the nations they are about to dispossess served their gods; then (12:5–14) the Israelites are told "you shall seek *the* place that the Lord your God will choose" (5) and that "only at *the* place that the Lord will choose in one of your tribes—there you shall offer your burnt offerings and there you shall do everything I command you."[6]

There is much literature on these matters, and I cannot claim more than limited acquaintance with it. But I am drawn to it as I try to imagine the interpretative communities from which Cultee or other survivors came. Of course, the strength of centers of authority and regulation was different. In communities of the Pacific Northwest each family might have recognized a different center. Denis Demert, a Tlingit educator, once remarked that the Tlingit knew there were different local versions of certain historical events, but that was not a problem until one version was written down and as a result taken as the true one.

Yet forces for diversity have been present in both Native and Judeo-Christian communities. It is well known that the several canons, Jewish and Christian, have existed within a large field of other works also representing part of what some thought should be authoritative.

If one recognizes "revisionism" (see Brisman 1998) and "interpretation" (Kugel and Greer 1986; Kugel 1997) as "creativity," then such creativity was in fact an ordinary feature of both kinds of community. Both had stories considered central to how they came to be as they are and to what might become of them, stories often instructive, sometimes amusing (Native Americans seem to have a considerable edge there), but taken for granted as sources of orientation in the world. Both experienced a need for renewal and reconciliation between stories and experience.

When Boas came to Bay Center, Washington, and met with Cultee, the only locus of myths in Kathlamet at the moment may have been in Cultee's head. But certainly Cultee did not think of himself as author or source of any, but as someone for whom the enabling event of performance was still potentially possible and for whom tradition was surely the enabling reference (to use terms of reference from Foley 1992). Despite his apparent day-to-day isolation, Cultee still was an embodiment of what Glassie has said folklore seeks to capture: "the relation of individual will to collective process" (1994:241), in sum, a nexus of the need to interpret and recreate a part of something not one's own.

I suggest three terms for what would occur when narrators like those in the Northwest, like those who transmitted Biblical tradition, wrestled with

figures and events in thinking about and conveying a narrative. These are not learned or stylish terms, but terms akin to what Indian narrators themselves might have used.

    a. Could have been
    b. Should have been
    c. Must have been

(a) *Could have been* is part of bringing a story to life or close to home by reimagining its details, as much for some historians (Alter 1995:71, passim) as for folk narrators. Indeed, when Hiram Smith tells "The News about Coyote," having just heard Louis Simpson's telling as taken down by Sapir a half-century before, there is no disagreement between the two as to what happened and where: Coyote did perform fellatio on himself on the Washington side of the Columbia across from Mosier. The difference is in how it happened.

Simpson tells it as straightforward fact. Smith tells it with extenuating circumstances—the sun was hot, he was tired, he sat down, sitting, he became aroused, then. . . . The two openings correlate with the two endings. For Simpson, Coyote is refused food by people, not once but twice. Each time they say what he had done. For Smith, Coyote, hoping to keep the news from getting out, first creates the rimrock that runs down to the river there, but he can't prevent the news from getting out. Smith says that wherever he goes, Coyote hears the people saying the news but quotes what they say only once. Simpson ends with Coyote admitting, "Truly now I am known." Smith ends with Coyote going off and leaving, a conventional start of a new adventure (see chap. 12 for more).

Reading a recent title by two leaders in the current quest for Jesus, Borg and Wright (1998), both of whom I respect, I cannot help thinking of a parallel for a study I might write: *The Meaning of Coyote: Two Visions, by Hiram Smith and Louis Simpson.*

The differences match other differences in treatment of Coyote's character by the two men (see Hymes 1996b). Perhaps "should have been" and "must have been" flow together here with "could have been." But the starting point would seem to be something like this: Given that it did happen (everyone knows the story), how did it happen? There is room for creativity in answering that question—creativity grounded in how one has come to conceive that actor, what possibilities would be in character.

(b) *Should have been* especially comes to mind when one finds a narrator wrestling with outcome. The Kathlamet Salmon myth has spring salmon, coming up river, endure insult from the plants along the river. "Without us,

your people would have died" (in winter). Telling the myth a second time to Boas a few years later, Cultee revised both form and ending so that that the complementary ascendancy in winter of the female domain (plants instead of fish) is overcome forever (Hymes 1985a; see chap. 6 of this volume).

Telling Melville Jacobs about the arrival of foods in spring, Victoria Howard (in Clackamas) has some of the same formulaic words as Cultee but turns a journey step by step upriver into the appearance, one after the other, of plants and other things. The tone is entirely pedagogic. There is an announcer, probably a fish person, who explains what each new thing is named and food for (Jacobs reports), but as the end of the series approaches, Howard breaks off. She has been treating each kind of food in sets of three. Now she is at the end of fish and, having treated sturgeon, has only salmon left as the culmination. But how can salmon be both announcer and announced? She breaks off and says that her grandmother said that it was Coyote who provided for all the things good to eat. That seems "should have been" for sure. Salmon (a male hero par excellence) as ordainer of foods is dismissed for good.

(c) *Must have been* is how I place Victoria Howard's telling of "Seal and Her Younger Brother Lived There," the first of her myths I interpreted thoroughly and one which I still perform (Hymes 1968, 1977, 1981b). I am moved by the daughter, the expressive heart of the telling. The telling has its origin in a story of revenge. On the Pacific Coast various versions are known of a plot in which a man (or two men) travel to another place to take revenge on its headman. To gain access, the avenger disguises himself as a woman of the headman's house. He may be almost discovered several times. At night, when he climbs up to the man's bed (still disguised as his wife), a young child calls out that he has a penis (or a knife) but is shushed. The "wife" goes uncaught, kills the man during the night, and escapes. All this to the satisfaction of the audience, presumably, the story having been told from the standpoint of the one who seeks revenge.

Among eastern Chinookans a version came to be known in which the child is a girl on whose face blood drips during the night. Victoria Howard told Melville Jacobs a version in which the entire story is told from the standpoint of that girl. She notices something odd about the "woman" who comes to her uncle and tries to warn but is shushed. When at night something drips on her face, she tells her mother but is told to shush. When she hears something dripping, she tells her mother and is told again to shush. She gets up, raises a torch, and sees her uncle dead. She reproaches her mother. Her mother begins a formal lament. Again the girl reproaches and weeps. Until now the word "to say" has been transitive. Now the word "to say" is intransitive. The two women no longer address each other.

In his useful account of canonical interpretation (taking the Bible as a whole), Sanders uses the term *dynamic analogy* for "re-presenting the tradition, consciously identifying with the character or characters in the tradition most *representative* of the new hearers or readers" (1984:70–71).

Surely this is how we come to have what Howard said. The "wife" and the husband slain in revenge are little more than props. All the dialogue is between the two women. And it is the girl who speaks last, to the audience, if not to her mother, in the place Chinookan myths provide for final evaluations. To account for the telling one must infer that someone, perhaps the mother-in-law from whom she heard the story, perhaps Howard, asked herself, what was it like for that child?

The three attitudes may be difficult to distinguish, may overlap. All three may come together in Cultee's envisioning of the destruction of his people, transforming a plot with the Sun as hostile father-in-law to be able to say so. To dramatize what might have been, then what became, was to keep the people still heroes of their own story, though tragic heroes, brought low by the hubris of one of their own. It is hard to understand the existence of the story except in such terms. It is hard to account for it except as a creative act, true to the tradition, new to the tradition.[7]

I suggest that the three attitudes make sense of continuing re-creation and creativity conducted in good faith. Recognition of narratives as traditionally organized throughout (*durchcomponiert*), sometimes in telling details, gives further confidence to an interpreter, as it may have given to a narrator. Such texts, though taken down at or near the end of a tradition, are not merely remembered, much less haltingly so. Louis Simpson's "The Deserted Boy," for example, as told to Sapir, in its middle act is a bravura display of identification with the guardian-spirit quest that it in effect becomes (see chap. 13, this volume).

In these cases, then, we are dealing with minds that tradition continued to inhabit, for whom a tradition continued to be "good to think." They were sustained in this by command of a tradition's technical resources of form.

Oral, Aural, and Anal

How can this be, some might seem to say. Karl Kroeber has recently written, "Because the Trickster story is oral, it exists solely in terms of its affects [*sic*] on a participating audience" (1998:233). Others have depreciated texts that exist only in writing in other ways. I hope to have shown, in relation to

Cultee's "Sun's Nature" and other texts, that such an attitude dismisses verbal art of value. It turns its back on materials of importance to those whose heritage they are. And it ignores that analysis of the form of such texts is possible and can "liberate" them. (On this, see the final chapter of Chappell and Bringhurst 1999.) Whether or not Cultee told the "Sun's Nature" to anyone before telling it to Boas, it would be ludicrous to suppose that until then it did not exist, being only in his mind. And that it did not exist in terms of its effect on Cultee himself.[8]

If we are to adequately respect and understand such narratives, we must think in terms of thoughtful, motivated minds, seeking narrative adequate to their experience, surviving and renewing.

My turning away here from speech events may seem surprising, given my effort to develop the ethnography of speaking. Texts that I know force me to it. And respect. Again and again, people whom some whites would have seen only as impoverished and uneducated have been found to be creative and articulate, to have rich minds, minds both retaining stories and continuing to think them.

To say that stories exist only in performance is to say that between performances narrators do not think. That they are prisoners of the presence of an audience. That they go about their daily lives, encountering nothing that makes them remember a story. Or think of how a story might or ought to have gone. That the stories they know never pose them problems, from perceived incompleteness to contradictions, with one another or with their own experience. That, in short, they have very limited minds. We should be embarrassed to denigrate them so. To do so seems to me intellectually constipated.

The same is true of views that only what can be heard (and perhaps seen) through recordings is worth attention. All this adds a final coup de grâce to the destruction of tradition through disease, disruption, and war.

Moreover, as we come to understand more clearly that the stories are not prose, not paragraphs, but lines, organizations of lines, we can recapture something of the actual artistry and creativity of the originals (see Hymes 1998a; chap. 5 and 13, this volume; Bringhurst 1999) and on occasion, given respect and understanding, speak them again.

A start has been made, but only a start. We are not yet able, for example, to speak with confidence about the perspective and style of any one narrator, grounding what is said in terms of that narrator's own language and the kinds of organization we can assume to be present. Nor can we compare and contrast the styles of different narrators and different traditions in such a way. That can only be done when all of a body of narratives has been analyzed ethnopoetically. Even if materials are limited, as for many traditions, there is much that can be learned.

Herder, Chomsky, and Others

What can be learned, indeed, speaks to an old tradition of our own, associated with such names as Herder. It is a tradition that sees languages and cultures as at least in part a result of creativity on the part of those who share them. Anyone who has taken delight in the particulars and patterns of another language will have a sense of this.

A dominant force in contemporary study of language and mind, to be sure, dismisses such delight: "The primary one [task at hand] is to show that the apparent richness and diversity of linguistic phenomena is illusory and epiphenomenal, the result of interaction of fixed principles under slightly varying conditions" (Chomsky 1995:8).

A different view would welcome establishment of fixed principles in the organization of verbal art (such as may prove true in ethnopoetics) but see such principles, not as an end in themselves, but as an aid in discovering richness and diversity. Those of us who have such a view welcome such evidence of community and personal creativity: I happen to be reading a book that delves deeply into what can still be seen of the Appalachian world the Cherokee once knew. One part recounts the return of peregrine falcons. Let me end with two quotations, taking them as analogous to narratives whose form we do not yet know: "[W]hen I stop here, to savor an old edge of the Cherokee country, I watch the sky bordered by this table mountain pine and replay the flight of falcons in my mind as I know it to be, a sight I could not have imagined if I had not seen it, no more than I could have imagined red wolves or a rock-loving pine that needed fire" (Camuto 1997:318). Earlier, watching birds but recently released: "After they learn to hitch rides of midday thermals, which take them to new heights and load their wings with possibilities the vultures and ravens cannot imagine, they begin to exercise the freedom of their wildness and create a fabulous order in the air no one would have imagined without them" (315).

in decorating fur coats from Siberia, and Roman stripes on modern ribbons, girdles, and silks. Letters are assigned elements to chart their occurrence. Boas is not mentioned, but probably his conception of rhythmic repetition was assumed as known.

Years later, Reichard (1944) dedicated her book *Prayer: The Compulsive Word* to Boas's memory. She remarks that her 1924 paper and one by Cora Stafford on Peruvian embroideries "were inspired and aided by Professor Boas, who had a perennial interest in the subject. He felt that similar elaborations could be found in the literary sphere of art, even as it had been demonstrated in the music of primitive peoples. The possibilities of adding new forms of rhythmic repetition in music forms suggested by Navajo chant setup of music, song and song sequence are limitless and they await a detailed and time-consuming analysis which is at present impossible" (Reichard 1944:35). She goes on to quote Boas on the possibility of complex rhythms being found in narrative literary forms (Boas 1927:310-11) and to say that there is little doubt Navajo has a great deal to offer on this question, much of it in prayers.[2] When she discussed this matter with Boas a short time before his death, he told her that he had "something of the kind" in Kwakiutl prayers, which, however, were not as complicated as those of the Navajo. "The obvious questions came up in our discussion: Does the person who uses the prayer realize its significance as a whole pattern? If he does, is that realization felt in the ways in which we might feel it? How would one proceed to answer such a question? In what way or ways does the Navajo memory function, for surely its demands are burdensome beyond any which our own culture furnishes? . . . Can we devise a method for answering these questions? The following analysis aims to present the material which arouses them and in part to answer them, but it could profit greatly by suggestions regarding procedure" (1944:35-36). Reichard treats the prayers as rhythmic prose, since they are intoned, but adds that if it later should be decided that the form is nearer to poetry (when the prosody has been worked out), there is nothing in her discussion to prevent its being classified as such (37). The grouping of lines on the page and problems of translation are taken up, together with the division of most prayers into three parts—invocation, petition, and benediction—and the patterning of individual prayers. She notes that four and its multiples are not as common as is often assumed (46). A prayer from the Male Shooting Chant Evil-chasing is presented in full with explanation (chap. 6).

Repetition and number were important to Reichard also in her book on Navajo religion (1990 [1950]), as shown in chapter 14 on "Number," in chapter 16 on "Word, Formula, and Myth," and in the many entries in the index under the heading "repetition" (792).

to printed literary style. The stylistic difference is considerable (491). And he speaks of "this pleasure given by the rhythmic repetition of the same or similar elements, in prose as well as poetry" (494). He concludes: "We have found the literatures of all the peoples about which we have information share one feature, namely rhythmic form" (502).

Near the beginning of Boas's essay is a statement that could be taken to anticipate ethnopoetics: "The investigation of primitive narrative as well as of poetry proves that repetition, particularly rhythmic repetition, is a fundamental trait" (491). But the continuation of the paragraph does seem to identify form with what is fixed or with what is musical: "All prose narrative consists in part of free elements the form of which is dependent upon the taste and the ability of the narrator. Inserted among those passages we do find others of fixed form which give the narrative to a great extent its formal attractiveness. Quite often these passages consist of conversation between the actors in which deviation from the fixed formula is not permitted. In other cases they are of rhythmic form and must be considered poetry or chants rather than prose" (491). In short, form must be recognizable either by fixity, or by rhythm in the sense that song or chant has rhythm.

Boas does recognize variation of contents within a pattern. Citing Kwakiutl speeches, for instance, a passage such as "I have come Northerners; I have come Great Kwakiutl, I have come Rich Side," he remarks: "The repetitions discussed so far are rhythmic in form, varied in contents. They may be compared to an orderly succession of decorative motives that agree in the plan of the unit, but vary in details," but continues, "In poetry rhythmic repetitions of identical formal units are frequent" (1927:314). In sum, the discussion never gets very far from identity.

Decorative Art

Boas's work on material art shows the generality of his conception of the role of aesthetic form in human life. It may also contribute to a conception of verbal form that, as it were, hugs the material ground. In this regard attention should be paid to the work of his student Gladys Reichard.[1] Boas himself cites her early article "The Complexity of Rhythm in Decorative Art" in his own discussion of rhythmic repetition in decorative form as the rhythm of time translated into space (Boas 1927:40; Reichard 1922 in Boas 1927: 41–42). Reichard states the question as, "Do primitive people have a definite plan in carrying out their ideas in headwork, embroidery and other handicrafts?" (Reichard 1922:183). She analyzes beadwork and embroidery from the Thompson River Indians of British Columbia, bands of skin used hitherto collected, we are hardly in a position to speak of *the literary form of the tales*. I am inclined to count among their formal traits the typical repetition of the same incident that is found among many tribes; or the misfortunes that befall a number of brothers, until the last one is successful in his undertaking. These have the purpose of exciting the interest and leading the hearer to anticipate with increased eagerness the climax. (478, emphasis added)

To be sure, Boas sets "poetry" apart: "The literary style is most readily recognized in the poetic parts of tales; but, since these fall mostly outside of the purely narrative part of the stories, I do not enter into this subject" (479). But having contrasted the style of poems (song texts) in the Northwest and the Southwest, he goes on to remark: "Equally distinct are the *rhythmic structures* that are used by the Indians of various areas" (479, citing Fletcher 1901 [emphasis added], presumably for patterns of repetition in the songs and chants of the Pawnee Hako ceremony).

In my own work, the recognition of thoroughgoing patterning in Chinookan narratives came through pursuing the hypothesis that a cultural pattern number ("sacred number"), five, and its correlate, three, played a part. It is striking to find Boas associating such numbers with literary composition, with rhythmic repetition as a source in his 1914 study, "Mythology and Folk-Tales of the North American Indians": "I am not inclined to look at these [so-called sacred numbers] primarily as something of transcendental mystical value; it seems to me more plausible that the concept developed from the aesthetic values of rhythmic repetition. Its emotional effect is obviously inherent in the human mind; and the artistic use of repetition may be observed wherever the sacred number exists, and where it is not only used in reference to distinct objects, but also in rhythmic repetitions of tunes, words, elements of literary composition and of actions" (1940:489). In his later paper "Stylistic Aspects of Primitive Literature" (1925), Boas continues to make statements that are strikingly suggestive. The goal of the article is "to discuss in how far general mental traits account for the development of poetry and of the art of narrative, and in how far special historical conditions have exerted an important influence" (1940:491). Again, the notion of poetry is equated with song: "Song and tale are found among all the people of the world and must be considered the primary forms of literary activity. It does not require special mention that primitive poetry does not occur without music, and that it is frequently accompanied by expressive motions or by dance. It is, therefore, more correct to speak of song rather than of poetry" (491). At the same time, Boas stresses that primitive prose is based on the art of oral delivery and therefore is more closely related to modern oratory than

What follows is not a full scale "sideshadowing" of Boas on narrative style. I do take up statements by Boas about literary form and "rhythmic repetition" that seem to imply a new kind of work. I analyze a text taken down in Kathlamet Chinook by Boas in 1894, the one chosen by Stocking to represent Boas's work of this kind, to show what results if one seeks regularities of kinds of repetition and rhythm throughout such a narrative. I also present a few examples from other Chinookan texts that in their ritual-like action and lyric suspension of time seem akin to Boas's own recognition of "repetitions . . . rhythmic in form, varied in contents" (1940:314). If Boas had followed up his own statements with more extended work, he might have come first to such passages.

In Boas's statements there was a seed, then, even if it did not take root. I shall consider why it did not and comment on an irony in that, an irony that in the long run dissolves.

Boas on Form in "Primitive Literature"

Boas was moved by verbal art in his earliest fieldwork (see Boas 1887a, b). In his introduction to the 1917 *International Journal of American Linguistics* he did not limit himself to questions of language in a narrow sense but declared, "The problems treated in a linguistic journal must include also the literary forms of native production" and observed, "The most promising material for the study of certain aspects of artistic expression are the formal elements that appear with great frequency in the tales of all tribes" (1917:7). He goes on to say: "Most of these are stereotyped to such an extent, that little individual variation is found. Even in poorly recorded tales, written down in translation only, and obtained with the help of inadequate interpreters, the sameness of stereotype formulas may sometimes be recognized. Conversation in animal tales and in other types of narrative, prayers and incantations, are probably the most important material of this character" (7). Early in "Mythology and Folk-Tales of the North American Indians" (1914) Boas remarks again on literary form (emphasis mine): "Even the best translation cannot give us material for the study of *literary form*—a subject that has received hardly any attention and the importance of which, as I hope to show in the course of these remarks, cannot be overestimated" (1940: 452). Later he elaborates:

> While much remains to be done in the study of the local characteristics of folk-tales in regard to the points referred to, a still wider field of work is open in all that concerns *their purely formal character,* and I can do no more than point out the necessity of study of this subject. On the basis of the material

one in 1962, two in 1968 (see Stocking 1968, 1974a, 1974b). It was in preparing to take part in a conference in his honor in the spring of 1995 that I returned to his paper on the Boas plan for American Indian languages, thinking about the relation between Boas's work with grammar and his work with texts. Stocking represented Boas's work with texts in his Boasian anthology by a Kathlamet narrative, "Swan's Myth," reproducing its initial page from the field notebook, its initial published page, and the full English translation. I found myself analyzing the narrative and rereading Boas on mythology, particularly on what he called style.

Reading Boas, one finds a number of statements about form. They seem to be calls for a new kind of analysis. If one recalls his "analytic" approach to grammar, describing languages in their own terms, their own processes and categories (cf. Stocking 1974b), an "analytic" approach to narrative form would seem a natural extension. Thoroughgoing analysis of a grammar in terms of its own processes and categories seems an analogue and starting point for thoroughgoing analysis of texts in terms of their own processes and categories.

This did not happen, of course. It was at least in some way a possibility, perhaps, a horizon now forgotten. Two recent experiences have made me especially appreciate such a horizon.

Some years ago I was asked to read an impressive manuscript on intellectual foundations for linguistic anthropology. I found myself slotted into a narrow genealogical niche. The manuscript was wide-ranging, for the most part, but for the period into which I was slotted for consideration omitted most of what I remembered as having mattered. I felt compelled to reconstruct for several pages what to me had been circumambient horizons of what to the writer was only a notch on a line from past to present.

A few months later I came upon a book on just this theme (composed in intellectual collaboration with a friend, Gary Morson). In *Foregone Conclusions,* Michael André Bernstein argues against histories and literature that assign people responsibility for outcomes they could not know while denying their sense of futures for them still open. He is first of all concerned with writing about the Holocaust, but he addresses as well Christian appropriation of the Hebrew Bible as merely preparation for a New Testament and explores Robert Musil's novel *A Man without Qualities* for its account of Austrians on the eve of the First World War (see the English translation [Musil 1995]), full of plans and expectations. Writing in terms of foregone conclusions is "foreshadowing." Writing in terms of actual horizons is "sideshadowing." It is concerned with the quotidian, what Bernstein and Morson call "prosaics," what an anthropologist would call ethnography.

2

Franz Boas on the Threshold of Ethnopoetics

History is part of what there is to be "theorized." Let me suggest that it has two aspects: what did happen, what did not happen.

As to what did happen, there is need to overcome stereotypes and misconceptions, not least on the part of linguists, for whom part of the past has become unintelligible. Today the contexts and climates of opinion in which linguistic work developed in American anthropology often are lost from sight. (See Hymes and Fought 1983:67–77; Hymes 1983b:118–19, 131 n.70). Saussure, for example, is likely to be generalized as an influence, when in fact he was hardly noticed in the United States until after the Second World War. Present-day comments on the formative period of the first half of the twentieth century often overlook major factors in the development of descriptive linguistics in the United States (it was not then "structuralism") such as sheer pleasure in the discovery of pattern for its own sake, desire to show that unwritten languages had pattern analogous to that of written languages, concern to void reductionist explanations in terms of psychology and biology, and concern for regularities that gave linguistics status in a horizon dominated by images of science.

To be sure, the need to recover contexts and actualities from documents and manuscripts is not recent. The initial stimulus to my own reading in the American tradition came as a graduate student, when history was mostly what a teacher could remember. Meaning then was under a cloud in American linguistics, a distant cloud, and my professor, a leader in linguistics in anthropology, asked in class, in a genuinely puzzled tone, "Why was Boas interested in grammatical categories?" I discovered that one had only to open the *Handbook of American Indian Languages* (Boas 1911) and read its introduction to find out.

Valuable work has been accomplished and continues, to be sure. For me, the start of serious sustained history of the Americanist tradition, with its roots in both linguistics and anthropology, is associated with its being taken up by George Stocking and with papers he contributed to three conferences,

Part 2. Overview

Gill's book on Navajo prayer (1981) takes its departure from Reichard (cf. xx and 3–5). "She is the first and only person to have attempted such an analysis" (4). He notes the origin of her interest in patterns of repetition in the Thompson River work (not mentioning the other bodies of data in Reichard's article or Boas). Examining prayer texts not included in Reichard's book but for which she prepared diagrams, Gill finds many errors and notes that the criteria for analysis of form and content are usually indeterminate. (See appendix A, "Critique of Reichard's Analysis of Prayer.") Still, he says, the vision she undoubtedly saw and followed is clear.

Gill himself analyzes Navajo prayers in terms of constituents, a set of twenty-two in all (1981:14). He discusses "Navajo Prayer as Oral Poetry" (180–83), with some observations on overlapping repetition within the performance, and notes that rhythm and repetition are essential elements. He presents diagrams of prayer texts (32–34, 211–35) in terms of their constituents (and catalogs). The constituents are kinds of act and topic. The status of the prayers as poetry seems to be assumed, rather than needing demonstration.

Some Navajo and Apache narratives have in fact been found to have the kind of poetic relations discussed later in this chapter (unpublished work by myself, Keith Basso, Mary Beth Culley, and Anthony Webster), but that is independent of the line of influence just described.

Poetry without Music

In contrast to statements that indicate universality for rhythmic repetition in verbal art, Boas at one point goes so far as to say: "Poetry without music, that is to say forms of literary expressions of fixed rhythmic form, are found only in civilized communities, except perhaps in chanted formulas. In simpler cultural forms the music of language alone does not seem to be felt as an artistic expression, while fixed rhythms that are sung occur everywhere" (1927:301). Again, recurrence is associated with fixity.

I like to think that if Boas had had time and opportunity to explore verbal form more fully, he would have discovered further dimensions of it in unsung language. Or if he were alive when such dimensions came to be recognized, especially in languages that he himself wrote down and knew intimately, such as Kathlamet Chinook (Hymes 1994b) and Kwak'wala (Kwakiutl) (Berman 1991), he would have accepted them.

Over the past thirty years it has become apparent that in many, perhaps all, communities there are oral narratives that are organized in terms of regularities of recurrence. Sometimes these regularities are obviously marked, as when the Wishram Chinook texts, dictated by Louis Simpson, commonly mark units that can be called "verses" by an initial pair of particles (usually, *aGa kwapt* 'now then,' sometimes *aGa wit'aX* 'now again,' or contrastively *kwapt aGa*).[3] Generally, where one can hear a narrative, such verse units are marked by potentially final intonation contours. Even without intonation contours, a variety of features enter into patterning—expressions of time, turns at talk, and, most of all, pattern numbers. Broadly speaking, there are two types: use of relations of three and five, as in Chinookan and American English, and use of relations of two and four, as in Kwakiutl, Takelma, and Zuni.

The recurrent regularities of such narrative for the most part are not within lines, that is, they are not metrical. Rather, they hold between lines or groups of lines and can be called *measured*. There can be variation in the way in which relations are deployed. A sequence of three may be a sequence of three pairs. A sequence of five may be a sequence of five pairs. Within sequences that answer to an expected cultural pattern, there may be more than one kind of internal rhythm. Five verses may constitute a rapid run or may consist of two pairs and an outcome (cf. Hymes 1992b).

The kind of repetition focused upon by Boas does, of course, occur. In "Swan's Myth," a "conjugal duet" between Swan and his wife about a roasting smelt ("my" versus "our," a pattern that occurs in Kathlamet Texts between a man and a woman in "Panther and Owl" as well) is formal in the first sense: similar pairs of repeated lines with, to be sure, a significant contrast. Repetition involves repetition of content. The relations among verses marked initially by *aqa* 'now' (see "The Deserted Boy" in the following section) are formal in another sense. The relations give rise to recurrent patterns that shape and express content, but the content need not be repeated.

Instead of "repetition" and "fixed," terms such as "recurrent" and "abstract" are appropriate. To stick to the recurrence of overt forms is to miss underlying relations. In terms of grammar, it is as if one could not recognize that the category of person-marker has occurred in three positions in a row in a Kathlamet verb, because the same person marker has not occurred three times in a row. This last, in fact, cannot occur, so far as first and second person markers are concerned.[4]

In sum, Boas pioneered in discovering recurrent relations among grammatical elements and the patterns of words constituted by them. A similar step is to discover recurrent relations among narrative elements and the patterns of texts constituted by them. The concept of rhythmic repetition is a step in that direction, but a limited step so long as it does not go beyond elements to relations.

Rhythms Change

If one extends Boas's phrase "rhythmic repetition," a text can be said to have a consistent rhythm in the sense of making use of an underlying principle. In Chinookan narratives the informing principle is not just of one pattern but of two: three- or five-step relations. Moreover, there is not just one level of organization but several: the number of verses within a stanza, the number of stanzas within a scene, the number of scenes within an act, possibly the number of acts within a myth or major part. Choice is possible at each point. And even with similar choices, the pace may differ.

The Deserted Boy. The three scenes of the second act of "The Deserted Boy," told by Louis Simpson to Edward Sapir in 1905, are a striking example (see Hymes 1994a). The first act has ended with the boy deserted. The second act begins with him facing winter, alone.

		(II) (i) (He survives)
Now then the boy wept.		(A)
Now then he heard,		
"TL' TL' TL'"		
Now then he turned his eyes,		35
he looked,		
he dried his tears.		

Now then he saw a *very* little bit of flame in a shell.   (B)
Now then he took that very same flame.
Now then he built up a fire.   40

Now again he saw fibre,   (C)
  again a little bit of it,
    straightway he took it.
Now again he went to the cache,
  he saw five wild potatoes.   45
Now then he thought: "My poor father's mother saved me potatoes,
  and fire was saved for me by my father's mother,
    and my mother's mother saved me fibre."

Now then the boy made a small fish-line,   (D)   50
  and he made snares with string;
    he set a trap for magpies.
Now then he caught them.
Then he made a small cloak with magpie's skin.
  He just put it nicely around himself.   55
Again he lay down to sleep.
Again he just wrapped himself nicely in it.

Now then he fishes with hook and line;   (E) (ab)
  he caught one sucker,
    half he ate,
      half he saves.
Again, morning, he ate half.

Now again he fishes,   (cd)
  he caught two,
    one he ate,   65
      one he saved.
Again, morning, he ate one.

Now again in the morning he fishes,   (ef)
  he caught three suckers,
    he ate one and a half.   70
Again, morning, he ate one and a half.

Now again he went to fish,
  he caught four suckers,
    two he ate,
      two he saved.   75
Morning, now he ate all two.

Now again did he go to fish for the fifth time.
  Now five times the boy had fished.
  Now he had become a grown man.

                                        (ii) (He sings)
Now then he examined his fish-line.   (A)   80
Indeed, ats' ə 'pts' ə p fills to the brim a cooking-trough.
  He stood it up on the ground.
Now then the boy sang.
Now then all the people watched him.
Now then they said: 85
  "What has he become?"

Indeed! he became glad,   (B)
  he had caught ats' ə 'pts' ə p.
Thus he sang:
  "Atséee, atséee,   90
    "Ah, it waves freely over me,
      Ah, my feathered cloak."
  "Atséee, atséee,
    "Ah, it waves freely over me,
      "Ah, my feathered cloak."   95

"Atséee, atséee,
    "Ah, it waves freely over me,
        "Ah, my feathered cloak."
Indeed! Ič'ɔ́xian's daughter had given him food.

Now then the boy had camped over four times;   (C)   100
    he camped over a fifth time.
Now then he awoke,
    a woman was sleeping with him,
    a very beautiful woman:
        her hair was long,   105
        and bracelets right up to her on her arms,
        and her fingers were full of rings,
    and he saw a house all painted inside with designs,
    and he saw a mountain-sheep blanket covering him,
        both he and his wife.
Indeed! Ič'ɔ́xian's very daughter had given him food,   110
            and plenty of Chinook salmon,
            and sturgeon,
            and blueback salmon,
            and eels,
            plenty of everything she had brought.   115

                                        (iii) (The two are together)
Now he married her.
    Now the woman made food.
        Now, morning, it became daylight.
            Now the two stayed together quietly that day.
            Now the two stayed together along time.   120

The opening act has moved precisely in threes and fives to the desertion
of the boy. Now in a scene of five stanzas, each of different formal complex-
ion, the boy's status changes. In (A) he weeps, hears, and finds. The three
verses are formally coordinated, each beginning with "Now then," describing an arc of onset, ongoing outcome, but the third verse has that same arc
again within its smaller compass (turn, look, dry his tears).

The second stanza has that arc (see, take, build a fire) in three lines, each
a verse. The third stanza is an outcome for seeing and finding. In one verse
of three steps, the boy finds fiber. In a second of two lines, he finds potatoes.
In a concluding third, he gives three lines of thanks.

In Chinookan narratives a sequence of five groups often has its third
group as an intermediate outcome. Having summed up what he is thankful
for at the end of the third stanza, the boy deploys his resources. In five verses

in the fourth stanza, he mainly provides himself with a cloak against the winter. In the fifth stanza, he fishes step by step, to a surprising result. Now the framework of the scene expands so that the fifth stanza itself has five parts, each of them having itself a pair of verses. The first of each pair begins "now then / now again." The second of each pair ends with "again, morning" except for the fifth. It ends with a couplet that counts as one unit, the two lines both marked ("Now . . . , Now . . ."), but together they are equivalent ways of making the same point. Notice that unlike in the preceding four stanzas, what he caught is not stated. That is held over to be the subject of an entire scene in itself. (I call such holding over "extraposition.") What we do learn in this ending casts what has preceded in a new light. Using his meager resources resourcefully, step by step the boy has become a man.

The second scene is ordinary at the level of number of stanzas and verses: three stanzas, of five, three, and three verses, respectively. In content it swells with what Russo has called "epic fullness" (1994:374).

The first stanza describes the boy catching, not fish, but a delicacy prepared for winter, a mixture of huckleberries and salmon. He sings because he knows that a spirit power has given it to him. Saving himself, he has been blessed. The people across the river who had deserted him watch and ask what he has become.

The second stanza is devoted to intensifying particles and the boy's song. The song can be repeated as long as desired. The food has come to him from the daughter of a being in the river, a being who causes whirlpools.

The third stanza swells its three verses with catalogs in the second and third (more "epic fullness"). The first verse locates the occasion—he sleeps a fifth time. The second verse expatiates on the woman he awakes to find with him, her beauty and ornament, the house they are now within, the blanket covering them both. The third verse itemizes the kinds of food she has brought, embracing four kinds of fish in two lines of generalization (had given him food, plenty of everything she had brought).

In the third scene, the tempo changes yet again. There are five verses, but none of them has "then" to indicate a succeeding step. The verses are for the staying together of the man and woman, each marked only with "now."

In sum, the act has three scenes, and each scene has three or five stanzas, or (in the last) five verses. Yet each of the parts is strikingly different in pace. The act of fishing is detailed in precise, parallel, incremental steps, day by day, only for its culmination to put the hearer on hold. The next scene reiterates a song in one stanza and swells with catalogs in another. The culminating scene suspends progression of time.

Such a *lyric moment* occurs also in the center of Charles Cultee's "Sun's

Myth" (Kathlamet Chinook), and its wording and form suggest a sense of shared pattern. (For the whole, see Hymes 1994b.) If the passage is taken to be prose and Englished as prose sentences, then it is understandable that recurrent relations might not be apparent. Here is how the published running translation appears: "He asked about all those things, and thought: 'I will take them.' When it was evening, the old woman came home. She hung up something that pleased him. It was shining. Every morning the old woman disappeared. At night she came back. She brought home all kinds of things. She brought home arrows. Sometimes she brought mountain-goat blankets and elkskin shirts. She did so every day. He stayed there a long time; then he grew homesick. He stayed there a long time; then he grew homesick" (Boas 1901:29).

The last line above begins a new scene and in fact a new act and the second half of the myth. The scene in question is itself an act, completing the first half. The relations of the scene in question are as follows:

A long time he stayed there;
   now he took that young girl.
They stayed there.
In the early light,   115
   already that old woman was gone.
In the evening,
     she would come home;
   she would bring things,
     she would bring arrows;   120
sometimes mountain goat blankets she would bring,
   sometimes elkskin armors she would bring.
Every day like this.

Notice the suspension of change in the first pair of verses (stayed, stayed there), departure and return in the second (was gone, came home . . . bring), and absence of any verb in the fifth, last verse. The corresponding scene in "The Deserted Boy" (Wishram/Wasco Chinook) also pairs morning and the rest of a day (lines 118, 119) and has "stayed there" twice (119, 120). There is perhaps another parallel, a woman providing (goods in "Sun's Myth," food in "The Deserted Boy").[5]

Stumbling Blocks?

Now that one can see such possibilities, one wonders why they were not seen by Boas or his students. What seems not to have happened is overcoming the received dichotomy of song and narrative as equivalent to poetry and prose. Some of this writing occurred in a time of experimentation in poetic form, experiments in the alignment of lines on the page. It is probably not surprising that what was put forward as highly modern in our own civilization would not be applied to what was studied as unwritten tradition in an ancient culture.

What *is* surprising is that no connection was made between the presentation of conversation in plays and conversation in oral narratives. It would have seemed an obvious convenience and clarification to distinguish turns at talk on the page. The turns themselves are there in the story and are not an intervention from without. Seeing turns at talk might have suggested other relations and recurrences within a text.

Perhaps there was a feeling that any change in the record of what had been dictated was an imposition; that once a text was taken down as carefully as possible, that written record took the place of the original speaking as guarantor of authenticity. Of course, one might notice slips of hearing or transcription or even, it might seem, of speaking. But change beyond scrupulous editing smacked of lack of rigor, lack of scientific observation.

The practice of alphabetizing the words of Native American languages in terms of the phonetic alphabet instead of the standard alphabet suggests such an attitude. The phonetic alphabet, of course, was no more a part of the Native American language than was the European alphabet. And if Native Americans used materials written by outsiders about their own language, the European alphabet would be familiar.

This is speculation, although I have encountered attitudes that suggest it. Perhaps an element of caution was involved. Everyone knows that songs have form, no intrusion there. Narrative form is another matter. There was no awareness of a single kind of patterning for that, then or, for the most part, now. Still, in some texts the recurrence of certain initial elements is constant and might have been taken as a mark of recurrence. But the past cannot fairly be criticized for not discovering what many today decline to recognize even when it is pointed out.

On Irony

There is irony here and an implicit contradiction. The Boasian goal was to represent languages in their own terms, free from distortion and overlay from the preconceptions of another culture. Nowhere are texts excluded from this goal. Texts, indeed, are explicitly included as indispensable to reaching the goal. In a letter of 1905 to W. H. Holmes, urging that all of Swanton's Haida texts be published, Boas stresses the connection: "I do not think that anyone would advocate the study of antique civilizations or, let me say, of the Turks or the Russians, without a thorough knowledge of their languages and of the literary documents in these languages; and contributions not based on such material would not be considered as adequate. In regard to our American Indians we are in the position that practically no such literary material is available for study, and it appears to me as one of the essential things that we have to do, to make such material accessible. My own published work shows, that I let this kind of work take precedence of practically everything else, knowing it is the foundation of all future researches" (1974: 122–23).

Boas remarks on the necessity of a mode of treatment appropriate to the features of the material: "The fact is nowhere more apparent than in our studies based on the old missionary grammars. In these the characteristic features of the languages treated are so entirely obscured by the mode of treatment, that without new and ample texts our understanding of the languages will always remain inadequate" (1974:123).

"The characteristic features of the languages": disclosing those became the starting point of an American tradition of synchronic grammar preceding and independent of European structuralism. If traditions were consistent, the texts that contributed to the linguistics ought themselves to have become the starting point of a tradition of analysis of narrative form. But "the characteristic features" of the texts were obscured by mode of treatment, a mode of treatment that persisted. Texts that are a kind of poetry in having an organization of lines were treated as prose and published as paragraphs. The ethos of an "analytic" approach and, indeed, concepts central to the grammatical work might have been extended into work with texts but were not.

IRONY IN TIME PERSPECTIVE (1)

If this is ironic, it is an irony that Boas helped provide a basis for overcoming. Arnold Krupat (1988, 1992) has written of such irony with regard to Boas, focusing on an apparent contradiction between anthropology's goal of being a science, concerned with laws, yet postponing the formulation of laws until a time when all (or enough) was known. Let me put that contradiction in the perspective of the long term.

First, it is not quite true that Boas was a positivist for whom the facts are "simply out there" (Krupat 1992:90). It is fairer to say that he was an empiricist who had to overcome the ways in which cultural assumptions could distort perception and interpretation. Of such distortion there was abundant evidence, from racial and cultural prejudice and in particular from failure to see that unwritten languages and cultures could have patterns of their own. (See Stocking 1968:59; 1974c:58–59)

Second, the laws that Boas thought it possible to find were, in important part, laws of the human mind, common to all yet accessible only through the diverse outcomes of specific cultural and linguistic histories. Such laws would not simply present themselves but would require informed comparison and sifting of many such outcomes.

In effect, three kinds of "laws," or generalizations, were involved. One kind was not far to seek: the respects in which human beings, as such, were creatures with certain common potentialities in regard to language and culture. Negative critique of evolutionary and racial theories had this positive result from early on in Boas's work.

A second kind of "law" would predict the course and development of an individual case. It may be worth clarifying what Boas actually said on this point, since Krupat has drawn attention to his 1932 presidential address to the American Association for the Advancement of Science, and in an otherwise valuable book, Jonaitis claims that Krupat says that "Boas explicitly asserts that laws governing culture cannot be found" (1995:35). But Krupat does not so assert. In his original article (1988:113), Krupat presents Boas's statement that "[t]he phenomena of our science are so individualized, so exposed to outer accident that no set of laws could explain them" (Boas 1940: 257) as the last of a series of partial quotations, intended to show pervasive skepticism. In the later version of Krupat's book, it is again the last of a long series of such phrases, a series he is careful to precede with the caution "without, to be sure, providing sufficient context to understand each of his remarks in itself" (1992:98). And he follows the list with the remark: "For all that aporia and antiphrasis structure Boas's text, still, the doubts and negations may yet imply some positive recommendations." For Krupat, the point is that throughout the text one finds "irony's ability to doubt and deny; the question for science is whether the doubt and denial are, once again, in the interest of alternative affirmations or whether they go so far as to deny affirmative statements of any kind" (1992:97).

Missing from all this is a sentence Boas puts after the one quoted to the effect that the situation of anthropology is in principle that of science as a whole. "It is as in any other science dealing with the actual world surrounding us. For each individual case we can arrive at an understanding of its determination by inner and outer forces, but we cannot explain its individuality in the form of laws" (1940:257). Boas cites astronomy and biology with respect to the present location of stars and the forms of individual species. On the next page he sums up his position, not denying possible general laws in anthropology, but saying that "general laws . . . , on account of the complexity of the material will be necessarily vague and, we might almost say, so self-evident that they are of little help to a real understanding" (1940:258). A multitude of affirmative statements as to determination by inner and outer forces are possible; but not "generalized conclusions . . . that will be applicable everywhere and that will reduce the data of anthropology to a formula which may be applied to every case, explaining its past and predicting its future" (257). Even so, Boas concludes his address with a universalizing goal: "It is our task to discover among all the varieties of human behavior those that are common to all humanity. By a study of the universality and variety of cultures anthropology may help us to shape the future course of mankind" (259).

This third kind of positive finding seems always to have been in Boas's mind with regard to language. At the time he wrote, generalizations valid for all languages and cultures in terms of how they became what they are were far to seek. It is fair to say that they are closer now. Shortly after Boas's death, indeed, a renewed concern for universals (in the sense of universal implications in the relations among features) was initiated by Joseph Greenberg while at Boas's institution, Columbia University. The concern for universals has been influential and, together with much other work in language typology, is directly in keeping with what Boas would have considered desirable (cf. Greenberg 1954, 1963, 1978). A generation and more of renewed work by many scholars can be said to have done much to carry forward what Boas (and his student Sapir) began. Indeed, although much work in generative grammar and cognitive linguistics sets cultural considerations aside, the methodological principle of seeking in language what could not be culturally motivated can be said to be Boasian. Boas more than once said that language was basic to the discovery of such laws, because, being out of awareness, it was not subject to secondary manipulation (e.g., 1911:63).

Work in "ethnopoetics" can be seen in this light as well. It can particularly be said to honor and justify the argument Boas made to Holmes in the letter of 1905, when he wrote: "As we require a new point of view, so future times will require new points of view, and for them the texts, and ample texts, must be available" (1974:123).

Boas's own Kathlamet texts, such as "Swan's Myth," "Salmon's Myth," and "Sun's Myth," all written down over a century ago, are examples. (See Hymes 1985a, 1994b.) They disclose organization that links particulars and general principles. They are part of the evidence for possibilities of form, which, if not innate, still are likely to prove universal (Hymes 1991d). They link such possibilities with ways of shaping specific to cultures, with resources that serve individual expression. As with universals of language, so with narrative form: materials preserved by the Boasian tradition and the ethos of its work connect the general and the particular. These discoveries are consistent with Boas's belief in the universality of "the craving to produce things that are felt as satisfying through their form and . . . the capability of man to enjoy them" (1927:9). That the implicit form is felt but often out of awareness may be part of its contribution to a sense of what is said as inherently warranted (see Urban 1996:183–86, 204). Ultimately there is no irony, only the fact that more than one lifetime is required.

IRONY IN TIME PERSPECTIVE (2)

One can wonder still further as to what may have conditioned the timing of a recognition of ethnopoetic form. I suspect that Boas himself was reasonably satisfied to assert that rhythmic repetition is fundamental in narrative art. He had found it in visual art and believed it to be present in all art. About the time he wrote "Stylistic Aspects of Primitive Literature," his classic book, *Primitive Art* (1927), asserted symmetry, rhythmic repetition, and form as foundations of aesthetic activity (cf. Jonaitis 1995:23, 28, 301, 304) and included similar pages on verbal art (chap. 7, "Primitive Literature, Music, and Dance," 299–340) Certainly Boas saw esthetic form as potentially universal in human life: "The very existence of song, dance, painting and sculpture among all the tribes known to us is proof of the craving to produce things that are felt as satisfying through their form, and of the capability of man to enjoy them. All human activities may assume forms that give them esthetic values" (1927:9). One can imagine what he concluded about mastery of the means of decorative art being extended to mastery of words: "From this we conclude that a fundamental, esthetic formal interest is essential; and also that art, in its simple forms, is not necessarily expressive of purposive action, but is rather based upon our reactions to forms that develop through mastery of technique" (1927:62).

Still, such extension did not happen. There is no study of narrative by Boas that pursues these properties with thoroughness, perhaps because for Boas the key trait of rhythm was close to music; when it came to narrative, rhythm was not considered an aspect of linguistics. In his 1925 essay "Stylistic Aspects of Primitive Literature," he remarks: "It is not easy to form a correct opinion regarding the rhythmic character of the formal prose; in part because the rhythmic sense of primitive people is much more highly developed than our own. The simplification of the rhythm of modern folk song, and of the poetry intended to appeal to popular taste, has dulled our feeling for rhythmic form" (1940:492). Recall the statement quoted earlier about form apart from music: "Poetry without music, that is to say forms of literary expressions of fixed rhythmic form, are found only in civilized communities, except perhaps in chanted formulas. In simpler cultural forms the music of language alone does not seem to be felt as an artistic expression, while fixed rhythms that are sung occur everywhere" (1927:301). Presumably "in civilized communities" alludes to explicitly written and taught forms, such as sonnets, sestinas, and the like. The irony here is that what was not yet recognized in preliterate communities was equally unrecognized in literate communities. The kind of organization of oral narrative considered here is present all around us and is commonly as invisible. (See the last two chapters of Hymes 1996b on narratives from New York and Philadelphia.)

Some of Boas's students certainly carried on his concern with style in the sense of characterizing in close detail the various aspects of a narrative tradition (see Reichard 1930, 1947; and Jacobs 1958, 1960, 1972). Correspondence with students and others may illuminate this continuity.

To my knowledge, none of their work suggests analyzing a text throughout for formal relations. None suggests that relationships of form might run throughout a text. None suggests that recurrent elements may stand in relations to one another that indicate points of equivalence in organization (see Jakobson 1960:358).

Recurrence and equivalence are at the heart of the kind of work in question and illustrated here. Perhaps there is a fundamental practical difference between recognizing rhythmic repetition in visual art and in oral narrative. The object of art—a box, a basket, a blanket—shows its formal repetition. One can walk around it to confirm one's sense of that. A narrative text, written in a notebook, framed by the pages of the notebook, begins and ends and proceeds in terms of an arbitrary external frame. Turns at talk, recurrent particles, expressions of change of time or location do not stand out against the rest of which they are a part. When such a text is typed and printed, it is paragraphed, but not on an analytic principle, and little else about it is presented so as to disclose recurrent relationships. Some persons may have an eye and a visual imagination able to reconstruct such a text in their minds. Most of us need to put it on a page and indeed experiment with ways of showing what recurs and succeeds.

I am not aware that any in the Boasian tradition experimented with modes of presentation alternative to paragraphs of prose. That may be a key to why there was a delay in being as "analytic" about narrative as about grammar. I can only suggest some enabling circumstances that may have helped a recognition of narrative as poetry defined by relations of equivalence, in keeping with Jakobson's generalization, make sense and take root in some Americanist work—circumstances not present for Boas and perhaps not for those who followed him.

(a) During the 1920s and 1930s and certainly after the Second World War, the notion of poetic form changed for many. Contemporary poetry experimented with a wide variety of kinds of line and relations among lines. Lines with internal metrics (as with lines in songs) were far from the only kinds. The boundary between prose and poetry became less definite. (Early in the century, contemporary poetics affected the translation of Native American song texts, but not, so far as I know, of texts considered to be prose.)

(b) The dominance after the Second World War of the New Criticism encouraged intense examination of poems and other works of literature for internal structure.

(c) In the same period, a thoroughgoing distributional perspective became familiar to American linguists, and approaches to the formal study of discourse emerged.

By 1960, then, when Jakobson's essay was published, it would not seem strange to consider as poetry lines that were not metrical but were connected to one another externally. It would not seem strange to trace the distribution of a grammatical element, say, a particle, and to suspect its recurrence of having an organizing function.

These are suggestions. In any case, looking back, one can see that the notion of grammatical process as "composition in definite order" (Boas 1911: 27) could have been extended to the relations of phonetic groups such as "lines" or "verses" (intonation contours) or their syntactic equivalent. An example would be the "Chinookan triplet" illustrated in "The Deserted Boy" and the relations of succession that emerge in Native American narratives, understood as sequences of lines.

As said, one could *imagine* the notion of grammatical categories as ideas expressed by processes extended to recurrent constituents of narratives. A number of them have been noticed by those writing about "style" (e.g., Jacobs 1972) as kinds of content, but not always as significant for organization. Change of location, change of time, change of participant, for example, are regularly indications of change at a formal level, such as change of scene.

No Boasian, so far as I know, analyzed a narrative throughout as a sequence of such units from introduction through scenes and turns at talk to, say, concluding pronouncement or remonstrance. Ends and beginnings received attention, but not much of what came between.

It is particularly striking that turns at talk were not set out as units. Even Jacobs, who considered Clackamas narratives dramas, did not see the turns at talk of the characters separately. Perhaps there was unwillingness to adapt a mode of presentation from our culture (separation of turns in printed plays). Yet one needs to *see* such things in order to recognize and think about their relations to one another. Often enough, ritual acts were obscured by failure to set them out as such and by failure to translate the same words the same way. Identity of words is often an essential part of larger organization (e.g., initial particles).

I cannot avoid the thought that, above all, an inherited sense of what poetry must be, over against prose, persisted, even though people might not have the same sense. Poetry had quotable lines, prose had sensible paragraphs. If this is true, then it is a deep irony indeed.

In any case, we do have what has been preserved, and because it was preserved, much of its internal form as narrative and as grammar can still be discovered. Transcending the irony requires that collections be redone. The original manuscripts and notebooks must be used if possible. (See the discussion of changes introduced by Sapir into the printed text of Louis Simpson's "The Deserted Boy" in Hymes 1981b, chap. 4, and that and other points in Hymes 1994a; and the indications of intention in unpublished details of Boas's Kathlamet notebooks for two versions of "Salmon's Myth" [Hymes 1985a].)

New editions, concerned with presentation as well as preservation, are one way in which scholarship can fulfill the tradition's ideal of taking Native American languages as seriously as texts in European languages are taken.

Boas was right in putting first the need to preserve texts for the future, texts that the future would not be able to obtain. We are now able to recover and repatriate them, as it were, in more adequate form. Thanks to preservation, we can explore presentation and help to realize a conception of the Americanist Tradition as governed by the demands of its materials (see Hymes 1976a). In the long term, we are able to adapt Boas's well-known statement about the grammars of the languages: "[T]he psychological groupings which are given depend entirely upon the inner form of each" (1911:81) substituting "narrative" for "language" at the end. We can do work of which it can be said that the narrative "has been treated as though an intelligent Indian was going to develop the forms of his own thoughts by an analysis of his own form of speech" (81).

3

Use All There Is to Use

My title is from Kenneth Burke.[1] I cannot now recall when I first learned it
from him—perhaps as long ago as the summer I met him, a student in his
class at the School of Letters at Indiana University in 1952. If there is a motto
that sums up and informs my work, it is this. To use Burke's pregnant vocabulary, it serves as a strategic, stylized answer to situations in which I have
found myself.[2] It names an attitude toward what counts as anthropology
(as against "that's not anthropology"); toward what counts as linguistics (as
against "that's not linguistics"); toward the scope of competence in the use
of language (as against "that's just performance"); toward administering a
school of education; toward ethnopoetics.[3]

Let me use this saying now as the title for an apologia. When even those
whose work one admires publish portraits one doesn't recognize, an attempt
at clarification may be justified. What follows, then, is part response to what
others have said, part a general view of work ahead.

I

Someone who studies narratives ought not to object when others construct
one that gives him a prominent role. Still, as a historian, I would like to re-
sign from the role of "Hymes" in the drama "Hymes versus Tedlock." To be
sure, there are differences in what we do and prefer to do. It might be a fair
summary to say that Dennis is concerned most of all with the moment of
performance, and I am much concerned with the competence that informs
it. Dennis trusts most of all the speaking voice, I evidence of recurrent pattern. That means I run the risk of finding pattern that isn't there (but I have
Virginia Hymes [e.g., 1987] to keep pointing that out). Dennis runs the risk
of missing pattern that is there.

What is not so is that there is a fundamental difference between us with
regard to the importance of the oral life of narrative. Dennis regarded his
Tulane dissertation (1968) on Zuni narrative as the first dissertation in the

ethnography of speaking, an enterprise I had launched, and correctly so. Both of us contributed to an issue of *New Literary History* with titles that stress oral performance (Hymes 1977, Tedlock 1977).

What is particularly not so is the equation Tedlock : Hymes = pause : particle. Dennis has sometimes attended to particles as relevant, and I have never attended to particles alone. The point of method is not to look for any single feature, but to look for what counts in the text and tradition. In the article just mentioned, I put it this way (1981b [1977]:318). "Verses are recognized, not by counting parts, but by recognizing repetition within a frame, the relation of putative units to each other within a whole. Covariation between form and meaning, between units and a recurrent Chinookan pattern of narrative organization, is the key." With regard to features that count, the principle is that which Roman Jakobson (1960) called equivalence. With regard to patterns of narrative organization, the principle is that which Kenneth Burke called "arousal and satisfying of expectation" (1925, 1941 [fifth paragraph of the foreword]). Lines, equivalence, arcs of expectation: these are the three keys (see Hymes 1987a:49–51).

What counts as equivalence is always to be determined. When Ralph Maud thrust a set of Bella Coola texts into my hand at the Vancouver airport some years ago, a little before I was to talk to his class at Simon Fraser, what counts turned out to be a non-final quotative suffix (Hymes 1983a). In the Koasati texts analyzed by Geoffrey Kimball, a small set of initial particles, turns at talk, and a word-final quotative string figure prominently (see Kimball 1989). When I turned from the Wishram Chinook texts of Louis Simpson to the Clackamas Chinook texts of Victoria Howard, Simpson's explicit pairs of initial particles were seldom to be found. The two varieties of Kiksht (the Native name for the language) are closely related; the two narrative styles seemed not to be. I was forced to discover something beyond overt signals. In Chinookan that something is a small set of alternative relations.

Not that there are no overt markers at all in Howard's stories. As put in 1977 (1981b:319): "Mrs. Howard often makes use of 'Now,' 'Soon now,' and other such elements, but often does not. To determine the organization of her narratives, one has to recognize and abstract features that co-occur with the use of initial particle pairs in the narratives of Louis Simpson. Especially salient and important are statements of change in what Kenneth Burke calls the 'scene-agent ratio'—indications of change of scene in either location or lapse of time, and indication of change among participants in the action."[4] The long myth that is the subject of the final chapter of *In Vain I Tried to Tell You,* "Grizzly Woman Deceives and Kills Women" (Hymes 1981b), shows the preponderant importance of these considerations. Reading it, one would see at once the recurrent marking of units by time expressions ("In spring," "In the morning," "It became evening," "At daybreak," "Now it was day") and the dramatic organization of scenes in terms of turns at talk.

If one organizes Howard's stories in the order of their dictation (Jacobs's notes identify the sequence of notebooks), her way of using initial particles turns out to have evolved in the course of her two seasons of work with Jacobs. What proves basic in her narratives is not any one kind of marker of units, but a set of rhetorical relations. It is a set shared with the other Chinookan narrators known to us, a way of accomplishing what Burke has called the fundamental principle of style, the arousal and satisfying of expectation. I have discussed the Chinookan pattern at length in other places (see chaps. 2, 6, 7). Suffice it to say that it offers narrators certain options for grouping sequences of incident, event, and image. The normal options are sequences of three or five. (Often enough a sequence of five is an interlocking double sequence of three, the third unit being a pivot, completing a first series and initiating a second.) My work with Howard's narratives has depended upon recognizing a variety of kinds of equivalent features in the identification of verses and recognizing the recurrence of rhetorical relations. These rhetorical relations pervade the narratives; they relate verses, stanzas, scenes, acts.

Particles, then, are not the alpha and omega of my work. Historically, they were the alpha, but no more than that, not even the beta.

II

There remains the general question: how should texts be put on the page? We have escaped a phase in which oral narratives were put on the page in paragraphs, because narratives were assumed to be prose. It is generally recognized that putting a narrative on the page implies an assumption as to its form, and that form involves lines. But in what way? And with what else?

A fundamental issue is the extent to which a presentation can combine different kinds of information. The issue arises in several ways. Let me consider first the relation between the kind of information focused on by Tedlock and others (e.g., Facey 1988), on the one hand, and the kind focused on by myself and others, on the other hand.

(1) A narrative involves pace shaped by pause and intonation and pace shaped by rhetorical proportion and point. There is the speed or slowness, the length or brevity of lines, their clustering or separation. There is speed or slowness of progression through a formal part, the length or brevity of verses, stanzas, scenes, their interconnection.

Can both be presented on the same page? Where the two dimensions coincide, as Bright has found them to do in Karok (1984:93–94) and as Virginia Hymes has found consistently in English, or complement each other, as Kroskrity (1985) has found them to do in Arizona Tewa, or intersect, as Sherzer (1982) has found in San Blas Cuna, there is, of course, little problem.[5] Where the two do not coincide, as appears to be the case in the Zuni text we have from Tedlock (and also in Hopi and Nguna), the two kinds of account may appear quite different on the page.[6] If one experiments with presenting both kinds of information, however, the degree of difference seems to depend on the starting point: lines shown in terms of pauses, or lines shown in terms of rhetorical patterns.

I have examined the one Zuni text published by Tedlock, "Coyote and Junco" (1978), and the Nguna (New Hebrides) story of "The Heron" (Facey 1988:250–53).[7] One comparison has been to put the texts on the page so as to show verses and rhetorical patterns, while introducing brackets to indicate the scope of the lines with which they were first published. The brackets permit recovery of the information as to what is part of such a line, but not an easy inspection of those relations (and possible insight from seeing them).

If one starts from the other side and introduces information as to verses into a presentation in terms of pause, my own impression is that this second experiment works better than the first with the Nguna "The Heron." The Nguna lines are usually short, and one can usually display relations of verse, scene, and stanza at the right. In two instances, a verse begins in the middle of a line so defined (8, 15).

When the two experiments are tried with the Zuni "Coyote and Junco," again the first result does not seem very effective. The lines as defined by Tedlock are too variable to be easily perceived as performance within the showing of underlying relations. Information as to rhetorical relationships is more intelligible, again, as with the Nguna text, with occasional exceptions in which a verse or stanza begins in the middle of a pause-defined line (20, 75, 81). Still, the lines defined by rhetorical relations are not easily perceived or taken into the mind for comparison.

Two texts, two narrators, two languages, accidentally chosen, are, of course, not adequate for a general conclusion. And others may form different impressions from the same presentation. On this showing, however, it seems to me that in those cases, perhaps exceptional, when the two kinds of information differ notably, then the foregrounding of one does allow one to document the other, but for interpretation it is best to provide each separately. If one mode of presentation must be chosen, it may be easier to show rhetorical relations within a presentation in terms of vocal lines than conversely.

These questions of mode of presentation arise because ethnopoetics involves not only translation but also transformation, transformation of modality, the presentation of something heard as something seen. The eye is an instrument of understanding. Still, questions of translation itself arise as well. When the purpose of presenting a text is to convey its rhetorical relationships, one translates in the service of that aim. Insofar as possible, signals that are the same in the original are kept the same in the translation. In "Coyote and Junco," for example, *Taachi* is always 'meanwhile' (as indicated in Hymes 1982), *Taas* always 'again' in my verse translation. When Sapir published Louis Simpson's Wishram Chinook myths, *Aga kwapt* was variously translated, according to context and taste, from "Now" and "Then" to "And" and nothing. In the verse translation it is always "Now then." That is a little awkward in English, but one asks the reader to come to take it for granted.

This, indeed, is a hallmark of the understanding of narrative structure that has emerged in the last two decades. When taken as ingredients of prose, such elements did not seem to matter. One would translate them ad hoc, certainly not always the same, and might often leave them out. If all that is of concern is what the story is about, and if one believes that what it is about is not affected by an original structure, of course, that is all right. Even if one knows that the point of the story depends in part on its shape, and on the marking of that shape, one may want to convey it in English that is idiomatically effective. Still, the translation may be a reader's only access to the original lines and relationships. If so, adaptation to the target language may conceal the otherness of the text and some of its interest. There is no single answer to the question, how much to adapt, how much to preserve, but some degree of teaching is often necessary. One must often ask the reader to learn.

(2) The question of "what else" arises because we must teach as well as show. Local hearers of a narrative usually share with the teller the idiom employed, along with knowledge of conventions of form and expression, of references and allusions, of a taken-for-granted world.[8] Readers generally do not and generally lack access to other sources of information. What they see, together with whatever else may be found in the publication, is what they get.

The kinds of information that may be helpful are diverse. Because much of ethnopoetics involves other languages and other cultures, information about those languages and cultures obviously has a part. Such information may be relevant as well for narratives from parts of the vast network of English use not one's own.

Many linguists incorporate linguistic information within a translation. At least one pioneer of ethnopoetics has incorporated contextual information. Let me consider each in turn.

(a) A way of presenting texts quite popular with linguists working on American Indian languages is interlinear translation. (Part of the popularity may have to do with the availability of a useful computer program.) Each phrase or sentence of a text is represented three times, as a triplet of lines—one the original language, one a morpheme-by-morpheme analysis with grammatical information, one a full translation. Here is an example from a Klamath text collected by Theodore Stern, as edited by Noel Rude.[9]

1 coy hok lmelamlis   cii-ya
   and the thunderbird   SG.live-IND
   And the thunderbird lived.

2 coy hok lmen-damn-a
   and the thunder-HAB-IND
   And he thundered all the time.

3 coy hok w'a-k'a   ho-n-k   domn-a   lmelamlis-as
   and the coyote-DIM   the-OBJ-   hearken-IND   thunderbird-OBJ
   And Little Coyote hearkened to the thunderbird.

4 coy w'a-k'a   g-en-a   hadakt-dal
   and coyote-DIM   go-TRL-IND   there-ALL
   And Little Coyote went there,

5 coy ho-n-k   sle-pga-pg-a   lmelamlis-as
   and the-OBJ-   see-DUR-DUR-IND   thunderbird-OBJ
   and watched the thunderbird.

6 coy hok lmelamlis   b-awal-lG-a
   and the thunderbird   throw.PL-upon-down-IND
        mna lolp blay-dal
        his eye up high-ALL
   And the thunderbird threw his eyes up toward the sky,

7 na?as   t'ikt'ik t t t hrrrrrr
   thus
   [saying] thus, "T'ikt'ik t t t hrrrrrr

8 coy hok lolp he-tGi-bli
   and the eye PL.fall-down-back
   And the eyes fell back down,

9 he-wy'aq-bli   lolb-at   lmelamlis
   PL.fall-into a container-back   eye-LOC   thunderbird
   fell into the eye sockets, thunderbird.

Such a presentation is helpful in making sure of the linguistic underpinnings of translation and interpretation. It is less helpful in detecting narrative form. It dictates pauses on the part of the reader, but for information or to pick out the line that continues the story. Picking out, it is hard to sustain a sense of rhetorical form, of the arousal and satisfying of expectation. And insofar as an inquiring eye must take the place of a cultural ear, there is not enough on a page. The passage just given runs over one manuscript page onto another, yet is just three pairs of verses. Here they are, the pairs identified by a closing brace at the end of each:

And the Thunderbird lives.
And he thunders all the time.}
And Little Coyote hearkens to the Thunderbird.
And Little Coyote goes there,
    and watches the Thunderbird.}
And the Thunderbird throws his eyes up toward the sky,
    (speaking) this way: "T'ikt'ik t t t hrrrrrr."
And the eyes fall back down,
    fall into Thunderbird's eye sockets.}

However useful the interlinear program and presentation for linguistic analysis, concordances, and documented lexicons, a separate presentation is needed to show rhetorical form.

(b) We tend to forget that the usual way of writing languages on the page is one that implies, or, one might say, conceals, linguistic information. It is phonological, or phonemic, in the sense that it abstracts from spoken qualities and represents words as part of a grammar. One who knows the grammar, one who knows the language, may be able to infer the spoken qualities from the abstract representation. Many may not be able to do so, and any reader who is not a user of the language may forget the spoken qualities.

We are concerned to convey the voice of performance in various ways, by indicating loudness, quietness, raspiness, and the like. It is in keeping with such concern to convey the words in a phonetic, rather than phonological, way as well. To do so is to reverse (for the purpose at hand) the accomplishment central to the rise of linguistics, phonemic analysis. But it is easier to

infer phonemic status from phonetic symbols than the reverse and, insofar as the quality of performance and its effects involve actual sounds, not
structural abstractions, desirable.

Here is an example (translation first) from Louis Simpson's "Coyote and
Deer" (see Hymes 1984a). As the myth ends, Coyote's wife reproaches him.

Then the woman told him:
"You are bad, Coyote.
"I for my part am not Deer.
"Look at the Deer;
"Everyone will swallow *his* meat   60
"I do not have good meat.
"Likewise you, Coyote, are different;
"You are a poor thing, Coyote.
"No one would swallow your meat.
"This is what people will say: 65
    " 'Dead things are Coyote's food.' "

A phonemic representation would be:

Kwapt gagiulxam agagilak:
"Imik'amla Isk'ulya.
"Našqi náit'a Ič'ánk.
"Yaxtau sik'lutk Ič'ánk;
"Kánawi šan luq ałgiuxwa iágiwaq.
"Našqi naika it'ukti Ičgiwaq.
"Daukwa maika Isk'ulya mxlúidat,
"Mguałilx Isk'ulya.
"Naqi pu šan luq ałgiuxwa imigiwaq.
"Qidau alugwagima idlxam,
    "Iłmimlušt iałxlm Isk'ulya."

Stress is marked only where it is an exception to the prevailing rule that stress
occurs on the next-to-last syllable. Length of vowel is not phonemic and is
not shown. The final [a] or [i] of a word is often elided before a word beginning with a vowel, especially [a] before initial [i], but all words are shown in
full. The back stops, palatal [k] and velar [q] are pronounced with an audible
fricative release [x], [x̣], respectively. When [l] and [m] follow a consonant,
a vocalic transition usually precedes them, written by Sapir (who recorded
the text) with schwa [ə], but that is not phonemic and thus not shown. Phonemic /a/ is sometimes heard as schwa. The language has two high vowels,
phonologically /i u/. When these vowels occur next to a velar consonant (q,
x̣), their quality is that of a midvowel (e, o). Next to a velar consonant, the

quality of [a] is commonly somewhat further back and higher [ɔ]. All these features are regular and not shown. Here is the text, then, with phonetic detail:

Kx̣wɔ́pt gagiúlxam agagílak:
   "Imik'ámǝl(a) isk'úlǝyǝ.
   "Ná·šqx̣i náit'(a) ič'ánk.
   "Yáx̣tau sík'ǝlutk ič'ánk;
   "Ká·nauwe· šan lúqx̣ ałgiux̣wa iágewɔq.
   "Ná·šqx̣i náik(a) it'ukt(i) Ičgéwɔq.
   "Dáukwa máik(a) isk'úlǝyǝ mx̣lúidǝt,
   "Mgoáłix isk'úlya.
   "Ná·qx̣i pu šan lúqx̣ ałgiúx̣w(a) imigéwɔq.
   "Qé·dau alugwagím(a) idǝ́lxam,
     "'Iłmé·mǝlušt iáłxlǝm isk'úlǝyǝ."

Much of this one could predict. Some of it is not regular and so not recoverable from a phonological presentation: the schwa in "Coyote" (5, 7, 11) and the last syllable of line 7, the [o] in the first word of line 8. The elision of vowels is expectable in a fluent style of speech but could have been otherwise.

Vowel length on the first syllables to lines 3, 5, 6, 9, and 10 is expressive. Notice the words it emphasizes: "Not," "all (every)," "not," "not," and "thus." The stress on the third syllable from the end of the last word in line 5 ('his-meat'), rather than the second from the end, is contrastive. Expressive length and stress can be shown in a phonological representation, as illustrated in the last example ('*his* meat'). Still, a phonetic presentation seems desirable, in that expressive features are inherently shown, along with other details that could not be inferred. One has the phonetic texture as a whole.

(c) Melville Jacobs preserved much of what can be known about several narrative traditions of Oregon and Washington (Northern Sahaptin, Miluk Coos, Santiam Kalapuya, Clackamas Chinook) and pioneered in conceiving of such narrative as dramatic performance. In presenting the Clackamas Chinook narratives of Victoria Howard, he sought to make clear the meanings by incorporating contextual detail. Footnotes served for information about the recording of the text, linguistic comments, comments on and from Howard, interpretive remarks, and so on. Some explanation of what was being said and done or referred to also appears in the footnotes, but much information of this kind appears in parentheses within the translation. For the myth of "Tongue" (Jacobs 1959a:369–75), one footnote comments on the recording of the story; the other recounts the opening (635 nn.314, 315). All other information is supplied in parentheses. Here are the opening scenes (Jacobs 1959a:369-70). (The numbers are those provided by Jacobs to link portions of translation and text to each other.)

> 1. Those persons who lived at their village right here (a little above Willamette Falls at Oregon City) were always playing. Now their wealthy headwoman died, and they put her away, they hung her up (on branches of a tree, inside a canoe with small holes punched in it). Then when it became nighttime now they saw something just like fire. It came out (from an island in the river) high up in that direction on one side from the river. At that place then they placed two of them (two Fish persons), they remained there, from both sides they watched that (fire-like) thing as it came there. 2. Their name was   Fish (a fish with some kind of sharp cutting edge) from the river.

Explanatory information is at hand as one goes along, but the rhythm of going along is not that of the story, even taking the story as prose. With a presentation in lines, one can key needed information to the pertinent point in the story in a separate set of notes. Victoria Howard's narratives, the fullest body of Chinookan narrative we have, have long been out of print. I hope eventually to be able to republish them, presenting them in lines, but without losing useful information provided by Jacobs. There seem to be two kinds of information. Some appears to reflect a sense on Jacobs's part of a need to help the reader make connections, as in "they watched that (fire-like) thing." Some, such as "a fish with some kind of sharp cutting edge" is from the notebooks, obtained from Howard. The first such item "a little above Willamette Falls at Oregon City" is telling for interpretation. The opening words and the supplementary remark identify the people of the story as predecessors of the Clackamas in their own place, as perhaps then representatives of the fate of the historic Clackamas. The opening words indeed have special force and an alliterative ring in Clackamas: dáyčka dába nux̱ílayt idálxam 'Those-people here they-lived, their-community'. Not the common 'they lived there' or 'they lived at X', but 'here'. (See the use of the opening scene as illustration of rhythm in the next section, under "Partial Parallelism within Pairs.")

In sum, both three-line interlinear translation and Jacobs's parentheses provide information that is useful. Neither could readily accommodate the information of the other, just as a translation shaped on the page by rhetorical form, by composition, may not be able to offer the eye and mind the sense of a translation shaped by pause and intonation, by overt performance, and conversely.

There is a way to show the composition of a narrative compactly, separate from the presentation of the narrative itself. One can show the relations, the verses, stanzas, scenes, and acts, their sequence and hierarchy in relation to one another and their lines. I myself have often wanted to present a story with little or no apparatus, so that the reader can experience it for its own sake and can perhaps detect relations independently of what I had found, relations perhaps that I had missed. To some extent, then, a profile might be an adequate complement to a story presented with no marking of relations other than those of lines. (For an example, see the profile of "Coyote and Eagle's Daughter" at the end of this essay.)

When one is interpreting a story, such a profile works well as a test of completeness and consistency. Missing lines, skewed relations become evident. One can see pattern or lack of it.[10] Providing the information is, of course, not the same as experiencing the unfolding of the story in terms of it. It may be hard to merge the two mentally. One may still want to see the story itself with relations explicitly marked.

One more important question remains regarding how to put a story on the page. Passages that are alike in general pattern may yet differ in internal rhythm, and one can find visual equivalents for such differences. This question can be addressed best toward the end of the next section. Let me end this section with a short peroration.

One often reaches a point at which more than one presentation of a story may be desirable, if not essential. Of course, it is difficult to publish such narratives at all, let alone in more than one form. The justification of our work is to make the narratives accessible, interpretable by others, and to make clear what we ourselves have done. Ours is the laying of foundations, and we should make them as secure as we can. Ultimately, others will be free to experiment, to recreate, to respond as the spirit may move them to what they can grasp of the often astonishing and moving oral literatures of other peoples. But much of the time an oral literature is not able to defend itself. The world's literatures are not on equal footing. If someone takes liberties with a poem by Verlaine, others need not depend on that willful version. Someone who cares can likely find the original, find even a bilingual edition. Someone who does not know French can likely learn it or pick up a dictionary and grammar to help make out what goes on. That is possible for several modern languages and for the languages our civilization has accepted as classical. A novice can find resources with which to compare and interpret translations of the Hebrew Bible and the New Testament. There are handbooks and dictionaries with information about places and persons and customs. There are diverse translations, interlinear translations, even guides to the assessment of the original manuscripts. It is not so for most languages with which ethnopoetics is concerned. Here the dialectic between original and adaptation is acute. The original text is normative, yet one wants it to speak to places and people not its own. One wants to establish a connection between different languages and settings, without reducing either to the other. In ethnopoetics we must do almost everything ourselves and with little support. Still, regardless of the compromises in presentation that are required, the goal of full accessibility to original texts can be kept as a standard.

III

The years have seen a step-by-step recognition of the architecture oral narratives can have. There has been a progression from overt markers to implicit patterns and from cultural uniformity to individual diversity.

(a) Writing in the fall of 1957, I recognized that initial particles had a structural role in Wishram Chinook (Hymes 1958). Commenting on the presentation of my paper in a symposium at the American Anthropological Association meetings that fall, Melville Jacobs declared that it would be impossible to pursue such an approach. In 1971, however, I analyzed one of the myths that Louis Simpson had told in Wishram to Edward Sapir in such terms, "The News about Coyote" (Hymes 1975a). Analysis consisted simply of recognizing initial particle pairs as identifying segments of the text.

(b) In the course of a year's leave in Oregon in 1972–1973, thanks to the National Endowment for the Humanities, I convinced myself that there was more than the marking of segments. There was systematic relationship among segments, relationships of a kind involving the Chinookan pattern number (five). At the time, Virginia Hymes thought I must be making it up, if not mad, but close analysis of another of Louis Simpson's dictations to Sapir ("The Deserted Boy") showed consistent and telling patterning, not just in groups of verses, but at levels beyond that (Hymes 1976b). I would now revise the last portion of that analysis, but the difference would not change the general finding, that of pervasive patterning. "The Deserted Boy" remains the first full-scale demonstration.

(c) At this point, narrative patterning appeared to have a strict correlation with cultural patterning. It has long been known that cultures have preferred "sacred," "ceremonial," pattern numbers and that in a story with a series of siblings, say, or repeated actions, the number of siblings and actions will accord with such a number. The ethnopoetic discovery showed such accord to exist within the formal organization of narrative itself. Where the pattern number of the culture was five, narrative units would occur in series of five. Where the pattern number was four, narrative units would occur in series of four. But narrative proved subtler than a single pattern. In narrative the pattern number was found to have a correlate. Five would have three, and four would have two.

This double correlation has been sustained. Five- and three-part relations go together in all the Chinookan varieties (Wishram-Wasco, Clackamas, Kathlamet, Shoalwater-Clatsop); in the narrative traditions of several of their neighbors along the Columbia River (Nez Perce, Sahaptin, Chehalis and Cowlitz Salish) and in the Willamette Valley (Kalapuya); in some other Native American traditions (e.g., Coos, Klamath, Tlingit); in Xhosa of southern Africa; in Nguna of the Pacific; and in much English-language narrative. Two- and four-part relations go together in Coos of the Oregon coast, Takelma of the Rogue River Valley in Oregon, Karok and Hupa of the Klamath River Valley, Zuni, Tonkawa of Texas, and elsewhere.

(d) The double correlation points to more than a reflection of cultural pattern generally. It appears to point to something in the nature of human narrative ability. In Chinookan, as said, the cultural pattern number is five and known by members of the culture to be so. They are not particularly aware, however, of three-part patterning, although certain forms of it are so salient as to have led Henry Morrison to call one of them "the Chinookan triplet" (as in "Coyote went, he kept on going, he arrived"). In English, of course, three is a recognized pattern number, but not five. It was a surprise to Charlotte Ross, an Appalachian storyteller, to find that her *Märchen* and legends had five-part relations as well as three.

It seems, then, that if one starts, as it were, from either five or three, one will get the other too. It seems that such patterning in narrative always involves alternatives. One can imagine the mind of the narrator at work in performance, coordinating two kinds of sequence, one of incident, the other of rhetorical form (see Hymes 1981b:327). Alternatives allow for flexibility and increase expressive possibilities.

The world has seemed partitioned almost between three and five, on the one hand, two and four, on the other. Empirically, of course, it is rash to say so. Only a small portion of the world's traditions have been analyzed. Theoretically, however, one can imagine grounds for it being so. Suppose that part of the point of narrative is not to provide news, but satisfying form. Surely this must be so for myths and tales told many times, as it is for music listened to again. The interest is not so much in what will happen as in how it will happen. As C. S. Lewis put it: "The re-reader is looking not for actual surprises (which can come only once) but for a certain surprisingness. . . . In the only sense that matters the surprise works as well the twentieth time as the first. It is the *quality* of unexpectedness, not the *fact* that delights us" (1947:16; cf. also 1961). And as Kenneth Burke put it in a seminal essay:

> The methods of maintaining interest which are most natural to the psychol-
> ogy of information . . . are [the fact of] surprise and suspense. The method
> most natural to the psychology of form is eloquence. . . . The contemporary
> audience . . . is content to have facts placed before it in some more or less ade-
> quate sequence. Eloquence is the minimization of this interest in fact, *per se,*
> so that the "more or less adequate sequence" of their presentation must be
> relied on to a much greater extent. Thus, those elements of surprise and sus-
> pense are subtilized, carried down into the writing of a line or sentence, until
> in all its smallest details the work bristles with disclosures, contrasts, restate-
> ments with a difference, ellipses, images, aphorism, volume, sound-values,
> in short all that complex wealth of minutiae which in their line-for-line as-
> pect we call style and in their broader outlines we call form. (1968:37–38)

At any point, then, the teller and re-teller, the hearer and re-hearer of a myth
may assume that in its smallest details it will again and again complete an
arc of culturally satisfying form and, at the same time, may choose or find
that there is more than one way to realize such form. If there are to be relations of form at all, indeed, there must be something to relate—two elements at least or three. These are the minimal relations for narrative art. Four
can be two taken twice. Five can be three taken twice, when, as often in Chinookan and independently, it appears, in other traditions, the third element
of five counts as a pivot, facing two ways, completing an initial three-part
arc and initiating a second. And if it is to be possible to subtilize surprise and
suspense, and point and emphasis as well, work them into the line-by-line
achievement of style, one wants the recurring relations to be, as these are,
the smallest possible.

I am suggesting that such relations arise in response to a use to which narrative is put, that they are the result of selective adaptation of an aspect of
language. It is only fair to acknowledge that they might be innate. After all,
such relations begin to appear universal; they take just a few possible forms;
that they occur and take the forms they do is not explained by common
historical origin. That is the sort of thing Noam Chomsky, Jerry Fodor, and
others would expect of an aspect of language with an innate basis. A child
could be imagined as born with the kind of ability, or relation, in question,
settling upon a specific form in response to the linguistic input it encounters. Verse relations may be innate in that sense. Still, the argument for innateness is most convincing when the property in question does not seem
something that can be acquired through experience and when there is no
consistent, current functional reason for it to be what it is, when it appears
independent of use. Since it seems possible that children could extract verse
relations from experience of stories, that such relations could be explained
in terms of current use, innateness is less likely.

(e) It was clear early on that narrators need not confine themselves to expected patterns and markers. If one analyzes a text entirely in such terms, it may fight back. Just counting particles, say, of threes and fives or of twos and fours can make hash of a text. The principle of method, after all, is not simply one of counting, but one of discovering form/meaning covariation.

In Victoria Howard's "Tongue" (Jacobs 1959a:369–75), the scene in which the chief's son recreates the people ends with what would have to be two verses, one ungainly, if only initial particles were considered. Freed from the cramped confines of a prose paragraph, the lines clearly express the repetition three times of a ritual outcome: "[T]hey became people." It would be foolish of an analysis not to show that.

Then now, he transformed them:
    they became people.
Those feathers there,
    bones,
        they became people
            those other feathers were for canoes.
Now they became people.

John Rush Buffalo's Tonkawa telling of "Coyote and Eagle's Daughter" was an early instance (first published in Hymes 1980c, revised 1987c). I analyzed Tonkawa to honor a late teacher, Harry Hoijer, in a series dedicated to him at UCLA, the institution at which he had taught for so long and where I had studied with him. Rush Buffalo made use of a kind of double initial particle, the base 'e- followed by another element, to mark verses. The myth opens with clear four-part relations. The first two stanzas have a common pattern of four lines: Coyote goes, goes up (down), arrives at a point, perceives something (sees a camp, hears weeping). Each of the next stanzas has a two-part exchange between Coyote and a woman in the camp. He says he will fight the monster that has destroyed the people and sets off to prepare ritually. The next stanza is patterned in, not four, but six lines:

When it was evening,
    he went down to the river, and
cutting off a piece of hard wood,
    he burned it black, and
putting it away,
    he went to sleep, they say.

The succeeding stanzas of this part have four or two lines. I know no reason for the intervening six, but there they are.

In Victoria Howard's "Gitskux and His Older Brother" (Hymes 1983d), the story proceeds in sets of three and five, as one would expect. At one point ten lines stand by themselves. Any attempt to subdivide them would destroy their unity. They occur in the second part of the myth. The older brother (Panther) is the only free survivor of the destruction of his village. He comes to a house, then sees someone enter at the other end, bringing a deer and going out. Later he sees a woman enter, who washes and twists her hair into braids. She allows him to stay and at night causes fleas to bite him and bring him from the corner to her bed and beside her, joining five nights together. She becomes his wife. He does not know that she was the one bringing deer.

Now the two stayed.
  She told him,
    "Now you will be doing the hunting.
    "You will have thought,
      Perhaps there is some man."
    "Here I have lived alone,
    "I would be the one hunting."
  "Indeed,"
    he told her.
Now that is what the two did.

The shape is that of a chiasmus:

the two stayed
  she told him
    you hunting
      you
        some man
      I alone
    I hunting
  he told her
the two did.

The shape seems a beautiful expression of interchange within duality. The man will be the hunter, not by right, but by gift.

(f) Some years ago I realized that the two kinds of basic pattern were not mutually exclusive. Both could occur in the same text. One would be the normal, "unmarked" kind of relation. The other would enter as a "marked" pattern, intensifying the action.

John B. Hudson's Kalapuya account of "Coyote Releases Water Dammed Up by the Frogs" (Hymes 1987a:50–57; see chap. 14 of this volume) contains three scenes. In the first (five verses), Coyote prepares to deal with the Frogs, who charge people to drink; in the second (three verses), he trades them a money bead. In the third, he drinks. The third scene has eight verses, organized as three sets of two, followed by two others. The three pairs correlate the three steps of a pair of actions, the denouement in which Coyote, on the one hand, drinks as expected, and, on the other, with his hands surreptitiously destroys the dam. The next (fourth) verse describes the result with regard to this water; the last (fifth) verse is the result with regard to water everywhere.

Now then indeed he drank, Coyote.
   Now then he put one hand down in.
Now then he drank.
   Now then he put his hand down in the water where it
      was dammed up.
Now then he stopped drinking water.
   Now then he got up,
     he scooped the dirt aside,
      he scooped it out.
Now then the water went through.
Now then Coyote said,
   "All the time water will be everywhere."

In Charles Cultee's two tellings to Boas of the Kathlamet Salmon myth (Hymes 1985a; see chap. 6 of this volume), intensification by pairing is at the heart of the difference between them. Both tellings have two parts, in the first of which Salmon and his party come up river in the spring, are hailed five times from the shore in an insulting way, recognize an elder relative, and go ashore to give gifts and place the plant where it will be. All this is a striking acknowledgment of the importance in winter of a woman's domain of food by a figure symbolic of male pride and men's role as suppliers of the food that made the people well off relative to others lacking direct access to the Columbia. In the second part, Salmon and his party continue, encounter an odd trio coming down river, whose claims he rejects, twisting their necks and, in the second telling, telling them where they will be. In the second telling, Salmon regains the upper hand, for the myth ends with his telling Flounder to be in the river. It will no longer be entirely true what the insulting relatives had said, "Without me your people would have died," that the people had to rely on plants until salmon returned upriver in the spring. There will be food from Salmon's domain, fish, in the winter as well.

The second telling proceeds unhurriedly with three- and five-part patterning throughout. Only the second telling has the placing of the trio, Flounder, last. The first telling has only the twisting and the insistence that the trio are wrong in saying it took them only a day to come from The Dalles. In the first telling, Cultee was evidently in a hurry to get to the second part, but not in the second telling. In the last scene of the first part, he omitted one line, one step of the action, and went right on. In contrast, when he omitted a line of quoted speech in that scene in the second telling, he paused to add it (so the field notebook shows).

The unhurried, rhetorically unmarked second telling goes, I think, with Cultee having remembered the second phase of dealings with the trio in the second act and knowing that so far as the emblematic dignity of Salmon is concerned, male versus female domains, he has a flounder up his sleeve. In the first telling, the part about the flounder in the river had not been remembered, was not in store. Salmon's dignity is restored by dramatic assertion of control, intensification by pairing, as soon as the first act is over.

(g) The use of patterns may differ in another way as well, by gender. Elizabeth Jacobs (1990 [1959]:116 n.21) noted that "four is the pattern number of feminine contexts, five of masculine contexts, in Tillamook folklore."[11] As it turns out, the contrast is not only a matter of four women in a set or series, but of five men. It obtains in the formal organization of a story (Hymes 1990b). In Clara Pearson's fine telling of "Split-His-Own-Head" there are nine scenes. The first five have to do with the younger brother of the title taking literally what his sister had told him and making a fool of himself as a result. That there must be five times is shown in the fact that in this telling to Jacobs five is achieved by having the fifth duplicate the third, whereas in an earlier telling to May Mandelbaum Edel, five is again achieved by duplication, although not the same duplication. The last four have a different theme, getting a wife, and each is distinct. (The two patterns are further interwoven in that they alternate as between levels of organization. In either part of the story, whether scenes are five in number or four, the number of stanzas within scenes is four or two, while the number of verses within stanzas is five, three, or one.)

Such an association of a most general level of patterning with gender may occur in Tonkawa also, but reversed. Four goes with male, five with female, at least in John Rush Buffalo's "Coyote and Eagle's Daughter" (Hymes 1987c). The first major part, in which Coyote restores the people destroyed by a monster, has four main sections, themselves paired: Coyote promises to defeat the monster, Coyote prepares; Wolves (actually) defeat the monster,

Coyote restores the people. The one woman is a source of information, but the action is focused on male actors. The second major part has five main sections. Having been given a wife, Coyote leaves her to go gambling; she follows, a young man is intermediary, one commands the other, she leaves. The five-part pattern is repeated, the difference being that the second time it is the woman who commands Coyote, and when she leaves, she leaves for good. Here the focus is on the woman, and a contrast is carefully drawn between the two acts as to her behavior toward Coyote.[12]

(h) The preferred relations may differ among individuals within a community and from one telling to another by the same individual. I discovered this some summers ago when working through Bright's fine Karok texts as a way of keeping sane in the Mount Hood National Forest while learning to use a computer. One and the same myth, "Coyote's Journey," is told with three- and five-part patterning by one of the women with whom Bright worked, Julia Starrit, but with two- and four-part patterning by another. Conversely, the narrator, Nettie Reuben, who used pairing pervasively in telling "Coyote's Journey," uses three- and five-part grouping in telling "Coyote's Homecoming" and "Coyote Trades Songs" (see Hymes 1985c:47–53).

In sum, one or the other of these two widely occurring matrices of relationship may dominate a cultural tradition, but that dominance cannot be taken for granted of the next story one hears or sees. One may contrast with another within the same tradition—to foreground and intensify a point in the story, as appropriate with one gender rather than another, as a difference among persons or occasions for which we may not have an explanation. Some cases of unexpected use of a pattern may be attributable to acculturation, as when Timothy Montler (personal communication) reports that his principal source for Saanich Salish patterns stories in terms of two and four, but her son, influenced by English, shows three. Probably there are many cases of Indian people having learned stories, and patterning with them, from one of their elders from a different tradition. I suspect that the prevalence of pairing in Victoria Howard's early dictations to Melville Jacobs have such a source, as does what seems a reversion in the midst of her telling of a Clackamas counterpart to Cultee's Salmon myth to four verses within a stanza, seemingly just by not making the effort to add the pro forma fifth turn at talk that she occasionally supplies.[13] Acculturation or some other factor may explain the presence of three- and five-part patterning in several Tlingit texts, despite the pervasiveness of even-numbered patterning otherwise in the culture.[14]

IV

There are further differences, differences that can affect the way one puts a text on the page. Two passages may have the same formal patterning, the same number of elements, at a given level and yet display a difference in balance and a difference in rhythm. One may find oneself wanting to reflect a sense of this in the way one places the lines. I have done so often enough in publishing texts in articles and books and want here to be more explicit and systematic.

Here we are very much in the midst of the transformation of something heard into something seen. The differences may or may not have audible characteristics. Often the differences have to do with composition, with balance of content. A verse with four lines, for example, might be balanced 3 + 1, 1 + 3, 2 + 2, or as a straight run of 4.

There is an example of the first possibility in the Tonkawa "Coyote and Eagle's Daughter." The sequence in which Coyote revives the people proceeds steadily in terms of stanzas each having a pair of verses. The verses, however, differ. The first has three lines, quite like a Chinookan triad. The second, describing the outcome (futile in each case until the fourth and last), has one. Possibilities of three-part patterning seem exploited here for a comic anticlimax. Here are the last two stanzas:

Then again he went off, and,   (D)
      coming at a run,
         "Hurry! This camp is on fire!" they say he said.
Then, they say, nothing happened.
Then the last time he went off, and,   (E)
      coming at a run,
         "Hurry! This camp is on fire!" they say he said.
Then, they say, many people ran out.

As I have noted, as one becomes more sensitive to a text, to local movement and rhythm, one senses that something of the "voice" of the narrator is lost if lines are aligned all the same way. This sense comes, not from hearing the voice itself, but from becoming intimate with the disposition of words, phrases, and markers in relation to one another. A desire to have a visual analog to one's sense of relations increases when one does want to display as little as possible of the machinery of analysis, explicit labeling of verses and stanzas, with the text. I would like to show several types of cases that have arisen in connection with Victoria Howard's dictations in Clackamas Chinook, types that may be suggestive and useful to others, and then to display the true complexity of the Tonkawa text just quoted, a complexity I failed to grasp in previous analyses of it.

VICTORIA HOWARD

Victoria Howard's Clackamas texts indeed exhibit a variety of local rhythms. Units may be formally equivalent (e.g., the stanza) and the principles of grouping the same (three- or five-part relations), yet the rhythm within such formal equivalence may not be the same.

Recognizing such differences among them, I find myself almost instinctively representing them differently on the page.[15] Here is an overview, citing instances. The examples are almost entirely from "Tongue" (Jacobs 1959a: 369–75), whose analysis is otherwise unpublished.

Step-by-Step Run

Sometimes in a stanza the sequence of verses seems to proceed in a "linear" fashion, rapidly, from first to third, or first to fifth. Each verse is a short step in a continuous sequence of action. It seems right to set such a stanza on the page with each unit successively indented. Lines 73–77 of "Tongue" are such a case.

Now to be sure,
   now she went into labor,
      now she brought out a baby boy.
         Now it dawned five times,
            now she bathed.

And (181–85):

Now he goes,
   morning,
      now he goes,
         now there . . . he is in the mountains,
            now he trains to the end.

Partial Internal Pairs

Sometimes in a stanza of an odd number of verses, the actions seem not to be a straight line sequence as a whole, but to have parts grouped in pairs. It seems appropriate to indent the second member of a pair. There are two kinds of case.

The usual case in Chinookan is one in which the final verse has no partner. The procession is pair, pair, singleton. Lines 105–13 (III ii A) of "Tongue"
are such a case. Each of the first four lines is marked as the start of a verse
by an initial particle. The paired alternation (Now again : now, Now again :
now) suggests the stepwise placement of these four verses.

Now again he goes about,   105
  now he hunts.
Now again he comes back,
  now he says to her,
    "Mother! If only my bow were a little bigger,
      "I could kill something big,   110
        spotted all over."
"O. . . ,"
  she told him.[16]

Sets of Pairs: Reported Action

Sometimes in a stanza, all the verses enter into pairs. Sets of three (or five)
pairs are not uncommon in Chinookan narrative. When the pairs of a stanza
are reported action, it is appropriate to indent the second member of each.
Lines 124–29 (III iii), in which each line is also a verse, marked as such, are
an especially clear and appropriate case.

Now again he goes,
  now the boy hunts all the time.
Now he would bring back deer,
  sometimes he would kill two deer.
Now she would take a little of it,
  now she would give all (the rest) to it.

Sequences of Quoted Speech

Sequences of quoted speech do not lend themselves to the indentation just
shown. In part that is due to a convention of indenting what is said. It is also
often because speech of more than a line or two obscures the visual relation
signaled by indentation. With such a convention, it seems best to put each
turn at talk flush left. The opening three stanzas of the first scene of act IV of
"Tongue" (131–53) illustrate the difference. The three verses of the first stanza
seem a run served by indentation. The three verses of the last stanza of talk
between the boy and his mother "Tongue" might be shown this way (and I

will do it as an example), but the three verses of the middle stanza would be
ill served.

Now they lived on there.   (A)
   Now that is the way the two did to him.
      Now her son became a man.
Now he asked his mother.   (B)
   "How does it happen we are the only ones?"
She told him,
   "Ahhh. I had not thought it would be so soon,
   "(but) a little later before I would tell you about it."
Now she told him all about it,
   she told him,
      "That thing you look at there is not a person.
      "He devoured our village,
    he ate all the people,
       when you were not yet a person."
Now he told her,   (C)
   "How could you not have told me about it already?"
     Now . . . she told him.
      He told her,
      "Now I will go from here.
      "I will not get back for a day or two.
      "I will camp overnight before I get back."

If quoted speech itself is not indented and is brief, then it might be possible
to indent verse in the same way as for reported action. Extended sequences
of paired verses, however, involving quoted speech, seem not to lend themselves to this.

Extended Sequences of Pairs: Reported Action and Quoted Speech Combined

The final lines of "Tongue" (286-308) are a moving example. Due to their
folly, the people of the village had all been eaten by Tongue. One woman,
the chief's other wife, survived, having been out digging roots. She copes
with Tongue and bears her son; he grows rapidly, and together they kill
Tongue. Then in the mountains he gathers feathers and bones from which
he recreates the people. On return to the village, where his father teaches
them to fish, they mock him. This scene follows. Its pairing is in terms of
the relation of actions to actors. The person in focus changes with each pair
of verses: son (286, 287-88), mother (289-90, 291-94), people; son (295-97,
298-99), son (300, 301), mother (302, 303-9). More precisely, the third pair

of verses (stanza C) are the pivot, the turning point. The two stanzas that precede (A, B) and the two that follow (D, E) are parallel. In the first of each, the son has bad feelings, then is in water (A, D). In the second of each, the mother responds and admonishes the people (B, E). In between, the people repent and call him, but he goes on (C). (Only with such analysis, in terms of lines, verses, and stanzas, can one recognize such formal artistry. And one needs to have in mind the normal role of the particle pair, "now then," that of initiating onset, to hear in what is last said, in their doubling, separately and alone, virtual drumbeats of decisive change, of the onset of something entirely new.

(V) (iii)

Now   his heart became bad.   (A)
Now he went,
     he waded.

Now his mother saw him,   (B)
     going.   290
Now she ran,
     she scolded the people:
     "It is he himself who has made you,
     "He brought you back here."

Now in vain he was followed,   (C) 295
     he was told,
     "Come back!"
No.
     He went further.

Now he wept.   (D) 300
Now there he stood in the water.

Now his mother wept.   (E)
Now she told the people,
     "Now then.
     "Had you not done like that to him,   305
     "You would have lived on here.
     "Now then.
     "Now we shall make our separation."
(See Penn 1997:145–49 for the entire myth in verse form.)

Another example is at the beginning of Victoria Howard's "Grizzly Woman Began to Kill People" (Hymes 1981b:356). There are five pairs of verses, the last three of which are turns at talk. Again the relationships of the scene

seem shown best by beginning each verse flush left. One could put space between each pair, but the presence of the pairs can also be shown by putting
a closed brace at the end of each.

Soon now,
    a woman reached him.
They said,
    "Some woman has reached our headman"}
Now they lived on there.
In spring,
    she went I don't know where,
        she came back at evening:
            Oh dear! she brought back camas;
                now she began to share it about.}
They told her,
    "Where did you gather them?"
She told them,
    "Well, I reached a burned-over place,
    it's just camas there,
        the camas stand thick."}
They told her,
    "Goodness, whenever you go again,
        we'll follow you."
"Very well,"
    she told them,
        "Perhaps tomorrow."}
"Indeed. We will follow you too."
"All right,"
    she told them.}

Coordinate Series

Sometimes in a stanza of marked verses, there is continuity without either a
run of action or internal pairing. For such a set of verses, it seems appropriate to set each verse flush left. Lines 67–71 of "Tongue" are such a case. Three
groups of lines are marked each with initial "now." The first is a general condition, the second has two quoted lines of thought and decision, the third
has a pair of actions.

Now the two stayed there, (she and) that thing.
Now she thought,
    "Now it's nearly time for my labor,

"now I'll carry in moss."
Now she carried in wood also,
   she filled up her house.

Partial Parallelism within Pairs

As we have seen, what is possible and desirable depends in part on how
much there is to accommodate line by line on the page. Victoria Howard
sometimes pairs verses one way, content another. She presents tristichs, two
of which are related as marked verses and two of which are related as semantic parallels or elaborations. The opening of "Tongue" has several. One could
choose to make the verses parallel on the page, or the semantic parallelism,
or neither. Here are the three alternatives for the second pair: (a-1, a-2) no
relation shown on the page, (b) pairs of verses aligned, (c) semantic content
aligned.

Now their head-woman died,
now she was put away,
she was hung up.

Now their head-woman died,
   now she was put away,
      she was hung up.

Now their head-woman died,
now she was put away,
   she was hung up.

Now their head-woman died,
   now she was put away,
   she was hung up.

In the case of "Tongue" and Victoria Howard's style of narration generally,
a choice is hard to make, but I have adopted the second possibility (b). It
seems important to make clear the presence of marked pairs within larger
sequences by putting them to the left, especially if space cannot be used
to separate them. To align such pairs also is consistent with aligning the
pairs that sometimes occur within five-element sequences within the same
longer sequences. The amplified third verse of the second scene of "Tongue"
is a case in point.

   Here, then, are the three scenes of the first act of "Tongue." End braces,
rather than space, are used to indicate the pairs of verses and the two ex-

tended five-member sequences that alternate with them in scene ii. To present them consistently in one of these ways has the virtue of showing the consequence of a practice, even if one's response is to want another.

It was here those persons lived,   (i)
  had their village.
Always they were playing.}
Now their head woman died.
Now she was put away,
  she was hung up.}
Now it became night.
Now a thing just like fire was seen,
  it came out high on one side of the river.}

Then now, two were gotten   (ii)
  they stayed,
    they watched from both sides
      (as) the thing comes—
        (their name was "Cut-fish" from the river).}
Soo ⋯ n while they are there
now something comes like fire.}
Now they are there,
  there they watch:
    straigh ⋯ t where ⋯that dead person hangs it goes,
    straigh ⋯ t there that thing gets,
    now its tongue,
    now it carries all of it.
      It is lying on its tongue.}
Now the two clip the tongue,
now that thing draws all the way back.}
Now the people go,
  they go to take the dead one;
now the dead one is put away again.}

Now they lived on (there).   (iii)
Now that thing,
  indeed its name is "Tongue,"
    now da⋯y,
      night,
        "Give me back my tongue."}
Now he made them tired.
Now they said,

"Let's give it back to him."}
Now then they gave it back to him.
Now he put an end to the village.
    he ate all···the people.}

In terms of rhythm we have here a case in which paired relations are not an intensification, against a background of three- and five-part relations, as in Cultee's "Salmon Myth" (Kathlamet Chinook), John B. Hudson's account of Coyote and the Frogs (Santiam Kalapuya), and elsewhere. Quite the reverse. The pairs are the norm in this passage. The five-part relations enter as intensification, a mode of elaboration that allows for additional marking. Notice that the second and third pairs of the first scene display the "this, then that," initiation and outcome, effect often associated with narrative pairing: died, put away; night, something seen. The same is true of the three pairs in the second scene: they are there, something comes; they clip, it draws back; people go, the dead one is put away, and of the pairs in the third scene: they live on, the thing pleads (elaborated in form, but with only one action in its five lines); he makes them tired, they say; they give it back, he eats them up.[17]

At the same time this prevalence of two-part rhetorical form and meaning is interwoven with the three- and five-part logic one expects in Chinookan. The three pairs of the first scene are an arc of ongoing, onset, outcome, the outcome being an object of perception, as is often the case in Chinookan narratives. The second scene, which begins with a marked reversal of the usual particle order, "then now" rather than "now then," has also a three-part sequence ending in perception in its five lines: the two are gotten, they stay, they watch the thing coming. The extended third group uses pairs in an elaborated three-part sequence: there, watch; goes, gets there; carries it, has it lying on its tongue. Pairs of lines that correspond to a step in the progression are marked in parallel fashion (straight, straight; now, now). The five parts of the scene are related by the rhetorical logic by which the third part completes one arc and begins another. The two who are gotten watch the thing coming, see it coming like fire, watch as it gets the corpse (onset, ongoing, outcome). The thing gets the corpse, they clip its tongue and it goes back, the people put the corpse away again (onset, ongoing, outcome). And the three pairs in the third scene have such a logic: "give it back," "let's give it back," eaten up.

Here we have something more than a question of segmentation into appropriate parts. We have an interweaving of rhythms. One might say that Victoria Howard was like Brahms in liking to play off three against two.

JOHN RUSH BUFFALO

Such complexity is not unique. In John Rush Buffalo's telling of "Coyote and Eagle's Daughter," an interplay between pairing and tripling is commonly marked within individual stanzas. I discovered that the initial particles that so often marked verses in pairs gave way at one point in the story to marking them in sets of three (Hymes 1980b; cf. 1987c). There could be no doubt; the form of the narrative was clear in a classical way. Coyote's wife, coming after him, stops at each of a series of camps, and exactly the same details are repeated. To insist on grouping verses in pairs would violate the obvious coherence of the story. But elsewhere I accepted the evident pairing as matrix and published the result. I noticed that a pair of verses often had three word-final quotative suffixes. That was striking, but it did not lead me to suspect three- and five-part relations as having any organizing role beyond their use to intensify one scene.

While preparing this essay and turning to my earlier analysis for that example, I noticed what might be a loose end in the fit between form and meaning: the way in which even-numbered relations had been posited might be forced in, for example, the first act when Coyote prepares to fight. Why did there have to be four groups? Why not five, one for the preparation by the river and one each for each of the directions in which he howled? And while Coyote comes running to revive the people four times, perhaps the scene really begins in the preceding verse and has five elements also. I had already revised analysis of the encounters between Coyote and his wife in the second and third acts, with success in recognizing a recurrent relation in regard to Coyote peering in. But the passage in which a young man acts as intermediary had not fitted easily. Perhaps there did not have to be four parts of an act. Perhaps there could be five. And having a single element in a unit at a large level makes some sense; it seems to occur naturally enough in three- and five-part (odd-numbered) patterning, but seemed unmotivated in the instance or two in which it had seemed necessary in this story.

All this led to a reconsideration and a recognition that three- and five-part relations are pervasive in the organization of the narrative. An incidental benefit was a neatening or tightening of the disposition of a line or two. Most importantly, whatever may have led Victoria Howard to interweave even- and odd-numbered patterning, such a phenomenon could be not explained (away) simply as mingling of traditions. Here it was in Tonkawa, intricately accomplished, explicitly marked, and, as mentioned earlier, having an apparent appropriateness also. The initiation of action in act I is on Coyote's part, which can be taken as befitting the sequence of five stanzas in each scene. The kind of action is in keeping with proper response to a woman and to the needs of a community, leading to it giving him a wife. Hence, one can infer that there are not three or five scenes, but four.

Once Coyote leaves the community and the wife at the start of the remaining two acts, the larger relations, including numbers of scenes, are in terms of three and five. But at a finer level, at a turning point of interaction, when the twice rejected wife refuses Coyote water, there are not three of five verses, but two pairs, four in all (111-18). (See the profile at the end of the chapter.)

Such a case makes one want particularly to display the relations and their marking in an abstract form. I have done so in an appendix at the end of this chapter. Here is the story itself, doing fuller justice, I hope, to John Rush Buffalo, its teller, and to Harry Hoijer, who sought him out and recorded it.

(I) (Coyote restores the people)

(i) (He discovers an empty camp)

They say Coyote was going along;   (A)
In doing so, he went up a mountain.
They say he stood there;
When he did, they say, there was a large camp at the mountain's foot.

Coyote went down,   (B)   5
he went to that large camp; and
when he went to the tipi on the edge,
there was weeping inside, they say.

Then Coyote went in.   (C)
    "What is it?" they say he said.   10
Then that woman,
    "Here all the people in this camp are gone," they say she said.
    "A fearsome being destroyed them," they say she said.

Then Coyote,   (D)
    "Now, do not weep," they say he said.   15
    "Tomorrow I shall fight it," they say he said.
Then that woman went outside, and
    "Coyote says he will fight it tomorrow," they say she said.

"Tomorrow when I fight it,   (E)
    "Do not run away," they say he said, Coyote.   20
    "Watch me closely," they say he said.
Then,
    "Yes," they say she said.

                                                         (ii) (He prepares to fight)
When it was evening,   (A)
   he went down to the river, and   25
cutting off a piece of hard wood,
   he burned it black, and
putting it away,
   he went to sleep, they say.

And at daybreak, arising,   (B)   30
he went outdoors, and
sitting to the east,
he howled loudly, they say.

And then again, to the south,   (C)
again he howled, they say.   35

And then again, to the west,   (D)
again he howled, they say.

And then, last, sitting to the north,   (E)
he howled, they say.

                                                         (iii) (He meets the monster)
This done, they say, Coyote joined some women going after wood.   (A)   40
As he did,
   "That one is coming!" they say was said.

As it did, that fearsome being from the waist up, they say, was red;   (B)
And there, from the waist down, they say, it was black.

Then, they say, those women were afraid.   (C)   45
Then, they say, Coyote hid.

As he did, it came in that direction at a run;   (D)
Coyote fought it, they say, that fearsome being.

As he did, a great many Wolves,   (E)
catching that fearsome being,   50
were fighting it, they say.
Doing so, they killed it, they say, that fearsome being.

                                                         (iv) (He restores the people)
And then, they say, those Wolves left.   (A)
Then Coyote went toward that camp that had no people.
   "Close all those tipis tight!" they say he said.   55
All those tipis were closed, they say.

And then Coyote went off from the place, and,   (B)
galloping,
   "Quick! This camp is on fire!" they say he said.
When he did, they say, nothing happened.   60

Then again he went off, and,   (C)
coming at a gallop,
   "Hurry! This camp is on fire!" they say he said.
When he did, they say, nothing happened.

Then again he went off, and,   (D) 65
coming at a run,
   "Hurry! This camp is on fire!" they say he said.
Then, they say, nothing happened.

Then, the last time he went off, and,   (E)
coming at a run,   70
   "Hurry! This camp is on fire!" they say he said.
Then, they say, many people ran out.

          (II) (Coyote goes gambling)
      (i) (He leaves his wife for another camp)
Then, they say, they made Coyote marry a beautiful girl.   (A)
Then, after staying a while, to that woman,
   "I'll go to the other camp over yonder," they say he said, Coyote.   75
Then that woman,
   "Oh!" they say she said.
   "Don't go!" they say she said.
Then Coyote,
   "I won't stay long," they say he said.   80
   "In two days I'll come back," they say he said.
Then that woman,
   "All right," they say she said.

          (ii) (She follows him)
Then, they say, Coyote went off.   (A)
And, getting to a large camp,   85
   they say he stayed for a long while.

It was then that woman went after them, they say;   (B)
getting to that large camp,
   "And Coyote?" they say she said.
Then,   90
   "He's joined a bunch of gamblers over there," they say they said.

Then she got to a place nearby, and   (C)
   entering the tipi,
    "Water," they say she said.
Then,   95
    "There is none," they say they said.

(iii) (Young man as intermediary)

Then she picked up the bucket, and,   (A)
   they say, she went to get water.
As she did so, one young man at the gambling place: —
    "Oh!" they say he said.   100
    "Coyote's wife!" they say he said.
    "She comes this way!" they say he said.
Then Coyote saw her, and,
   they say, he was laughing.
Then the young man,   105
    "We heard that you left her," they say they said.
Then Coyote,
    "No," they say he said.
    "Watch me!" they say he said.
    "She'll give me water to drink," they say he said.   110

(iv) (She refuses him water)

And then, getting to where that woman was,   (A)
   they say, he touched her.
Then that woman, seeing Coyote,
    "Leave me!" they say she said.

Then Coyote,   (B)   115
    "Give me water to drink!" they say he said.
Then, that woman, not giving him water to drink,
   went off, they say.

(v) (She decides to go)

When night came he came to that woman,   (A)
   and as he talked with her, the young men,   120
    "Let's not let Coyote sleep tonight," they say they were saying.
    "Let's steal that woman," they say they were saying.
And then that night, they say, they danced with him.
And, they say, they didn't let him sleep until daylight, Coyote.
Then, they say, that woman was angry;   125
And,
    "I'll go," they say she said.

(III) (Coyote goes gambling again)

(i) (He goes north to gamble)

Then Coyote,   (A)

   "I'll go to gamble in the north," they say he said.

And, they say, he went away, Coyote.   130

And he got to a large camp, and   (B)

   "I go to gamble in the north," they say he said.

And then, going away,

   they say, he got to a large camp.

And the next day,   (C) 135

   "I go to gamble in the north," they say he said, Coyote.

The next day, they say, he went off;

   getting to a large camp,

   they say, he joined a bunch of gamblers.

(ii) (She follows him)

While he did, that woman,   (A)

   "I'll go after Coyote," they say she said.

And, they say, she went after him;

   getting to a large camp,

   "And Coyote?" they say she said.

Then,   145

   "He's gone to gamble in the north," they say they said.

Then, they say, that woman went after him.   (B)

And again, getting to a large camp,

   "And Coyote?" they say she said.

Then,   150

   "He's gone to gamble in the north," they say they said.

Then, they say, that woman went after him.   (C)

And getting to a large camp,

   "And Coyote?" they say she said.

Then,   155

   "He's gone to gamble in the north," they say they said.

Then, they say, that woman went after him.   (D)

And getting to a large camp,

   "And Coyote?" they say she said.

Then,   160

   "He's gambling here," they say they said.

Then,   (E)
  "Go to him, and
  "Tell him,
  "Come!" they say she said.   165

          (iii) (Young man as intermediary)
Then, going to him,   (A)
  "Your wife is summoning you," they say he said.
Then Coyote,
  "You're lying," they say he said.
Then,   170
  "I speak the truth," they say he said;
  "Now come!" they say he said.

     (iv) (He refuses her command to come in)
Then Coyote went with him, they say;   (A)
the two got to the tipi, they say;
  "She is staying here," they say he said.   175
Then, they say, Coyote peered inside.

Then that woman,
  "Come in!" they say she said.
Then Coyote, they say, not going in,
  was laughing.   180

Then again,
  "Come in!" they say she said.
Then Coyote, they say, not going in,
  was laughing.

Then again, that woman,   185
  "Come in!" they say she said.
Then Coyote, they say, not going in,
  was laughing.

Again as he peered in,
  "Come in!" they say she said.   190
Then when Coyote laughed, that woman,
  "I shall go away," they say she said.
  "Back," they say she said;
  Going outside, she flew away, they say.

            (v) (She goes for good)
Then Coyote peering in,   (A) 195
  "And my wife?" they say he said.

Then,
   "She has gone away," they say they said.

Then, they say, Coyote came running,
   back.   200
As he did, that woman was getting home;
   "I left him," they say she said.

Then her father and mother,
   "You are doing the right thing," they say they said;
   "Let us go," they say they said.   205
And, they say, she flew away with them up into the air.
   She was an Eagle, they say.

So it is.

Composing this narrative, John Rush Buffalo used all there was to use, I think. His words were not fitted to a simple, single template, his verses and stanzas not a sequence of verbal cookies, all the same. Nor were they words simply off the cuff, darted out in the excitement that congenial performance can have. These words were dictated slowly to a linguist, writing them down to preserve what has proven to be all we know of the verbal heritage John Rush Buffalo had survived to share. It is a heritage, we can now see, that could vary shape and texture so as to indicate differences in the role of an actor, and particularly the role of a male or a female. Thus, early on, Coyote acts in four scenes when taking the part of the community (perhaps identifying with women as well as men) but then acts in five scenes when he goes off on his own. At another level, the two pairs of verses in scene iv of act II, amid groups of three and five, show decisive action that highlights a forthcoming break by a woman (cf. the triplets of verses in scene ii of act III, where pairs prevailed). A plot can be doubled, as between acts II and III, with the second played off against the first, so as to let details of interaction show a wife, given by a community as a reward to its reviver, loyally seek her husband but respect herself and, in the end, take charge. Perhaps anyone in the Southwest could have said that a Coyote cannot keep an Eagle for a wife. This narrative shows that truth as something learned and earned.

Would we not want to know these things because there is no tape recording? Or for that reason, not use this narrative? Some schools of linguists have rejected information about language because it was not obtained in an approved way: "That's not linguistics." Are we to say of all we can ever know about the imagination of people like John Rush Buffalo, "That's not ethnopoetics"? Philology, I submit, can do something to make known a voice worth knowing.

V

The worth of the texts makes worthwhile our concern about how to present them.[18] More fundamental than how it is done is whether it is done. Means are scant in relation to need. Texts published years ago should be edited in the light of the field notebooks and republished in ethnopoetic terms. There are texts collected years ago that have never been published at all (Frachtenberg's Molale from Oregon, Swadesh's Chitimacha from Louisiana, to name two). There are texts collected in recent years that have not been published for lack of funds and series in which to place them (the native-language originals of Tedlock's Zuni, Ellen Basso's Kalapalo, for example, and who knows whether the unique Apache myth cycle recorded fifty years ago by Hoijer and now prepared in close collaboration with Apache speakers by Keith Basso can find a publisher?). Computers make it possible to do many things that would once have been impossible or a matter of lifelong labor. Perhaps ethnopoetics will be a field in which the basic materials are privately published and distributed—a field for the elderly and established, since younger people could not expect to gain recognition and employment through such endeavors. Texts, of course, are not important to the hungry and homeless, although there are those of us who love them, and descendants who would value having them in appropriate form. If the funds of the country all were going to meet the needs of children, women, schooling, health care, one could have no complaint.

Let me close with a plea as well for readers of such narratives. Fieldwork with ongoing traditions is vital. Documentation of living performance is absorbing. But reading matters too. It is the way we can recreate something of the imaginative world, the intertextuality, in which a given telling arose and so recognize and appreciate a teller's aesthetic and moral imagination. If all one has is the one occasion, one may miss important aspects of what is there. Narrators create in performances but also between performances. Stories are good to hear, but also good to think. John Rush Buffalo's "Coyote and Eagle's Daughter" did not come to him as an inspiration as Harry Hoijer opened his notebook. Surely "all that complex wealth of minutiae which in their line-for-line aspect we call style and in their broader outlines we call form" (Burke 1925:38) had a history, marked by moments of reflection as to how such a relationship between a woman and a man, an Eagle's daughter given as wife to Coyote, might be true to inherent natures and lived experience.

The resources in such moments are not one's voice and audience, but experience reflected upon, stories reflected upon, experience and stories acting upon each other. We need to recover as much as possible of that experience, of that horizon of stories. Other stories may inform us of meanings, possibilities, inventions, and transformations, even though new performances are not to be heard. It is here that Lévi-Strauss stands as a permanent example, however one may criticize particular interpretations. He has read widely with close attention to detail and so approaches particular stories with a sense of alternative possibilities and sources of creative change.[19]

Such reading is essential because the standard sources of comparison and context are fundamentally inadequate. One does learn from them. The contributions to naming of recurrent plots by Kroeber (1908) and Lowie (1908a, 1909) early in the century are still something to read, as are comparative studies by them and Boas (notably, his *Tsimshian Mythology* [1916]) and the next generation (e.g., Lowie 1908b; Reichard 1921; Demetracopoulou 1933; Gayton 1935). The notes to Thompson's 1929 *Tales of the North American Indians* are still indispensable. There are insights and comparisons in a great many publications (e.g., Demetracopoulou and Du Bois 1932; Adamson 1934; Reichard 1947). One needs to be acquainted with the classificatory schemes of motif and tale type (see Thompson 1955–1958, 1961; Wycoco [Moore] 1951) and with what Lévi-Strauss has proposed (1964–71, 1979 and other works) as transformational relationships. The critical point, however, is that for a given starting point, what proves relevant but comes into view may not have been brought together by anyone else. What one can discover regarding informing context and intertextuality will depend on one's own reading and recollection—and chance.

This situation could be improved by new guides. Motifs and tale types are helpful, but knowing that a story is about Coyote, say, is about as useful as knowing that a statue is one of Jesus. Is it Jesus lying in a mother's lap as a baby, Jesus erect upon his mother's knees as Pantocrator, Jesus as an emaciated corpse? More specifically, the fine details, the explicit frames, the implicit themes that are relevant are often not mentioned in the comparative guides available. Part of the problem is that their scope is not sufficiently local, not sufficiently fine. Part of the problem is that their sources may exclude nonprofessional material that yet provides crucial information.

Let me briefly offer four cases in point: two have to do with framing sequences of action, one characterizes tricksters in relation to one kind of act, and one validates two kinds of transformational relationship in the recasting of a myth.

Sequence of Action (1)

In 1975, Donald Bahr published an analysis of ritual oratory among the Pima and the Papago (Tohono O'odham) Indians. I first saw it at the Cultural Center at Warm Springs Reservation, Oregon, when visiting its then director, Nathan Jim. Bahr found a pattern he summarized as DTAX: departure, travel, arrival, outcome. In the orations the pattern governs whole texts. In John Rush Buffalo's telling of "Coyote and Eagle's Daughter," it governs two opening stanzas (and confers pattern on the second stanza, which itself is without markers). In the midst of a myth of Eagle and Grizzly Woman that France Johnson told Edward Sapir in Takelma (Rogue River, Oregon), the device governs that stanza in which Eagle first discovers the Grizzly girl.

Three separated cases lead one to inquire. It becomes evident that frames for the moments of a sequence of travel may be characteristic of every tradition. The ingredients may differ. Moments may be recognized in common but kept as distinct steps in one tradition, combined in a single step in another (not unlike the relation between distinctions that enter into aspect categories across languages). In Saanich Salish (Vancouver Island) preparation can be a major element. (See the discussion of these matters in Hymes 1990a.)

Sequence of Action (2)

By accident of reading, again, I know a recurrent device for getting people together in bed. In the Clackamas Chinook myth "Gitskux and His Older Brother" (Willamette Valley, Oregon), Victoria Howard tells how the woman to whom Panther comes allows him to sleep inside her lodge far in the corner. At night he is bitten by fleas until step by step (five steps in all) he comes to her bed and then beside her. Jarold Ramsey called my attention to Clara Pearson's account of brother-sister incest in a Tillamook myth (Oregon coast). The sister takes the initiative in a step-by-step progress involving leaks in the roof (E. Jacobs 1990 [1959]: 48–49; Ramsey 1983:96–126). Working through Tonkawa to honor a late teacher, I discovered that this device is not peculiar to Oregon. John Rush Buffalo knew it as well. In the partner to the myth given earlier in this chapter, "Coyote, Jack Rabbit, and Eagle's Daughter," when Eagle's daughter and Rabbit are in bed, Coyote makes his way there step by step by pretending he is being bitten. The result is that the couple leave (Hoijer 1972:16–17). Such step-by-step biting must have been a narrative device over a wide stretch of North America.

Characterizing Tricksters

Working on a notebook of texts that Philip Kahclamat dictated in Wishram Chinook to Sapir's student Walter Dyk in 1933, I came upon one new to me. The trickster Coyote has killed his partner, Deer, intending to eat him, but has propped him up as if sick but still alive and calls on Owl to lead singing to cure him. Owl's song says that the curing is a waste of time, but it is in Chinookan. Then Coyote laments for Deer in Sahaptin. Evidently the truth in Chinookan is not to be understood by those to be taken in by the falsehood in Sahaptin. The narrative assumes a Sahaptin-speaking audience for Coyote, a bilingual audience for itself.

At first I thought the story unique. Working through texts in Quileute (from the northwestern corner of the state of Washington), I found a story, evidently popular, since different narrators told it to three different collectors over the years, in which the trickster Q'wati kills the chief of the Wolves; when confronted by other wolves, Q'wati sings first in Makah, then in Quileute, about what he has done. Like Coyote, his choice of language cannot conceal the death (Andrade 1931:46–50, 94–98; Clark 1953:121–22). As it happened, I found a copy of the narratives collected by Barbeau and Beynon (Cove and MacDonald 1987:20) in the bookstore in the Hoodland Shopping Center near Rhododendron. In it I discovered a Tsimshian story in which the trickster Raven has his slave speak for him when he comes as a great chief to visit another chief. Officially, Raven does not understand the local language. As a result, he loses out on the food his hosts provide. And rereading Clark (1953:100), I rediscovered a story that Melville Jacobs's Kalapuya collaborator, John B. Hudson, had told to Clark in English. It explains why the falls that make a rich harvest of salmon possible on the Willamette are in the territory of the Clackamas, not further upriver in the territory of the Kalapuyas. When Meadowlark called across to Coyote to make the dam, she spoke in Clackamas, and Coyote did not understand, since he knew only Kalapuya. Later she used sign language too. Clark was an amateur who did not always publish full versions of what she was told (David French, personal communication) and who focused on the kinds of things local whites thought romantic about Indian legends: the origins of mountains, rivers, waterfalls, and the like. But perhaps her asking in terms of that interest is why she obtained a story that Hudson did not tell Jacobs in all the years he worked with him.

The hypothesis that emerges is association of a trickster figure with bilingualism, but with bilingualism that does not benefit. In Kalapuya (Willamette Valley, Oregon) and Tsimshian (Alaska), the trickster loses out on food because of someone else's bilingualism. In Wishram (Columbia River, Washington) and Quileute (northwest corner of Washington), the trickster cannot conceal death and loses out on food, despite his own bilingualism, presumably because of the bilingualism of other people. The nature of things, it would seem, is not monolingual. Not to be or to pretend to be bilingual is to lose out; to presume that others are not is to lose out. One can see a connection between the trickster's inability to control such language skill with the widespread premise that a trickster cannot control a song (songs being serious also, a source of power and sign of status).

Validation

The figure of Salmon is of central importance to the narrative imaginations of those who lived along the Columbia and its tributaries, just as the food salmon was of central importance to the sustenance of life. Salmon proves a contested figure, as between the Kathlamet Chinook narratives of Charles Cultee and the Clackamas Chinook narratives of Victoria Howard. In the latter, Salmon is displaced, once in the very course of dictating a story (Hymes 1984a), whether by Victoria Howard alone or by the tradition she acquired from her mother-in-law and mother's mother (see chap. 7 of this volume). Most remarkably, there is the story of "Tongue." The association of the father with teaching others to fish and the pride of the son suggest a chiefly actor such as Salmon. As it happens, Ramsey (1977:94–95; cf. Lyman 1900) has reprinted an early account, taken down by a local historian and antiquarian from a mixed-blood, Louis Labonte. Although not authentic performance, it offers authentic information. The man who goes into the river is indeed Salmon, and where he goes explains which streams have salmon today and which do not. But he is shamed, not by the people, but by his father. Victoria Howard has changed a story focused on a father and a son into one in which the active parent is the mother—the only one to survive the destruction of the people by Tongue, doing so through her diligent provision of food (digging roots). She fends off Tongue and bears and raises the heroic son.

In the story first mentioned, the Clackamas counterpart to Cultee's Salmon myth (Hymes 1985a), the contested role is that of pronouncer of the foods that will be provided for the people. It is in that role that Salmon is explicitly supplanted by Coyote in the Howard telling. In the story of Tongue, something else is going on. It appears that the virtuous son of a virtuous mother can be Salmon and the source of salmon. The role is not contested, although the name is suppressed: neither Salmon the actor nor salmon the food is named as such.

There is a second transformation, one of the Lévi-Strauss type. The opening of "Tongue" is a transformation, partly the same in details, partly inverted, of a major part of William Hartless's telling of Coyote's attempt to copulate across a river with a long and borrowed penis (Hymes 1987a). Why? For some time I could think of no reason. The formal relation was there, but not a motivation. I now think that the transformation and inversion have to do with chiefly status. Coyote attempts to copulate across the river (the same river, the Willamette—the Kalapuyas were up river from the Clackamas, as the story of where the falls were put indicates) with the daughter of a chief. When he subsequently pretends to be a shaman who can cure her (the tip of the penis has been cut off and is still inside her), much is made of the way in which he deceives the chiefly father, by pretending to be old, experienced, famous, and reluctant. When he crawls inside the place in which the girl lies, he deceives and humiliates the chiefly father. Coyote has a cohort of raucous birds sing to help him with his song, while he copulates, gets the penis parts to rejoin, and runs away.

"Tongue" has quite another view of chiefs and chiefly families. It begins with Tongue wanting the corpse of one chiefly wife. The other wife (chiefs in this area often had two wives) is the only virtuous survivor, and because of that, the only survivor at all. Her son is a chief's son and the restorer of his people. When at the end of the story he enters the river and all must change into what they will be in the next age, it is the people who have injured his pride. The story suggests that the Clackamas themselves, who lived at the same spot, the spot highlighted in the story's first words, might still be there if they had heeded their chiefly family.

One myth mocks chiefly honor, as ordinary people might, and one sustains it against the foolishness of ordinary people.[20] The formal connections are detailed, and a meaning can be given to the transformation. Because the Coyote story is so widespread in the region and the story of Tongue unique so far as we know, the former is presumably the starting point. And in this case the interest of an antiquarian provides a validation. Lyman reports (1903:126–27) the Clackamas version of a widespread story in which Coyote creates a fish trap. Coyote offends the trap, and it will work no more: "So the people were left to simply spear the fish. The story, which is also a continued one, proceeds then to tell of the great tribe that flourished on the shore, one great man being chief. The village was on the right bank. In his days there came a monster, or Skookum [Chinook jargon for 'strong'] from the mountains, and devoured all the people but the wife and unborn son of the chief." Now the Hartless Kalapuya story ends with a brief scene in which Coyote marries, has children, and makes a fish trap. It ends, that is, with an allusion to just the story that in Clackamas, according to Labonte, precedes the story of Tongue. The two stories are related not only by transformation. According to Labonte, they are related by succession.

Others can no doubt supply similar examples, and no doubt there are many more to be discovered. One has to read all there is to read, whatever its source. Each fresh venture will require fresh reading, because what is relevant now may not have been relevant when the story was originally documented. Much will have been forgotten and is not to be recovered from secondary guides. Only by fresh reading can we reconstruct the imaginative narrative resources and surroundings of the stories we give attention. Through such reconstruction, we can bring analysis to the focal point it must have, the named narrator, not the named tribe. Perhaps doing so, we will create guides for others that begin with the frames and characteristics that emerge from such close reading, the workings of style that emerge from the analysis of rhetorical form we can now undertake.

Each time we seek to understand a particular myth, we find ourselves tracing a new path among what we can remember and can find. We can be guided by expectations as to rhetorical form, but the workings of the particular text may always surprise us. And each text attracts to itself its own constellation of analogues. In this regard, the slogan *use all there is to use* is vital. Scholars are likely to be prejudiced for and against certain sources, may value certain kinds of relations and not others. But in the name of all that is oral, when there is so little, who can refuse any part?

The true work of ethnopoetics, certainly as it addresses the many and manifold oral traditions of Native Americans, is barely begun.

Appendix: Profile of "Coyote and Eagle's Daughter"

At the right side of the page are the indications of the three acts (I, II, III) and of the scenes (i, ii, iii, iv, v).

At the left side of the page the columns show stanzas (A, B, C, D, E), verses (a, b, c, d, e), lines, and markers other than initial particles. Line numbers for different verses are separated by a comma. Markers that belong to different verses are separated by a semicolon; here, a comma indicates separate lines. The indications of markers usually are P for initial particle, - for no marker, " for quoted speech, Q for quotative. Occasionally "-and" indicates a connective ending to a line, and "Time" indicates an initial time word.

			(I) (Coyote restores the people)
			(i) (He discovers an empty camp)
A	ab 1–2, 3–4	Q, P	Q, PQ
B	ab? 5–6, 7–8	-and;	-Q [same framework as A]
C	ab 9–10, 11–13	P, "Q	P, "Q, "Q
D	ab 14–16,17–18	P, "Q, "Q	P -and, "Q
E	ab 19–21, 22–23	-, "Q, Q	P, "Q

			(ii) (He prepares to fight)
A	abc? 24–25, 26–27, 28–29	-and, -and	-Q
B	ab 30–31, 32–33	P, -and	-and, Q
C	ab 34, 35	P, and	Q
D	ab 36, 37	P;	PQ
E	ab 38, 39	P, -and;	Q

			(iii) (He meets the monster)
A	ab 40, 41–42	PQ;	P, "Q
B	ab 43, 44	PQ;	PQ
C	ab 45, 46	PQ;	PQ
D	ab 47, 48	P;	-Q- [fearsome being final]
E	ab 49–51, 52	P, -Q;	P -Q- [fearsome being final]

A	ab 53, 54–56	PQ;	PQ, "Q, Q
B	ab 57–59, 6O	P -and, -, "Q;	Q
C	ab 61–63, 64	P -and, -, "Q;	Q
D	ab 65–67, 68	P -and, -, "Q;	Q
E	ab 69–71, 72	P -and-, -, "Q;	Q

		(II) (Coyote goes gambling)
		(i) (He leaves his wife for another camp)
A	abcde 73	Q
	74–75	P, "Q
	76–78	P, "Q, "Q
	79–81	P, "Q, "Q
	82–83	P, "Q

			(ii) (She follows him)
A	ab 84, 85–86	PQ;	P -and, Q
B	cd 87–89, 90–91	PQ, -, "Q;	P, "Q
C	ef 92–94, 95–96	P -and, -, "Q;	P, "Q

		(iii) (Young man as intermediary)
A	abcde 97–98	P -and, Q
	99–102	P, "Q, "Q, "Q
	103–4	P -and, Q

105–6	P, "Q	
107–10	P, "Q, "Q, "Q	

(iv) (She refuses him water)

| A ab 111–12, 113–14 | P -and, Q; | P, "Q |
| B cd 115–16, 117–18 | P, "Q; | P, Q |

(v) (She decides to go)

A abcde 119–22	Time, -, "Q, "Q
123	PQ
124	PQ
125	PQ
126–27	P, "Q

(III) (Coyote goes gambling again)
(i) (He goes north to gamble)

A ab 128–29, 130	P, "Q;	Q
B cd 131–32, 133–34	P, "Q	Q
C ef 135–36, 137–39	P, "Q	P, Q

(ii) (She follows him)

A abc 140–41, 142–44, 145–46	P, "Q;	P, -; "Q;	P, "Q
B abc 147, 148–49, 150–51	PQ;	P, "Q;	P, "Q
C abc 152, 153–54, 155–56	PQ;	P, "Q;	P, "Q
D abc 157, 158–59, 160–61	PQ;	P, "Q;	P, "Q
E 162–65	P, ", ", "Q		

(iii) (Young man as intermediary)

| A abc 166–67, 168–69, 170–72 | P, "Q, "Q |

(iv) (He refuses her command to come in)

A ab 173–75, 176	PQ -Q-, "Q;	PQ
cd 177–78, 179–80	P, "Q;	PQ
ef 181–82, 183–84	P, "Q;	PQ
gh 185–86, 187–88	P, "Q;	PQ
ij 189–90, 191–94	P, "Q;	P, "Q, "Q, Q

(v) (She goes for good)

A ab 195–96, 197–98	P, "Q;	P, "Q
cd 199–200, 201–2	PQ, -"	P, "Q
cf 203–5, 206–7	P, "Q, "Q;	PQ, Q

(A related narrative is presented in chap. 11.)

4

Variation and Narrative Competence

Gender in Focus

In recent years an increasing number of narrative traditions have been found to make use of organization in terms of lines and groups of lines. The majority of studies so far have been of Native American traditions, but many examples have been analyzed in other languages as well, especially English. It seems likely that the competence of skilled narrators everywhere will include this.

Organization in terms of lines is a general characteristic of the diverse kinds of poetry found in the world. Oral narrative performances also have been called "dramas" (e.g., by Melville Jacobs), and the kind of organization of lines being discovered in them fits that notion. Indeed, terms familiar from poetry and drama fit at several levels: verses, stanzas, scenes, acts (sometimes groups of acts, which can be called parts).

In oral performance it seems that final intonation contours identify a line or lines as constituting a verse. Even without a record of intonation contours, other features often identify verses—initial particles, especially time-related words, such as "now," "then," "meanwhile," and conjunctions. Turns at talk seem always to count as verses. Other kinds of recurrence particular to a story may indicate patterning as well.

In shaping stories, narrators have been found to make use of relations of two and four or of three and five. Four scenes in an act, say, four stanzas in a scene, four verses in a stanza, on the one hand, three or five, on the other. American English narrators, for example, appear to group lines and verses and stanzas in sequences of three or five. So did narrators in the Chinookan languages along the Columbia River between the states of Oregon and Washington. On the other hand, at least some narrators in Irish English prefer groupings of two and four or three and four (as evidenced in texts from Northern Ireland collected by Henry Glassie), as do narrators in Hopi, Navajo, and Zuni in the American Southwest. (See my papers, "Sung Epic and Native American Ethnopoetics," prepared for the Conference on Textualization of Oral Epics, Turku, 1996b, and Hymes 1998b, chap. 4.)

Variations, of course, are possible. A sequence has a rhythm, and the rhythm can vary. The number of verses in a stanza may be, not three or five, but three or five pairs. In Chinookan languages and perhaps others, a sequence of three commonly has the force of an onset, ongoing, and outcome: he went, he kept on going, he got there. A sequence of five may also be a straight run from beginning to end; or it may balance as two, two, one; or it may show interlocking in that the third, middle element may be the outcome of an initial three-step sequence, and at the same time the onset of a final three-step sequence.

Especially interesting are cases in which a usual pattern, either threes and fives or twos and fours, is replaced by its alternative. In a number of Native American narratives in the western United States, such alternation has been found associated in one way or another with gender. This is not to say that such alternations do not occur elsewhere. These traditions are those with which I am most familiar.

I have mentioned cases from Tillamook, Takelma, and Tonkawa narrators in "Sung Epic and Native American Ethnopoetics" (Hymes 2000) and remarked on the phenomenon elsewhere. What follows is the most complete account, and it attempts to be systematic, abstracting as headings the aspect of organization in which the shift occurs and what it expresses.

(1) *Different patterns for the same story: relation with audience.* Among the Tillamook Salish of the northern Oregon coast, when a sequence of incidents and actors focused on a woman, there would be patterns of four; when it focused on a man, there would be five. Such alternation in patterning could occur within a single story. Such is the case with Clara Pearson telling a story called "Split-His-(Own)-Head." In each telling there is a first part with five scenes; in it a younger brother consistently misunderstands what his sister tells him (ironically) to do. A second part has four scenes. Here again the younger brother misunderstands, but the focus now is how to get a wife, and he finally succeeds.

Pearson told the story to two different women, in English to one, in Tillamook to the other. The number of stanzas within scenes differs between the two tellings. The difference is not due to the language or to the gender of her audience. It is in telling the story in English, where one would expect threes and fives, that Pearson grouped stanzas within scenes as two and four. It is in telling the story in Tillamook that Pearson grouped stanzas within scenes as three and five.

The alternations seem to be due to her relationship with the women to whom she told it. In Tillamook she was telling the story to a young woman, unmarried, reportedly brash. In English she, was speaking to a white woman, married, nearer her own age, with whom she could identify. It seems that the difference is due to a sense of social distance, far or near. It seems that the pattern associated with males (five) is associated with greater social distance, while the pattern associated with women (four) is the one associated with closeness (see Hymes 1993).

(2a) *Different act or scene in the same telling: characterization.* Frances Johnson, a speaker of Takelma, a language of southern Oregon, used relations of two and four in those texts she dictated to Edward Sapir, which have been studied. She does so throughout all but one of the eight acts, or scenes, of a myth Sapir christened "Coyote Goes Courting," and which I refer to as "Coyote and Frog." In the second act she uses relations of three and five. The change is dramatic. The preceding act has a peaceful stillness, depicting Coyote's characteristic activity, going to get gophers every day and coming back at night. Suddenly he hears the sound of a girl's puberty dance and rushes toward it. The dance signals that the girls will be available sexually (presumably through marriage). The act is elaborated with a repeated rhetorical question ("How long did he not run!") as Coyote keeps telling himself he must be almost there (Hymes 1995c, 1998a).

(2b) *Different act or scene: response to a woman.* The best recorded texts we have from Tonkawa, a language of Texas, were told to Harry Hoijer by John Rush Buffalo. His "Coyote and Eagle's Daughter" has three acts. In the first act Coyote finds a woman at a deserted camp, weeping for its people, who have been killed by a dangerous being. He pretends to drive the being away and does revive the dead. This act has relations of two and four.

In the second and third acts, having been given a wife as reward, Coyote immediately leaves her to go where there is gambling. Each time she follows and in the end leaves him. These acts have relations of three and five (one stanza has even-numbered relations). (See Hymes 1987c, 1997a, and "different stanzas" in [3a].)

2c) *Different act or scene: man's, then woman's domain or control.* In 1927, Marion Davis, who grew up among Upper Chehalis Salish in western Washington, told stories he had learned from his mother to Thelma Adamson, a student of Boas. In "Crow, Her Son, Her Daughter," the patterning is in terms of three and five, except for the second scene.

In the first scene the son's mistake has caused his sister's death; this scene has patterning of three and five. In the second scene the mother persists in uncovering the truth and then as a doctor (shaman) sings until the girl is restored. This scene has four stanzas, and each stanza has four verses. The scene mentions that the mother questions the son five times, but it shows only four instances. After this scene, the story reverts to relations of three and five.

(3a) *Shift within a scene: woman's control.* In "Coyote and Eagle's Daughter," discussed in (2b), the second act, as said, has relations of three and five overall, but one stanza has four verses instead of three or five. The verses show two exchanges. Coyote touches his wife, and she tells him, "Leave me!" He tells her, "Give me water to drink!" (a wifely duty), and she does not, does not even answer, but goes off.

The wife's rejection of Coyote and assertion of herself is twofold, once in each pair. It is the beginning of the end of the relationship. In the third act she does come after him again but summons him to come to her. When he only looks in and laughs, she leaves for food, rejoining her family (Eagles). Her parents tell her, "You did right."

Here and in (2b) we have use of four-part patterning in the same story by the same narrator for what seem somewhat distinct reasons. Both have to do with a male protagonist's relation to a woman, both supportive and non-supportive. In the first act, he responds supportively. In the second act, she responds assertively and determines the outcome.

(3b) *Shift within a scene: woman's control explicit, but that of a young man as intermediary allowed; the common element appears to be shift in relationship.* (Cf. the stanza in "Coyote and Eagle's Daughter" discussed in [3a].) John Rush Buffalo told Hoijer another narrative involving Coyote and Eagle's daughter. It has a young man, Jack Rabbit, as a mediating figure. Indeed, it was published as "Coyote, Jack Rabbit, and Eagle's Daughter." Here again the usual relations are three and five, but there are four passages in which they are two and four. Coyote encounters the young man, finds out he is going to Eagle's daughter, and pretends that he is going there too. When they arrive, Coyote lies on the bed and tells the young man where to be. Eagle's daughter then enters, and in two stanzas, each of four verses, she tells Coyote where to be (G) and when to eat (H). Apparently her authority is established, for in the next stanza (I) she tells Coyote where to lie in five verses.

Now there are again two stanzas with four verses. In each, Coyote repeatedly calls out that he is being bitten by ants, and the young man tells him to come up (onto the bed where he and Eagle's daughter are) (J), then to lie on one side of him (K). The stanza ends with the woman getting up and going to the far side. When Coyote calls out again, the woman has the young man take her away; this stanza has three pairs of verses.

There follows a pair of contests between Coyote and the young man, first as to how far each can shoot an arrow, then as to how long each can stay under water. Coyote proposes that the winner of the second contest will marry Eagle's daughter (perhaps this holds for the first contest as well). Coyote comes up first. Jack Rabbit does not hear the woman tell him so and is drowned by Coyote. Coyote then tells the woman to stand at a distance for him to shoot toward, and he kills her. He cuts the woman's body at the waist and carries the lower part with him. He is found out by a little girl, an older woman beats him on the lower part of his body to drive him away, and he runs off, defecating all around. The portrayal of Coyote as despicable is complete.

When the relationship is between just Coyote and Eagle's daughter, the four-part stanzas parallel those in the other story, establishing Eagle's daughter as in charge.

When the relationship is mediated by the young man, Jack Rabbit, the four-part stanzas show Coyote gaining advantage. The woman thus becomes dependent on the actions of the young man and ultimately becomes a victim. The second set of four-part stanzas seems to indicate woman's authority as now having come into question. Perhaps the four-part relations imply that the young man is not equal to a man's role. (See Hymes MS b. This discussion supercedes the paragraph in Hymes 1997c:238.)

I have found instances of part of a scene shifting from three- and five-part relations to two and four in narratives in three languages of the Columbia River. In each case the shift goes together with explicit indication that what happens is now within the control of a woman. These shifts do not depend on the narrator being a woman. Two of the narrators are men.

(3c) *Shift within a scene: woman's control.* The Clackamas myth, "Gitskux and His Older Brother," told to Melville Jacobs by Victoria Howard, is about two kinds of woman, one alternately petulant and aggressive, the other properly assertive when necessary (see Hymes 1983d). Almost all the story is in relations of three and five, as one would expect in Chinookan. At one point there is a shift.

Grizzly Woman, a complex and significant figure for Howard, who had grizzly power herself, comes to a chief to be his second wife. (Two wives are standard for chiefs.) Angry about a small matter, she destroys all the people of the village, except for the chief (presumably Panther) and his younger brother, Gitskux (presumably Marten). Gitskux she takes away with her as a slave and uses his head to wipe her anus, making him bald. (The anus-wiper motif is found widely.) Panther escapes alone. He reaches a house and goes in. He sees someone enter the other end, carrying a deer, and assumes it is a man who has brought it back from hunting. The person goes out, returns, and washes and braids her hair. It is a woman. She butchers the deer and feeds him. So far, relations of three and five.

Panther is allowed to stay the night, first sleeping on the floor. The woman brings him beside her in bed in five steps (by causing insect bites). She then joins five nights together, after which they rise as husband and wife. Then comes the third, concluding scene of the act.

Now the two stayed.
She told him,
   "Now you will be doing the hunting.
   You will have thought,
     'Perhaps this is some man.'
   Here I have lived alone.
   I would be the one hunting."
"Indeed,"
   he told her.
Now that is what the two did.

There are just four verses: an opening and a closing, both marked by "now," which frames two turns of talk. The quoted speech at the center is itself framed by placement before and after the terms of speaking (she told him, he told her).

Of course, it would have been taken for granted that a hunter would be a man. Here a man has the role of hunter conferred on him by a woman, one who does not need him to hunt.

(3d) *Woman's authority, although already known, and explicitly stated, now formally implicit as ultimate ground.* It is hard for me not to reach for analogies from music for the effect of the shift to relations of two and four at the very end of the "Sun's Myth," as told by Charles Cultee to Franz Boas in Kathlamet Chinook in 1891 (see Hymes 1994b:285).

The story makes use of three and five, as is characteristic of Chinookan, until that shift. Five is a reference point throughout. A chief with people in five towns (i.e., an important chief) goes out early to see the sun and cannot. He insists his wife make him ten sets of leggings and moccasins. He travels to where the sun rises, wearing out all his footwear, through places where there are no people. He finds a house and a young girl, about to become eligible for marriage at menarche, in a house with all imaginable human wealth on its walls. She explains that when she marries, the wealth will be given away. He stays. The third act is a lyric moment in which time does not go forward but recurs. The old woman who bears the sun goes out each morning and returns each night, bringing valuables. The text says, every day like this. If the story stopped here, one would have a happy ending, a reward for intrepidity.

The chief becomes homesick. That in itself is not unexpected in the culture, and the old woman offers him gifts to take back to his home. He refuses every human gift; he wants only the shining thing she carries during the day. Since he is now a relative, she cannot forever refuse him. She gives him the shining thing to carry and an ax as well and warns him. As he reaches each of the towns of his people, what he carries sings. He loses consciousness, then revives to see that he has destroyed the town and the people in it. He tries to rid himself of what he carries, one way after another, and cannot. His own town is the fifth. He tries to stand still but is pulled forward, and it too is destroyed.

Now come the last lines, in an act with three stanzas. In the first stanza the old woman addresses him in three verses. Such a remonstrance is common at the end of Chinookan myths and always right. The final two stanzas are not in terms of relations of three and five, but of two and four: a stanza with two verses for the old woman, a stanza with two verses for the man. Here is that act.

(VI)

He looked back.   (A)
Now she is standing near him, that old woman.
"You,"
   she told him,
     "You."
     "In vain I try to love you,
       in vain I try to love your relatives."
     "Why do you weep?"
     "It is you who choose."
     "Now you carried that blanket of mine."

Now she took it,   (B)
   she lifted off what he had taken.
Now she left him,
   she went home.

He stayed there;   (C)
   he went a little distance.

There he built a house,
   a small house.

The tragedy seems Greek in its display of the working out of the consequences of hubris. In this it is very rare among narratives of the Native
American Northwest Coast. The only analogue to the plot itself known to
me is a Wasco Chinook myth with a different ending. A young man sets out
on a journey with several pairs of moccasins and finds a young woman in
the house of the Sun. But the Sun is a male and not benevolent, but rather
someone who brings humans back to his house to eat them. The young man
changes this, so that the Sun eats only animal flesh. The teller did not finish
the story at the time it was being written down but assured the transcriber
that it had a nice ending (Hines 1998:183–85 with notes; Trafzer 1998:44–
46). See also, closer to Kathlamet territory, the narrative told in Klikitat
Sahaptin in 1928 to Melville Jacobs by Joe Hunt, "Sun and His Daughter"
(Jacobs 1937:28–34, 1934:33–39; cf. Seaburg and Amoss 2000:146–53).

    Such a plot is familiar on the Northwest Coast—a hostile father-in-law
who is overcome. Cultee's narrative transforms such a framework as a way
of making sense of historical experience. His and other peoples on the lower
Columbia were devastated by disease, beginning late in the eighteenth century and reaching catastrophic proportions in the 1830s. The Sun's myth
interprets the destruction of the people, not as coming from outside, but
as brought about by one of their own. In the same way the Israelites interpreted the Assyrians as agents of their own God, punishing them for their
misdeeds. In each case, the ultimate power of the world, as found in the
story, continues to exist. Here the chief's hubris is a desire for power beyond human ability to control. Perhaps desire for things brought by whites
seemed like that in retrospect. But an insatiable chief was already known
in the myth of one who allowed only girl babies to live, keeping all women
for himself, until one wife disguised her infant boy, who returned as a man
to overcome that chief (Boas 1901:155–65 [Kathlamet]; Jacobs 1959b:108–16
[Clackamas]; Curtin 1909:248–53 [Wasco]; Curtis 1911:150–53 [Wishram]).

    In any case, the lines with which the myth ends leave behind three- and
five-part relations. They take on the two- and four-part relations associated
with women. Nothing announces the change; there is only the pairing of
"Now, . . . Now" and verbal repetition.

    Sometimes this seems like the effect of a change of bar measure, perhaps
a change of orchestration, even a final chord, integrating notes struck in
what has gone before. There has been the trio of warnings by women: the
first wife's doubtful question (do you think it is near, that sun?), the second
wife's rebuke about wanting the shining thing the old woman carries (she

will never give it to you), the old woman's admonition when she does give it to him (take care). There is the natural symbolism of sight. At home the chief could not see the sun when it came out. That is normal near the coast (because of mist), but it motivates him to go where the sun is. There he finds that he can see the Sun as a person, as kin, but not look at her power. When he looks at the shining thing she brings back each evening, his eyes close. But he does not learn what this means until the end.

(3e) *Different parts and shift within a scene: woman as ground.* Larry George, a narrator and artist, has told and illustrated many narratives of the Yakama, Sahaptin speakers north of the Columbia River in Washington. He has also composed an eloquent elegy for what was once a central part of life in the region, salmon fishing, focusing on the great center for such fishing at Celilo (above The Dalles, Oregon). He told and recorded it in English, but the patterns are Sahaptin. Especially striking is that four-part relations occur just at three points.

The narrative has an opening and a coda, framing the whole. The first has to do with the beginning of the world, and the other bids farewell. Each has two pairs of lines, four lines in all. These frame the whole.

Near the end of the fourth of the five framed parts is a verse invocation. The narrative has told of the coming of salmon, the coming of Indians, then the coming of whites, who built dams and changed the world. Yet the people continue to thank the Almighty, pray, feast, laugh, and sing. Two communities known for maintaining tradition are named. Then there is this:

The earth,
　　the earth is my mother.
The Almighty made her so.
How could I trade my mother?
How could I sell my mother?

Fish there,
　　people.
Fish there
　　for all time.
Fish for
　　as long as the mountains stand.
Fish
　　for as long as the river flows.
Fish as long
　　as the sun shall shine.

The last stanza's five verses invoke eternal continuity of the people's relation to salmon. What precedes, four verses, two pairs, invokes a woman as grounding of the world.

(4) *Shift of relations between stanzas and verses: women in control in the sense of initiators.* Two myths from California use pairing in connection with women's control in a more intricate way. Both myths involve the figure of Night-Hawk-Man. In each myth two women come to obtain an admirable man as husband, Salmon in a myth from the Karok along the Klamath River in northwestern California, a great hunter (unnamed) in a myth from the Maidus in mountain valleys of northwestern California. The women are misdirected to Night-Hawk-Man, discover the mistake, and leave. In the Karok myth, they leave ashamed and quarreling. In the Maidu myth, they break Night-Hawk's neck and transform him into the bird he is to be, predicting that in the world to come men will lie to the women they marry. They then go back to the right house.

In each narrative there is an interplay between patterning of stanzas and patterning of verses within stanzas. Let me display profiles of the relations between scenes, stanzas, and verses for each for reference.

(a) Phoebe Maddux, Spring Salmon Stays Single (Karok)[1]

Scene	Stanza/	Verses	
i	A	abc	Introduction
	B	abc	
	C	abc	
ii	A	abcde	The two girls meet Whippoorwill
	B	abcde	
iii	A	abc	Night-Hawk in the house
	B	abcde	
iv	A	ab	Night-Hawk disclosed
	B	ab	
	C	ab	
	D	ab	
	E	ab	
v	A	abcd	Salmon revealed
vi	Close	abcde	

Scenes ii and iii each have a pair of stanzas; each stanza has three or five verses. In these stages the two women arrive and initiate what happens. They arrive and find a man. In (ii), they arrive in search of Salmon and meet Whippoorwill, who instructs them where to find him (B). They go to the house to which they were directed and find a man (as yet unnamed) who actually is Night-Hawk.

Scene iv has an odd number of stanzas; each stanza has a pair of verses. In these stages the two women respond to what happens around them. People in the community act first. They holler for Night-Hawk to come and clean (A); then Night-Hawk pretends to the girls that he is being called as host (B). Only in the middle of the scene do the girls act, deciding to go see for themselves (C). They see Night-Hawk, not dividing food for others, but cleaning up scraps (D), a menial job further developed in the next stanza (E).

Scene v parallels iv in three respects. It also begins with talk outside by someone other than the girls (ab); in the middle the girls decide to go (c). (In [d] they do go and in [e], can still be heard going.) And just as in (ii) and (iii), the girls successively meet men (Whippoorwill, Night-Hawk), so in (iv) and (v) the true Night-Hawk and the real Salmon are disclosed.

In sum, the four narrative scenes (ii–iv) describe an arc of initiation and its reversal on the part of the two girls. When they come and find men, initiating action themselves, the superordinate pattern, that of stanzas, is one of pairs. When they find out the truth about the men in contexts initiated by others, voices of the community, the superordinate pattern, that of stanzas, is one of odd numbers.

It is likely that the subordinate pattern, that of verses, goes with gender as well. Certainly the pairs of verses in (iv) show the situation of the two girls reversed. They decide to go, not at the outset of the scene, but in the midst of it, the third stanza (C). And the same is true of the next four verses, where they decide to go in the third verse (c).

Indeed, scene v probably should be considered to have just four verses. (This corrects the presentation in Hymes 1997c.) The last verse (e) is not part of the narrative action, but a formal close.

Even-numbered relations, then, are associated with women, odd-numbered with men. (Notice also that the story has two women, three men.) But although the named actors all are men in the community to which the women come, the contrast informing the story has to do less with women versus men than with outsider versus community. Community rankings are stated in terms of men, to be sure, but if Salmon is most highly valued, Night-Hawk is least valued. Insofar as control is expressed, it is in regard to initiation of action only. The girls have it for two stanzas, then voices of the community for two.

(b) Tom Young, Night-Hawk-Man (Maidu)
(adapted from Dixon 1912:192–97)

Act	Scene	Stanza/	Verses
I	i	A	abcde
		B	abc
	ii	A	abcde
		B	abc
	iii	A	abcde
		B	abcde
II	i	A	ab
			cd
			ef
			gh
			ij
	ii	A	ab
			cd
			ef
		B	ab
			cd
			ef
			gh
			ij
		C	ab
			cd
			ef
			gh
	iii	A	abcde

In this Maidu myth there is again an inverse relation between pairing of stanzas and pairing of verses. The three scenes of act I each have two stanzas, while the stanzas themselves have three or five verses. The three scenes of act II each have odd numbers of stanzas (one, three, one), while the stanzas themselves, all but the last, have pairs of verses.

The relation between this inversion and initiative or control by women, however, is the opposite of that in the Karok myth. In that narrative pairs of stanzas and odd numbers of verses went with women initiating action. Odd numbers of stanzas and even numbers of verses went with others initiating action. The two women first took the initiative, then left in disgrace.

Here pairs of stanzas and odd numbers of verses go with others taking the initiative; odd numbers of stanzas and even numbers of verses go with women taking initiative. First the women are sent; then they become shapers of something of the world to come. Initiative and control extend far and are formally grounded with four-part relations unique in the story.

In act I, scene i, Night-Hawk lives opposite a great hunter (A). A father sends his two daughters to gain the latter as husband, telling them they will see black bear skins beside the smoke hole of his house (B). In (ii), Night-Hawk sees the women and puts the hides on his own house (A). The two women arrive, enter, and sit beside him as he plays the flute (B). In (iii), the real hunter returns and recovers his hides (A). After Night-Hawk has slept with the two women, they wake to see that the hides have been moved (B). In this act stanzas are paired; verses are in series of three and five.

In act II, there is a reversal. In scene i, the two women discuss their situation and decide to go across to the other house, where they sit down on each side (A). In scene ii, Night-Hawk sings, probably in lament, causing the wind to blow and water to rise (A, B). Then the two women cross over, break his neck, and pronounce what he actually is and will be (C). Having done these things, they go back to the same place (the hunter's place). The rain stops and stays stopped, and they remain in that house, presumably with the hunter.

It is in the reversal of the second act that the two women take control, and this is formally signaled by the four pairs of verses in the third stanza (C).

Then at last they,
   the sisters of these many men,
      having arisen,
         went across.
Then having gone in,
   by a blow they broke off the neck of the one who was always singing.

The evil Night-Hawk-Man not long ago,
   angry because of women,
   made water everywhere to rise in flood.
"That is what you are," they said.

Now, "You are not to disturb mortal men," they said.
"You are Night-Hawk,

you shall be a bird,
   unable to do anything," they said.

"Lying to women,
   men marry them,
   that shall be the world."
So they made it be.

From these examples, one might infer a pattern in northern California of having inverse relations between stanzas and sets of verses as to odd and even and also of inverting the relation as between the first and second part of a myth. With just two cases, however, such a conjecture would be rash. Based on other Karok myths I have analyzed, I doubt such is the case. Perhaps this particular myth-frame carried with it certain formal traits. Again, I would be surprised if this proved true.

Comparison of the two myths does show clearly two things:

(1) Such intimate covariation between levels of organization makes it difficult, I would say impossible, to doubt that control of such patterning is part of the narrative competence of the tellers.

(2) Four-part patterning has been available to Native American narrators in what are now the states of Washington, Oregon, and California, as well as Texas and possibly a larger area, as an alternative that marks significance of women. The meaning of the significance can range from that of a feminine ground for the life of the world to that of initiating action and even of feminine authority coming into question (Coyote, Jack Rabbit, Eagle's daughter in Tonkawa).

(3) The examples brought together here have come to hand by chance. To understand such marking of gender more fully will require making verse analysis a normal step in the interpretation of narratives. It will be particularly important to discover the characteristics of individual narrators. Very likely there are occasions of such variation and the kinds of meanings it may have that are not yet known.

5

When Is Oral Narrative Poetry?

Generative Form and Its Pragmatic Conditions

I want to persuade the reader of three things:

1. Spoken narrative has a level of patterning that is likely to be found everywhere, or nearly so, but that has been missed in most research (in the common kinds of entextualization [Blommaert 1997:15–24]).

2. We are only beginning to grasp the complexity of such patterning as a part of narrative competence.

3. Such patterning may be present to different degrees, or even absent, in ways dependent upon personal and community circumstances and concerns.

A fair amount has come to be known in regard to the first point (see the discussion later in this chapter). Something has begun to be known in regard to the second. What it would be like to know something about the third can be suggested.

The first point has to do with transcending two conventional practices. One is the long-standing assumption that narratives consist of paragraphs. Of course, one knows that epics such as the *Iliad* and the *Odyssey* and many other long narratives are organized in terms of lines. We readily recognize their lines because they are organized internally. There are patterns in terms of which a line has a certain number of stressed syllables, alliterating initial consonants, feet of types defined by a tradition. We have a name for such lines, metrical.

When metricality is absent, internal organization has been taken to be absent. Even those devoted to avoiding imposition of alien frameworks on languages, to describing the organization of languages inductively in terms of relations within the languages themselves, scholars such as Boas and Sapir, have left that devotion behind at the sentence's edge. Much of the traditional oral narrative of the world is published only in terms of paragraphs.

Today there is a great deal of work that transcribes oral narratives in terms of lines. The working assumption is to attend to pauses, phrases, tone groups, and the like. Such features are noted to divide a narrative. Largely ignored are features that enter into relationships to organize a narrative (see discussion of John L.'s story later in this chapter).

In recent years it has become clear that in many languages, perhaps all, there is an organization of lines in terms of which the shape of a narrative can be discovered inductively and shown on the page. The relations are not internal to lines, not metrical, but among lines, "measured." There are regularities in the relations among measured lines, just as there are regularities in metrical lines.

These regularities have to do with cultural patterns, but also with the explorations and skill of narrators. In terms of cultural patterns, communities appear to build upon one of two alternatives: relations in terms of two and four or relations in terms of three and five. English narratives in the United States appear to work in terms of three and five, but in parts of Ireland in terms of two and four. Among Native American groups, Navajos, Zunis, and others build in terms of two and four, while the narratives of Chinookan and Sahaptin peoples build in terms of three and five. In a flourishing narrative tradition, one may find a variety of ways of making use of such relations and of varying their aesthetic effect. A set of three or of five may be a set of three or five pairs. A sequence of ten lines may be a single rhetorical unit. A set of lines may be balanced internally, or a run from start to end. Uses of quoted speech and of catalogs are variables also (see chaps. 11 and 13 of this book; see also Hymes 1994c, 2000b; Hymes and Hymes 2002).

For many narrative traditions, discovering lines and relations is pretty much all that we can do. Such an endeavor can lead to understanding and interpretation otherwise not possible. We can recognize artistry and subtleties of meaning otherwise invisible. For a true account of the human capacity for verbal art, this is crucial. But as with the *Iliad* and the *Odyssey*, there are no people to observe and question, only texts.

The second and third points concern when and where and to what degree narrators are conscious of such relations or are sensitive to them, vary in their deployment of then, as in regard to gender, and are perhaps unconsciously affected by their presence. Pragmatic research should not be ignorant of the first point when dealing with narrative. It can make major contributions to the second and the third ones.

Introduction

Oral narrative is recognized as poetry when it is sung (ballads, many epics). That it is organized in lines and groups of lines is clear.

It has become increasingly clear that unsung, spoken narrative is also organized in lines and groups of lines, that it also is poetry. Such organization has been found in some seventy-three Native American languages, twelve languages of the Old World, three of the Pacific, and one Caribbean Creole (see appendixes 2 and 3.) It is abundantly true in English in both Great Britain and the United States.[1]

If this kind of organization is common, why has it been missed? With regard to earlier work and still often enough today, it is missed because for a long time *only* oral narrative that is sung or chanted has been considered poetry. Other narrative has been assumed to be prose and presented in paragraphs. As a result, the form of much of what has been preserved of the verbal art of the peoples of the world remains hidden. The first task with such material is to discover that it has lines.

It is common in several lines of work today to transcribe narratives as sequences of lines. The task with such material is to discover that it has shape. Syntax is not simply a sequence of words. Sentences have parts and internal relations. The same is true of stories. They have parts and internal relations. The parts and internal relations frequently are signaled. Yet much valuable work proceeds as if it did not notice the signals. (See the second example, John L.'s story from Labov's work in New York City, and the last two examples, one from work in South America, the other from work in California.)

Any account of a spoken narrative should provide the equivalent of a "profile," an overview of the relations among lines within it. Descriptive adequacy requires no less.

Such relations have been missed, no doubt, because we have not been used to considering spoken narrative as a level of linguistic structure, as having consistent patterns—patterns far less complex than those of syntax, but patterns nonetheless.

Missed also perhaps because lines in a spoken narrative may not announce themselves as part of a poem. We recognize lines as poetry when there are defining features internally, when they are lines (verses) that are metrical in having a certain number of syllables, stresses, alliteration, or have certain sequences of feet and tones. Or when they are part of a sequence of recurrent parallelism (including rhyme).[2] Even in isolation, such lines can be heard as poetry.

The constituent units of spoken narrative can usually be heard as units; probably they will have sentence-level intonation contours. (This remains to be tested widely.) Such contours allow them to be heard as units. It does not show them to enter into sequential relations. Yet in unrhymed spoken narrative such relations constitute organization.

Often indeed the unit that counts as a constituent of pattern has more than one line. That happens particularly with a sequence of turns at talk. In my experience a turn at talk counts as a single unit in the patterning of the next level, the stanza, even though the turn at talk itself may contain several lines. That is a reason for distinguishing between lines and constituent units. For units, the term "verse" can serve.

The relevant units, then, the parts of pattern, are verses within a stanza (and stanzas within a scene and so on). These make up the architecture of the story. In this respect a spoken narrative is, as one says in music, *durchcomponiert*. One can speak of "measured verse" (relations counted among lines) as against metered verse (relations counted within lines). To be sure, in spoken narrative there may be continuua between poles of meter and rhythm, as in the Hebrew Bible (cf. Gammie 1989), and rhythms, characteristic of particular authors and works, but I cannot explore that here. When recognized as poetry, Native American verbal art and vernacular traditions in communities of Europe and the United States may contribute to a deeper understanding of such things (cf. Fabb 1997; Meschonnic 1982).

A PLEA FOR THE UNSPOKEN

A basic definition in terms of spoken lines is a characterization in principle. It does not mean that nothing can be learned about narratives for which current performances or past recordings do not exist. One merit of verse analysis (as this work can be called) is that it helps recognize the worth of oral traditions for which we have only written evidence. Most of the Native oral traditions of the part of the world from which I come, the Pacific Northwest, are in that state, and much of my effort over the years has been devoted to recovering them. When lines, verses, and relations are recognized, one can venture to perform the narratives again, given appropriate circumstances.[3]

Much of the oral narrative of the world's peoples is in such a situation. The primary documents have line ends determined by edges of pieces of paper. Intonation is not marked. Yet the pages can reveal lines that enter into relations that give regular, sometimes powerful shape. Intonation is not the only clue. Verses are often overdetermined. Often they are marked by lexical elements initially, conjunctions and expression of time ("then," "now," "again," "next day," "a long time"). A turn at talk counts as a single unit, a verse, in the makeup of stanzas. When a tradition uses a quotative element ("they say"), its presence marks a verse. And as patterning emerges, it contributes to interpretation. In my experience, a lack of patterning shows a lack in interpretation. Often I have come back to an unsatisfactory result and discovered something new.[4]

Here we engage the principle Roman Jakobson (1960:369–62) christened *equivalence*. Speaking of Finno-Ugric and Russian folk poetry and referring to all the levels of language, he remarked: "[W]e learn what elements are conceived as equivalent" (369). The statement holds generally. Working with a text, a tradition, a narrator as source, one learns what enters into relations that give shape. One works back and forth between details and contexts, nearer and farther relations. The work cannot be mechanical. A tradition provides resources, but a resourceful narrator can put them to fresh use. In the event, one both interprets and analyzes, doing justice as fully as one can to the original.

This kind of work corresponds to a concern of importance to native peoples, *repatriation.* The term came to attention first with regard to human remains and material goods taken to museums and other repositories. In the United States many such things are being returned to the descendants of those from whom they came. It has strengthened sensitivity to the right of people and their cultures not to be treated merely as objects of science and scholarship. I think of this kind of recovery of the implicit form and meaning of texts as repatriation (Hymes 1991b, 1994a:353–54; cf. Alter 1985:214).

Most work so far has been undertaken in the spirit of early work with unwritten languages: to show that what is only spoken has order too. The goal of the first case was to make universal the scope of general grammar. The goal of the second case is to make universal the scope of poetry.

TWO EXAMPLES

Let me present two examples, one Native American from a language no longer spoken, one contemporary African American from New York. Discovery of intrinsic form heightens effect and meaning in each.

To recognize the value of oral narratives, one must recognize patterning of lines. Often enough, one must also recover the wording of the original.[5] A story may be translated in words that are felt respectable, but that conceal its artistry.

Two Native American examples have become fairly well known: "Seal and Her Younger Brother Lived There," told in Clackamas Chinook by Victoria Howard, and "Sun's Myth," told in Kathlamet Chinook by Charles Cultee.[6]

Example 1. Victoria Howard, "Tongue" (Clackamas Chinook)

Here is a passage from another narrative from Victoria Howard. The accompanying material shows the text as it was first translated and displayed in publication, then as patterned lines. In wording and shape, the first translation conceals the presence of a three-part reiteration of a transcendent moment, resurrection of the people themselves.

The people known as the Clackamas (they called themselves "people having vine maple") lived along the Willamette River just south of what is now the city of Portland, Oregon. Almost all that is known of their narratives (smidgens apart) comes from one woman, Victoria Howard, who told a great many stories in the months before she died (1929, 1930) to Melville Jacobs, who was trained by Boas and able to transcribe them in her language. Like others of his generation and many scholars today, Jacobs assumed the narratives were prose and presented them in paragraphs. Like others, he tended to avoid repetition in English.[7]

Howard grew up on Grand Ronde Reservation near the coast, but this story takes place on the Willamette River, where the Clackamas originally lived. A chief's wife had died and her body put out in a tree. Tongue comes from the river and starts to take the body. Two watchmen (Cut-fish) cut off its tongue and put the body back. Tongue cries day and night, "Give me back my tongue." The watchmen tire, give it back, and Tongue eats everyone. Only one woman survives. Other people played all the time, but she had gone to dig camas plants. When she returns to her house, there he is. She is (already) pregnant and has a son who grows swiftly, a fine hunter. Told what happened to the people, he trains in the mountains for power, then turns rotten wood into quantities of deer. Tongue brings them in and eats until he falls asleep in a stupor. Mother and son set the house afire, and he burns with it.

Now comes the moment in question. The son goes again to the mountains, where he collects feathers and bones, as many of each as the number of people Tongue had killed. The climax comes in lines 265–71. A ritual act is reiterated verbatim three times: "They became people" (in Clackamas, *idálxam núxax̣* 'people they-became').

As first published, the lines constitute a paragraph (no. 27). The reiteration is not distinct, in lines or wording: "He wished them to become persons. . . . Those feathers and bones became people. . . . Now there the people were." (The word for his act means, not 'to wish', but 'to transform (by power)'.)

More than that, the first two words are markers of a structural unit and inverted from their usual order: "then now" instead of "now then." That inversion signals a turning point. The three repetitions of "they became people" show three parts. "Then now" marks the first as a turning point; "now" without "then" shows the third to be a summing up.

Then now, he transformed them,
  they became people
Those feathers,
  bones,
    they became people
      those different feathers were for canoes.
Now *they became people.* (Jacobs 1959a:375)

The remaining part of the story now begins. The restored people are un-grateful. When the young man comes where the people are working in the river, fishing as instructed by his father, they scold him for not working. His mother scolds them for not realizing it is he who revived them, but, already insulted, he continues into the river. He weeps but continues. Such pride is associated in other Chinookan stories with Salmon, and a version of this story told in English by a man partly of Clackamas descent indicates that it is Salmon here. It is not a chief who returns each spring, but one who leaves. The last words of Howard's text indicate that the people in the story are of the myth age. Because Salmon leaves, so must they, to be what they will be in the age to come.

Had you not done like that to him,
You would have lived on here.
Now then.
Now we shall make our separation. (Jacobs 1959a:375)

One can imagine association of this outcome with the outcome in histori-cal time when the Clackamas could not stay in their own place but were forced to Grand Ronde Reservation, those that had survived disease. The im-plication is that the cause lay in not heeding their chief. Such a difference in outcome is the interpretive voice of the narrator.[8]

Example 2. John L., "Well, One Was with a Girl" (New York City)

William Labov's path-breaking work in New York City has included influ-ential work on oral narrative. Himself a storyteller, he sought to show the worth of narratives that many in the society disregarded, often because of the variety of English in which they were told. The starting point of the method was contrast between clauses that carry a narrative forward in time and those that do not. Those that do not are interpreted as evaluation. Over-all shape has been interpreted in terms of six general categories derived from rhetoric (abstract, orientation, complicating action, evaluation, resolution, coda). A text is presented in lines, taken as syntactic clauses but as a continuous series, not as having internal organization in terms of verbal form.[9]

The limitations of such an approach appear with a principal example, a story from a narrator highly regarded among the African-American young men with whom Labov worked, John L. (see Labov 1972:358–59). The relations among the lines are not governed by sequence alone. There are relations of equivalence as well. A variety of words and phrases both say what they say for the content of the story and by recurrence convey its form.

Here is John L.'s story in terms of lines and verses, followed by a profile that makes relations and features explicit.

What was the most important fight that you remember,   (i) (A) [Question]
   one that sticks in your mind. . . .

Well, one was with a girl,   (B)
Like I was a kid, you know,
And she was the baddest girl,   5
   the *baddest girl in the neighborhood.*
If you didn't bring her candy to school,
   she would punch you in the mouth;
And you had to kiss her when she'd tell you.

This girl was only about 12 years old, man,   (C)   10
   but she was a killer.
She didn't take no junk;
She whupped all her brothers.

And I came to school one day,   (ii)
   and I didn't have no money.   15
My ma wouldn't give me no money.

And I played hookies one day.
[She] put something on me.

I played hookies, man,
so I said, you know,   20
   I'm not gonna play hookies no more
   'cause I don't wanna get a whupping,

So I go to school   (iii)
and this girl says, "Where's the candy?"

I said, "I don't have it."   25
She says, powww!

So I says to myself,
    "There's gonna be times my mother won't give me money
        because a poor family
    And I can't take this all, you know,   30
        every time she don't give me any money."
So I say,
    "Well, I just gotta fight this girl.
    She gonna hafta whup me.
    I hope she don' whup me."   35

And I hit the girl, powww!
and I put something on it.
I win the fight.

That was one of the most important.   (Answer)

Profile

Scenes/Stanzas/Verses			Lines	Features	Contexts
i	A	a	1–2	*Turn*	(Framing question)
	B	abcde	3, 4, 5–6, 7–8, 9	*Turn, Well*	(the girl)
	C	abc	10–11, 12, 13	*man*	(the girl)
ii					(Ma and me)
	A	ab	14–15, 16	*And, one day, no money*	
		cd	17, 18	*hookies, one day*	
		ef	19, 20–22	*hookies, man, said*	
iii					(Girl and me)
	A	ab	23, 24	*So, says*	(he, she)
	B	ab	25, 26	*said, says*	(he, she) (1st round)
	C	ab	27–31, 32–35	*So+says, So+say*	(deliberation)
					(he as to she$_1$,
					he as to she$_2$)
	D	abc	36, 37, 38	*And I . . .*	(second round)
	E	a	39		(answer)

There are a variety of recurrent features in the story. Several show that it has three scenes. After an introductory answer to the question that prompts what John L. says, there are two changes of location and time. These begin the second and third scenes. The thematic word "whupped" occurs in each scene. In each of the first two scenes, it is in the last line. In the third scene, it is in the last two lines of the third stanza, a turning point. The first line of the last stanza in each of the first and second scenes each end with the term of address, "man." The second scene is organized in part by interlocking repetitions of the phrases "one day" (stanzas A, B) and "played hookies" (stanzas B, C). In turns of theme, the worth of the opponent is built up in the first scene; moral constraint on the narrator is established in the second scene; the resulting dilemma is faced and overcome in the third.

One parallel corrects Labov's statement that the narrative proper does not begin until line 23 ("So I go to school"). Line 14 begins "And I came to school one day." Each line indicates change of location, indeed, the same change. As it turns out, each introduces a consistent pattern of verses as well (see the profile).

A particular feature of this narrative is emphasis and evaluation of action, not by non-temporal clauses, as Labov would have it, but by doubling (see Hymes 1996b:202–3). Particularly important is the doubling of initial "so" at the midpoint of the last scene. The two verses complete a sequence of three pairs. Both are reflections, spoken by John to himself. The first recalls the situation at home, as to his mother and money, while the second considers the immediate situation, facing and fighting the girl. Each leads to a moral decision.[10]

The narrative departs even further from linearity. It is a sequence of actions, of course; it is also a sequence of doublings, and moreover, a series of enclosing circles.

Some scholars think traditional stories should be expected to have ring-like structure, the end returning to the starting point. That is not generally true in my experience, but it is true of John L.'s story when seen in its context. The first line is an interviewer's question, and the last line is an explicit answer, capping the narrative that comes between. Moreover, question and answer enclose two other circles. The initial account of the girl as a fighter follows the opening question; the dramatized fight precedes the concluding answer. This is the second circle. It encloses the account of the boy and his mother, the second scene. This central scene is highly marked. It initiates grouping of verses in pairs and has three pairs of verbal repetition. It establishes John L.'s moral resolve in relation to his mother. And it has a double within the third and final scene. The central stanza of the third scene is to it what the second scene is to the story as a whole. It is intensified (initial "So" twice) and doubles the theme of moral resolve, with John thinking first of the mother, then of the girl.

In sum, the story begins by enhancing the opponent as a fighter and ends with victory in a fight against her, but John's resolve to fight has his mother at its heart.[11]

Two Principles for Relations (Two and Four, Three and Five)

An example of a text with each kind of principle is presented in Hymes 1982 (reprinted in Kroeber 1997).[12]

INNATE?

If the two kinds of relations continue to be found throughout the world, one might ask, are they in some way innate? I suggested that they might be in commenting on a paper by Newmeyer (1991) in which he sought to extend the scope of what might be considered innate in generative grammar (Hymes 1991b). Newmeyer rightly resisted any temptation to agree. Universality would not be enough. One should be able to show that exposure to the relevant data would not be enough for the feature in question to be learned (105). And from a functional standpoint, it is easy to argue that the kinds of relations involved could come about through cultural adaptation.

Assuming that patterned organization beyond the sentence or line would be found rewarding, the two kinds of relations would seem to be just what would make pervasive patterning of texts possible. Two and three seem to be the minimal bases that could provide a variety of perceptible and manageable sequences and effects. Four is a multiple of two. Five seems everywhere associate with three. Six is found, but as a grouping of three sets of two. Seven is found ceremonially (e.g., the number of required drums in a ceremony), but not as a regularly repeated basis for verbal organization. (I am considering only spoken narrative.) Eight again is a multiple of two. Nine is a multiple of three. Ten is twice five. Eleven apparently is too large to be a minimal starting point, as is the case for other larger numbers (see Hymes 1991b:51).

This argument obviously only indicates a possibility; it is not a proof. The likely universality of internal organization of spoken narrative in terms of lines (verses) points to a grounding in human nature. One can hope that future work will clarify the precise nature of that grounding.

CHOICE AND MOVEMENT

Common patterning allows for choice, for particular effects and personal styles. When one becomes familiar with a tradition, this becomes clear. If a tradition makes use of relations of three and five, there is a choice of either three or five at any point. A stanza may have three or five verses. For elaboration or emphasis, it may have three or five pairs of verses. And there are options as to the kind of movement within a sequence, what Kenneth Burke called "arousal and satisfying of expectation."[13]

Often a sequence of three has a movement of onset, ongoing, outcome, as in Wishram Chinook: *Gayúya, gayuyá:, gayuyám* 'he went, he kept on going, he got there'. (cf. Caesar's *veni, vidi, vici*).

Sometimes a sequence of five is an *interlocking* of two sets of three. In John L.'s story, the third scene has five stanzas. The third is a culmination in relation to the first two stanzas in the scene and a beginning for the final two (see Hymes 1996b:202–3). In Louis Simpson's "The Deserted Boy" (Wishram Chinook), the same is true of the opening scene (see Hymes 1994a:336–37). A narrative taken down in a Philadelphia department store by Nessa Wolfson has interlocking at several levels of organization ("She's a Widow" in Hymes 1996b, chap. 10, "Inequality in Language: Taking for Granted"; see especially p. 215). The middle point of a sequence of five both completes one three-step series and is the onset of another.

A five-part sequence may thus have a variety of internal relations: interlocking, as just described (ab(ɔ)de); a run from first to last (abcde); two pairs completed by a fifth element (ab cd e). (For examples of other possibilities, see chaps. 3 and 15 of this volume.)

ALTERNATION

Recently it has become clear that there is a further kind of choice, choice of underlying principle itself. Even if a tradition is pervasively one kind of relations, three and five or two and four, a narrator may not be limited to a single kind. I have summarized several examples and presented one in detail in articles (Hymes 1997c; chap. 4 of this book). Let me call attention here to the example that first compelled me to recognize such alternation in terms of *gender*.

SOCIAL DISTANCE

In the narratives of the Tillamooks of the northern Oregon coast, four is the pattern number in feminine contexts, five in masculine (Jacobs 1990 [1959]:116 n.21). A story taken down twice from Clara Pearson, "Split-His-Own-Head," has this pattern. An older sister tries to tell a younger brother how to do things but speaks ironically and is misunderstood. The first part of the narrative has five scenes, the second part four. The first part has to do with activities proper to a male, such as building a canoe; the second part has to do with getting a wife. (At the end the sister speaks plainly, and the effort succeeds.)

For patterning of parts, each telling is the same. For patterning of stanzas within scenes, the two tellings differ. In one, Pearson used three or five stanzas within scenes. In the other she used two or four.

This alternation cannot have to do with gender in the sense of what a part of the story is about. In both tellings the parts are the same.

Nor can it have to do with the language in which the story is told. Patterning within scenes is commonly in relations of two and four in Tillamook, in terms of three and five in English. With these two tellings of "Split-His-Own-Head," the opposite is the case. The version in Tillamook, a Salish language, has relations of three and five, while the English telling has relations of two and four.

The telling in Tillamook was taken down by May Mandelbaum (Edel), the telling in English by Elizabeth Jacobs. Comments by both and other information indicate that Pearson felt closer to Elizabeth Jacobs, who, like her, was a married woman and was nearer her own age. May Mandelbaum was young, unmarried, and reportedly brash.[14] Evidently Pearson associated closeness with the relations linked with focus on women (two and four) but associated social distance with those linked with focus on men.

TRANSFER OF CONTROL FROM ONE GENDER TO ANOTHER

Sometimes alternation of underlying principle of pattern is associated with change of control from one gender to another. When Frances Johnson told Edward Sapir a story involving Coyote rushing to a girl's puberty dance, the opening act is a brief portrait of what he did every day, catch gophers. The second act shifts from moderato to agitato. He hears the sound of the puberty dance and rushes toward it. He keeps pausing to listen, thinking he is almost there, when he is not. Now in Takelma (a language of the Rogue River in southern Oregon) narrative relations are usually in terms of two and four. The almost bucolic first act is such. The second act changes to relations of three and five. After it, relations of two and four are resumed.

Certainly the interval of three and five fits the expression of energetic, if fitful movement. Coyote keeps stopping, thinking he is almost there, when he is not. Perhaps relations of three and five, used this way, indicate masculine control, mocking it.

In the Pacific Northwest examples are coming to light in which alternation between the two kinds of relations goes with alternation in controlling gender. A succinct instance is a scene in the myth of "Gitskux and His Older Brother," as told in Clackamas Chinook by Victoria Howard.

Example 3. Victoria Howard, "Gitskux and His Older Brother" (Clackamas)

This myth is in essence about two kinds of women, one properly assertive, one alternately petulant and aggressive (see Hymes 1983d). The latter, a Grizzly Woman, comes to a chief to be his second wife. In anger, she destroys the people of the village, all except Gitskux (probably Marten) and his brother. She takes them away with her as slaves and uses their heads to wipe her anus. The older brother (presumably Panther) escapes alone. Eventually, he reaches a house and goes in. There he sees someone enter the other end, carrying a deer. He assumes it is a man. Then the person goes out, returns, and washes and braids her hair. It is a woman. She butchers the deer and feeds him. (All this is in relations of three and five.)

Panther is permitted to stay the night, and during the night the woman causes him to come beside her in her bed. (Five steps are involved; for the first three, she has him bitten by fleas.) She joins five nights together. They rise as man and wife. Then comes this scene (part 3, act I, scene iii):

Now the two stayed.
She told him,
   "Now you will be doing the hunting.
   You will have thought,
     'Perhaps there is some man.'
   Here I have lived alone.
   I would be the one hunting."
"Indeed," He told her.
Now that is what the two did.

There are four verses, not three or five. The opening and the close are marked by initial "now." In between are two turns at talk. A role that would have been taken for granted to be that of a man, that of hunter, is conferred on this man by a woman who does not need him for it.

Example 4. Charles Cultee, "Sun's Myth" (Kathlamet Chinook)

I have become convinced that a scene in Charles Cultee's Kathlamet Chinook "Sun's Myth" also shows transfer of control to women, in form as well as in content.

The myth tells of a chief who has five towns of relatives. He becomes determined to travel to the sun. His wife tries to dissuade him, but he persists. He
travels ten months to where the sun rises and reaches a large house. Inside
is a young girl. On each side of the house are many kinds of wealth (human
goods), and he asks the girl about them. The wealth all belong to her father's
mother, who will give it away when she matures and is eligible to marry. He
decides to stay and eventually takes the young girl. Every day the old woman
is gone by the early light; every evening she brings home wealth.

Eventually he feels homesick. The old woman asks what he would like to
take with him on his journey home. He refuses human wealth. He wants
only the large shining thing she puts away at the end of the house. His wife
tells him she will never give it. But at last the old woman's heart becomes
tired (one cannot refuse a relative forever). She warns him and gives him the
shining thing and an ax.

At each of the five towns, that which he has taken makes him lose consciousness. He recovers to see he has destroyed the town. He tries to rid himself of what he carries and cannot. At the last town, his own town, he tries
to stand and his feet are pulled.

Here is what the myth says next:[15]

He looked back. (act VI) (A)
Now she is standing near him, that old woman.
"You,"
    she told him,
    "You.
"In vain I try to love you,
    in vain I try to love your relatives.
Why do you weep?
It is you who choose.
Now you carried that blanket of mine."

Nothing explicit is said as to an alternation of form at this point. But
already with the woman's speech, pairing appears. The stanza itself has three
parts: he looks, she stands, she speaks. But when she speaks it is first, "you.
. . . you" and then "in vain. . . . in vain." And the two final stanzas are entirely in terms of two and four, not three and five, as the myth has been until
this point.

The first of these stanzas (act VI, B) has two parts, each introduced by
"now." The second also has two parts, partly indicated by parallel occurrence of "there." Each of these parts is a semantic couplet.[16]

The action of the myth is driven by the desire of the chief. Three women attempt to divert him without avail. Only at the end of each part is there a steady state—when he has first married the Sun's granddaughter and she brings them goods in her large house, and when having destroyed all his people, he builds a small house. The change from threes and fives accompanies a shift from a male domain of hubris and terror. The final pairs suggest a recognition of the limits of human control with which the women of the story have been in touch all along.

Future research most likely will extend the range of purposes for which alternation may be used. Such alternation in type of relation among narrative elements is analogous to the kinds of alternation called style-switching and code-switching. General explanations are clearly premature, even more so in this regard than with regard to code-switching, as Cheshire and Gardner-Chloros (1998) have shown. Both phenomena may have different meanings within different communities and different meanings within the lives of individual speakers (Cheshire and Gardner-Chloros 1998:29).[17]

Variation

I have stressed the need to recognize the presence of patterned relations. It is important as well to recognize variation in their presence. Narrations differ in the degree to which patterning is present and what its role is.

One dimension of variation is elaboration and intensification. This may involve devices that are more than temporal sequence and that need to be recognized as such. Let me give a rich example.

DEVICES OF ELABORATION

Rhythm of movement may change dramatically despite regularity of patterning. An expected number of verses in a stanza, of stanzas in a scene may be maintained, but weight and expressive effect take the center of the stage. (Just as the count of beats in a measure of music may be constant across a range from one whole note to a run of sixteenths.) Five ways in which this focusing within a regular frame can occur are *itemization, extraposition, catalog, inset,* and *lyric moment.* All occur in one act of a widely known Native American narrative, "The Deserted Boy," as told to Edward Sapir by Louis Simpson in Wishram Chinook (cf. Hymes 1994a—the analysis in that article supersedes that in Hymes 1981b, chap. 4).[18]

The frame of the narrative in the first part is that a child is deserted and left to starve. In the last part it is now the people who lack food and the child who has much. Discovering that, the people set out. A narrator's sense of justice will determine whether all, some, or none of them arrive.

Louis Simpson's second act first shows the boy being self-reliant, making a cloak against the winter cold and finding a way to catch fish. Each step of his effort each day is *itemized*—how much he caught, how much he ate, how much he saved, each time. One more of each, each day. The fifth day, however, we do not learn what he has caught or what he does with it. The scene ends with telling us that having fished five times, he has become a grown man, something not before mentioned.

The food he has gotten the fifth day is carried over to a second scene. I call this *extraposition* (see Hymes 1981b:167).

What he has gotten is not fish, but a prepared food (a mixture of fish and berries). When he finds the delicacy, he sings. The plot stops for this *(inset)*.[19]

The daughter of a spirit-power in the river has given food, and when he has camped over five times, he wakes to find her beside him. There are just three verses here (marked by "now then"), but seventeen lines. The second marker introduces the woman, first that she is beautiful, then her hair, bracelets, and rings, a painted house, and a mountain-sheep blanket. The third marker lists kinds of food she has brought, naming fish from the river. In short, two *catalogs*.

The scene ends with five verses, marked only with "now." No "then" for succession of time, just "now." Such a moment in which time is not marching, a *lyric moment*, seems to have been well known to Oregon narrators. When the chief seeking the Sun first stays with her daughter, there is such a moment. In the Takelma myth of "Coyote and Frog," Coyote's opening catching of gophers has similar character. Indeed, both are told in terms of "every day." (In "Gitskux and His Older Brother," Howard reports such a moment for Panther and the woman to whom he comes, a single night extended to the length of five nights.)

The ending of a story of desertion characteristically varies in how others are treated. Here, when the village that deserted the boy finds out he has food, the people set out across the river toward him. First come the grandmothers who had left the boy food and fire, and he lets them arrive safely. As to the rest, he raises an east wind in which they drown. He comments on his reasons in each case. In Victoria Howard's telling of the story, a motive of remorse is added to those of gratitude and revenge. The wife who came to the boy is the one who has had power to deal with the people of his village. The story continues after his revenge. She leaves him, ashamed of having used her power in such a way.

It would be a mistake to recognize motives only in what happens, not also in how it happens. Gratitude and revenge complete Louis Simpson's story, but at its center is exultation. The central act is a virtuoso display of traditional ways of modulating action. They adorn the boy's accomplishments like an accumulation of fine blankets at a potlatch. The final act enacts moral judgments. The central act displays identification.

ROUTINES OF VERBAL INTERACTION

Verse patterning may serve metalinguistic and metapragmatic purpose by giving shape to a reported routine of verbal interaction. Victoria Howard dictated several cases to Jacobs. Each is built on quoted speech ironically deployed. (See discussion of "Perennial whistling," "Laughing at missionaries" and "Maybe it's Milt" in D. Hymes 1987b; Ramsey 1995 adds to understanding of the last.) These seem to be well-known routines, repeated for amusement. (See also the account of Kilipashda's joking, to which quoted speech is central [D. Hymes 1987b:313].)

Such examples of the modeling of interaction are especially interesting because there is little other evidence of conscious analysis of the organization of narrative in the materials with which I have worked. People may comment on pattern numbers, such as four and five in the Tillamook case presented earlier in this chapter. They certainly evaluate narrators in terms of such traits as verbosity or conciseness, ability to use uncommon words or to bring a story alive with gestures and voices. It may be that when Native American traditions were part of flourishing communities, comments about patterned organization occurred as well: "So-and-so really knows how to get a lot into a stanza." I have not heard them, nor do I know of them among contemporary narrators in English. It seems that the skill deployed, like that of syntax, is productive, but out of awareness, or at least not given explicit terminology.

BREAKTHROUGHS IN PERFORMANCE: FRAMING AND REFRAMING

Narrators may differ in their relationship to the stories they tell, and the relationship may change in the course of telling. In the cases I know from Chinookan languages, verses are always present as constituents of organization, but their explicitness by marking may vary. Observations on differences among several Chinookan narrators in relation to personal outlook and situation are given in Hymes 1981b, chapters 3 and 6.[20]

Especially interesting are cases in which a narrator may intervene in what he or she is saying to frame or reframe it. An instance memorable to me occurred when I was working on the Wishram-Wasco lexicon with Philip Kahclamat, once a source for Walter Dyk and Edward Sapir, in a restaurant booth. Discussion of the word for "crier," someone who announces to the village, led Kahclamat to assume the role and perform it (see Hymes 1981b: 87ff., 203–5). The words are perfectly organized throughout in five stanzas, of three, and, in one instance, five, verses. Having broken into performance, Kahclamat ends by breaking from English into Wishram.

Verse patterning may be a factor when the unfolding of a narrative brings a narrator to a halt. This occurred when Victoria Howard told Jacobs a myth in which foods that appear in spring are noted, one by one. They are asked about, named, and described, and something is said about where they will be or how they will be used. As told by Charles Cultee to Boas in Kathlamet (the language downriver from the Clackamas), the foods are encountered by people traveling upriver in a canoe with Salmon as headman (see Hymes 1985a). As told by Howard, there is no journey. Foods appear in place. (See chaps. 6 and 7 of this volume.)

The two accounts share a verbal tradition. The first formulaic line in Howard's telling is a frozen, incomplete version of a line in Cultee's. The change from journey to encounter in place is part of a transformation of male adventure into a recital of domestic instruction.[21]

Howard presents a series of three kinds of food—plants, birds, and fish—in sets of three members each. There are two sets for fish, which are last. When the series reaches the fifth set, and the second one of two for fish, the third (and last) fish is to be named, Howard gives no name. Instead she says:

All the things in the water like that,
I don't know their names.
I (can't) think what their many names were.
They all spoke that way.
I think I remember only up to there now.

She continues with a shift in gears.

My mother's mother would say,
  "Coyote did like that,
  all the things we eat here.
On the other hand, my mother-in-law would say,
  "I don't recall who made the things that are good to eat here."
My mother's mother would say,
  "Coyote did like that to all these things here.
  He went past all the things that are berries.

She continues with a humorous encounter with berries, in which each kind of berry addresses Coyote by a special proper name, *štánkiiya.*

The narrative breaks off because the course of its telling has given rise to contradiction. For Chinookans the culminating name for a series of fish would be salmon. (Possibly sturgeon for some, but the series has already included sturgeon: mudfish, chub, trout; eel, sturgeon.) But at the start Howard indicated that the one who encounters the foods is a fish person, maybe Salmon. If the series is to culminate in salmon, however, it cannot be (or have been) Salmon who announces. If the announcer is (and has been) Salmon, salmon cannot be what he announces.

To be sure, myths can have an actor who is also an ordinary source of food, but the roles are separated. The actor becomes a food at the end, after the action of the myth is over, when those within it separate to become what they will be when human beings arrive. Here the two stages confront each other. It seems an incomplete transformation of a male-centered version such as that of Cultee. Perhaps Howard was thinking through the transformation as she spoke. In the event she leaves the conflict unresolved and resorts to another tradition altogether.

VARIATION AND ITS EVALUATION: SOCIAL LEVELS

Marking of verses may play a part in distinguishing levels of a language. One example comes from "Frontier Norwegian" (see Hymes 1997b).

In the summer of 1929 in southeastern South Dakota, the young Einar Haugen took down dictated narratives that his mother then used in an annual publication for settlers from Oppdal, Norway. He did not think the materials could be published as linguistic texts, given their imperfections, but did hope to publish them for content. Years later, Haugen published and compared two versions of an incident as told by a principal source, Halvor O. Aune (Haugen 1980).

Both versions tell of two men on a long trek. They reach a host who gives them whiskey in which to bathe. They fear the cost, but in the end he does not charge them at all.

Haugen prefers the version in local idiom. Although it omits some details, it "has a narrative directness and cohesion that is far superior: It establishes the rancher-saloonkeeper as a man with a heart beneath his crude exterior and dubious mode of life . . . a small study in character, an encounter between two cultures, a true frontier exemplum" (1980:26).

The text in local dialect does have an explicit evaluation as outcome, gratitude for a kindness to strangers that could not have been taken for granted. That personal touch seems to encourage or reinforce a prior attitude on Haugen's part toward the two levels of language. He goes on to say that the two versions offer "evidence of how radically the speech situation can alter a speaker's language, inducing a virtual diglossia that can inhibit even a practiced and skillful narrator when he believes be must elevate his language" (1980:27).

In point of fact, when the two texts are compared in terms of analysis into verses, the first text, the text in a nearly standard Dano-Norwegian of the time, is the one that is consistently marked and integrated, more so than the text in the local idiom. The concern for the host's reputation found at the end of the text in local idiom is framed by that text's one switch to the literary code.

In sum, verse analysis shows the version in the literary code to be more consistently marked and integrated, shaped neatly toward the end of a dramatic telling. As with grammar, so with narrative: one needs to discover implicit relations and form. Labov has often remarked that many narratives in standard speech are in fact poorly told. This is not one of them.[22]

CONTINUA, CONTINUA

There must be many dimensions of variation and contrast in explicitness and elaboration of verse form in oral narrative. I should like to discuss one that may reflect development of a relationship between narrator and audience. In this case the audience is an inquirer.

Victoria Howard and Melville Jacobs worked together twice, in the summer of 1929, then again for two months, from January to March 1930. Early on, she told Jacobs a story that at its end she unwittingly told him again. (The first text is in his second field notebook, the second in the eighteenth and last.)[23]

The second version expands the title of the story. Howard first called it "They Died of Hunger" (literally, 'hunger killed-them'). The second time she specified the place by name: 'K'ašxə́kšix / 'its-name / where / they died of / hunger.'

Memory enhanced by working with the language and traditions may explain that difference. Increased confidence in her command of the fullness of her narratives is likely a factor as well. During the course of her work with Jacobs, she began to use a formal close. She does so at the end of the second telling of this story: k'ánik'áni ···! 'Story! Story!' (Formal endings may have words before 'story story' that explicitly say 'That is all (complete)'.)

The second version is more fully performed as well. It includes the onomatopoetic expression for the sound the headman makes when he hits something to call his people (dək·dəl·dəl·dəl·). When the headman goes to find out why his people are covered by snow, the second version elaborates his actions five times with quotation of his inner speech.[24]

The surprising difference between the two versions is that it is the first that marks verses again and again with an initial particle (*aga* 'now'). This occurs in a number of the narratives Howard told Jacobs early in their work together. All her narratives are couched in relations of verses, but later initial particles are uncommon. This stands in sharp contrast to the earliest narratives we have in the language itself from a speaker of Kiksht (Clackamas and Wishram-Wasco), Louis Simpson, where particularly the initial pair, "now then," is standard. Simpson varies his use of initial particles for effect, as we have seen in the second act of "The Deserted Boy." When Howard comes to use them sparingly in what she tells Jacobs, her use seems analogous to the variation for effect found with Simpson. In this instance, they seem alike.

Why then the superabundance of "now" in Howard's early dictations? I think it is a sign of uncertainty about her command of the device, of a formal style. At the outset she sprinkles "now" as if it is a token of reassurance. Later she has no need for tokens.[25]

Continua in the use of devices are likely to appear in all manner of circumstances. This will be true as well for genres other than narrative (speeches, sermons, some kinds of writing). The Senecas (an Iroquois group) have been shown by Chafe (1993) to have three speaking styles, conversation, preaching, chanting, that are on a continuum, reflecting "decreasing responsibility of the speaker, or an increasing responsibility of a remote authority for the content being expressed." If the styles involve the kinds of relations considered here, as speeches in the Native Northwest do, a continuum in formal marking might show degrees of responsibility both across and within genres. When narratives are recognized as having verses and relations among verses, one can recognize such variation as evidence.

ABSENCE?

There may be cases in which one pole of a continuum, of variation, is absence of any evident marking. Over the years, Virginia Hymes and I have seen many narratives brought to class by students, and nary a one without verse form, but these narratives have been valued by those who took them down. Whatever the reason for valuing them, they have form. But it is quite possible that they acquired form in the course of repetition.

The fact that children's narratives give evidence of the same kind of form encourages the thought that such form is natural, in that it will emerge among members of a community if not hindered (see Hymes 1996b, chaps.

7 and 8). Nonetheless, it may be hindered or perhaps avoided. Verbal art attracts for its own sake and as an attribute of those who possess it, but research needs to consider its absence. Absence may tell something as well. Perhaps the narratives of communities and individuals vary from thoroughgoing patterning to rudimentary presence, even virtual absence. Two recent studies suggest one factor that may contribute to such variation.

VALUATION AND REPETITION

(a) The presence of patterning and its degree may be governed by valuation, particularly as to centrality to a group or person, and consequent repetition, rehearsal. The anthropologist Greg Urban provides an example from his work with a Brazilian Native American group, the Shokleng. Urban (1996) stresses the importance of ceremony and assemblage. At one point he touches on repetition of lines:

> [G]roup assemblage is one way of heightening nonreferential communication—the relatively more direct experience of social reality. It is one way of making nonreferential communication salient, and, simultaneously, of backgrounding the referential, of backgrounding language-based consciousness. The mechanism for doing this is the repetition of units, such as the line, which brings discourse as sound into prominence. Repetition is the basis for such phenomena as chanting and singing. It is the basis also of dance and dancelike kinesic forms. Repetition does not require group assemblage, but when the group does assemble, repetition tends to occur. (1996:185)

In other words, ceremony and some narratives "embody" experience and weave a spell that engages participants in community.

In this context, Urban presents a narrative that he says brings the sensible, perceptible qualities of discourse into awareness more than any other from the community with which he is familiar, because it is the only one that endeavors to represent a ceremony in words (1996:182). He remarks: "In representing communication within the ceremony as taking place largely beneath the level of consciousness, this narrative captures the opposition I have been positing—the world of ceremony is built out of contextual, nonreferential meanings. Such meanings I understand to be aligned more closely with the unconscious than with reflective consciousness . . . a modality of experience of the world that is distinct from reflective awareness" (1996:184). Analysis of the narrative in terms of relations among lines and groups of lines does indeed show the kind of patterning I have discussed (Hymes MS c).

(b) Centrality and repetition may be an attribute of a personal story. In their important book, *Constructing Panic*, Capps and Ochs (1995a) investigate the development of narratives in the life of a woman suffering from agoraphobia.

Clinical literature has not recognized such narrative accounts, Capps and Ochs report. There is attention to responses from questionnaires, but not to what patients formulate for themselves. Patients' accounts may show underlying patterns and help therapy to overcome them.

Capps and Ochs consider a number of linguistic characteristics of the stories told by Meg (a pseudonym for the narrator). They refer to the *architecture* of the major narrative on which they focus and to the *structure* and *structuring* of a story (1995a:39, 40, 47). They remark that meaning arises as much from how something is said as from semantic content (28). A verse analysis (see Hymes and Hymes 2002) brings out dimensions of this phenomenon, while showing that this much-rehearsed story is patterned in verses and stanzas throughout.

Jill McRae (1995) has explored the presence of such patterning in a long, moving narrative from a victim of rape. The narrative is presented in terms of relationships of the kind found in other English-language narratives. In certain respects the analysis is a step removed from verbal detail—single word answers and most initial affirmations or denials are omitted. One might also question some details of the assignment of lines to patterned units, but further reflection of that sort is normal in the course of interpreting a complex narrative. The full account is impressive.

Jan Blommaert (1998) explores the emergence of narrative pattern in interviews with Belgian missionaries who had a spent a significant portion of their lives in Africa. Patterns like those of verse-relations appear to be present.

One can hope that others will take up this kind of analysis and thereby enrich understanding of the part language plays in the understanding of both community and individual lives.

Part 3. Stories Twice-Told and Complemented

6

Language, Memory, and Selective Performance

Charles Cultee's "Salmon's Myth" as Twice Told to Franz Boas

Introduction

I want to show that the shaping of a story in performance may disclose something of personal voice. No news there, of course. The news is in the nature of the texts and perhaps in the bringing to bear of the point on a common kind of structural analysis.

The texts are two tellings of the "Sun's Myth" in Kathlamet Chinook, recorded not quite a century ago. Thus, interpretation depends not on tape recordings and interviews but on philology. As data we have the published texts and behind them the field notebooks. Yet careful attention to details of language in the context of a theory of the poetics of Chinookan narrative makes evident the presence of a narrator.

Such texts have not usually been seen in such a light. They have been considered evidence of history, ethnology, and language, not of performance. The words of a single speaker have been glossed in the name of an entire culture, Victoria Howard as "Clackamas" and so on. Claude Lévi-Strauss's discovery of transformational relationships in myths has been associated with interpretation in terms of a single original configuration for the entire New World. Now, poetic analysis illuminates the cultural meaning of the myth, and transformational relationships obtain within it and between it and a neighboring (Clackamas Chinook) version. But the evidence is in the first instance what the narrator chose to say. In so choosing, he or she communicated something personal as well as cultural, if we have the skills to recognize it. The personal meaning is especially clear here because two tellings can be compared. The second telling was recorded to test memory; similarity was what was wanted, but the differences show individual artistry as well. And the differences show that a structuralism that relies on units of propositional content alone as the basis of analysis will fail. The commonalities so identified prove to be, not the structure of the text, but only ingredients. Each telling makes use of common ingredients, but it is precisely in the difference in the way they are deployed and shaped that the meaning of each is disclosed.

Here is the background of the data.

In 1890, Franz Boas, seeking to rescue knowledge of languages and traditions in the Pacific Northwest, could find on the Oregon coast no one who could dictate texts in the language of the Chinook peoples, who had dominated that very place at the beginning of the century and hosted Lewis and Clark. Referred to Bay Center, Washington, Boas found there three other survivors, one of whom, Charles Cultee, proved "a veritable storehouse of information" (Boas 1901). Cultee quickly grasped Boas's purposes, even though their only medium of communication was the Chinook jargon, and enabled him to understand the structure of the language. Boas made three trips in all, in 1890, 1891, and December 1894. On the last trip he sought to test the accuracy and validity of his Kathlamet data, as he himself explains:

> Cultee was my only informant [for Kathlamet]. This is unfortunate, as he told me also Chinook texts, and is, therefore, the only source for two dialects of the Chinookan stock. In order to ascertain the accuracy of his mode of telling, I had two stories which he had told in the summer of 1891 repeated three and a half years later, in December 1894. . . . They show great similarity and corroborate the opinion which I formed from internal evidence that the language of the texts is fairly good and represents the dialect in a comparative pure state. Cultee lived for a considerable number of years at Cathlamet, on the south side of the Columbia River, a few miles above Astoria, where he acquired this dialect. His mother's mother was a Kathlamet." (Boas 1901:5)

This is all that Boas ever published about the "great similarity" of the two tellings of the two stories, the "Salmon's Myth" and "The War of the Ghosts."[1]

Sixty years later, Boas's finding about the state of the dialect was abundantly confirmed. His texts provided the basis for an account of Kathlamet phonology, morphology, and lexicon (Hymes 1955). But little has been said about the state of the tradition. Its contents have simply been cited from time to time as evidence. Today we can ask in a fundamental way about it. Many Chinookan narratives and narratives from other American Indian traditions have been found to show organization in terms of lines and groups of lines (see Hymes 1975b, 1980c, 1981b, 1982, 1983c, 1983d). Narrative competence of this kind can shine through even a text both brief and somewhat garbled dialectally (Hymes 1984c). What, then, about Cultee's two tellings of the "Salmon's Myth"? ("The War of the Ghosts" shows something of interest about tradition and performance also, but lack of space precludes inclusion of it here.)

These narratives show the general Chinookan patterns of organization. Closely compared, they show details that bear on the stability of tradition and that can be taken to have to do with memory and its refreshment. The narratives also show details due to selective performance, to focus on one implication of a myth rather than on another. Once pointed out, such details sometimes seem obvious, yet often they are not visible in texts as usually published and perused. It takes presentation in line and verse to make them available to the eye. Above all, my understanding of the meanings of the two tellings arose only as an answer to the question posed by discovery that they differ in form. Without the verse analysis, I could have said that in 1894 Cultee added an ingredient at the end. I could not have seen how he shaped his telling to different effect in each case nor brought appropriate evidence to bear on the differences. Such a conclusion must emerge from consideration of the evidence for the form each telling is taken to have. Let me insert first some methodological reflections.

"Practical" Structuralism

Current discussion in ethnopoetics sometimes loses sight of the basic question of descriptive method. Whatever else "ethnopoetics" may be, it is first of all continuous with the description of other aspects of language. Its starting point must be what might be called "practical structuralism." The term "structuralism" here does not refer to what has been made of linguistic analysis in anthropology, semiotics, and the like. The term here refers to the elementary task of discovering the relevant features and relationships of a language and its texts. One should think of the work of Kenneth Pike, Eugene Nida, and H. A. Gleason Jr., rather than that of Claude Lévi-Strauss and Roland Barthes. Such work is continuous with Boas's establishing a certain essential level of adequacy and accuracy earlier on and the kind of work from which "structuralism" as a theory is an abstraction. If Zellig Harris had not decided to change the name of his 1951 book from *Methods in Descriptive Linguistics* to *Methods in Structural Linguistics,* his student Chomsky might not have taken "structural" as an epithet for everything preceding him that he rejected, and the lineage of practical work might be clearer today.

"Practical structuralism," then, or "descriptive structuralism," has to do with the elementary task that Hockett (1955) called "gathering," as distinct from "collation." Linguistic controversy today usually presupposes the results of "gathering." The argument is not about what exists (in one sense at least), but about how what exists is to be understood in terms of a model or general theory. Of course, a theory directs attention to some facts and away from others. Transformational generative grammar has directed attention away from the prosodic facts that are vital to discourse and narrative patterning whenever they can be ascertained. But there is a large area of presupposed agreement. Linguists have not disagreed as to the fact that /p/ and /b/ contrast initially in English words ("pill":"bill") and do not contrast after /s/ and before vowels; there is a labial stop in that position, which we write with *p* in "spoon," but only one. Argument has been concerned with the way in which to relate the facts about initial position to the fact about occurrence of a labial stop after /s-/. (Is it /p/? Is it /b/? Is it common core? Is it part of a sequence of dental fricative and labial stop that is voiceless /sp/ or voiced /zb/ as in "asbestos" as a whole?)

The situation in ethnopoetic analysis is parallel. It is not difficult to recognize lines and local groups of lines. In Chinookan, at least, and some other languages, each predicate phrase is distinct as a line. Certain other constructions show, through predicate import or parallelism, that they can be regarded as lines. Certain sets of lines are readily recognizable as belonging together: they share content, show verbal repetition, and contrast with what precedes and follows them. In some styles, such as that of Louis Simpson in the Wishram-Wasco texts recorded by Sapir (1909b; cf. Hymes 1981b, chap. 4), an initial particle pair, translatable as "now then," consistently marks a unit at a level above that of line, which can be called the verse. (Other particles sometimes substitute, notably "now again.") In other styles, such as that of Charles Cultee, initial particles occur, and when they do, they mark larger units, but do not occur initially with every unit larger than a line. To be sure, certain other kinds of word turn out to be consistent signs of demarcation: temporal words, such as statements of season, time of day, or the passage of time, are notable instances. A turn at talk, a change of location by the movement of the actor focused upon, or a new actor are commonly signals of units. Beyond such indications of individual units is the matter of relations among units.

Some local relations are recurrent and consistent evidence that the lines showing them belong to a common unit: three or five lines in a common sequence of travel, such as "he went, he went on, he arrived"; a sequence of two actions leading to something perceived as a third element and outcome.

Beyond these immediate relations are relations of longer scope. Here patterns of repetition and parallelism play an essential part. On the one hand, there is the known Chinookan principle of grouping actions in sequences of three and five. On the other hand, there is the way in which this flexible

principle has been implemented in a particular case. Sometimes the boundary of a larger grouping is indicated by an accumulation of initial markers:
particles, time words, a turn at talk, even a change in tense-aspect; but often
it is not. There can be some room for uncertainty and disagreement at this
level. My experience with Chinookan leads me to have confidence in de-
marcating lines, verses, and some local groupings of verses, which is equivalent to what Hockett called "gathering," that is, establishing the elements
that occur with contrastive significance in a position, in the paradigmatic
set within a slot. Larger relations depend in important part upon accumulated intimacy with a text and the rhythm it seems to have, and they inevitably depend in part on criteria of consistency and, sometimes, on an inference as to expressive intention. (As mentioned, in the texts in this article,
expressive intention was inferred from patterning already established, but
the "spiral" or dialectical back-and-forth between both kinds of inference is
often unavoidable.)

The local relationships usually can be simply noticed and presented. The
larger relationships must sometimes be argued. Alternatives must be explored in a quasi-experimental fashion. The choice will be the larger patterning that best accounts for all the data, that best fits the covariation of form
and meaning in the text. In this respect, "texts fight back" (to put quotes
around what should be taken as a slogan). A pattern that is formally feasible
may do violence to content, forcing reconsideration of what the possibilities
of marking and patterning are. At the same time, the hypothesis of pervasive
patterning may bring out aspects of content otherwise missed.

These considerations are familiar, and I have mostly mentioned them
elsewhere (Hymes 1981b, esp. 150–52, 176–77, 192–93, 313–20). Yet if they
were obvious and compelling, the landscape of recent debate and activity in
ethnopoetics, and with regard to American Indian texts, would have a different appearance. Some seem to think that the discovery of such patterning
is reserved to poets. Some seem to think that emphasis on the importance of
one kind of marker must imply the exclusion of other kinds. And a passion
for mind or a passion for performance may lead some to ground structure
in just one of the two traditional planes of language, meaning or sound. To
be sure, there is valuable work that strives to integrate the two planes (as in
the concern of Anthony Woodbury and Joel Sherzer for the place of prosody
in both grammar and performance). Such integrative work helps transcend
the traditional polarity, opening up a necessary third plane not reducible to
the usual spheres of sound and meaning, namely, the plane of act and event.
But many students of texts seem to perceive the field as grounded in just one
traditional plane and even only a portion of that.

On the one hand, a great deal of work informed by structural principles, the work best known to our general culture, has grounded itself in units of propositional content in abstraction from text as a sequence of words. Now, such abstract relationships have a place. The kind of analysis given in this chapter often enough yields results that partly conform to, partly confirm, broad relationships of content, relationships that might be noticed without its aid. But without such aid, the perceived relationships may turn out to be superficial or even transverse to the actual purport of the text, closely read. There may be emphases and implications that only attention to verbal form enables one to notice. I yield to no one in my admiration of Lévi-Strauss for his discovery of relationships of transformation, but it is a strange tribute to linguistics to ignore language. And the meaning of a text is controlled not only by local norms of phonology and syntax but also by local norms of the point and patterning of stories. One must work out a "grammar" of the local world of discourse and work out the internal relations of a text in relation to that grammar before proceeding to analytic comparison and interpretation in terms of relationships found elsewhere.

On the other hand, Dennis Tedlock's admirable insistence on the vocal realization of texts has given rise to the impression in some quarters that pauses alone, not other kinds of markers as well, let alone interdependence of signals with content and function, are the foundation of units in a text. I have even known a folklorist to determine significance of pause with a stop-watch. But pause or any other feature of sound is in itself a physical, not a cultural, phenomenon. It becomes an aspect of structure only in terms of the basic principle of "practical structuralism," contrast and repetition, the use of form/meaning covariation to establish what counts as the same and what as different. In a single case, one cannot be sure which features are accidental, which are conventional in the style of one narrator, which are conventional in the community. What contrasts in the sense of covarying with a difference in significance? What counts as repetition, as the same, despite the observer's ability to detect physical difference?

This general perspective applies to all features, of course, and to comparative analysis as well. The convincing discoveries of Lévi-Strauss are those that show close covariation of elements as between texts. The claims that assimilate a text to a series on the basis of a superficial likeness or a distorting selection of a single feature without close internal analysis are unconvincing, even misleading, as in the case of the texts treated in this paper.

"Practical structuralism" has to see the main task before us as a descriptive task. We simply do not have many instances of narratives presented and analyzed in an adequate way. The elements, devices, patterns, relationships, and meanings present in these texts remain to be discovered for the most part. We have only begun to give grounding to models of what the narrators were up to.

The First Telling (1891)

Following is my new translation for the 1891 telling. I should have liked to present the story simply as a sequence of lines, so that one could read it without prejudice to a particular analysis of its parts. When this was done in a first draft, it proved difficult for a reader to relate the subsequent discussion to the story itself. In order to follow the argument, one has to locate portions of the story in terms of parts identified by the analysis. In consequence, the various levels of the analysis are identified at the left of the lines, but if one wishes one can cover them up and read without attention to them.

The translation is followed by a profile, which summarizes the analysis of the structure. Covariation of form and meaning is indicated by summary labels for incidents and markers. The units are keyed to the story by the roman numerals and letters that label them at the left and by the numbers for the lines they comprise at the right.

Most everyone would recognize the presence of the two acts and of the five scenes composing the first act. It does not prejudice interpretation to identify these levels in the same central column as the translation itself. The level at which judgment may differ and change is that of the stanza, both as to the grouping of stanzas into scenes and as to the grouping of verses into stanzas.

Most everyone would recognize the predicate phrases, turns at talk, and parallelisms that define the lines and groups of lines. Others might settle on other visual alignments on the page. Some of the alignments, to be sure, are aesthetic choices on my part. A tape recording of Cultee's performance, if one existed, would add to our understanding, but it would not much affect the form/meaning relationships discoverable through the words themselves. These relationships would still obtain, whatever the tone of voice, intonational contour, and distribution of pause. Cultee's voice might be found to reinforce some relationships, clarify others, override and play off against still others. Or his voice might demonstrate the pace at which Boas had instructed him to dictate. In any case, the text still permits inference as to what he meant, and the field notebooks, as will be seen, even preserve some indications of spoken continuity.

The verses of act II are lettered sequentially through the act as a whole, to facilitate discussion of alternative groupings of them.

Salmon's Myth I (told 1891)

	(I) ("If I were not")		
	(i) (Skunk Cabbage)		
The people of myth times died of Hunger.	(A)		1
Large arrowhead root was all they had to eat,			2
and small arrowhead root,			3
and skunk cabbage,			4
and *tqanapSupSu* root they would have to eat,			5
and rush root.			6
Spring came,	(B)	(a)	7
now Salmon went up river.			8
First Salmon would arrive,		(b)	9
the companion of many.			10
Somewhere he arrived,		(c)	11
now Skunk Cabbage said:			12
"At last my brother's son does arrive.			13
"If I were not,			14
"Then your people would have died."			15
Salmon said:		(d)	16
"Who is it who talks that way?"			17
"Ahh, Skunk Cabbage,		(e)	18
"he talks that way."			19
"Let us go ashore.	(C)	(a-1)	20
"Let us go ashore!"			21
They went ashore.		(a-2)	22
He was given an elk-skin armor,		(b-1)	23
five elk-skin armors were given him.			24
Under his blanket was put a club,		(b-2)	25
and one was put under his blanket the other side of his body,			26
two bone-war-clubs were put under his blanket.			27
He was carried inland,		(c-1)	28
he was put in the midst of willows.		(c-2)	29
	(ii) (Small Arrowhead Root)		
Now again Salmon and his party went upriver.	(A)		30
Now again another person made itself heard:	(B)	(a)	31
"At last my brother's son does arrive,			32
"the one with maggots in his buttocks.			33
"If I were not a person,			34
"then your people had died."			35
"Who is it who talks that way?"		(b)	36
he said.			37
"Ahh, your father's sister Small Arrowhead Root."		(c)	38

He put small dentalia at her buttocks,	(C)		39
he gave her a woodchuck blanket,			40
he gave her three woodchuck blankets.			41

(iii) (Large Arrowhead Root)

They left her,	(A)		42
they went a little distance.			43
Now again another person made itself heard:	(B)	(a)	44
"At last my brother's son does arrive,			45
"the one with maggots in his buttocks.			46
"If I were not a person,			47
"then your people would have died."			48
Salmon said:		(b)	49
"Who is it who talks that way?"			50
"Ahh, your father's sister Large Arrowhead Root,		(c)	51
"she talks that way."			52
"Let us go ashore!"	(C)	(a)	53
He put long dentalia at her buttocks.		[b]	54
Five woodchuck blankets he gave her.			55
He carried her to mud.		[c]	56
He put her down.			57

(iv) (Rush Root)

Now again they went upriver.	(A)		58
They arrived some distance.			59
Now again a person made itself heard:	(B)	(a)	60
"At last my brother's son does arrive,			61
"the one with maggots in his buttocks.			62
"If I were not a person,			63
"then your people would have died."			64
He said:		(b)	65
"Who is it who talks that way?"			66
"Ahh, your father's brother Rush Root."		(c)	67
"Let us go ashore,"	(C)	(a)	68
said Salmon.			69
He was given an elk-skin shirt.		(b)	70
Feathered head regalia were given him.			71
He was put down in soft ground.		(c)	72

(v) (Greens)

Now again they went upriver.	(A)		73
Where they arrived,	(B)	(a)	74
now again a person			75
"At last my brother's son does arrive,			76
"the one with maggots in his buttocks.			77

"If I were not a person,   78
  "then your people would have died."   79
"Let us go ashore.   (b)   80
  "Who is it who talks that way?"   81
"Ahh, Greens," your father's brother,   (c)   82
  "he talks that way."   83
Five raccoon blankets were given to him.   (C)   84
  He is set down at the shoreline.   85

(II) (Blue Jay, Crow, Flounder)

Now they went upriver up above.   (A) (a)   86
  They met a canoe.   87
    Salmon said: 88
      "Ask that canoe."   89
In the canoe were three people.   (b)   90
  A man was steersman (in the stern).   91
    The one put in the middle made itself heard: 92
      "Laq'alaki:awa:,   93
      "Laq'amo:Sq'amo:S,   94
      "Laq'apa:wapawa."   95
Salmon said: (B) (c)   96
  "What does that woman say to us?"   97
That steersman said: (d)   98
  "Ahh, she is saying,   99
    "it was floodtide,   100
      "now they went upriver,   101
    "they arrived at the Cascades,   102
      "now it was ebb tide,   103
      "now again they came downriver."   104
"Stop their canoe.   (C) (e)   105
  "Why then does a Lie always move her?   106
    "How long should they (take to) return,
      those going to The Dalles?"   107
They stopped their canoe.   (f)   108
  They were reached.   109
In the bow was Flounder.   (D) (d)   110
  Her head was seized,   111
    the (throat) was held down,   112
      that is the way her face was twisted,   113
      that is the way her mouth became crosswise.   114
Crow was seized,   (h)   115
  she was grasped around the nape,   116
    her face was twisted.   117

Blue Jay was seized,	(i)	118
he was grasped around the nape,		119
his neck was held down,		120
his face was twisted.		121
They were told:	(E) (j)	122
"How long should they (take to) return going to the Cascades?"		123
They were left.	(k)	124
"Future generations	(l)	125
"shall camp five times until		126
"then they shall reach the Cascades."		127

PROFILE

A way to make clear what is entailed by "practical" structuralism is by a profile of a text (cf. Hymes 1980c:46–47; 1981b:225, 227, 232–33, 238; 1983d: 134–35). Such a profile commits one. It expresses an analysis of the entire text, thus answering to the linguistic criterion of "total accountability" at this discourse level. It states all the relationships and units found in the text, from lines to acts and major parts. Such a profile is a check on the adequacy of one's own analysis for oneself and a concise statement for purposes of alternative analysis and comparison.

In previous presentations of profiles, I have shown mostly the "form" in the sense of the lines and groups of lines. Content has been indicated chiefly in labels for sections, if at all. It is easy enough to include indications of content at every level, and to do so makes the form/meaning covariation that underlies the analysis much more evident. The indications do not touch all that is to be found and said about meaning. They represent a minimal abstraction from the content, a low-order labeling of it.

Such a profile permits precision in statements of difference and similarity, whether between alternative analyses, between performances, or between different narratives. I have suggested some conventions for tagging points of alternative analysis (Hymes 1981b, chap. 5) and mentioned this contribution of verse analysis to comparison (Hymes 1981a) with regard to a Clackamas and Kalapuya version of "The News about Coyote." Here I give such a profile, incorporating form/meaning relationships throughout for the first time.

Notice that the fact of presentation in lines itself facilitates alternative analysis and comparison. Cumbersome phrasings, complicated footnoting, and the like can be avoided. One need simply cite the line numbers to identify the data in question.

With such a profile and the analysis that underlies it, one can show precisely what is at issue in arriving at an analysis of the overall patterning of a text; one can specify what is invariant in the style of a narrator or a story; one can hope to lay the basis for systematic comparative understanding of American Indian narratives. A motif-index, the ingredients of Boas's 1916 *Tsimshian Mythology,* and the analyses of Lévi-Strauss garner insights and aspects of the truth.[2] Yet in the light of verse analysis they come to seem as partial in the light they shed as would a grammar of one of the languages encased in a Latin model. The true inner "economy" (as the great French missionaries to Algonquian groups in the sixteenth century might have put it) is missing. Most strikingly of all, perhaps, is that no comparative method based on translation and content alone has ever, so far as I know, brought to attention the speech acts and other devices that enter into the arousal and satisfaction of expectation in these stories. The "speech of remonstrance" that culminates Victoria Howard's "Seal and Her Younger Brother Lived There" (Hymes 1981b, chaps. 8–9); the withholding of an expected final element to constitute an entire scene in Louis Simpson's "The Deserted Boy," a device of "extraposition" that recurs in Chehalis Salish, Zuni, and Tonkawa (Hymes 1981b, chap. 4); the specific pattern of arrival on the scene that is shared by Pima (Akimel O'odham)-Papago (Tohono O'odham) texts of a certain genre, certain Tonkawa Coyote myths, and a Takelma myth (Hymes 1980c, 1982)—such devices and their import are hardly to be seen except after analysis has liberated a narrative into verses and lines. In consequence, the artistry involved in their deployment cannot be perceived nor the element of personal voice discerned. One cannot cross the gap between comparative analysis and performance, between common inventory and emergent configurations of form.[3]

The analysis underlying the profiles depends on control of the language of the Kathlamet original, not only as published (1901) but also as first recorded in Boas's field notebooks.[4] Each telling has been retranslated, and the Kathlamet edited in the light of the notebook transcriptions. All of this would far exceed the scope of a single essay. Here I present only the fresh translations, but not the supporting notes nor the texts and the notes on the choices of orthography and analysis involved. I retained one paragraph from the notes to the retranslation of the 1894 telling, having to do with line 94, because it bears significantly on the form the telling is taken to have and the necessity of philology. In the last analysis any text is partly established, not found. A discussion of the cognate myth in Clackamas from Victoria Howard is also omitted (see the chap. 7 of this volume). Only let me note here that it shows both verbal continuity with the Kathlamet tradition and also an opposed perspective. Analysis of the Clackamas text and its post-script narration suggests a process by which the figure of Salmon was characterologically eviscerated, then replaced, in a line of Clackamas women, and that the process can be glimpsed being enacted at the end of Howard's own narration.

Not all indications of structural units can be included in the column headed *Markers*. Repetition of incidents in a consistent pattern itself establishes expectations and structural relevance, as in the three recurrent incidents in stanza C: going ashore, gifting, placing. As often happens, the first sequence is elaborated (stanza C in scene i), establishing it, and successors are briefer.

Abbreviations include: Fa: = "father"; loc. = locative or locational word; vb.: = verb. "Turn" replaces the fuller phrase "turn at talk" after its initial appearance. "To gift" is used as a transitive verb by Indians in the region, hence "gifting" for the recurrent incident in stanza C of each scene.

Profile: Salmon's Myth I (told 1891)

Act	Scene	Stanza/Verse	Incident	Markers	Lines
I	i	A	Myth people hunger	Scene/agent frame set of 5 names, 3 vbs.	1–6
		B a	Upriver (1)	season word, now, travel (1)	7–8
		b	Upriver (2)	ordinal, travel (2)	9–10
		c	"If I were not"	loc., travel (3), now turn at talk	11–15
		d	"Who?"	turn	16–17
		e	"Your Fa's sibling"	turn	18–19
		C a-1	Ashore (1)	turn	20–21
		a-2	Ashore (2)	change location	22
		b-1, b-2	Gifting (1, 2)	pentastich (2; 3)	23–24, 25–27
		c-1, c-2	Placing (1, 2)	distich	28,29
	ii	A	Upriver	"Now again," travel	30
		B a	"If I were not"	"Now again," turn	31–35
		b	"Who?"	turn	36–37
		c	"Your Fa's sibling"	turn	38
		C	Gifting (1, 2)	tristich (1; 2)	39–41
	iii	A	Upriver	travel	42–43
		B a	"If I were not"	"Now again," turn	44–48

		b	"Who?"	turn		49–50
		c	"Fa's sibling"	turn		51–52
	C	a	Ashore	turn		53
		[b]	Gifting			54–55
		[c]	Placing	(C = pentastich)		56–57
iv	A		Upriver	"Now again," travel		58–59
	B	a	"If I were not"	"Now again," turn		60–64
		b	"Who?"	turn		65–66
		c	"Fa's sibling"	turn		67
	C	a	Ashore	turn		68–69
		[b]	Gifting			70–71
		c]	Placing	(C = pentastich)		72
v	A		Upriver	"Now again," travel		73
	B	a	"If I were not"	loc., "Now again," turn		74–79
		b	"Who?", ashore	turn		80–81
		c	"Fa's sibling"	turn		82–83
	C		Gifting, placing	distich		84–85
II	A	a	Upriver, ask	"Now," travel, turn		86–89
		b	Answer	turn (3 + 3)		90–95
	B	c	"What?"	turn		96–97
		d	Answer	turn ("Now" 3 times)		98–104
	C	e	Alongside (1)	turn		105–7
	D		Alongside (2)	change of loc.?		108–9
	E	g	Twisting (1)	loc., name (Flounder) pentastich		110–14
		h	Twisting (2)	name (Crow), tristich		115–17
		i	Twisting (3)	name (Blue Jay)		118–21
	F	j	Pronouncement (1)	turn		122–23
		k	Departure	turn		124
		l	Pronouncement (2)	turn		125–27

The Second Telling (1894)

Here is the translation of the 1894 telling. As in the 1891 telling, letters are assigned to stanzas and verses in act II on a different basis than in act I. In act I the series of letters for stanzas (A, B, C, etc.) begins anew in each scene (i, ii, iii, etc.). The series of letters for verses (a, b, c, etc.) begins anew in each stanza. That practice is consistent with the usual practice in plays and other literary texts. The line numbers remain available for identification of a particular point whenever they are more convenient for the purpose.

In act II of both tellings the letters are assigned to verses in a continuous series throughout the act (a–k), (a–o). This is done because the relationship among the verses is in question. Discussion of alternative patterns of relationship among the verses is facilitated, and prejudice to one or another alternative pattern is avoided.

In act II of both tellings the letters are assigned to stanzas in a continuous series as well. There is no apparent difference, since there are five stanzas, and the series ABCDE would be a normal pattern.

Were it not for the analytical purpose being served, the stanza and verse lettering in act II of the 1891 telling might be presented as A ab; B ab; C ab; D ab; E ab. The stanza and verse lettering in act II of the 1894 telling might be presented as i A abcde; ii A abc; iii A abc; B; C abc. (There would be no need to assign lowercase letters where there is only one verse in a stanza.)

Salmon's Myth II (told 1894)

	(I) ("If I were not")		
	(i) (Skunk Cabbage)		
The Spring Salmon was going upriver.	(A)		1
First he came,			2
and he was going upriver.			3
Now a person is standing:	(B)	(a)	4
"At last my brother's son does arrive,			5
"the one with maggots in his buttocks.			6
"If I were not a person,			7
"then your people would have died."			8
He said:		(b)	9
"Who is it who talks that way?"			10
"Ahh, your father's brother, Skunk Cabbage,		(c)	11
"he is talking."			12
"Quick, let us go ashore."	(C)	(a-1)	13
Salmon landed (out of the canoe).		(a-2)	14
He was given an elk-skin armor,		(b-1)	15
five elk-skin armors were given to Skunk Cabbage.			16
Under his blanket was put a club,		(b-2)	17
beside his arm,			18
and beside his (other) arm			19
another one,			20

a bone war club.   21

He was carried inland,   (c-1)   22

  he was put in the midst of willows.   (c-2)   23

                     (ii) (Small Arrowhead Root)

Now again they were going upriver.   (A)   24

Now again a woman was seen,   (B)   (a)   25

  standing: 26

    "At last my brother's son does arrive,   27

      "the one with maggots in his buttocks.   28

    "If I were not a person,   29

      "then your people would have died."   30

He said: (b)   31

  "Who is it who talks that way?"   32

"Ahh, that is your father's sister, Small Arrowhead Root."   (c)   33

Now: (C)   (a-1)   34

  "Quick, we go ashore."   (a-2)   35

A double deerskin blanket was given her,   (b-1)   36

  two deerskin blankets were given her.   37

Small dentalia were put at her buttocks.   (b-2)   38

"Later on you will be bought,   (b-3)   39

  "you will wait for small dentalia,   40

    "you will be exchanged for them."   41

She was carried inland to mud.   (c-1)   42

  She was set down.   (c-2)   43

                            (iii) (Rush Root)

Now again they were going upriver.   (A)   44

Now again a person was seen   (B)   (a)   45

    "At last my brother's son does arrive,   46

      "the one with maggots in his buttocks.   47

    "If I were not a person,   48

      "then your people would have died."   49

Salmon said: (b)   50

  "Who is it who talks that way?"   51

"Ahh, that is your father's brother Rush Root,   (c)   52

  "he talks that way."   53

A buckskin was given to him,   (C)   54

  two buckskins were given to him.   55

                 (iv) (Large Arrowhead Root)

Now again they were going upriver.   (A)   56

Now again another person was seen:	(B)	(a)	57
"At last my brother's son does arrive,			58
"the one with maggots in his buttocks.			59
"If I were not a person,			60
then your people would have died."			61
Salmon said:		(b)	62
"Who is it who talks that ways"			63
"Ahh-that-is your father's sister Large Arrowhead Root		(c)	64
talking that way."			65
"Quick, let us go ashore."	(C)	(a-1)	66
Now they went ashore.		(a-2)	67
A woodchuck blanket was given her,		(b-1)	68
three woodchuck blankets were given her.			69
Long dentalia were put on her,		(b-2)	70
they were put at her buttocks.			71
"When you will be bought,		(b-3)	72
"you will wait for long dentalia,			73
"you will be put up for woodchuck blankets."			74
She was carried to mud,		(c-1)	75
she was put down.		(c-2)	76
		(v) (Greens)	
Now again they were going upriver.	(A)		77
They went some distance.			78
Now again they reached someone,	(B)	(a)	79
there is a person.			80
"At last my brother's son does arrive,			81
"the one with maggots in his buttocks.			82
"If I were not a person,			83
"then your people would have died."			84
"Who is it who talks that way?"		(b)	85
Salmon said.			86
"Ahh, your father's brother "Greens,"		(c)	87
"he talks that way."			88
"Quick, let us go ashore."	(C)		89
Five raccoon blankets were given to him.			90
He was set down near the water.			91
	(II) (Blue Jay, Crow, Flounder)		
	(i) (Encounter)		
They were going upriver.	(A)	(a)	92
Now they went above,		(b)	93

they arrived at Saint Helens.		94
[*They arrived.]		[*94]
A canoe was seen coming downriver.	(c)	95
The canoe came near.		96
Ahh, Blue Jay (is one of) those coming downriver,		97
and Crow,		98
and Flounder in the bow.		99

	(ii) (Colloquy)	

"Ahh, from where have you come?"	(B)	(d-1)	100
they were asked.			101
They did not make themselves heard.		(d-2)	102
Again they were asked,		(d-3)	103
twice they were asked.			104
Now Crow made herself heard,		(e)	105
she said:			106
"łaq'ala:kiwa:,			107
"łaq'amo:Sq'amo:S,			108
"łaq'apa:wapawa."			109
Salmon said:		(f)	110
"What did she say?"			111
One person said:		(g)	112
"It was flood tide early,			113
"now they were going upriver,			114
"They arrived at the Cascades,			115
"now it was ebb tide,			116
"now again they came downriver."			117
"Crow's lies.		(h)	118
"A canoe never returned from the Cascades (in one day)			119
"A canoe sleeps over five times,			120
"(as) it goes upriver,			121
"then it can arrive at the Cascades.			122
"Quick, let us go alongside."			123

	(iii) (Outcome)		

Now they went alongside Blue Jay.	(C)	(i)	124
Blue Jay was grasped around the nape,			125
that is the way his face was twisted.			126
Crow was seized,		(j)	127
she was grasped around the nape,			128
her face was twisted.			129
Flounder in the bow was grasped around the nape,		(k)	130

that is the way her mouth was put crossways.		131
"Future generations	(D) (l)	132
"will never return (in)		133
"one day from the Cascades."		134
Blue Jay was thrown inland.	(E) (m)	135
There Crow was thrown inland.	(n)	136
"Your name is Crow,		137
"You shall never speak the Wasco language."		138
Flounder was thrown in the water.	(o)	139
Flounder was told:		140
"Go down river to the beach.		141
"You shall put your face down there (lie down flat).		142
"Your name is Flounder."		143

PROFILE

In this version of "Salmon's Myth," the field notebook has an additional *iLōyam* 'they arrived' after the word for "Saint Helens." I have shown it with an asterisk for the line number [*94] and have indicated that it would require an additional line, giving rise to a triplet. This is the only instance of a word recorded in the field notebook being omitted in the printed text. A consideration of the alternatives for alignment of lines in verses and stanzas, induced by the additional line, has led me to include it in the text established here. The addition introduces some awkwardness into the sequential phrasing of the added verse that its inclusion requires. Yet the addition is consistent with a coherent account of the ensuing stanza and scene. Groups of three are common in Chinookan tradition. A group of two, a couplet, on the other hand, would be isolated here. Couplets usually occur in a series of three or five couplets.

Perhaps Cultee himself was not entirely certain of what he wished to do at that point (line *94), and that is why the place name, Saint Helens, is not as one would expect the culminating explicitness of the verse. It seems most likely that with this added word, recorded but not published, we catch a hesitation in performance, a moment of awkwardness, and that Boas was aware of such grounds for omitting the word in print.[5] One can believe that he would correct a recorded word, but not that he would delete it without reason. Yet the subsequent organization of the scene makes splendid sense when the word is counted in. Here philology provides evidence and ethnopoetics a hypothesis, such that the two combine to provide a fuller understanding of performance.

Profile: Salmon's Myth II (told 1894)

Act	Scene	Stanza/Verse		Incident	Markers	Lines
I	i	A		Upriver	3 vbs. of travel	1–3
		B	a	"If I were not"	"Now," turn	4–8
			b	"Who?"	turn	9–10
			c	"Fa's sibling"	turn	11–12
		C	a-1, a-2	Ashore	turn, change of location	13, 14
			b-1, b-2	Gifting (1,2)	distich, pentastich	15–16, 17–21
			c-1, c-2	Placing	distich	22, 23
	ii	A		Upriver	"Now again," travel	24
		B	a	If I were not"	"Now again," turn	25–30
			b	"Who?"	turn	31–32
			c	"Fa's sibling"	turn	33
		C	a-1, a-2	Ashore	"Now," turn	34, 35
			b-1	Gifting (1)	distich	36–37
			b-2	Gifting (2)	38	
			b-3	Gifting pronouncement	turn	39–41
			c-1, c-2	Placing	distich	42, 43
	iii	A		Upriver	"Now again," travel	44
		B	a	"If I were not"	"Now again," turn	45–59
			b	"Who?"	turn	50–51
			c	"Fa's sibling"	turn	52–53
		C		Gifting	distich	54–55
	iv	A		Upriver	"Now again," travel	56
		B	a	"If I were not"	"Now again," turn	57–61
			b	"Who?"	turn	62–63
			c	"Fa's sibling"	turn	64–65
		C	a-1, a-2	Ashore	turn, "Now"	66, 67
			b-1	Gifting (1)	distich	68–69
			b-2	Gifting (2)	distich	70–71
			b-3	Gifting pronouncement	turn	72–74
			c-1, c-2	Placing	distich	75, 76
	v	A		Upriver	"Now again," travel	77–78
		B	a	"If I were not"	"Now again," turn	79–84
			b	"Who?"	turn	85–86
			c	"Fa's sibling"	turn	87–88
		C		Ashore, gifting, placing	turn	89–91

II	i	A	a	Upriver	92	
			b [*b]	Arrival	3 vbs. of travel, "Now"	93-*94
			c	Canoe met	pentastich	95–99
	ii	B	d-1	Canoe asked (1)	turn	100–101
			d-2	Canoe silent	implied turn	102
			d-3	Canoe asked (2)	"Again," "Twice"	103–4
			e	Answer	"Now," turn	105–9
			f	"What?"	turn	110–11
			g	Answer	turn ("Now" 3 times)	112–17
			h	"Alongside"	turn (pentastich)	118–23
	iii	C	i	Twisting (1)	"Now," name (Blue Jay)	124–16
			j	Twisting (2)	Name (Crow)	127–29
			k	Twisting (3)	Name (Flounder)	130–31
		D	l	Pronouncement	turn	132
		E	m	Placing (1)	Name (Blue Jay)	133–35
			n	Placing (2), Pronouncement	Name(Crow), turn	136–38
			o	Placing (3), Pronouncement	Name (Flounder), turn	139–43

As before, expectations based on parallel repetition of incident affect the patterning beyond what can be indicated in the column of markers. Not all groupings of lines in sets of three and five have been noted (especially in act II, scene iii). Notice also that the number of pronouncements in this last scene comes to three, and that the last sequence of three incidents, the three placings, builds from one line through a tristich to a concluding pentastich with the most important character, Flounder.

The First Act: Variations on a Ritual Journey

Let me now discuss the relationships that have been summarized in the profiles. The discussion will further explain the analyses and the nature of the narrative competence that informs the texts.

Discussion of the first act will elaborate and clarify what is fundamentally a clear pattern. Discussion of the second act will bring us to an analytic crux: interpretation of the two tellings depends upon the conclusions reached as to this act's form. I shall argue that the second act has a distinct configuration in each telling, one emergent in the telling. Neither is reducible to the other nor to a pattern shared with the first act, except with loss of meaning.

Even a casual reading shows that the story has two acts, one concerned with plants, one concerned with a trio in a canoe. It is the same with the five scenes of the first act. Salmon and his party reach five different roots in turn, engaging in the same pattern of interaction each time. What requires closer attention is the organization within scenes. There is a common pattern within the variation of detail, but a knowledge of the conventions of Chinookan narrative is necessary to grasp it. Early in the nineteenth century, a Kathlamet audience would have assimilated that knowledge inevitably in the course of growing up. We have to work for it.

Each predication is a line. Sometimes parallelism within a sentence suggests that phrases that are not explicit predications should be distinguished as lines as well.

Lines are grouped into verses, verses into stanzas, stanzas into scenes, scenes into acts in terms of a narrative logic that organizes sequences again and again in terms of three and five. Five is the ritual number in the culture, and three is its narrative partner. Several neighboring groups have the same twin principle of three and five: Sahaptin, Kalapuya, and the Salish languages of the lower Columbia (Chehalis, Cowlitz). The numerical patterning is not mechanical. It commonly involves a sequence of meaning as well as form. The meaning sequence can be glossed as "onset, ongoing, outcome." In a sequence of five elements, the middle element is pivotal, completing an initial series of three as the outcome and initiating the second as onset. Given the basic matrix of three- and five-part grouping, sometimes pairing emerges within it. I think that this may intensify the moment in which it occurs, either for clarity or for emphasis.

Given the flexibility of the use of the basic matrix in practice, units within the story cannot be determined simply by counting and sometimes depend upon a sense of parallelism within the story and general conventions. New units are commonly signaled by change of location, change of speaker for a turn at talk, and the presence at the beginning of a line of particles such as "now" and "now again." The ends of units often enough are culmination of a sequence in an object of perception or a turn at talk. Obviously, a clear beginning and a clear ending establish boundaries for what has preceded or is to follow.

With these regularities in mind, we can see how each of the five scenes of the first act is organized. A scene after the first one, such as the second scene in the 1891 telling, shows the format. Each use of "again" here shows that a relevant unit is being noted. The first is for the travel upriver (30); the second is for the colloquy initiated by the plant and ending with its identification for Salmon. Notice that the dialogue has only three turns in this second scene. In other scenes of the act, the identification of the plant to Salmon by a spokesman (presumably of his own party) as to name and kinship is followed by Salmon's command, "Let us go ashore." The absence of the command in this scene is one indication that it is not part of the central stanza, which is intact in all its parts through both tellings. (It is the third, following stanza that varies.) Another indication is that the command goes together lexically with the going ashore, a change of location and hence a new start. And the rhetorical logic that informs the narratives gives unity to the three steps of announcement, question, answer, on the one hand, and the three steps that follow of going ashore, gifting, and placing the plant in question.

The most salient difference among scenes of the first act comes at the beginning. Here there is an expectable weighting of the start of the story as a whole with information and fullness of action. In this first scene, indeed, the first stanza is just a statement as to a set of people in a certain location (myth times) and condition (hunger). Narratives commonly begin in just this way. (There is indeed a serious pun on such beginnings here. The root -ɬait and its etymological partner, -lait, in the meaning 'to stay, remain, live', frequently introduce the community that is the context of the story. Here -ɬait also occurs but with the preceding reflexive element -x̣ua, constituting a theme with the meaning 'to die'.)

Parallelism with the succeeding scenes of the act might lead one to take lines 1 through 10 as all part of the first stanza. That is, the travel of Salmon's party would be in the first stanza, and the second would not begin until the colloquy. In point of fact, lines 7 onward very heavily mark and establish the onset of the second stanza. The sequence begins with a seasonal word, "spring came," first of a triad of locational expressions (spring, first, somewhere). It has a sequence of three verbs of traveling (went upriver, would arrive, arrived), of which the third is the culmination. All this combines to make the verse beginning in line 11 a local culmination, not a start. It is the pivot of the scene, third in the series just described, and first in the series of turns at talk shared with succeeding scenes.

In the remaining four scenes of the act, the initial element of travel is indicated briefly, and the central scene of colloquy follows a constant pattern. Both stanzas are typically introduced with "now again," and, as noted, the middle stanza always has a three-part exchange. The third and concluding stanza begins with a turn at talk, or a change of location, or both, but not with a particle. The character of the third stanza seems especially strongly established, however, in the first scene. The stanza has ten lines in the first scene, as against three, five, three, two, respectively, in the four scenes that follow. No succeeding scene has more than half that number of lines. Moreover, a rhythm of pairing within each of the three actions of the stanza seems to be present. Salmon twice says, "Let us go ashore" (the only instance of this in either telling), and that is followed by a report that they go ashore. There are two gifts, and the account of the second seems to swell into a five-line passage. So framed, the two steps of carrying the plant inland and placing it among willows seem to have a rhythm of pairing as well. (By contrast, the two steps in the third stanza of the third scene seem simply to complete a five-line sequence of the stanza as a whole.)

The fullness of the first and third stanzas in the first scene, as against other scenes (keeping in mind that the middle stanza remains quite constant), illustrates two principles important to accurate analysis and interpretation. The precision made possible by analysis into lines and verses may tempt one to be too precise. To be sure, it is difficult to imagine the kind of interpretation of the Salmon myth presented here as being at all possible without an analysis into lines and verses. Cultee's performances and intentions depend upon close accounting of them. On the other hand, Cultee's performances and intentions are flexible enough, one might say subtle enough, that mechanical precision will distort them. The two principles are familiar, but since I do not now recall names for them I should like to christen them here.

Rank shift. The greater fullness of the first scene, in identifying places and actors, makes Salmon's travel and arrival part of the second stanza in the scene, whereas thereafter in the act it is the initial element. One might adopt Michael Halliday's grammatical notion of "rank shift" to label this phenomenon.

Fading explicitness. The greater fullness of the first scene with regard to the third stanza might be called an example of "fading explicitness." The one element that is constant through succeeding scenes is gifting (showing its ritual importance as response to the ritual-like core of the central colloquy). Scene ii lacks either explicit going ashore or placement. If there is a difference in the number of lines assigned to one of the three elements of the stanza, gifting has more lines (scenes i, ii, iv).

The treatment of the third stanza suggests another principle. Put in general terms, a segment that holds a certain place in a hierarchy of structure may be elaborated so as to have constituent parts within its own level. We have seen that with regard to the rhythm of pairing within the third stanza of the first scene. There the internal elaboration flows through the entire stanza. In other scenes only the element of gifting is so treated, a fact that again underlines its importance. In scenes iii and iv in the 1891 telling, to be sure, the elements of gifting and placement are caught up with going ashore in single five-line units. (Thus they are not independent verses, and their status as analogues to verses elsewhere is indicated by square brackets ([b] and [c].) Quite the opposite is true in certain stanzas of the first act in 1894. While iii has only gifting and v is a quick three-step verse of ashore, gifting, placing, i, ii, and iv elaborate the actions. The number of lines shows the relationship: eleven, ten, two, eleven, three. The greater detail in the first scene, with its pairing rhythm, no doubt is to be again explained as initial establishment of a pattern and its contents, a frame extending in scope over subsequent scenes (fading explicitness). The elaboration of the second and fourth scenes has to do, I think, with their subjects, the two Arrowhead Roots, which are the two roots that are feminine in gender and the two most significant as sources of food. (More will be said of this later on.) Notice that these two instances are the only ones in which the third stanza has "now" in its beginning verse. In scene iv there seems clearly to be a two-step motion (direct speech, now with change of location), differentiating a-1 and a-2. The "now" before direct speech in scene ii seems a gesture in that direction. In these contexts, as in the 1891 telling, I take the internal elaboration to extend to carrying and placing in the third verse of the stanza.

Notice that with this elaboration it is the central element of gifting that is most elaborated. With the two Arrowhead Roots, gifting swells into three internal units, two gifts and a pronouncement (39–41, 72–74).

Amplification. It would be possible to determine a status as independent verse units for each of these constituents designated by hyphenated numbers within verses. I spent some hours attempting to do so. The result seemed to me to obscure rather than to clarify the story. One becomes involved in a series of inconsistencies, or awkwardnesses, or hairline judgments that are not much supported elsewhere by parallel and overall pattern. What is abundantly clear is that the third stanza of each scene in the first act has in principle the three elements of going ashore, gifting, and placing, and that Cultee varies his handling of the three considerably, sometimes reducing the stanza just to the gifting (ii in 1891, iii in 1894) and sometimes elaborating the presentation and the environs as well. This practice might be called "amplification," bearing in mind that the elaboration is not of number of units but within a unit. That is, not of number of verses but within verses. (One might designate the numbered subunits *versicles* and speak of their presence and numbers.)

I am the more persuaded of this analysis because there is an analogue in the grammar of the language. The Kathlamet verb has a very large number of morphological positions. Were every distinguishable position presented on the same level, the structure of the verb would be obscured. Some distinctions are at the level of the verb as a whole: tense-aspect, subject, direct object, indirect object, relational, directional, root, continuative, stative. Some distinctions are within units of that level. Thus within the positions of subject (ergative agent), object, and indirect object, there are positional distinctions involved in the marking of number, agency, and reflexiveness. The latter differentiations are analogous to the amplification of the verse positions in the third stanza. They cohere as a unit in relation to the rest of the structure.

In the 1894 telling, the first act does not show the initial elaboration of the 1891 telling, and a motive for this will be suggested later on. The differences in general belong with an account of the intentions involved in the two tellings. The common pattern of five scenes, each of three verses, is clear.

Incident and stanza. We can conjecture that any performer of act I, sharing Cultee's tradition, would know and perform it as a sequence of five scenes, each corresponding to a root. He or she would know and perform each scene as a sequence of seven incidents, grouped in three stanzas. Setting apart the first stanza of the first scene as a frame for the act as a whole, the sequence of seven incidents would comprise (using brief labels for each) the following:

1. travel upriver
2. "If I were not . . ."
3. "Who?"
4. "X, your father's Y"
5. "Ashore!"
6. gifting
7. placing

The seven incidents would be grouped in stanzas as follows:

(A) travel upriver (1)
(B) colloquy (2, 3, 4)
(C) disposition (5, 6, 7)

This pattern of joining the sequence of incident and a proper sequence of form would be the invariant part of narrative competence, together with the set of roots and much of the wording. Evidently the travel, the quasi-formulaic colloquy, and, out of the third stanza, the gifting would be most invulnerable to slips of memory and attention and to selective emphasis and intention.

The Second Act: Emergent Configurations

Whereas the scenes of the first act have the same pattern in both tellings, the scenes of the second act do not. It is necessary to test alternative hypotheses as to what Cultee is *doing* in each second act.

Let us examine the three kinds of hypothesis that can be entertained: equivalence of the two acts (in general); equivalence of the two acts within a given telling; equivalence of the two second acts across tellings.

Act II as complement of act I. It is easy to see act II as a complement of act I in terms of a sequence of incidents and as a transformational inversion of it.

The sequence of incidents in act I can be given a counterpart in act II.

Act I	*Act II*
(1) travel upriver	(1) travel upriver
(2) "(identification)"	(2) "(identification)"
(3) "Who?"	(3) "What?"
(4) "(interpretation)"	(4) "(interpretation)"
(5) "Ashore!"	(5) "Stop"/"Alongside"
(6) gifting	(6) twisting
(7) placing	(7) (placing) (absent in 1891)

As inversion, the three formal groups of the first act each have a contrast with something corresponding in the second act.

Act I	*Act II*
(A) Salmon comes to a person upriver	(A) Persons come downriver to Salmon
(B) The person announces itself	(B) Salmon demands the others identify themselves
(C) The person is gifted and placed so as to be useful to the people along the river	(C) The others are twisted, and, when placed, two are placed so as to be deprived of fish and use

There is something to the idea that the three main groups of the first act figure in the second. As we shall see later, however, the three groups figure as semantic relationships that are mapped into the form of the second act. Neither telling of the second act is organized in just that way. When we try to match the actual organization of each second act in terms of verses and stanzas to a first act, we find the second act distinct.

Act II in the shape of act I? (1891 telling). If the verses of act II in the 1891 telling are grouped together so as to parallel the three-part organization of act I, the result would be as follows:

| *Scene i | (a) (upriver) |
| *Scene ii | (b) (identification) |

                   (c) (what?)
                   (d) (explanation)
*Scene iii   (e) ("Stop")
                   (f) (stop)
                   (g) (disposition: twisting [1])
                   (h) (disposition: twisting [2])
                   (i) (disposition: twisting [3])
                   (j) (further outcome: pronouncement [1])
                   (k) (further outcome: pronouncement [2])

Such a grouping, if imposed, ignores, one might say violates, the relationships and proportions that the act itself displays. The act makes evident a pairing of initiation and response. The first verse is a standard type of onset, ongoing, outcome sequence with the outcome direct speech. So is the second verse. Together they form a pair: in (a) Salmon asks the canoe, and in (b) it responds. Again, in (c) Salmon asks for explanation, and in (d) explanation is given. The two turns at talk are paired. In (e) Salmon calls for the other canoe to be stopped, and in (f) the response is compliance. (The root for 'stop' occurs at the beginning of the first line of each of the two verses.) Content dictates a three-part pairing next (ghi), as each of the three in the canoe is disposed of, but the pronouncements that end the myth are presented in two statements, each paired with an action.

The evidence of pairing as a principle of grouping seems compelling. The set of five stanzas that results fits neatly the recurrent logic of Chinookan narrative. The middle group (ef) is outcome to the sequence of the first three pairs and is onset to the remaining two. (Were the putative three-stanza organization that would match act I imposed, the fit to Chinookan narrative logic would be gross. In particular, it would divide paired turns of talk (a, b) that belong together.)

Act II in the shape of act I? (1894 telling). If the verses of act II in the 1894 telling are grouped together so as to parallel the organization of act I, the result would be as follows:

*Scene i   (a) (upriver)
                   (b) (arrival)
*Scene ii   (c) (encounter)
                   (d) (ask)
                   (e) (response)
                   (f) (what?)
                   (g) (explanation)
*Scene iii   (h) (alongside)
                   (i) (twisting) (1)

    (j)   (twisting) (2)
    (k)   (twisting) (3)
    (l)   (pronouncement)
    (m) (placing) (1)
    (n) (placing) (2)
    (o) (placing) (3)

(This discussion assumes the analysis explained in the presentation of the 1894 translation in this chapter. If verse (b) were not distinguished from (a), the points made here about the putative scenes *ii and *iii would not be affected.)

If such a grouping were imposed, it would violate the normal Chinookan patterns of grouping. To start with the third scene, corresponding to stanza C of act I: the scene would have not three or five stanzas, but four. That is, the internal unity of the three verses concerned with twisting (i, j, k) is clear, and so is the internal unity of the three verses concerned with placing (m, n, o). The verse of pronouncement between them (l) is thus distinct, and so in relation to them is the verse of Salmon's speech (h) that precedes them: in short, four stanzas.

In the first scene, separation of verse c, in which the trio are met, from the preceding steps of travel and arrival, runs counter to what is perhaps the most frequently recurring three-step pattern in Chinookan literature, a pattern of three-step travel, including its outcome, at the beginning of a scene or story.

The internal coherence and linkages of the middle verses have been discussed in the notes to the 1894 translation. Here we might simply recall the unity of each verse: a five-line sequence of approach and resulting object of perception within (c), with the middle line beginning "Ahh, Blue Jay" as outcome of the first three lines and simultaneous onset of a last three; the threefold lexical repetition ("asked") within (d); the marking of (e) with initial "now" and its turn at talk, a feature (turn at talk) that separates (f) and (g) as well.

Why not, one might think, assign (h) to the middle scene? Now the third scene would have a clear three-part coherence. Perhaps the six verses now present in the middle scene could be grouped in pairs. There is a certain alternation with Salmon's party speaking in (d), (f), and (h). Such a grouping would make the act a pair-wise progression through eight verses, only to be suddenly changed to a three-part grouping for the remaining seven verses. One might say that the change was required by dealing with the trio, but there is no motivation (except imposed pattern), unlike the sequences of turns at talk that motivate pairing in act II of 1891. Verse c goes as object of perception as outcome of (a) (b), not as initiation of colloquy. And pairing denies the unity of the three verses (f, g, h) in which Salmon individually takes part, asking, being answered, and giving an evaluation. And in any case the assignment of (h) to a scene or stanza preceding the last is already a departure from the model of act I, wherein "alongside" does not end the middle group but begins the last group.

Why not decide that it is a mistake to take the identification of the trio in the canoe in verse c as the beginning of the middle section? Perhaps the crucial point in act I is not the appearance on the scene of another party, but the beginning of the colloquy, the first direct speech. That makes good sense. One would now have (abc) (defgh) (ijk-l-mno). But that is the three-part pattern already arrived at for act II in the 1894 telling, and, as noted, it departs from the three-part patterning of act I crucially in the place of (h).

Second telling in the shape of the first? If the principle of pairing found in the 1891 telling of act II were applied to the 1894 telling, the following would be the result:

*A	a	travel (92)
	b	arrival (93-*94)
*B	c	encounter (95-99)
	d	ask (100-104)
*C	e	response (105-9)
	f	What? (110-11)
*D	g	explanation (112-17)
	h	alongside (118-23)
*E	i	twisting (1) (124-26)
	j	twisting (2) (127-29)
*F	k	twisting (3) (130-31)
	l	pronouncement (132-34)
*G	m	placing (1) (135)
	n	placing (2) (136-38)
*H	o	placing (3) (139-43)
	?	

Unless one is prepared to argue for the equivalent of a significant musical rest as a silent *Hp, one has seven sets of pairs and an orphan. An argument to reduce the anomaly by, say, taking the three verses of twisting together applies equally to the three verses of placing and leaves one with seven sets of pairs and an orphan. In either case, the result is a pair-wise progression through the first eight verses that has a certain plausibility but loses all plausibility and coherence with the remaining seven verses. The considerations that apply in this regard are the same as just mentioned in regard to putting act II of 1894 in the shape of act I (following the hypothesis of assigning verse h to the middle section). This version lacks the motivation of paired speech acts that the 1891 telling itself provides.

In summary, one either has immediate failure (an odd number of pairs and an orphan) or an awkward attempt to ascertain five groups, presumably (*AB) (*CD) (*E plus *Fk) (*Fl) (*G plus *Ho), which transgresses the evident expectations of coherence, especially in severing the response of (e) from the asking of (d).

First telling in the shape of the second? If the principle of three-part patterning found in the 1894 telling of act II were applied to the 1891 telling, the following would be the basis of any result:

A a, b   ask, response
B c, d   What? explanation
C e, f   "Stop," stop
D g, h, i   twisting (1, 2, 3)
E i, k   pronouncement

The five groups (A B C D E) themselves conform to Chinookan patterning. To arrive at a three-group pattern, one would seek a sequence of three among the five. The three logical possibilities are: (A) (B) (CDE); (A) (BCD) (E); (ABC) (D) (E). One would want the middle term to make sense as an "ongoing" step between the first and the third and, of course, the three units grouped together to be coherent.

The pattern (A) (BCD) (E) does not make much sense. The twisting of D and the final pronouncement in (E) either go together in a larger unit or belong alongside each other as parallel units. One could conceive of (CDE) as outcome to the preceding units or of (ABC) as colloquy that precedes two steps of outcome. Either choice falls short on the criterion of sensible middle term. The sensible middle term in the act is obviously (C). It completes the colloquy and initiates the outcome. But a grouping of (AB) (C) (DE) is anomalous. The initial grouping of A B C D E is transparently normal in Chinookan narrative. A further classing together of its units seems to be unmotivated superstructure.

Overview, incident, verse, and stanza. In summary, it seems clear that both tellings of act I agree in general pattern and that the two tellings of act II do not. If we align the verses of act II of the two versions, we can see this rather clearly.

Incident	1891	1894
(travel, encounter, ask)	a	abcd
(response)	b	e

(What?)	c	f
(explanation)	d	g
("stop," alongside)	e	h
(stop)	f	—
(twisting)	g, h, i	i, j, k
(pronouncement)	j, k	l
(placing)	—	m, n, o

The entire first scene of the 1894 telling (verses abc), one-third of the act at that level, is encompassed within the first verse of the 1891 telling. The 1891 telling moves in two verses to the point at which the 1894 telling arrives in five. It moves in four verses to the point at which the 1894 telling arrives in seven. These comparisons make clear that the two tellings are organized differently, the one in terms of even-numbered groups, the other in terms of odd.

The narrative competence involved can be made clearer by examining more closely sequence of *incident,* as we did with act I. Sequence of incident and grouping in lines and verses are the two tracks along which performance travels. Put loosely, they are the twin strands of meaning and form that weave the narrative. (One has to say "loosely," because incident conditions and contributes form, and choice of form has connotations of meaning.)

Although the contents of act II can be aligned with the contents of act I, as we have seen in discussing act II as a complement of act I, they are more numerous—some fifteen elements instead of seven. The narrative competence of Cultee, and presumably that of anyone who shared his tradition for the myth, included that fifteen-element sequence. It also included in principle the alternative possibilities of verse alignment realized in Cultee's two tellings and the alternative orders of the trio in the scene of their disposition.

Here is the series of incidents, together with their position in the two tellings.

Incident	1891	1894
(1) upriver	line 86	verse a, verse b (92, 93-*94)
(2) meet canoe	line 87	verse c (95–99)
(3) ask	lines 88–89	verse d (1, 2, 3) (100–101, 102, 103–4)
(4) Crow speaks	verse b (90–95)	verse c (105–109)
(5) Salmon, What?	verse c (96–97)	verse f (110–11)
(6) Steersman, "—"	verse d (98–104)	verse g (112–17)
(7) Salmon, stop	verse e (105–7)	verse h (118–23)
(8) stop	verse f (108–9)	—(part of line 124)
(9) twist (1)	verse g (110–14)	verse i (124–26)

(10) twist (2)	verse h (115–17)	verse j (127–29)
(11) twist (3)	verse i (118–21)	verse k (130–31)
(12) pronouncement	verse j (122–24)	verse l (132–34)
	verse k (125–27)	
(13) placing (1)		verse m (135)
(14) placing (2)		verse n (136–38)
(15) placing (3)		verse o (139–43)

Differences of emphasis and alignment can be clearly seen. We must imagine the narrator choosing to express the first three incidents each as a line within a single verse (a) in 1891, and each as a verse (or more than a verse [a–b]) in 1894. In contrast to the 1891 treatment, both the initial element of travel upriver and of asking the encountered canoe are doubled. Conversely, the 1891 treatment doubles, as its final element, the pronouncement that has a single intermediate verse in 1894.

The most striking difference in alignment is the way in which the 1894 telling conflates in a single line the action of accosting the trio's canoe and the initiation of disposition of its occupants, name by name: "*Now* they went alongside Blue Jay." The initial *now,* with emphatic stress, leaves no doubt as to the beginning of a new section. Yet the accosting was separate in 1891. I take this difference in alignment to be the result (and clear indication of) the difference in pairing versus "tripling" between the two tellings of the act. The incident of stopping completes the third pair before disposition begins in 1891. In 1894 a separate status for it would disrupt the three-part progression of verses at that point.

Differences in emphasis and alignment appear also when one steps back from the specific sequence of incident and imagines the narrator as also guided by a sense of grouping of larger scale in that regard. As we have seen, the three-part pattern of act I does not structure act II, but it can be taken to inform it. Each act makes use of a sequence of incident, distinct in content and number, that answers, broadly speaking, to (A) travel upriver, (B) colloquy, (C) disposition. In effect, the "syntax" of verse gives form to the "semantics" of incident in this instance. A comparison between the two tellings shows the following:

Incident	1891	1894
(A) travel upriver	verse a (A)	verses a, b, c (A)
(B) colloquy	b (A)	d, e, f, g, h (B)
	c, d (B)	
	e, f (C)	

(C) disposition	g, h, i (D)	i, j, k (C)
	j, k (E)	l (D)
		m, n, o (E)

In terms of emphasis, one sees that the 1894 telling elaborates both (A) and (C) in comparison with 1891 — three verses as against one for the travel upriver and encounter, seven verses as against five for the disposition. Both tellings, however, have exactly five verses for the middle part, the colloquy. This pattern is strikingly identical to the middle part of act I in both tellings and suggests that the central speech acts are, as event, a stable core in both acts.

One gets a further sense of a reality for the larger scale relationships when one notes that the 1891 telling has eleven verses distributed across the three parts in the proportion one, five, five, and that the 1894 telling distributes its fifteen verses in the proportion three, five, seven (where seven is three, one, three). The proportions, in other words, are made up of pattern numbers (counting one alongside three and five). Yet the larger scale relationships clearly are not fixed molds. The 1894 telling has a neat allocation among them, to be sure: travel upriver (A), colloquy (B), disposition (CDE). But the 1891 telling does not; the division between travel upriver and colloquy comes within its first stanza (A), and the further allocation is not in pattern number units or multiples. Altogether, it is travel upriver (A-), colloquy (A-, B, C), disposition (D, E). Insofar as this last pattern again reflects a pair-wise orientation in the 1891 telling, it seems clear that "informed by" is the right expression for the role of such larger scale relationships. They inform but do not entirely determine performance, in which emergent configurations of form, spurred by attitudes of the moment or of considered reflection may obtain. But an intuitive sense of such larger scale relationships must be a part of narrative competence. It must lie behind the fact that two sequences, one of seven incidents, one of fifteen, converge so closely on a pattern of travel, colloquy, disposition.

Indeed, the two tellings indicate that the closer one comes to the level of the wording itself, the greater the fact, and one may infer, the scope, of variation. The two tellings are identical at the two higher levels of organization. Each has two acts, with five scenes in the first act and five stanzas in the second (constituting there the equivalent of a single scene). And each scene in the first act has three stanzas. It is with the distribution of verses in relation to stanzas in the second act that diversity appears at this third level; to recapitulate, 1891 has (ab) (cd) (ef) (ghi) (jk), whereas 1894 has (abc) (defgh) (ijk) (l) (mno). And whereas the allocation of verses to stanzas (or, put the other way around, the diversification of stanzas into verses) is parallel in both tellings in act I, it is not identical, and in act II the variability is greater.

Numbers of verses and of lines themselves show something as to the balance between the two acts in each telling. Here are the numbers of verses:

	Act I	Act II	
1891	29	11	(40)
1894	25	15	(40)
	(54)	(26)	

Put in percentages:

	Act I	Act II
1891	72.5%	27.5%
1894	62.5%	37.5%
	(67.5%)	(32.5%)

Here are the numbers of lines:

	Act I	Act II	
1891	85	42	(127)
1894	91	52	(143)
	(176)	(94)	

Put in percentages:

	Act I	Act II
1891	66.9%	33.0%
1894	63.6%	36.3%
	(65.2%)	(34.8%)

One sees that the 1894 telling has greater balance between the two acts, but the difference between the two tellings in this regard in number of lines is very small and unlikely to be significant. The organization of lines into verses shows a clearer difference. In the 1891 telling the proportions between the two acts are about 3 to 1 (3/4 to 1/4). In 1894 the proportions are about 5 to 3 (5/8 to 3/8). The number of verses overall is the same (40).

The locations of the difference are clear. Both tellings are alike in the first act, except for the larger number of verses (four) with which the 1891 telling begins. Both are alike in the middle portion of the second act, which contains the colloquy (five verses in each). The 1891 telling has two fewer verses in both what precedes and follows the colloquy, hence a total of eleven verses as against fifteen for the telling of 1894. It is precisely at these points that one finds the more deliberate introduction of the plants in 1891, as against the more deliberate introduction of the encountered trio in 1894 and the more decisive disposition of the trio in 1894.

Such observations bring us to a consideration of the differences between the two tellings in substance and motivation. But before attempting an overall interpretation, we need to attend more closely to differences in verbal detail. To do so, we need to sort out differences that may reflect slips of memory and attention in order to assess what may be attributable to choice of wording and device. This brings us back for a moment to the question that led Boas to ask for the second telling.

Verbal Detail: Remembering and Intending

Insofar as Boas sought a second telling of the myth as a check on Cultee's linguistic competence and consistency in Kathlamet, he must have been satisfied with the results. There is no evident inconsistency or variation, so far as command of phonology, morphology, and syntax are concerned. Even the three unintelligible words uttered by Crow are repeated word-perfect.

What of differences in narrative competence, particularly in command of the particular myth? There do seem to be differences of this kind. By and large, they point to a fuller command of the content of the tradition in the second telling. One can guess that Boas's earlier visits (1890, 1891) had activated Cultee's memory of the story, and that his last visit (1894) may have found the story more to the fore in Cultee's mind. But one must distinguish between differences that seem to be of this kind and differences that appear systematic. Let us notice first the differences that seem the result of recollection and attention. Differences in the initial framing of the acts, the use of verbs of speaking, and certain other features seem to stem from intention and will be taken up later.

(1) In the verses of the first act in which a root announces itself, every scene in both tellings has the appellation of Salmon, "the one with maggots in his buttocks," except the first scene in the first telling. It would seem that Cultee did not think of it until after the pertinent moment in that first scene but never forgot it afterward (1891 telling, lines 33, 46, 62, 77; 1894 telling, lines 6, 28, 47, 59, 82).

Let me mention that more than memorization of a formula is involved. There is an allusion in two respects. The first allusion is to the scene and season of the myth itself, the spring after winter, when the only salmon available, if any, would have been dried from the year before and when the last male salmon seen in the river the preceding fall would have been fading, even rotting, after having fertilized eggs. The second allusion is to a dramatic enactment of the theme of Salmon's annual return, (recorded from Cultee in Chinook proper by Boas, from Victoria Howard in Clackamas by Jacobs, from Louis Simpson in Wishram-Wasco by Sapir, and from an unnamed source in Wishram-Wasco by H. H. St. Clair [unpublished]). In this myth the Salmon has been killed. An egg from his body survives (thus underlining the respect in which Salmon expresses a male principle) and is found and tended by Crow (by two Crows in one version), from whom the young Salmon eventually learns of his history and implicit duty to avenge. Having rescued his father's widow from those who had taken her, he is asleep with his head in her lap as she paddles them home. When maggots appear on him, she brushes them aside and pushes him away, awakening him. He flings her high on a cliff. Later, reminded of her by birds who have seen her, he has them rescue her and restores her beauty (in Clackamas and Wasco; in Chinook, he goes on to other women). Apart from the implication that a man may have inner worth that a woman fails to recognize, the maggots, like the plot of which they are part, express the cyclical death and return of the fish on which the Indians were dependent for their standard of living, one that was high for people without horticulture. (Notice that such a young Salmon might need to have someone name his father's siblings to him.) At the specific stage in the story, maggots may also express another kind of "death" and "rebirth," a stage of life in which the young avenger, having been nurtured and advised and successful, is now to become an autonomous chief and protector in his own right.

In this second rebirth, the Chinookan versions contrast sharply with an Upper Chehalis version (Adamson 1934:110–12), which ends with the appearance of the maggots! And a gloss about spring salmon from the narrator, Peter Heck:

> The body was covered with maggots. She wept and wept over her husband who had left her so quickly.
>
> K'walale:::i—and that's the way it is with spring salmon; they don't last long. They soon become full of maggots. They must be watched very carefully while drying. Unless properly taken care of, they do not last long. Other salmon last longer. (Adamson 1934:112)

This fact about the spring run of salmon is well known, but the reference to it by the plants in the Kathlamet myth seems a deliberate and gratuitous insult. After all, the fresh salmon is available, now that it has come; its coming signals that other foods will be available as well; and spring salmon *can* be dried properly to last. Perhaps the roots are implying both: here we are already, while the salmon from last year have rotted, and you yourself won't last long. What from the standpoint of Salmon, and the culture itself in other contexts, is a miracle of renewal and return is derided here as inadequacy and absence.

Note that the traditions of the region show a scale of sensitivity to the vulnerability of the spring salmon in relation to women. The Chehalis myth ends with the recovered wife lamenting her new husband's loss. The Chinookan traditions have the husband wake and punish the wife, who herself almost dies before being restored to him. A Sahaptin tradition (Jacobs 1934: 47–83) doubles the wife's punishment; after she is rescued by birds from the rocks, her husband pulls out in his canoe as she is about to board so that she has to be rescued again from beneath the water. (Turtle succeeds and gains her as his reward.)

(2) When the roots announce themselves, all scenes in both tellings have a line that is literally "If not I I-became I-person," except the first scene in the first telling, which lacks the word for "person." Again, the implication would seem to be that the word did not come to Cultee until after that point but was not forgotten afterward.

This phrase also has a moral import. The reference is to a sense of "person" as a kind of being in the world in whom power can be found. In ordinary discourse the word could be used for "human person" in the sense of merely that, thus "poor, poor fellow," someone with nothing to be said of him, no status as kin or chief or hunter or whatever, except personal existence itself. Here the generic sense is doing ontological duty, expressing participation through the category of personhood in the reciprocity that maintains the world.

(3) When the first root is reached in the first telling, it is identified by name, Skunk Cabbage. Thereafter in both tellings the identity is withheld until the spokesman explains. I suspect remembered or chosen artistic intention account for the withholding, putting the hearer in the position of Salmon with something to wait to learn.

(4) Each root after the first is initially identified as a "person" (thus confirming in advance what each will say of itself, but in 1894 in the second scene it is identified as "a woman." This is the only time that the gender of the nominal prefix of a root figures in the immediate context. It goes together later with kinship as "uncle" and "aunt.") The root here is feminine, Small Arrowhead Root, and the use of "a woman" reflects not only that but the association of the domain of plants (quite apart from grammatical gender) with women. The two arrowhead roots are the two roots among the five with feminine prefix and also the two of most importance as sources of food. They are closely associated in the telling of 1891: after

scene ii with the small root, the phrase of going upriver is absent (lines 42–43), and instead the party is said to have left the small root, to have gone a little distance. The prominence of the two roots as representative of the domain of plants is shown in the 1894 telling by the fact that only they receive speeches of pronouncement (39–41, 72–74), along with dentalia (a form of wealth analogous to money), and are said in the pronouncement to be something people will trade. Moreover, in the 1894 telling, Large Arrowhead Root is the only one of the five to be introduced with the full form of "now again" (*Aqa wit'ax*), and to be explained with an expressively prolonged pronoun, *ay—ax—ka* (line 64), the only such instance in the tellings, and it is in her speech that the diacritic expressive prefix *wi-* occurs, on the word for "your people" (line 61). That gives to her the expression of the survival of the people, Salmon's people, as the focus of concern for the outcome of the myth. In summary, the use of "woman" here may be a slip from the regular use of "person," but if so, it anticipates and reflects symbolic significance.

(5) In Salmon's query as to the person speaking, there are three elements: verb of speaking, name, the direct speech. The full form is *igékim Igúnat, "ɬan ɬáxi ákua ɬxóla?"* Both preface and statement have a rhythmic and alliterative ring. (Each of the first two words is technically an amphibrach.) In the 1891 telling, the full form occurs in the first and third scenes. Salmon's name drops out in the other scenes (ii, iv, v), which seems an instance of what I have called "fading explicitness," and the verb of speaking drops out in the fifth scene, which seems a slip, since it occurs all nine of the other ten possible times (1891 telling, lines 16, 37, 49, 65; 1894, lines 9, 31, 50, 62, 86). The slip in the fifth scene in 1891 seems part of a general character of that scene, to be discussed later in this chapter.

(6) When the spokesman tells Salmon who is speaking, he usually ends with the phrase "he (or she) talks that way." In the 1891 telling this phrase is present in the first, third, and fifth scenes (Skunk Cabbage, Large Arrowhead Root, Greens) but is missing in the second and fourth (Small Arrowhead Root, Rush Root, lines 39, 67). The alternation suggests either lapse of memory and recovery or a form of "fading explicitness" in which attention is focused on the "cardinal numbers" of the rhetorical pattern, first, third, and fifth. The same explanation may hold for the omission in the second scene of the 1894 telling (Small Arrowhead Root, line 33). If omission is a slip, the second scene seems to favor it. The phrase does not seem to have the import of the line that precedes it, naming the plant and its kinship tie.

(7) When Salmon initiates the third stanza of the scene with the roots, he commands, "Hurry, let us go ashore." The word "to go ashore" is established

with threefold repetition in the first scene in 1891 and occurs in every other parallel scene in both tellings (cf. 1891 telling, lines 20–22, 53, 68, 80; 1894, lines 13, 35, 66, 89) except one in each. It is missing in the second scene of 1891 (line 39) and in the third scene of 1894 (line 54). The two omissions seem to be slips or else part of an overall abbreviation of the third stanza in each case to its minimal core, the gifting.

(8) The gifting of the roots is variously amplified in different scenes (see discussion in the notes on translation earlier). The differences are taken as intended. But the omission of the placing of a root in one scene in each telling, as just mentioned (scene ii in 1891, scene iii in 1894), occurring as it does with a different root in each case (Small Arrowhead Root, Rush Root), the first of which is of special note, reflects impatience. This conjecture is suggested in part by the fact that it is in scene ii of the 1891 telling that a gift with the verb "to put" comes before gifts with the verb "to give" (line 39; cf. by contrast 25–27 in 1891, and 17, 38, 70 in 1894). But since the same order ("put," "give") occurs also in scene iii of the 1891 telling, the connection here may be that the placing of "to put" first in the second scene goes together with the omission there of "ashore" and the omission also of the placing that the line with "put" would have triggered; and the partner of Small Arrowhead Root in scene ii is brought into parallel ad hoc in scene iii. In 1894 all three roots with which "to put" is used, Skunk Cabbage, both Arrowhead Roots (the three most important roots), have "to put" after "to give," as does Skunk Cabbage in the first scene in 1891. As to placing, for the three roots whose placement is stated in both tellings, it is the same: willows for Skunk Cabbage, mud for Large Arrowhead Root, shoreline or water for Greens.

(9) The same set of roots appears in both tellings, but the order is reversed at one point. In the 1891 telling, Large Arrowhead Root is third, Rush Root fourth. The opposite is the case in 1894. If there is any significance to the difference, it would seem to lie in the fact that the 1894 ordering has a symmetry in alternation of gender: male, female, male, female, male (uncle, aunt, uncle, aunt, uncle).

(10) The gifts to each root are partly the same, partly different as between tellings. The first and fifth persons receive the same gifts in both: elk-skin armor and bone war clubs to Skunk Cabbage and in the same amounts; Greens gets five raccoon blankets each time. In both tellings, Large Arrowhead Root receives long dentalia and woodchuck blankets, but the order of presentation is reversed. The same is true for Small Arrowhead Root, who gets small dentalia and blankets in 1891 but the reverse in 1894. In effect, dentalia is first for both in 1891, blankets are first for both in 1894. If there

is a significance, it is that blankets and other garb are either the first or the only type of gift throughout all five scenes in 1894. That may reflect a more controlled telling. So may the increased individuation of gifts in 1894. In 1891 both Arrowhead Roots receive woodchuck blankets, but in 1894 Small Arrowhead Root is given deerskin blankets. In 1891 both Rush Root and Skunk Cabbage receive elk skin, but in 1894 Rush Root is given buckskin.

In summary, quite a few details seem to reflect differences in recollection and attention that point toward the second telling as more complete and in that respect more fully performed. An additional feature of this kind has to do with the occurrences of the initial particle, *aqa* 'now'. It occurs more frequently in both acts in 1894, a fact that is also true of the 1894 telling of the other story Boas had Cultee tell again, "The War of the Ghosts." Here is the number of occurrences for "Salmon's Myth":

	Act I	Act II	
1891	7	1	(8)
1894	11	3	(14)
	(18)	(4)	

The greater frequency of the structural marker in 1894 suggests a fuller performance.

The differences in both tellings as between acts, however, seem to reflect more than a difference in scale and length. They seem to reflect the greater ritual formality of the first act, over against a second act that is in some sense an inversion of the first, less sacrosanct in pattern perhaps, more open to adaptation. This difference has been seen in the different shapes of the two tellings of act II. Altogether a number of differences between the two tellings go together either in giving the second act a distinctive character in itself or in preparing for it differently. The contrast in the order of the trio encountered in the canoe, involving as it does the one of the three on whom the myth will end, cannot be accidental. That the 1891 telling ends with Blue Jay, the 1894 telling with Flounder, is part of the shaping of the whole. The absence of a placing of the trio in the 1891 telling, while it deprives that telling of a final symmetry between acts, is hard to assign to failure of recollection. It seems consistent with *a difference in attitude and concern.*

Deliberate detail. The difference in emphasis and concern is evident in the different ways in which the beginning of act II is reached and then begun. In both tellings and presumably in the structure of the tradition, the second act gives Salmon an initiative, having the encountered trio asked, at the outset. In this way the second act in both tellings asserts an authority for Salmon in relation to the trio that he does not have in relation to the roots.

In the first act, they speak first, and he asks about them. In the second act, he speaks first or has his party do so, preceding the sequence common in both acts for the rest of the colloquy. *In the 1891 telling, Cultee seems in haste to reach this point and to establish it. In the 1894 telling, he seems to prepare for it in a more considered way and to establish it more deliberately.*

Salmon's query. One detail in this regard is the variation in act I in Salmon's query. In the 1891 telling, as we have seen, the full three-part formula occurs in the first and third scenes only, an instance of "fading explicitness" common to such narratives. In the 1894 telling, just the verb of speaking and the query itself occur in the first two scenes, but then the remaining three scenes have the full formula, containing Salmon's name. This contrast seems a considered focusing on Salmon's presence approaching the second act.

A small chart may help show this; (a) is verb of speaking, (b) is Salmon's name, (c) is what is said.

Scene	1891	1894
i	a b c	a b c
ii	a c	a c
iii	a b c	a b c
iv	a c	a b c
v	c	a b c

Verbs of speaking. Again, when each root speaks in the 1891 telling, there is an associated verb of speaking: *-kim* for Skunk Cabbage, a verb with a sense of speaking broadcast, announcing (it is inherently intransitive), and "to make oneself heard" for the succeeding four. In the 1894 telling, no root has a verb of speaking. Rather, each is encountered and introduced simply as standing (i), as seen and standing (ii), as seen (iii), as seen (iv), and as simply being there (v). Verbs of speaking imply a status, both in their presence and in their choice. The roots are silently demoted in standing in relation to Salmon's party by this absence in the 1894 telling.[6]

Listing. The 1894 telling lacks the initial statement of the situation of the myth people and the listing of the roots to be encountered as found in the 1891 telling. The difference does not seem to be the result of forgetting between the two tellings, for in 1894 such a listing occurs at the beginning of the second act, when the trio encountered in the canoe are named to complete a five-line verse: "Ahh, Blue Jay. . . ., Crow, Flounder." This contrast seems to show that such an initial listing is a deliberate device. The listing's presence in 1891 in act I indicates focus on the plants, and its presence in 1894 in act II indicates focus on the outcome with regard to the trio. The order in each list is significant. In 1894 the order prefigures the order of outcomes, ending with Flounder. The 1891 order puts first the two Arrowhead Roots, the two roots of feminine gender, showing that the domain is understood as under the sign of the feminine.

Gifts and pronouncements. It seems in keeping with such a difference in focus that the giving of feathered regalia (a symbol of guardian spirit power) to Rush Root in 1891 is absent in 1894. It seems also in keeping that in 1894 the two Arrowhead Roots are given speeches of pronouncement as part of their gifting. To select them for this role is to single them out as especially representative and valuable. To have such speeches is to put Salmon in the first act more firmly in the role of one who determines future destinies. In both tellings, Salmon's gifts and placements of the roots provide for the future, but the direct speech twice in 1894 heightens the role by enacting it in speech. All this seems in keeping with the contrast in form of the onset of act II in the two tellings in other regards and the evidence of transitional haste in the immediately preceding scene (act I, scene v) in 1891.

Transitional haste. In the 1891 telling, the authority of Salmon as leader and chief is made paramount at the outset. What others do in each of the first three pairs of verses is in response to Salmon. He is named as the speaker in each of the first two pairs, whereas in 1894 the party in the other canoe is asked impersonally (and only a little later on). Again, Salmon is the only person named throughout the first three verse pairs in 1891, whereas in 1894 the other party is not questioned until all three of its members have been identified by name. In 1891 the speaker in the other party is identified only by position in the canoe, but in 1894 Crow is named. Once past the establishment of Salmon's authority as initiator in the first three pairs of verses in 1891, the telling proceeds rather rapidly to its close. The other characters are named individually in the course of being disposed of, pronounced upon, and left. The repetition of question form in the first of the concluding two utterances probably expresses irony and condescension on the part of the true chiefly party. The second concluding utterance, coming after the trio has been left, probably is implicitly addressed to the audience, stating the true proposition and leaving no doubt as to the wrongness of the trio.

This intensity is emphasized by beginning each of the two verses in the third pair with "stop," the first time in Salmon's direct speech. By contrast in the 1894 telling, Salmon responds to the interpretation of the other party's remarks in five lines of his own statements, including the information as to the requisite time for going to The Dalles, which is held to the very end in 1891. And Salmon says last, not "Stop," but "Quick, let us go alongside," a remark quite parallel to "Quick, let us go ashore" in the five scenes of act I. Altogether, Salmon is more deliberate in 1894, his words more in tune with his words in act I. Whereas in 1891, after his initial "stop," the comment in question of the trio's veracity is followed quickly by a "stop" that marks the actual halting of the other canoe; in 1894 there is no explicit stopping, and going alongside is conflated with the onset of the disposition of the trio (line 124).

Salmon's assertion of authority at the outset of act II is anticipated in the abbreviation of the preceding scene v of act I. Six details cohere in two sets of three each in this regard.

1. In 1891 the formulaic speech of the plant is reached after three lines, but in 1894 after four. Both telling's begin with "Now again they went up-river," but in 1894 the first stanza is amplified with a second line that forms a distich: "Far they went." Such amplification is lacking in 1891. The second stanza begins immediately.

2. In 1891 the second stanza shows subordination in both lines that precede the plant's speech. The stanza's first line "Where they arrived" is itself subordinate, and the particle pair associated with marking the stanza is subordinated by not occurring until the beginning of the second line, "Now again a person was heard." The 1894 telling proceeds deliberately: "Now again they arrived at, reached someone;" "there is a person." And the arrival is more fully marked. In 1891 a suffix of completion is added to the root for 'to go, travel' (-ya-m), whereas in 1894 a distinct root of 'to arrive' precedes the suffix (-qoa-m).

3. The person's speech is reached in the verb of saying in the third line of the scene in 1891, but not until the quoted speech in the fifth line of the scene in 1894.

4. Salmon's statement, "Let's go ashore," is *prematurely placed* in 1891, before the question "Who is it that talks that way?" This is a clear sign of anticipatory haste.

5. The 1891 telling quotes Salmon without a verb of saying, whereas the 1894 telling adds "Salmon said."

6. The 1891 telling simply has the verb, "Let's go ashore," whereas the 1894 telling also has "quick." The word proposes haste but also lengthens the saying.

The 1894 telling has one slip akin to these points. In the fifth scene of the first act, the second line of the formulaic statement by the root, "the one with maggots in his buttocks," does not occur *until the end of the speech. At least it occurs there in Boas's field notebook.* Knowing the consistent pattern of the four-part speech, Boas put the line where it belongs when he printed the text. I have followed Boas in this regard. If a motive is sought for the slip, perhaps a wish to suppress the insult involved in the allusion to maggots is to be invoked. In any case, the change of position does not change the pace of the scene, unlike the anticipatory placing of "let us go ashore" in the same scene in 1891. In 1894, the change seems clearly something passed over and remembered in time to include before the turn at talk is over. *In 1894, it would seem, in contrast to 1891, there is no haste.*

The individual details of the fifth scene of the first act in 1891 altogether convey a sense of a narrator eager to reach the next act. The next act, we have seen, brings immediate assertion of Salmon's authority in word and configuration.

The Shape of an Ending

The differences between tellings in the second act, past the onset, revolve around the ending. The choice of order for the trio determines that the telling will end with Blue Jay in 1891 and with Flounder in 1894. The significance of the ending is shown by a verb of speaking. The transitive stem -*lxam* 'to tell', conveying direct address, occurs just once in each telling and does so at the end. In 1891 the stem is used to tell the trio about travel time to the Cascades (line 122). In 1894 it is used to tell Flounder where she will be (140).

The path to the ending is prepared quite differently in the two tellings. In 1891 Salmon's voice is heard three times in succession at the onset (lines 89, 97, 105-7) before the impersonal agent, the voice presumably of the party (and community) declares the final judgments about travel (123, 125-27). In 1894 the voice of the party is heard first (100), and Salmon speaks only after Crow (111), and again in response to Blue Jay (118-23). The voice of the party (and community) returns for the rest of the act three times, regarding travel time and the fates of Crow and Flounder (132-34; 137-38; 141-43). In summary, Salmon speaks first and three times in 1891, being named as speaker the first two, but speaks third and twice in 1894, being named as speaker only once. His authority is not so much on stage in 1894 but more pervasive and far-reaching, for it reaches past travel time to the permanent provision of food.

This lower profile for Salmon goes together with a higher profile for the trio. In 1891 the opposite was true. Salmon was announced at the start, but a hearer who did not know the story would have to piece together the identities of the three until almost the very end. In verse b such a hearer would learn that there are three persons in the canoe, a man in the stern and someone in the middle who speaks. In (c) the hearer would learn from Salmon's question that the one in the middle is a woman. In (g) the hearer would learn that the third party, the one in the bow, is Flounder (a woman). In (h) the hearer would learn that the one in the middle must have been Crow, she being the only other woman. And in (h), just before the final pronouncement, the hearer would learn that the name of the man in the stern is Blue Jay.

In 1894, as we know, each person in the trio is identified by name in the first stanza. When Crow speaks, she is named (line 105). The spokesperson is not named (112) but cannot be Crow and probably can be inferred to be Blue Jay. The names of the trio each recur twice again, once each in each of the dispositions. The sheer frequency of names is telling: once each in 1891, for a total of three, but fifteen times altogether in 1894: Blue Jay four times, Crow six, Flounder five (lines 97, 124, 125, 135 for Blue Jay [plus an unnamed turn at talk in 112]; 98, 105, 118, 127, 136, 137 for Crow; 99, 130, 139, 140, 143 for Flounder).

The highlighting of Salmon and ending with Blue Jay in 1891 goes together with a *metalinguistic element* that is missing in 1894. Notice the presence of words about speaking in the speech itself. In 1894 the trio is simply asked, but in 1891 the same action is initiated by Salmon saying, "Ask that canoe" (lines 100–101, 1894; 89, 1891). In 1894 Salmon says directly, "What did she say?" (111), but in 1891 the expression refers to a continuing process of speech (97). In 1894 the steersman simply reports what Crow has said, but in 1891 he prefaces the report with "Ahh, she is saying" (99). And in 1894 the steersman's words are directly contradicted by assertion ("Crow's lies"). In 1891 ironic questions are used three times (106, 107, 123). All these factors seem to point to a metalinguistic interest in the wording of the 1891 telling. And such an interest seems to fit a telling that highlights response to the immediate action and situation. The wording, like Salmon's action and the configuration of the act, focuses on quick righting of wrong—wrong felt, if suppressed, in Salmon having to subordinate himself five times to the plants and compounded, insult added to injury, with the pretensions of the trio.

To have Blue Jay, the one who makes chiefs unhappy, third and last to be punished fits all this. We must examine, though, the details of the punishment. On the face of it, one aspect involves a typical explanatory motif. The story ends by telling something about the physical identity of one or more of its characters. This story has something to explain, to be sure, but not that, or that in only a subordinate way. The only line in either telling that has to do with the physical traits of one of the creatures is the line that says that Flounder's mouth is crosswise (1891, 114; 1894, 131). The handling and twisting of Blue Jay and Crow are symbolic. It does not seem possible to connect the handling of Blue Jay with his distinctive crest, and there is nothing about Crow even to be considered. Twisting symbolizes reversal of the reversal, enacted by the trio, and, in the explicit placing of the 1894 telling, the further punishment of being thrown inland, away from the river and its food. (This placement of Blue Jay and Crow is symbolic; both can be seen along rivers.)

This significance of the verses of twisting perhaps is reflected in their structure. To see this, we must align the actions mentioned for each of the three.

	1891			1894		
	Flounder	Crow	Blue Jay	Flounder	Crow	Blue Jay
seized	+	+	+		+	
grasped	—	+	+	+	+	+
held down	+	—	+			
twisted	+	+	+	+	+	—
mouth	+			+		

All three are seized and twisted in 1891. Perhaps the absence of being grasped at the nape for Flounder and of being held down for Crow are slips, since in each case the other two have that happen to them. One might think that one possible step is omitted for Crow to yield a total of three, but both Flounder and Blue Jay are left with four, not five. I suspect that Flounder shows the potentially full series, in which the fifth element is the actual physical transformation, and that the other two fall short because no such transformation applies. A crosswise mouth is inapplicable and no other trait is substituted for Crow or Blue Jay. Blue Jay's role as third in the series of outcomes may explain his having four, as full a series as possible. Crow here can be kept to a pattern number, three.

In 1894 the corresponding verses are abbreviated. Cultee's attention is devoted to the second disposition of the trio. Each of the three is grasped around the nape; Blue Jay and Crow are twisted, while Flounder's mouth is made crossways. The additional element for Crow at the outset, that of being seized, again gives her a three-step verse and may reflect her importance (shown in the frequency of her being named) to the action.

The subordination of Blue Jay in the outcome of 1894 and the relative importance of Crow are clearly shown in the final disposition, that of being placed. Blue Jay is disposed of inland in one line. Crow has three lines, two of which address her. "Your name is Crow" has the force of saying your nature, your character, is that of Crow. Flounder has five lines, three of which address her. Where Blue Jay is named once, Crow is named twice, and Flounder three times. Altogether this ending to the 1894 telling is a carefully crafted culmination.

The end of this craft is a transcendence of the inherent contrast between the two acts to which the 1891 telling is confined. Not only is mockery of the

serious journey punished, but the acknowledged claims of the roots in the
first act are offset. Flounder is told to go downriver to the beach, that is, into
the territory of Salmon and his companions, whence they have just come
further upriver.[7] Flounder, as a fish, is one of Salmon's people in the specific
sense—not in the broad sense of the community, addressed by Large Arrowhead Root, as the people who depend on fish, but one of the fish people
on whom the larger community depends. And Flounder is female. Thus the
1894 telling ends with Salmon asserting control over two women, the two of
the other canoe. Salmon asserts control over Crow with regard to external
territory (she is to go from the river and is not to speak the upriver variety
of the language) and over Flounder with regard to internal territory. As the
final outcome of his travel, Salmon himself provides a food of his own kind
for his people. Since Flounder can be found in the river all year round, her
availability matches and goes beyond the role of the plants in the first act. In
Salmon's absence, his people are not dependent wholly on foods of another
kind.

These factors of gender and boundary acquire resonance when the other
version of this myth known to us, recorded in Clackamas Chinook, is considered (Jacobs 1958:75–80, cf. discussion in Jacobs 1960:58–64). The verbal
continuity between the two versions, yet dialectic opposition in character,
cannot be taken up here. Suffice it to say that the ritual journey of the Kathlamet tellings is replaced by a pedagogical panorama of foods of all kinds,
each introduced with a verbal formula analogous to that of Salmon's journey. The likely history of the Clackamas version in a line of women fits a view
of the figure of Salmon as one that embodies tensions as to assertion and
subordination, deference and demeanor, between men and women, amid a
necessary mutual dependence.

7

A Discourse Contradiction in Clackamas Chinook

Victoria Howard's "Coyote Made the Land Good"

Old texts, transcribed by hand, are static. New texts, tape-recorded, are dynamic. If one wants material that shows the active working of the narrative mind, shows negotiation of what is said, what was written down long ago will not do. Or so it would seem.

Tellings of myths about Salmon in Chinookan languages show that old texts may still sometimes answer such questions. Linguistic detail shows shaping and reshaping of performance in relation to tensions bound up in the figure of Salmon himself.

The Context in Cultee

This chapter focuses on a Clackamas myth told by Victoria Howard to Melville Jacobs in 1930 (Jacobs 1958:75–80, text 8 [from field notebook 16]). Its context is the preceding chapter, in which two tellings of "Salmon's Myth" in Kathlamet Chinook are compared. The two tellings, both by Charles Cultee to Franz Boas, one in 1891, one in 1894, contrast in poetic form, especially in their second acts. The contrast cannot be explained by, indeed, would not be noticed by, analysis in terms of ingredients of content, whether of the kind traditional in folklore or of the kind developed by Lévi-Strauss. The one kind of form cannot be reduced to the other. Linguistic detail, including selection of verbs of saying, presence or absence of ironic questions, and contrasting treatment of memory slips, show Cultee to have paced the two tellings differently. In both cases, his concern evidently is to assert in the second act the authority of Salmon and the male domain of fish, after a first act in which Salmon has been shown acknowledging the claims of the women's domain of plants.

The Crux in Victoria Howard's Telling

Cultee's 1894 telling appears to be an assertion not only of a masculine domain but of a Chinookan domain as well. When Crow is thrown away from
the river at the end, she is ordered also never to speak "the Wasco language"
again. And the first word said by Crow is in fact the name of button-root
camas in Clackamas, close linguistic kin of Wasco. The term "Wasco" may
have served the Kathlamet for all the varieties of Chinookan upriver from
them, including that from which Crow and her companions have come.[1]
Moreover, in this upriver territory a line of women narrators appears also to
have found in this myth of reciprocity a source of ambivalence and to have
made it a contested terrain. Victoria Howard, like Cultee, tells of the provision of the foods on which the people depend. Like Cultee, she finds the
figure who encounters the foods problematic. As we have seen, Cultee has
a second act that in 1891 reasserts the authority of the male figure, Salmon,
and, in 1894, a partial lack of dependence on the domain of women as well.
Victoria Howard has a second part that does away with Salmon altogether.
The process of Salmon's elimination occurs before our very eyes.

Howard unfolds a series of plants, birds, and fish, each in sets of three.
The fourth and fifth sets are those for fish. She reaches the point at which
the third of the set is to be named. The obvious culminating name of the
series would be a salmon, sturgeon having already been encountered. No
name is given. The narrative is broken off. Metanarrative commentary takes
its place. A sort of close is given to the accounting for fish, acknowledging
incompleteness. What her sources, her mother's mother and her mother-in-
law, had said is recalled, particularly that her mother's mother said that the
one who made the foods good was Coyote; a myth of Coyote encountering
berries is sketched, with a bit of quoted speech, what each berry would say to
him, including his special name, Štánk'iya.[2] The dictation ends with further
quotation of her mother's mother as to the theme of the myth, the making
(provision) of food for the people.

The narrative is broken off, apparently because its telling has led to a
contradiction. Is "salmon" a food or an announcer of foods? To Chinookans salmon was of course both. In the tellings by Cultee, however, the importance of salmon as food, returning in the spring, and heralded as that,
is background knowledge. The male figure Salmon, named as such, strides
the stage as symbol for a wider change that comes with spring, embracing
plants. In Victoria Howard's telling, the issue of background or foreground
for salmon, announcer or food, is not resolved in the story itself. No word
for "salmon" occurs in either role. Rather, the identity of the announcer is

addressed outside the narrative; the need to name the culminating fish (as food) brings the narrative to a close.

Continuity and Transformation

Behind this crux is a transformation not quite complete. The pattern followed by Cultee for encountering foods has been recast, and the identity of the announcer of foods put into dispute. It would seem that Howard's mother's mother must not have been the only one from whom she knew of the story; otherwise she would not have begun the story as she did. She must have heard, or heard of, the story, from someone for whom the announcer of foods was not a Coyote but a fish person. Notice that Howard's mother's mother is said to have told her the myth only at the very end, and the knowledge gained is qualified. To quote from the interlinear English of Jacobs's notebook:[3]

> Only thus, that way would she tell me. Maybe, I don't know if she'd tell me the whole myth.

Followed by a bracket, presumably an interpretation by Jacobs:

> [She'd only recount the story in this outline form to me.]

And then:

> but not do I remember it all/everything.

And the final comment (following the Clackamas word order):

> When it ripens, the berries, then he'd tell me now at this time, now he went there, everything, and good to eat, he made it, Coyote.

It seems clear that it was particularly the part about berries that Howard remembered hearing from her grandmother, together with a general attribution to Coyote — not the step-by-step appearance of other foods, including fish.

Again, introducing the role of Coyote, Howard explicitly says that her mother-in-law would say, "Not do I remember what (who) here he did them good things to eat" (again following the literal translation).

Apart from her mother's mother and her mother-in-law, then, there must have been at least one other person from whom Howard heard the framing with which she herself begins. Whether or not such source(s) were female, and they had already reshaped the role of Salmon, we do not know. My guess is she knew of a version in which Salmon is announcer, but not explicitly food, and knew also of a version in which foods are not reached by travel but appear. Perhaps they were one and the same version. Perhaps she herself, thinking about the myth to tell it to Jacobs, was the source of that stage in its development, not quite complete. (For more on Victoria Howard and her work with Jacobs, see chaps. 4 and 5 in Senier 2001.)

From Cultee to Howard

To understand this contradiction, emergent in performance, and the changes that lie behind it, we need to consider what links Howard's narrative with the two of Cultee and what contrasts them. Such examination requires a retranslation of the Clackamas text—some details of the published translation are incorrect, and some pose puzzles. The examination depends also on analysis of the text into the lines and groups of lines of which it is composed. Both the translation and the Clackamas text are given at the end of the paper. Most of all, the examination and ultimate interpretation depend on close comparison of linguistic detail. Some of this is taken up in the chapter text, while much of it is given in notes keyed to the lines of the translation.

A SCENE FROM CULTEE

Let me repeat here the first scene of Cultee's 1894 telling (Hymes 1985a: 403–4, chap. 6 here). It will be useful for reference.

The Spring Salmon was going upriver.
> First he came,
>> and he was going upriver.
Now a person is standing:
> "At last my brother's son does arrive,   25
>> "the one with maggots in his buttocks.
> "If I were not a person,
>> "then your people would have died."
He said:
> "Who is it who talks that way?"   10
"Ahh, your father's brother, Skunk Cabbage,
> "he is talking."
"Quick, let us go ashore."
> Salmon landed.
He (the plant) was given an elk-skin armor,   15
> five elk-skin armors were given to Skunk Cabbage.

Under his blanket was put a club,
  beside his arm,
  and beside his (other) arm,
      another one,   20
        a bone war club.
He was carried inland,
  he was put in the midst of willows.

LINKAGE

There is evidence here that Kathlamet narratives lie behind the Clackamas.
The formulaic first line for food in Howard's narrative is an incomplete, frozen version of a corresponding line in Cultee's. In Howard's text, the lines
(7–9) with which the first food hails the announcer are (in Clackamas):

Gałə́kim:
"Adi:::! Kinîkštx̣ náyka.   7
"Nagə́lgat adáłutk.   8
"Idmîlxam á::nga Wakádaču ikdúdina."   9

The second word in line 7 is a frozen form of the construction that begins
line 7 of the Kathlamet, *Qe: ne:kštx̣ naîkainə'x̣ox̣ ngoałé:lx* 'If not I I-became I-
person'. The negative form *nikštx̣* is not otherwise known in these Clackamas texts, nor is a conditional prefix *ki-*. Howard indeed replaces this construction once with a productive Clackamas equivalent, *qama nešqi* (stanza
C, line 36).

Another lexical link suggests Kathlamet awareness of Clackamas tradition. The first root named in Howard's text, the button camas, is *ił-k'álak'iya*.
(The word is the same in Wasco). This is the first word spoken in Cultee's
texts, there rendered *ła(their)-q'alakiawa* but untranslated. To put this word
first in Crow's recital, as she comes downriver past the mouth of the Willamette, below which the Clackamas lived, shows awareness that an upriver version of the myth might start with this name.

PATTERNING OF INCIDENT

The connection and at the same time contrast between the tellings by Cultee
and Howard is illuminated by the patterning of incident in each encounter
with a food. In Cultee's narratives, the invariant part in each of the five encounters with a root consists of seven incidents, grouped in three stanzas.
(After the first scene in each telling, the grouping is marked by the initial
particle pair, "now again.")

1. Travel upriver
2. Hailing ("If I were not")
3. Question ("Who?")
4. Answer ("Name, your father's aunt/uncle")
5. Command ("Go ashore")
6. Gifting (including pronouncement with the two Arrowroots)
7. Placing (1894 telling only)

Howard's narrative shows just the core of the colloquy:

2. Hailing ("If I were not")
3. Question ("What is it like?")
4. Answer ("Like . . .")
6. Pronouncement ([a] "It is a person"
                   [b] "Name"/"Use"
                   [c] "Use"/"Name")
8. Response ("Indeed") (stanzas B, C, J, L only)

The shared core of turns at talk is essentially fourfold: a food declares itself, hailing the announcer and appointer of foods; who or what is asked; identification is made; the announcer responds.

Cultee's narratives have the framework of a journey, recognizing reciprocal obligations among kin and communities. Howard's narrative has the framework of a pedagogic panorama, identifying beings that share the status of persons in a common world.

With Howard there is no explicit statement of travel from one point to another between scenes (Cultee's [1]) or within them (Cultee's [5], "Go ashore" and [7], placing the roots). With Cultee there is no account of what foods look like, framed as such. The only explicit statement as to future use has to do, not with bodily ingestion (eating, medicine), but with external trade (the two arrowhead roots).

PATTERNING OF VERSE, SCENE, AND ACT

The absence of an initial marked verse, concerned with travel, and of action subsequent to the colloquy makes Howard's narrative seem incompletely formed. Like Cultee's narratives, it has four turns at talk in the central colloquy. Unlike Cultee's narratives, it only occasionally maps the four turns at talk into a pattern for the scene as a whole that fits the Chinookan convention of grouping in terms of sets of three and of five. Where Howard does have five units within a stanza, it is accomplished once by having the four turns at talk follow the introductory frame (A), once by adding a metanarrative comment, "All done" (D), and three times by adding a verbal acknowledgment, "Indeed" (B, J, L).

Clearly it is the core of talk that is remembered or wanted, and it is in terms of an additional turn at talk that the three- and five-part conventions for groups of verses are sometimes realized. (The initial frame itself is stated in terms of quoted speech.) Pairing can serve intensification, as in the second act of Cultee's 1891 telling, but there it is organized in terms of the usual patterning at the next higher level (there are three sets of pairs).

One might argue that where there are four verses, Howard's narrative shows intensification by means of pairs of pairs, but that seems unlikely. One would have to judge that scenes that have five verses are not marked for intensity or importance. If anything, the contrary seems to be the case. The first scene is obviously important as a frame; the next two scenes with five verses are within the series of roots; in the fourth instance (J), the concluding acknowledgment can be taken as underscoring the importance of knowing that mudfish is not a food, parallel to the metanarrative comment at the end of the scene with the root that is not a food but a medicine (D); the fifth instance comes with the one fish of feminine gender, Trout (L).

The placement of the five scenes that have five parts also suggests that attention to five-part patterning was distributed across the several sets of foods and would-be foods. Five-verse patterning is found at the outset (A B); at the beginning of the second set of three (D); and at the beginning (and end) of the fourth set of three (J L).

Relations between scenes and groups of scenes are another matter. Each food or would-be food is part of a set of three. There are five such sets: three camas, three other roots, three birds, three minor fish, three major fish. The narrative is clearly conceived in terms of such patterning, and it is the presence of such patterning that pinpoints the final scene of the final set as a culmination and crux. And when that crux arrives, the lines that follow in a metanarrative epilogue are, if less overtly marked, still part of a sequence of five stanzas.

Here is a table of these relationships.

Roots

A	prologue	+	4 turns
B	4 turns	+	"Indeed"
C	4 turns		

Other Roots

D	4 turns	+	"All done"
E	4 turns		
F	4 turns		

Birds
G   4 turns
H   4 turns
I   4 turns

Fish 1
J   4 turns   +   "Indeed"
K   4 turns
L   4 turns   +   "Indeed"

Fish 2
M   4 turns
N   4 turns
O   4 turns

It appears that organization of the narrative in terms of the foods and would-be foods themselves was clear and consistent for Howard, and also that at a larger level the usual conventions of grouping were maintained both before and after the crux at the end of the main narrative. Within the main narrative, however, dialogue is of primary importance and mostly at the expense of expected form.[4]

PEDAGOGY

To be sure, there is more congruence between the tellings by Cultee and Howard than might at first appear. The instruction made explicit by question, answer, and pronouncement in Howard's text as to the appearance and use of foods is conveyed through reported action in Cultee's. Each gift to a root establishes physical features by which it henceforth will be recognized, and each placement indicates where it is to be found. Thus, the elk-skin armor and bone war club given to Skunk Cabbage become the yellow brown bract and elongated stalk of that plant in its spring pride. To place Skunk Cabbage inland among willows is to teach a listener where to look for it.

TRAVEL

Conversely, travel is not wholly absent from the Clackamas text. Howard begins, like Cultee, speaking of something arriving in the spring—only it is a root (button camas), not an announcer (whether Salmon or Štánk'iya). Each subsequent scene begins with two or more particles (usually the pair, "Soon now" [*Kwálá aga*]) that express passage of time and may imply change of location, as if the announcer or the announcer's party were coming upon the foods of the Clackamas world one after another. The common particle pair *kwálá aga* 'soon now' almost exactly parallels the first words with each root in Kathlamet, *Koala ščáqa*. (Translated there by Boas as 'at last', but *koala* is often translated not only as 'at last' but also as 'soon', and *aqa* is cognate with Clackamas *aga* 'now'.)[5]

Yet "soon now" in Clackamas begins a line that says, not that someone traveled, but that someone spoke. The one possible exception reinforces the point. When the series of fish is begun, "someone spoke" is the second line (122). The first line says, "Now again soon they are" (121) (cf. note to line 154, [b]). The line may imply that they (the party of the announcer) have come to a new location, thus the next individual now speaks; if so, a word of motion or travel is avoided for a word of state. Again, the first spoken line in each scene says that someone is to be seen (see note to line 18 of the translation). This also implies arrival, a change of location by the party of the announcer. But again, that is implicit in Clackamas, while in Kathlamet the first words say "he has arrived."

A further indication of travel is that the specific use mentioned of a second kind of wild carrots is a use not practiced by the Clackamas themselves, but by people upriver from whom the Clackamas obtained the cakes in question. One can readily imagine a Clackamas audience taking the myth to have moved upriver into the territory of those carrot-cake trading neighbors (see note to line 86 of the translation). But again, the indication of travel is implicit—one might almost say suppressed—in favor of an ecological inventory.

Howard's narrative transforms the role of travel. In Cultee's narrative, the relation between the other foods and Salmon is a relation between winter and spring. There is recognition that roots of the women's domain have sustained the people in winter before the arrival of the salmon (and other fish) in spring. In Howard's narrative it is almost entirely spring.

There are indeed *two* kinds of arrival: that of "things in the ground coming out" (line 2) and other foods and would-be foods, and that of Salmon. Only the first of the things in the ground, button camas, is spoken of explicitly as having arrived. The foods to be surveyed are not specifically winter foods at all, but foods of all seasons.

In suppressing Salmon's travel, Howard both suppresses the dramatic image of his much awaited return each spring and denies its special importance. Chinookan men, like modern ethnologists, may think first of salmon when they think of what made the peoples of the Northwest Coast so remarkably prosperous for peoples without cultivation of plants. Howard's narrative makes salmon but one of many foods (even if Salmon remains announcer/recognizer of the others). With Cultee, each of the other foods announces that without it Salmon's people would have died. In his 1894 telling, Cultee subverts the proposition that without roots (women's domain) the people would have died in winter by ending the second act with provision of a fish in winter as well. Howard subverts the proposition that in waiting for spring the people were waiting for salmon by having the myth begin with them waiting for things in the ground.

One finds in Howard's text indications that its perspective is that of the arrival of all the main kinds of food, birds and fish as well as plants. The male grouse is the first bird, and with it the statement "He is to be seen" is followed in the translation by the parenthetic remark "about April" (line 88). The remark evidently derives from Howard. The reference to appearance is parallel to the statement in the narrative about things in the ground. Again, the first fish is Mudfish, and the verb in the initial line can be taken to refer to the appearance of these fish ("being there"). As Howard recalls further what her mother's mother said about Coyote and berries, she concludes with lines about arrival that are very much like those with which the series of roots begins: "Things will ripen, the berries/ Now she will tell me at that time" (229–30). All this indicates a pervasive orientation to the arrival of the several kinds of foods.

That Howard saw the narrative from the standpoint of the foods and would-be foods being what arrive is indicated as well by the puzzling ways in which the first line of the opening formula of each stanza are translated. With the medicine of stanza D, the printed translation is explicitly from the standpoint of the would-be food, "Now I am." With the staple camas (C), the translation refers in the third person, "she is," to the root, not to the announcer. Yet the Clackamas expression in these cases and throughout is *not* "I" or "she" but "he (see note to line 18). And although the translation in the rest of the scenes that contain the expression are with "he" or "it," all those for roots and birds, except (D), which has "I am" in the main text, have "(I am)" inserted.

The stimulus for insertions of "(I am)" probably comes from Howard. The regularity of the insertion throughout stanzas B–I, followed by the regularity of complete absence (J–L), may have resulted from Howard ceasing to indicate in the course of the translation that for her the perspective was that of the food or would-be food. Perhaps the unceasing march of the formulaic lines themselves affected her. After stanza D in which "Now I am" is given, she settled on third-person pronouns to render the lines. Perhaps by stanza J and the advent of the series of fish, the lines themselves have convinced her of their perspective or discouraged her from insisting on her own.

All this underscores the status of the opening lines of each stanza as, for Howard, formulaic lines, perhaps incompletely recalled. It underscores the presence of two perspectives in the narration itself. In the dominant perspective, the arrivals that frame the story are those of foods. Remembered words recall a perspective in which the arrivals are those of someone else. (These paragraphs are adapted from the conclusion of the detailed analysis in the note to line 154, [b] and [c].)

PERSON

The congruence and contrast in the category of person are in keeping with all this. Each time a root is reached in Cultee's narrative, it is identified as a person at the outset, before speech begins (e.g., "Now a person is standing" in line 2 of the scene quoted from Cultee's 1894 telling; in the first scene of the 1891 telling, Skunk Cabbage is named (and thereby identified as a person at the outset; in the second scene of the 1894 telling, Small Arrowhead Root is identified as a woman [and therefore a person]). The spoken question is "Who?" and the answer the name of a root and a kin term, aunt or uncle. The question, in the event, is inclusion in the rights and duties of kinship relation.

In Howard's narrative, a food is referred to as a person only after speaking (speech evidently entitles it to that status) and then only occasionally (Button-Camas (A, line 11), Wild Carrot (E, line 71), Wild Carrot 2 (F, line 80), the unnamed last fish (O, line 193). The spoken question is "What," and the answer a description. Only then is it stated whether or not the speaker is a definite person (singular noun with gender prefix) and then only if it is a food.[6] The unnamed medicine (D) is not so identified; neither is Mudfish (J), which is not food, nor the Chub (K), which some people will eat and some will not. (The omission of the identification for Eel (M) seems an accident, but in keeping with Howard's depreciation of the fish series (see discussion later in this chapter). Whether or not the speaker is within the category of person, in the sense of being a participant together with the people in the maintenance of their common world, is at issue. (On such a Native American conception of person, see Hallowell 1960.)

There is in fact an expressive gradation in the form of the stem for "person" itself. When a food is being asked about as a person, the form (with indefinite prefix *ił-*) is *-gwəłilx* (with the schwa that often merely holds a place for stress). When a food is declared to be a person, the form (with feminine or masculine gender prefix *a-/i-*) is *-gwa:łilx* (with full, lengthened vowel). (See discussion of these forms and their translation in note to lines 11, 14.)

The schwa under stress is a reduced form of phonemic /a/, while the long /a:/ under stress is expressively emphatic: "person indeed."

MASTER-SERVANT

For such persons, participants, to be useful to human beings is a reward (see note to line 11). A variety of myths embody this theme, and mythologies regularly tell how the world has been changed from a earlier state for the benefit of the Indian people who are near and about to arrive. It will be their part in turn to respect and observe the ways of their new world and to realize that they depend on its powers for their survival. It is to this fundamental level of reciprocity that Howard takes the myth. In neither Cultee's narrative nor hers is the announcer a creator in the sense of a creator ex nihilo. The announcer is more a sort of Moses, recognizing and promulgating for people ways inherent in the nature of things. But as we have seen, in Cultee's narrative reciprocity between beings accompanies a tension between genders for which Salmon is a focus. Salmon is first servant, then master. Howard's narrative eliminates the master-servant dialectic.

That elimination goes together with the absence in Clackamas of the insult with which Salmon is hailed in Kathlamet ("maggots in his buttocks"). The insult might seem agreeable to anyone wishing to diminish Salmon as dominant symbol, but it alludes to another myth (also told by Howard) in which Salmon is dominant male par excellence. He survives his father's death as an egg from his father's body without feminine participation; he avenges his father's death; he kills his mother's new husbands while forcing them to drink from beneath her legs; when he sleeps as she paddles him to their home, and she takes fright at maggots that appear on him (spring salmon spoil easily), thus mistaking appearance for true worth, he throws her up on a cliff to die alone. (Later he does restore her.) (Cf. the preceding chapter of this book, Hymes 1985a: 422–23.) Absence of the insult is also absence of the heroic figure who is insulted.

There seems to be another pertinent allusion to that other myth of Salmon. Howard's telling of that myth has the salmon egg found and tended by grandmotherly Crows. In Cultee's telling of the myth in question here, Crow is the central figure of the trio presented as parodying and pretending to supplant Salmon. That seems a change of relationship from one of dependence for survival to one of contest for dominance. Salmon's twisting of Crow and (in the second telling) throwing her away from the river seems a rejection of the dependence that the other myth relates, an assertion of dominance. Once past the aunts of act I, women figures either serve (Flounder) or are expelled (Crow). All this seems further expression of the violence associated with Salmon as symbol of gender tension, further indication of what Howard's narrative has eliminated.

It is not that no trace of concern with relations between genders remains. Changes in the conception of the myth as a whole remove a heroic conception of a male protagonist. And certain details of Howard's narrative show sensitivity to gender.

(a) There is a gender-linked polarity in the sequence of foods and would-be foods, as disclosed in the pronouncement at the end of each scene.

The sequence is: *Roots:* she, she, she; *Other roots:* she, he, he; *Birds:* he, she, he; *Fish 1:* he, he, she; *Fish 2:* he, he, he. The polar sets are the most valued roots (camas) and the most valued fish (eels, sturgeon, [salmon]); the one is entirely feminine, the other entirely masculine.

(b) The choice of initial particles for each scene reflects a polarity as well. The standard sequence within both the series of roots and the series of fish is *Kwála aga ɬgúnax̱* 'Soon now another (spoke)'. This is case for all five of the roots after the first (except that the sixth adds *wît'ax̱* 'again' after "now") and for all five of the fish after the first. The first root has no initial particles, being embedded within the initial frame of the myth; the first fish is specially marked with *Aga wît'ax̱ kwála* 'Now again soon (they are there)/ someone spoke'.

The birds that come between the roots and the fish are disparately marked. The first bird has an expectable "Soon now (someone spoke)"; the absence of "another" goes together with being the start of a new set. The second bird has "another" indeed, but extra initial marking as well: "Now again soon another (spoke)." The third bird lacks "another" and also has "now again" but in a different order: "Soon now again (someone spoke)." The marking of the second bird, the one feminine bird, seems special attention to it. The diversity of marking for the birds as a set seems to show an individuation of interest in them and a lack of attention to them as a set. The roots and fish are treated as opposed sets.

(c) The order of the three key elements of the final pronouncement in each scene changes, as between the series of roots and the series of fish. Here is a chart to show the relationships.

Camas

(A)	person	name	eat
(B)	person,	name	dig, eat, bake

		speak truth		
(C)	person	name		eat: boil, bake, cook

Other roots

(D)	—	medicine	name is ?
(E)	person	name	speak truth
(F)	person	name	eat: boil, mashed cake

Birds

(G)	person	name	eat: soup
(H)	person	eat, eggs, all sorts	name
(I)	person	name	eat

Fish 1

(J)	just says so	not food	name
(K)	—	eat/not eat	name
(L)	person	food: soup	name

Fish 2

(M)	—	food: roast, smoke-dry, eat	name
(N)	person	food: boil, smoke-dry, eat	name
(O)	person	food: all sorts	—

All roots that are foods are named, and then their use is given. All fish that are foods have their use given, then their name. The first and third (male) birds agree with the roots: name, use. The second (female) bird agrees with the fish: use, name. (It is exceptional in regard to its initial markers as well; see the discussion later in this chapter.) Clearly there is a contrast, and the main break is between the fish and the rest.

(d) The chart in section c further shows that all six of the roots have uses, five as foods and one (D) as medicine. All three birds are foods. Only among the fish are found beings without use. The first fish pretends to be a food but is not (and therefore not declared a person); the second fish may be eaten by some, but not by others (and therefore is not declared a person). The fourth fish, Eel, is a food and in the culture a quite desirable one, as the elaboration of its use (parallel to that for Sturgeon next) shows; but Howard omits to say that it is a person.[7]

These details seem to show attention to gender and some diminution of the foods that are linguistically and culturally masculine.

YOUNG MAN/GRANDFATHER

The authority of the announcer in Cultee's tellings is that of the young leader of a traveling party. He must learn. He knows how long it takes to travel to the Cascades but does not at first recognize some of his own senior relatives. The authority of the announcer in Howard's narrative is that of someone with knowledge. It is an authority that in the culture increases with age. The announcer asks for information and, receiving it, identifies and explains. In pronouncing names and uses, he teaches what children should learn.

All the myths were told with the assumption that children should hear them. But in Cultee's tellings, as in many myths, action is foremost, pedagogy implicit. In Howard's narrative the pedagogic function dominates; movement and action are only implied. Both announcers affect the world to come in which the Indian people will be present. Cultee's announcer does so as a young man who accosts and shapes the world. Howard's announcer is an older man who discriminates and instructs. He is in effect a grandfather. A relation between genders has become a relation between generations.

Coyote Made Everything Good

(I) (Announcing foods)

(i) (Camas)

(A) (Button Camas)

It must be at this time that they would say,
   now things in the ground are coming out,
     perhaps this moon,
     perhaps (when) the next will stand,
       the very first button camas have arrived.   5
Someone spoke:
   "Gee! Were it not for me,
   "I keep them alive [lit. I hold their breath]
   "Long ago Starvation had killed your people."
Someone said: 10
   "Indeed. What does the person talking look like?"
They said:
   "Sort of flat (and) grayish white."
[—] "Indeed. She is a *person*.
   "Her name is Button Camas.   15
   "That's what they will eat soon."

(B) (Cat-Ear Camas)

Soon now another spoke:
   "(Now) he can be seen.
   "Were it not for me,
   "I keep them alive [lit. I hold their breath]   20

"Long ago Starvation had killed them."
They said:
  "What is talking?
  "What kind of looking person is it now?"
They said: 25
  "To be sure. Seems to be long faced and flat."
[−] "Indeed. She is a person.
  "She speaks the truth.
  "Her name is Cat-Ear (camas).
    "She will be dug out,   30
      "she will be eaten (raw),
        "she again will be baked in ashes."
[−] "Indeed."

                                  (C) (Staple Camas)

Soon now another spoke:
  "(Now) he can be seen.   35
  "Were it not for me,
  "Long ago Starvation had killed your people."
[−] "Ohh. What is speaking?
  "What is its appearance?"
Someone was told: 40
  "To be sure. Her head is kind of round."
[−] "Indeed. She is a person.
  "Her name is Camas [the staple type].
  "Everyone will eat her.
  "She will be boiled (with hot rocks),   45
    "she will be baked,
      "she will be cooked (underground on hot rocks)."

                                (ii) (Other Roots)
                                (D) (Medicine [?])

  Soon now another spoke:
    "(Now) he can be seen.
    "Were it not for me,   50
    "I hold their breath.
[−] "Indeed. What is speaking?"
[−] "To be sure. Its hair is kind of black,
      "it's tied in a bunch on top,
      it's a widow."   55
[−] "Ohh! She is just saying that,
  "she will not be eaten,
    "she's bitter.

"You put her down your mouth,

  "you vomit.   60

    "She is just medicine.

"Sometimes a person will become ill,

  "now she will be mashed,

    "they will drink her juice.

"Her name is . . ."   65

All done.

                     (E) (Wild Carrot 1)

Soon now another spoke:

  "(Now) he can be seen.

  "Were it not for me,

  "I hold your people's breath."   70

[−] "Ohh. What does the person speaking look like?"

[−] "Sort of lengthened."

[−] "Ahh. He is a person.

  "His name is Wild Carrot.

  "He speaks the truth."   75

                     (F) (Wild Carrot 2)

Soon now again another spoke:

  "(Now) he can be seen.

  "Were it not for me,

  "I hold your people's breath."

[−] "Ohh. What does the person speaking look like?"   80

[−] "To be sure. Their legs are long."

[−] "Indeed. To be sure. They are persons.

    "Their name is [another] Wild Carrot.

  "They will be eaten,

    "they will be boiled,   85

      "they will be made into boiled mash cakes."

                     (iii) (Birds)

                     (G) (Male Grouse)

Soon now someone spoke:

  "(Now) he can be seen.

  "Were it not for me,

  "I hold your people's breath."   90

[−] "Indeed. What is speaking?

  "What is its appearance?"

The one was told:

  "To be sure. Its appearance is kind of gray."

[−] "Indeed. He is a person.   95

    "His name is (Male) Grouse.

    "He will be eaten,

    "Soup for a sick person will be made,

    "That one will drink it."

                                 (H) (Female Grouse)

Now again soon another spoke: 100

   "(Now) he can be seen."

[—] "Indeed. What is speaking?

   "What is its appearance?"

[—] "To be sure. That way again."

[—] "Ohh. She is a person.   105

   "She will be eaten,

     "she also will have her eggs eaten,

       "all sorts of things she's good for.

   "Her name is (Female) Grouse."

                                   (I) (Quail)

Soon now again someone spoke: 110

   "(Now) he can be seen."

   "Were it not for me,

   "I hold your people's breath."

[—] "Ohh. What is speaking?"

[—] "Something kind of stretched out,   115

    "it is standing on its head.

     "It's a small person."

[—] "Indeed. He is a person.

    "His name is Quail.

   "He will be eaten."   120

                               (iv) (Fish 1)

                               (J) (Mudfish)

Now again soon they are there.

   Someone spoke:

   "(Now) he can be seen.

    "Were it not for me,

   "Long ago Hunger had killed them."   125

[—] "Indeed. What is speaking?

    "What is its appearance?

[—] "To be sure. It is small,

    "Its head is very large."

[—] "Ahhh. He just says so.   130

   "It's not food.

   "His name is Mudfish."

[—] "Indeed."

(K) (Chub)

Soon now another spoke:

   "(Now) he can be seen.   135

   "Were it not for me,

   "I hold your people's breath.

   "Long ago Hunger had killed them."

[—] "What is speaking?

   "What is its appearance?"   140

[—] "To be sure. Its mouth is small, sharp."

[—] "Indeed. To be sure.

   "Sometimes they will think they will eat it,

     "but others will not eat it.

   "His name is Chub."   145

(L) (Trout)

Soon now another spoke:

   "(Now) he can be seen.

   "Were it not for us,

   "We hold your people's breath."

[—] "Indeed. What is its appearance?   150

[—] "To be sure. Its mouth is kind of sharp.

   "It is good-looking."

[—] "To be sure. She is a person.

   "She is food,

     "They will boil her soup for a sick person,   155

      "he will drink it.

   "Her name is Trout."

[—] "Indeed."

(v) (Fish 2)

(M) (Eel)

Soon now another spoke:

   "(Now) he can be seen.   160

    "Were it not for us,

    "we hold your people's breath."

[—] "Indeed. What is speaking?

   "What is its appearance?"

[—] "To be sure. They are long,   165

   "Kind of blackish people."

[—] "To be *sure*. He is food.

   "It will be gotten,

     "it will be roasted (on spits beside the fire),

      "it will be smoke-dried,   170

      "they will eat him.
    "His name is Eel."

(N) (Sturgeon)

Soon now another spoke:
    "(Now) he can be seen.
      "Were it not for me,   175
      "I hold your people's breath."
[−] "Ohh. What is speaking?
    "What is its appearance?"
[−] "To be sure. It is very large,
    "Its body is white."   180
[−] "Indeed. He is a person.
    "He is food.
    "He will be boiled,
      "also that one will be smoke-dried,
        "that one will be eaten."   185
    "His name is Sturgeon."

(O) [?]

Soon now another,
    he too said:
      "(Now) he can be seen.
      "Were it not for me,   190
      "I hold their breath."
[−] "Indeed. What is speaking?"
[−] "To be *sure*. A good person.
    "Indeed. He is a person.
    "He is food.   195
      "They will make all sorts of things with him."

(II) (Epilogue)
(A) (Close on fish)

All sorts of things in the water like that,
    I do not know their names,
      I don't know what kinds of names.
All spoke like that.   200
I think I remember only that far now.

(B) (Mother's mother,
mother-in-law)

My mother's mother would say,
    "Coyote did like that,
    "*All* those things that feed us."
But my mother-in-law would say,   205
    "I don't remember them,
    "those things he made good as food."

My mother's mother would tell me:
    "Coyote made those things like that."

                                          (C) (Štank'iya and
                                             berries)

He went past all the things (that are) berries.   210
They told him:
    "I am going to stab you, Štank'iya!"
He would pluck it:
    "To be sure. You are good eating!
    "Now our people are near."   215
First wild strawberries,
    now those blackberries,
        Raspberry,
    little gray huckleberry,
        mountain huckleberry,   220
    serviceberries,
        crabapples,
           chokecherries.
All those things told him like that,
    "I am going to stab you, Štank'iya!"   225
                                        (D) (Mother's mother,
That is the only way she told me.   Štank'iya, berries)
I don't know (that) she made the (whole) myth to me,
    I don't remember all.
Things will ripen, the berries,
    now she will tell me at that time,   230
        "Now he went past,
        "He made the things food,
        "Štank'iya."

                                        (Mrs. Wacheeno)
Soon she is telling the myth,
    now she will say,   235
        "All the things that were made good,
            "it is those that feed us.
        "But those bad things that are not food,
            "those do not feed us."

Profile of "Coyote Made Things Good"

This profile presents "Coyote Made Things Good" in terms of one extended act and an epilogue (act II). The principal act is taken to have five scenes, each concerned with a particular type of food: (i) camas, (ii) other roots, (iii) birds, (iv) small fish, and (v) large fish.

An alternative would be to consider each kind of food as constituting a scene, and each of the five groups as an act. I tried that, and it seemed heavy-handed.

The second part of the narrative, however, includes three stanzas about Coyote and berries that evidently constitute a scene. The two stanzas that precede it are distinct from each other, but the second appears to lead into the sequence about berries. Still, notice that the closing remark of the second stanza gives Coyote his common name, *It'alapas*, while in the sequence about berries Coyote is addressed by the name particular to this myth, *Štan-k'iya*, and named so at the end (the last word of the myth). That seems to make these three stanzas distinct. But some readers may prefer to treat all five stanzas as a single scene. The last stanza, however, is separate, as indicated in the notes to the text. Although the episode is included in the text, it was not part of the original telling.

Usually it makes sense to identify each set of stanzas separately. That is, just as each act will consist of scenes, beginning with scene i, so each scene will consist of stanzas, beginning with (A). In this myth one sequence seems so much to continue throughout the main act that I have lettered its stanzas in one sequence throughout (A–O).

Acts/Scenes		Stanzas/Verses	Lines
I	i Camas	A abcde	1–5, 6–9,10–11, 12–13, 14–16
		B abcde	17–21, 22–24, 25–26, 27–32, 33
		C abcd	34–37, 38–39, 40–41, 42–47
	ii Other roots	D abcde	48–51, 52, 53–55, 56–65, 66
		E abcd	67–70, 71, 72, 73–75
		F abcd	76–79, 80, 81, 82–86
	iii Birds	G abcd	87–90, 91–92, 93–94, 95–99
		H abcd	100–101, 102–3, 104, 105–9
		I abcd	110–13, 114, 115–17, 118–20
	iv Small fish	J ab cd ef	121, 122–25; 126–27,128–29; 130–32, 133
		K abcd	134–38, 139–40, 141,142–45
		L abcde	146–9, 150, 151–2, 153–7, 158
	v Large fish	M abcd	159–62, 163–64, 165–66, 167–72
		N abcd	173–76, 177–78, 179–80, 181–86
		O abc	187–91, 192, 193, 194–6
II	i Epilogue	abc	197–9, 200, 201
	ii Coyote did it	abc	202–4, 205–7, 208–9
	iii Berries	A abc	210, 211–12, 213–15

	B abc	216, 217–23, 224–25
	C a	226, 227–28, 229–33.
[Mrs. Wacheeno's comment]		234–39

Notes to the text (Identified by line)

5: Jacobs notes parenthetically "(flat like buttons)." The same camas figures significantly in the myth of Tongue (Jacobs 1959a:370). Jacobs comments: "Spier and Sapir (*Wishram Ethnography,* 182) refer to this root as a large wild onion, and on the next page describe it as a flat bulb of a plant with small grayish flowers" (1958:272 n.64). But the comment confuses *ił-q'láuwaitk* 'wild onion' (182) and *ił-k'álak'ia* 'a flat root bulb' (Spier and Sapir 1930:183).

6a: I follow Jacobs in translating the first occurrence of *-kim* in each stanza as "spoke," although other occurrences are translated "said." "Spoke" (suggesting "spoke up") seems apt for the initiating speech act of each scene.

-kim is intransitive and can have the sense of speaking broadcast; it is the root of the term for a "crier" or "announcer." Here it seems to have the sense of announcing to the world.

6b: This first food, when it speaks, does not use the opening formula found hereafter, but simply "Goodness!" (*adí* 'Oh my goodness! Dear oh dear!' has also been in use among Wascos at Warm Springs Reservation. The notebook has "gee!" and I use it here). The consistency with which Howard subsequently uses the formula suggests that it just had not yet come to mind.

8: "breath," equivalent to "spirit, life."

9: Capitalized "Starvation," because the notion is personified. The word is *wa-* (feminine singular prefix) *-kádaču* 'Starvation', then immediate past-she-them-kill. The pattern, shared with Wasco, is also found with 'Hunger' *Wa-lu* (see lines 125, 138). Cf. the unidentified transitive feminine agent *g-/k-* discussed in regard to lines 128–29.

10: Omission of the name of the announcer here and throughout act I is probably because Howard was not sure what name to use. Jacobs identifies the announcer in parentheses at line 6: "It (this camas) said (to a fish person, maybe Salmon, which also appears at the same time of year)" (1958:75). The information that the addressee is a fish person must have come from Howard. Jacobs eschews any cross-reference to Kathlamet materials in the volumes of texts from Howard. Had he identified this addressee with the protagonist of Cultee's myth, he would have simply said "Salmon," adding a reference note. (Cf. the reference noted with line 5 above).

Jacobs regularly provides two kinds of parenthetic information with these texts: substantive information that must derive from Howard in the course of translation and clarifying words, such as referents for pronouns and occasional amplifications (e.g., a copula in a nominal sentence). Thus line 10 is printed as

"He (Salmon) said." Howard probably provided all the parenthetic information quoted above; "maybe" seems her idiom, not that of Jacobs.

In sum, that the announcer is a fish person is taken to be the case. There is reservation as to which fish person it is. Coyote is not in question. Salmon is the only specific suggestion. In confirmation, note Jacobs's third parenthetic clarification when Howard turns to recollection of her sources at lines 202-4: "My mother's mother would say, 'Coyote (the Coyote named *Štánk'iya*) did (named creatures) like that (not Salmon as indicated), to absolutely everything we eat here'" (1958: 79, paragraph 21).

10-15: There is a regular pattern to indication of gender, so far as Howard's Clackamas text is concerned. When the announcer asks about the food that has appeared, the indefinite third-person pronouns are used (*ɫ-* subject or object, *ɫa-* possessive). The same is true when people tell the announcer one or more characteristics of the food. *Only* then does a gendered person-marker appear, as the announcer pronounces.

The published translation obscures this pattern. It may anticipate the gender by using "she" or "he" in English for what in Clackamas was "it." That is unfortunate. The consistent Clackamas pattern reserves disclosure of gender to the announcer, no doubt as part of the announcer's role (and right). This pattern fits nicely the framing of the situation as one of teaching and learning.

11, 14: Jacobs translates "person" when the stem occurs in the form *-ɫgʷəɫilx* in the announcer's question, as in line 11 here, and lines 71, 80, 194 (also in line 62). He translates "poor fellow" or "poor thing" when it occurs in the form *-gwá:ɫilx* in a culminating pronouncement (lines 14, 27, 42, 73, 82, 95, 105, 118, 153, 181, 194). The stem can have the meaning of "(mere) person" in ordinary speech, hence someone "poor," but the structure of the discourse rules this out. Jacobs himself shows awareness of a different force: "I am uncertain whether the denotation is specifically 'pitiable' or 'person-to-be-pitied because he will be eaten and used,' or whether the comment implies essentially gratitude, or merely hails him so that the apt translation would be 'good fellow!' or 'generous fellow!'" (1960:60). The status of the thing as a person at all is initially in question each time, then its nature as a definite and known kind of person. The announcer's use of *-gwá:ɫilx* is, I believe, an affirmation. As a number of myths show, to be eaten and used is not to be pitiable but is a reward, for which people are to show appropriate respect.

Jacobs himself indicates this a few lines later on the page just cited: "Foods wished to become people even as people wished for foods" (1960:60). All the participants in the cultural world, Indian and others, are persons. In these pronouncements the context of the word is not a matter of social hierarchy but of ontology. (Cf. A. I. Hallowell's analysis of Ojibwa ontology [1960].) I translate the term as "person" in both contexts.

Cf. the note to line 23 and discussion in the text.

18: Literally, "his" plus nominalization of the stem "to see" followed by "he-has-become." Jacobs translates variously: "It is (I am) visible now here" (18); "She is (I am visible) now" (35); "Now I am visible" (49); "It is visible now (I am visible)" (68); "He has become (I am now) visible" (77); "He is (I am) visible (about April)" (88); "He is (I am) to be seen now" (101); "He is (I am) visible" (111); "He is to be seen" (123); "He is to be seen" (135); "He is to be seen" (147); "It is visible" (160); "It is visible" (174); "He is visible" (189).

If Howard's intention had been to express "*I* am visible, *my* seeing," that could easily have been done (*i-č̣-gikl*). If her expression referred to each of the foods in turn in the third person, it would vary with their gender and be feminine in the case of the three types of camas, the female grouse, and the trout (*-ga-*), and show concord with a dual prefix in the case of eel (*-šda-*), rather than be constantly masculine (*-ya-*). Evidently the expression does not identify the one speaking, but the one addressed, the leader of those who encounter the foods. The sense could be either "he can be/is seen" (by the food) or "he can/does see it" ("his seeing *by* others" or "*of* others"). The former is by far the most likely, and addition of the continuative suffix *-im* makes the expression refer to "his appearance" (see line 39). Either in any case implies the other, Chinookan being pervaded by mutual relationships between two poles (see Hymes 1975c). One might render the expression "he can be seen," or better, with the phrase used sometimes by Jacobs, "he is to be seen," which matches the Clackamas pair of words, in which the pronominal prefixes all are masculine (*i- ~ y-*).

23: *łan* 'who, what,' indefinite, as distinct from *šan* 'who,' definite and only in regard to persons. The foods are sometimes referred to as a person before being fully identified, but that is always with the indefinite gender marked by *ił-*. A full sequence develops to a close in which the leader typically announces three things: that the food is a person (assigned a male or female identity through gender), its name (containing gender marking), and its mode of use. This is in keeping with the fact that the leader makes things good, not in the sense of bringing them into existence, but in the sense of performing an act that confirms their natures. Like a creator shaping a world from existing material, the leader recognizes properties that roots, birds, and fish already have, once they are described to him. In announcing their personhood, he confers or confirms their status as participants in mutual reciprocity and maintenance of the world (cf. note to lines 11, 14).

24: *qa* 'what, how,' interrogative of manner.

37: Notice that "Starvation" occurs only in the first three occasions. The first two times it has the feminine singular prefix *wa-*, the third time *a-*. *Wa-* would seem to confer special potency. (see Hymes 1981b:353 for alternation of *wa-* and *a-* in a Grizzly Woman myth told by Howard). I take its use here, and the use of the word for "starvation," as rhetorical emphasis. Presumably after the first three occurrences, the threat of starvation is taken to be established.

39: Literally, "what its-seeing" with continuative *-im* of steady state or process.

45, 47: The verbs in these lines specify the ways of cooking that are indicated in the parentheses.

60: The tense is aorist, immediate past continuing into the present: "You (have just) put her down your mouth, you (have just) vomited."

65(a): Jacobs reports (1958:274 n.65) that "Mrs. Howard never recalled the name of this emetic root."

65(b): In the culminating announcement, all of the edible plants (A–F) begin with a statement as to status as person. (I take the remark "she just says so" in D (56) to be a negation of "She speaks the truth" (cf. B [28] and thus a part of the person component). Five (A, B, C, E, F) have altogether the order person, name, use. Thus it may be structurally significant here that the one case in which the description of use precedes the name (D) involves something not eaten. It may also be that Howard withheld the position for a name in hopes of remembering it.

Notice that among the birds, two of the three (G, I) have the order that the plants do, while Female Grouse (H) again has the order person, use, name. This order, inverting that for name and use found with plants, is the constant order for all six fish (J–O), although a person element is missing (K, M) or not clearly present (*x*) in three of them.

72: Jacobs records *q-ł-u-λqt* 'someone-it-longs (makes long)' the first three times this construction occurs (72, 115, 128), but then *k-* twice (141, 165). The later recordings might represent more accurate perception. Also, line 129 has both *q-ł-ú-k'ayts* 'it is small' and *g-y-u-qbayλ i-łá-q'akstaq* 'it-makes-it-big its-head' (with augmentative *qb* for unmarked *g*). It is difficult to imagine Jacobs mishearing *g-* for *q-*, but there is nothing to indicate that *g-*, transitive feminine subject, is intended. The fish in question, mudfish, has a masculine prefix, *wi-*. Nor does the impersonal marker *q-* ever enter into voiceless-voiced alternation with velar *g*. Cf. note to lines 210, 229. I conjecture that the element is *q-* in all cases.

75: A third element, describing use, is evidently missing here. The line, "He speaks the truth," appears elsewhere as part of the first component, positively with Cat-Ear Camas (28) and by negation, with regard to medicine (56) and Mudfish (130). Its occurrence as second and last element here seems out of place, a substitution for failure to remember what to say about use.

86: Jacobs reports (1958:274 n.66) that the Clackamas themselves did not make these hard cakes of mashed boiled carrots, which had to be soaked in water before eating, but obtained them from Chinookans upriver. Thus the location (unstated) for perceiving this kind of wild carrot is probably not in Clackamas territory, but further east up the Columbia. (Not up the Willamette, on which the Clackamas lived, since there are no Chinookans there.) This strongly suggests that this version of the myth derives from one like Cultee's, in which the sequence of foods involves a sequence of travel. Upriver, the name (cf. *id-'inxt* in Sapir 1909b 78: line 6 and n.1), while involving wild carrot, appears to have a different reference: "This is an Indian stew made of two roots (*a-dwaq* 'wild carrot' and *a-mumal* 'wild potato') to which dried fish was sometimes added."

88: Note the parenthesis at the end of the printed translation of this line: "He is (I am) visible (about April)" (Jacobs 1958:77).

96–97: At this point the notebook has "[comes about April] and "[grouse will be shot with bow and arrow]."

115–16: Jacobs writes of the verb in the first line: "This word has the same meaning, 'it is standing', as the following word. Mrs. Howard indicated her preference for the second of the two" (1958:274 n.67). In fact, the first verb root, *-nxa,* has the sense "to stretch, extend"; only the root in the second line, *-tx^w,* has the sense "to stand."

The notebook has: "At this point Mrs. Howard apparently said first *iɫgə́nxát* 'they are standing', and then said *iɫktxwí·la* 'it is standing', commenting that she dislikes the first word, preferring the 'full' word." The words differ between a state that is immediately present state (*-t*) and one that is continuing (*-la*), but also have distinct roots. Jacobs gives the sequence in his notebook as "they are standing, it is standing on his head," and in the published text as "something is standing, it is standing on its head." I have translated it more literally, as "something sort of stretched out, it is standing on its head."

119: Jacobs reports that "Mrs. Howard then said that for 'quail' her grandmother said *idəlxg^wl.* Her mother-in-law said *idsüx̣^wabwala* (the term used in Wasco)" (1958:274 n.68).

128, 129: The constructions for "it is small, its head is big" are parallel: transitive actor-transitive object-transitive verb prefix u-verb stem (small, big). But in the text the initial element is *q-* in the first case, *g-* in the second. I can think of no reason for feminine singular *g-* here and infer a slip in perceiving the sound or the letter *q* as *g* somewhere along the way (cf. note to 72).

154: Jacobs comments at this point: "I deduce that by the time Mrs. Howard got this far in each successive paragraph, she anticipated consciously the gender prefix to be used for the food she was about to name [*a-* feminine, *i-* masculine]. Hence the inconsistent employment and translation of 'he' and 'she'" (1958:274 n.69).

(a) In fact, there is no inconsistency "this far" within a scene—that is, within the concluding turn at talk, the pronouncement, as to the correlation, in both Clackamas and English, between "he" or "she" on the term "person" or "food" and the corresponding gender prefix on a name that follows.

(b) There is, to be sure, some anticipatory inconsistency of translation in the preceding turn at talk, where someone reports the appearance of the plant, bird, or fish. In the case of the second grouse (H), the report on appearance is "same again." In the case of eel (M), whose gender-number prefix is inherently dual, the report of appearance uses a plural person-marker prefix to refer to them. In *all* the other thirteen cases, the person-marker prefix used to refer to the being in question, when it is identified, is the indefinite singular (*ł-; ła-* possessive in such a case as "long its-legs [F]"). There is no pronominal translation in (B), and in (E) "(He is)" appears to be supplied by Jacobs. In the eleven cases in which there is a pronominal translation, it is "it" in just one (J, lines 128, 129, 131)(Jacobs 1958:76). Here the use of "it" may be in anticipation of the outcome that Mudfish's claim to be a food for the people will be denied, so no status as a person is to be granted. The translation is "his" at first in (L) (Jacobs 1958: 78), although the gender and name in the pronouncement to follow is feminine. That is perhaps because the fish are usually masculine.

In the nine remaining cases, that is, most of the eleven in which a pronominal translation of the indefinite prefix is given, it is gendered in translation, and the gender anticipates the gender to be marked in the pronouncement: "she," "her," "her" and "she" in (A), (C), (D); "he," "he," "his," "his," "he" and "his," "he" in (F), (G), (I), (K), (N), (O).

It seems likely that Jacobs had this phenomenon in mind in his note, and that in typing the texts for publication (they were printed from his typing) footnote number 69 was inappropriately placed.

Here is a table that shows more clearly the facts in question.

Pronominal and Translational Gender and Point of View

There is no inconsistency within the concluding turn at talk,
the pronouncement: x is a person, x is food, its name is x.

Let me summarize the grammatical genders of the foods.

A	button camas	*a-*	feminine
B	cat-ear camas	*wa-*	feminine
C	staple camas	*a-*	feminine
D	[a medicine]	no name	referred to as feminine
E	wild carrot 1	*i-*	masculine
F	wild carrot 2	*id-*	plural (no gender marked)
G	grouse	*i-*	masculine
H	grouse	*a-*	feminine
I	quail	*i-*	masculine
J	mudfish	*wi-*	masculine
K	chub	*i-*	masculine
L	trout	*a-*	feminine
M	eel	*iš-*	dual (no gender)
N	sturgeon	*i-*	masculine
O	?	?	(referred to as indefinite, then masculine)

There are three points preceding the pronouncement at which pronominal elements sometimes are translated with gender. First is with the statement by the

food in question as to "visible" and "were it not for me." The second is in response to "What is its appearance?" and the like. The third is when appearance is
described.

How do possibly anticipated genders (before pronouncement) agree with the
preceding turn, in which appearance is described? In the following table, I indicate the gender of the Clackamas name with # for feminine, + for masculine,
S for dual, P for plural; then spell out the method of reference used in the notebook translation, then that used in the published version. Parentheses indicate
wording supplied in parentheses by Jacobs.

Clackamas Gender	Notebook	Published
A button camas #	indefinite	(she is)/ "she"
B cat-ear camas #	feminine	indefinite/no pronoun
C staple camas #	indefinite	"her"/"her"
D a medicine #	indefinite	"her," "she's"/"her," "she"
E wild carrot 1 +	indefinite	"(she is)"/("he is")
F wild carrot 2 P	plural	"(he has)"/"he"
G grouse +	indefinite	"he," "he"/"he"
H grouse #	no pronoun	"it"/ no pronoun
I quail +	indefinite	"his"/"his"
J mudfish +	indefinite	"it"/indefinite
K chub +	indefinite	"his"/"his"
L trout #	indefinite	"her," "(she is)"/"her"
M eel (dual)	plural	"they," "(they are)"/"they"
N sturgeon +	indefinite	"his"/"He," "his"
O ? +	indefinite	"(he is)"/"He"

In sum, description of appearance is almost always treated as indefinite in
translation at this point, as it is in Clackamas. This holds for twelve of the fifteen
cases: (A), (C), (D), (H), (L) (feminine in gender) and (E), (G), (I), (J), (K), (N), (O)
(masculine in gender). Two cases are not marked for gender but are marked for
number (dual [M], plural [F]). The one real exception is B, cat-ear camas, rendered
as feminine in the notebook translation. Why Howard did this, I do not know.
The published translation treats it as indefinite (evidently recognizing a general
pattern).

When the name is feminine in gender, the published translation as to appearance has "she" in just three cases, (A), (C), (D). (B), (H), and (L) do not. (B) and
(H) receive no gender in the published translation. With trout (L), perhaps this is
because for Jacobs the domain of fish was predominantly masculine. For cat-ear
camas and feminine grouse, I have no idea.

When the name is masculine in gender, G, I, K, N, O are masculine in the published translation as well. Wild carrot 1 (E) has both "(she is)" and "(he is)" supplied. Mudfish (J) has "it." In addition, plural wild carrot (F) becomes masculine. Again, I have no idea why.

Clearly, one cannot rely on the published translation for inferences as to the role of gender. It is mostly consistent, but not always. One has to consult the Clackamas words.

(c) There is inconsistency in pronominal translation at the very beginning of these scenes, one already addressed in part in notes to lines 11 and 14.

In (C) the printed translation is "She is (I am) visible (now)"; the name at the end is feminine in gender, but the term translated at the outset as "she" is the masculine possessive prefix. Similarly, in (D) the printed translation is "Now I am visible," and the being at the end is feminine, but the Clackamas word at the outset again has the masculine prefix. Stanza L, to which Jacobs appends his note 69 (quoted at the beginning of this discussion), accurately translates "he is" at the outset, although the eventual name ("trout") is feminine. So also with stanza H (Female Grouse).

(But the expression "by the time Mrs. Howard got this far" in note 69 rules out reference to these beginning lines. If the use of "she says" in translation at the outset of (C), or "I am" at the outset of (D), instead of "he," is due to Howard, Jacobs does not tell us.)

Howard may have been uncertain of perspective and interpretation herself early on. The first scene, about Button Camas, does not have "he is to be seen" at all; that, however, may indicate that the camas, whose arrival has just been stated, is brought on the scene with status equal, both temporally and culturally, to that of the announcer.

The second stanza (B) has "It is," and in (E) the printed translation settles on use of "It is" (occuring altogether in five stanzas (A, B, C, D, E) or "He is" (G, H, I, J, K, L, O). The use of "it" may reflect the uncertain, indefinite identity of the announcer.

In Cultee's tellings, each root initially greets Salmon with third-person expressions, "At last my brother's son does arrive,/the one with maggots in his buttocks," before turning to "I" and "thine." The "he" and "it" on which Howard settles are parallel.

In sum, the initial variation in pronominal translation is most likely due to Howard. Howard seems initially unsure in translation of the relationship between participants and words within the speech event, of the initial deictic perspective, one might say, but settling, *in translation at least,* on one consistent with Cultee's.

(d) There remains a further puzzle, a revealing one. After the first root, with which "to be seen" does not occur, all the roots (B, C, D, E, F) and all the birds (G, H, I) have parenthetic "(I am)" in the printed translation of the initial formula "He is to be seen" (*i-ya-gikl igíxux̣*) (as in the note to line 88). None of the fish (J–O) do. Invariance throughout roots and birds, variation in the English translation, suggest the hand of the editor, Jacobs. But a change is already to be found in the notebook.

Mudfish   : now I'm/she's to be seen (circled)
Chub   : now it's to be seen (circled)
Trout   : to be seen he is (with circle around "en he is")
Eel   : now it's seen (circled)
Sturgeon   : now it's to be seen (circled) above now-just-now-see-you
             (circle around the whole)
?   : now to be seen (circled)

Such consistency in the notebook points to Howard. My conjecture is that Howard interpreted the initial formula in English in terms of the first person, because that is what it implies, and gave a translation to make matters clear. But perhaps after six plants and three birds, she tired of that mode and turned to a more literal expression. Or perhaps the advent of the fish led her to translate more literally, because the third-person expression conveys an indirectness befitting status, due respect, appropriate to all foods from nature, but de rigeur when it comes to fish.

Another possibility: could it be that Howard took the fish as not being seen, because they are in water? The extra line at the beginning of the set of fish, "Now again soon they are (there)," probably refers to the existence of the fish in the water. But they must be seen in order to be described in the turn at talk that follows.

There is an additional bit of information. With the male grouse the statement "He is to be seen" is followed in the translation by the parenthetic remark "(about April)" (line 88). The remark evidently derives from Howard. Her first stanza has framed the myth in terms of a time at which things in the ground arrive. Following the roots, Male Grouse is the first bird, and a reference to its appearance (showing up) would be parallel. Again, the first fish is Mudfish, and as just noted, the initial line can be taken to refer to appearance ("being there"). As Howard recalls further what her mother's mother said about Coyote and berries, she concludes with lines about arrival that are very much like those with which the series of roots begins: "Things will ripen, the berries/ Now she will tell me at that time" (229-30).

All this underscores the status of the opening lines of each scene as formulaic lines for Howard, perhaps incompletely recalled. It underscores the presence of evolving perspectives within the narration.

Quite possibly, as indicated in the main text, it is tacitly the very nature of birds and fish themselves that is at work. They *do* travel and can be seen doing so, not just appearing in place.

187-88: With simply "another he-said" one would have a single mention of a speaker (the verb requires a subject pronoun). With "he too" (*yáxt'ax*) also, the doubling of subject pronouns gives two lines at the outset of a scene instead of the usual one. In addition, the verb is not marked as usual with the remote past prefix, *ga-,* characteristic of myth, and the indefinite person marker *q-,* but with a generic past prefix *ni-* and masculine singular *i-.* The generic past prefix has a generalizing quality; note its use in lines 200, 202, 203, and 205 in what follows. There seems to be particularly a parallel to its use in 203, "Coyote like-that he-did (in relation to himself)," where the scope is the entire myth. This suggests a perhaps unconscious sense in line 188 that the scope of the entire myth is involved with the actor of this scene. Unique use here of a definite gendered person-marker, rather than the indefinite *ł* used hitherto invariably, further indicates anticipation of an identity that is to constitute a narrative crux. Recognition seems to emerge with the emergence of the second line. Not "Soon now someone (*ł*)-other remote past-someone (*ł*)-said" in one line, but "Soon now someone other/ he-too (*y-axt'ax*) generic past-he (i)-said."

193: In this culminating scene, the published version shows three turns at talk: 187–91, 192, 193–96. This may be a typographical error. "Indeed" (*âw*) at the beginning of 192, and *ə'··* at the beginning of 193 are both response-initiating expressions. The stanza has, not three turns at talk, but four (187–91, 192, 193, 194–96).

The third turn at talk, responding to the query of the announcer, "He is a good person" (in the printed translation) has the role of a description of appearance. The stem in question is used not only of conduct, but also of appearance. One uses this term to say that a man or woman is "good-looking," "handsome," or "beautiful." Hence the translation here "A good-looking person." Cf. line 152, where Jacobs did render *i-t'úkdi i-łá gigliw* as "He is good-looking."

194: The printed text shows only one turn at talk for lines 193–96. The general structure of the interaction shows 193 to be the description offered in response to the query of 192, and 194–96 to be the announcer's response to that description. The particle of recognition and assent with which 194 begins, *aw,* is regularly the beginning of a turn at talk in this text. For *ə* as the beginning of the reported description and *aw* as the beginning of the pronouncement, see lines 26 : 27 (B), 41 : 42 (C), 81 : 82 (F), 94 : 95 (H), 141 : 142 (K). (Both vowels have ^ (circumflex), as does *u* in line 177.) Jacobs (1958:4–6) does not indicate his intention in using this diacritic, but from what I have heard from older women at Warm Springs, "rise and fall" seems very likely. Jacobs seems to have marked the circumflex in Clackamas only with such self-standing initial particles. This text shows three options for them: no mark, stress (´), and circumflex (^), with or without length.

201: Cf. the closing words of Howard's "Seal and Her Younger Brother Lived There," discussed in relation to closings in general in Hymes 1981b:330–31. The presence of the pronoun *yaymayx* 'that-only' indicates specific forgetting, lack of completeness. Without the pronoun, the rest of the phrase would indicate only that the actors may also have other adventures in a myth world that is open, beyond any one person's knowledge.

204, 207, 237, 239: The word in 204, 237, and 239 is *d-l(x̣)-x̣i-lax̣* 'they-us (inclusive)-in relation to-is eaten, feeds'. In 207 it is *q-u-x̣i-lax̣* '(impersonal transitive)', that is, 'it is eaten, feeds', or in this context, '(they are) good to-be-eaten'. The stem *-łx̣əlm* used in the nouns for "it, he, or she is a food" is in basis a verb, "to eat, eating," commonly translated by Jacobs in this text as "edible." I have rendered the first construction always with "eat" and the second always with "food," keeping the two distinct. (Jacobs gives the first as "our foods" in 237, as "we eat" in 239.)

205–7: The printed text translates "On the other hand my mother-in-law would say, / "I do not recall / who made the things that were good to eat here." If the Clackamas indicated "who," the verb would have a singular pronoun (*ł-* or *i-*) followed by *łan* or *šan* (indefinite or definite). In fact, the Clackamas verb has *d-*followed by *dan*. The construction is "not they-I-in relation to myself-recall *what/thing* those past-he-them-make good one-eats them." In Clackamas the mother-in-law is disclaiming, not knowledge of the announcer, but of the proper list of foods.

208, 226: "Will" reflects use of the future tense in Clackamas. This future is probably a "perfective" future of certainty, as in Wasco (cf. Hymes 1975c).

210, 229: *k-d-u-k'anxa-t* 'she-them-weave?-s'. In Kathlamet *-k'anx-ti* is the noun-stem for "gill net," and in Wasco the stem for "weaving material." It is a nominalization by *-k'a-* of the root *-nxa* 'to stretch, extend' (cf. note to lines 115–16). As a generic term for berries, it is attested only here. Apart from a term or two, for "wild animal" and "quadruped," the Chinookan practice is to have the chief instance of a category, the category par excellence, stand for the set, as in the use of "eagle" for "bird" and of "Chinook salmon" for "fish." Perhaps this Clackamas term, drawing attention to the uses of the plants apart from eating them, highlights Coyote's accomplishment in making them available as well for food.

214–23: The printed text encloses 214–23 in quotation marks within a larger paragraph. The names of the fruits seem actually to be a three-part sequence, from earliest and most valued to last and then least.

214–15. "Now our Indian-people are near" is a frequent remark at the end of a myth (see note to line 215 just below). Lines 216–17 begin a distinct concern, a sequence that implies ripening (cf. 229): "first . . . , now . . ." (strawberries do precede raspberries). The sequence appears to lead to summing up by "all those things" in line 224. These ten lines (216–25) are in effect a sketch of the myth, an expansion of the gloss in lines 210–12.[8]

215: Notice that the noun for (Indian) people, the people proper who are to enter and possess the land, is not "the people," "my people," or even "our people" with exclusive first-person plural (*nša*), but "our people" with inclusive first-person plural (*łxa-*). It includes those spoken to, in this case, berries—a pronominal expression of what Robert Redfield termed "participant maintenance." The implication is that the time has come for the participants in the teller's world to take the form they are to have in it. Cf. Jacobs 1960 where this recurrent expression is the title of a book commenting upon most of Howard's narratives, including this one. (See his discussion on pp. 58–64 concerning a relevant myth.)

216: The inclusion of "wild" in the English implies recognition of cultivated strawberries introduced by whites. Cf. "wild carrot" (E, F).

224: I take *k'ʷáɬqî* 'like that' as going with *kánawi dán* 'all things', as in line 197 ("all things like that in the water"), rather than with the verb (not, that is, "they told him like that").

227: Jacobs inserted "(entire)" where I insert "(whole)." Neither gloss is an expansion of the meaning but rather a way of conveying in English the sense of the expression "to make (-*x*-) a myth" (used by Louis Simpson in Wishram also). Howard's remarks in lines 227–28 and elsewhere indicate that "to make a myth" is to make (tell) a myth completely. Otherwise it is not, as such, "made."

228: The form of the negative particle here is emphatic *néšqi*, distinct from *nîšqi* in line 198. Cf. lines 238 and 239: *néšqi, nîšqi.*

8

Bungling Host, Benevolent Host

Louis Simpson's "Deer and Coyote"

The term "Bungling Host" has long been established as a label for a kind of story told by Indian people throughout North America (Boas 1916:694–702; Thompson 1929:310 n.103). A trickster, as guest, is given food; the food is provided by remarkable means. Later, the trickster attempts to reciprocate by using the same kind of means but fails. The means vary from story to story but often include the use by the host of a part of his own body or else the body of a wife or a child. Parts are restored, the dead revive, unharmed. But whomever the imitator cuts or kills is injured or dead.

In this article I draw attention to an aspect of such stories that seems to be neglected. In doing so, I focus on a text in Wishram Chinook (Sapir 1909b: 145–46). This short text makes it possible to illustrate a general method for the presentation of such texts, one that makes it possible to see readily the way in which the form and verbal features of the story convey its meaning.

The established label, "Bungling Host," focuses attention on the would-be imitator. Moreover, it invites us to focus on the imitator's failure, often as something humorous. Sometimes the incident is humorous, as when Coyote thinks he can get fish by diving into the water, just as Fish Hawk does, only to do damage (temporarily) to himself.[1] In other cases, such as a text told in Wishram Chinook by Louis Simpson, presented here, there is perhaps an aspect of black humor in Coyote's thinking that he can emulate Deer, but attempting to do so by cutting his wife instead of himself. The dominant tone, however, is one of averted horror. We are invited not to laugh so much as to learn.

Our delight in the humor of many of these stories may lead us to bring an expectation of laughing to all of them. Say that Coyote is in the story, and one is ready to laugh. But the figure of Coyote is a very complex one, as Luckert (1984) has shown. We have to attend closely to the particular instance. Louis Simpson's stories about Coyote's escapades several times express a degree of scorn for Coyote. One case is his version of the story of "The News about Coyote," in which Coyote performs fellatio on himself. Simpson elaborates the subsequent punishment, in contrast to the light-hearted way in which Hiram Smith of Warm Springs Reservation deflects that part of the story (see Hymes 1981b:238–42). And in another story Simpson has Coyote himself acknowledge that he is subordinate, not a chief, unlike Eagle and Salmon.

Another point to bear in mind is that the stories about Coyote that are obviously humorous show the consequences of his misjudgment as inflicted only on himself. And even when the result is death, Coyote is immortal and revives. Not so with stories in which the death is that of another person. In Clackamas Chinook there is a myth, "Seal Took Them to the Ocean," in which the trickster Blue Jay seeks to emulate Sturgeon, who has provided food from the flesh of his wife. Sturgeon's wife died only temporarily and returned to life. Thus the story teaches that sturgeon will always be provided to the people (as fits various rites and beliefs about the return of such sources of food). Back home with his own people, Blue Jay slices his own wife. She dies and remains dead forever. The leading actors of the myth, Canoe-maker and Seal Hunter, are said in the myth itself to be shocked by what Blue Jay has done. The horror was not averted.

Careful attention to the choice and placement of words in Louis Simpson's story of Coyote and Deer indicate that he took the same view toward the attempt to kill Coyote's wife. I will try to show this toward the end of this paper. Differences in verbs of speaking associated with Coyote; differences in the ways and places in which actors are named; and the organization of groups of lines all work together to treat Coyote as isolated morally in the story as someone not part of the relations of reciprocity it reflects.

Our fascination with the figure of the trickster may lead us to overlook other dimensions of meaning. The fundamental lesson of a story may be more than the futility of trying to be something that one is not. I want to argue that the success of the first host, the benevolent host, may reveal a deeper meaning.

Earlier comparative studies of stories of the Bungling Host have missed this point. In his comparison of such stories, Franz Boas focused on the initial host but reduced the significance of the host to a question of the means by which the host provided food and called such means "magical" (1916: 694).[2] The great folklorist Stith Thompson followed Boas's basic study in the case of this story (1966 [1929]:301). But the underlying premise of such stories is a conception of the world, not as a place of magical means, but as providential. Powers exist to provide the food that people need. People need only show the proper respect and understanding toward such powers. From this standpoint, such stories might equally well be called stories of a "Benevolent Host."

No doubt we should attend to both primary participants. The contrast between them conveys lessons about the nature of both. The nature of the initial host, who has the ability in question, is displayed in contrast to the nature of the would-be host, who does not. That is why both kinds of host are named in the title of this article. And there is a warrant for focusing on both kinds of host in the culture from which this text comes. In Chinookan myths one actor may be named first in the title used to refer to a story and so be the focus of the "pedagogical" lesson of the story (see Hymes 1981b, chap. 7). A second actor may be a focus as well, one with whom the narrator shows identification by describing in detail the sensory experience he or she has. In this Wishram text, Coyote seems an actor of the first type, and the story ends with his wife telling him his proper place. But the sensory detail associated with Deer shows an identification with him as well. Indeed, the form and verbal features of Louis Simpson's telling bring the responsive acts of Deer to the fore and even may take an element of dramatic color from Christian rite.

Insofar as the dimension of meaning expressed in Deer is spiritual and may need to be inferred, it can be called "anagogic." Insofar as it reflects a way of life, it could be called "socio-anagogic," to adopt a term invented by Kenneth Burke (1950; cf. Rueckert 1982:141–42, 202–8). Burke has in mind the way in which nature and what lies beyond nature are interpreted through language in terms that reflect patterns of human relationship in a community.

The Text and Its Presentation

This account of "Coyote and Deer" was told by Louis Simpson to Edward Sapir in the summer of 1905, during their work together on the Yakima Reservation, where Simpson lived. The name "Wishram" is in origin Sahaptin. It came to be applied to the Chinookan-speaking people living at what is now Spearfish on the Washington side of the Columbia River, a few miles above the present site of The Dalles, Oregon. Their own name for their community was Nixlúidix and for themselves, Iláxluit.[3] They and their kin on the Oregon side, the Wasco, were the easternmost representatives of speakers of the Chinookan family of languages, which extended to the mouth of the Columbia, with occasional interruptions, on both sides of the river. The Wishram were moved north to the Yakima Reservation in 1855, the Wasco south to the Warm Springs Reservation. Today Indian people usually use "Wasco" for the descendants of both groups. Simpson indeed includes himself in the term in his personal narrative of the Paiute War (Sapir 1909b:255).

The published title probably was supplied by Sapir. At least no Chinookan title is recorded. In the language, "Coyote and Deer" would be "Isk'úlya kwádau Ič'ánk, " or perhaps, "Isk'úlya k'ma Ič'ánk." A full form of title, on a model found in Victoria Howard's Clackamas (Jacobs 1958, 1959a), however, would juxtapose the proper names without a conjunction.[4] (Clackamas was spoken in the Willamette Valley and is a dialect of the same language; both varieties were called *kikšt* by their speakers.)

Three tasks are involved in presenting a text recorded earlier in the century: retranscription, retranslation, realignment. *Retranscription* has to do with decisions as to how the words and phrases are to be spelled. *Retranslation* involves reconsideration of the English equivalents for the Indian words and phrases. *Realignment* is a name for discovery of the ways in which words and phrases are actually organized in relation to each other.

Let me begin with an explanation of the way in which the text and other Chinookan words in this study are written. Next comes the retranslation, together with the information and notes pertaining to it, some of which makes reference to words in the original text. Third comes an account of realignment and of the "profile" that summarizes it. The profile entails a discussion of the organization of the story and how that organization was discovered. With this before us, we can consider more closely the artistry of the story and its implications.

Retranscription

Sapir recorded Louis Simpson's words in a phonetic orthography. Thirty years later he no doubt would have changed the transcription. He and his colleagues had adopted somewhat different symbols for writing American Indian languages, and linguistics had discovered the principle of the phoneme (largely because of his insight, so far as the United States is concerned). When first recording an unfamiliar language, one writes down everything one hears, not knowing precisely what features of sound are significant. The phonemic principle leads to a method for discovering just which differences count. In Wasco, *nawit* and *na:wit* (with long *a:*) both represent the same word, 'straight, straightway, immediately'. *Kwapt* and *kxwapt* (with strong local friction after the *k* in the second form) both represent the same word, 'then, at that point'. In short, vowel length, the difference between a vowel like that in English "hate" and one like that in English "hit", and the difference in strength of aspiration in the release of a voiceless stop such as *k* do not differentiate one word or sentence from another for users of the language.

These kinds of difference, however, are not the only kind of difference. Some differences have to do with what one is talking about ("referential" or "propositional" meaning). Some differences have to do with the way one is talking about it. The long *a* in some pronunciations of *nawit* is a conventional form of emphasis in Wasco. Just because vowel length does not make *nawit* into a different word (meaning, say, '*I am going' [which actually would be *nuit*]), a vowel length can convey an attitude or emphasis ("expressive" or "presentational" meaning).[5]

Descriptive linguistics developed on the basis of the kind of contrast that underlies the phonemic principle. Only differences in referential or propositional meaning were addressed. The general term "language" was reduced to that one, basic dimension of language. The phonemic principle is vital. Some variation in pronunciation is accidental or mechanical, not affecting what is meant or conveyed in either way. Establishing the minimal referential code of sounds has been valuable in education and literacy. But in the telling of stories people draw on both dimensions.

The phonemic principle led many linguists to omit features of the second sort from their recordings of texts from the 1930s onward. Recordings that included nonphonemic features were even thought of as "old-fashioned" and of no scientific use. Fortunately, the phonetic transcriptions from earlier in the century were innocent of this kind of scientific advance. They preserve a number of expressive features.

In presenting such a text today, then, we have to consider two things. We want to be sure that the symbols represent the phonemic (and grammatical) structure of the language adequately. If, for example, actual speech elides one of two adjacent vowels, as happens often in Wasco and Wishram, we may want to show the elided vowel (in parentheses) so that the reader can be sure of the identity of the words. Sometimes such elision omits a syllable that is grammatically essential (as when *aga* 'now' and a verb beginning with the remote past tense prefix *ga-* may coalesce, so that one has just *a() ga-* or *aga ()*). At the same time, we want to be sure that features that were part of the teller's performance, conveying emphasis and attitude, are represented also. In Wishram and other Chinookan languages, these features especially include vowel length, shift of stress, and vowel color.

Length of vowel does not ordinarily distinguish words in Chinookan, and variation in length is often a concomitant of other factors. Thus, the vowel quality *e* (as in English "hate") normally occurs next to velar consonants (*q*, *x̱*), as a variant of the high front vowel phoneme usually written /i/, and this *e* is always long. But *a* (as in English "hot") is not usually long, and when it is, the length is shown here as an expressive feature (see lines 3, 9, 16, 22, etc.). Sapir's use in them of numbers for exceptional length is retained.

Stress is usually on the next to last syllable of a word. A few affixes cause
exceptions, and sometimes the rhythm of a sentence is a factor (see Dyk and
Hymes 1956). Shift of stress, especially to the final syllable, is expressively
meaningful. Thus, the final stress on *k'wá* in line 15 contrasts with the normal stress of the word in line 52 and emphasizes the return at the turning
point of one scene just before the beginning of the next. The final stress on
wit'á in the next line is contrastive as well (cf. lines 17, 18, 19, 20, 23). Together
the two contrastive stresses seem to underline the fact of return and repetition of what has happened in the first scene. Again, the final stress on the
first word of the text, together with the vowel length conveys, not just 'he
went' or 'he traveled', but 'he went on and on'.

Wishram does not normally have a low front or low back vowel in its
words. When these occur (ä as in English "hat," a as in some pronunciations
of "haughty"), they convey expressive emphasis. Such is the case with the
verb of line 3, where stress, length, and vowel color, all three, combine.

Most occurrences of such features in "Coyote and Deer" have been shown
in the translation either by italics or by repetition ("on and on," "sat and
sat").

Other details of the transcription include the use of parentheses to indicate a sound elided in speech and a hyphen to separate vowels not part of a
semivowel but distinctly articulated (thus, the first syllable in *naika* would
rhyme with English "nigh," but *na-i* would indicate two separate syllables).
The obscure central vowel schwa is phonemic in the language in only a few
stems, one of which, *-gəč* 'nose', occurs in this text. Other occurrences are
concomitants of stress or syllabic rhythm, or the syllabic status of the con-
tinuants *l, m, n.* These occurrences are retained, because they are helpful to
an appreciation of the rhythm.

Changes from the published transcription include the following:

(1) Sapir wrote *L* instead of *ł* for the lateral fricative in lines 9,18, 42, and
48 (*łq'oab, łq'up*). Since all instances are word-initial before *-q'u,* that environment seems to explain the difference in what he heard. (In his phonetic
notes, Sapir observed that *L* is the same as *ł,* but with an initial stop (dorsal *t*)
quality and that it either is derived from a combination of *t + ł,* or is merely a
phonetic variant of *ł.*) Subsequent work with Wishram-Wasco indicates that
the latter is the case.

(2) Sapir sometimes wrote the reciprocal-reflexive prefix as palatal *x* (as
in German *Ich*), but it is in fact a velar *x̣* (as in German *ach*). Hearing the
difference is often difficult for anyone.

(3) The stem 'blood' was written *-g̣awulqt,* but the second vowel appears
to be a concomitant of *l,* heard as a rounded *u* in the environment *w-l.* It is
written here with schwa.

(4) The printing of *-xəł* in the last word in line 20 is a typographical error. There is no such element in this grammatical position. The form is actually the common reflexive-relational element, *-xəł*.

(5) Sapir typically writes *kx* and *qx* in certain words, such as *kwapt* 'then', *kwadau* 'and, before', *naqu* 'not'. *qx* occurs in this text also in *aq'ewiqe* (8), *gaqilud(a)* (10), *luq* (60, 64), but not, in this text, in *quidau* (34, 65). The palatal and velar fricatives (*x, x*) actually are the form taken after *k* and *q* by the strong aspiration with which voiceless stops are released in the language. These automatic occurrences of the fricative sounds are omitted.

(6) The symbol *ô* represents a back rounded vowel, short as in German *voll;* *â* is the equivalent long vowel, as in English *saw.* The short vowel occurs here after a labialized back consonant (such as *kw-*) and between labial *w-* and velar *q-*, as in *-gewaq* 'meat, flesh'. (Sapir heard the effect on the vowel, but missed the velar position of the following stop and so wrote *-gewôk.*) Sapir also wrote *ô* before the stem *-qł* 'house'.

This low back rounded vowel position is a difficulty in Wishram-Wasco, because both Boas and Sapir heard and wrote it for vowels that are, phonemically, sometimes /*a*/ and sometimes /*u*/. In line 3, *štâ2xt* shows lowered vowel quality, together with exceptional length. The ordinary form would be *stuxt*. Such a case seems parallel to another expressive feature of the language, the lowering of a high front vowel (*i*) to *ä* as in English "hat." When *o* or *a* represents phonemic *a*, in other words, the cause would seem to be the phonetic environment. When the basic sound is phonemic *u*, the cause would seem to be expressive emphasis.

Isk'úlya kwádau Ič'ánk

	(i)
Gayuyá: (I)sk'úlya.	1
Ná:wit gayúyam Ič'ánkb(a) idiáqł.	2
Aga kwápt štâ2xt.	3
Aga kwápt galíkim Isk'úlya:	4
"Ag(a) anxk'wáya."	5
"Á-u,"	6
gačíux Ičánk.	7
Aga kwápt gačagálg(a) aq'éwiqe;	8
a-iłq'oá2b gačíux igéwaq iáłqba.	9
Aga kwápt gaqílud(a) Isk'úlya.	10
Kwádau išiágəčb(a) ik'ámunaq galixəlúqłkwаčk.	11
Aga kwápt głigálb(a) iłágawəlqt;	12
pá2ł at'íwat.	13

Aga kwápt Isk'úlya gaqłílut. 14

Aga kwápt itqułiámt galix̣k'wá. 15

(ii)

Aga wit'á2 gayúy(a) Isk'úlya; 16

Ná:wit aga wit'(a) Ičánkba. 17

Aga wít'a łq'úp gačiux̣ igéwaq iáłqba; 18

Wít'a gaqílut igéwaq Isk'úlya. 19

Kwádau wít'a išiágəčb(a) ik'ámunaq galix̣əlúqłkwačk; 20

  gałigálb(a) iłiagáwəlqt; 21

    pá2ł at'íwat. 22

Aga wít'a Isk'úlya gaqłílut. 23

Aga kwápt gačiúlxam Ičánk Isk'úlya: 24

  "Šmáni pu wál(u) agmúx̣wa, 25

  "p(u) amdía naikába." 26

  "Á-u," 27

    galíx̣ux̣ Isk'úlya. 28

Aga kwápt galíkim Isk'úlya iáx̣'ax̣: 29

  "It'úktix amdía náikaba máit'ax̣." 30

  "Á-u," 31

    gačiux̣; 32

  "Ag(a) anúya náit'a Isk'úlyab(a) idmíqł." 33

Qédau gačiúlxam. 34

(iii)

Aga kwápt gayúy(a) Ičánk Isk'úlyab(a) idiáqł yáx̣t'a. 35

Ná:wit gayúyam. 36

Aga kwába p'á:la gayúłait Ičánk. 37

Aga kwápt galix̣łúxwa-it Isk'úlya: 38

  "Aga yáx̣t'ax̣ igéwaq anilúd(a) Ičánk ts'únus." 39

Aga kwápt gačagəlg(a) á:gikal, 40

  gačax̣ímaču wílxba. 41

Aga kwápt łq'úp gačúx̣wa; 42

Kwápt gašax̣əlqíłx agagílak. 43

Kwápt gatssúbən(a) Ič'ánk; 44

Kwápt gačiulxam: 45

  "P'ál(a) áx̣(a) agagílak. 46

  "Náik(a) ayáməlud(a) igéwaq." 47

Aga kwápt a-i-łq'oá:b gačiux̣ igéwaq iáłqba; 48

Kwápt gaqíšəlut igéwaq Isk'úlya ayágikal. 49

Kwádau iłgáwəlqt išiágəčiamt gačlúx̣; 50

  gačłšəlut iłgút iłgáwəlqt Isk'úlya ayágikal. 51

Aga kwápt galíx̣k'w(a) Ič'ánk idiáqłiamt. 52

Aga kwápt gačšúlxam: 53
  "Šmáni pu wál(u) agəmḍúx̣wa, 54
  "P(u) amdúya náikaba." 55
Kwápt gagiúlxam agagílak: 56
  "Imik'ámǝl(a) Isk'úlya. 57
  "Ná:šqi náit'(a) Ič'ánk. 58
  "Yáxtau sík'ǝlutk Ič'ánk; 59
  "Kánauwe šan lúq ałgiúx̣wa iágewaq. 60
  "Ná:sqi náik(a) it'úkt(i) ičǵéwaq. 61
  "Dáukwa máik(a) Isk'úlya mx̣lúidat, 62
  "Mgoáłilx Isk'úlya. 63
  "Ná:qi pu šan lúq ałgiúxw(a) imigéwaq. 64
  "Qédau alugwagím(a) idǝlxam, 65
    "'Iłmémǝlust iâłxlǝm Isk'úlya.'" 66

Retranslation

One needs to review the original translation, not take it as gospel because it is the earliest. Louis Simpson spoke little English, and the English words associated with his text are the product of collaboration between Sapir and the mixed-blood interpreter, Peter McGruff. Both were brilliant men, but, thanks in part to their contributions, we now understand the language more fully than was possible when these texts were recorded. The main concern of retranslation, however, is stylistic. The conventions of English prose have dictated against exact repetition, yet exact repetition is a major structural device of the traditional stories. It shows the ways in which the story is organized and underlies many of its particular effects, not unlike the patterning that is coming to be recognized in the Hebrew Bible (Alter 1981). In Chinookan such initial particles as *nawit, aga, kwapt, kwadau, wit'a, qidau* must be translated each time they occur, not omitted as boring, and they should be translated each time in the same way. Here they are rendered, respectively, as 'straightway,' 'now,' 'then,' 'and,' 'again,' 'that (this) is what.'

The basis of the method of presentation here is a recognition that such stories are a kind of poetry. Although usually published and studied as sentences and paragraphs, they are in fact lines and groups of lines. When their true shape is seen, the stories display effects of literary artistry that usually escape notice when they are read as prose.

The retranslation is presented in terms of the lines of the original text. Generally speaking, each line is a separate predication. The way in which the lines go together is not shown here but later in a "profile" (under realignment) in order not to prejudice a reader's experience of the relationships. I am confident that the groupings indicated in the profile are the true ones, but to show them in the translation now would prejudice a different experience. And the original audience would have heard only a sequence of lines without headings, although they would have been able to interpret the sequence in terms of shared understandings as to narrative form.

By presenting the text in lines with numbers for each line, as in editions of major poetry from the English past, one makes it possible to comment easily on features of the translation or text. In the notes that follow the translation, the expressions in quotation marks are literal translations, intended to help make clear the force of the original and the reasons for the English equivalent. Some explanations are of translations published by Sapir without comment (lines 1, 3); others are of changes from the published translation (13, 63). Not all modifications of the published translation are mentioned in the notes. Thus, as stated, I render particles always the same. Also, I strive to match word order. English word order cannot always be made to parallel Wishram word order, but when lines have a common word order in Wishram, the translation lines have a common word order also. When contrast in order seems significant in Wishram, there is a contrast in word order in the translation. (Cf. lines 10, 19, 49 to lines 14, 23, and line 51.)

Here then is the new translation, followed by the notes. The notes necessarily make references to the language of the original text; it follows immediately after the notes. The italics in the translation reflect expressive features in the original text; those features are discussed as part of the discussion of retranscription.

Coyote and Deer

	(i)
Coyote went on and on;	1
Straightway he arrived at Deer's house.	2
Now then the two sit and sit.	3
Now then Coyote said:	4
"Now I'll go home."	5
"All right,"	6
Deer responded to him.	7
Now then he took a knife,	8
he just sliced meat from his body.	9
Now then it was given Coyote.	10
And he pushed wood up his nose.	11
Now then his blood flowed out;	12
filling a bucket.	13

Now then Coyote was given it.	14
Now then he went home to the house.	15

Now again Coyote went;	16
Straightway now again to Deer.	17
Now again he cut meat from his body;	18
Again the meat was given Coyote.	19
And again he pushed wood into his nose;	20
his blood flowed out,	21
filling a bucket.	22
Now again Coyote was given it.	23
Now then Deer told Coyote:	24
"If you should be hungry,	25
"You should come to me."	26
"All right,"	27
responded Coyote.	28
"Now then Coyote in turn said:	29
"You in turn ought to come to *me*."	30
"All right,"	31
he responded to him.	32
"Now I shall go in turn to your, Coyote's, house."	33
That is what he told him.	34

Now then Deer in turn went to Coyote's house;	35
Straightway he arrived.	36
Now there Deer sat *quietly*.	37
Now then Coyote thought:	38
"Now I shall give Deer a little meat in his turn."	39
Now then he took the *wife*,	40
he threw her down on the ground.	41
Now then he cut her;	42
Then the woman burst into tears.	43
Then Deer jumped;	44
Then he told *him*:	45
"Let that woman alone.	46
"I shall give you meat."	47
Now then he just sliced meat from his body;	48
Then meat was given Coyote and his wife.	49
And he produced blood from his nose;	50
he gave blood to Coyote and his wife.	51
Now then Deer went home to his house.	52

Now then he told the two:	53
"If you two should be hungry,	54
"You should go to *me*."	55
Then the woman told him:	56
"You are bad, Coyote.	57
"I for my part am not Deer.	58
"Look at that Deer;	59
"Everyone will swallow *his* meat.	60
"I do not have good meat.	61
"Likewise you, Coyote, are different;	62
"You are a poor thing, Coyote.	63
"No one would swallow your meat.	64
"That is what people will say:	65
"'Dead things are Coyote's food.'"	66

Notes on the Translation

1: "On and on" renders the rhetorical stress and length on the last syllable of the verb. Contrast *gayúya* in line 16.

2: 'Deer-at his-house'; cf. lines 17, 33, 35; emphatic length on first word; cf. 36.

3: 'Now then the-two-are' with rhetorical length and vowel color (the underlying vowel is *u*) that are rendered "sat and sat" by Sapir.

7: *a-u* conveys acknowledgment and agreement. It is perhaps not as positive or assertive as its mate, *ai,* often translated 'yes.' The associated verb is not a verb of saying or telling, but the factotum root *-x* 'do, make, be.' Thus *au* is expressed almost as a gesture. Since 'say' and 'tell' are used uniformly for two other stems, *-kim* and *-lxam*, "respond" is used here; cf. 27, 31, 33.

9: Sapir comments: "*a-i-* denotes the ease with which the cutting was done; the over-long a in *Lq!oa2b* implies the continuous slice-like character of the cut" (1909b: 145 n.3.).

10: Impersonal subject prefix *q-;* cf. 14, 19, 23 and contrast 51.

12: Verb theme *-gəl-ba* 'out from an enclosed space'; "flow" is added because of its occurrence with "blood" as noted by Sapir; cf. 21.

13: 'Full (emphatic length) bucket'; cf. 22.

16: Emphatic stress on "again."

25: 'If condition Hunger she-you-does.'

26: 'Condition you-shall-come me-to.'

29: *ia-x-t'a(x)* 'his-third-person pronominal base-also, too, for his part, in his turn.'

30: *m-ai-t'a(x)* 'you-participant pronominal base-also, too, for his part, in his turn', as in 28; cf. 58.

30: 'Good you-will-come me-to you-for-your-part.'

34: *Qedau* is regularly translated "thus" by Sapir.

37: *p'ala* 'quiet, still, to cease to move or do'; cf. 46. Verb stem *-łait* 'stay, re-side, sit.'

40: *a-ya-gikal* 'his-wife' would be expected. The form with only gender-number prefix *a-* and stem is exceptional, almost ungrammatical. Cf. the expected form in 49, 51; but cf. the use of 'woman' in 43, 46 to show lack of relationship. Emphatic stress on first syllable; one would expect *a-gíkal.*

45: Emphatic stress on *-i-* 'him'; cf. normal stress on *-u-* in 24, 34, 56.

46: '(Be) still (in regard to) her the-woman.'

55: Emphatic stress on *n(a)-* 'I', as in 31; cf. 26.

60: Emphatic stress on *ia-* 'his'. Cf. normal penultimate stress in 9, 18, 19, 39, 47, 48, 49, and especially the possessed forms in 61, 64.

63: *-goa-łilx* is 'person; poor' (that is, mere person, lacking relationship or status can convey in context being poor). Sapir has "person" here, but Coyote and Deer are equally actors of the myth age in this story, equally persons as well as proto-types of the animals that are to bear their names. The explicit content of this speech of remonstrance and pronouncement is a contrast in the quality of flesh to be provided for the people: Deer's is good, Coyote's not (poor).

66: 'Dead-ones his-food Coyote.'

Realignment

Let me now present the "profile" of the story. (See figure 1.) It shows the way in which lines are grouped together in verses, stanzas, and scenes.[6] Con-versely, it shows scenes, stanzas, and verses in relation to one another and to lines. The profile identifies the hierarchy of units in the story.

The profile represents an analysis of the text. It will be easier to discuss the criteria used in the analysis, once the profile is in view. At this point let me make just a few general observations.

In this short text there are no separate acts, but there are three scenes. These might themselves be readily recognized, since each begins with one actor going to the other. Often enough, the results of an analysis such as this are not surprising, so far as broad patterning is concerned. What is surpris-ing is that the results are certain. One can show that the three parts, say, as in this story, are justified as part of a consistent patterning at every level of the story. With such analysis, one can speak precisely of the parts of a story: how many there are, where they are. One can compare different tellings and stories precisely. And given the use of line numbers, one can cite relation-ships and features easily and exactly.

The first two scenes in this text have three stanzas, and the last has five. The stanzas vary in the number of verses comprising them, whether one,

Figure 1. Profile of "Coyote and Deer"

Act/	Scene/	Stanza/	Verse	Incident	Marker	Lines
	i	A	a	traveled	standard frame, Coyote went	1
			b	arrived	*nawit*	2
			c	stays	*AK (Aga kwapt)*	3
			d	"Go back"	*AK*, turn at talk	4–5
			e	"assent"	turn at talk	6–7
		B	f	takes knife, cuts flesh	*AK*	8–9
			g	gives Coyote	*AK*	10
			h	wood in nose	*Kwadau*	11
			i	blood	*AK*	12–13
			j	gives Coyote	*AK*	14
		C	k	return	*AK*	15
	ii	D	l	C. went	*AW (Aga wit'a)*	16
			m	arrived	*Nawit AW*	17
		E-1	n	cuts flesh	*AW*	18
			o	gives C.	*W*	19
		E-2	p	wood in nose, blood	*Kwadau W*	20–22
			q	gives C.	*AW*	23
		E-3	r	tells C.	*AK*, turn	24–26
			s	"assent"	turn	27–28
		F	t	invitation	*AK*, turn	29–30
			u	"assent"	turn	31–33
			v	he said	*Qidau*	34
	iii	G	w	D. went	*AK*	35
			x	arrived	*Nawit*	36
			y	stayed	*A kwaba*	37
		H	z	C. think	*AK*, turn	38–39
		I	aa	take wife	*AK*	40–41
			bb	cut her	*AK*	42
			cc	woman cry	*K*	43
			dd	Deer jump	*K*	44
			ee	Tell C.	*K*, turn	45–47
		J	ff	cuts flesh	*AK*	48
			gg	gives C & wife	*K*	49
			hh	blood, give	*Kwadau*	50–51
		K	ii	return	*AK*	52
			jj	tell C & wife	*AK*, turn	53–55
			kk	wife tells C.	*K*, turn	56–66

three, five, or six, but the verses in the middle stanza of the second scene are in fact three groups of pairs (total, six). In general, a unit at one level will comprise one, three, or five units at the next lower level, or, exceptionally, ten. Seeming exceptions, such as that just mentioned, turn out to involve an intermediate grouping of pairs in a set of three or five.

The profile shows the relations of form and content. Elements of content are indicated under the heading of "Incident." Elements of form are indicated under the heading of "Markers." Together the two kinds of element show the story to have a structure in terms of the elementary principle of linguistic structure, covariation of form and meaning.

I have assigned capital letters to stanzas and lowercase letters to verses in a continuous sequence throughout the story. One might start the sequence over again in each scene (whose first stanza would always be A, whose first verse would always be a). It would be easier to show certain parallels that way. (Thus, the first and third scenes have parallel first stanzas: A : A, would be more obvious than A : G). But since the grouping into stanzas is an analytic decision, it seems best to offer a labeling that could be revised. Given the verses, one can consider different ways of grouping them.

Markers and Rhetorical Logic

The grouping of lines into larger units is based on the occurrence of several markers, on the one hand, and on underlying relationships known to obtain in the language, on the other. The kinds of markers that distinguish groups of lines vary from language to language. In Wishram-Wasco, initial particles are central. In this text they include *aga kwapt* 'now then'; *nawit* 'straightway'; *kwadau* 'and, before'; *aga wit'a* 'now again'; *qidau* 'that is the way'. Turns of talk are always distinct units. A change in actor or in scene, especially when a verb of travel is involved, is always a new unit. Units are related to one another in terms of an underlying "logic" of discourse. In Chinookan the basic matrix of relationship makes use of sequences of three and five units. It is well known that five is the pattern or ceremonial number in Chinookan. If there is a set of brothers or a number of times something is to be done, it will be usually five. The pattern number five seems always to go with three as a partner in the organization of a narrative, not only in Chinookan but also in neighboring Sahaptin, Kalapuya, and Chehalis and Cowlitz (Salishan languages).

The use of the numbers is not mechanical. The narrator always has the choice of one or the other. The pacing of the story by means of these relationships may be fast or slow. Initial particles, marking units in a sequence, may come in rapid succession or be separated by long speeches or inventories. Notice the rapid succession in lines 40–45, as against the ten lines of speech in the last verse (56–66). The relations of verses to one another in such a sequence is analogous to the use of bar lines in musical scores. The bar lines define a relation of equivalence. One bar may include a single note (a whole note); another bar may include sixteen sixteenth notes. The underlying equivalence allows the composer or narrator to gain effects by varying what occurs within the formally equivalent units.

The use of the numerical sequences is not merely formal. In Chinookan there is a semantic sequence as well, one that can be called "onset, ongoing, outcome." When the sequence has five parts, the third part is a pivot, serving as outcome of the first set of three and onset of the second set of three: 0-1, 0-2, 0-3/0-1, 0-2, 0-3. Each of the three scenes of "Coyote and Deer" has three or five main parts, or stanzas, and this logic seems to hold in each of them. Coyote comes to Deer, Deer gives him food, Coyote goes back (ABC in scene i). Coyote arrives; Deer gives him food and a general invitation, Coyote gives an invitation in return (DEF in scene ii). Scene iii is more complex: Deer comes to Coyote; Coyote thinks of reciprocating; he takes his wife, cuts her; she cries, Deer jumps up, commands Coyote to stop and restates his offer; Deer gives food, returns, tells Coyote and his wife again of his general invitation; the wife reproaches Coyote at length (GHIJK in scene iii). It helps to notice that Deer is the pivot in each scene. In the first two scenes he links beginning and ending actions of Coyote, standing at their center. In the third scene, with its five stanzas, what Deer does resolves the action within the middle stanza, and the action of the first three stanzas as a group, while initiating the action of the two stanzas to follow.

Pairing against a Ground of Three and Five

The pattern of narrative logic helps one recognize relationships in cases where one might otherwise be puzzled. When I first drafted a profile of this story, the two-part stanza of travel in scene ii (l, m), which is identical in form to the first two verses of the other two stanzas (a, b; w, x), led me to think of each scene as beginning with a two-part frame. Such an opening is certainly formally in keeping with what follows in scene ii. The verses of Deer's giving of himself that follow the opening are grouped in pairs: cut flesh, give; produce blood, give; invitation, assent. Indeed, the three verses in the final stanza (t, u, v) seem something of a fillip intended to restore a sense of three-part patterning. And the fact that Deer's giving is so patterned here seems significant. That is why I take the three pairs of verses to belong together in a common stanza. One might take each pair to be a separate stanza and label the pairs EFG, instead of E-1, E-2, E-3. But the pairs belong together, as continuous action on Deer's part and as continuous expressions of Deer's nature. The three pairs seem to go together as one immediate constituent of the scene in relation to what precedes and follows (16–17, 29–34). Notice that Deer's actions culminate in the issuing of his general invitation. The pairing, which is unique here in the story, may be taken to highlight that culmination, one in which *his* nature, what he stands for in the story, is announced.

In this regard, two things more may be said about pairing. On the one hand, its presence shows that the principle of three- and five-part grouping is that of a basic *matrix,* not something that slices everything into threes and fives regardless. A variety of relationships and effects may occur within the matrix. On the other hand, pairing may have its own connotation. Analysis of the full corpus of narratives from Louis Simpson and other Chinookan sources may provide a definitive answer. My sense of the matter is that pairing has a heightening effect, perhaps even an effect of lyric intensity. It is the analysis into verses and stanzas that brings out the presence of such an effect.

More on Organization

Let me return to the earlier assumption of a constant two-part opening frame for all scenes. Such an assumption led to a different grouping of the subsequent verses in scenes i and iii. Rereading the draft profile, I was abashed at having amputated the three-part travel sequence each shows, for it is a sequence pervasive in Chinookan narrative. It is a very common form of the three-part logic of onset, ongoing, outcome, taking the form of "go, travel, arrive," or, as here, of "go, arrive, stay." Once one remembers the common pattern, it tells one to recognize the first three verses of scenes i and iii as going together. In the one case it is Coyote, in the other Deer, who travels, arrives, and stays. In the third scene, the stanza ends with staying, because there is a change of actor from Deer to Coyote. In the first scene, the staying is a pivot, concluding the initial sequences of three verses and beginning a second (still connected with travel) in which Coyote says he will go back, and Deer assents.

This recognition shows scenes i and iii to be more consistent in their stanzas than had hitherto been apparent. Previously, I had taken scene i to have five stanzas: (ab), (cde), (fg), (hij), (k). Why the parallel content of (fg) and (hij) should not be parallel in form was quite unclear. Now that the first

five verses were seen to belong together, as concerned with Coyote's travel,
the next five clearly belonged together, concerned with Deer's actions of
giving (fghij).

Again, the correction with regard to the opening stanza led to correction
of an awkward grouping of stanzas in iii. Given a (mistaken) opening stanza
of two verses (wx) and a sense of a three-part sequence of onset, ongoing,
outcome in (aa, bb, cc), the rest seemed to make up a scene as follows: (wx),
(yz), (aa, bb, cc), (dd, ee, ff, gg, hh) (ii, jj, kk). Again, now that the opening stanza was seen to include staying (y), Coyote's thought (z) was seen
to begin a new stanza. Here another pattern, Louis Simpson's use of particles, led to further correction. For Simpson, it seems, the particle pair, AK,
takes priority in the marking of stanzas over the single particle, K. Now, if
we were to group together the three verses beginning with Coyote's thought
(z, aa, bb), the next question is taken to have five verses (z, aa, bb, cc, dd),
with Deer's command and renewed invitation (ee). In either case, the third
stanza of the scene would begin with K. A stanza beginning with verse ee
seems wrong, since it would subordinate AK to K as stanza initiator (whether
the stanza ended with the third verse, the one having AK [ff] or continued
through five verses). It would make more sense to think of (z, aa, bb) as one
stanza and (cc, dd, ee) as another (let us label it *I), the latter marked curiously throughout with K alone. But at this point the trees may make one
forget the forest. This is a story about hosts. In the first two scenes, the action
of the host is central and constitutes the middle stanza (B, E). So also here,
the host now being Coyote. He takes his wife, parallel to Deer having taken a
knife (8), and the ensuing four verses tell what happens. It is a recurrent pattern in Chinookan for what actors say to culminate a unit, and the pattern
applies here. The report of the woman's cry (cc) concludes the first sequence
of three verses and initiates the second, which in turn ends with Deer's command and offer (ee). The next three verses present for the third time Deer's
use of himself as source of food (ff, gg, hh), shifted to the position of the
fourth stanza in this scene in which Coyote is the host. The last three verses
begin, as did the last stanza of the first scene, with a statement of return. All
the stanzas of the scene begin with a verse that begins with AK. (Notice the
fit with scenes i and ii, in which Deer's cutting himself also begins a stanza.)

Coyote's thought (z) fits the pattern of speech as culmination (reported
thought patterns in the same way as quoted speech in these myths), for
it is the end as well as the beginning of its stanza. It is the only stanza to
consist of only one verse. Recall that the middle stanza of the middle scene
was the only one to contain a set of three pairs of verses. These two stanzas are the only exceptions to the grouping of sets of three and five verses

in a stanza. The exceptional status seems no accident. The formal uniqueness goes together with revelation of character. Deer's nature is revealed in a special form of elaboration. Coyote's nature is revealed in formal isolation.

Coyote's isolation must be discussed further, but let me first conclude this discussion of the relationships summarized in the profile with a general remark. One's understanding of a text grows with attention to it and draws upon interlocking relationships within it, informed by patterns and conventions encountered in other texts from the narrator and the culture. One can easily fall into the trap of relying entirely on linguistic features, expecting them to provide a formal segmentation of a text, or into the trap of ignoring linguistic features, expecting one's judgment of the elements of content that are relevant to be a guide to structure. The only adequate standpoint is one of imaginative sympathy with the narrator, who is telling the story to a purpose, using content and language together in covariation to serve that purpose. Again and again, the narrator uses conventional understandings and emergent patterns to arouse and satisfy expectations of form. Patterns such as the travel triad and the culmination of a unit on something said or thought are standard in the community. Other relationships emerge in the narrative itself, as when the aborting of the travel triad in scene ii goes together with use of pairing for subsequent verses about Deer. Other expectations adopted or developed within the one narrative include the placing of Deer's cutting of his own flesh always initial in a stanza; the introduction of Deer's producing of blood always with *kwadau* 'and' (not often used as an initial particle); the implicit contrast in scenes i and iii marked by a verb of taking, when Deer takes a knife, Coyote a wife; the placing of Deer's repeated offer of himself as food, not final in a stanza as before (r, ee), but medially (jj) in the last scene. The return, parallel to Coyote's return in the first stanza, has already been stated (ii); the words seem a parting reminder and are topped by the one long speech of the story, the wife's remonstrance (kk). In effect, Deer restates the basic reciprocity and providence of the world, then allows the wife to put Coyote emphatically in his place within it. From a would-be peer of Deer, using his wife instead of himself, Coyote is demoted to mute object of the wife's reproach.

Coyote's Isolation from Reciprocity

To return to Coyote's isolation: there is a striking pattern in the verbs associated with speaking (and thinking). When a verb of saying is used, Deer and the wife "tell" someone, using the inherently transitive stem *-lxam*, preceded necessarily by person-markers for both the one who addresses and the one who is addressed: *ga-č-i-u-lxam* (24, 34, 45), *ga-č-s-u-lxam* (53), *ga-g-i-u-lxam* (56), where *č-* is 'he,' *g-* 'she,' *-i-* 'him,' and *-š-* 'the two.' But when Coyote speaks, an inherently intransitive stem is used, *-kim* 'to say' (4, 29), with *i-* as intransitive subject prefix 'he' but without expression of an object. When Deer responds with "au" in assent, the accompanying verb again is transitive: *ga-č-i-u-x* (6, 32) (where *-x̱-* is a factotum verb stem 'to do, make, be'). But when Coyote responds with "au" (28), the construction is not transitive but reflexive; he himself is the object: *gal-i–x-u-x* (ga(1)- 'remote past'; *i-* 'he', *-x̱-* 'reflexive, reciprocal marker'). Again, the verb construction with the stem 'to think' is necessarily reflexive in the language, and it is used in this story only with regard to Coyote: *gal-i-x̱-łuxwait* (38).

Each of the words involves a common construction. No expressive marking is involved. (The only expressive emphasis in on 'him' in line 45, and that is distinct from the choices just indicated.) But the consistent selection of one kind of verb and construction, transitive, for Deer and the wife, and of another, intransitive and reflexive, treats Coyote as outside the reciprocal communication in which the others engage. The expression of speaking in the story is an expression of the underlying theme. Coyote does not comprehend the true nature of reciprocity in food in the world and of his place in regard to it.

Speaking includes the taking of turns, and turns at talk are handled in a way that shows the same concern with reciprocity and Coyote's separation from it. There are ten turns of talk in the text. The first six are exchanges. One party says something, the other responds with *au* in assent. The next is Coyote's thought, or internal speech, which, of course, is without response. The last three turns of talk are addressed to Coyote or to Coyote and his wife, but Coyote is given nothing to say in response. Deer commands him to leave his wife alone and repeats his standing invitation, applied to the situation; Deer tells both again of his invitation; the wife remonstrates with Coyote. *In sum, the story begins with exchanges, three of them, and ends with three statements that lack response. In between comes Coyote's isolated thought. That line seems to be the point at which a pattern of reciprocity is changed into a pattern of unresponded address. It is as if Coyote has lost his right to have a turn, even of response.*

A further expression of Coyote's isolation from reciprocity is in the terms for his wife. When she first appears, Coyote is said to take a "wife," not "his wife": *á:gikal*, not *a-ya-gíkal*, as would be expected And the *a* is stressed; one would expect *agíkal*. Moreover, the *a* is long. In short, there is a concentration of emphasis on the beginning of the word, underlining the point that the woman is at this point "a wife," not "his-wife." Presumably, this is because of what Coyote intends to do to her, "imitating" Deer, not by using his own flesh and blood, in the literal sense, but by using his wife. The hearer would anticipate the consequence as her death. (Cf. Blue Jay's attempt to emulate Sturgeon's use of his wife to provide food in "Seal Took Them to the Ocean"; Sturgeon's wife returns whole, Blue Jay's wife dies (Jacobs 1958:222, 225–26).) And she is "a woman" when first mentioned by Deer and when she remonstrates to Coyote (46, 56).

The story does not end with Coyote alone. In effect, Deer reconstitutes Coyote as part of a relationship, by thrice addressing his gifts and words to the pair, Coyote and his wife (49, 51, 53). The first two instances name "Coyote (and) his-wife," while the third marks the two as a unit by dual object prefix š-. Perhaps Deer's doing so is an expression of male-female partnership and reciprocity as a proper part of the larger order of things. Within that relationship, the woman apparently has the right to be a person in her own right, not merely an adjunct of her husband. Perhaps we can take the sequence of terms for her to imply that Coyote's taking of her to cut cancels his right to regard her as "his"; she is "wife" still, but not now an adjunct. Deer recognizes this in referring to her as "woman" in his command to Coyote to leave her alone. The narrator confirms this status for her in designating her "woman" in introducing her long speech and underscores her importance by giving her the longest and final word, making her the voice of general cultural authority at the end.

Deer's role in reconstituting the Coyote and wife pair is part of an emergence of Deer as the commanding figure. This pattern is reflected in a shift in the circumstances in which actors are named. If we note four types of circumstance in which Coyote and Deer are each named, as initiator or as recipient and, in speech, as addressee or as someone referred to, the following pattern appears.

Coyote

	i	ii	iii	Total
Outside speech				
initiator	1,4	16,28,29	38	5
recipient	10,14	19,23,24	35,49,51	8
Within speech				
addressed by name			57,62,63,66	4
referred to		32		1

Deer

initiator	7	24	35,37,44,52	6
recipient	2	17		2
addressed by name	0			
referred to			58,59	2

If one groups together *recipient* and *addressed by name,* as indicating a role as object, then Coyote is evenly both object and subject, recipient and initiator, in the first two scenes (twice each in scene i, thrice in ii), but then overwhelmingly put in the role of an object of action in scene iii (7:1). Like Coyote, Deer is evenly both object and subject in the first two scenes (once each in each scene), but then overwhelmingly put in the role of named initiator in scene iii.

Notice that to be addressed or referred to by name in speech is almost entirely an aspect of the third, final scene. Deer's reference by name to Coyote at the end of scene ii seems to anticipate and lead into the next scene. I take this concentration in scene iii to be a function of the heightening of dramatization in this, the climactic scene, bringing with it at its close the story's longest speech, the wife's remonstrance, in which all the naming in speech in the scene occurs.

Deer's taking charge is indicated early in scene iii by the expressive length of the word for "quietly" in line 37. Chiefly behavior is ideally nondemonstrative, composed of confidence and self-control.

Of the two gifts with which Deer demonstrates his nature, it is the giving of blood that is highlighted linguistically. This is done in three ways. First, the initial particle *kwadau* 'and' occurs in such a structural role only and always with the line in which Deer produces blood (11, 20, 50). Second, there is a change of word order. The first gift, that of meat, has the common word order of verb preceding noun (10, 19, 49). (The verb indicates the subject, direct object, and indirect object by prefixes; the adding of nouns makes the identity of one or more explicit.) The second gift, that of blood, has the less common word order of verb following noun in the first two scenes (14, 23). In the third scene, the word order is verb preceding noun, but the giving of the blood is distinguished by a third feature, a change in the subject prefix. In each of the five preceding verbs expressing giving, the subject has been impersonal *q-,* translated here with a passive 'it was given'. With blood in the third scene one has the third person masculine subject, *č-* 'he.' The morphological pattern is the same in all the verbs, but this time an expectation developed in five preceding instances is reversed, emphasizing, it would seem, Deer as the actor and source.

Christian Influence

The analogy of Deer's provision of meat and blood from his own body to the Christian sacrament, wherein bread and wine are symbolically body and blood, is striking. Yet the meaning of the Christian rite is a promise that an inherent state of sinfulness will be overcome by the sacrifice of the provider. In stories of the benevolent host, such as this, the provider is not sacrificed. That is the point. The provider's power is such as to be able to continue without permanent injury or death. The analogy with Christianity is not soteriological (having to do with redemption and salvation), but ontological (having to do with the nature of the created world). However much some varieties of Christianity may act in practice like the ancient Manichean heresy, taking the world as the domain of another, evil power, Christianity has to maintain in principle that the world, being God's creation, is good. This myth of Deer and Coyote and many other myths maintain that the dominant powers of the world intend humanity's good. The powers of the world and humanity are participants together in maintaining the world. If human beings do their part, not killing more than they need, respecting the other forces in the world, seeking personal relationships with them, then those other powers will continue to provide what humanity needs. And this basic need, which sacramental relationships maintain, is, so far as the myths tell, not salvation but subsistence. (Needs for health and curing seem to be dealt with in legends and personal experience stories among Chinookans, not in myths.) Whatever the interpersonal relationships and adventures in a myth, again and again the subject of food is present: getting, sharing, having the right kind.

As for Coyote in this story, presumably he learns his lesson, but he is not "redeemed." The Christian rite holds that an inherent state of sinfulness will be at last overcome. Not so for Coyote. Other characters may change at the end of myths to become what they are to be (for good or bad) in the world to follow, when the people will have come. So far as I know, that is never said of Coyote. There is an aspect of it in this story. The wife's harangue drives home the point that his meat is not good like Deer's, that it will not be wanted, that people will say Coyote is an eater of dead things. All that points to the forthcoming presence of the human beings, the Indian people, and draws on the fundamental ethos of participant maintenance, in terms of which it is a punishment not to be useful to the people. But what Coyote experiences in one adventure makes no difference to the next or to his ultimate status. He never goes somewhere to be a particular creature but remains the same, always Coyote. Indeed, one might think that it is Coyote who embodies the principle of sacrifice in such stories. Through his embarrassments, others learn.

In sum, the two principles, creation of a good world and sacrifice for the benefit of humankind, which orthodox Christianity unites in the figure of Jesus as Christ ("through him all things were made"; "God gave his only begotten Son") are here apportioned to separate figures, one benevolent, one bungling.

It is necessary to address these questions because Louis Simpson was a Methodist. Indeed, he perceived an analogy between Coyote and Jesus, since both had lived many generations ago and had appeared in this world to better the lot of humankind (Sapir 1909b:xi). Now, given knowledge of the communion service, Simpson might have been led to highlight the giving of meat and blood. If so, the effect is to sharpen the story, but not to change its doctrine. Its doctrine is traditional Indian still. It is in keeping with Sapir's report that Simpson "implicitly believes in the truth of all the myths he narrated" (1909b:xi).

A Providential World

Other myths moderate the providence dramatized in this myth. Coyote, seeking food, is given flesh by an old woman or an old man, which he finds disgusting, just sores. Later on his way, he smells good fish and discovers that what he has packed with him is salmon (Sapir 1909b:32–34) or sturgeon (Jacobs 1958:84–86). He hurries back, but the old person will not give more, because of the bad treatment he received from Coyote the first time. Coyote decrees that in the future people will not just be given such food but have to catch it. What changes in this "fall" from Eden is not the provision of the food, however, only the ease of getting it. The underlying providential relationship is still present. A Chinookan myth that makes this point about deer is not known in the literature, but the point is clearly made about elk, which makes itself available to those who treat it with proper respect but denies itself to those who do not. (A short Clackamas text recorded by Boas, "The Boy Who Lied about His Scar", mentions deer, but apparently as a slip for elk, which is named (correctly, it seems) in the next line or two. See my discussion of the linguistic features and poetic form of the story (Hymes 1984c).)

One can infer a parallel between myths about such matters and legends about human beings. There are stories about misrepresentation of one's own nature: (1) claiming by imitation a power one does not have (Bungling Host); (2) claiming a relationship with a guardian spirit one does not have ("The

Boy Who Lied about His Scar" and "The Hunter Who Had an Elk for a Guardian Spirit" (Curtin 1909:307–9).[7] There are stories about failure to recognize the true nature of others: (3) Coyote's failure to recognize sturgeon or salmon, mentioned just above; and (4) stories about a boy whose disrespect for taboos with regard to the moon or other matters causes severe weather, which would prevent the obtaining of food (cf. the consequences of snow investing a village uniquely ["A Boy Made Bad Weather"] in Jacobs 1959a: 458–61, 462–65). The consequence of the first kind of story is a reaffirmation of the true or proper natures of each part. Only the misguided actor bears the consequence. The consequence of the second kind is a danger or difficulty to the whole community: salmon must now be caught, are no longer simply given; the boy responsible for bad weather must be drowned to remove the threat to all. In tabular form:

	myth	legend
own nature	1	2
other's nature	3	4

Underlying these distinctions remains the provident nature of the world, expressed in Deer's thrice-repeated statement that he will provide.

9

Coyote, Polymorphous but Not Always Perverse

I. Whose Coyote?

Coyote is the best known Native American trickster, but he is hard to pin down. Stories vary so much. He and the figure of the trickster generally often are celebrated for just that duality of being now this, now that.

The trouble with such celebration is that it diverts attention from those who tell the stories. It is not Coyote but the narrators who are diverse, as are the issues they use Coyote to think about. On a given issue, two men, speaking the same language and telling the same story, may come to different conclusions. Louis Simpson and Hiram Smith did. Their Indian language was the same (called "Wishram" on the Washington side when Simpson worked with Edward Sapir in 1905, "Wasco" then and now at Warm Springs Reservation where Hiram Smith worked with David French and myself from 1950 on). Simpson generally condemned Coyote; Smith sympathized with him.

When Simpson told a story of Coyote as bungling host, trying to imitate another in providing food and failing, Coyote is despicable. He visits Deer, and Deer feeds him with his own flesh and blood. Having invited Deer to visit him in return, Coyote attempts to cut flesh off his wife. Deer stops him, reiterates that they should come to him, and provides again.

Throughout the story, Deer and the wife use verbs that mark what they say as addressed to another. When Coyote speaks, the verbs are intransitive or reflexive, that is, not addressed to another. And when he starts to cut his wife, the word for wife is ungrammatical. It lacks the prefix of relationship (in this case, "his") that kin terms require. The very language of the story isolates Coyote. And the story's last lines are a long speech by his wife, reproaching him to the point of his very Coyote nature (no one would want to eat your flesh).

When Smith told the popular story of Coyote and Fish Hawk, Coyote also bungles as a host. He fails in his attempt to reciprocate, but the only harm is to himself. Fish Hawk again provides food for him and his wife, while Coy-

ote worries about the danger to his friend in doing so (diving through ice).
He is not an isolate, only incapable.

In Simpson's version, Deer is almost Christlike in providing flesh and
blood ("come to me"). In another context, Coyote may prove a savior of
deer, as will appear later in this chapter, in two myths from the Nez Perce of
Idaho, myths that can be used to show that such narratives have not only
imaginative power but also poetic form—form that is part of what they say.
But let me first sketch the place of deer in the myths of the region.

II. Being Deer

Different characterizations of a trickster or a figure such as Deer may reflect
different attitudes or the handling of different problems. Two great spheres
of narrative reflection can be distinguished. *One has to do with setting the
world right, the other with keeping the world right.* In the world of the North
Pacific Coast and Plateau, Deer, the most important animal food on land, is
pervasive in both.

Some languages have specific devices for marking a statement as contrary
to fact. People whose languages do not are sometimes suspected of being unable to reason in such terms. Native American myth is a refutation of such
notions. It predicates conditions contrary to fact, exploring them with zest,
humor, and sometimes a tragic sense. The present world (as Indians lived
before others came) was not fallen from a Golden Age but set right. The first
stage, before the Indian people came, had much ignorance, many dangerous
beings. Often the figures in myth were ways of exploring relationships and
problems still real. But the fundamental premise was that of transformation
between then and now.

Something in the myth world may need to be transformed for two reasons: a trait it should not have or a trait it should have.

As to traits it should not have: The Thompson Indians of British Columbia
told of a time when deer were the only animals on earth and plentiful, but
people could not kill them because they were so fast and jumped so far, from
one mountain top to another in a single bound. At last a woman changed
them to ordinary deer by throwing her breechclout on their hindquarters
(Teit 1898:51).

Various Salish groups of Puget Sound and southern Washington said that
Deer heard that the Transformer was coming along, changing things. Not
wanting to be changed, Deer sharpened a point with which to kill him.
After a bit of conversation, the Transformer (perhaps Moon) nonetheless
changed him into what he would be for the people to come (Ballard 1929:

75, 81; Adamson 1934:336). Pike Ben of the Upper Chehalis gave the part of Transformer to Jesus (Adamson 1934:139).

Myths may include human beings who are predecessors of Indians. Joe Hunt, a Klikitat of south central Washington, told of five brothers, four of whom went in turn to hunt a certain deer, which put them under a spell and took them to its place within a lake, where there was much food. The youngest brother had the power to kill the dangerous deer and restored his brothers. He pronounced that henceforth it would not be like that, the people who are coming are nearby, and deer will be food for people (Jacobs 1934:14).

Myths of transformed uncatchable or dangerous deer speak to the main concern as to traits Deer should have: Deer should be food. A favorite kind of story has Deer gullible enough to be tricked. In one type, Coyote tells Deer to watch out for a (fictitious) enemy, then pretends to be that very thing, shoots Deer, and having pretended to care for Deer, eats him when he dies (Jacobs 1934:54). In a story told by Philip Kahclamat, a Wishram Chinook, Coyote pretends to try to cure Deer, calling Owl to lead the singing to cure him, although Deer is already dead (Kahclamat MS).

Another favorite story has Coyote and Skunk pretend that Skunk is desperately sick and needs the help of other animals to be carried out of his underground house. As they lift him up from within, Skunk discharges his musk sac, they die, and both Coyote (who has been outside in the lead) and Skunk have food for some time. Eventually Deer, Elk, and the other animals get wise (Adamson 1934:134; Boas 1901:79; Jacobs 1934:98, 177).

If the main concern about Deer in stories is for it as food, there is yet a polarity, perhaps ambivalence. There are stories whose point is that Deer gets away—from Cougar (Adamson 1934:191), from wolves (Reagan and Walters 322). If Raven tricks and kills Deer, pushing him over a cliff (Boas, *Mythology* 704, Reagan and Walters 1933:299), a version may have Deer get up and escape (Reagan and Walters 1933:318).

Perhaps the escaping implies that deer should continue to be available, but when that is the point of what happens, myths normally specify that one out of a set escapes, which is why there are still such beings. Here one sees sympathetic imagination for the figure of Deer. In one case, a Quileute myth about the trickster and wolves even has the trickster replaced by Deer! (Reagan and Walters 1933:322; cf. 307, where it is the trickster K'wáiti). Deer is killed at the end but in the meantime has been given a dynamic place at the center of the mythology of the people. And there is a Klikitat myth about helping deer, not to be food or to escape, but just to be deer. Deer goes to the Mountain Goats and marries their sister. Warned not to follow them onto rocks, he nevertheless does so and cannot get back. The Goats then give him a moccasin so that he (and all subsequent deer) can travel on rocks and bad places without falling (Jacobs 1934:19).

Myths, of course, have lessons about keeping the world right in the future. With Deer, they concern the ways in which Deer can and cannot be successfully hunted. Coyote has to learn this lesson (Jacobs 1934:57, 59, 199). In the transformed world, hunters must as well (Jacobs 1934:5, Ramsey 1983:60, Hymes 1984a:195).

Among all these myths the one that seems to me most remarkable for sympathy with Deer is one in which this lesson is made necessary for the sake of Deer as well. Before the changes, Deer was too innocent, too unsuspecting. He would not have survived being hunted. He must change, so that people will have him to hunt for food, but also, I think, so that they will have him as Deer. The story begins with Deer, not dangerous but at peace. Coyote speaks with wonder at it. In this myth, at least, Coyote is a cause of conservation and of ritual purification for men who hunt. (The one parallel known to me, also remarkable, is in Kroeber's *Ute Tales*.)

III. A Nez Perce Myth: Coyote and White-Tailed Buck

Let me compare a respectably presented translation of this myth with a translation in what can be called "ethnopoetic" terms, a translation that takes the myth to have implicit poetic form. I present the two translations, then discuss the basis for difference, and present details, as evidence of the way of working and also of the character of the myth itself. Here is the published running translation:

> When the different kinds of deer were created, there was White-Tailed Buck. Coyote used to see him sitting there. Nothing disturbed him, even when Coyote came over and tried to scare him by shouting in various ways. He was just peaceful and chewing his cud. For a long time Coyote studied the matter, wondering, "How can he become more alert? He is too indifferent. Anyone, even a woman, could club him to death." In this way Coyote contemplated now.
>
> Then he thought, "Maybe this will do it," and pointed his genitals at White-Tailed Buck's nose, almost touching it. Buck got the scent and gave a warning snort. After that, whenever Coyote showed up, Buck snorted. "There, you reacted in the right way," Coyote said. "That's what will make you wary. Only a man who prepared himself, taking a sweat-bath and cleansing himself, will be able to kill you. But not those who do not bathe. You were just too complacent, so much so that even women could kill you. That's the way you were. But this is the way you will be from now on."

From that time on, white-tailed bucks became difficult to approach. Only those who are prepared properly have a chance to kill them. (Aoki and Walker 1989:100)

Here is an analyzed and revised version:

Coyote and White-Tailed Buck
As told by Samuel M. Watters

When all the different kinds of deer were created,
Then there was White-Tailed Buck.
Then Coyote used to see him simply sitting there.

Just so, not alarmed by anything.
Just so, even though he came over,   5
   tried to scare it (by shouting) one way after another.
Then it simply sat peacefully,
   chomp, chomp,
     chewing its cud.

Then for a long time he thought about it—   10
   "How in the world can it have become that extreme?
   Simply so it is,
   just so,
   Simply anyone, even some woman,
   Simply could knock it down."   15
Then he thought about it exactly this way.
   Now,
     "Maybe this will do it!"

Then he took out his genitals.
Then he pointed them at its nose.   20
When they just touched,
   just almost smack there against the nose,
     then White-Tailed Buck got the scent of them.
That's it: it snorted.
The moment he (Coyote) shows up,   25
     then it snorts.

From that time on that (has been) just exactly this way.
"Yes, you are finally right.
   That's the way you will be.   }
Only a man who will prepare himself completely,   30
     will train himself,

will take a sweat bath,
    then will finally cleanse himself,
      then these will kill you.
  And not those who do not bathe.   }   35
You were extreme
  Simply so much so that even women could kill you. }
  That is the way you were.
  And you will be right this way,   }
  from now on,   40
    from this time forward."   }
From that time on White-Tailed Buck deer became hard to catch.
In no way (are they) easy to approach.
Only the man who prepares completely, for that reason, can kill them.

Putting a story on the page implies decisions about its organization. The running translation reads well, but the interlinear translation and Nez Perce text, which precede it, suggest a different organization, when considered in terms of what has been learned recently about oral narratives in the same region and elsewhere. The text appears to have, not three parts, as published, but five. These five parts begin and end at points that do not coincide with the paragraphs of the running translation. The paragraphs of the running translation are reasonable but ad hoc. The alternative parts are inferred from the language of the original in terms of a general assumption about the shaping of oral narratives.

The assumption is that narrators organize what they say by weaving together two threads. One has to do with *what*. The other has to do with *how*. The shape of the told story has to do with both. In effect, a competent narrator knows two kinds of sequencing. One sequence consists of what happens, what must happen if the telling is to count as an instance of the story. The other sequence consists of relationships among lines and groups of lines, relationships that must pattern in certain ways if the story is to count as well told.

Until recently, study of oral narratives, such as those of Native Americans, focused mostly on the *what*. That was what could be studied by those unacquainted with the languages or working with materials for which the original languages were not available. Observations as to characteristic ways of telling stories might be made but did not much affect how stories were presented. Now it is possible to discern the *how* in a thoroughgoing way, a way that requires presenting stories in its terms. Such a way makes explicit recurrences and relations among elements. In effect, it makes it possible to see what someone versed in the original tradition could have heard. With a certain effort, we can learn something that narrators and audiences tacitly knew.[1]

Such analysis of the *how* depends upon three principles.

(1) The first is that oral narratives consist of spoken lines, which need not be equivalent to written sentences. Often a line is marked by a final intonation contour. (In English there are three: falling contour, rising contour [question intonation], and a sustained level contour). Sometimes such a contour contains more than a single line. In either case the unit so marked enters into patterned relations with other such units. A name for such a unit is needed ("line" will not do, since it may be more than one line), and "verse" has been adopted.

Verse, of course, is a term for poetry. It fits, because one trait that the many different kinds of oral poetry in the world appear to have in common is that they consist of lines, of ways of organizing lines. Oral narratives, then, are not prose but poetry. Often enough, they are not poetry in the familiar sense of having lines with internal measurement, meter, as do the sung epic traditions of India, classical Greece, Egypt, Turkey, Slavic peoples, Anglo-Saxons, and so on. They are lines that are regular, not internally but externally, in the ways in which they go together. These regular ways are patterned by a kind of external measurement. One can speak of "measured verse," as distinct from metrical verse.

(2) Therein is the second general principle. It is an instance of what the great linguist and student of poetry Roman Jakobson considered basic to all poetry, namely, "equivalence." With metrical verse, equivalence may be in terms of syllables alone, syllables and stresses, alliteration, rhymes, sequences of types of feet, and so on. In sequences of intonation contours in oral narrative, each contour is equivalent as an element of larger organization.

Often enough, verses are marked by words as well. They often begin with time expressions ("one day," "that night," "for a long time," "the moment," etc.) or with markers of succession of time ("then," "now," "again," "From that time on," "pretty soon"). In some traditions, quotatives ("they say," "it is said") are such markers. A turn at talk seems always to count as a unit in relation to other verses, as part of a stanza or a scene, though it may itself contain what amounts to several verses, especially in Native American narratives when it is a pronouncement. Relations among verses are often indicated by parallelism and repetition.

(3) The third principle is one discovered in recent years. The lines and verses of a narrative succeed one another at more than one level. There is an architecture whose levels can be distinguished as verses, stanzas, scenes,

and, sometimes, acts. The elements of one level make up another in terms of conventions as to their number. In much of the region of which the Nez Perce tradition is a part, the basic convention is that elements will occur in sequences of three or five. A further possibility is sequences of three or five pairs of verses. In other communities not far away, the basic convention is that elements will occur in sequences of two and four. Narrative communities everywhere seem to choose among these alternatives. (Sometimes both may be known and used, as among the Tillamook of the Oregon coast and the Karok of northern California.)[2]

Speakers of a language are unaware of many of the relationships that enter into what they say. Often they can tell if something is or is not done in an acceptable way but cannot analyze why. So it is with these narrative relationships. If not part of language proper, they appear to be part of a level of use interdependent with it. The elements themselves, after all, are elements of a language. What distinguishes them is a mode of relationship.

IV. Translating the Nez Perce

We can go beyond the prose paragraphs of the running translation of Watters's story, because of the tradition in which Aoki works and his great contribution to it. He has provided not only a running translation but also an interlinear translation, showing the connection between each Nez Perce word and a translation meaning (Aoki 1970). He has provided as well a substantial dictionary of the language, so that one can discover the range of meanings for a word and contexts and patterns of its use (Aoki 1994). And he has provided a grammar for the analysis of the words into their elements (Aoki 1970).

When the English words that follow differ from those in the running translation reprinted in this chapter, it is the result of examining the range of meanings of the Nez Perce words in the dictionary.

One concern is to carry over the repetitions and constants of the Nez Perce, for they are part of the sense of form it conveys. Thus, the initial particle *ka··* can be either 'and' or 'then', and I have consistently adopted 'then'. Again, I have settled on 'thought about it' in both lines 10 and 16, since the Nez Perce word is the same. (The interlinear translation has "thought" and "contemplated," while the running translation has first "studied the matter, wondering," then "contemplated . . . thought.")

Again, in lines 11 and 36 the word *tamawin'* is translated 'too' in the interlinear text, while explicated differently in the running translation, as 'too indifferent' and 'too complacent.' The dictionary shows that *tamawin'* has the meaning 'extreme, excessive,' and I have adopted 'too extreme' in both contexts.

In one case I could not think of a constant English equivalent. The root of the verb in lines 4 and 6 has a sense of 'be alarmed, surprised' in the dictionary. The interlinear and running translations have it as 'disturb' in the one case, 'scare' in the other. I have substituted 'alarmed' in line 4.

The dictionary also implies that 'by shouting' is not part of the Nez Perce verb but a concomitant in this story, and so I have put it in parentheses.

Sometimes one needs to work the other way, making sure that distinct Nez Perce expressions are present and distinct in the English. Two recurrent forms in this text, *kál'a* and *q'ó*, are both translated 'just' at the start of the interlinear translation (lines 4 and 5). The first continues to be translated 'just' in the interlinear translation, while the second is usually 'quite' and once 'still'. In the running translation both are often unrepresented. It is awkward to carry them over into the English, but it is part of the purpose of an analysis such as this to be as literal as possible and in effect teach, if necessary, something of an unfamiliar style. Without these two forms, the force of the stanzas about the initial peacefulness of the deer would be almost lost (together, they occur seven times). Consideration of all contexts of both forms suggests that 'simply' can serve for *kál'a*, 'just (so)' for *q'o*.

Another point at which it is important to render expressive force is line 24. The interlinear translation has just 'that' for *ke yóq'o'*; the running translation has nothing. The dictionary (under *yoq*) shows that the second form has a sense of 'that's it, correct' (Aoki 1994:954). Just such a sense fits this climactic moment!

In the final speech (lines 30 and 44), both state in general terms what the successful hunter must do: prepare. These lines bracket the rest, as a sort of inclusio. The word translated 'prepare' in both lines in the interlinear translation is distinguished as 'prepare' and 'prepare properly' in the running translation. According to the dictionary, it has a sense also of 'completely', and "completely" fits Coyote's insistent, bracketing instruction. (Similarly, I have made explicit the sense of "exactly" that the word translated 'in this way' [16, 27] may have.)

In a tradition such as that of the Nez Perce, a sequence of three steps with a sense of outcome in the third is common. The specific steps of preparation are such a sequence: train, sweat, cleanse himself. The running translation, perhaps inadvertently, omits the first of the three.

The interlinear translation has the first as 'cleanse,' but the verb is not the same as that rendered 'cleanse' at the third step. It has a sense of 'exercise, get in shape, train,' and that meaning makes the sequence both culturally and rhetorically cogent.

In this concluding stanza, *kawánnax* 'finally' occurs twice in Nez Perce. It is missing in the running translation, yet it doubly underscores the getting right of things: the deer (28) and the hunter of the deer (33). In line 33, moreover, it emphasizes the status of the third step of preparation as an outcome.

One temporal expression poses a problem, not of translation, but of placement. *Koni·x* 'from that time on' occurs twice, once after the second time the deer is said to snort (line 26 here), once in the third line from the end (42). The difficulty is with the first occurrence. Evidently, Aoki was unsure how to construe it in context. He did not include the next three words in the running translation. By themselves they can be glossed 'just exactly-this-way that.' They do not seem to be part of what follows, Coyote's speech of pronouncement. Most likely they complete a sentence introduced by *koni·x*. *Koni·x* indeed introduces the antepenultimate line of the story (42), and its relative, *kínix* 'from now on,' occurs twice in the preceding lines at the end of Coyote's speech. It makes sense to see here a concluding stanza that emphasizes three times (a pattern number) what will be "from now/then on."

In the running translation, however, such a relation for the first occurrence is abandoned. *Koni·x* is translated 'after that,' and put at the beginning of the preceding sentence: "After that, whenever Coyote showed up, Buck snorted." This position seems very unlikely. While *koni·x* need not be the first word in a sentence, the other examples in this text and those in the dictionary all show it preceding a verb, not following (as it would in a Nez Perce equivalent of the English sentence). Nor does the preceding Nez Perce sentence need it. It already has an introductory word with temporal reference, rendered 'still' in the interlinear translation but glossed 'first' in all the examples in the dictionary (Aoki 1994:614) and followed by a change of tense to the present to indicate a recurrent state. (I use "the moment" to convey "the first time," "as soon as.")

The kind of patterning one finds in such narratives reinforces the conclusion that *koni·x* is the first word of what follows. There are five verses in the concluding stanza. The first three, as mentioned, express the notion "from this time on," two as they begin, the intervening speech twice as it ends (27, 40–41, 42). There is a second triplet as well. The last three lines (42, 43, 44) all express the notion that the deer became and remained hard to catch. The two triplets intersect in the middle verse, which ends one series and starts the other. I call this "interlocking." It turns up in a number of traditions, including English.

The other stanza with five elements, the preceding stanza (D), has two interlocking series as well. The first series has to do with three steps taken by Coyote: take out genitals, point them at the nose of Deer, touch the nose (19, 20, 21–22). The second series has to with Deer's response: get the scent, snort, snort whenever Coyote shows up (23, 24, 25–26).

Finally, an oral narrative ought not to lose its oral effects. In line 8, the Nez Perce has a reduplicated element for the sound of chewing cud, followed by the verb and noun for doing so. The interlinear translation merely identifies the element: ["sound of chewing"]; the running translation has nothing to represent it. English "chomp chomp" seems close as actual sound.

These examples first of all explain and justify departures from the published translation. They show as well that the questions of translation interact with questions of the shape, the patterned form, of a story. Close translation can be more than a linguistic exercise. It can be an exploration and explication of expressive and rhetorical force.

V. A Comparison

Of course, it is possible to tell a story in a different form and to use form to a somewhat different point. Thanks to Dell Skeels, we have a version from Owen Gould (Skeels 1949:148). Gould spoke in English, but with the kinds of narrative pattern one finds in Nez Perce. Here is the story in terms of relations of lines and verses. As before, space separates stanzas.

Coyote and White-Tail Deer
As told by Owen Gould

Coyote was worried   (A)
   because White-Tail Deer was so tame
      and was so easy to kill,   5
and he wanted to make the White-Tail wild
   so he would be hard to kill
      or get in sight.
He had thought of many ways
   that he might make him wild,
but none of his plans seemed to work out
   that he had tried.   10
And he thought of one particular scheme,
   thought it might work
      so that the White-Tail would be wild.

And he went around to the White-Tail,   (B)
   and he walked up to him,   15

and he said,
   "Here's my chance
   and I'm going to try
   if this will work."
He walked up to him   20
   and he pulled back his foreskin
   and hit him over the nose with his penis.
The White-Tail snorted,
   and away he packed his tail on his back,
      and he flagged it   25
   and wiggled his tail,
      and away he went snorting into the timber.

Coyote said,   (C)
   "Now I have in mind what I wanted White-Tail to be,
      wild instead of tame as he has been before.   30
   Now I'll go and look for him again
      to see what he'll do this time.
   Maybe I can walk up to him again."
He went about looking for White-Tail Deer again.
He never even got in sight of him,
   and White-Tail got the scent of him,   35
      and White-Tail began to snort at him from away   (D)
         off in the timber,
and he said to himself,
   "That's what I want him to be, a wild deer."
He said,   40
   "The human people are coming after me.
   From now on, you White-Tail Deer,
      you'll always be that way.
   When you get scent of a human being
      you'll always snort   45
         and be a wild animal hereafter."

Gould emphasizes Coyote's effort, from initial worry to testing to make sure of the result. Much of this emphasis comes at the end, in the testing.

Watters focuses on change in the nature of the Deer in a different way, mostly at the beginning. There he dwells on the Deer's initial pastoral peace, describing it with "just so, just so, simply" (in his second stanza) and having Coyote repeat "simply so, just so, simply, simply" to himself (in the third). Gould pictures the deer once but afterward, flaunting its tail as it snorts and disappears into the timber.

The two versions suggest elements essential to any Nez Perce version—what one would know who could be said to know the story. They also suggest what is optional, what is open to a narrator for personal emphasis. Here is a comparison. Parenthetic letters identify stanzas in each. When a narrator dramatizes a point, has an actor speak significantly about it, or only names it, I use the terms "shown," "spoken," and "named."

	Watters	Gould
(1) Introduction (who, where)	named (A)	—
(2) How Deer is	shown (B)	named (A)
	spoken (C)	
(3) Attempts to change	named (B)	named (A)
(4) Scheme conceived	end of (C)	end of (A)
(5) Scheme carried out	(D) (snort)	(B) (snort, tail)
(6) Test of success	shown briefly end of (D)	shown at length (C)
(7) What hunters must do	spoken, named again at	—
	end of (E)	
(8) Pronouncement	spoken at length mid (E)	spoken end of (C)

Both narrators have essentially six elements in three parts: an opening in which the mildness of White-Tailed Deer (Buck) is identified, attempts to change him are noted, and a scheme conceived; a middle in which the scheme is carried out; and an end in which Coyote pronounces what will be. Both have testing before pronouncement, but Watters at the end of the middle part, Gould at the beginning of the third. Presumably, any competent version would have these elements in this order.

Both narrators organize their stories within a culturally appropriate number of stanzas, three for Gould, five for Watters.

Only Watters has an introduction, identifying the characters separately. Many narratives have such, but Gould merges identification with motive. His opening begins immediately with that.

Gould names White-Tailed Deer's state ("tame and so easy to kill"). Watters elaborates it in depiction (B) and report (C). These elaborations of Deer's initial state (plus an introduction) account for the difference between the two tellings in formal length. In effect, Watters extends part one, so as to bring him at the end of a third stanza to the point (scheme conceived) at which Gould arrives at the end of a first.

Both detail Coyote's act in the center of the story. Watters's Deer snorts (twice); Gould's Deer snorts, then packs, flags, and wiggles his tail.

Both test. In the last verse of Watters's fourth stanza ("The moment Coyote shows up / then it makes its snort") the words and change to present tense imply at least one later test. (The deer did not snort the moment Coyote first showed up but let him reach it.) Gould elaborates most of his last stanza around testing (four verses out of five).[3]

Both have Coyote pronounce how things will be. Only Watters describes the former state of Deer as so tame a woman could kill it; he does so twice, before and after the change, implying that only men can kill Deer now. Only Watters speaks of the consequences for hunters, how they must train and purify themselves. He spells it out and ends with it as well.

Neither Watters nor Gould mentions that most of the work of preparing deer, once killed, is done by women.

We cannot now hear Watters or Gould, but analysis of their stories into lines and verses and the relations among them makes it possible to perceive much of what they intended and did in the telling of them.

VI. Two Profiles

It is helpful to summarize the relationships involved in a story in such a way that one can see that nothing has been missed, gain an overview, and perhaps see inconsistencies of patterns not otherwise noticed. Here are profiles for the two stories. "−" represents quoted speech. Notice that both Watters and Gould sometimes use runs of what appear to be verses within a unit equivalent to other verses within a stanza (Watters[D (c), E (b)]; Gould [B (abc)]).

This apparently is available in Nez Perce as a resource, as it is in Kathlamet Chinook (Hymes 1985a:402) and some other traditions.

Coyote and White-Tailed Buck
Samuel M. Watters

Stanzas	*Verses*	*Lines*	*Features*
A	abc	1, 2, 3	When . . . , then . . . , then . . .
B	abc	4, 5–6, 7–9	Just so, just so, then
C	abc	10–15, 16, 17–18	Then, then, Now "−"
D	abcde	19, 10, 21–23, 24, 25–26	Then, then, When . . . then, That's it, The moment . . . then.
E	a[b]cde	17	From that time on
		[28–41]: [ab cd ef gh ij]	
		[28, 29; 30–34, 35; 36, 37;	
		38, 39; 31–32] 37, 38, 39,	
		40–41] 42, 43, 44	

Coyote and White-Tail Deer
Owen Gould

A   abcde   1-3, 4-6, 7-8, 9-10, 11-13
B   abc   [14, 15, 16-19] [20, 21, 22] [23, 24, 25, 26, 27]
C   abcde   28-33, 34, 35-37, 38-39, 40-46

IO

Helen Sekaquaptewa's "Coyote and the Birds"
Rhetorical Analysis of a Hopi Coyote Story

This chapter shows that one facet of a Hopi narrative may involve relations among verses and stanzas. The quotative is a principal marker of such relations. The spoken lines of the narrative in question vary greatly in length and makeup, and the same is true of a Zuni telling of a related story. Perhaps one might generalize that this aspect of Hopi and Zuni narrative is also characteristic of other languages in the Southwest region, in contrast to much of Native North America. In such a case the contours of performance cannot all be represented together. Vocal and grammatical marking of relations must be shown separately. The latter show a formal coherence that reflects a deep-seated competence.

Quotatives as Discourse Markers

In his valuable account of the narrative considered here, Andrew Wiget remarks:

> The most obvious hallmark of Hopi narrative style is the recurrent /*puu yaw*/, or sometimes simply /*yaw*/, which is a reportative feature signifying that the events being narrated were not personally witnessed by the narrator but were reported to him by someone else. Usually translated as "it is said," the phrase lends to things purely imaginative a verisimilitude associated with things actually seen while disclaiming personal responsibility. Its superabundant use, as in this text, is so frequently a mark of storytelling throughout Native America that many ethnographers simply didn't record it, or if they did record it in the source-language text, they did not bother to translate/transcribe it in the English text. (1987:329)

This last omission is the case in the published texts of another language of the Southwest, Tonkawa, where Hoijer indicates the presence of the quotative suffix in English translation simply by a capital *S* (Hoijer 1972). Further study of one Tonkawa myth (cf. Hymes 1987c, 1992b) has shown that the suffix occurs in sets, usually three in number, which play a part in the organization of the narrative. In a Bella Coola myth (Hymes 1983a) a quotative suffix again proves a key to narrative sequence, in this case in sets of four. The same may be true of Maidu, to judge from an analysis begun by William Shipley (Hymes 1991e: 173), and is clearly true in an Arizona Tewa text connected with this one, where the evidential "hearsay" particle *ba* distinguishes all but the final line of a verse. (The verses themselves turn out to cohere in series of three and five [Hymes MS a].)

Whether or not quotative markers always play such a role, I do not know, but evidently they can in Hopi. When pairs of the two initial particles cited by Wiget occur together, they group lines in what can be considered pairs of verses, as in lines 115 and 116 of the text that follows:

Now, they say, indeed he sat down with them.
Now, they say, they provided him with a plaque.

So also in lines 38 : 39, 130 : 131, 150 : 152, 167 : 168.

Initial pairs, however, are not the only way in which the two particles figure in the narrative. In one line *yaw* may not be contiguous with *pu'* (43 : 46).[1] In one set the initial pair is followed by three other verses each with just *yaw* (47 : 48 : 49 : 51). An initial pair with *piw* 'again' may be coupled with *piw* (64 : 65), or with a song (66 : 69). An initial pair may be coupled with *Pai* 'Well' and *yaw* (143 : 148, 218 : 219).

It appears that several particles enter into marking verses and that they may occur together in a variety of ways. Study of a variety of texts may show that particular combinations have certain expressive effects, at least for some narrators, and that certain narrators have individual preferences. Accumulation of markers in a single line is emphatic in some traditions and may be here. Consider the series of three elements *Pu' yaw piw'* 'Now they say again' in lines 64 and 66, and the same three elements in lines 178 and 183. These could be instrumental to the circumstances. *Pu'pai piw* (29), *Niqw pu' yaw* (117), and *noqw. . . . pai yaw piw* (141), however, do seem emphatic. Comparison of performances and consultation with narrators would clarify these matters.

The usual pairing of verses contrasts with what seem sets of three, triplets, at two points. Lines 101, 102, 103 begin with *niqw pai yaw, pu'*, and *pu' yaw*, respectively. The marker *yaw* occurs but twice (101, 103), which might be taken to define just two verses, but it is hard to overlook the initial *pu'* of the intervening line. The three lines together seem to intensify Coyote's hesitation and act.

Lines 112, 113, 114 begin with *pai yaw . . . yaw, pai*, and *pai yaw* respectively.

Again just the first and. third of the lines have *yaw,* but it is hard to overlook the initial *pai* of the intervening line. As with the preceding case, the middle line of three has an initial particle that occurs with *yaw* in the line that follows. Perhaps the two cases reflect a conventional pattern. The two triplets indeed correspond. The first has to do with Coyote's uncertainty and act, while the second has to do with uncertainty and act on the part of the birds.

The possibility of such covariations of form and meaning encourages attention to such markers.

The occurrences in this text are shown in the profile that follows the text and translation. For reasons of space, most markers are abbreviated:

I	*Iisau*	'Coyote' (Sometimes such a name is a marker, although not clearly here.)
N	*niiqe*	'that's why', 'because'
	niqw	'and'
P	*pu'*	'now'
Pai	*pai*	'well' (written out)
piw	*piw*	'again' (written out)
Y	*yaw*	'it is said', 'they say'
"—"		quoted speech or song

In this text quoted speech or song usually is preceded or followed by a line that frames it and is itself marked. In some traditions a turn at talk or song is itself marked as a verse, and such seems to be the case here in lines 186–90.

The presence of such elements does not in itself show rhetorical shape. For that, a hypothesis regarding relations among such elements is needed.

Dimensions of Performance

Experience of a number of Native American traditions and of narrative traditions in some other languages, including English, has led to a conception of a narrator as weaving together two threads. One is a thread of incident, what is going to happen, and the other is a thread of form, how what happens is to be given shape.

The ways in which shape is marked are instances of what Roman Jakobson (1960) called "equivalence," singling it out as basic to poetry. Intonational contours, or tone groups, are such an indication of equivalence, showing what counts as a line and what line or lines count as a structural unit, or verse. When one does not have the evidence of the voice, as so often is the case with valued Native American materials, written down but not recorded, other linguistic elements may serve.

In many cases the evidence of the voice and the evidence of other elements is in harmony. What one would regard as a verse in an English narrative, because of falling final contour, will agree with what one would regard as a verse because of an initial marker, such as "well," "so," "now," and the like.

Hopi and Zuni appear to be exceptions. The one Zuni narrative for which Dennis Tedlock (1999 [1972]:75–84) has published the original text has been argued about in just this regard. The argument has given rise at times to the impression that there is a conflict between recognizing pause (and implicitly, intonation contour) and recognizing particles (since markers of verses are so often initial particles such as "now then," "again," "soon," and the like). The argument can even be taken to involve a fundamental difference between what is actually said and true of Native performance, on the one hand, and imposition of an alien literary template, on the other.

The real question is simply, How does the text in question work? What gives it form? The answer to those questions again and again involves more than one level. There are relations indicated by pause and intonation. There are relations indicated by grammatical markers, lexical repetition, turns at talk. There are relations of cohesion and proportion of yet larger scope, extending to the whole.

The traditions I have examined not only distinguish segments but also group them together. Grouping is, first of all, based on one or a few conventional patterns. Along the lower Columbia River in Oregon and Washington and along its Oregon tributary, the Willamette, the principle of patterning is, first of all, based on relations of three and five. In many traditions the principle is one of relations of two and four. These patterns are not mutually exclusive. The story of "Coyote and Frog," recorded by Sapir in Takelma from Frances Johnson early in the century, makes use of relations of two and four. There are eight acts, balanced in four pairs and two halves, and acts and scenes have four stanzas, four pairs of stanzas, or the like. In the extravagant second act, by far the longest, Coyote runs and runs to a girl's puberty dance; he keeps hearing the sound and keeps thinking he is almost there. This act is organized, intensified, I would say, by relations of three and five. At moments of climax in Kathlamet and Kalapuya myths, a three-part relation may obtain, but the verses related are pairs (Hymes 1985a, 1987a).

This kind of relation answers to the principle of style that Kenneth Burke (1925) long ago called arousal and satisfying of expectation. One has a sense of arousal and satisfying of expectation, according to one or the other kind of relation, again and again, at every level. Recognizing the possibility of such relations, one gains a deeper sense of placement and proportion. These relations are active in the mind of a narrator in giving shape to sequences of incident.

The Zuni text alluded to earlier in this discussion, Andrew Peynetsa's "Coyote and Old Lady Junco," is a fine example. This brief story is beautifully told. Its spoken lines, as transcribed by Tedlock (1999 [1972]:76–84; 1987:58–61), vary a great deal, are often very long, and may seem to show no movement other than that from line to line. When one attends to turns at talk and recurrent particles, such as "then," however, pairings and parts emerge. On the premise of two- and four-part relations, the story has four scenes. Coyote and Old Lady Junco are introduced in four alternating verses. Then Coyote comes upon her while she is singing her winnowing song, asks about it, asks to learn it, and goes off. Soon he forgets it and comes back to ask again. When he comes to ask a fourth time—the point at which by pattern the scene could end—it does not tell what happens. Rather, it has Old Lady Junco say what she thinks and put a rock inside her shirt. The outcome has a whole scene to itself, eight verses in all, the longest scene of the story. Coyote asks twice with no response, then begins a count, threatening to bite if she does not sing by the time he reaches four. When he reaches four, there is still no response; he jumps to bite her and breaks his teeth on the rock. Such holding over to a separate scene can be called *extraposition* (to borrow a term from syntax). (See Hymes 1982.)

The general point is that what Tedlock says about the line-to-line expression of the story is true and that what I show about the organization of the story is true. There is grouping of words and lines by means of the voice, and there is grouping of incident by means of a cultural logic. Both can be used to heighten effect. To ignore either would be to fail to do justice to Andrew Peynetsa's art.

We are familiar with the difference between the phrasing of action in performance by the voice and movement of an actor and the relations, local and extended, implicit in the text. It should be easy enough to accept the presence of both in oral narratives.

Such narratives can be considered poetry, inasmuch as they consist of lines and organization of lines. They differ from traditional poetry in much of the world in that the first level of organization is not within the line. One does not count syllables, or stresses, or initial alliterations. One keeps track of relations among lines or, more strictly, verses. Organization within the line is usually called *metrical*. Organization among lines can be distinguished by calling it *measured*.

The relations of measured verse often have a sense of formal meaning—of action proceeding with a sense of "this, then that," of initiation and out-

come, when relations are of two and four, and of action proceeding with a
sense of initial condition or onset, then ongoing, then outcome, when relations are of three and five. Insofar as such relations establish an expectation of outcome, a sense of the rightness as outcome of what comes second
or third, they are persuasive, and it can be appropriate to speak of them as
rhetorical. The term *rhetorical* is useful in two ways. It fits the criterion of
"arousing and satisfying expectation," and it easily accommodates relations
of larger scope (e.g., among stanzas, scenes, and acts). I use it here to distinguish this analysis from that by Wiget, focused as it is on performance in the
sense of observable detail.

Wiget's article (1987) should be read for its variety of insights, attention to
other versions of the story, photographs of gestures by Sekaquaptewa, and
to see how the text appears when pause and intonation are the guides to presentation on the page. Wiget (1987:315) touches on display of competence
as well. The relationships explored in this chapter also involve competence.
It is a competence that probably is largely out of awareness, like the competence that enables us to deploy complexities of syntax we could not ourselves analyze. Again and again, an analysis of form leads to recognition of
larger relationships, to deployment in the service of balance and point. One
is able to recognize with some degree of accuracy just what parts a narrative has.

Wiget himself distinguishes two major parts. The parts stem from the recurrence of the two songs, that of winnowing and that of flying. The winnowing song occurs four times, the flying song (based on the name of the
birds) twice, but since Sekaquaptewa goes from the first to the fourth occurrence, Wiget (1987:330) notes that a second and third repetition are implied.
In effect, then, part 1 consists of scenes with the four occurrences of the winnowing song, and part 2 of scenes with occurrences of the flying song.

The parts distinguished here have arisen after the fact. The analysis began
with recognition of verses and of immediate relations among them. Stanzas were recognized on the hypothesis that they would consist of pairs and
pairs of pairs. There was the constraint that the groups make sense in terms
of the content of the story. Scenes and acts were recognized by an extension
of the same reasoning: pairs or, in this case, sets of four, as it turned out, that
make internal sense in terms of the content of the story.

It was only in writing the final account that scenes and acts were given
attention in their own right. I wanted to provide brief headings for them.
That brought their relations into focus. Clearly enough, the two scenes of
act I introduce the birds and what they are usually doing, (scene i) gathering
seeds and (ii) preparing seeds.[2] The two scenes of act II introduce Coyote,
(i) coming to the birds and (ii) joining them.

The next two scenes show Coyote unable to do what the birds can do. They sing, but he cannot (III, i), they fly up, but he cannot (III, ii). The next two acts address these lacks. The birds give him feathers and again sing their winnowing song (III, iii), which he now learns quickly; they fly up, and Coyote flies up with them (III, iv).

These four scenes go together in terms of two parts that manifest a well-known folkloric sequence, lack and lack liquidated, one emphasized by Dundes (1964:61–64)(here, lack of ability to sing and fly).

The transition between the two parts seems to have been affected by an interjection from the audience, "Coyote was happy?" (line 164) and the narrator's response (lines 165–66). Notice the apparent hesitation in the lines that follow the scene (178–80).

I am troubled by an intuition that the interjection—the single instigating interjection—affected Sekaquaptewa's sense of evolving form; that the interjection counted as part of telling the story, together with the two verses that follow it, that answer it (165, 166). It would seem that after the winnowing song (lines 160–64) Sekaquaptewa was going to let Coyote's joining the song remain implicit and move on directly to flying up (with the song in lines 169–73 and 186–90). Apparently, someone in the audience sensed something missing and asked about it.

On this assumption, the interjection might still be taken as something intrusive, and bracketed. But the interjection and response are fitted neatly into a four-verse fourth scene of the act. The scene is not developed, to be sure, beyond its essential element, the song the birds sing, ululating their own name *(tsiroot)*. Sekaquaptewa seems eager to get to the denouement, Coyote's downfall (literally).

The fourth time constitutes the fourth act, a scene for Coyote's success in flight and a scene for his fall. All this rings an interesting change on the widespread theme that a trickster, such as Coyote, cannot master a song of power and cannot sustain flight with birds. Here he manages to do both. Failure is not due to his own carelessness or other fault. It is due to the birds. They know what he is up to and undo him.

In sum, the scenes and relations among scenes that emerge at the end of an analysis of verses make sense. They suggest a pairing at the level of the story as a whole, between a part 1 and a part 2, but at a different place than matching numbers of songs (actual and implied) would give. Part 1 introduces the protagonists to the audience and each other. Part 2 has the birds accept Coyote and provide for him (act III), then undo him (IV). The disposition of the songs does not mechanically match broad structural divisions. The winnowing song is introduced toward the end of act I, which is about the birds alone. In act II it occurs at the beginning, seemingly as a reprise of the world of the birds just before Coyote comes. In act III it occurs twice, once as something Coyote cannot do (i), once as something he can (iii–iv). The flight song occurs each time as something Coyote can do (III, iv; IV, i), but the first time as part of his success, the second time as prelude to his downfall (as the birds indicate in lines 181–82).

(One might guess that the flight song could have occurred in act III, scene ii in tandem with the winnowing song in the stage at which Coyote fails. If it did, III would be nicely balanced, each song twice as he fails, each sang twice as he succeeds. But the one occurrence of the flight song in the fourth act would make it occur three times in the story as a whole, and the story as a whole would have seven songs, not six. It may be too much to infer that a narrator would tacitly keep track of such a thing and have the occurrences of each song come out in even numbers, but it seems to me possible.)

Presentation and Translation

This presentation is analytic. It is designed to bring out the elements and relations to which it calls attention. For this purpose, it departs from Wiget's presentation and the transcript with which he worked. The result is not a model of vocal performance and does not take the place of one. It may be taken as a hypothesis about performance at another level, as an inquiry into ingredients of narrative competence integral to performance.

The translation that follows is not identical with either that of Emory Sekaquaptewa and Allison Lewis, which accompanies the Hopi transcript (see the acknowledgments in endnotes to this chapter), or the revision published by Wiget. In keeping with the goal of bringing out the relations among verses, I have kept constant the relation between Hopi markers and English equivalents. *Pu'* is always 'now', *pai* always 'well', and so forth. Markers are translated wherever they occur, for example, *yaw* in lines 16, 26, 31, and so on. Other words are translated that are not translated in the sources, no doubt for idiomatic reasons, for example, *nen* 'and so' in line 39. (I have depended upon Albert and Shaul 1985 in this effort). The result, as has been said, is not an idiomatic English version of the story but what might be called an analytic English version.

Some additional points: Wiget retains Hopi *I'isau,* a nice effect, but I give 'Coyote'. Likewise, while he retains the Hopi for "tale" in the opening lines, the English is given here. Finally, "they say" seems to me a more flexible and idiomatic equivalent for the quotative than the usual "it is said."

I'isau Tuutuwutsi

(Opening of the situation)

Diane: Um qa hiita tuuwutsi'yta, itaaso?
Helen: As'a, pai nu' hiitawat,
        hiisavawyat umumi tuutuwutsni, um . . .

Audience: Aliksa'i (prompting)
Helen: ALIKSA'I   5
Rest: Owi.

Helen: "Oo'" uma kitotani, louder.
        ALIKSA'I,
        uma qa hingqakwa.
Rest: Owi.   10

Helen: Taqpi tuuwutsi'ytaka qövisaningwu.
        hakiy qa hu'wutoinayakw,
           pai hak qöviste'
           qa tuutuwusngwu.
Rest: 'Wi.   15

(I) (i) (Introduction)

YAW Oraive yeesiwa.   (A)

             'Wi

Pai sinom pep pi YAW yeesiwa

niqw
ayam   20

Pai tsiroot piw, YAW, ang naavinta, hal puma   (B)
pai tuwat sumiyankyaa,
    kyang puuyawnumyangwu, (gestures)
pai puma tuwat tomongmiq hoitaqw
    hiita nöösiwqat, na'sastotangwu   25

           Owi....'wi

Niiqe oovi hiihita tuusaqat YAW tuqwsiqw.

PU' puma pang akil . . akii . . kii'atkye,   (C)
PU['] pai piw pang hikis oova pi pai tuuwi'ytaqw (gestures)
panq himu pai hinurs wungwungwu   30
put poosi'at tuqwsiqw

PU' YAW puma put ang ayan/ mawtinumyangwu.   (D)
Yungyaphooyat YAW himu'yyungge,
put YAW aw yan mawtotangwu.

Ang put / sivo . . . *(gestures)*   35
halowi, pos'humiyat.

                 (ii) (The birds gather and winnow seeds)
Wuuhaq tote, *(gestures)*   (A)
PU' YAW puma suuvo tsovaltotingwu haqam
nen PU' YAW yan, umun
qön . . .   40
                         qönikiw[3]
qönikiw kyaakyangwu yesvangwu.

Pu' puma put YAW ep pi ini'yyunge   (B)
put ep maamapriyaqw pam pingngwu *(gestures)*
                        owi, 'wi,. . . .   45
PU' YAW puma put soosoyam yan yungkw. *(gestures)*
PU' YAW puma tawkyaakayngwu put wunitotangwu.   (C)
YAW paipi hiita tumalai'ytaqw maqsoni.

Niqw oovi pai YAW puma qa öönatototingwu
                        Owi, 'wi. . . .   50
OOvi YAW soosoyam ang yesve.

PU' YAW tawlalwangwu, YAW.   (D)
put pai uma sonqe taawi'yyungwa:
                        Owi

   "Pota, pota, pota, *(gestures throughout)*   55
   pota, pota, pota,
   yowa'ini, yowa'ini,
   ph, ph, ph, ph."

YAW yantsaklalwaqw
PU' YAW ang naapi'at ayo' puuyaltotingwu. *(gestures)*   60
                        Owi
Hoiyaqw,
PU' YAW hiita aw o'oyat.

                    (II) (i) (Coyote comes)
Pu' YAW piw peehut ang tsovalaye,   (A)
piw put piingyayat.   65

Pu' YAW piw[-]yangwu,
teevep puma pantsakyaqe,
   pi'ep tawlalwangwu: *(giggling, gestures throughout)*

   "Pota, pota, pota,
   pota, pota, pota,   70

yowa'ini, yowa'ini,
ph, ph, ph, ph."

YAW puma pantsaklalwaqw, (B)
YAW kurs Iisau angkw taavangqöngahaqaqw wuuvi.

        'Wi 75

Niiqe YAW pep Oraivi, wuko'owa.
Uma put qa tuwi'yyungwa, Oraivi? *(leans forward)*
        (a head shakes)
Pam hapi Oraivi,
  pep wuko'owa yanta,
a-village, 80
  hah-kiihut,
aataavangqöive
  pangqaqw YAW
kurs pam na'uyi'kyanhw,
  amumi taita 85

        Um, hm...

    noq puma pantsaklalwaqw.

Pai pi puma hiitu sutsep tsöngmokiwnumyangwu, (C)
  niqw pai kyapi as pam kwaingyavo hiita pai hepto,
pai[-]pi hiita, öö'öqat pi pai 90
  sinom maspitotangwu.
Niqw put YAW pam heptoqe,
  oovi aw wupqw,
YAW puma pep pantsatskyaqw.

YAW pan wuuwanta: (D) 95
  "Is as nu'imui hisa' niiqamui qo'ye,
  kwanga nösni."
YAW yan wuuwankyanqw
  am amumi taita.

        'Wi 100
      (II) (ii) (Coyote joins them)
Niqw pai YAW as oovi amumi namtsiknat (A)
PU' pas qa nam'gui 'qe,
PU' YAW amumi nakwsuqw.

YAW tutwaqe, (B)
PU['] YAW pai as watqani. 105

"Nu' pai, pam um, son umui hintsan'ni," (C)
  YAW amumi kita. *(smiles)*

"Pas hapi uma sosonkiwyaqw oovi;
    nu' angwk umumi nakswu.
"Ya . . . ya sen nu' son umumumni?"   110
    YAW amumi kitaqw.

Pai YAW—YAW naanami yoirikya, yantoti,   (D)
pai songyawnen naanami maqaptsitota.
Pai YAW soosoyam sumataq nannakwhaqw.
                                    (III) (i) (They sing, Coyote cannot)
PU' YAW pi oovi amumum qatuptuqw.   (A) 115
PU' YAW pai oovi aw yungyaptoinaya.

Niqw PU' YAW oovi nuutum pantsaklawu, pep pami'i.   (B)
                                                         Um...'wi
YAW. . . .
    piw oovi aw intotaqe,   120
    piw naat tawlalawaqw.

Paapi Iisaw sonpi naat pu'niqw taawi'yta YAW *(smiles)* (C)
Niqw, pai oovi qa su'amun kyapi pai yantsaki.

Piw tawlalwaqe: *(gestures throughout)*   (D)
    "Pota, pota, pota,   125
    pota, pota, pota,
    yowa'ini, yowa'ini,
    ph, ph, ph, ph." *(giggles)*
        ep yantotit.
                                    (III) (ii) (They fly up, Coyote cannot)
Puu' YAW, ang himui yang o 'oyat,   (A) 130
PU' YAW puyaltotingwu oomiq haqami. *(gestures)*

Hiisavo YAW ange yan'numyat,   (B)
PU' piw han'ngwu.

Noq Iisaw, pi qa hiita masai ytangwu,   (C)
niiqe pai YAW okiw pantotiqw qa nuutum,   135

puuyaltiqe amumiq YAW,
    yan taita—
Paipi haqtotiqw,
    kurs hin PU' ngu'ataniqe.
                                                         'Wi   140
Noqw . . . pai YAW piw hanqe,   (D)
    piw naat antotiqw.

(III) (iii) (They give Coyote feathers)

PU' YAW   (A)

   "Sen, nu'sen, son uma nui anqw umuu masay,

     umuu pö höy maqayaqw,   145

   "sen nu' umumum puuyaltini,"

    amumi kitaqw.

                           'Wi

Pai YAW sunanakwha.

PU' YAW hak oovi,   (B)   150

   puma tsiroot hinui naapa tsotspilalwakyanqw. *(gestures)*

PU' yaw Iisawui,

   haqami, hak masay tsoope'

   panqso tsur YAW—

   ang put tsurumnaya Iisawui anga'. *(gestures)*   155

Anga paas YAW oovi aptsinayat   (C)

PU' YAW piwya,

piw aw intotaqe   (D)

PU' YAW pantatskya: *(gestures throughout)*

   "Pota, pota, pota,:   160

   pota, pota, pota,

   yowa'ini, yowa'ini,

   ph, ph, ph, ph"

              (III) (iv) (Coyote flies up with them)

                          (A)

              ....I'isau tsoni'?....

Tsoni' yta YAW nuumum,   (B)   165

pai YAW pi suutawi'va YAW niiqe.

PU' YAW oovi ang o'oyat,   (C)

PU' YAW *(gestures throughout)*

   "Tsii

    ii   170

      ro

        ro

          rooo"

YAW kitotat,

PU' oomiq pu.   175

Pai hapi YAW Iisaw nuutum puuyalti. *(giggles)*   (D)

Pai YAW oovi qa suus amumum puuyaltit.

(IV) (i) (Coyote flies with them the last time)

Pu' piwyaqw . . . YAW . . . nuutungh,   (A)

Hal pai / kya naalös haqamtotaqw, *(gestures)*

nalösni'wisqw, *(gestures)*   180

PU' YAW puma tsiroot naami na'ui hinqaqwa,   (B)

  "Pu' hapi aw pitu," YAW kitota. *(giggles)*

Pu' YAW oovi puma piwya,   (C)

piw panto pantotiqe,

piw YAW aqwhaqami: *(gestures throughout)*   185

  "Tsii

    ii

      ro

        ro

          rooo"   190

Kitotat anqe yan'numyaqw,   (D)

  Iisaw YAW nuutum yan'numa. *(gestures)*

            (audience giggles)

(IV) (ii) (Coyote falls)

PU' YAW tsiroot sumitsovaltiqe   (A)

  "Nam ta'a tuma, aw pitu,"

    YAW kitaqw;   195

Puu YAW aw homikmaqw,   (B)

  hak hiita himuy YAW angkw tsoopangwu, *(gestures)*

masay hak maqe, put tsoopangwu, *(gestures)*

  suruy,

    pöhöy,   200

soosok YAW ang tsospitota.

Puu' YAW okiw Iisaw,   (C)

  angaqw yantsakma

    namtototimakyangw, *(gestures)*

  atkyamiq haqam yeevaqe,   205

YAW okiw mooᵒᵒoki *(giggles all round)*

YAW hanqe puma aw,   (D)

tsuiti YAW:

  "Paipi.

  "Naap uu'unangwainiaqw'ö,   210

    naapas himu hin.

  "Itamui um sowaniqey

    wuuwankyangw yep itamui pitu,"

YAW aw kitotaqw.
"Oovi pai itam ung niinayqw,   215
pai um itamui qasowani,"
    YAW aw kitota.

PU' YAW apiy pai puma naanalt pantsaklalwa.   (iii) (Finis)
Pai YAW son oovi hiita puma
    qa wuuhaq tunös na'sastota pep taawat epe.   220

Pai yuk pölö. *(smiles)*
            (audience reacts)
            (she giggles)   (iv) (Close)

It was quite long,
    I thought it was short.

Coyote and the Birds

                                    (Opening of the situation)
Diane: Do you not have a tale for us, our grandmother?
Helen: Yes, well a short one,
            I will tell a short tale to you, um . . .

Audience: *Aliksa'i (prompting)*
Helen: ALIKSA'I   5
Rest: Yes.

Helen: "oo" you must say, louder.
            ALIKSA'I,
            you are not answering.
Rest: Yes.   10

Helen: It is known the storyteller is touchy,
            If you do not answer,
                she may pout
                and not tell a story.
Rest: Yes.   15
                                        (I) (i) (Introduction)
They say at Oraibi they were living.   (A)
                                            Yes

Well as a matter of fact, there, they say, they were living

and
over there   20

Well birds also, they say, were abundant there, I mean they,   (B)
well likewise flock together in their usual way,
   while flying about like so, *(gestures)*
Well they likewise, when it got to be toward winter,
   would prepare to store some food   25
                                               Yes....yes
And that's because all kinds of grasses, they say, would mature.

Now they would go along below their vill . . vill . . village,   (C)
now then also even along above where there is a ledge, *(gestures)*
along where things grow up in abundance,   30
when the grass seeds matured.

Now they say they would go about like picking them.   (D)
They say they had small plaques,[4]
into that they say they would harvest.

Like this the bean . . . *(gestures)*   35
I mean the seeds of maize.
                       (ii) (The birds gather and winnow seeds)
When they had a lot, *(gestures)*   (A)
now they say they would gather together in one place somewhere,
and so now, they say, like you,
round . . .   40
                                     in a circle
round in a circle they would sit themselves.

Now they say with enough in them [their plaques],   (B)
they would rub them, grind them *(gestures)*
                               yes, yes,....   45
Now they say they would all move them like this. *(gestures)*
Now they say they would sing while dancing them [winnowing].   (C)
They say it is a fact that working at something is tiresome.

And so that, they say, they not get tired out,
                                 Yes, yes....   50
for this, they say, all of them together would settle around.

Now they say they would sing, they say,   (D)
and perhaps you most likely know this song:
                            Yes

  "Pota, pota, pota, (gestures throughout)   55
  pota, pota, pota,
  yowa'ini, yowa'ini,
  ph, ph, ph, ph."

They say as they were doing this
now they say the seed coverings would fly away. *(gestures)* 60
Yes
This done,
now they say they would put them down in something.
(II) (i) (Coyote comes)
Now they say again they would gather some more around there, (A)
again they would grind them. 65

Now they say they would repeat,
all day they did that,
   each time they would sing: *(giggling, gestures throughout)*

   "Pota, pota, pota,
   pota, pota, pota, 70
   yowa'ini, yowa'ini,
   ph, ph, ph, ph."

They say they were doing that, (B)
they say evidently (as) Coyote from the southside somewhere climbed up.
Yes 75
And they say that's because that was Oraibi, the big rock.
Are you not familiar with it, Oraibi? *(leans forward)*
(a head shakes)
That in fact is Oraibi,
   at the big rock (standing) so,
ah, the village. 80
   hah the village,
toward its southside,
   from there, they say,
he was hidden,
   watching them 85
Um, hm...
   while they were doing that way.

Well, as we know, those (creatures) always go around hungry, (C)
   and probably he was headed for the trash pile to look for something,
well, whatever, bones or something, 90
   people are apt to throw away.
And that, they say, is what he was looking for,
   why he climbed up,
they say, when he came upon them that way.

They say he thought this way: (D)   95
   "**I wish** I could kill some of these,
   and so (have a) good tasting snack."
They say this is what he was thinking
   as he watched them.

                                Yes   100
            (II) (ii) (Coyote joins them)
And, at first they say he decided not to show himself to them,   (A)
now quite unable to restrain himself,
now they say he approached them.

They say they saw him,   (B)
now they say at first they wanted to flee.   105

"I wouldn't do anything to you,   (C)
   they say he said to them. *(smiles)*
"Very truly you are delightful (to watch);
   that is why I have come to you.
"May, may I not join you?"   110
   they say he said to them.

Well, they say—they say they looked at each other, like this,   (D)
well, as if seeking approval from one another.
Well, they say, everyone apparently agreed.

          (III) (i) (They sing, Coyote cannot)
Now, they say, indeed he sat down with them.   (A)   115
Now, they say, they provided him with a plaque.

And now, they say, he joined in what they were doing, there. (B)
                          Um...yes
They say . . .
   so again they went to fill them [their plaques],   120
   yet again they sang.

Coyote could not yet know the song, they say. *(smiles)*   (C)
And that's why he could not do the same as they.

Again they sang: *(gestures throughout)*   (D)
   "*Pota, pota, pota,*   125
  pota, pota, pota,
  yowa'ini, yowa'ini,
  ph, ph, ph, ph." (giggles)
   on like this.

(III) (ii) (They fly up, Coyote cannot)

Now, they say, they would put their things down, (A) 130
now, they say, they would fly high up somewhere. *(gestures)*

For a while, they say, they would go around like this, (B)
now again they would come down.

On the other hand, Coyote was not a feathered creature, (C)
that's why, they say, being that way the poor thing could not be with the 135
others,
flying together, they say,
   looking on like this—
Well, they were so far away, they say,
   evidently there was no way now to catch them.
                                        Yes 140
On the other hand, when, they say, they came down again, (D)
   again they did the very same thing.

(III) (iii) (They give Coyote feathers)

Now, they say, (A)
   "Maybe if, I maybe, couldn't you give me some of your feathers,
      your down, 145
   maybe I could fly up with you,"
      he said to them.
                                        Yes
Well, they say, they consented.

Now, they say, since that was so, (B) 150
   they, the birds, began plucking feathers from themselves. *(gestures)*
Now, they say, on Coyote,
   wherever they had plucked the feather out,
   there (they) stuck in, they say—
   there they stuck it on Coyote. *(gestures)* 155

After, they say, they had done enough to take care of him, (C)
now, they say, they started again,

again they filled them, (D)
now again they say they did this: *(gestures throughout)*

   "Pota, pota, pota, 160
   pota, pota, pota,
   yowa'ini, yowa'ini,
   ph, ph, ph, ph."

                                      (III) (iv) (Coyote flies up with them)
                                                          (A)
                                  ....Coyote was happy?....
He took great delight, they say, with them,   (B)   165
well, they say, because he learned the song quickly, they say.

Now they say they put them down,   (C)
now they say *(gestures throughout)*
    "Tsii
        ii   170
            ro
                ro
                    rooo"
they say they said,
now they would be above.   175

Well indeed they say Coyote flew up with them, *(giggles)*   (D)
Well they say he flew up with them not just once.
                          (IV) (i) (Coyote flies with them the last time)
Now again they say . . . they say . . . after that,   (A)
Oh I mean for about the fourth time, *(gestures)*
on the fourth time, *(gestures)*   180

now they say, those birds whispered among themselves,   (B)
    "Now enough! It's time," they say they said. *(giggles)*

Now, they say, again for the last time,   (C)
again they flew up,
again they say they went higher: *(gestures throughout)*   185
    "Tsii
        ii
            ro
                ro
                    rooo"   190

As they said this, gliding along and about,   (D)
    Coyote, they say, glided about with the others. *(gestures)*
                                      (audience giggles)
                                      (IV) (ii) (Coyote falls)
Now they say the birds came together,   (A)
    "Let's . . . , okay, let's start, the time has come,
        they say they said;   195

Now they say they closed in on him,   (B)
    each plucked off, they say, his own from him, *(gestures)*

the feather that he gave he plucked, *(gestures)*
  tail feathers,
    downy feathers,   200
they say they plucked off them **all**.

Now, they say, poor Coyote,   (C)
  down he came,
    turning over and over like so, *(gestures)*
  and landed somewhere far below,   205
they say the poor thing died. *(giggles all round)*

They say they came back down,   (D)
they laughed at him, they say:
  "See how it is.
  "Your own heart (is at fault),   210
    it's because of your wrong doings.
  "Thinking to gobble us up,
    you came among us here,"
      they say they said.
  "That's why we thought if we killed you,   215
    you would not eat us up,"
      they say they said to him.

From then on, they say, they worked and gathered alone.   (iii) (Finis)
So, they say, it is very likely
  that they gathered a lot of food there that day.   220

So it is drawn to the end. *(smiles)*
                    (audience reacts)
                    (she giggles)   (iv) (Close)

It was quite long,
  I thought it was short.

Profile

	Stanza	Verses	Lines	Features
Opening				
		ab	1, 2–3	[Narrator responds in b, d,
		cd	4, 5, 6	but d seems to initiate also]
		fg	7–9, 10	
		hi	11–14, 15	
Act I, scene i. Introduction				
	A	ab	16-(17)-18, 19–20	Y, Pai…Y

B	abcd	21, 22–23, 24–25, 27	Pai, Pai, N…Y
		24–25, 27	Pai…Y,
C	ab	28, 29–31	P, P pai piw
D	abc(d)	32, 33, 34, (35–36)	PY, Y,…Y (gesture)

Act I, scene ii. The birds gather and winnow seeds

A	ab	37–38, 39–40…42	PY, PY
B	ab	43–44, 46	P…Y, PY
C	abed	47, 48; 49, 51	PY, Y; Y, Y
D	ab cd	52–53 55–58; 59–60, 62–63	PY…Y, Song; Y…, PY;…PY

Act II, scene i. Coyote comes

A	ab cd	64, 65	PYpiw, piw
		66–68, 69–72	Pypiw-, Song
B	ab	73, 74	Y, Y…Iisau (Coyote)
	cd	76 [77], 78-[86] 87	NY,…. Y…
C	ab cd	88–89, 90–91, 92–93, 94	Pai pi (N pai), Paipi;…Y, Y
D	ab	95–97, 98–99	Y "—", Y

Act II, scene ii. Coyote joins them

A	abc	101, 102, 103	N . . Y, P, PY (Coyote)
B	ab	104, 105	Y, PY (Birds)
C	ab	106–7, 108–11	"—" Y, "—" Y (Coyote)
D	a(b)c	112 (113), 114	PaiY (pai), Pai Y (Birds)

Act III, scene i. They sing, Coyote cannot

A	ab	115, 116	PY, PY
B	a(b)cd	117, 119, 120, 121	NPY, (Y), piw, piw
C	ab	122, 123	Paipi I…Y, N pai
D	a	124–29	Piw + song

Act III, scene ii. They fly up, Coyote cannot

A	ab	130, 131	PY, PY
B	ab	132, 132, 133	…Y, Ppiw
C	ab cd	134, 135, 136–37, 138–39	Noq I, (Niiqe)…Y,…Y; Paipi
D	ab	141, 142	Noq . . paiYpiw, piw

Act III, scene iii. They give Coyote feathers

A	ab	143–47, 149	PY "—", Pai Y
B	ab	150–51, 152–55	PY I, PY
C	ab	156, 157	Anga . . Y, PY
D	ab	158, 158–63	Piw, PU + song

Act III, scene iv. Coyote flies up with them

A	a	164	Audience question
B	ab	165, 166	…Y, Pai Y…Y
C	abed	167, 168–73, 174, 175	PY, PY + song, Y, P
D	ab	176, 177	Pai . . Y, PaiY

Act IV, scene i. Coyote flies with them the last time

A	ab	178, 178-80	PpiwY . . Y . ., . . pai(4th)
B	ab	181, 182	PY, "—" Y
C	abed	183, 184, 185, 186-90	PY . . piw-, piw, piwY, song
D	a	191-92	. . . , I Y

Act IV, scene ii. Coyote falls

A	ab	193 194-95	PY, "-" Y
B	ab (c)d	196, 197, (198-200), 201	PY, Y, (. . .), Y
C	ab	202-5, 206	PY, Y
D	abcd	207, 208, 209-14, 215-17	Y,. . .Y "—" Y, "—" Y

Act IV, scene iii. Finis

	ab	218, 219-20	PY, PaiY

Act IV, scene iv. Close

	221	Formula

II

John Rush Buffalo's "Coyote, Rabbit, and Eagle's Daughter"

This narrative is another exploration by John Rush Buffalo of the relation between Coyote and Eagle's daughter (cf. chap. 3). Both stories assume the same thing, that Coyote cannot be the husband or partner of Eagle's daughter. But although they explore the same theme, they do so in quite different veins. One is comic throughout. The other begins with some humor, but if it ends in humor, the humor is black. Of the three actors, two are killed, and the third, having kept the lower half of a woman's maggot-ridden corpse to use it sexually, is discovered and sent packing in the midst of his own defecation.

I can think of no explanation of the presence of both stories in the mind of the same man, except a desire to explore alternative characterizations through narrative. I know no better demonstration of the practice of accounting for the world through stories. Granted, in both narratives the world is such that Coyote cannot have Eagle's daughter, but Coyote's nature is such that there is more than one way in which that may have come about. In the first story, his trickster character can have some positive outcome (part 1). In the second story, his character is ultimately evil. Hoijer comments: "This is an unusual Coyote story, in that Coyote is pictured as a vicious killer and a pervert" (1972:100 n.18 [chap. 3]).

There may be a clue to John Rush Buffalo's thinking in the use of a suffix. Throughout most of the story, the ending -wa:'a:la 'that one aforementioned' is used only with the other two characters, the young man and the young and beautiful woman. Near the very end (line 186) the ending is used with Coyote's name. Hoijer comments: "The ending -wa:'a:la 'that one afm' is not usually added to ha:csokonay since there is, in the myths, only one Coyote. Occasionally, however, the ending is used; the reason is not clear" (1972:100 n.13 [chap. 3]). The place at which the ending is used suggests a reason. That this Coyote is a killer and pervert, to use Hoijer's words, has now been shown. The use of the ending, 'that one,' here can be taken to indicate *that* one, not the only one. Or, given that John Rush Buffalo acknowledged only one myth Coyote, it can be taken to indicate that aspect, that possibility, of one who for John Rush Buffalo "was a kind of divinity. His name, *ha:csokonayla*, is, literally, 'the owner of the earth,' a divinity who owns in particular all the animals on which the Tonkawa depended for food. In this capacity, hunters always requested Coyote's permission to hunt and always left a portion of the game killed for Coyote. Failure to observe this rule resulted in failure both to find and to kill food animals" (Hoijer 1972: 1–2).

Another use of the "aforementioned" suffix with Coyote's name occurs in a version of the "benevolent host, bungling host" story (cf. chap. 8). In "Coyote, Tiger, and Buzzard" (Hoijer 1972:25–28), Tiger has killed animals that provide food for Coyote, but Coyote violates Tiger's instruction not to eat the liver. Then, having become quite fat, he meets Buzzard, who has not eaten for a long time, and offers to provide for Buzzard. He tells Buzzard to search for game but twice rejects what Buzzard sends (cattle, buffalo). When Buzzard sends horses, Coyote says in effect, "Watch me!" and catches a mule. But the mule bucks him off and kicks him to death. Again, a foolish Coyote, one who rejects the kinds of game (cattle, buffalo) that the Tonkawa kill for food and that he, Coyote, presumably provided.

Just as many believe in a monotheistic source of all that is and have stories, even epic poems, that wrestle with reconciling the evil part with such a source, so, evidently, did John Rush Buffalo with regard to the world of which Tonkawa myth was a part. If not a separate name, identity, for an evil aspect, then separate stories and a distinguishing suffix. I take the marked use of "aforementioned" with the name of Coyote to imply "the one in this story," "that particular one." (Cf. the four names for Coyote in Clackamas Chinook provided by Victoria Howard [chap. 7]).

There is an analogue in treatment of Rabbit and Jackrabbit. In the text of "Coyote, Rabbit and Eagle's Daughter," the word "Rabbit" does not occur. There is only a young man. Evidently, this is a myth in which the physical identity of the actor is at a distance. In contrast, in the immediately preceding myth, "Coyote and Jackrabbit," the physical identity of Jackrabbit is salient: Coyote saddles and rides him, turns him too sharply, is thrown off, falls over a bank, and is killed.

Order of telling might offer clues as to interpretation, but at present it is not possible to interpret the order in which the stories were told. In *Tonkawa Texts*, Hoijer did put "Coyote, Rabbit, and Eagle's Daughter" before "Coyote and Eagle's Daughter" (chaps. 3 and 4, respectively). Whether John Rush Buffalo told them in this order, I do not know. Field notebooks would tell,

but Rudy Troike, once a student of Hoijer, like myself, told me that he has
not been able to locate them.[1]

I regret that I have not had the years of experience with Tonkawa texts that
I have had with texts in the Chinookan languages. Further study is much to
be desired. In Tonkawa there is a complex interplay of markers of relationships, of form: initial particles, such as *'e:kla, 'e:kwa, 'e:ta* 'then'; time words,
such as *taxso:kla* 'next day'; the quotative *-lakno'o,* a recurring logic of action
(see chap. 4 of this volume and Hymes 1987c). Interpreting the recurrent
quotatives, for example, is not entirely clear. The fifth stanza of the first act
(E) seems almost to show organization in terms of pairs of quotatives, four
pairs in all. Yet the second pair of verses, consisting of reciprocal turns at
talk (28–30, 31–33), has two quotatives in each turn. I have taken the turns
at talk and the initial markers (then, and; this done, then; then, then; then,
and) to outweigh the quotatives, treating the quotatives at that point to be
in effect doubled.

In the profile I have noted multiple occurrences of the quotative in a verse
by raised exponents (e.g., a^2). Detailed experience of all the texts, living with
them for a while, will be needed to be confident in interpreting the interplay
of the quotatives and other elements. On the assumption of the presence of
coherent form, simply counting quotatives will not suffice.

A thorough account of John Rush Buffalo's uses of poetic form would be
an important contribution to wider understanding of oral narrative.

In any case, these two narratives involving Eagle's daughter are especially
intriguing. "Coyote and Eagle's Daughter" (Hoijer 1972: chap. 3) appears to
interweave two-part and three-part relations. At the most general level there
are three acts. (Earlier I considered the two acts in which Coyote goes off
gambling to be part of a single part 2. Now they seem to be equivalent, in
length and organization, not only to each other but to the first act. Three
parts, three acts, each a stage in the relationship between Coyote and Eagle's
daughter.

Pairing of verses in a stanza, on the other hand, goes together with good
relationships (all the stanzas in part 1 have pairs of verses) and assertive actions by Eagle's daughter: she follows him when he has gone gambling (act
II, scene ii), she refuses him water (II, iv), she tells him what he must do (his
last chance) (III, iv), and she goes for good (III, v).

The three pairs of verses in which Coyote goes north to gamble a second
time (III, i) are an exception; perhaps they unconsciously anticipate the outcome of the act.

A possible exception are the five verses at the end of the preceding act (II),
at the end of which the woman decides to go. The outset and most of the

lines are concerned with Coyote and young men. Coyote has come to talk to the woman, but the young men disrupt them, dancing with Coyote, not letting him sleep. It is in response to that episode that she becomes angry and decides to go.

The two other instances in act III of scenes having five verses (i, iii) concern Coyote leaving (i) and a young man as intermediary (iii). And in act III, the third scene has a young man as intermediary, with three verses. Clearly three and five here are associated with men.

What then of the fact that in act I, where verses come in pairs throughout, stanzas come in fives (ABCDE)? And that acts II and III each have five scenes?

These larger relations, together with taking the story as a whole to have three parts, go with Coyote as primary, Coyote as one who keeps going along. Three- and five-part relations overall, then, with a counterpoint of pairing. The counterpoint pervades part 1, in which Coyote shows what could be called sympathy for a woman in distress and a community orientation. It enters into parts 2 and 3, where a strong woman asserts herself.

The role of the young man as intermediary in acts II and III is central to both their form and the outcome. In act II he conveys Coyote's order to the woman, which in the next scene, iv, she refuses. In act III he conveys the woman's order to Coyote, which he at first calls a lie (scene iii), then, in the next scene, having come to where the woman is, refuses by laughing. (Note that she gives the order four times.)

These central events show expectations on the part, first, of Coyote, then of Eagle's daughter, that prove mistaken. He misjudges her as submissive; she misjudges him as trustworthy. Or, one could say, she follows him twice to twice give him a second chance to prove himself a husband who is responsive, a partner, not a boss. As an Eagle might well expect. In the end they go their separate ways. Not partners, but apart.

"Coyote, Rabbit, and Eagle's Daughter" is quite different. It is a striking example of myths as narratives in which to explore alternatives, of thinking out possibilities of natures and relationships. The first myth dramatizes incompatible natures. The second dramatizes a demonic nature, a nature that reduces another and itself to death and defilement. It uses motifs associated with a trickster elsewhere, of carrying a woman's sexual organs about and of eating something, or so much of something, that he defecates helplessly. The two are combined at the end of this narrative to express this trickster's ultimate nature.

Notice the parallel in the way trickster and woman end. Both are reduced to something the trickster can do with the bottom of each.

If this is so much an account of one trickster's nature, why are not relations of three and five pervasive? After the first two acts (of five stanzas, three stanzas, respectively), the larger relations are four stanzas (act III), four scenes (IV), two scenes (V). The last act has five stanzas in its first scene, but four in its second and pairs of verses throughout. I think that early moments of four-part relations express efforts toward normal order, but that four-part relations at the end are a way of expressing judgment.

A trickster who stops by and goes off again is unreliable, but sometimes a benefactor and frequently entertaining. One kind of nature among others.

A trickster obsessed with possessing a woman and just the part of her of sexual use, who gains possession by destroying a normal relationship by killing both parties, one after the other, is not entertaining. He is to be beaten and sent packing in shame. Tonkawa mythology and Western theology (I am thinking of Paul Tillich) both recognize demonic power.

Such an interpretation suggests that narratives and narrative minds among Native Americans can have a deeper grasp of human reality than is sometimes recognized. Part of that grasp finds expression in relations of form. Relations that can lend a depth akin to orchestration.

Thanks to Hoijer, Tonkawa is a language for whose further study there are resources at hand—grammar, dictionary, texts (Hoijer 1933, 1946, 1949a, b, 1972). I hope use will be made of them.

Coyote, Rabbit, and Eagle's Daughter
John Rush Buffalo

> (I) (Coyote makes himself partner
> to Rabbit's journey to a bride)

They say Coyote was going along.   (A)
In doing so, he went up a mountain and
   they say he was sitting there.
This done, there was a camp at the foot of the mountain,
   a large camp, they say.   5

Coyote, they say, went down.   (B)
And he went to the center of the camp,
    to a tall tipi,
      to a long one, and
   he lifted up the entrance curtain,   10
    and he peered inside, they say.
When he did so, a young man, they say, was making arrows.

Then Coyote went in, they say, (C)
and "What are you doing?" they say he said.
Then that young man, 15
    "Over yonder at a big camp yonder,
      they have called me to a woman wanting to marry me," they say he said.
Then Coyote,
    "Oh," they say he said.
    "They have spoken that way to me too," they say he said. 20

And then Coyote went down to a small river and (D)
    he was making an arrow, they say.
And then he came up and
this done, he told that young man,
    "Let's go," they say he said. 25

Then, they say, the two went off, (E)
    and, they say, the two went up to the top of a mountain. }
This done, that young man,
    "Let's go," they say he said.
    "To what place did they call you?" they say he said. } 30
Then Coyote,
    "*You* say," they say he said.
    "To what place did they call *you?*" they say Coyote said. }
Then that young man,
    "All right. 35
    "Over there to the center of that camp yonder,
      to the big tall tipi yonder,
      to that place yonder,
        I have been called," they say that young man said.
Then Coyote, 40
  "Yes. To that place yonder they have called me also," they say he said. }
Then,
    "Let's go," they say he said,
and they say the two went down that mountain. }
                    (II) (Coyote preempts the bed, but
                      the woman maintains control)
And the two arrived at that large camp, they say, (A) 45
    to that big tall tipi.
When they did, a bed,
    a very big one, was there, they say.
Coyote lay down on that bed, they say,
and then to that young man, 50

"You go over there," they say he said.
Then that young man sat down, they say.

As he did, that woman came in, they say.   (B)
When she did, they say, she was a very beautiful woman. }
To Coyote she said, "Get up!" they say.   55
    "Yours is over there!" they say she said. }
Then Coyote,
    "All right," they say he said.
    "Yes," they say he said.
Getting up, he sat down in the other place, they say.   60
Then that young man lay down, they say, on that bed.

As they did so, that woman, they say, prepared and brought in food.   (C)
Then, they say, she said to Coyote,
    "Go ahead!
    "Eat!"   65
Then Coyote, they say, was eating.
And then as soon as he had done so,
    she took away the dishes, they say.

                                          (III) (He shams pain to get to her
                                                in bed; she has Rabbit take
                                                her away; he catches up)
And then that woman, they say, came in.   (A)
As she did, it being night,   70
    the two lay down, they say.
And then that woman, making a bed, they say,
    gave it to Coyote on the ground.
To Coyote, 'Lie down!" she said,
then Coyote, they say, lay down.   75

He lay down and   (B)
    after lying a while,
    "Ouch!" they say he kept saying.
    "Oh!" they say he kept saying.
    "Ants are biting me!" they say he kept saying.   80
Then that young man,
    "Come up," they say he said.
Then Coyote got up, they say,
    and he lay down, they say, on that bed.

And after lying a while,   (C)   85
    "Ouch!" they say he said.
    "Oh! There are lots of ants!" they say he said.

"They are biting me again and again."
Then that young man said, they say,
   "All right! Lie down on this side!"   90
Then Coyote got up,
   toward the other side,
   toward where the woman lay, he lay down, they say.
Then that woman got up, they say,
   she lay down on the far side.   95

Then Coyote   (D)
   "Ouch!" they say he said.
   "Oh! There are lots of ants!
   "They are biting me again and again," they say he said. }
Then that woman said, they say,   100
"He will not let us sleep."
   "Take me away from this Coyote
     when he falls asleep," they say she said. }
When he did,
   when morning was about to come,   105
     Coyote, they say, fell asleep.
Then, "Let's go!" they say she said. }
He took her away, they say, that woman.
He went far away with her, they say. }

                  (IV) (He catches up again; three contexts;
                     he kills Rabbit on purpose,
                     the woman by mistake)
As he did, Coyote woke up   (i)   (A) 110
   and (there was) no one.
He went out outside,
   and he went after them, they say.
And although the two had gone far away,
   they say he ran and caught up with them, }   115
and they say he said,
   "Why did you not tell me?"
Then that young man,
"*You* were sleeping," they say he said. }
                  (ii) (Shooting arrows)
Then Coyote,   (A) 120
   "Let's have a shooting contest with these arrows," they say he said.
Then,
   "All right," they say he said.
   "Let's do it," they say he said.

Then that young man shot off an arrow, they say,   125
and he shot it, they say, so that it stuck in the ground toward the far
                                        side of the mountain.
Then Coyote, they say, shot an arrow so that it stuck into the ground
                          at the near side of the mountain.

Then they went there, they say.   (B)
Coyote said, they say, "Here is your arrow."
Then that young man said, "No," they say.   130
  "It isn't mine," they say he said.
And then they went on and
  when they came to the other side of that mountain
  that young man picked up his arrow, they say.

                            (iii) (Diving)
And then when they went down to a river,   (A)   135
  Coyote,
    "Whoever defeats the other in diving
      marries this woman," he said, they say
Then that young man said, they say,
    "All right."   140
And then going down to the water,
    the two dived, they say.

Almost at once Coyote, they say, came up.   (B)
Then that woman said, they say, "He came up!"
When she did, that young man did not hear her, they say.   145
Then Coyote, getting angry, caught hold of him, they say,
and, they say, drowned him.
                       (iv) (Target practice)
And then Coyote said, they say, "Let's go!"   (A)
  He took that woman away, they say.
When the two went off to the prairie,   150
Coyote said,
    "I generally shoot those arrows well," they say.
    "Stand over there.
    "I'll shoot at you," they say he said. }
Then that woman going off,   155
  standing at a distance,
    Coyote shot at her, they say,
and, they say, killed that woman. }

Coyote, going to her,   (B)
  pulled out his arrow and   160

they say he was weeping.
And then from the waist down he cut off that woman's body, they say.
And carrying it,
    he went off, they say, to an encampment.

                  (V) (He pretends she is alive but is
                        discovered and driven away)

When the sun was going down,   (i) (A) 165
    he arrived at that encampment, they say.
And "I have been married," they say he said.
    "Put up a tipi," they say he said.
    "I'll be going to bring her here.
    "My wife is bashful," they say he said.   170

And then when he went away,   (B)
    they put up a tipi, they say.
And almost at once, this done,
    in that tipi he was making laughing sounds, they say.

Then the old man said, they say,   (C) 175
    "He has gotten there with her."
During that night he prepared and
    brought in something to feed him.

Coyote, they say, ate it all,   (D)
    the sweet potatoes.   180
And then when morning came,
    "Where are those sweet potatoes found?" they say he said.

Then,   (E)
    "They are over that way at the creek," they say he said.
The next day *that* Coyote, taking a gunny sack and   185
    going off,
        filled that sack with sweet potatoes and
            carried it back home, they say.

And then they say Coyote would be urinating.   (A) (ii)
And (he) going out some distance while urinating,   190
    a little girl ran over to that place, they say,
        to that tipi.

And when she lifted up the entrance curtain,   (B)
    that woman was there, they say, covered with maggots.
The little girl ran away screaming, they say.   195

They say she told her mother about it.   (C)
Then taking her club, they say she ran over there.

When she did so, Coyote was sitting there.   (D)
    That woman beat Coyote, they say, on the lower half of his body.
Then Coyote ran far away, they say, defecating all around.   200
Thus they have always told those night stories.

Profile

Scene/Stanza	Verse	Line
\multicolumn{3}{l}{Act I. Coyote makes himself partner to Rabbit's journey to a bride}		
A	abc	1, 2–3, 4–5
B	abc	6, 7–11, 12
C	a²bc²	13–14, 15–17, 18–20
D	abc	21–22, 23, 24–25
E	ab c²d²	26, 27; 28–29, 30; 31–32, 33;
	ef gh	34–39, 40–41; 42–43, 44
\multicolumn{3}{l}{Act II. Coyote preempts the bed, but the woman maintains control}		
A	abcd	45–46, 47–48, 49, 50–51, 52
B	ab c²d² ef	53, 54; 55–56, 57–59; 60, 61
C	abcd	62, 63–65, 66, 67–68
\multicolumn{3}{l}{Act III. He shams pain to get to her in bed; she has Rabbit take her away;}		
\multicolumn{3}{l}{ he catches up}		
A	ab cd	69, 70–71; 72–74, 75
B	a³bcd	76–80, 81–82, 83, 84
C	a²bcd	85–88, 89–90, 91–93, 94–95
D	a²b² cd ef	96–99, 100–103; 104–6, 107; 108, 109
\multicolumn{3}{l}{Act IV. He catches up again; three contexts; he kills Rabbit on purpose,}		
\multicolumn{3}{l}{ the woman by mistake}		
i A	ab cd ef	110, 111; 112–13, 114–15; 116–17, 118–19
ii A	ab²c²d	120–21, 122–24, 125–26, 127
B	abc²d	128, 129, 130–31, 132–34
iii A	abc	135–38, 139–40, 141–42
B	abcde	143, 144, 145, 146, 147
iv A	a²b²cd	148–49, 150–54, 155–57, 158
B	abc	159–61, 162, 163–64
\multicolumn{3}{l}{Act V. He pretends she is alive but is discovered and driven away}		
i A	ab	165–66, 167–70
B	ab	171–72, 173–74
C	ab	175–76, 177–78
D	ab	179–80, 181–82

	E	ab	183–84, 185–88
ii	A	ab	189, 190–92
	B	ab	193–94, 195
	C	ab	196, 197
	D	ab	198–99, 200
(Close)			201

12

Coyote, the Thinking (Wo)man's Trickster

Trickster figures are part of tradition throughout the New World, but for western North America and, increasingly, American literature, the trickster par excellence is Coyote (Bright 1993). He reaches Virginia both on the ground and in stories and poems.[1]

The first white people to encounter Coyote were often shocked. Since Coyote sometimes made things to be as they would be thereafter, some called him an Indian god. Since he might stop at nothing for the sake of food or sex, such a god symbolized a vulgar way of life that ought to be replaced. (Though a Yahweh who lies in wait to kill his messenger because of the state of his penis [Exodus 4:24] might seem a distant relative.)[2]

Today, Coyote has become a favorite symbol, even a patron saint, for a good many writers and artists, admired as a mocking, resourceful outsider, often down but never out. Still, unstinting admiration is as misleading as denigration if the purpose is to understand what Coyote and other tricksters have meant to those who told about them. Evidence will be given later in this discussion. A relevant observation at this point is that Coyote and other Native American tricksters are almost always unable to learn or remember a song.[3] That mode of power is beyond them.

There is a tendency to take differences in characterization as part of a common essence and to define the trickster as a protean amalgamation of them all. Often the focus is upon what is comic, irresponsible, and unsocialized. There are stories that fit such traits. There are also stories in which the trickster ends in domesticity, matures, shows concern for others, subordinates himself, and goes to the land of the dead rather than be separated from his daughter. There are stories in which the trickster is despised.

Some narrators rank Coyote as the supreme source of a way of the world, as did two Oregon narrators, Stevens Savage (Molale) and Linton Winishut (Sahaptin) of Warm Springs Reservation, while others rank him high but not highest. Some stories from the Thompson River people of British Columbia show him finding himself less powerful than Old Man. Among the Upper

Cowlitz Sahaptin of Washington, Jim Yoke understood Coyote to have ordained all the places in the land, but for Lewy Costima, he acted as the agent
of Jesus, and was a second choice at that, after Crow was found incompetent.
Among the Wishram Chinook of Washington, Louis Simpson had Coyote
himself acknowledge at the end of a story that, even though a transformer,
he ranked below those with the qualities of a chief.[4] Coyote has just changed
Antelope and his sons to how they will be when the Indians have come:

Now then they started to run away, all gray.
Now they had no gold on their bodies.
Now then he told them:
   "You should not be chiefs.
   "I am Coyote.
   "Now this is what people will say:
      'Now these are the ones Coyote transformed,
         Antelope and his two sons.'
   "Indians shall be chiefs;
      you for your part are Antelope.
   "They will say,
      'This Antelope was transformed by Coyote.'"
Coyote said:
   "Salmon is a chief,
      Eagle is a chief,
         and people will be chiefs.
      I am Coyote,
         I am no chief."

The heart of the matter is that a trickster such as Coyote is "good to think"
(to apply Claude Lévi-Strauss's phrase about animal figures generally). What
is good can differ from one person to another and even from story to story
of the same narrator. It is a mistake to characterize all tricksters, or even the
trickster of a particular society in all stories, in the same way. If the trickster
answers to a Platonic idea, it is an idea that is a starting point, not a realization.

This is not to say that there are no recurrent characteristics associated
with cultural areas and evolutionary complexity. It is to say that one must
beware what the sociologist W. R. Robinson called the ecological fallacy,
which attributes to individuals a property observed across a group. Tricksters and traditions about them were and are resources that reflective people
have drawn upon in different ways. We realize that a Shakespearean play,
even a canon like the Hebrew Bible, is internally diverse and open to diversity of interpretation. Just so, Native Americans have found in their tradi-

tions resources that admit of different interpretations. Their tellings select and group together what is meaningful to them, enacting personal attitudes. In principle, they transmit, but in practice, they may transcend and transform.

The theme of this study, then, is that stories of a trickster must be read, first of all, as the stories of those who told them, not as expressions of a constant culture, let alone as expressions of a single nature. If all trickster stories are thrown into a common pot, it is not surprising that the supposed trickster will taste now of one nature, now of another. But narrators, having relative autonomy of interpretation, can themselves be consistent. Let me illustrate this with a pair of comparisons between two narrators of the Pacific Northwest and then extend the first comparison in terms of other narrators as well.

"The News about Coyote": Simpson versus Smith

"The News about Coyote" was known along the Columbia River, in the Willamette Valley, and perhaps more widely. The premise is that Coyote performs fellatio on himself, seeks to conceal the fact, and fails.

Let me present the story as told by Simpson and by Hiram Smith and say something about their versions. I compare them further in terms of a continent-wide type of story, "The Bungling Host" and then consider what three other narrators from the same region have made of "The News about Coyote."[5]

Simpson and Smith lived on reservations to which their people had been removed in the nineteenth century, Simpson in Yakima, Washington, Smith in Warm Springs, Oregon. The original communities were almost opposite each other on the Columbia River, the one on the Washington side becoming known as Wishram, the one on the Oregon side as Wasco. The two communities had the same language, and the two men told the story in that language. Yet the Coyote of their stories is different, different in a way consistent with other of their stories.

Here are the tellings. Each is followed by a profile of formal relationships. Chinookan speakers give shape to narratives in terms of successions of three and five, and it is helpful to see them.[6]

The News about Coyote
Louis Simpson

Now then he went,   (A) (Coyote makes news)
   he went and went,

he sat down.
Now then Coyote looked all around
Now then Coyote sucked himself.   5
Now then he did thus:
   he put up his penis,
   he put down his head.
   Someone pushed him down.
Coyote said: 10
   "You've done me no good."

Now then he locked up the news—   (B) (The news gets loose)
   he did not want it to be made known.
Now then someone made the news loose.
Now then everyone came to know   15
   what Coyote did to himself.
Now then he had headed the news off.
Now then they made the news break loose.

                                        (C) (The news goes
                                            head of him)
Now then Coyote became hungry.
Now then he thought: 20
   "Now I shall eat."

Now then he ran among the people
Now then they said:
   "He did badly to himself, Coyote,
   "He sucked his own penis."   25

Now then again Coyote ran.
He thought:
   "Over there I am not known.
   "Truly now I will not be made known."

He ran again to a house.   30
Now again they are laughing:
   "Now Coyote sucked himself."

The people again are telling one another.
Now then he thought:
   "Truly now I am known."   35

Simpson Profile

Stanza	Verse	Line
A	abcde	1–3, 4, 5, 6–9, 10–11
B	abcde	12–13, 14, 15–16, 17, 18
C	ab	19, 20–21
	cd	22, 23–25
	ef	26, 27–29
	gh	30, 31–32
	ij	33, 34–35

The News about Coyote

Hiram Smith

He was running along again,   (A)
   then the sun was shining hot.
He was tired,
   then he sat down.

He was sitting,   5
   then he got a hard-on,
      then he sucked himself.

Just got started,   (B)
   somebody pushed down on his head,
      "Hey, what you doing again?"[7]   10
He looked all round:
   nobody.
But he heard them.
He thought,
   "They'll make news."   15
Then he did his hands like this: *(sweeping gesture)*
   it was rimrock straightway to the river,
      this side and that.

He got afraid,   (C)
   it might make news.   20
But already it blew the down up over the rocks,
   already the news got ahead of him.]
Wherever he goes,
   there at a camp,
      straightway he hears the people.   25

They're saying,
  "You folks hear now,
  'Coyote sucked himself?' "}
Wherever he goes again,
  he hears the same thing again.   30
Then he went off and left.}

Smith Profile

Stanza	Verse	Line
A	abc	1-2, 3-4, 5-7
B	abcde	8-10, 11-12, 13, 14-15, 16-18
C	(ab)(cd)(ef)	19-20, 21-22; 23-26, 27-29, 30-31, 32

The line-to-line form of the stories manifests their difference. Simpson's Coyote marches to action. Three lines of a common triad of travel (go, continue, arrive) begin a triad of verses (Now then . . . , Now then . . . , Now then . . .). He sits down, he looks around, he sucks himself. Smith uses three verses also, but each step is coupled with an explanatory (exculpatory) detail—he was running along (but) the sun was hot; he was tired (so) he sat down; he was sitting, he got a hard-on, (so) he sucked himself.

Notice the differences in the ending points of the three stanzas. With Simpson, the focus throughout is on the consequence and cost for Coyote. He acknowledges, "You've done me no good" (end of [A]). In (B) the intermediate ending point (third verse of five) has everyone know; the remaining two verses double the opening pair, that Coyote wanted to conceal the news and that it got loose. In (C) both the intermediate and final ending points have Coyote acknowledge that he is known (26, 27-29, 33, 34-35). Twice he has been shamed and denied food. (The story is the second of a set of three in which Coyote fails to obtain food.)

In his middle stanza, Smith dramatizes Coyote's response to the pushing down of his head. In contrast to Simpson's story, the news is not yet loose. Rather, Coyote creates a long ridge of rimrock (still to be seen on the Washington side of the river, across from Mosier). And in Smith's concluding stanza, Coyote is not hungry. True, twice he finds that the news has gotten ahead of him, indeed is all over ("wherever he goes"). But whereas Simpson has the news spoken twice, Smith does so only once. Smith's Coyote does not confess, "I am known." Instead, his last line has the style of the first line of another story.

For Simpson, Coyote is twice punished, gets his just deserts. For Smith,

Coyote is almost a victim of circumstances, embarrassed but on his way. Nor is the difference between the two tellings accidental. I read Simpson's telling to Smith, asking him to explain bits of it that were unclear (as first published—see Hymes 1981b:134–38 on the difference made by restoring the field transcription). I read Simpson's version to him in the Chinookan language. Smith went on to tell it in his own way. That bespeaks a firmly rooted conception of Coyote of his own.

Simpson versus Smith: Providing Food

The same sort of contrast, punitive as against sympathetic, appears in a use by each narrator of one of the most popular themes of Native American tradition, that of the bungling host. One person provides food by a remarkable feat or power, perhaps by cutting himself or killing a family member; the apparent victim is restored unharmed. The guest invites the host in return, seeks to emulate him, and fails. Simpson tells it in terms of Coyote and Deer, Smith in terms of Coyote and Fish Hawk (Osprey).[8] Here is an English version of Simpson's narrative:[9]

Coyote and Deer
Louis Simpson

	(i) (Coyote visits Deer)
Coyote went on and on.	(A) (Coyote comes)
Straightway he arrived at Deer's house.	
Now then the two sit and sit.	
Now then Coyote said:	
"Now I'll go home."	5
[—] "All right,"	
Deer said to him.	

Now then he took a knife,	(B) (Deer gives Coyote
he just sliced meat from his body.	food)
Now then it was given Coyote.	10
And he pushed wood up his nose.	
Now then his blood flowed out,	
filling a bucket.	
Now then Coyote was given it.	

	(C) (Coyote goes)
Now then he went to the house.	15

		(ii) (Coyote visits Deer again)

Now again Coyote went;   (A)
Straightway now again to Deer.
Now again he cut meat from his body;
Again the meat was given Coyote.
And again he pushed wood into his nose;   20
  his blood flowed out,
    filling a bucket.

Now again Coyote was given it.   (B)
Now then Deer told Coyote:
  "If you should be hungry,   25
  "You should come to me."
[—] "All right,"
  agreed Coyote.

Now then Coyote in turn said: (C)
  "You in turn ought to come to *me*."   30
[—] "All right,"
  he said to him.
  "Now I shall go in turn to your, Coyote's, house."
That is what he told him.

		(iii) (Deer visits Coyote)

Now then Deer in turn went to Coyote's house.   (A)   35
Straightway he arrived.
Now there Deer sat *quietly*.

Now then Coyote thought: (B)
  "Now I shall give Deer a little meat in his turn."
Now then he took the *wife*,   40
  he threw her down on the ground.
Now then he cut her.

Then the woman burst into tears.   (C)
Then Deer jumped.
Then he told *him:*   45
  "Let that woman alone.
  "I shall give you meat."

Now then he just sliced meat from his body;   (D)
Then meat was given Coyote and his wife.
And he produced blood from his nose;   50
  he gave blood to Coyote and his wife.

Now then Deer went home to his house.   (E)
Now then he told the two:
   "If you two should be hungry,
   "You should go to *me*."   55

Then the woman told him:
   "You are bad, Coyote.
   "I for my part am not Deer.
   "Look at that Deer;
   "Everyone will swallow *his* meat.   60
   "I do not have good meat.
   "Likewise you, Coyote, are different;
   "You are a poor thing, Coyote.
   "No one would swallow your meat.
   "That is what people will say: 65
      "'Dead things are Coyote's food.'"

Simpson Profile

Scene	Stanza	Verse	Line
i	A	abcde	1, 2, 3, 4-5, 6-7
	B	abcde	8-9, 10, 11, 12-13, 14
	C	a	15
ii	A	abcde	16, 17, 18, 19, 20-22
	B	abc	23, 24-26, 27-28
	C	abc	29-30, 31-33, 34
iii	A	abc	35, 36, 37
	B	abc	38-39, 40-41, 42
	C	abc	43, 44, 45-47
	D	abc	48, 49, 50-51
	E	abc	52, 53-55, 56-66

In Chinookan myths, a final speech of reproach is always right, and here Coyote's wife is right in her condemnation. Deer has twice enacted the principle of the world as providential. The other beings of the world will provide for those who respect their natures and the ways that govern both. Deer has power to offer himself inexhaustibly; Coyote does not. Coyote, indeed, tries to use, not himself, but his wife. The isolation of Coyote is expressed in verbal choices as well. When Deer and the wife speak, it is to another person; the verb requires or has an object. When Coyote speaks, the verbs used do not. The forms of speaking express the theme of reciprocity. Deer and the wife speak reciprocally; Coyote does not. Coyote's isolation is remarkably expressed in a second way. The terms of the relationship require a "possessive" prefix indicating the other person: not "son," but "my son," "your son," and so forth. The first use of the term for "wife" here is actually ungrammatical; it has no relational prefix.

Coyote and Fish Hawk[10]
Hiram Smith

(I) (Coyote seeks food from Fish Hawk)[11]

There was a Coyote living.	(A)
He had six children.	
They were starving.	

Coyote goes hunting (in vain)   (B)
  He brings nothing.   5
    They're really starving.

He was wandering (was around).   (C)
Then he thought,
  "I'll go see my friend, Fish Hawk."

He went toward him (to visit him).   10
He saw the Fish Hawk's children.
  laughing, raising the dickens (kids usually).

He sat down.
He thought,
  "My children will be laughing and doing the same."   15

He went down the hill to the Fish Hawk's home.   (D)
  He got there.
    He went in.

The Fish Hawk asked him,
  "What brings you here?"   20
But Fish Hawk knew
  Coyote was hungry.

Fish Hawk and his wife were eating.
Then they fed the Coyote.

He told them,   25
  "I came to mooch food off of you."
Fish Hawk told him,
  "Okay."

(II) (Fish Hawk provides)

Then they went down toward the river.   (A)

  Close to the riverbank a big pine tree was standing.   30

    Down in the ice was a big hole.

Fish Hawk he flew up, sprang up, in the tree.   (B)

  He looked down.

    [In a little while] he flew down [fast] into the hole in the ice.

Coyote sat there.   (C)   35

He thought,

  "Gee! I wonder if I risked my partner?"

Coyote thought,

  "I might as well go home."

They might think,   40

  he killed his partner.

He was about to go home.

Then Fish Hawk appeared.   (D)

This side strings of fish,

  other side salmon,   45

    he laid up on the ice.

He told Coyote,

  "This your children will eat."[12]

He took it,   (E)

  and was on his way.

(III) (Hungry again, Coyote tries)

(i) (He fails)

It lasted them for a while to eat, Coyote's children.   (A)   50

Then they started to go hungry again.

The Coyote thought,

  "I can do the same as the Fish Hawk did."

He ran down to the river.   (B)

  He climbed up the pine tree.   55

    He sat up there, like the Fish Hawk.

Then he jumped   (C)

  and he missed the hole.[13]

    He flopped down on the ice:

      Dead.   60

(ii) (Fish Hawk provides again)

Fish Hawk was watching him.
He went down to the river,
   he got there to him:
      Coyote, he was dead.
He felt sorry for him.   65
He dove down, Fish Hawk.
   The same as before.
      He lay by his side salmon and fish — trout.
Then Fish Hawk went on home.

(iii) (Coyote recovers)

He was dead still for quite a while.   70
He come to.
   He set up.
      He looked around:
      he saw salmon and fish.
Then he got them.   75
Then he said,
   "That's just what I thought
      the Fish Hawk would do for me."
Then he was on his way home.

Smith Profile [14]

Act	Scene	Stanza	Verse	Line
I		A	abc	1,2,3
		B	abc	4,5,6
		C	ab cd ef	7, 8–9; 20, 21–12; 13, 14–15
		D	abc	16, 17, 18
		E	ab cd ef	19–20, 21–22, 23, 24, 25–26, 27–28
II		A	abc	29, 30, 31
		B	abc	32, 33, 34
		C	abcde	35, 36–37, 38–39, 40–41, 42
		D	abc	43, 44–46, 47–48
		E		49
III	i	A	abc	50, 51, 52–53
		B	abc	54, 55, 56
		C	abc	57–58, 59, 60
	ii		aBcDe	61, 62/63/64, 65, 66/67/68, 69
	iii		aBcde	70, 71/72/73–74, 75, 76–78, 79

Both Simpson's Deer and Smith's Fish Hawk are benevolent. Deer offers himself to a vain and thoughtless Coyote, self-isolated from discourse and family. Fish Hawk helps Coyote, who considers himself a friend, thinks of how his children will be happy, worries that he may have risked his friend in asking help. Fish Hawk knows without being told that Coyote is hungry; Coyote's characteristic presentation of himself as having known in advance emerges at the end but is linked to the partnerlike relationship. Whoever told stories to Jeremiah Curtin also saw Coyote and Fish Hawk as partners; but in this story, Coyote is thoughtlessly greedy and, at the end, when he fails, angry.[15] Smith's characterization of Coyote is not collective Wasco but rather his own (or in a tradition he adopted as his own).

Stories of a bungling host are a resource that can be put to diverse uses. Conventional scholarship has classified them in terms of the different ways in which the first host produces food (Boas 1916:694–702; Thompson 1966: 301–2; Faber 1970). The differences in the relationship between the two hosts have been ignored. Yet as these two narratives indicate, such differences may reveal characteristic differences in the views of the one who bungles. The heart of the story has to do, not with magical devices, but with reciprocity and solidarity. Sometimes the relationship has to do with the relation between what tricksters are and do and the human community as a whole.

"The News about Coyote": Other Views

"The News about Coyote" was probably known to many communities north and south of the Columbia River.[16] Randy Bouchard has heard a version of it several times from Louis Pichette of Inchelium, both in English and in Colville, a variety of Colville-Okanagon (southern branch of Interior Salishan in northeastern Washington and southeastern British Columbia).[17] Pichette's story has a different frame from those of Simpson and Smith. In theirs, there is no other actor (Lynx) to spread the news; it gets out by itself (as a feather, according to Smith), but as against the Willamette Valley versions, all these versions share having Coyote's head pushed down. One might speak of an Interior Columbia type.

Versions have survived from speakers of the three languages of the Willamette Valley, Clackamas (closely connected to Wishram-Wasco), Santiam Kalapuya, and Molale. All share the feature of Coyote himself asking for news, only to find that the news is about him. This frame of finding that the news is oneself was a resource in the region beyond this story. It is known from the Oregon coast in stories of a young man copulating with his grandmother, knowingly and enthusiastically in Tillamook, just south of the Columbia, deceived and ashamed in Miluk Coos, some distance to the south; and it occurs in a quite uncomic Colville-Okanagon story of Coyote confronted by the wife he has abandoned.[18]

The Clackamas, Kalapuya, and Molale versions might owe their similarity to the fact that all three groups shared the Grande Ronde Reservation in the latter half of the nineteenth century and had interacted with one another before then. Victoria Howard had Molale relatives and knew enough Molale to have understood stories told in it. John B. Hudson remembered Savage and told Melville Jacobs a dream about him. The versions by Howard and Hudson are almost identical in substance, although different in form. They exploit the humor of Coyote finding out that the news he asks for is about him. The discovery is made just once, unlike the other version, in which finding that the news is known happens twice. The focus here is on Coyote's role as an example, learning from his mistake and announcing how things will be.

News about Coyote
Victoria Howard

He went,   (A)
   he was going along,
      now he thought:
         "I shall suck myself."

He went on,   5
   off the trail, he covered himself with five rocks,
      now *there* he was.
He sucked himself,
   he finished,
      he came out.   10

He was going along,   (B)
   he saw a canoe going downriver;
      he thought,
         "Let me inquire of them.
         "Perhaps something is news."   15

He hallooed to them.
They heard him,
   they told him,
      "Ehhh what?"}[19]

He told them,   20
     "Isn't something news?"
[—] "Indeed! Come a little this way."}

He went close to the river.
[—] "Yesss,"
       they told him,   25
     "Coyote was coming along,
     "Now he covered himself with rocks.
     "He sucked himself.
     "That's the kind of news that's traveling along."}
He thought,   30
     "Hmmmm! Wonder who saw me?"
He went back   (C)
     where he sucked himself at;
He saw
     the rocks are split.   35
That was where the news had rushed out.
He thought,
now he said:
     "Indeed, even though it was I myself,
       the news rushed out.   40
     "Now the people are near.
     "Whatever they may do,
       should they suppose,
         'No one will ever make me their news,'
     out it will come."   45

Howard Profile

Stanza	Verse	Line
A	abc	1–4, 5–7, 8–10
B	a	11–15
	bc	16, 17–19
	de	20, 21–22
	fg	23, 24–29
	h	31
C	abcde	32–33, 34–35, 36, 37, 38–46

The News Precedes Coyote
John B. Hudson

Coyote was going along [down the Willamette River].	(A)	(i)
he wanted to go to the falls here [at Oregon City].		
Now then he made camp,	(B)	
now then it became morning,		
now then he went on again.		5
Now then it became dark,	(C)	
now then he camped again,		
now then at morning he went on again.		
Now then it was dark,	(D)	
now then he camped again,		10
now then at morning he went on again.		
Now then at dark he camped again,	(E)	
now then he slept in a sweathouse,		
now then he turned the sweathouse into rock.		
Now then he was licking his penis,	(F)	15
now then he came out:		
"This sweathouse will be a rock."		
Now then he went along,	(A)	(ii)
now then he was going along,		
now then he saw a lot of people in a canoe.		20
Now then Coyote called out,	(B)	
"What's the news?"		
Again he called out,		
"What's the news?		
"What's the news?"		25
Now then one of those people said,		
"*What* can be calling out?		
"Oh it's that Coyote!"		
Now then that person called back to him,		
"Hello!"		30
Coyote said,		
"*What's* the news?"		
Now then that person said,		
"There's no news at all.		
"The only news (is) Coyote was sucking his penis."		35

"Ah! But where was the one who saw me standing?"   (C)
  "Ohhh. I'll go back.
    "I'll see where he could have been standing."[20]

Now then he went back,   (iii)
  now then he got to the sweathouse here   40
Now then he examined his sweathouse,
  now then he saw where the rock had been cracked apart.
"Ohhhhh! I suppose this is where the news came out from it.
      That is how it is going to be.
        That is the way it will always be.   45
      Nothing will ever be hidden.
        That is the way it will always be."

Hudson Profile

Scene	Stanza	Verse	Line
i	AB	a abc	1–2; 3, 4, 5
	CD	abc abc	6, 7, 8; 9, 10, 11
	EF	abc abc	12, 13, 14; 15, 16, 17
ii	A	abc	18, 19, 20
	B	ab cd ef	21–22, 23–25; 26–28, 29–30; 31–32, 33–35
	C	a	36–38
iii	A	ab cd e	39, 40; 41, 42; 43–47

As just seen, Hudson elaborates the narrative, marking each line as a verse
(with the particle for "now then") for a very long stretch (3–20). He then
turns to three pairs of dialogue (21–35) and one verse of inner speech (36–
38) before four lines that again are each a verse (here paired: 39–40, 41–42)
and a concluding pronouncement (43–47).

   Howard's and Hudson's tellings are alike in that the covering up of the
news by rock(s) is in the first of the three parts (stanza A for Howard, scene i
for Hudson); for Simpson and Smith, the covering up is in the second (stanza
B for both). As mentioned, the latter two have Coyote twice discover that
the news is out, in a third, last part; Howard and Hudson have it once, in
a second, middle part. The Coyote of Simpson and Smith makes the discovery while going on. The Coyote of Howard and Hudson discovers and
goes back. He finds how the news got out and pronounces a moral. For the
Wishram and Wasco narrators, the end is one of going on with personal
shame, rubbed in or shrugged off. For Howard and Hudson, it is an occasion
to return and point out a moral for everyone.

Savage adds a twist. Like Hudson, he elaborates the form of the story, deploying scenes instead of stanzas. Like Hudson and Howard, the sucking and covering up (in that order now) are in the first of three parts, but so is finding that the news is out. Savage's Coyote goes back to find how it got out in the second of three parts. He finds out from his "lawyers." (That is an original designation, so far as I know, for a narrative device found throughout the Northwest, turds Coyote carries along with him and turns to for advice when he is at a loss. To have Coyote ask them is de rigueur for Savage; it happens in story after story.)

Another small characteristic on which Savage insists is that Coyote foretell the end of the world (of myth), pronouncing what will be. Savage is so fond of this closing scene that in one story, when the actors are beginning to disband, he has Coyote arrive (out of nowhere, so far as the myth is concerned) and tell them to go back so that he can address the assembly with a pronouncement.

Here is Savage's story:

The News about Coyote
Stevens Savage

(i) (The news gets out)

Coyote . . .
After he had gone a little way, he got hungry
He was talking to himself,
   "O! I am hungry."

Then he built a house, a rock house.   (B)   5
   He patched up the walls in the house tight.
Then he went in.
Then he began sucking his penis.

After he sucked it,
   then he went out.   10
     He was going now.
Then he saw three people drifting downstream in a canoe.
He shouted at them,
   "Do you know anything?"

Then they answered him.   (D)   15
   They said,
   "Yes, we know something."

[—] "What do you know?"
[—] "Coyote has been sucking his penis."

[—] "O what do they tell me. . ."   (E)   20
They were going, those people,
   going downstream in a canoe.

                                        (ii) (Coyote finds out who saw him)
Coyote went back.   (A)
   He went in where he was sucking.
      He was looking around after he got in.   25
Then he saw a hole in the east side.
Then he said,
   "There's where the news went out."

Then he began thinking about it   (B)
   and couldn't make (out?) anything.   30
Then he let out his lawyers.
Then he asked them,
   "You tell me."
Then he told them,
   "Tell me something."   35
Then they said,
   "Yes, we will tell you.
   "A little ways from here people are living.
   "Thus we tell you."

Coyote said,   (C)   40
   "How did they know what they told me about
      when I was sucking it?"
Then they said,
   "There was a hole in the rock (house).
   "There is where they looked in."   45
Coyote said,
   "Who looked in?"
[—] "She saw,
      Duck saw you,
      while you were sucking it.   50
   "Now that's all we tell you.
   "Whatsoever you want to do,
      do as you please now."
[—] "I am satisfied .
      as you two told me about it."   55

	(iii) (Coyote transforms the informers and pronounces)
Then he put them back in now.	(A)
Then he started.	
Then he came to them, to many people.	

While traveling,	(B)
he was shouted at	60
He was shouted at,	
"Don't you cross this way."	
Coyote kept on going.	

Then he arrived there alongside one man.   (C)
He looked down,   65
  he said,
  "What are all these people doing here?"
Then that one began telling him,
  he told him,
  "They are telling one another about something."   70
Coyote said, he was told,
  'Coyote has been sucking his penis.'
  "Now that's what the people are telling one another."
Then he answered, he said,
  "Ah, I understand now."   75

He said,   (D)
  "Now I am glad since you told me about it.
  "Now I am going to make an end of this earth.
  "Now I am going to kill you all."
To Duck he said,   80
  "Never will you carry news.
  "You will (just) be a duck now."
Now he killed them all.

Then he was alone.   (E)
He said,   85
  "Now people thus will tell this story,
  those who will come here."
  "Now that's all.
  "I am going now East."
That's the end of the history.   90

Savage Profile

Scene	Stanza	Verse	Line
i	ABCDE	abc	1, 2, 3-4
		abc	5-6, 7, 8
		abc	9-11, 12, 13-14
		abc	15-17, 18, 19
		a(bc?)	20 (21-22)
ii	ABC	abc	23-25, 26, 27-28
		abcde	29-30, 31, 32-33, 34-35, 36-39
		abcde	40-42, 43-45, 46-47, 48-53, 54-55
iii	ABCDE	abc	56, 57, 58
		abc	59-60, 61-62, 63
		abc	64, 65-67, 68-70, 71-73, 74-75
		abc	76-79, 80-82, 83
		abc	84, 85-89, 90

Conclusion

A table may help bring out the similarities and differences among the several tellings. All these narrators share a tradition in which (1) Coyote sucks himself and (2) covers the spot with rock, but (3) the news gets out. Along the middle and upper Columbia (compare Pichette's Colville-Okanagon version in note 18), Coyote twice goes on to places that know the news before he gets there (4a) (twice also in Molale; three places in Colville-Okanagon). In the Willamette Valley, Coyote discovers he is the news by asking for news (4b). There he goes back to find out what happened (5) and makes a pronouncement (6) (so too in Colville-Okanagon). In Savage's telling, he also punishes the one responsible (7).

The table uses the narrators' initials and letters for the stanza, roman numerals for the scene in the story, except for Colville-Okanagon, which has not been analyzed ethnopoetically:

	LS	HS	LP	VH	JH	SS
(1)	A	A	+	Ac	iF	i
(2)	B	B	?	Ab	iEF	i
(3)	B,C	C	+			
(4a)	C	C	+			
(4b)				B	ii	iCDE,iiiABC
(5)				Cabc	iiC,iiiabcd	ii
(6)			+	Cde	iiie	iiiDE

In these versions of a common situation, Coyote is portrayed as a culprit doubly punished by shame and denial of food (Simpson); as one who could plead extenuating circumstances, is lightly punished, and continues along (Smith); as someone caught in public embarrassment, who then takes on the role of transformer, pronouncer of what will be ever after (Howard, Hudson); as someone who takes revenge as well as makes pronouncement (Savage).

If narrative attitudes toward Coyote lie on a single dimension, here we have polar ends. Simpson's Coyote is punished; Savage's Coyote punishes others (his is the only version in which Coyote takes revenge). Smith's Coyote performs (creating a landmark) and goes off, Howard and Hudson have Coyote learn from experience and pronounce a useful moral, while Savage, like Winishut of Warm Springs Reservation some sixty years later, has Coyote in charge of a world. For Savage, it is a world that at the end of almost every story is about to be transformed forever. For Winishut, it is a world in which there are precedents for the world that follows as well (for example, jet travel).[21]

Despite all that has happened to suppress their languages, traditions, and original communities, there are Native Americans in the Pacific Northwest who continue in the twenty-first century to interpret and characterize Coyote in distinctive, congenial ways. (Smith and Winishut died only within the last quarter century.) We honor their thought best, not by extravagant generalization, but by close attention to the detail of their narrative skill.

Part 4. Contexts and Perspectives

13

Ethnopoetics, Oral-Formulaic Theory, and Editing Texts

John Miles Foley (1992) has opened up a consideration of the connections between oral-formulaic theory and work that has come to be called "ethnopoetics." This is much to be desired, for until recently the two have seemed to occupy different worlds, yet a general view of oral poetry requires both. Foley focuses on a major thrust of folklore today, the interaction between performance and tradition. Here I want to focus on two older concerns, the structure of texts and manuscript sources.

Constraints within and among Lines

Oral-formulaic theory and ethnopoetics are both concerned with composition in the course of performance and with constraints that must be met in doing so. In the epics and other poetry studied in terms of oral-formulaic theory, the constraint is a metrical line, commonly a sung metrical line. In oral narratives the constraint is commonly a relation among lines.[1]

When constraint is internal to the line, we do not hesitate to speak of poetry. In the oral narratives of many Native American peoples and many speakers of English, perhaps universally, there is a constraint external to the line. It has to do with relations among lines that count as "verses." A "verse" is usually easily recognized in speech. It is marked by one of the main intonational contours of the language. Such verses form sequences and do so in terms of a small set of alternatives. There appear to be two fundamental principles. The usual (unmarked) alternatives may be sequences of two or four. Many Native American communities (such as those of the Kwakiutl, Takelma, Zuni, Hopi, and Navajo) make use of such sequences. Many others (such as those of the lower Columbia and Willamette Rivers) and many speakers of American English, so far as is known, connect verses in sequences of three and five.[2]

Narrators are not restricted to just these alternatives. Some command both principles and may adopt one or the other for a particular story or situation, or part of a story, or level of organization (cf. Hymes 1993, 1995c).

If organization in lines is a general definition of poetry, then these narratives are poetry. In one kind of poetry, what counts first of all is a relation within the line, a relation among syllables, stresses, alliterations, tones, conventional feet. In another kind, what counts first of all are relations among lines (more properly, verses) themselves. If the first kind is metrical, the second kind can be called "measured." It is sometimes called "measured verse" and its analysis, "verse analysis."[3]

Such analysis depends upon three principles. One is that just discussed. It implies that narratives transcribed and published as prose paragraphs are in fact organized in lines. The second principle is one Roman Jakobson considered basic to poetry and called "equivalence" (1960). Sequences, however diverse, may count as equivalent in the organization of a narrative, if some recurrent feature marks them as such. As already noted, intonation contours are usually such a mark. Sometimes intonation contours appear not to be such a mark, and verses are signaled by a grammatical feature, such as the quotative, or a combination of grammatical elements and patterning itself (cf. Hymes 1982 on Zuni, 1992b and chap. 10 of this volume on Hopi). For texts for which we do not know the intonation contours, there still are indications of equivalence. Sometimes a certain word or words mark the beginning of units. Turns at talk seem always to count as verses. Other forms of repetition and parallelism occur.

The principle of equivalence implies a text that is a sequence of units. In addition to equivalent units (and repetition and parallelism), there is *succession*. Succession is not a matter simply of linear sequence, of counting. Successive units give shape to action.[4] In particular, patterns of succession can be ways of coming to an ending point. As suggested, one common way is by sequences of two and four, the other by sequences of three and five.

Sequences of two tend to give to action an implicit rhythm of "this," then "that." Pairs of pairs may have the same relation (although other internal relations may obtain). Sequences of three tend to give an implicit rhythm of onset, ongoing, outcome. A development of this last, found as far apart as the Columbia River, Philadelphia, and Finland, integrates two sequences of three within a sequence of five. It is possible (although not necessary) to have the third unit a pivot, completing one succession of three and beginning another.[5] I call this "interlocking." There are other possibilities of rhythm within each type of sequence, and their representation on the page calls for a variety of solutions and a willingness to experiment (see Hymes 1992b).

The principle involved in succession became clear to me in rereading a remarkable essay by Kenneth Burke, "Psychology and Form" (1925). Let me summarize its theme as "the recurrent arousal and satisfying of expectation." Not a straight line, but a series of arcs. What Burke writes of works accepted as literature is pervasively true of oral narrative and often enough deserves the connotations of his other term for it, "eloquence" (34–35, 44).

INTERLOCKING IN PHILADELPHIA AND YAKIMA (THREE AND FIVE)

Here are two examples of interlocking that illustrate the arousal and satisfying of expectation and the difference that verse analysis can make. The first is from Philadelphia. It is from one of a number of narratives collected by Nessa Wolfson in a study of the use of the historical present. The narrative has five scenes. Their foci, successively, are a situation (i), the seizing of an opportunity (ii), acceptance of a bid (iii), acceptance of a demand for certificates (iv), acceptance of a settlement date (v). The first three scenes show an initial condition, development of it, and a proximate outcome. The series could be taken as complete. The third scene, however, turns out to be the first of a second series of three, concerned with stages of acceptance. The two series of scenes interlock at the level of the narrative as a whole. (The narrative is discussed in Hymes 1996b, chap. 10, but the text itself is not included.)

Interlocking also obtains within two of the scenes (iii and iv). In each there are five pairs of verses. The first four are turns at talk between the real-estate agent and the narrator's wife. The fifth relates an outcome, acceptance. In each series, the third pair of verses has the couple's offer. It is outcome to what has preceded and at the same time onset to what follows (she won't accept, she does accept).

Wolfson presented the text in one block paragraph. The lines of the relevant scenes are shown below between brackets, within part of the paragraph.

"She's a Widow"

So he says, "That you have to do in any house." So she says, "Yes, we have to lay down new floors, the rugs are no good [the rugs happen to be in good shape], we have to—there's too much shrubbery, we have to tear out some of the shrubs." [The shrubbery around the house is magnificent if it's done right, if it's done right.] So really we made up everything. [So he says to my wife, he says, "Well, what would you bid?" So she says, "It's stupid for me to talk," she says, "You got a bid for thirty-three, thirty-four," she says. "Why should I even talk to you? It ain't gonna be anywheres near." So he says to her, he says, "Well," he says, "the person at thirty-four backed out." So she says, "Oh yeah?" He says, "Yeah," he says, "What would you bid?" So she says, "Twenty-eight." He says, "Oh," he says, "No, that she'll never go for." So she says, "Okay, that's my bid, Mr. Smith. You want it, fine; you don't, fine." Got a call that afternoon. It was accepted! So I go to see the house—I go to sign the contract, I look at the contract and I says, "I ain't signing this." He says, "Why?" I says, "I want a plumbing certificate, I want an air conditioning certificate, I want a heating certificate, and I want a roof certificate!" So he says, "Really, we won't guarantee . . ." I says, "I don't want guarantee, I want certificates, from certified people that it's in good shape, and I want the right to bring in any of my guys." So he says, "She won't go for it . . . this, that . . ." So I says, "Aah, don't be silly," I says, "Look, you just take it to her." So I get a call back about a day later, "Okay, she's accepted."] So then I get a—now what I do is, I pick up this thing, I take it to my cousin, he goes to someone, he says, "Settlement's no good. She's got us for forty-five days." In October she wanted to settle.

Here is how the bracketed passage appears when displayed in terms of lines, verses, stanzas, and scenes.

		(iii) (Bid accepted)
So he says to my wife, he says,	(A)	60
"Well, what would you bid?"		
So she says,		
"It's stupid for me to talk," she says,		
"You got a bid for thirty-three, thirty-four," she says,		
"Why should I even talk to you?		65
"It ain't gonna be anywheres near."		
So he says to her, he says,	(B)	
"Well," he says,		
"the person at thirty-four backed out."		
So she says, "Oh yeah?"		70
He says,	(C)	
"Yeah," he says,		
"What would you bid?"		
So she says, "Twenty-eight."		
He says, "Oh," he says,	(D)	75
"No, that she'll never go for."		
So she says,		
"Okay, that's my bid, Mr. Smith.		
"You want it,		
fine.		80

"You don't,
    fine."

Got a call that afternoon.   (E)
It was accepted!

                                                    (iv) (Certificates accepted)
So I go to see the house—   (A)   85
I go to sign the contract,
    I look at the contract
        and I says, "I ain't signing this."

He says, "Why?"
I says, "I want a plumbing certificate.   90
    "I want an air conditioning certificate,
    "I want a heating certificate,
    "and I want a roof certificate."

So he says, "Really, we won't guarantee . . ."   (C)
I says, "I don't want guarantee,   95
    "I want certificates,
        from certified people that it's in good shape,
    "and I want the right to bring in any of my guys."

So he says, "She won't go for it . . . this, that . . ."   (D)
So I says, "Aah, don't be silly," I says,   100
    "Look, you just take it to her."

So I get a call back about a day later,   (E)

"Okay, she's accepted."

The same relations open a narrative told to Edward Sapir in Wishram Chinook by Louis Simpson at Yakima, Washington, the summer of 1905. Here are the lines as published in prose paragraphs (Sapir 1909b:139–45.)

The Deserted Boy

Some time long ago the [people] said to the boy: "Now let us go for reeds." The boy was [considered] bad. So then they said: "Now you people shall take him along [when you go for] reeds." And then they said to them: "You shall abandon him there." So then the people all went across the river. They went on and arrived where the reeds were. And then they cut off the reeds and said [to them]: "If the boy says, 'Are you people still there?' you shall answer him, 'U'uu'."

And then they all ran off; straight home they ran, went right across the
river. No person at all (was left) on this side; they were all on the other side.
And then that boy said: "Now let us all go home!"—"U'uu," said the reeds
to him. He looked about long, but in vain; there was nobody. And then he
too started to go home, he too went following behind them; he ran until he
arrived [at the river], but there were no people to be seen. So then the boy
cried. And then he heard [something].

Here is the opening in terms of lines, verses, and stanzas:

Now then they told a boy,	(A)
"Now let us go for reeds."	
Long ago the boy was mean.	
Now then they said,	
"Now you will take him for reeds."	5
Now then they told them,	
"You shall abandon him there."	
Now then the people all went across the river,	(B)
they went on,	
they came to the reeds.	10
Now then they cut them off.	
Now then they said,	
"If the boy should say,	
'Are you there?'	
you shall answer,	15
'U'uu.'"	
Now then they ran off,	(C)
straight home they ran,	
straight across they went,	
not a person on this side,	20
all on that side.	
Now then the boy, too, said,	(D)
"Now let's go home."	
"U'uu,"	
went the reeds.	25
In *vain* he searched about:	
no person.	
Now then he too started home,	(E)
he too followed behind them;	
he arrived running:	30
now, no people.	

Stanzas A, B, C tell of the people deserting the boy. These stanzas are linked by having the people, "they," as agents throughout.

Stanzas C, D, E tell of the boy finding himself deserted. These stanzas are linked by their endings:

not a person on this side, / all on that side.
no person
now, no people

Stanza C is the pivot. The preceding stanzas (A, B) are linked by the plan to abandon the boy, first by instructions to take him for reeds, then by instructions to the reeds as to how to deceive and delay him. The following stanzas (D, E) are linked by the boy's search for the others. Stanza C is outcome to the first pair and the onset for the second. It realizes the plan and provides the condition for the discovery of absence.

Around (C) indeed there is a chiasmus-like symmetry. The immediately adjacent stanzas (B, D) involve the instructions to the reeds, their being given (B) and their being carried out (D).[6] The outer stanzas have to do with the state of abandonment, its initiation by the people (A) and its realization by the boy (E).[7]

INTERLOCKING IN ALASKA AND COCHITI (THREE AND FOUR)

Native American narratives taken down in English can display Native form. In the summer of 1924, Ruth Benedict took down a number of tales from interpreters from the Cochiti Pueblo in New Mexico. In pursuit of a type of story involving Coyote, birds, water, and songs and names imperfectly mastered, I analyzed one titled by Benedict "Coyote Imitates Crow" (Benedict 1981 [1931]:149; cf. Hymes 1992b). The sequence in terms of actions, verses, and scenes seems clear, probably because it was carefully translated.[8] The story has one of the two examples known to me of interlocking within four-part relations.

For a five-part sequence to contain two interlocking sequences of three seems possible wherever three- and five-part relations are used. Until early 1993, I knew of but one example with two- and four-part relations. Early in this century the missionary John W. Chapman recorded some sixteen narratives in the language of those he served (the language has since been referred to as "Ingalik" and now, "Deg Hit'ana"). The texts have been re-elicited (Kari 1981:1–15). One is the widely known story of Raven obtaining the light of the sun (Chapman 1914:22–26, 109–15).

The patterning of verses and scenes uses relations of two and four, and the story as a whole has four acts. The four acts integrate two distinct plots. Each involves three acts (Hymes 1995c).

In the first plot, act I establishes that no young man can marry a certain woman, act II has Raven succeed in entering her, act III has her discovered to be pregnant and Raven born as her child. The woman who would not marry has been overcome.

In the second plot, act II introduces Raven, who flies in darkness, act III has him born to the daughter of the man who controls the light, act IV has him make off with the light. The world has been set right.

In the narrative as a whole, act I involves the young woman but not Raven. Act IV involves Raven but not the young woman. Each plot is in three acts, and they share the central acts II and III.

In the Cochiti narrative, there are two scenes. The first is about Coyote's attempt to imitate a bird, the second about what happens after he fails. Both scenes involve interplay of relations of three and five with relations of four but differ in internal form.

The first scene has three stanzas, the second four. In the first scene, the first and third stanzas each have four verses. The first elaborates pairing in each verse in terms of opposition between what is high (a bank of paper bread) and what is low (a pond of sweet-corn milk). The first pair of verses have to do with what is there, the second with what Crow does (sing, then bite and fly down to drink). The third stanza also has two pairs. Coyote eats and wishes to drink in one, prepares to jump and jumps (to his death) in the other. The middle stanza has five verses. They interlock with Crow's song as pivot. Coyote comes along and asks for the song, Crow agrees, Crow sings. The outcome of one three-step sequence is onset to a second: Crow sings, Coyote listens and learns, says he is ready to start.

Only after long consideration of this first scene did I realize that it is analogous to the second if the two interlocking sequences are counted together with the stanzas on either side. In the first stanza there is only Crow, in the last stanza only Coyote. In the two interlocking sequences, there are both Coyote and Crow. Three for Crow, then, and three for Coyote, in a series of four.

This interplay of three and four complements an obvious interplay in the four stanzas of the second scene. Crow takes Coyote's eyes herself, then summons those who use fur, then those who eat meat. Finally, an old man comes and takes the bones for soup for his wife. The first three stanzas show Crow in charge; the last three are about the use of Coyote's body. The first stands apart from the practical uses of the rest, because Crow simply plays with the eyes, shaking them so that they sound like bells. (An audience would recognize a popular incident, often the frame of an entire story, in which a bird takes Coyote's eyes.) The last stands apart because the old man comes without reference to Crow. The second and third stanzas belong to both sequences, involving both Crow and usefulness.

The story's two scenes are alike in beginning with Crow and ending with Coyote, each having a three-step sequence that overlaps the sequence of the other. They differ in expressive shape in ways that further analysis of Cochiti may clarify. It may be accidental that these two instances of interlocking sequences of three in a set of four—one from Alaska, one from New Mexico—are the only ones known. The device may not be as rare as it now seems.

Ethnopoetics and Editing

If organization in groups of lines is pervasive in oral narrative, then the editing of oral narratives for publication should take that into account.[9] Any presentation of a narrative on the page implies a hypothesis as to its form (cf. D. Hymes 1987a). Yet it is still possible to encounter oral narratives presented as block paragraphs (see "She's a Widow" in this chapter). Often, oral narratives are presented as sequences of lines, carefully transcribed and edited (Tedlock 1999, Wiget 1987, Parks 1991), but the possibility of organized relations among the lines is not considered. Even when verses are identified, relations among them may not be (Kroskrity 1985).[10] In general, we should realize that complex artistry in the organization of lines may be natural to users of language and flourish wherever language does.

Presentation in terms of lines and verses makes visible the shaping artistry of narrators, "all that complex wealth of minutiae which in their line-for-line aspect we call style and in their broader outlines we call form" (Burke 1968:38). The reading is slowed, which makes it far more possible to perceive repetition, parallelism, and succession in the particular text, and what is constant and variable among texts (cf. Hymes 1981b, chap. 6; 1985a). Such analysis contributes to a general theory of the competence and practices involved in oral narrative itself.

Verse Analysis and Manuscripts Interact

Relations among verses interact with the details of manuscript sources. Manuscript evidence may clarify what is otherwise puzzling about such relations. The presence of such relations may indicate the integrity of an original source and the failings of a published one. It is fair to say that all the published sources for Native American narratives need to be examined and reedited in the light of the original manuscripts and verse analysis for the choices and changes that have been made.

"THE DESERTED BOY"

This text, dictated to Edward Sapir in 1905, has three instances of such choices and changes. The third leads to a discovery in the one text that is remarkable for poetics comparatively. (As indicated earlier, the story is given in full in an appendix at the end of this chapter, because of its importance to more than one part of the discussion.)

(1) The first lines of the story were published as follows:

Some time long ago the (people) said to the boy:
"Now let us go for reeds."
The boy was considered bad.
So then they said.

The field notebook shows that "some time long ago" does not actually start the story. The story starts with "Now then" (*aGa kwapt*). The word rendered "some time long ago" (*GanGadix*) precedes "the boy was bad (mean)." Nor is that fact accidental.[11]

The second statement in a Chinookan myth often enough describes the character of one of the actors. Usually this is done through a characteristic activity, understood to be virtuous or not. An actor characterized as virtuous will not come to harm at the end. Here the boy is characterized as bad, but the badness is displaced: "long ago."

Another of Simpson's texts, one about "Clothing" in the section on customs (Sapir 1909b:182), does begin with this time expression, translated there "in olden times." A second paragraph in the same text (but about tools) begins the same way. Perhaps this is why Sapir thought the expression should be first in this story, and it seems right there, given our familiar "once upon a time." In "The Deserted Boy," however, "long ago" has structural work to do. The boy will not end badly, but as a wealthy hero, taking revenge. His meanness is a once, but not a future, thing. Louis Simpson keeps faith with the convention of a statement of character in second place, letting a hearer know that what follows upon it in this case is the immediate action, not the final outcome.

As always, one has to take seriously the exact detail of what was said. Formal analysis need not displace the manuscript but may underscore its integrity. The two together provide as sure as possible a basis for interpretation.

(2) A second instance also has to do with a formal anomaly. The narrator, Louis Simpson, marks verses regularly with an initial pair of particles, translatable as 'Now then' (*aGa kwapt*), as we have seen. The common alternatives are regular too: a second sequence may have another pair, 'Now again' (*aGa wít'a*) instead of 'Now then'.[12] A turn at talk is always a verse, however it begins. Simpson builds stanzas and scenes again and again with sets of such verses. At one point in "The Deserted Boy," however, this regularity fails. Nor can it be taken to have expressive point. Where there ought to be a third pair, there is just one particle, "then." Some narrators do use this single particle as a marker of verses, but not Louis Simpson.

Sapir's field notebook (no. 3, pp. 94–97) shows that at this point of formal irregularity there is an irregularity in transcription. The words of one line are inserted above the words of a line that follows. Either the inserted words were initially missed by Sapir, who went back to write them, or they were retroactively supplied by Simpson. The latter seems more likely. The verse with a single particle completes an expected sequence of three; the discrepancy suggests recovery in the midst of distraction. (Hymes 1981b:156–58 indicates what the content and context suggest was intended.)

(3) The third example involves recognition of conventions of patterning that had been missed. In the final act, the published text has the following five lines (published as prose):

Now snow, lightly, lightly.
There is no food among the people,
the people are hungry.
Now then the people said,
"Let us go to the boy."

That is a reasonable sequence. The field notebook, however, shows that for publication Sapir changed the order of the lines. If the order in the notebook is identified as *abcde,* then the printed lines are in the order *ecdab*. The change appears to be an interpretation. The field notebook shows no insertions. What it does show are carets and parentheses. These indicate transposition in two steps. This fact and the fact that the translation remains continuous in the original order suggest a result of editorial attention, not of interaction with a narrator (see Hymes 1981b:161 for details).

When the relevant lines are considered in the order in which they were written down and presumably spoken, they lead to reconsideration of the organization of the act as a whole. One gains a richer sense of the ways in which initial particles are used, of their motivation and consistency, a further confirmation of "traditional referentiality" and the premise that "poetic meaning depends fundamentally on poetic structure" (Foley 1991: 6, 14).

Here is the notebook order:

Now then the people said,
    "Let us go to the boy."
There is no food among the people,
the people are hungry.
    Now snow, lightly, lightly.

Notice that the published order puts the last line at the beginning. This may be because it has initial "now." A single initial "now" (*aGa*) is sometimes used by Louis Simpson. It is used in each act of this narrative, but the circumstances are different and revealing.

(a) The last line (30) of the first act is "Now, no people." That sums up the outcome of the desertion of the act and the condition of the act to follow. (This "now," however, does not mark a new verse. It does not begin a predication but completes one. See note 17.)

(b) The first scene of the second act ends with lines each beginning with a single "now," two of them. These lines conclude the fifth of a strict sequence of verses. The boy fishes five times. Four times we are told that he has caught one (two, three, four) fish, eaten half of what he has caught, and saved half for the morning. The first time begins with "Now then," the four that follow with "Now again." The fifth time we are not told what he has caught; rather:

Now five times the boy had fished.
Now he had become a grown man.

A sequence of five is a standard pattern that arouses expectation of completion, but the expected completion—what he has caught—is held over for a scene of its own, an extravaganza in which the boy, discovering that a being in the river has given him, not fish, but prepared winter food, sings and waves a feathered cloak. Three of the verses indeed begin with the emphatic particle *quStíaxa* 'behold! indeed!'

The lines at the end of the fishing scene sum up what has occurred (he has fished five times) and what will be the condition of what follows (he has become a grown man).

(c) The third scene of the second act ends with five lines (116–20) that each begin with a single "now." Lacking a following "then," the onward push of the narrative is suspended. There is a moment of lyric unity between the boy and the woman who comes to him. (Such moments for a man and woman occur, variously marked, in a Clackamas narrative from Virginia Howard and one Kathlamet narrative from Charles Cultee.) The lines culminate and sum up the reward of what the boy has done (food, a wife, power). The food and power are a condition of what is to follow. (In Victoria Howard's Clackamas version, so is the wife.)

(d) The last line (167) of the story is "Now only the two old women remained." It sums up the outcome of revenge.

(e) In the notebook order of the five lines in question, "Now snow, lightly, lightly" occurs at the end of a stanza (act III, stanza B). It does not sum up a state of affairs, but it anticipates what is to follow. Perhaps in this respect it complements the other instance in act III. The uses of a single "now" at the end of a unit in act I (31) and act II (78, 79; 116–20) both sum up and anticipate. In act II one anticipates (31), the other sums up (167).

Another pattern intersects this one. There are three mentions of "snow" in the narrative. In each of the others, "snow" is the third element in a sequence of three lines.

Then now he raised the east wind,
    the east wind became strong;
        and it snowed
Now again he treated them this way,
    a strong east wind blew,
        moreover now there was snow.[13]

It seems reasonable to take the first mention of "snow" as participating in that pattern. The people who abandoned the boy twice drown in the midst of wind and snow. Here the condition of that outcome, snow, has begun.

(4) *Couplets: Act III.* Notice that the two lines preceding the first mention of snow (141–42) are odd in terms of Chinookan patterns of verse marking. What precedes is marked as a verse by initial "Now then" and a turn at talk (139–40). What follows is marked as a verse by initial "Now." What intervenes has no initial particle, no turn at talk, yet it seems to have the position of a verse.

One might think of the lines "There is no food among the people, / the people are hungry" as part of a preceding verse, "Now then the people said, / 'Let us go to the boy.'" But Chinookan quoted speech always is the end of the verse of which it is a part. If the two lines in question are to be a verse, they ought to begin with a marker. Instead, they begin literally 'Nothing food people-at'.

It has taken me twenty years to notice that the two lines are a couplet, a semantic couplet. Each says much the same thing:

There is no food among the people,
the people are hungry.

With this recognition it was a matter of a moment to consider two other lines about people as a couplet as well:

All died in the water,
the people were drowned. (156–57).

So to consider these lines was to provide an answer to longstanding dissatisfaction with the form of the act. The way I had published it, after much wrestling, had never seemed quite right, and I had tinkered with it in the interval. Lines that should be structurally parallel were not. Now they could be. Now the recognition of lines 156–57 as a couplet *and thereby a single unit* seems inescapable.

The context is this. Line 144 is strongly marked as an onset, beginning as it does with three particles in a row, "Now then again. . . ." A few lines later "Then now" is strongly marked as an onset, as an inversion of the usual sequence, "Now then." If each is the beginning of a stanza, then each also ends in parallel fashion. At the end of each, the boy recalls of the people, "they abandoned me." Such coming round to the same point is an important device in the tradition. These two sets of lines, then, make perfect sense as stanzas, with strongly marked beginnings, parallel endings essential to the theme, series of verses, five and three, fulfilling a pattern number—if and only if "All died in the water, / the people were drowned," the "people couplet" in the second of the two (156–57), is a structural element.

As with the preceding couplet, these lines express a common theme in varied form and stand apart from what precedes and follows. What follows counts as a separate verse because it is a turn at talk (and thematically parallel with the ending of the preceding stanza). What precedes it is itself formed on a model repeated in the stanza that follows: he did this, a strong east wind, snow (162–64). (I set the lines apart in the earlier analysis but did not reach the point of counting them as a verse.)

Act III, then, has three instances of a three-step sequence ending with snow and three instances of a psalmlike pair of lines involving people (141–42, 156–57, 165–66). Recognition of these patterns makes possible a coherent, pointed shape for the act as a whole.[14]

As said, I missed this shape in my published article on the story. (It was one of the first texts I analyzed in terms of verse patterning.) To discover the original order of the lines involving "Now snow," as I had done, was not enough. I was not intimate enough with Louis Simpson's style, not sure enough of its constants and those of other Chinookan narrators. Not recognizing the structural role of these two patterns (a triad ending with snow, couplets), I could not reconcile the different kinds of repetition and marking in the act with an overall expectation of three- and five-step sequences.[15]

Now a clear working out of implicit narrative logic, explicitly marked, can be seen. The first five verses form a stanza with interlocking: The third verse, the grandmothers crossing to the boy, is outcome of the preceding two and onset of the two that follow. The next verses can be seen as a sequence of three pairs of verses. Such sequences are common enough in Chinookan narrative. The implicit rhythm of expectation within each pair is "this, then that." The first pair of verses (131-32, 133) has to do with the two old women: they go across, they are there a long time. The second pair (134-38, 139-40) concerns the news and what is said: there is much food at the boy's, let us go across. The third pair juxtaposes the couplet: the people are hungry, and now there is snow. A rhythm of "this, then that" joins irresistible motivation (no food) to incipient danger.[16]

The third stanza is the peripety: the grandmothers come, they get close to the boy's house, other people start across. The boy turns, looks, sees. Doing so, he echoes the triplet in which he discovered the fire his grandmothers left him and remembers his abandonment. By implication, he resolves how to act.

This memory is doubled (stanzas C, D), and so is the drowning of the people (D, E). All this is part of an interlocking relation among the five stanzas. The first two stanzas (A, B) have the presence of food at the boy's house discovered. The last two stanzas (D, E) have the people who come for it destroyed. The middle stanza (C) has the people start across and the boy resolve. That is the outcome of one three-step sequence (discovery, wider discovery, confrontation) and the onset of another (confrontation, outcome, further outcome).

The texture of the scene includes other three-part relations as well. The grandmothers cross three times (A, B, C). Snow comes three times (B, D, E). There are three couplets about the people (B, D, E). Each of the last three stanzas (C, D, E) actually ends with the theme of the abandonment, two with memory of those who did abandon, the third with the safety of the grandmothers who did not.

(5) *Couplets: Acts I, II.* Such couplets occur in each act. In act I, they have to do with the people's abandonment of the boy:

straight across they ran,
straight across they went (18-19)

not a person on this side,
all on that side (20–21).[17]

The parallelism of the lines was readily seen and expressed from the start,
and the organization of the act is not affected by counting the pairs as single
units.

In act II, on the other hand, the recognition of couplets forces recognition of relations that had been ignored. The fifth stanza of the first scene
is clearly strictly patterned in terms of going to fish five times, so much so
that presenting it as just that seemed obvious. But if the last two lines are a
couplet and hence a unit with the status of a verse, matters are different. If
lines 77 and 78–79 are a pair of verses, what precedes them does not fit in a
consistent pattern with them, unless also consisting of pairs. And, of course,
it does.

In any other narrative sequence of successive days, the occurrence of
"morning," let alone "again morning," that is, of initial markers for recurrence and a new point in time, would have automatically been seen as marking a new verse. Here the obvious sequence of five days induced a false
security, and the lines about eating the next day were tucked in with the
catching. Five days, five verses.

Now it is evident that the stanza is expressively elaborated with, not five
verses, but five pairs of verses. The first four pairs have fishing one morning
and eating the remaining half of the catch the next. The fifth pair has going
the fifth time and a dramatic change of perspective in a concluding couplet,
the sudden disclosure that all along the boy had been achieving adulthood
(78–79).

I know no other instance of such narrative couplets in the region. Such
may be found, but at present it is impossible to think in terms of diffusion.
Perhaps the couplets are an indigenous development of the pairing that is
widespread in the three- and five-part patterns of the region, often to highlight a focus of action. They can be seen as an intensification of it. I have no
hypothesis as to why they occur only here in what is known of Louis Simpson's narratives. They may be a sign of how much it meant to him to etch
with decisive strokes, as a triumphant guardian spirit quest, the story of an
abandoned boy.

Significance of What Is Missing: Salmon's Myth

Manuscripts may show a published text to be missing a line or two, and restoration of the missing line(s) may show the structure of the narrative to be

different (cf. Hymes 1985a:406–7, Hymes 1995c). In one case, missing lines reinforce interpretation by the fact of where they are omitted.

In the last decade of the last century, Franz Boas searched for speakers of the Chinookan languages spoken near the mouth of the Columbia River. He found Charles Cultee, with whom he intended to stay a day or two, but whose intelligence and ability caused him to return several times. Cultee was the only person from whom Boas could obtain connected texts in either Kathlamet or Chinook proper (which I call "Shoalwater" to distinguish it). Wanting to check the accuracy of Cultee's command of Kathlamet, Boas asked him in 1894 to tell again two stories he had told in 1891. With one, "The War of the Ghosts," he got a variant about people on the other side of the river. With the "Salmon's Myth," he got a version elaborated in the service of a theme.

Both versions have two parts. In one, Salmon returns upriver in spring and is hailed five times by plants along the bank. They insult him and assert that (in his winter absence) the people would have starved if not for them:

"At last my brother's son arrives,
    the one with maggots in his buttocks.
"If I were not a person,
    your people would have died."

Salmon shows no offense but recognizes each plant as an aunt or an uncle, gives it a gift, and places it where it will be in times to come.

In the second part, Salmon and his company meet three people coming down the river toward them. They claim to have gone all the way upriver to the Cascades and to be returning in a day. The leading person is a woman. Her spokesman implies the truth of the claim by speaking the upriver language, Wasco, and naming in Wasco (untranslated) a major woman's food, camas. Salmon takes umbrage at these characters, twists their necks, and denies their claim. It will take five days to reach the Cascades.

In this 1891 telling, the first part begins somewhat leisurely; several lines explain the situation. The second part begins dramatically, with Salmon issuing directions three times in succession, and using ironic questions. It is accomplished in five stanzas, one scene. In the 1894 telling, it is the second part that begins somewhat leisurely, as Salmon's company moves on upriver. The verses are ordinary threes and fives; no dramatic pairs of Salmon's behests end responses to them, no ironic questions but questions in the passive at first ("they were asked"). There are three scenes, not one.[18] A second section deals with the three who have come downriver: Salmon pronounces what they will be. And the order in which they are dealt with is reversed, so that the last one is Flounder, whom Salmon tells to remain in the river in the winter.

Salmon is a contested figure in terms of gender. In other narratives, he is shown as proud and peremptory with women. Victoria Howard transforms and ultimately excludes Salmon from a version of this very story. Here he is made to acknowledge the importance of women's food (plants) to the survival of the people. One can see his behavior in the second part as a result of suppressed anger at the insults he must suffer silently in the first part. In the 1891 telling, the anger is overt. In the 1894 telling, it is not. Evidently, the reason is the further ending. By having Flounder be year round in the river, Salmon forever undercuts the claim of the plants to be the only winter source of food.

The field notebook makes a minor difference to the number of lines in the 1894 telling (one notebook line appears to have been missed in the printed text). What is revealing for interpretation is the fact that in both tellings Cultee skipped a line in the scene just before the second part. In the first telling, he went right on. In the second telling, so the notebook shows, he remembered the omission and inserted it a moment later. What Cultee did is invisible in the printed text, because in editing Boas put the remembered line where it should have been.

The notebook indicates that Cultee was quick to get to the second part in 1891 but not in a hurry in 1894. In both tellings, one can infer, he wanted the second part to offset the humiliation of Salmon in the first. In 1891 he hurried to the part in which Salmon can be in command and dramatized that commanding role (a marked pattern of verses, ironic questions), letting go a line along the way. In 1894 he did not hurry but paused to restore an omitted line; nor did he mark the new part expressively. He had Flounder up his sleeve.

The two tellings convey a common concern on Cultee's part. The notebooks underscore it. Differences in response to a slip in performance covary with different ways of accomplishing a purpose.

Editing and Value

Discovering Cultee's handling of omissions, discovering Louis Simpson's ordering of lines, are examples of recovering intention (cf. Gorman 1989:194, discussing Parker 1984). One is concerned with what the narrator actually said, with authenticity. That has been a primary value for many.

In these cases the recovered intention supports a form of the text that has greater aesthetic value, if, as I believe is the case, there is aesthetic value in the shape the narrators have given what they say. But what gives value is not always obvious or agreed upon. Folklorists sometimes conflate versions, choosing what appears a better passage or wording from each (eclectic editing). If each version has its own shape, however, the result may be a mixture partly without shape. Suppression of a line may suppress indication of a verse; addition may add one. Either may distort a local configuration and produce puzzling irregularity. From the standpoint of verse analysis, such a practice is to be shunned.

To be sure, a particular performance may be both authentic and inferior. Here is where a value other than the aesthetic enters. Verse analysis is analysis of language and contributes to linguistics as well as to folklore, anthropology, and literature. Noam Chomsky has led many linguists to consider it their concern, at least in principle, to analyze, through language, the abilities that underlie it, competence. For abilities in a broad sense, beyond grammar, the term *communicative competence* has been adopted by many (cf. Hymes 1974a, 1984d). Imperfect narrations may shed light on the competence that underlies narrative, on how it works.

Even with splendid narrations, aesthetic value and analysis can easily be at odds. Being unfamiliar with the conventions of another tradition or unconscious of effects deployed in our own language, we may need to have what goes on called to our attention, pointed out, in order to see it. Where alternative interpretations of form are possible, the alternatives must be shown in order to be discussed. If analysis is to contribute to understanding of competence, it must be explicit. For all these reasons, narratives must be presented in a format that makes their analysis recoverable and clear.

I call this "showing the bones of the narrative." There is analogy to an edition of *Gilgamesh* that presents precisely what is there on a certain set of tablets, as distinct from a translation that presents a continuously readable story (see Kovacs 1989, Sandars 1972). In some cases, it is clear that one is displaying relationships that, though marked, are not salient in the flow of words, what might be called the "flesh" (see Hymes 1992b).

At this stage of our knowledge of many traditions, such as those of Native Americans, "showing the bones" is required. When what is there is not yet publicly known, it must be presented first. After that, surrogates of all kinds, retellings, imitations, dramatizations can proceed. But bones come first. To do otherwise would be to regard Pope's *Iliad* as Homer, Lamb's *Tales* as Shakespeare, and Bible stories for children as Genesis, Job, and the Gospel according to John.[19]

Recovery of the Old

This concern is linked to the notion of *repatriation*. The notion has come to the fore in connection with the recovery of burial goods and other objects taken from Native American communities. There is a textual parallel. For many Native American communities, texts in the traditional languages are no longer told. What remains is what has been written down. Important as it is that Native Americans speak for themselves, texts do not. The relations of form and meaning explored by verse analysis are like other relations of form and meaning in language. Mostly we are not aware of them. Analysis is necessary to make them explicit. It is a kind of repatriation, then, for those of us fortunate enough to be able to do so to help recover in older texts their lineaments of shaping artistry.

This may go against the grain of a focus on performance and theory of a certain kind. When I spoke about such work some years ago at the Smithsonian, using a text from a now extinct language of Oregon, someone asked why work with such (limited) materials? Why not work with materials in which one can hear and see the performance? The short answer is that I am from Oregon. It matters to me and to people I know to recognize the value of what textual record there is. From this standpoint, recovery of the old as such matters. A few scholars are pursuing this kind of work. Let me illustrate its value with a few examples.

MULTILINGUAL SOURCE?

About a century ago, Franz Boas recorded some stories from the now extinct Salish people known as Pentlatch. Some of the stories exist now in manuscript in Pentlatch, some in published translations in German, but not all in both. It is likely that some narrations in Chinook jargon were translated directly into German. In any case, Kinkade (1992) is able to clarify the relation between the two kinds of source, comparing a manuscript text in Pentlatch and its published German translation with the help of verse analysis.

RECOVERING VERBAL PLAY

Berman (1992) provides a notable example of recovering the value of a text. She notes that it is not the original texts in Kwakw'ala ("Kwakiutl") but Boas' translations of them that have become the primary source for generations of scholars. Berman observes: "Lévi-Strauss to the contrary, the meaning of a myth lies within the narrator's use of language, not outside it. Boas knew this, which is why he left us eleven volumes of Kwakw'ala texts. If Boas' translations to those texts are unreliable, I believe it is at least in part because he did not intend for them to be relied on. For Boas, the texts were in and of themselves the end products of ethnography, and the translations a necessary evil, an aid to those without fluency in Kwakw'ala" (1992:257). Berman herself commands the language and sources scattered over a number of years, so that she is able to reconstruct choices that Boas made, not only in translation but also in composing a dictionary. She is able to show that a text is couched in verbal play that escaped Boas and that has escaped everyone since.[20]

There is in general a need for anthropologists and folklorists to understand their field as philology—to return to manuscript sources, to discover what has been excluded, rearranged, normalized, misunderstood (cf. Foley 1992:276, 290). What can be known can be expanded in the archive as well as in the field.

PERFORMANCE REGISTER (1)

The manuscript sources of Boas's two volumes of Chinookan texts (Boas 1894, 1901) show an allegro style of dictation. Boas appears to have normalized elisions and published full forms. The easy style suggests that the narrator, Cultee, was not much affected by the process of dictation and that something of a relatively spoken style can be recovered. That is the good news. The bad news is that the published texts cannot be confidently relied upon until the uncorrected originals are studied. The sources of some titles and incidents, published in the language by Boas, have not yet been located in the notebooks. (There are also many supplementary verbal forms, never published, which I did not learn about until I had written a dissertation grammar on the basis of the published material alone.)

PERFORMANCE REGISTER (2)

Even with narratives told in English, the English style of the narrator has probably been revised. Here is one scene from a narrative in Tillamook Salish that has attracted attention.[21] There are four stanzas, separated by space. Verses begin flush left. Closing braces indicate pairs of verses that go together in a pattern of three such pairs.

Later on his sister said to him,
  "You are getting grown now,
  you should hunt a woman for yourself.
  You are old enough to get married.

Any old thing, a dead person, is perhaps better than no wife at all."
"Huh! I can do that all right, sister."
He went to look for a wife.

He returned late at night.
His sister was already in bed
  and did not see him.
Presently she heard him say,
  "Oh! My wife is sticking me with her scratcher."
His sister thought,
  "Why, he must have a maiden bathing after her first menstruation."

Daylight came.
  The sister arose
    and built the fire.
  Split-His-Own-Head got up,
    he had no wife.
"Where is your wife?"
  his sister asked. }
"In bed."
"Is she not going to get up?" }
He told her,
  "No. You told me to obtain a dead person for a wife.
  That is a dead woman I went and got."
She said to him,
  "Now you take that dead body
  and put it right back where you found it." }

He took it back.

Here are the words in the field notebook (in verse analysis):

Next, she told him,
  "You're getting big enough now,
  you can hunt yourself a woman,
  you can get married.
  Any old thing, a dead person."
"Huh, I can do that, all right, sister."
He went to look for a wife.

He came back in the night.
  His sister was already in bed,
    and didn't see him come.
Presently she heard him say,
  "Oh! My wife is sticking me with her scratcher."

His sister thought,
   "Oh he must have found a maiden
     just bathing after her first mensis."

Daylight came.
   The sister arose
     and built the fire.
   He got up,
     he had no wife.
"Where's your wife?" }
"In bed."
"Isn't she going to get up?" }
"No, you told me to get a dead person for a wife.
   That's a dead woman I went and got."
"Oh you take that dead body
   and go put it back where you got it." }

Most changes are the sort a teacher would make to dress up spoken style for appearance in print: eliminate contractions, substitute "returned" for "came back," "obtain" and "found" for "get" and "got." The expansions in the fourth and fifth lines, like substitution of proper name for pronoun in the third stanza, are evidently to make sure the reader does not miss the point. A third kind of change, found in another scene, eliminates direct naming of body parts and functions. Such changes are probably widespread in what one is invited to read as a native voice: written norms, explanations, propriety. But unedited wording has more the flavor of a told story and sometimes shows a different number of lines and local shape.

ORDER OF NARRATION

Presumably, fundamentalists and higher critics alike recognize that the order in which Paul's letters appear in the New Testament is not the order he gave them, or the order in which they were written, but editorially determined by length, longest first, shortest last. Students of Native American collections may forget that the order in which myths and tales appear is not likely to be the order in which they were told and that inferences based on the published sequence are suspect. Recovering actual order can indicate something about style and interaction.

The order in which Victoria Howard dictated Clackamas texts to Melville Jacobs in 1929 and 1930 indicates two ways in which her style changed (see Jacobs 1958, 1959b, and the footnotes therein). On the one hand, the earliest recorded narratives show a great deal of pairing of verses marked initially by "now" (*aGa*). That practice drops out to be replaced in favor of far less pairing and far less explicit marking of verses by any initial element. On the other hand, it is only a certain distance into the relationship that she begins to end a narrative with the formal close "story, story" (*k'áni k'áni*). The first change seems to indicate that she was used to a style in which two- and four-part relations were very prominent, a style not otherwise known in Chinookan and which she may have experienced in hearing Molale (which she knew) or some other language at multilingual Grande Ronde Reservation, where she was born and grew up. The second change seems to reflect a growing confidence in her narratives as complete. (Various comments show awareness of some narratives as incomplete.) Both changes may reflect also a growing ease in her relationship with Melville Jacobs.[22]

COOS BAY: REPEATED TELLINGS

Let me end with a few lines from an obscure manuscript that are for me a sign of grace. I had been working on a collection to make visible to others the pervasiveness of this kind of poetic structure in the words of Native Americans of the Northwest and hit upon the title, "River Poets of Native Oregon." Some years ago, just as my wife and I were setting out for the coast of Oregon, we picked up a forwarded letter from a man we did not know. He was director of cultural heritage for the Confederated Tribes of Coos, Siuslaw, and Lower Umpqua Indians; he knew we had visited such people many years before (the first summer of our marriage in fact). Experience had taught him that linguists did not answer his letters, but how about it? We went and found that he had patiently assembled every known bit of documentation of the languages, cultures, and histories of these people (including an old letter of mine). In the course of collaboration subsequently, he sent me a xerox of the field notes of Harry Hull St. Clair 2d, who in 1903 had recorded texts in Coos that had later been published by another Boas associate who had worked with the same man (Frachtenberg 1913).

Scrutiny of the manuscript discloses that it contains two unpublished texts. Each is an earlier version of a text that was published. St. Clair recorded two versions of a text titled "The Country of the Souls," and Frachtenberg published the second (1913, no. 23). St. Clair recorded a version of "The Ascent to Heaven," but Frachtenberg obtained a fuller version and published that (1913, no. 3). The unpublished versions have details not present in the versions published. As in many cases, so little of Coos tradition is known to us that details are precious. And in these cases there is the opportunity to compare tellings (performances) by the same narrator.[23] The opportunity has remained unknown throughout most of the century and comes to light now through the efforts of a man of Coos descent who has made himself a scholar.

COOS BAY: RIVER POETS OF NATIVE OREGON

But the special serendipity has to do with a notebook page preceding the narratives. On page 25, numbered lines 8–12, St. Clair wrote down a few sentences that seem to have been volunteered by Jim Buchanan, perhaps elaborating in answer to a question. The sentences are eight in number and group in sets of four (as one would expect in Coos oral narrative).[24] They seem a perfect epigraph for a collection conceived as representing river poets of native Oregon.[25]

That's the only way they've been talking.
    They didn't come from any place.
That was their only place.
    They didn't know where they came from.

Every stream has people on it.
    That's how they all had a stream.
That's the way they know themselves,
    All other tribes had their stream as their land.

The Deserted Boy

	(I) (The people and the boy)
Now then they told a boy,	(A)
"Now let us go for reeds."	
Long ago the boy was mean.	
Now then they said,	
"Now you will take him for reeds."	5
Now then they told them,	
"You shall abandon him there."	
Now then the people all went across the river,	(B)
they went on,	
they came to the reeds.	10
Now then they cut them off.	
Now then they said,	
"If the boy should say,	

'Are you there?'
you shall answer,   15
    'Uu.' "26

Now then they ran off,   (C)
    straight home they ran,
    straight across they went,
        not a person on this side,   20
        all on that side.

Now then the boy, too, said,   (D)
    "Now let's go home."
"Uu,"
    went the reeds.   25
In *vain* he searched about:
    no person.

Now then he too started home,   (E)
    he too followed behind them;
        he arrived running: 30
        now, no people.

                                    (II) (The boy, deserted)
                                        (i) (He survives)
Now then the boy wept.   (A)
Now then he heard,
    "TL' TL' TL'."27
Now then he turned his eyes,   35
    he looked,
        he dried his tears.

Now then he saw a *very* little bit of flame in a shell.   (B)
Now then he took that very same flame.
Now then he built up a fire.   40

Now again he saw fiber,   (C)
    again a little bit of it,
        straightway he took it.
Now again he went to the cache,
    he saw five wild potatoes.   45
Now then he thought:
    "My poor father's mother saved me potatoes,
        and fire was saved for me by my father's mother,
        and my mother's mother saved me fiber."

Now then the boy made a small fishline,   (D)   50
  and he made snares with string;
    he set a trap for magpies.
Now then he caught them.
Then he made a small cloak with magpie's skin.
  He just put it nicely around himself.   55
Again he lay down to sleep,
Again he just wrapped himself nicely in it.

Now then he fishes with hook and line;   (E) (ab)
  he caught one sucker,
    half he ate,   60
      half he saves.
Again, morning, he ate half. }

Now again he fishes,   (cd)
  he caught two,
    one he ate,   65
      one he saved.
Again, morning, he ate one. }

Now again in the morning he fishes,   (ef)
  he caught three suckers,
    he ate one and a half.   70
Again, morning, he ate one and a half.

Now again he went to fish,   (gh)
  he caught four suckers,
    two he ate,
      two he saved.   75
Morning, now he ate all two. }

Now again he goes to fish for the fifth time.   (ij)
  Now the boy had fished five times.
  Now he had become a grown man. }

                                                (ii) (He sings)
Now then he examined his fishline.   (A)   80
Indeed, *ats'E'pts'Ep* fills to the brim a cooking-trough.[28]
  He stood it up on the ground.
Now then the boy sang.
Now then all the people watched him.
Now then they said: 85
  "What has he become?"

Indeed! he became glad,   (B)
  he had caught *ats'E'pts'Ep.*
Thus he sang:
  "*Atséee, atséee,*   90
    "Ah, it waves freely over me,
      "Ah, my feathered cloak."
  "*Atséee, atséee,*
    "Ah, it waves freely over me,
      "Ah, my feathered cloak."   95
  "*Atséee, atséee,*[29]
    "Ah, it waves freely over me,
      "Ah, my feathered cloak."
Indeed! ICE'xian's daughter had given him food.

Now then the boy had camped over four times;   (C)   100
  he camped over a fifth time.
Now then he awoke,
  a woman was sleeping with him,
  a very beautiful woman:
    her hair was long,   105
    and bracelets right up to here on her arms,
    and her fingers were full of rings,
  and he saw a house all painted inside with designs,
  and he saw a mountain-sheep blanket covering him, both him and his wife.
Indeed! ICE'xian's very daughter had given him food,[30]   110
    and plenty of Chinook salmon,
    and sturgeon,
    and blueback salmon,
    and eels,
    plenty of everything she had brought.   115

                                                 (iii) (The two are together)
Now he married her.
  Now the woman made food.
    Now, morning, it became daylight.
      Now the two stayed together quietly that day.
        Now the two stayed together a long time.   120

                                                 (III) (The boy and the people)
                                                          (A)
Now then it became spring.
Now then the people found out.
Now then his father's mother and his mother's mother went straight to his
Now then he thought: house.

"The two old women are poor.   125
    "My father's mother and my mother's mother took pity on me in this way."
Now then he fed them,
    he gave the two old women Chinook salmon
        and he gave them sturgeon.

Now then the two old women started home,   (B)   130
    they went across.
A long time they were there. }

Now then it became news,
    they said,
    "Oh! there is much salmon at the boy's,   135
        and much sturgeon,
        and eels,
        and blueback salmon."
Now then the people said,
    "Let us go to the boy." }   140

There is no food among the people,
    the people are hungry.
Now snow, lightly, lightly. }

Now then again first went his father's mother, his mother's mother.
Now then they were close to the house.   145
Now then a great many people went across toward the boy.
Now then the boy turned,
    he looked,
        he saw many people coming across in a canoe.
Now then he thought: 150
    "It was not good the way they abandoned me."

Then now he raised the east wind   (D)
    (there became a Walla Walla wind),
    the east wind became strong,
        and it snowed.   155
All died in the water,
    the people were drowned.
With a bad mind the boy thought:
    "This is the way they treated me,
    they abandoned me."   160

Now again others went across.   (E)
Now again he treated them this way,

a strong east wind blew,
   moreover now there was snow.
Now again they died,   165
   twice the people died.
Now only the two old women remained.
Thus the ways.

14

Anthologies and Narrators

I

I want to address the relation between anthologies and ethnopoetics. I want to argue that ethnopoetics provides a foundation on which anthologies should as much as possible be based, and to say that this is not for the sake of those who practice ethnopoetics, but for the sake of those who first performed the stories that anthologies and ethnopoetics address. Whatever else ethnopoetics may be taken to be, it is first of all a matter of taking seriously the ways in which narrators select and group words. It is through attention to such choices that individuality of attitude and style can be recognized.

This relation came forcibly to my attention when I was asked to review a new anthology. I will discuss that anthology as an indication of the current situation. While criticizing it, I will also provide an index that makes its original material more accessible. Then I will discuss the difference that ethnopoetics makes to two of the texts and narrators in the anthology. By doing so, I hope to reveal the interest and value of a body of material from Oregon—texts in Kalapuya—that has hitherto been little noticed.

II

The anthology in question is *American Indian Myths and Legends,* selected and edited by Richard Erdoes and Alfonso Ortiz. The collaboration itself is significant and admirable. Erdoes, born in Frankfurt, Germany, and educated in Europe, has lived in the United States for some time and published a number of books on the American West, including *Lame Deer, Seeker of Visions.* Alfonso Ortiz was a Tewa from San Juan, New Mexico, holder of a doctorate in anthropology from Chicago, and, after 1982, a MacArthur Fellowship. He was a professor of anthropology at the University of New Mexico and a leader of the Association on American Indian Affairs, a man for whom I had the greatest respect. In what follows, I take Erdoes, the senior author, to be primarily responsible for the characteristics of the anthology.[1]

The collaboration is admirable, because one point of view would be that only persons of Indian descent should use such materials. (Let us set aside the fact that some who claim Indian identity are only partly Indian in descent or sometimes even discovered not to be so at all.) The fact is that the underlying patterns revealed by ethnopoetics are not available in consciousness, even to those who enjoy an uninterrupted heritage. Like the beautiful and complex patterns of the languages themselves, the patterns that make so many Indian narratives a kind of poetry are acquired and employed without awareness. They are not topics of analytic discussion. The languages lack terms for them. Where continuity in the ancestral language has been broken, for Indian and non-Indian alike, the patterning has to be brought to awareness by the discovery of an appropriate method. Even where continuity has not been broken, transformation of an oral artistry to what is seen on a page requires conscious choices of the same kind. For the present, most work of this kind is done by persons trained in the kind of attention and discovery required by descriptive linguistics. One must hope that the activity of Indian participants in this endeavor will grow, but the contribution that such work can make to proper appreciation of Indian tradition and to educational efforts must depend for the time being to a great extent on persons not of Indian descent. Even when the present imbalance is righted, it will always be desirable to have both "insiders" and "outsiders" share the work. Accuracy and depth of insight require a dialectic between both groups (cf. Tedlock 1987). A world in which knowledge of each people was owned exclusively by that people itself would be culturally totalitarian. Just as it is indefensible to have an anthropology in which only outsiders know and insiders are only known, so it is to reverse that inequity. None of us is able to stand outside ourselves sufficiently to know ourselves comprehensively. The European-derived cultures of the United States need an ever-increasing amount of analysis by Indian people. Conversely, the disciplines that contribute to ethnopoetics are in principle not the prisoners of any one ethnicity.

Another point of view might be that anyone can do anything at all with Indian materials. To a great extent, this is the case: a great deal is in the public domain. Nor is such total openness ultimately a bad thing. Certainly one does not want to treat each original text as a perfection from which every other use is a falling off. That was not the nature of the original tradition itself, and many contemporary Indian authors themselves demonstrate the vitality in transformation of the original traditions in their stories, novels, poems, plays, and films. And various retellings make the material available to those who might not otherwise encounter it.

Still, if a distinction between Indian and scholar is to be made, here a worthwhile division of labor might be maintained. Let scholars of whatever ancestry contribute what they can to the analysis and understanding of traditional materials. Let those who are not Indian leave the continuing reworking of traditional materials to Indian people. They can be used as inspiration for poems of one's own, yes, but let those of us who are not of Indian descent not act as if the texts of Indians themselves are ours to change. Modern equivalents of the Brothers Grimm, presenting as authentic tradition what they have rewritten, perform a disservice (see Ellis 1983). A century from now, perhaps, it would not matter, but probably it will be a century before the basic work of making available original texts in accurate editions is even halfway complete, resources and scholars being so few. Once it is possible to consult an original that has been verified against the original field recording, whose translation has been reconsidered for consistency and in the light of all that is known about the language, and whose lines and alignments are visible on the page, then other handlings of the text will not be confused with the original, as now they may be. (Such is the case with some stories in the anthology discussed here.) No one mistakes Robert Lowell's imitations for the poems in other languages from which they derive, but we have yet to reach that stage for much American Indian tradition.

In suggesting a division of labor, I do not imply a divorce. The anthology in question here tacitly assumes that the enjoyment of Indian stories has nothing to do with scholarship or literature. None of the Indian writers making fresh use of tradition is mentioned—Peter Blue Cloud, James "Gogisgo" Arnett, Ed Edmo, N. Scott Momaday, Duane Niatum, Simon Ortiz, Leslie Marmon Silko, James Welch, and others. None of the attention to the traditions and modern writings by literary scholars is mentioned—nothing of the Association for the Study of American Indian Literature, or the work of Karl Kroeber, Jarold Ramsey, Andrew Wiget, and others that is represented in *Recovering the Word* (Swann and Krupat 1987), the volume in which this essay first appeared, and its predecessor, *Smoothing the Ground* (Swann 1983). And nothing is said of the comparative and analytical literature, from the essays of Franz Boas and the works of Stith Thompson to the more recent studies by Alan Dundes, Melville Jacobs, Claude Lévi-Strauss, and others.

Let us infer that theories, methods, studies, have been set aside as of no relevance to the life of the stories themselves or to the living sources. That kind of "populism" is a form of segregation. The public, including the Indian public, is kept at one end of the bus of the mind, allowed to enjoy stories, but prohibited from entering the conversation about them that is going on at the other end of the bus. Even if it is a question of enjoyment only, the public, including the Indian public, may enjoy knowing how other versions go and having the chance to reflect on the differences. A sympathetic public may welcome the knowledge that some of the best scholars of the century have devoted themselves to such stories. One may judge Lévi-Strauss's interpretations, in terms of structural transformation, to overshoot the mark at times; but if one wants to show the worth of such stories, why not mention that the world's most famous anthropologist has devoted years of his life to them?

Neither scholars nor Indian people who wish to use an anthology such as this to gain further access to the traditions are well served. On the whole I want to stress that it is the public, including the Indian public, that is the worst served. A scholar may be annoyed by a citation such as "Based on a tale from 1901" (Erdoes and Ortiz 1984:385) for an Alsea story but will know that the only possible sources for such a story are Frachtenberg's 1920 monograph and four texts published separately in 1917. Finding the story in question to be absent from the former, he or she will know it must be in the latter; but an Indian at Siletz or Grand Ronde—recently reinstituted reservations of western Oregon—aware of some Alsea ancestry and wishing to trace some content for it, would be stopped. And everyone will be frustrated by citations such as "Based on four fragments dating from 1883 to 1910" (45) or "Based on fragments recorded in the 1880s" (47).

Scholarship serves the public as well as scholars. People of Indian descent, deprived through history of fluency in an ancestral language or tradition, often seek to regain something of it. Much of the scholarly literature is not as accessible to nonscholars as it might be, and that includes writings of my own. If wanted as more than a symbol of a heritage, it may not serve, but many Native people are scholars themselves, and others can make use of scholarship and go beyond one book.

Being able to go on matters because a good many of the stories in *American Indian Myths and Legends* are said to be "retold," "based on," "from," "reported by." I have not been able to infer consistent meanings for the various phrases, but "retold" seems to go with the integration of more than one original, while "from" and "reported by" seem to go with the close following of a single source. Even in the latter cases, there appears to have been some reworking. The issue is not that the original translations are sacrosanct. Of course, they are not (see Hymes 1981b, chap. 1, and the retranslation of Kalapuya texts in this essay). The issue is whether or not the changed version does justice to the principle recognized in the introduction, that the stories "are embedded in the ancient languages" (Erdoes and Ortiz 1984:xi). Sometimes yes, often no.

Some of the reworking is advantageous, in that it liberates separate turns at talk into separate units on the page (e.g., the Cochiti "Crow and Hawk," given in the anthology as "The Neglectful Mother" [Erdoes and Ortiz 1984: 417-18]). Even here some lines of the original are omitted. There appears to be a parallelism, a doubling, at the end of the story that the omission of lines destroys. The content is present but not the shape. The same is true of the beginning of the Cochiti "Salt Woman is Refused Food" (61). While introducing conjunctions not present in the original, the telling here omits the second time that Old Salt Woman is refused food, a time that includes direct speech from her. Direct speech and the pointing up of significance by repetition are vital features of American Indian narrative. To omit them suggests an insensitivity to the traditional style (see Benedict 1981 [1931]).

Even stranger is the inclusion in this anthology of versions from other anthologies in which the stories have been freely rewritten. The Alsea story included here is taken from its retelling by Lopez (1977). The actual story does not begin, as it does in the anthology, with the mention of Coyote by name. Its narrator, Thomas Walker (not named here), tells such stories from the standpoint of women Coyote is trying to deceive. He brings such a story around at the end to a question on their part, Who was that? Must have been Coyote. Only then does Coyote's name, dramatically, occur.

Every North American Indian tradition has a trickster figure, but not every one has Coyote. Some have Rabbit, some the Stellar Jay, some Raven, some Mink. And just as Christians have struggled and disagreed as to the relationships between the major powers of their tradition, especially with regard to the attributes of omnipotence and goodness, so Indian people have resolved in various ways the ambiguity of figures who can be both benevolent and buffoonish. The Kwakiutl of British Columbia assign one series of adventures to the trickster, Mink, and another to a separate Transformer, who has no animal form and whose name, "born to be *q'ani*," is not further interpretable. The anthology reprints a Transformer story (362-65) but from Lopez, who substitutes "Coyote"—a trickster and not even the Kwakiutl trickster (1977). If I were a Kwakiutl, I'd be angry.

III

The great virtue of the anthology is that it demonstrates the vitality of the narrative traditions. For anyone who may think of such traditions as extinct, it will be surprising to find that so many of the stories were collected in recent years and not only at reservations. Of the 166 narratives, a good third are published here for the first time. Ortiz contributes seven from his native Tewa (the tellers' identities are properly kept confidential). Erdoes recorded one Cheyenne story at the Crow intertribal fair (392) and a Brulé Sioux story around a powwow campfire in Pine Ridge, South Dakota (374). One Zuni story was told in several versions during a sacred clown dance and pantomime at Zuni in 1964 (280), and a Cherokee story at a Cherokee treaty council meeting in New York City (107). Leonard Crow Dog told Erdoes stories both in New York City (496) and on Rosebud Reservation (499). David Red Bird, identified as a young Green Bay Indian (151), is the source of new Ojibwe tellings (151, 161) as well as of a Winnebago telling (166).

Sometimes we are told that a Cheyenne story was interpreted by someone (Erdoes and Ortiz 1984:37, 485; see reference to translation on 247). Otherwise, we are perhaps to assume that the stories were told in English. Certainly, it is important to recognize that the traditions may be maintained in English and in diverse localities. The Coos traditions of Annie Miner Peterson that Melville Jacobs recorded in Coos (1939, 1940) were also transmitted in English to a descendant, George Wasson, later a dean at the University of Oregon, who maintains this knowledge.

There are some 57 new tellings, then, scattered among some 109 others. There is no index, however, to lead one to them or that would lead one to stories from a particular people. The one index is of titles and not necessarily the titles that the stories had in the original. The editors indicate that they set no store by titles (xiii). Yet titles can be scholarly aids, as in the case of the standard catchphrase "Bear and Deer" for what is represented here in a Miwok version as "The Coming of Thunder" (216). And when recorded in the Native language, titles can express Native orientations toward the narrative (see Hymes 1981b, chap. 7). Thus one of the series of Chinook myths that has the Native title "Blue Jay and Ioi" (the name of Blue Jay's elder sister) here becomes "Blue Jay Visits Ghost Town" (Erdoes and Ortiz 1984:457). That is not a bad way to differentiate the one story from two others of the same title, but it eliminates the frame that the Chinook title provides. Naming and order of naming in titles covary with outcomes, and the type "X and elder sibling" is central to a part of Chinookan tradition.

To facilitate access to the new material, I have prepared an index of the names of tribal groups, which gives the initial page of the story. The index may be found at the end of this chapter. In certain cases, I have provided additional information as to linguistic affiliation (e.g., Chinookan, Iroquois, Salish). The affiliation of the story on page 385 is uncertain, as the heading says "Cheyenne," but the postscript says "Retold from several North Californian fragments." The new material is in italics.

IV

The great virtue of the Erdoes and Ortiz anthology is also part of a contradiction: The fifty-seven tellings are identified as coming from persons; the stories that come from other books are identified only as coming from tribes. We learn the names (with one shy exception) of the tellers visited by Erdoes and something interesting about them. Not so with the rest. With them, the only names are the names of tribes or occasionally of someone who is not an original source or an Indian at all. A Kalapuya myth is said to be "told by Barry Lopez in 1977" (Erdoes and Ortiz 1984:356). Lopez, of course, is the editor and rewrite-man of another anthology (1977). The myth was told in Santiam Kalapuya (there are three Kalapuya languages) by a man I once had the privilege of meeting in his home, John B. Hudson. In this particular case, one could not get back to Hudson even by finding the reference for the story in the back of the book. One has to know to look under Jacobs for *Kalapuya Texts* (1945), and the page numbers given there are for a myth in another language, Tualatin Kalapuya, recorded in the nineteenth century by A. S. Gatschet, probably from Wapato Dave. A scholar, again, can find such things out and trace the location of the actual original and its source, but why should an anthology preserve a rewriting by a white person and let the name of the Indian storyteller be lost? Someone aware of some Kalapuya ancestry, perhaps through Hudson, would like to find his or her name here.[2]

Should one care about the identities of Indians now dead, even if one is not descended from them? Yes. The stories told long ago, just as those told today, came from individuals. Creative personal use of tradition did not begin in our lifetime; it is as old as the narrative art itself. True, collectors in the pass often obscured the fact. Usually they gave credit to their sources by name and thanked them, but typically they published stories from a single person as though that person represented an entire community. Thus, the myths we have in the language of the Clackamas Chinook, who lived near Oregon City, Oregon, and whose survivors were removed to the Grande Ronde Reservation to the west, come from a single woman, Victoria Howard, who dictated them near the end of her life in 1929 and 1930. Her narratives reflect the line of women from whom she learned them and their experience of a shattered culture. Plots of male adventure are told from the standpoint of their effect on women and children. But the collector published and discussed them all as expressive simply of "the Clackamas" (Jacobs 1958, 1959a, 1959b, 1961).

The narrators, then, create as well as preserve. When what they have said is adequately recorded, and the devices and designs they have employed are understood, we can recognize both a tribal art and a personal voice (see

Swann and Krupat 1987, chap. 1). It is this exact art that must be the foundation of our attention and interpretation.

V

Three universal principles inform this art. The first is that the narratives consist, not of sentences, but of lines. Typically, though not always, a line is a phrase. The second principle, formulated by Jakobson (1960), is that of equivalence: A variety of means is employed to establish formal equivalence between particular lines and groups of lines. The third principle is that formulated by Burke (1925), the arousal and satisfaction of expectation. In other words, the stories are to be heard or seen in lines and thus are a form of poetry. There is a grouping, or segmentation, internal to the tradition not only of lines but also of groups of lines, sometimes at a series of levels. In addition to a segmentation and an architecture, there is also an arc or series of arcs to the story, governed by conventional understandings as to the logic or rhetorical form of enacted action.[3]

These principles appear to be universal in that indications of them can be found in oral narrative, even where it survives surrounded by other modes of verbal presentation, some inimical to them, such as those of the prose of schools. Where there is no competitor, where oral narrative is the central art—as among American Indians—the principles can inform accomplishments that deserve a place in any account of literature.

The three principles can be seen to apply to the Kalapuya text included in the Erdoes and Ortiz anthology. First, I will present a retranslation and realignment of the story. Retranslation is necessary because published translations typically do not preserve the repetitions and parallelisms that establish equivalence. Thus, the recurrent marker of a line or group of lines as a unit ("verse"), the compound particle *lau'mde,* is variously translated in the source as 'and', 'and then', 'now', 'now then', 'then', and 'and when'. Here it is translated invariably as 'now then', which fits the independent occurrence of *lau* as 'now'. The notes, keyed to the retranslation by line numbers, indicate other points of revision.

The realignment recognizes the recurrence of "now then" as the marker of significant units. In the Pacific Northwest initial particles of this kind are frequently the central marker of units, together with turns at talk (but other features can be involved or replace them, such as the quotative suffix in Bella Coola). The logic of grouping involves series of three or five, in keeping with other peoples of the same area, the Chehalis and the Cowlitz Salish on the Washington side of the lower Columbia River; the Chinookans along the river from its mouth to past the present city of The Dalles; and the Sahaptins, also along the Columbia, overlapping the Chinookans and east of them. I have found such grouping in all sources of Kalapuya tradition: in what probably is the earliest text transmitted in Kalapuya, a war talk delivered by a Tualatin headman, Xiupa, circa 1844; in a text about Yonkalla Kalapuya shamans changing into grizzlies to eat Tualatins, dictated by Dave Yechgawa (both of these were recorded by Gatschet and are published in Jacobs 1945: 185–86); in the myth of the four ages of the world, probably also dictated by Wapato Dave Yechgawa (Jacobs 1945:173–78); in the fine narratives in Mary's River collected from William Hartless in 1914 by L. J. Frachtenberg; and in texts in Santiam collected from John B. Hudson by Jacobs over a decade in the late 1920s and the 1930s (all these in Jacobs 1945).

The architecture implicit in the grouping provides a framework for recognizing elaboration, emphasis, proportion, pace. Yet two things must be said:

First, the grouping is not mechanical. On one hand, the narrator always has options within the principles of patterning. He or she must be understood as mapping sequences of incident, event, and image into sequences of line and verse. On the other hand, the underlying patterning is a grounding, a matrix, but not the exclusive kind of pattern available. Where the matrix is one of three or five, as in Kalapuya, the alternative of pairing may be used for intensity. (Conversely, where the matrix is one of two or four, as in Tonkawa of Texas, the alternative of three-part grouping may be used for intensity [Hymes 1980c; see chaps. 3 and 10 in this book].) Hudson employs such intensity in this text, when the action reaches the climax in which Coyote is using his hand to break the dam.

Second, the grouping is a matter not only of structure but also of process. The formal relationships have a semantic sense. In a matrix of pairing there is a sense of this, then that, of initiation and outcome, initiation and outcome. It pervades the architecture, so that one pair of initiation and outcome stands as initiation to the outcome of a succeeding pair. (See the Tonkawa study just cited [Hymes 1980b; see chaps. 3 and 10 in this book], and the Zuni narrative in Hymes 1982.) Where the matrix is three or five, there is a sense of premise or onset, ongoing, outcome, for a three-unit sequence. For a five-unit sequence, the third unit is often pivotal. It stands as outcome to the first three and as onset to a second sequence of three. Thus in the first scene of this Kalapuya myth, the first three verses have Coyote find a small deer, set aside a small rib, make a money bead.

The making of the money bead stands as onset to a sequence that describes the Frogs' monopoly of water as ongoing information and Coyote's intention to drink their water as outcome, both of the sequence and the

whole scene. The five verses together express an intention and preparation
on Coyote's part that is already introduced with the setting aside of a small
rib in the second verse. Similarly, the five verses of the third scene consist of a
three-part sequence in which Coyote drinks and uses his hand, interlocking
with a three-part sequence in which the outcome of the first triad is onset
to the water going through and Coyote's culminating pronouncement.

Since the narrator has options, the interpreter does also. More than one
formal segmentation is usually possible. One's sense that the right alignment has been discovered is dependent on being able to read the story consistently in terms of the logic of action, the arousal and satisfying of expectation locally as one goes along. Where formal markers are few, the implicit
logic itself may be the decisive factor. A further test of an alignment is that
other features cohere. It is rewarding to note that the colloquy with the Frogs
stands as a distinct ongoing scene (lines 13–21) and that the other turns at
talk, by Coyote alone, each culminate the other two scenes, that of preparation (i) and that of outcome (ii).

Segmentation, in other words, is inseparable from meaning and interpretation. It is rewarding to press a principle of segmentation as far as it will go;
one discovers new possibilities. The result, however, must be controlled by
a sense of the narrator's intentions and of the coherence of the whole.

The present narrative provides an example. If one were to count instances
of the initial marker "now then" as always forming groups of three and five,
one would be led to consider the five lines of Coyote's drinking (22, 23, 24,
25, 26) as constituting a stanza. The remaining three verses (27–29, 30, 31–
32) would evidently form a stanza as well. The three verses of the colloquy
with the Frogs (13, 14–17, 18–21) are clearly a distinct stanza. The material
preceding the colloquy (1–12) would then have to have two stanzas as well,
if the narrative as a whole is to have a total that conforms to a pattern number (here, five). Yet there are just five instances of verse-marking "now then."
That would constitute just one stanza, giving the narrative a total of four.
One could reason that the chiasmus of lines 8–9 ("all the time . . . all the
time") is striking; perhaps such a device could be taken to constitute a verse.
Then there would be six verses, assignable three each to the required two
stanzas (1–3, 4–5, 6; 7, 8–9, 10–12).

This is not an implausible conclusion, and it is the one to which I was
led in 1981 when I first analyzed the text. By dividing the parts preceding
and following the colloquy each into two, however, this analysis interrupts
the unity of setting and topic in each. It lessens the symmetry by which
each as a whole ends with Coyote's direct speech and all three scenes with
someone's speech. It lacks the integration that comes from recognizing in

each an interlocking five-part relationship, in which the third unit is simultaneously outcome of one triad and onset of another. These considerations are preferences; the text does not quite require them. Two things, however, can be said to be required: (1) not to promote stylistic devices to the status of markers of verse units, unless overall patterning makes such status clear; (2) not to overlook parallelism of form and content (form/meaning covariation). This first analysis does both those things. It promotes a stylistic device (chiasmus in lines 8–9) to the status of marking a verse ad hoc, departing from the otherwise consistent marking of verses by Hudson always with "now then." It overlooks the parallelism of form and content that runs beyond lines 22–26 to include lines 27–29.

There is an incremental repetition of content in the six verses of these lines. After the colloquy with the Frogs, two actions by Coyote are paired and repeated: drinking, use of the hand. Lines 27–29 are the third and concluding instance of the use of the hand. Two tracks of onset, ongoing, outcome of action run in tandem here: he drank, he drank, he stopped drinking (22, 24, 26); he put one hand down in, he put his hand down in the water where it was dammed up, he got up, scooped the dirt aside, scooped it out (23, 25, 27–29). (The elaboration of the third use of the hand gives use of the hand a five-line sequence overall.) The drinking and handiwork that to Coyote are satisfaction and service, to the Frogs' deception and dirty work, go together for two pairs of verses; then the deception is ended (26) and the work completed (27–29). The threefold pairing is an intensification of the climax of the action (see Hymes 1985c).

Here is the retranslation and realignment, together with the Kalapuya text, also realigned (the orthography has been slightly revised):

Coyote Releases Water Dammed Up by the Frogs

	(i) (He prepares)	
Coyote was going along.	(a)	1
A small deer had died.		2
Now then Coyote found it.		3
Now then he ate it all.	(b)	4
He set aside one small rib.		5
Now then he made a money bead out of the small rib of the deer.	(c)	6
Now then together the Frogs had the water.	(d)	7
All the time they stood guard over the water.		8
The people bought it all the time.		9
Now then Coyote said:	(e)	10

"I am going to drink water,   11
   "The Frogs' water."   12

                   (ii) (He buys water from the Frogs)
Now then he arrived.   (a) 13
Now he told the frogs: (b) 14
   "I want to drink water.   15
   "I have a large money bead.   16
   "I want to drink a lot of water."   17
Now then they told him: (c) 18
   "Do that!   19
   "Drink!   20
   "We will hold your head."   21

                    (iii) (He releases the water)
Now then indeed he drank, Coyote.   (a) 22
   Now then he put one hand down in.   (b) 23
Now then he drank.   (c) 24
   Now then he put his hand down in the water where it was dammed up. (d) 25
Now then he stopped drinking water.   (e) 26
   Now then he got up,   (f) 27
      he scooped the dirt aside,   28
         he scooped it out.   29
Now then the water went through.   (g) 30
Now then Coyote said: (h) 31
   "All the time water will be everywhere."   32

Coyote Releases Water Dammed Up by the Frogs

                        (i) (He prepares)
Asní gum'í·did.   1
   í·sdu-amú·ki' gum'ála'.   2
      Láu'mdé Ašní gumdá'ts.   3
Láu'mdé gumhú·k má·dfan,   4
   táu'ne i·-sdu-di'na gump'í·.   5
Láu'mdé giŋge'ts angawetsad guš-í·sdu-di'ná amú·ki'.   6
Láu'mdé Antgʷágʷa gʷiník ginip'í·ne ambgé'.   7
   Din'á·wi gini'lé·dgʷane ambgé'.   8
      Amím' giniyándan din'é·wi.   9
   Láu'mdé Ašní gum'nag: 10
      "Cŭm'í-čumkʷít ambgé',   11
      "Gus-Antgʷágʷa-dinibgé'."   12

                          (ii) (He buys water from the Frogs)

Láu'mdé ginthʷúq.	13
Láu gum'níšdini Antgʷagʷa:	14
"Čumhuli-dumikʷí'd ambgé'.	15
"Tsump'í·ne ubéla' aŋgáwetsed.	16
"Tsumhúli-dumikʷí't lúi-ambgé'."	17
Láu'mdé gidi·ni'níšdini':	18
"Gé'ts!	19
"Dekʷí'd!	20
"Čindugʷíndubu bugʷa."	21

                               (iii) (He releases the water)

Láu'mdé wi·neš-wí gindikʷí'd Ašní.	22
Láu'mdé gint'múi táu'ne-dilágʷa.	23
Láu'mdé gidikʷí'd.	24
Láu'mde gint'múi dilágʷa guš-ambgé' gidehefúgeče'.	25
Láu'mdé gidi·péslau' duŋkʷítye-bgé'.	26
Lau'mdé gidi·gódga,	27
giŋgáwi guš-amp'lú' qʷáčefan,	28
giŋgáwi.	29
Láu'mdé ambgé' giŋdengán.	30
Láu'mdé Ašní gum'nág:	31
"Din'é·wi ambgé' gamtí mátfanču."	32

Notes on the Text and Translation

Line 1 A conventional opening that marks Coyote stories in many groups.

2, 5, 6 Notice the threefold recurrence of "small."

3 The line initial particle pair, "now then" (*lau'-mde*) is withheld until the third line, at which point the narrative action properly begins. Lines 1–2 set the stage. Each verse throughout the story will begin with this pair, except for line 14, which has only *lau*.

8 "all the time" usually has *e·* as its stressed, middle vowel, as in lines 9 and 32 of this text. Thus *a·* seems marked, and the translation is underlined (italicized) to show this.

9 Notice the chiasmus begun and ended by "all the time."

7 The original publication shows no translation in this text for *gʷinik*. Other occurrences show a sense of collectivity, "together." Thus there are at least two frogs here (as in an Alsea myth of Coyote and two frog women). Hudson has Coyote encounter five frog women in another story (the Kalapuya counterpart to the Alsea story just mentioned [Jacobs 1945:96–97]), and William Hartless has five frogs in his version of the present story (Jacobs 1945:236–37); thus the number here probably is also five.

11-12 The first instance of direct speech culminates the first scene.

13 Travel with change of location commonly marks a new scene.

14 The marker now is simply "now."

14-21 First Coyote, then the Frogs, have three lines of direct speech. Note the eagerness of the Frogs. This excited colloquy in midpassage is the Frogs' only turn at talk. The first and third scenes, the preparation and outcome, have each one, final turn at talk, reserved for Coyote.

22 The initial particle pair lacks a second stress in this one line, most likely accidentally.

23 The line is indented, as are 25 and 27-29, because of the threefold binary grouping. The action proceeds by incremental repetition in three steps. He drank, put one hand down in; he drank, put one hand down where it was dammed; he stopped drinking, scooped out (by hand) the dirt damming the water. The pairing in the context of an organization in terms of three- and five-unit patterns is an intensification. The sequence has three parts, and the last member of the last pair is elaborated in three lines, though containing a pairing (he scooped).

28-29 It is not possible to translate *giŋgawi* identically in both lines idiomatically; the "out" that seems required in line 29 is omitted in line 28 because of the presence of "aside" (*qʷačefan*). Notice that there is no "aside" in the Kalapuya in line 29, though Jacobs has it there, and that the two verbs are identical, though translated differently by Jacobs.

30 The third pair of actions (drink, use hand) is the pivot of the third scene. It is outcome to the sequence (22, 23) (24, 25) (26, 27-29) and is onset to the concluding sequence (26, 27-29) (30) (31-32): the dam is broken, the water goes through, Coyote pronounces its universal presence henceforth.

32 It is not beyond the subtlety of such narratives that "all the time" in this line completes a trio begun in 8, 9.

VI

Let us compare this analysis of ethnopoetic form with the version of the story published in the anthology under discussion. Here is the initial portion, corresponding to the first thirteen lines:

"Coyote Takes Water from the Frog People"

Coyote was out hunting and he found a dead deer. One of the deer's rib bones looked just like a big dentalia shell, and Coyote picked it up and took it with him. He went up to see the frog people. The frog people had all the water. When anyone wanted any water to drink or cook with or to wash,

they had to go and get it from the frog people (Erdoes and Ortiz 1984:355;
Lopez 1977:177).

As we have seen, John Hudson had in mind a somewhat different story.
He began by framing it as a Coyote story with the widespread convention of
"Coyote was going along" (missing here). His Coyote was *not* out hunting.
He did not just *pick up a big* dentalia shell but ate all of a deer he found, setting aside one *small* rib. Both deer and rib are appropriately small ("small" is
repeated three times). It is out of chance and his own appetites, as so often
happens—here, through his eating the whole deer and at once—that Coyote has a chance to benefit humanity. The rib did not *look* like a dentalium
(money-bead) shell; Coyote *made* it so. Hudson's Coyote does not immediately go to the Frogs; he announces his intention. Nor do the Frogs simply
have all the water; they *sell,* making the people *buy* what should be available
freely. (This point is elaborated partly in relation to this myth by Lévi-Strauss
1981:255–84].)

The retelling loses the *purposefulness* of Coyote's behavior. Hudson has
Coyote reserve the deer rib, make the rib, announce his intention. Not so in
the retelling. And Hudson reserves the force of direct speech for just three
points: the colloquy of the middle scene and the two statements by Coyote
that end each of the other scenes, stating his intention and pronouncing
the future. The retelling turns most of the story into a dialogue as Coyote
drinks, some nine additional turns at talk in all, four for Coyote, five for the
Frogs. Here is an excerpt:

> Coyote began drinking. He drank for a long time. Finally one of the frog
> people said, "Hey, Coyote, you sure are drinking a lot of water there. What
> are you doing that for?"
>   Coyote brought his head up out of the water. "I'm thirsty."
>   "Oh."
> After a while one of the Frog People said, "Coyote, you sure are drinking a
> lot of water: Maybe you better give us another shell."
>   Just let me finish this drink," said Coyote, putting his head back under-
> water. (Erdoes and Ortiz 1984:355)

This elaboration of dialogue reads well enough; it just is not Kalapuya tradition. In the other version known to us, William Hartless elaborates the
striking of a bargain between Coyote and the Frogs, but once it is struck, he,
like Hudson, has no more talk, only action. It is accurate, then, for the anthology to say "Told by Barry Lopez in 1977" (356). But we were promised
Kalapuya and should have been given what was told by John B. Hudson.

VII

All this is not to say that an anthology can safely stick to whatever translation appears in the original source. As has been shown in the preceding discussion, the original translation fails to translate one word (line 7) and does not consistently render the structure-marking particles or the repetition of a climactic verb (lines 28-29). And the arrangement on the page of any translation is an implicit analytical claim, an implicit theory of underlying organization. Jacobs, in fact, proposes such a claim by dividing the text into five parts, marked by (1), (2), (3), (4), and what precedes (1). Here is the text as presented in the original publication:

1. Coyote Releases Water Dammed Up by the Frogs

Coyote was going along. A small deer had died, and coyote found it, and then he ate it all. He set aside one small rib, and he made a money bead (dentalium) of the little rib of the deer. (1) Now the frogs (at that time) kept the water. They stood guard over the water all the time. The people always bought it (from them). Now then coyote said, "I am going to drink water, the frogs' water." (2) Now then he arrived, and he said to the frogs, "I want to drink water. I have a large money bead (a valuable dentalium). I want to drink a lot of water." Then they said to him, "Do that! drink! We will hold your head." (3) Then indeed coyote drank. And he put one hand down in, and then he drank. Now he put his hand in the water where it was dammed off. (4) And when he ceased drinking water, and when he arose, he scooped the dirt away to one side (he channeled an egress for the dammed up water), he cast it aside. Now then the water went on through and out. And coyote said, "There will be water everywhere for all time."

The organization corresponds to the text as analyzed ethnopoetically as follows:

Jacobs	Hymes
1–6	1–12, (1, 4, 6/6,7,10)
7–12	
13–21	13–21
22–25	22–32 (22–23, 24–25, 26–29, 30, 31)
26–32	

This is not far from the ethnopoetic analysis discussed earlier and reflects the components of the story fairly well. However, it implies that the culminating point of the culminating action (lines 26, 27–29) is disjunct from the two steps that lead up to it. And it suggests no consistent principle for the grouping of verses in larger units. The five units demarcated in the text consist of 3, 2, 3, 4, and 4 verses, respectively. Such divisions of the story are ad hoc, reflecting a certain sense of the story; but they are either merely conveniences for reading and reference, or invitations to attribute openings, closings, and sequences on the basis of one's own unexamined impressions. Ethnopoetic analysis that liberates the lines of a story on the page and allows their disposition to have aesthetic effect also opens up the sources of effect to cumulative scientific study.

VIII

An anthology must almost inevitably conceal the qualities of a narrator. This is because an anthology typically presents only one telling of a story. The reader cannot discover what is due to the tradition of the community and what is due to the particular performance. The depths of the art, the interplay of convention and option, are thus hidden from sight.

The Kalapuya story of Coyote and the water dammed by Frogs permits a deeper view, because we are fortunate enough to have more than one telling. William Hartless told the story to L. J. Frachtenberg in 1914 in Mary's River, a dialect entirely mutually intelligible with John B. Hudson's Santiam —Jacobs indeed checked Hartless's dictations with Hudson in 1936 (Jacobs 1945:204; the text of this story is in Jacobs 1945:236-44).

Hartless told the story as the first act of a five-act sequence, and I will take up the implications of that later. Here let us compare the first act to Hudson's account of the same tradition.

In Hartless's account, the alignment of the narrative in verses, stanzas, and scenes is for the most part readily apparent. In the first scene, Coyote decides to travel (lines 1-8), does travel (9-14), and becomes thirsty (15-20). The first stanza (1-8) uniquely pairs Coyote and his wife. The second stanza (9-14) uniquely reports the travel in a three-part arc: he goes, goes on, camps; morning, he goes again, he camps again; he goes five days (the five indicating a summative statement). The third stanza (15-20) uniquely recounts his thirst and a colloquy about satisfying it.

The next three stanzas establish the bargain with the Frogs. Each begins with travel by Coyote (21-22, 31, 37-38). In the first and third stanzas (D, F), the travel frames a four-part colloquy with the Frogs, five verses in all. In between comes the report of Coyote's going off to make himself appear wealthy. Thus, both these first two scenes make reported travel intermediate to initial and closing turns at talk. So, in a sense, does the third and last. It begins with Coyote's beginning to drink, including further dialogue with the Frogs (G). Then there is a report of the action of drinking, tearing the earth, being hit, releasing the water and the fish (H). The third and final stanza again has speech, but now only Coyote speaks, pronouncing to the Frogs. (This pattern suggests a style distinct from Hudson's reserving direct speech for the end of the first and the last scenes.)

All verses begin with a time expression ("one day," "in the morning," "five days") or an initial particle marker ("now then," "to be sure") or consist of a distinct turn at talk. The exception is at the beginning. As with Hudson's telling, the narrative action proper does not start the story. First, the story is framed. Here there is a parallelism: Coyote stayed there / There stayed his wife. It matches the parallelism that follows in what he says, first by himself, then to his wife. Such initial framing seems part of a general practice of bracketing the action off from the immediate setting and everyday life (see the discussion of closings as a renewal of that relationship in Hymes 1981b: 322–27). Openings and closings together seem the devices for making narration of myth participate in what Marcuse considers the power of art to contradict and transform reality (1978). Such power requires the autonomy of aesthetic form. In these initial lines of myths, lacking narrative tense or narrative particle, often formulaic ("Coyote was going along"), we have signals of such autonomy. To omit or revise them is an aesthetic blunder or even a crime.

"Buy it" is italicized for emphasis in line 26 because the form (*da'yanda*) contrasts with later *de'yanda* (42) in the same way as the form in line 8 does with the forms in lines 9 and 32 of Hudson's story. Notice that the particle in line 47 stands as a line and verse itself and seems to be a placeholder in the pattern. The pairing of lines 1, 2; 3–4, 5–6; 12, 13; 33, 34; 64, 65, 68–69 within the three- and five-part patterning remains always subordinate to that patterning. Thus lines 55–63 (H abc) correspond in purport and length to lines 22–29 of Hudson's telling (iii abcdef) but do not have the intensity of pairing raised to the level of verses. Something like that intensity does occur at the end, where the final pronouncement interweaves two topics— you are not to keep the water (71–73, 74, 78); you will be frogs (75–77, 79)— with three occurrences of the main, first topic formulaicly (71, 74, 78) but only two turns for the second topic. The formulaic lines suggest three sets of pairs (ababab), but the content suggests a five-part sequence (aabab). Note finally that (H) (e) unites three dispersions: Coyote, water, fish.

Here is Hartless's narrative:

Coyote Releases Water and Salmon Dammed by the Frogs

(i) (He travels and become thirsty)

(A)

Coyote stayed there.	(a)	1
There stayed his wife.	(b)	2
One day he said,	(c)	3
"I'm going to take a look around the country."		4
Now then he told his wife.	(d)	5
"I'm going to take a look around the country."		6
His wife said,	(e)	7
"All right. Go."		8

(B)

To be sure, Coyote went,	(a)	9
he went on and on,		10
he camped overnight.		11
In the morning he went off again indeed,	(b)	12
he camped overnight again indeed.		13
Five days he went.	(c)	14

(C)

Now then he got thirsty for water.	(a)	15
Now then he was told,	(b)	16
"Over there is water:		17
"Oh, there's a big price for the water."		18
(—),	(c)	
"Oh, I am thirsty for water.		19
"I will just have to drink."		20

(ii) (He deceives the Frogs
into selling him water)

(D)

To be sure, he went,	(a)	21
he got there.		22
"I want water,"	(b)	23
he said.		24
Frog said,	(c)	25
"No. *Buy* it."		26
"Oh, I am thirsty for water,"	(d)	27
Coyote said.		28
Frog said,	(e)	29
"You cannot drink it now!"		30

	(E)
Now then Coyote went off.	(a) 31
Now then he dug camas,	(b) 32
he took the camas's tails,	33
he took a lot.	34
He made them (appear to be) money dentalia.	35
Now then he changed himself (to appear rich).	(c) 36

	(F)
Now then he went back again indeed,	(a) 37
he got to where the water was.	38
"I want water,"	(b) 39
said Coyote.	40
Frog said,	(c) 41
"Buy it.	42
"How much now do you want?"	43
Coyote said,	(d) 44
"Give me that much now."	45
(−)	(e)
"All right. I will give it to you."	46

(iii) (He frees the water and the fish)

	(G)
To be sure.	(a) 47
Now then Coyote put on five hats.	(b) 48
Now then Coyote kneeled down to drink.	(c) 49
Frog said,	(d) 50
"Swallow five times,	51
"Then stop."	52
Coyote said,	(e) 53
"All right."	54

	(H)
To be sure, Coyote drank.	(a) 55
He put his hand down into the earth,	56
he wanted to tear it open.	57
To be sure, now then Coyote was hit.	(b) 58
Another came again indeed,	59
she hit Coyote.	60
There were five indeed of the Frogs,	61
they hit and hit Coyote.	62
Now then Coyote tore open the water.	(c) 63
To be sure it broke through,	(d) 64
the water broke through.	65

Now then Coyote ran in flight.   (e) 66

 The water went,   67

  all the salmon went out,   68

   all sorts of things.   69

                    (I)

Now then Coyote said,   (a) 70

 "You are not to be keeping the water!   71

  "Everyone will drink,   72

  "They will not buy it.   73

 "You must not be keeping the water.   74

  "You will be bullfrogs,   75

  "You will live on the riverbank,   76

  "That is to be your place.   77

 "But you must never keep the water.   78

  "You are to inhabit the riverbank."   79

Let us note that the implicit alignment in the original publication (Jacobs 1945:236–37) scarcely approximates Hartless's organization of the story. Plain Arabic numerals are used to divide the story into two main parts: 1. (lines 1–14) and 2. (lines 15–80). The division corresponds to the first two stanzas of the first scene and then all the rest. Within the rest, the alignment is as follows:

(−)   15–22   (overrides travel in 21–22)
(2)   23–34   (overrides travel in 31)
(3)   35–43   (interrupts colloquy)
(4)   44–52   (interrupts one colloquy, does not reach end of other)
(5)   53–60   (interrupts sequence of Frogs' hitting Coyote)
(6)   61–66   (interrupts triple dispersion)
(7)   67–74   (interrupts pronouncement)
(8)   75–79

Now let us compare the actual alignments of the two tellings. Both have three scenes with analogous roles: Coyote intends to drink; he strikes a bargain with the Frogs; he frees the water. Within this common frame of what appears to be Kalapuya tradition, the two tellings further share as incident that Coyote is going along; that he deceives the Frogs by substituting something else for dentalia; that while he drinks he tears open the dam with his hand; that he pronounces the general availability of water. A common strand, or matrix, of incident can be inferred, granted a certain degree of abstraction: (1) appetite; (2) deception as to identity or possession; (3) trade; (4) deception in action; (5) detection and bodily punishment; situation is righted (6) by freeing the water and (7) by establishing that it will stay free. The two tellings can be summarized as follows (Hudson above Hartless):

(1)	(2)	(3)	(4)	(5)	(6)–(7)
hungry	deer rib	trade	drink, dig		free water, pronounce
thirsty	camas, rich	trade	drink, dig	head hit	free water, fish, pronounce

In terms of alignment of line and verse and other basic dimensions of narrative comparison, however, the profiles of the two tellings are quite distinct. There are two standard beginning frames for a Coyote story: He was going along, he was staying somewhere. Hudson uses the first, Hartless the second. Coyote and Frogs are the core of the actor matrix in both, but Hartless parallels Coyote at the outset with a wife (and at the end of his five-part sequence, refers to Coyote's children). Thus, Hartless devotes a first stanza to Coyote's decision to leave a domestic setting to look around (scene i, stanza A) and a second stanza (B) to travel itself, which Hudson simply announces at the outset with a conventional line. Hudson proceeds at once to the provision of false dentalia, by way of an accidental encounter conjoined with Coyote's appetite. Hartless holds the provision of false dentalia to be a response to unnatural monopoly in the second scene. Hudson reports here that the Frogs make people buy water, but Hartless withholds identification of the Frogs until the next scene. He does have someone tell a now thirsty Coyote that there is a high price for water. The two tellings converge at the end of the first scene, in that both have Coyote say he will drink.

In the middle scene, for Hudson, Coyote arrives, offers, and the deal is struck. His Frogs are eager at once. Hartless has the Frogs enact their turning of the communal resource into private property by refusing Coyote at first, since at first he has no money. Then comes a stanza of the making of false dentalia (from camas plants) and of his own appearance as being someone rich. A second colloquy (I want water: Buy it) leads to an agreement, couched in quite specific terms (that much). All told, there are two colloquies and three stanzas, instead of one.

In the final scene, Hudson's Coyote proceeds immediately to drink and dig, and the outcome is immediate as well. Hartless has Coyote prepare for attack when he digs (a full, fivefold round), and the Frogs display further their penny pinching, before the action starts. Where Hudson intensifies the climax by poetic form, pairing verses, Hartless does it by having Coyote persevere while being attacked five times. (We are to infer that each Frog, hitting Coyote, broke one of the five hats—this device is elaborated that way in Columbia River versions.) When the water breaks through, this Coyote runs in flight, perhaps having no remaining defenses, or perhaps to get out of the way of the water, or both. Flight in parallel circumstances in the fourth myth of Hartless's sequence is to escape community outrage, and so that is presumably an element here. Where Hudson's Coyote proceeds directly to pronouncement, Hartless's Coyote must perhaps return to speak from a distance, but in any case takes not one, but nine lines, both remonstrating against the Frogs in establishing freedom of water and assigning them their place in the world to come. Again, two colloquies and three stanzas instead of one.

What unites all this difference most of all, formally, is *doubling*. Hartless doubles the common ingredients some seven times. His initial frame has both a domestic setting and then travel, not travel alone. His Coyote has an appetite of the mind (curiosity), not just of the body (thirst, hunger). When deception as to wealth is called for, his Coyote dissembles both dentalia and personal appearance, not the bead alone. The colloquy negotiating for water is doubled: a no to the moneyless Coyote, a yes to the seemingly rich one. The deception involved in digging with the hand while drinking is extended, and in a sense doubled, by the detection and reprisal of the Frogs, beating Coyote on the head one by one. (Hudson here doubles poetic form.) When the situation is righted, there is doubling at three levels. When the water breaks through, it does so in two parallel lines (64–65); Coyote goes as well as the water, and the going of water is also the going of fish. Finally, the establishment of what is to be speaks not only of water but also of Frogs.[4]

What unites and motivates these differences in terms of theme and attitude is clarified by the rest of Hartless's myth, but one element is clear in these two tellings themselves and connects with the display of the differences in alignment and elaboration. The conceptions of Coyote are linked to the use of *turns at talk*. In the outer scenes, Hudson's Coyote speaks only at the end, alone. He is a transformer at his task, stating his purpose and his conclusion. In between he and the Frogs do use a transitive verb (-*niSdini* 'told him') with each other in their one exchange. But that suggestion of reciprocity only serves to heighten the immediate downfall. This is a foresighted Coyote but not one much for talk.

Hartless's Coyote is quite different. One aspect of the elaboration of his telling is the elaboration of turns at talk. His Coyote speaks alone at beginning and end, announcing his curiosity (line 4) and pronouncing, but the first is immediately repeated to his wife (6), with the one occurrence in the telling of the transitive verb (-*niSni* 'told'), and the last has the Frogs as audience, even if they are given no turn at talk. In between come two exchanges in scene i (Coyote and wife, someone and Coyote); two pairs of exchanges (Coyote and Frog) in (ii); and one exchange in (iii). The relations among the exchanges express the point of the story. The two in the first scene show Coyote in relations of freely given advice and concurrence. The remaining scenes each show an initial pair in which Coyote is rejected (ii) or told what to do (iii) and a final pair in which Coyote, having dissembled, gains the day: water to purchase (ii), water for all (iii). And this pattern of outer stanzas with talk, an inner stanza without talk, in each scene is characteristic of Hartless's first act, as against Hudson's reserving of speech for the end of each of the outer scenes, which are essentially reported action, the only colloquy being in the middle scene. All in all, Hartless's Coyote is embedded in a social world of frequent talk, both in this first act and in the rest of the myth.

Here is a display of the differences in alignment and elaboration, with Hudson's telling to the left and Hartless's to the right. Verses containing direct speech have their line numbers italicized. The order in the Hartless telling is broken in order to show the parallelism of the double colloquy in the first and last stanzas of scene ii:

Scene i

		A abcde	(1, 2, 3–4, 5–6, 7–8)
a	(line 1)	B abc	(9–11, 12–13, 14)
a	(2–3), bc (4–5, 6)		
d	(7–9)	C b	(16–18)
e	(10–12)	Cac	(15, 19–20)

Scene ii

		Da/Fa	(21–22)/(37–38)
a	(13)	Db/Fb	(23–24)/(39–40)
b	(14–17)	Dc/Fc	(25–26)/(41–43)
c	(18–21)	Dd/Fd	(27–28)/(44–45)
		De/Fe	(29–30)/(46)
		E abc	(31, 32–35, 36)
		(F: see D above)	

Scene iii

		G abcde	(47, 48, 49, 50–52, 53–54)
ab	(22, 23)	H a	(55–57)
cd	(24, 25)	b	(58–62)
ef	(26, 27–29)	c	(63)
g	(30)	de	(64–65, 66–69)
h	(31)	I	(70–80)

IX

Perhaps the doubling by Hartless stems from the dual outcome, release of both water and fish, pointing toward it. Certainly, the doubling establishes a narrative framework for the rest of his five-part myth and, I think, has the purpose of doing so. The doubling seems to underscore a frame of reference, in terms of which otherwise disjunct Coyote adventures will be connected in order to explore, through narrative, a common theme from a certain point of view or attitude. Four well-known and widespread adventures are so organized: loss of eyes, trading anuses, trading penises, making a fish trap.

This integration is unique to Hartless, so far as our knowledge of the region permits us to judge. Of course, the knowledge that we have is no more than the scattered tips of what was once an ever-renewing armada of icebergs. Within Kalapuya itself, we have only one other principal source, Hudson, who "heard Santiam and other Kalapuya dialect myths frequently when he was a youngster . . . but . . . the few that he remembers are the ones he heard with especial frequency" (Jacobs 1945:85). In any case, no sequence or cycle of Coyote stories is attested to. Besides the story of the release of water from the Frogs, Hudson did know another story in which Coyote encounters Frog women and then loses his eyes (Jacobs 1945:96–103); so did Hartless (Jacobs 1945:231–35). The encounter with Frog women involves salmon, but is distinct: they ask the passing Coyote for some; he deceives them with hornets (as in the Alsea story rewritten in the Erdoes and Ortiz anthology [384–85]). The women revive and cause snow that leads Coyote to enclose himself in a tree. Unable to get a woodpecker to release him, he throws out his body parts, and one eye is taken in the process, which people use to play shinny or gamble; Coyote retrieves it and escapes by disguising himself. The versions by Hudson and Hartless are distinct in a variety of details. Together with the first two parts of Hartless's cycle, they show a broad Kalapuya tradition of an encounter with Frog women followed by loss of eyes.

Hudson also told a story of Coyote trading anuses (Jacobs 1945: 113–15), but with a man. The motive, to stand out at dances, is the same, and the consequence, inability to catch game, is the same, but the game here is not birds, but gophers; after the trade back, Coyote is shown successful in catching a gopher and saying that is what he will always do when hungry. Catching gophers is associated with Coyote in the myths of the Takelma and the Maidu as well. No story of trading penises or making a fish trap is attested from Hudson, although probably he heard such things as a youth, as both narrative themes are popular in the region. Also, as I have said, there is no sequence.

The Coyote cycles that we do know from the region nonetheless suggest that Hartless's integration is unique. The sequence dictated to Franz Boas by Charles Cultee in both Shoalwater and Kathlamet Chinook has integration, but an integration of repetition. In one after another place, Coyote discovers through failure the customs for successful fishing that are part of the locality's nature. He is constant while the customs change. A geographical framework also prevails in the Clackamas and Wishram-Wasco Chinook Coyote cycles. The adventures Hartless organizes are known in Clackamas. The release of salmon, kept by two women (Grizzly Bears), is the second half of a myth of Raccoon and Coyote. The other four elements of the Hartless sequence are present and occur close to one another (eighth, ninth, seventh, eleventh in the series), but the only framework is that Coyote is going along, twice explicitly upriver. The cycle known to the Wasco and Wishram speakers does start with the release of salmon kept by two women (Swallows); trading penises with subsequent curing of a girl and making a fish trap are included. But again, there is no apparent linkage other than travel upriver from west to east.

Deliberate selection and grouping on Hartless's part seem all the more likely because he is the source of another Coyote sequence that emphasizes traveling along (Jacobs 1945: 222–26).[5] Its frame is similar: Coyote tells his wife he wants to go look around the country, but his curiosity is elaborated in speech:

Now then one day he said,
   "I am lonesome."
Now then he said,
   "I will go away,
   "I will look around the country.
   "I wonder what the people are doing.
   "Maybe some person is living up that way.
   "I will go look at the people.
   "I do rather want to see the country."
Now then he told his wife,
   "I am going to leave you.
   "I am going to look around the country."

The frame is doubled: he stays a year where people are playing shinny and gambling, again marries, and again goes along, saying, "I will really get back again." Three incidents follow; two double the situation of people lacking water because they are ignorantly afraid of something in the water. The same theme is part of the Clackamas and Wishram cycles involving white salmon, which Coyote shows the people how to catch and eat. Here the white salmon is preceded by crawfish. There follows an adventure with mouthless people, for whom Coyote cuts mouths. They ask him to remain and offer him a wife, but he replies, "Oh, no. I will be going along first. If when I do get back again, then I may do that. But I will rather still be going along now." Hartless provides as a formal close:

Now then to be sure Coyote went along.
Maybe indeed he is still coming. (Jacobs 1945:226)

The third decision not to stay for a woman, the rounding out again with the desire to go along (twice said), and the epilogue itself certainly highlight the traveling Coyote of other sequences. It is as if Hartless kept the traveling aspect of Coyote for this one sequence; in the other sequence, which concerns us here, Coyote goes along only to connect actions, ending at a place where he gets children.

In another myth (Jacobs 1945:236–44), Hartless uses the canonical pattern of five parts and a common narrative framework to do more than link picaresque and explanatory adventures in a geographical sequence. He explores the nature of Coyote as trickster-transformer; the adventures are selected and ordered to this purpose. The sequence of adventures is woven together in several ways. From one standpoint, there are an inner layer and an outer layer. The outer pair of acts involves provision of food (fish, fish trap) and domestic setting (wife, children). The inner trio involves exchange of body parts (eyes, anuses, penises). But this is only one of four ways in which the stories form an interwoven set. A second way groups the first three against the rest. Each of the first three involves trade with women who are creatures in the world to come (Frogs, Snail, Nightingale). The rest can be taken as a second, complementary triad, since the fourth part has two internal parts: attempted intercourse and successful copulation. The fifth mentions children, and while the copulation and the children are not causally connected, the post hoc placement suggests a narrative propter hoc. All the other actors in this second triad are simply people, as if the world to come, that of the people, were now near, brought near by casting alone.

From a third vantage point, the sequence constitutes a three-part structure, pairing the first two acts, then the third and fourth, before the fifth. The first two acts show Coyote as a normative trickster-transformer, as in Hudson's story: his own bodily appetites and capacity to deceive serve authentic need. We have seen communal need for water and fish served in the first act. In the second, Coyote, having fallen asleep in a warm sun, wakes to find that Blue Jay has stolen his eyes. Making imitation eyes out of rose hips, he convinces an old woman that he can see a louse crawling along a hair in the sky; he persuades her to trade eyes and to give him her eyes first. Leaving, despite her protest on discovery, he says:

You are not to have eyes!
You will be a snail!
You will barely go along.

In the third act, going along, Coyote finds a woman sewing and breaking wind. He prevails upon her to trade anuses, thinking of the laughter and attention he will get with hers in an assemblage. But envy and desire for attention prove his undoing. Whenever he tries to catch a bird, the anus makes its noise and the bird escapes. Hunger forces him to trade back.

In the fourth act, going along, Coyote finds an old man with a gigantic penis that must be fed wood chips, and he then sees five girls swimming in the river. He prevails upon the old man to trade and puts his new penis in the river, raising it under the girl he wants so that when she jumps, it fits inside her. Her companions come to her aid and pull her back, thus pulling Coyote in. He has to call to them to cut it off and then has to trade back with the old man.

The second part of this fourth act—a fifth unit in some respects—begins with Coyote again in need of a body part, the tip of his penis. Notice especially that the widespread sequel of Coyote pretending to be an old shaman (medicine man, doctor) unfolds here with a structure that closely parallels the first act. There, Coyote was told that there was water; here, he tells an old woman that there is a capable shaman (himself). There, Coyote dissembled as a wealthy man; here, as the old shaman. There, the Frogs refused to deal when first asked; here, invited by the headman of the village of the sick girl (who lies abed with the penis tip still in her), Coyote first declines, then says tomorrow, then agrees to come today. And, extraordinarily, and it would seem intentionally, the deception in action at the end has *the same five elements in almost the same order.* There, Coyote dug while drinking; here, he inserts his penis while singing. In both he reaches and removes the obstruction (the dirt of the dam, the tip of his severed penis); in both the result is the release of stopped up water. In both Coyote is detected. There, it was while digging before the release; here, it is when he arrives. Another coyote warns that he also is a coyote; the attempted detection is rebuked but then undertaken by the people themselves, after the water's release, when Coyote inside is copulating, while the birds he called upon conceal the girl's screams with loud singing. A louse, a flea, and finally, successfully, a water spider are sent across the flowing water to find out what is happening. Here, as in the first act, Coyote goes in flight. The angry people kill the birds that had helped Coyote sing, including ducks and geese, two of the kind that had escaped him when he had Nightingale's anus—perhaps implying that he now can compass their deaths, even if indirectly.

The fifth part is just three lines:

Now then Coyote came on downstream.
  He fixed a fish basket trap;
    at that place there he got his children.

All four full acts end with the establishment of the nature of one or more actors: the Frogs, who are to live on the river bank; Snail, who is to go slowly; Nightingale and Coyote, restored to anus equilibrium; the girl and Coyote, restored to equilibrium with regard to the tip of his penis. (The fourth act doubles the incident of penis restoration, first with the trade back with the old man.) Notice that the Frogs and Snail bespeak the world to come, when their natures will be different. The actions with Nightingale and the girl— the two motivated by needs neither necessary nor authentic—do not. Each restores an equilibrium. In each Coyote must trade back to regain that equilibrium, motivated in the second trade by a self-inflicted, authentic need (hunger, injured penis).

It is as though the successful joining of need and ability to deceive in the first two acts has inspired hubris in the second two. A pair of pronouncements for the world to come is succeeded by a pair of lessons leading simply to restoration of a previous balance—though the successful copulation that rounds off the fourth act is a bonus. Perhaps it is a bonus because Coyote is now in a state of actual bodily need, and his ability to deceive serves not only himself but also the sick girl and her community and headman. Restored to an action with an ingredient of common good, Coyote is ready to proceed with other necessary acts of setting the world right for the people to come. The well-known incident of making the first fish trap is briefly mentioned as an indication. But the real story—the exploration of Coyote's own nature in the context of the natures of others—is over.

The third act is pivotal in such a sequence, serving equally as outcome of the first series of three acts and as onset of the last three. This pivotal act is of course that with Nightingale, the one that first enacts the lesson of equilibrium restored. The third act equally has this pivotal role when the sequence is regarded from the standpoint of the fourth act having two parts, the second completing a five-part sequence within the four full acts. (The fifth act epilogue, functionally completing the fourth as an establishment for the future [fish trap], in this way also completes a trio with the first and second acts.) The explicit parallelism between the first act and the second part of the fourth act, including the detailed elaboration of release of water and flight, suggests this aspect of five within four, plus epilogue. The second part of the fourth act seems to be a rounding out of a cycle of exploration, through narrative, of Coyote's nature.

We are shown, then, a Coyote who has to "return to the place to know it for the first time" (to adapt T. S. Eliot's *Four Quartets*). He can use deception to trade for a body part when he truly needs it (eyes); when he trades for the sake of popularity or sex, he is thwarted and has to trade back. The underlying, organizing attitude seems to be this: *Coyote's nature, just as much as the natures of those he transforms, is already written in the scheme of things.* However, being Coyote, he can explore the truths of this nature through experience. (The presence of a second coyote, warning about the deceiving Coyote, seems further to build into the narrative the polarity of Coyote nature.)

The architecture of the five-part sequence weaves the actions together, as we have seen, in four ways:

(1) 1 (2-3-4) (5) (outer, inner) (*exchange body parts*)
(2) (1-2-3) (4a-4b-5) (*trade with women*)
(3) (1-2) (3-4) (5) (+/- *normative coyote*)
(4) (1-2-3-4a-4b) (5) (*motives established*)

This multiplicity of relationships seems to strengthen the integration of the whole.

The utilization of the framework of incidents can be summarized as follows. The elements are: (A) appetite or need; (B) deception as to identity, body part, or possession; (C) a trade; (D) a deception in action; (E) sometimes a detection and bodily punishment; (F) a righting of the situation; (G) an establishing of what should be.

Act I shows ABCDEFG: thirst; deception with false dentalia and as rich man; trade for water; digging while drinking; detection and hitting on head; freeing of water and salmon; establishment of principle as to water, location of frogs.

Act II shows ABDCFG: blind; deception as to eyesight; deception in trade (you first); trade for eyes; restore own eyesight; eyesight and pace of snails.

Act III shows ABCDEACF: envy; self-deception in expectation of control; trade anus; self-deception in action (hunting); self-punishment (slaps anus); hunger; trade back; restoration of own anus.

Act IV(a) shows ABCDEC: lust; deceives self as to expectation (control); trade penis; deceives girls underwater; tip cut off (directed by self); trade back.

Act IV (b) showsABCDF: tip lacking; deceives as old shaman; negotiates to come as shaman (involving payment in the culture); deceives underneath cover of singing to cure; girl and Coyote restored by recovery of tip.

Act V shows G: establishment of fish trap.

X

If an anthology may, by absence of comparison, conceal the qualities of a narrator, at times an analysis dedicated to comparison may also do so. Such is the case with this myth in the fourth volume of *Mythologiques* by Claude Lévi-Strauss, *L'homme nu* (trans. *The Naked Man,* 1981). Structural analysis, of which Lévi-Strauss is the preeminent representative, takes its inspiration in important part from the linguistic principle that structure can be validated *internally.* That is, relationships within the object of analysis show its proper structure. This "emic" perspective developed in contrast to a perspective that could find organization in cultural materials only from the outside, "etically." In the first part of his *Mythologiques* (1964–1971), Lévi-Strauss shows very detailed analysis of myths. The close covariation of details gives the analyses credibility; certainly, transformational relationships do obtain between myths. It is Lévi-Strauss's historical accomplishment to have discovered this.

As he nears the end of his analytical journey, however, Lévi-Strauss often approaches new myths too readily in the light of the old and without the concern for close covariation of detail that informed his initial work. The respect for the integrity of the object of analysis, which must be the first concern of structural analysis, seems to disappear. Myths are selectively cited, retitled, conflated. In the present case the two tellings by Hudson and Hartless are thrown together as "Kalapuya."

Lévi-Strauss correctly says of the Kalapuya tradition, "It is clear that this version stresses the release of *drinking water* rather than that of *edible fish*" (1981:256). However, this statement fails to note that Hudson's telling mentions only water, while Hartless's telling mentions *fish* as well, and that the place of fish in Hartless's telling is shown to have significance by its framing of the longer myth (fish in the first act, fish trap in the last).

By omitting the connection of Hartless's telling to the further acts of which it is a part, Lévi-Strauss contradicts the very point he uses the story partly to make! In these pages he criticizes Sapir for failing to recognize that parts of a myth, even if found elsewhere as separate entities, together constitute a coherent whole (Jacobs 1958:255, 261). Yet, he ignores the coherent whole of the Hartless myth, attending to just the first of the five acts and conflating it with Hudson's separate version.

The difficulty is compounded when Lévi-Strauss relates the first part, not to the rest of its own myth (in Hartless's telling), but to another Kalapuya myth, which is said to make it possible to suggest why there is stress on release of drinking water. He turns to Hudson's telling in Santiam Kalapuya of "Panther, Coyote, Whale's Daughter, the Flood, Obtaining the Fire" (Jacobs 1945:103–13; the myth has a Clackamas Chinook analogue [Jacobs 1958:52–67] not cited by Lévi-Strauss; see also "Flint and His Son's Son [Panther]" [Lévi-Strauss 1981:166–79]). The point of the comparison is that the preceding myth "is concerned with the *obtaining* of drinking *water* by the *demolition* of a dam, and that the Kalapuya have an exactly symmetrical myth explaining the *loss* of cooking *fire* resulting from the *erection* of another dam" (Lévi-Strauss 1981:256). But this latter myth, retitled by Lévi-Strauss "The Fire Which Was Lost and Found Again" (which is not the main point of the story), has no dam in it at all. To be sure, there is a dam that causes loss of fire (cooking is not mentioned) in the Mary's River version told by Hartless (Jacobs 1945:215–21; see p. 221). Lévi-Strauss notes it in these words: "[It] adds the detail that he [Coyote] built a dam downstream in the hope of recovering his children, who were being swept along by the current. This created the flood which is also mentioned in [the preceding myth], although its precise cause is not stated there" (1981:258). The preceding myth, Hudson's telling in Santiam, is in fact explicit. The cause is not a dam, but hair. Water pursues the people up a mountain (all this is after the main action involving the matrix of Panther and Coyote as alternate spouses of the same woman). Fire is carried along by Copperhead Snake. Here are the relevant lines from Hudson's text:

Now then the people said to Panther,
    "What have you taken?
    "This water does not want to go back."
Now then he said,
    "I took nothing.
    "I took only my child,
    "and I took that woman's hair."
"Oh,"
    the people said,
"Throw away that hair of hers.
"Maybe it is that which it is pursuing."

Panther tells small Chicken Hawk to throw the hair into the water, and to be sure, the water goes down. When the people then say that there is no fire, Copperhead Snake explains that he has it in his mouth and trades it to Panther for a deer-hide blanket.

In short, no dam and no loss of fire. Hudson and Hartless here, as before, do not tell the same story, at least not at the level of precise detail assumed by such analysis.

The problem of conflation of tellings is compounded when Lévi-Strauss goes on to contrast the myth with the withholding of water: "Conversely, one individual is able to deprive the community of fire and to appropriate it, because a newly built dam prevents water from flowing, holds it back and creates a flood" (Lévi-Strauss 1981:258). Earlier, he speaks of "a myth which conjures up an era when even indispensable possessions like fire could be monopolized by a selfish minority, and enjoyment of them had to be negotiated" (1981:258). Now, the dam occurs only in one of the two tellings (Hartless's), and it is built by Coyote *to try to save his children.* In the story with the dam, there is neither monopoly nor negotiation. After the flood, first Hummingbird is sent to get fire from where the sun rises, then, successfully, Copperhead Snake. He simply brings it to Panther, and again they have fire.

The negotiation for fire with Copperhead Snake is in Hudson's version, which has no dam. And the trading is amicable; no deception is required. Copperhead is delighted, once he gets a skin dry enough to produce the sound (x̣ax̣ax̣ax̣x̣x̣····) he will make as he goes along. To be sure, the lower-class people are left out. They have to capture fire by dancing with pitch wood in their regalia around the fire that the upper-class people want to keep as their own. But that is class struggle, not individual appropriation or subsequent negotiation.

Throughout his work, Lévi-Strauss tends to focus on the origin of culture out of nature—fire, cooked food, water as a resource. No doubt that is why the elements of fire and water in these myths attract him. Now, Hartless's story could be said to end with an explanatory incident that has to do with nature versus culture. Coyote's dam causes a flood that causes a general loss of fire, which is restored, as we have seen, from a natural source (where the sun rises). But Hudson's story ends with an epilogue that concerns social structure. It follows the in-law conflict of the main plot (Panther versus his wife's people). Trade with the one who has preserved fire benefits only the upper class, so that the lower-class people (Coyote among them) have to dance for their tinder, deceive, and flee. The identification of Coyote with a lower class, scorned by an upper class that identifies with chiefs like Panther, is explicit. It fits Coyote's getting the better of a headman's daughter in the fourth act of Hartless's cycle. It suggests a use of myth as social criticism, as a contested territory in cultural hegemony. But to pursue such questions, one would have to treat Hartless's Mary's River myths and Hudson's Santiam myths each as distinct traditions and performances, having each an expressive and therefore verbal integrity of its own. Before speaking of what the "Kalapuya tradition" is, one would therefore have to speak of William Hartless and John B. Hudson.

To sum up, two tellings are conflated to present a picture in which the following is true of Kalapuya tradition:

dam causes flood
flood causes loss of fire
fire is regained through trade

The facts of the matter are these:

	Hudson	Hartless
flood caused by	hair	dam
fire is	saved	lost
fire regained by	trade	quest

As to the dam, it seems no accident that all the stories in the region of Coyote, releasing fish, or water, or both have him releasing it or them from monopoly by *women*. Fish and the mythical figure of Salmon are connected with ambivalence and tension between the genders, the necessary mutual dependence and reciprocity going together with a projected struggle for dominance or even elimination of the other (see Hymes 1985a). It also seems no accident that Coyote twice releases water by deceiving women in Hartless's myth, both times to the discomfiture of the women, but both times to the general good and, the second time, to the good of the woman herself. There within Hartless's own myth is a second obstruction that illuminates the first.

Structural analysis generally ought to be based on ethnopoetic analysis, for meaning may depend upon shape (see chapter 6), and the careful attention to verbal detail required in ethnopoetic analysis is also a requisite of convincing structural analysis. Without respect for the specific text and the individual narrator, apparent precision casts forth an imprecise blur.[6]

The one lesson that seems difficult to learn is that myths are performed and thereby shaped, both in performance and in reflection between performances, by individuals. Even the heroic collector and preserver of what we reliably know about Kalapuya tradition, Melville Jacobs, succumbed to the ethnological habit of dissolving individual lives into processes labeled with group names. In his monograph, Jacobs comments on the French-Canadian stories of Petit Jean known by Hartless in terms of a general French-Canadian influence in the region. His original notes disclose that Hartless had a specific French-Canadian family connection (Zenk 1984). Perhaps the unreflecting practices of anthologies, structural analyses, and ethnology can at last be overcome by the simple fact that ethnopoetics requires one to start with language, and starting with language will at last make clear that the first literature of the continent is known to us through shaping minds that bear names such as Hudson and Hartless.

Index of Tribal Groups in Erdoes and Ortiz

15

Notes toward (an Understanding of) Supreme Fictions

My topic is change in oral narrative and, more particularly, in those serious oral narratives we commonly call myths. My examples come from the Indians of North America, mostly from the North Pacific Coast. My theme is that understanding change and whatever else one may wish to understand about these narratives involves the fact that they are literature. Not in the sense of being "literate," of course, but in the sense of being literary, of having characteristics in common with what we accept as literary art. Three authors afford a useful framework for establishing this: Robert Alter, on biblical narrative; Michael Riffaterre, on nineteenth-century novels; and A. J. Greimas, on narratology.

I take a title from Wallace Stevens, because, when asked to write, it struck me that if the tellers of the myths I have most studied had had the chance to reflect on their art, to look at it, as is were, with sympathy and distance, they might well agree that Stevens got it right: it must be abstract; it must change; it must give pleasure. After considering the three authors, I turn to these three "musts." Much of what is said in regard to literary art has to do with change, but my view of it will be put forward under the Stevens rubrics (Stevens 1947:115–48).

Ong and Alter

Literature that is oral is often set apart. One may read, for example, that orality implies oral-formulaic composition. For hundreds of oral traditions in the world, that is not so. In particular, it is not so for the traditions of the North Pacific Coast of the New World, which I have studied for forty years. The oral-formulaic approach, while it has usefulness for many traditions of the Old World, does not easily fit all of them, and a recent survey, although it tends to identify the approach with "orality" itself, mentions not a single New World case. Work of the kind I draw on here, done under the heading of "ethnopoetics," goes unmentioned.[1] In sum, one who says "oral" need not say "formulaic."

Another writer with a conception of what orality must be, Walter Ong, describes oral narratives as necessarily "prolix" (1982). But the narratives of the North Pacific Coast are remarkably terse.[2]

A terse style is illuminatingly discussed by Robert Alter, who speaks of "the reticence of the biblical narrator" (1981:184) and credits Erich Auerbach (*Mimesis*) with having shown more clearly than anyone before him "how the cryptic conciseness of biblical narrative is a reflection of profound art, not primitiveness" (17). It is therefore disappointing that Alter considers such art to begin with the Hebrew Bible, as against not only the verse epics of neighboring societies but also folklore generally. Folktale serves as a foil in his account, a genre where one would not expect morally problematic interiority, where one finds fixed figures, where a pattern of repeated actions is mechanical (28-29, 32, 106). Others may share similar assumptions. Yet features that Alter singles out are features of oral narrative among Indian people of the North Pacific Coast.

Let me show respect for Alter's work by using it to suggest what one might call a Noachic covenant of narrative. Biblical narrative always will have a special place, but other traditions know something of the art it discloses.

Alter's Overviews

Alter provides two overviews (1981:95-97, 179-85). Let me first consider features brought out only in the concluding overview, then take up the features of the first (having to do with kinds of repetition).

(a) "Everything in the world of biblical narrative ultimately gravitates toward dialogue" (Alter 1981:182). So also in oral narrative generally. In Indian narrative, when activity and quoted speech are combined, what is said is almost invariably the culmination of the series, the endpoint of a formal unit. (See scenes i, ii, iii of the appended text).[3]

(b) Alter calls attention (1981:187) to alteration of a single term across turns of speech as often finely significant and part of a larger pattern of definition of character through contrastive dialogue. A favorite set form in Indian narratives is one in which a series of questions is pursued, all answers being rejected but the desired last. Two girls bathe, only to find their clothes taken by two men. They address the men through the range of kin terms, beginning with courtesy kinship, but at last give in and address them as "my husband."[4] A girl comes seeking a great hunter as husband, but he is not at home, and his unworthy partner pretends to be he. In bed at night, he touches the girl on her head, asking "What is this?" "My head." "No, our head." (The effect is particularly nice in Chinookan, where "our" can be expressed not only as plural, but as dual ["just you and I"].) And so on down to private parts.[5] In the Kathlamet "Sun's Myth," the chief who has found the house of the Sun asks a young girl about each of the kinds of valuable goods on the walls of the house. Each time she answers "whose" with "ours": they belong to her grandmother and herself and will be given away at her puberty rite. The contrast is both local and cumulative: each time, there is a contrast between men's wealth and the amazing answer that women own it and, ultimately, acceptance.[6]

(c) "In the Bible . . . the narrator's work is almost all *récit*, straight narration of actions and speech, and only exceptionally and very briefly *discours*, disquisition on and around the narrated facts and their implications" (Alter 1981:184). So with Indian narratives. Tellings to outsiders, especially in English, may be more elaborate, because they make explicit motives and details a Native audience could be expected to know. Sometimes a practiced source may even take on the role of collaborator, carefully interspersing ethnographic and linguistic explanation.[7] A revitalization movement, such as the Feather religion, and long solitary pondering may in old age produce a Coyote cycle in which Coyote inveterately intervenes to foretell and so explain. But these respond to the presence of anthropology and Christianity, and other narrators regard them as poorly told. Alter's words can stand as a criterion of traditional form.

(d) Alter calls attention to repetition of single words or phrases that often exhibits a frequency, saliency, and thematic significance not found in other narrative traditions. Exploration of the semantic range of a root and play with phonetic relatives is indeed distinctive. Its prevalence in the Hebrew Bible is not matched in Indian narrative.[8] Significant repetition of words and stems as such, however, is common. Word repetition is often a key to the boundaries and coherence of a formal unit. Repetition across units may be thematic, something that can be called a keyword (*Leitwort*). In the appended text ("Seal and Her Younger Brother Lived There"), each of the first two scenes has the mother twice respond to the daughter with "Shush!" (*Ak'washka);* the second response ends each scene. In the third, final scene, the daughter remonstrates, throwing back the very word. The point of the story, signaled by a title in which the mother (Seal) is named first, is the consequence of acting as does the mother, insisting on what is proper at the expense of what is apparent, something her "Shush!" sums up.

(e) Alter writes: "Where the narration so abundantly encourages us to expect this sort of repetition, on occasion the avoidance of repetition, whether through substitution of a synonym or of a wholly divergent word or phrase for the anticipated recurrence, may also be particularly revealing" (1981:

180; see 97–103 on varied repetition). In the appended text, it is in the moment of transformation and remonstrance, when the daughter assumes responsibility, that the explicit word "urination" is first used, as against the recurrent euphemism in the preceding scenes, "go out." Again, each speech by daughter and mother in the first two scenes and the beginning of the third is framed by a transitive verb, here translated 'told' (-*lxam*). But the mother responds to the first remonstrance by a formal lament, addressed, not to her daughter, but as if to the world at large, framed by the intransitive verb of speech that is not directly addressed, but broadcast (-*kim*). Though the daughter's final remonstrance cites the "told" of earlier exchanges, it is itself framed with the same intransitive word. This simple substitution defines the two as separate.

(f) Alter observes that a relational epithet generally tells us something substantive without recourse to explicit commentary (1981:180). In the appended text, the man to be murdered offstage is introduced in relation to the mother, "her younger brother," but throughout the action of the story both daughter and mother refer to him in relation to the girl, as "uncle." Therein is one indication that there is a second focus—not only the consequences of acting as the mother does, but also the experience of the girl.

(g) The term *motif* is used by Alter to indicate a recurrent "concrete image, sensory quality, action, or object," one without meaning in itself without the defining context of the narrative, which may be incipiently symbolic or primarily a means of effecting formal coherence (1981:95). In the appended text, there are two sequences of imagery and sensory quality. One is of darkness to light. Although the narrator says that the action of the first scene happened throughout a long, long time, the scenes together have implicitly the unity of a single evening and night. Families go outside to relieve themselves before retiring for the night (scene i); they go to bed, mother and daughter below close to a (presumably smoldering) fire (ii); the daughter rises and raises a torch. A second sequence is of perceived wetness, from without to within. The daughter hears urination (i), feels dripping upon her (ii), which proves to be not semen but blood, and ends in weeping (iii). The two sequences are interwoven around the story's second theme, that of the emergence into maturity, through her own initiative, of a girl whom customary guides and values have failed. The sequences, together with that of speaking, converge on her maturation and apartness. The evening and urination are outside; the low fire and dripping are within; she herself makes and raises the torch, she herself weeps.

(h) Alter uses *theme* for an idea that is part of the value system of the narrative and made evident in some recurring pattern (1981:95). This is the common device of Indian oral narrative. Again and again, a theme is not stated, but shown by its place in a pattern. Thus, a spontaneous illustration of the speech of a man who would go about the camp in the old days has five stanzas (of three, three, three, five, and five verses, respectively), and the ending point of each stanza has to do with the theme of continuity of tradition.[9] It is often by noticing the recurrence of an ending point that one recognizes in the prose paragraphs of published myths the formal relationships concealed within them.

A moving example, associated with repeated words, is found in a Takelma myth. The narrator, Frances Johnson, did not much remember the second part, in which the two men go upriver, question two women, find out what the women do when they return to their village across the river, kill them, don their skins, and impersonate them (so as to gain access to the village and the chief's lodge in which their father is prisoner, his body hung above a smoking fire for which the girls have been gathering pitch). What Johnson remembered clearly was what the girls say in fearful anticipation, "Paddle a canoe over here, Strong-digging-dog / We fear Otter's children." We are told what the girls say, the first line or both, seven times: twice that the girls say it, twice that the brothers are advised on their way that the girls say it, so that they should too, once when the brothers, disguised as girls, do say it, again that the girls would say it, again that the brothers now say it.

Why did Johnson remember just this element of the story so well? Perhaps because people often remember a memorable song or set of words from a myth, but here, I think, because the words sum up a theme. In the first part, two young men have an unreliable caretaker, their grandmother, but overcome her. In the second part, two girls have an unreliable caretaker but are overcome. Whatever the point of the myth in earlier times, for Johnson it is remembered in terms of caretakers who fail children and, in the doubling of the theme, especially fail girls. Narrative falters, but not their cry.

(i) Alter notes patterning of sequence of actions, most notably in "the folktale form of three consecutive repetitions, or three plus one . . . usually concluding either in a climax or reversal" (1981:95–96). Of course, this is worldwide. Still, it can be important to recognize its relation to theme. In Victoria Howard's "Seal Took Them to the Ocean," a band of men engage in a series of contests underwater. One would expect the Chinookan pattern numbers, three, five, or ten, but there are eight. The narrative collector, Jacobs, considers that the next two scenes, in which Sturgeon is observed in quite different behavior, must be intrusive from some other unknown story. But if one considers the structural signals of the theme of the story, the two scenes are a culmination of a series of ten. The story is a woman's elaboration of a male adventure into a parable of the fundamental value of reciprocity. In this version (but not others), the adventure is launched when one brother refuses any longer to supply another. The older brother then causes the seal to attract them and, when harpooned, to take them ineluctably to the bottom of the sea. They survive the series of trials, with advice from a sister-in-law living there, and return despite a harrowing test (Symplegades). But then the narrator says that the younger brother and his people remained poor. Why, and why say it? Because the opening scene has shown him as one who violates reciprocity. Such indications at the opening of a story of moral worth or lack of it always correlate with outcome.

Together, the opening and the closing point to reciprocity as theme. So do the ninth and tenth encounters underwater. In one Sturgeon kills and bakes his wife to provide food, but she is magically restored. In the other Sturgeon steals a comb and spoon from a woman and puts them in his head. The first is an instance of the continentwide story of the benevolent host, an expression of an underlying value, that of participant maintenance.[10] Nature, or better, the controlling powers and persons of the world, are benevolent and provide of themselves to human beings so long as human beings respond with respect and proper behavior themselves. Human beings participate in the maintenance of this world. This fundamental reciprocity is shown to one of the younger brother's partners, Blue Jay. Sturgeon is the greatest fish in the river and shows that as he offers himself as food. The objects put in his head are, as it were, "stigmata," by which he will be recognized. But Blue Jay does not report and accept this mutual dependence. Rather, he seeks to emulate it and kills his own wife, who does not revive. The younger brother and his men have survived a great adventure, then, but nothing is said to show that he has learned the lesson of personal reciprocity, and one of his men is shown to have been offered the lesson of fundamental reciprocity and failed to understand. The scenes with Sturgeon are not intrusive from another (unknown) story, but, numerically and morally, the final test.

(j) Alter defines *type-scene* as "an episode occurring at a portentous moment in the career of the hero which is composed of a fixed sequence of motifs" (1981:96). There are striking examples in the oral traditions of the North Pacific Coast. In each case a standard frame may integrate an extended sequence in a different way.

A trickster myth in the Kalapuya language of the Willamette Valley is integrated by recurrent motifs of a generic kind (appetite or need, deception, trade, and so on) in each act (see my discussion in chap. 14 of this volume). It is further integrated by the fact that the deceptions that begin and complete its dramatic events have five elements, three of them in specific detail, in almost the same order. The first act is a version of a major story of the region. To break a dam and free water and fish kept from people by sisters, Coyote digs with one hand while pretending only to drink with the other. In the last dramatic act, he inserts his penis in a chief's daughter while pretending only to sing to cure her. In both, he reaches and removes an obstruction (a penis tip in the case of the chief's daughter); in both, stopped-up water is released; in both he is detected; in both he goes in flight.

A stock opening is turned into dramatic suspense in the middle of a Clackamas Chinook myth told by Victoria Howard. Some of these myths start with a dangerous being, Grizzly Woman, arriving at a village, seeking out its chief and making herself his wife. Indeed, Howard comments upon this as a characteristic of Grizzly Woman. Many die before Grizzly Woman is overcome.

Now, in the myth that begins with two men (bears) forcing two young women bathers to become their wives ("Grizzly and Black Bear Ran Away with the Two Girls"), the one who becomes Grizzly Bear's wife has a son and a daughter. The son is all bear, like his father, the daughter half-human, half-bear. While the mother and daughter are out digging for roots, one by one four uncles come in search of the woman and are killed by the bears at home. Only then does the mother understand why the daughter has asked that they go back early. Together they burn up both bears.

The daughter now says they should go to her mother's people, but, ashamed of her mother for having lost one eye, she throws her off a cliff and goes alone. The old woman nonetheless follows her, and the girl throws her into a fire. She comes to a village, asks for its chief, and goes to his house to be a wife, but the old woman arrives again, calls her by a name that alludes to her part-bear nature (her feet), and warns people. The girl goes on to another village, the old woman comes, the girl kills her and throws her in the fire. The fourth time the old woman comes and names her, the girl gains advice from Meadowlark that her mother's heart is not in her body but in her hat. When the old woman comes again, the girl throws the hat in the fire as well. At the fifth village, no old woman comes. The girl marries the headman, raises two sons, then in the menstrual hut sharpens claws, turns into a dangerous being, and eats everyone, both there and in the villages she had passed through.

This last episode is told briefly. What the central part does is to use the arrival of Grizzly Woman at a village to marry its chief, otherwise an opening frame, as an instrument of suspense. The male bears had killed the uncles. Will the bear's daughter now kill their people? Four times the mother keeps such a story from starting. Conversely, in the appended text such a story has already started. The bare beginning, that a woman comes to a chiefly man to be his wife, echoes this same frame, casting an expectation of horror over what ensues.

This central sequence is complex in its use of the type-scene, interweaving, but not in lockstep, several strands of recurrent elements. And although one would think one would want the mother to succeed, Howard deploys significant detail to another end. To have the mother's heart separate in her hat is to identify her with the pursuing old women in hundreds of stories across the continent (among them, Grizzly Women). To have Meadowlark help the girl is to treat the girl as favored protagonist. In the first part, mother joined girl to destroy Grizzly males. When the two separate, it is because of the girl. And it is not the pursuing mother, but the escaping girl, who will become Grizzly Woman and eat other people. There is a cultural logic here: Grizzly nature, even partial, will out. Yet that eventuality did not deter Howard from casting the mother as pursuing ogress, the daughter as one pursued and in need of help. This much, it seems, she identified with a daughter whose mother failed to respond to the danger of an uncle's death. (See also the appended text.)[11]

A third dramatic use of a type-scene is what I have called "extraposition." A series establishes that something will happen a certain number of times. When the last time is reached, the last outcome is not given. Something holds its place, and the outcome is given an entire scene of its own. In Louis Simpson's telling of "The Deserted Boy" in Wishram Chinook, the rhetorical number is five, and in one scene it is incrementally accumulated and divided with exactitude—almost to the end. The boy makes a line for fish from sinew left him by his grandmothers. The first day he catches one fish, eats half, saves half for morning. The second day, two, eats one, saves one. The third day, catches three, eats one and a half, saves one and a half; the fourth day, four (two and two); the fifth day—he has become a grown man. It is in the next scene that he examines his line and finds, not fish, but a delicacy, a mixture of huckleberries and salmon. The daughter of the power in the river has taken pity on him; he stands and sings.[12]

In the Zuni language of New Mexico, the rhetorical number is four. In Andrew Peynetsa's telling of "Coyote and Junco," Coyote has Old Lady Junco teach him her song, runs off, forgets it, and comes back to learn it again. The fourth time ends, not with his learning it again, but with Old Lady Junco putting a rock inside her blouse and saying, "He may come, but I won't sing." What happens becomes the fourth and final scene, and the expected four verses are doubled. Two times Coyote asks but gets no response. Then he says he will give her four chances. When there is no response, he leaps to bite her and cracks his back teeth on the rock (stanza 7). The final stanza (8) wraps up.[13]

A close-knit pattern can be deployed with telling effect. Chinookan narrators often enough present an action as a triplet, a sequence of three steps. Not "Coyote went to X," but "Coyote went, he kept on going, he arrived." In "The Deserted Boy," the first act ends, hammering in three times that there are no people. The second act begins with the boy alone. In the first stanza he weeps, he hears a sound, he dries his tears.[14] This triplet marks a turning point. In the second act he will survive, step by step, with what his grandmothers have left him and, rewarded, prosper. In the third act the tables are turned. It is the people who lack food. His grandmothers come to him, and he repays them. When the rest of the people come, he turns, he looks, he sees them; he thinks how they abandoned him, he raises an east wind in which they drown. The triplet marks the turn to revenge.

Other oral traditions would provide other examples of this kind of literariness, showing that its characteristics are not limited to the Hebrew Bible, or to written compositions of literate cultures, or to the North Pacific Coast. Alter does at one point qualify the uniqueness of the traits in his first synopsis. He observes that motifs, themes, and sequences of actions abound in other narrative traditions, and that while keywords and type-scenes are distinctively biblical literary conventions, one can find approximate analogues of these in other traditions as well. He goes on to say: "What most distinguishes repetition in biblical narrative is the explicitness and formality with which it is generally employed, qualities that . . . support an unusual proportion of verbatim restatement" (Alter 1981:96). In traditions in which there is great density of data, repetition may be partly camouflaged, something we are expected to detect. "When on the other hand, you are confronted with an extremely spare narrative, marked by formal symmetries, which exhibits a high degree of literal repetition, what you have to look for more frequently is the small but revealing differences in the seeming similarities, the nodes of emergent new meanings in the pattern of regular expectations created by explicit repetition" (1981:97). Just so must American Indian and many other oral narratives be heard and read. (And for just this reason, interpretation without access to the language of the original, interpretation dependent on translation, that is to say, most published interpretation, must fall short.)

At another point, Alter suggests that these ways of using repetition may have their origin in biblical poetry, "which, as in most cultures, antedates prose as a vehicle of literary expression" (1981:97). Whatever the role of poetic parallelism in the specific case, we see that societies without it yet have ways of using repetition. Such literary expression probably is ancient in the world, a potential concomitant of narrative in any language.

Alter also suggests that such use of repetition, individuating characters, has its roots in the biblical view of humankind (1981:115, 189). This may be true. And an Indian view of the world in terms of participant maintenance, of mutual obligation between human beings and other powers, is not so far from that of the Bible. Still, I would suggest that individuation through repetition is a potential resource generally in oral narrative. Some tales and myths are rather stereotypical (as are some segments of the Bible), but many are rich in implication of motive and feeling. It is perhaps a matter of the extent to which a narrative has been fed on, lived with, in the mind. Thinking narratives through in the light of the fate of one's community and self is human.

Riffaterre

One might accept the evidence just given and conclude, not that American Indian narratives are literary, like the Hebrew Bible, but that the Hebrew Bible in origin is oral, like American Indian narratives. Let me consider a theorist with no intention of addressing anything oral. The narratives he treats are nineteenth-century novels, and he discusses narrative entirely in terms of reading.

In his concise and penetrating book *Fictional Truth,* Michael Riffaterre holds that fiction is truthful, not by reference to reality, but through verisimilitude based in language. Not information, but form, provides a sense of truthfulness, and form does so by means that often call attention to themselves as form, as artifice. Riffaterre locates verisimilitude in devices that repeat and presuppose a given. In particular, "any verbal given will seem to be true when it generates tautological derivations that repeat it in successive synonymous forms" (1990:xiv–xv). The given, the situational and linguistic starting point of a narrative, has a semantic structure. Its components may be implicit or only incompletely explicit. The text substitutes explicit and developed descriptions. These must conform to a consensus about reality already encoded in language (be "grammatical"). The combination of multiple references to the given, of the verifiability of each against the accepted idea of reality, of the bulk of detailed translations of each into actual descriptions, of convergence on one initial lexical or phrasal expression, conveys the impression of truth. At the same time, fiction relies on codes, arbitrary conventions, that can be identified independently of the narrative, assigned to a viewpoint exterior to it, or perceived as irrelevant to the motivation of the narrative events. Fiction therefore emphasizes the fictionality of a story at the same time that it conveys the story as true: "Narrative verisimilitude tends to flaunt rather than mask its fictitious nature" (1990:21). In fact, "more can be learned about fiction from those indices that point to narrative truth by seeming to flout it. Far from being the exception, these signs are much used, an indication of their importance. Indeed, they differentiate between literary and nonliterary narratives, and may even be a locus of fiction's literariness since all of them are tropes" (1990:xv).

Three chapters develop three aspects of the argument: (1) the veridictory effect of multiplying representations; (2) commentary or gloss that presupposes the reality of the language in which the topics are broached and thus functions as if it presupposed the reality of what it glosses (metalanguage); (3) two kinds of clues to truth suppressed in subtexts—constants perceived through comparison of versions of a subtext and "ungrammaticalities" (things that do not fit), indicating an intertext as their source.

The richness of fiction, of nineteenth-century novels, affords many interesting examples and interpretations. In their spareness, the narratives of concern here are another world. Yet the dimensions addressed by Riffaterre are present, as I shall indicate. Whether or not Riffaterre's thesis can be sustained for fiction generally, I do not know. He cites interesting examples, but they are few in relation to the universe of novels. It will be enough for my purpose if his argument holds for what he does cite.

(1a) To multiply representations is a kind of repetition, as Riffaterre himself points out (1990:45), and examples of repetition offered in connection with Alter could be offered again. Indeed, it is very Chinookan to say that "repetition does not become a trope before the third time" (1990:21). There is a further important respect in which Indian narratives employ repetition as a meaningful trope, one that is both explicit and persuasive.

In brief, Indian myths and perhaps oral narratives generally are found to consist of lines, marked by intonation contours, and, second, of units (one or more lines) marked in speech by particular contours, notably in English by a sentence-final fall.[15] It is by virtue of being an organization of lines that one can consider them, not prose, but a kind of poetry, and the units that enter into relation can be called "verses." Lines and verses need not be equivalent internally (in terms of numbers of syllables, stresses, alliterations, or the like). Their equivalence is external, in terms of relations they enter into with other lines according to a few types of pattern. One can say that this is a kind of verse that is "measured," rather than metrical.

The units that enter into relation are often marked in other ways in addition to intonation, notably by initial words and phrases, such as particles translatable as "now," "then," "so," "well," and expressions of temporal change. Turns at talk count as units of this kind. In the text at the end of this chapter, the verses are shown flush left.

A particular oral tradition has conventions as to the grouping of such verses. In Chinookan there are two unmarked, or "default," options, a set of three, a set of five. Three or five verses, then, may form a "stanza" (two in an introduction); three or five "stanzas" may form a scene. In the appended text there are three scenes. The first two have three stanzas, the third has five. In the appended text, stanzas are shown by marginal (parenthetic) capital letters. (The two sets of five lines that open the third scene seem each to have the weight of a stanza.) In many traditions the unmarked relations have to do with two and four. Combined possibilities occur also, as in the Algonquian language Ojibwe, where sets of three pairs are prevalent. The possibilities of such organization are more diverse than can be considered here. Suffice it to say that there is meaning that covaries with the form, is one of "this, then that; this, then that." When Chinookan narratives have three units in a series, the pattern is one of "onset, ongoing, outcome." This sense obtains from three verbs in a row ("he was going, he kept going, he arrived") to three major units in a row. Where there are five units, the convention is that the third is pivotal, completing one series and beginning another, the two interlocking in it.

That lines and groups of lines are conveyed in terms of intonation contours (and, but only secondarily, pauses) and that the lexical and syntactic matters are often at the beginning of lines can be taken as aspects of orality (although end-rhyme oral epics, as in Egyptian Arabic, are not unknown). That the traditions analyzed so far make use of just a few types of pattern may suggest an innate basis, along the lines of Chomsky's view of language. Perhaps human beings are "wired" in terms of a few alternatives and, hearing narrative around them, select the option present in it. But an adaptive, functional explanation cannot be ruled out. An art that is to disclose itself in perceptible relations, that maintains interest for those who already know its story by news of form, not information, is likely to build from the minimal possibilities of two or three.[16] Two with four or three with five give consistency and options. Larger numbers would be multiples or harder to perceive.

Some narrators mark the verse units boldly and without exception. One such is Louis Simpson, whose Wishram narratives begin every verse with the double pair, "Now then," or an occasional substitute ("Now again; "Indeed"). Other narrators are less explicit. In either case the effect is both to frame what is narrated and to lend it a sense of necessary consequence. Such narration continuously arouses and satisfies expectation (to use the apt phrase of Kenneth Burke for the persuading work of literary form [1925: 34–46]).

Such conjunction of artifice and verisimilitude may be specific to oral narrative (and to writing derived from it) and may show that Riffaterre's argument extends beyond the fiction he addresses. The myths are preeminently "fictional truths," conveying truths important to life, yet fictional to us and sometimes to Indians. The Santa Clara Tewas of New Mexico introduce some stories with words such as these: "In a place that never was, in a time that never was, this did not happen." The Nootka Indians of Vancouver Island insist upon the literal truth of stories of how the founder of a kinship group obtained its prerogatives. Those stories are true because the initial adventure did happen and the story has been transmitted ever since in a known chain of succession. But myths can be referred to in English as "fairy stories." Inheritance, in short, is historical fact; the truths of myths may be of other kinds.

(1b) Riffaterre himself singles out humor as the primary trope of his first kind. It is said to betray a narrator's viewpoint, while presupposing the existence of that about which it speaks humorously (1990:xv–xvi, 41). On the one hand, repetition, in the sense of the maintenance of a uniformly humorous slant from one moment in a narrative sequence to the next — "this is the index of fictionality." On the other hand, verisimilitude requires adjustment to each successive context. And although humor as an index of fictionality is not necessarily repetitive, this type is the most important in narrative, says Riffaterre, for the intertwining of the two linear developments highlights the contrast between the adjustments of verisimilitude and the fictionality of repetition (1990:45).

The thesis fits the examples Riffaterre advances, and certainly it fits some sequences in Indian myths. A favorite scene in stories of the trickster-transformer Coyote, sometimes repeated in the course of a cycle of his coming upriver or the like, is one in which he has "died" or otherwise completely failed in an effort. He slaps his buttocks, or defecates, for his "sisters" (or "nieces") to come out and asks them what to do: They refuse, saying he will just say that he knew already. He threatens to make it rain and wash them away. They tell him then the truth of his situation, and he says, "Ah, that is just what I was thinking." The scene doubly presupposes what has happened, viewing it with a repeated form of humor and embedding a partial replay in its explanation.

(1c) Riffaterre's second case in point is that of emblematic names for characters (1990:xvi, 33 ff.): the faithful father of many, Mr. Quiverful (Trollope), the Barnacle family encrusted on the ship of state (Dickens). Such names are blatantly conventional yet function as givens repeatedly verified, at least in the stories addressed. Such imitative naming is hardly to be found in the Indian narratives considered here. Chinookan personal names have the

look of ordinary words but are not; they are titlelike, their significance accruing through a line of bearers, confirmed with each new conferral (see the last
section of Hymes 1966). Yet the names of actors in myths do what Riffaterre
says emblematic names do. They posit a truth, because they designate, not
a person, but a type (1990:35). Such names may be considered emblematic,
accruing through stories, as personal names through lives, features of expectation. They are the aspect of myths that fits Riffaterre's notion of stories
traceable to a single expression (sememe) as germinating source.

Not always quite the same type, to be sure. The type and name may be
contested. Where Native titles are known (they seldom are), they point in
the languages I know best, those that once prevailed along the Columbia
River from its Pacific mouth past the Cascades into treeless plateau, to exploration as well as elaboration. The term for myth itself, -k'ani, means 'nature'.
To refer to a myth as I-gunat i-ya-k'ani is to say 'Salmon his-nature'. That indicates that the point is to show the consequences of having that nature, of
acting as does Salmon in the story in question.

As a named figure, Salmon is constant in being chiefly, proud, and tense
in relation to women. His enacted nature varies. A myth known from all
the Chinookan peoples along the river shows him avenging the killing of
his father by Wolves, aided by Coyote. One egg floats in the river from his
father's death and is found by Crow and nurtured by her. (The myth imagines a birth without need of women.) He finds his mother wife to the Wolves,
dries up all water but a spring beneath her feet, and when each in thirst
comes to it, kills them. He takes the woman as his own wife, but, going
upriver, she exclaims when she sees maggots on his sleeping body. (Spring
salmon are prone to spoil.) Angered, he throws her up on a cliff and goes
on. Later, he hears birds squabbling as to who will get what body part, sends
them to carry her back, restores her, and they live on.

When Franz Boas revisited Charles Cultee in 1894, he asked him to tell
again a Salmon myth that Cultee had told in 1891. The first act is a ritual
journey upriver. Five times the returning Spring Salmon is hailed from the
shore: "At last you come, you with maggots on your buttocks; if it had not
been for me, your people would have died." Salmon asks who it is, is told
it is an uncle or an aunt, and goes ashore with gifts. Plants are a domain
of women, fish of men. The culture rightly heralds the return of salmon in
the spring as life giving, but in this myth the claims of women as food pro-
viders are asserted; even Salmon accepts insult and shows respect. But in the
second part, encountering another canoe coming downriver, whose trio of
passengers claim to have gone even further in just one day, he refutes their
claim and wrings their necks: Flounder, then Crow, then Blue Jay, the one

who makes chiefs unhappy. In 1891, Cultee rushed to the second act, not pausing to correct an omitted line. The second act begins with Salmon in command, and the grouping of verses is not unmarked three or five, but intensifying pairs. Salmon uses sardonic, metalinguistic questions. In 1894, Cultee paused to insert an omitted line of the last insult at the end of the first act and began the second act in ordinary three- and five-part sequences. Sardonic, metalinguistic questions are absent. When he disposes of the trio in the canoe, he does so in opposite order, Blue Jay briefly, then Crow (she is forbidden the river), then Flounder. She is told to go downriver. No need to rush to reassert the authority of Salmon, once past the plants. The story now ends with the claim of the plants (and women) ("Without me, your people would have died") forever falsified. In the winter there will be fish in the river as well as roots on the banks. (To be sure, the fish, flounder, is feminine in gender. See chap. 6 of this volume.)

Victoria Howard told this story in Clackamas, recognizable as such through the frozen formula "Without me your people would have died," but transformed. Travel upriver becomes a rehearsal in season of the appearance of plants and other foods, birds and fish as well, a pedagogic exercise. Question and answer identify the appearance and name of the food, and then its use is explained. The one who pronounces on such things is taken to be a fish person (that is, Salmon), as the telling proceeds in threes, plants, more plants, birds, fish, more fish. But when the third of the second trio of fish is reached, evidently the most important, Howard breaks off the narrative. My mother's mother said, she says, it was Coyote (the coyote called Štank'iya) who ordained the foods. Salmon loses his ritual journey, then even his place in the story.

Another of her myths, "Tongue," is known from independent versions to be about Salmon, explaining at the end why salmon come to some tributaries of the Willamette River and not to others. Not so in Howard's poignant story. The foolish Clackamas people allow themselves to be eaten by Tongue. One chief's wife, out gathering roots, survives to bear and rear her late husband's son. He grows rapidly, gains spiritual power in the mountains, stupefies Tongue by gorging him with deer created from rotten wood, and, with his mother's help, burns him up. Then he goes to the mountains to recreate the people ritually out of bones. When all have returned to the river, and his restored father is teaching the people to fish, he watches; some insult him, saying he is not working; he walks into the river forever. The pride, the river, echo Salmon. But the son goes unnamed; the motherless avenger of another myth has become the type of a mother's precocious, chiefly son.

Similar analyses can be made of other major figures, notably the trickster-transformer Coyote. Coyote is popular among many writers and artists, for his countercultural ways and picaresque indestructibility, but just as he is not a god (as early white settlers in the West sometimes mistakenly said), neither is he necessarily a hero. In the serious business of guardian spirit power and headmanship, Coyote was marginal, a figure through whom to mock such things, but not to obtain them. And within the limits of his germinating features, stories make him what he is. It is rather like the complexity inherent in a deity all-powerful and all good or a deity that is both one and three. One narrator may emphasize and punish Coyote's irresponsible acts, as does Louis Simpson, who has Coyote himself state that Eagle and Salmon are chiefs, but he is not. Simpson's version of the news about Coyote (who has performed fellatio on himself and tried to keep the news from coming out) ends with punishment: the people, having heard, twice refuse him food. Victoria Howard's version has Coyote embarrassed but quick to learn and end as pronouncer of things to come, saying that even he could not keep such news quiet and it will always be that way. Hiram Smith sympathizes: the sun was hot, he'd just awoken from falling asleep; the power with which he throws up a wall or rimrock to keep in the news is dramatized with gesture; and at the end, Coyote just runs off. (See detailed comparison in chaps. 3 and 6 of Hymes 1981b.)

A narrator may integrate several myths to explore the nature of Coyote and, through him, that of the world. William Hartless does so in the Kalapuya myth mentioned earlier. Twice Coyote meets needs of his own (for water, for eyes) in a way that serves others and the way things are to be (water and fish are to be freely available, Snail is to have weak eyes). Perhaps out of hubris, he then trades for body parts from vanity and lust (for Nightingale's anus because its sound will make him the cynosure of gatherings, for an old man's lengthy penis so as to reach girls bathing across the river). In the first two adventures, he succeeds and goes on; in the second two, he fails and has to trade back. He goes hungry because the birds he stalks always hear him farting; the penis gets stuck in the girl, and he has to call to the other girls to cut it off. The tip stays in. The girl's father, a chief, seeks a shaman to cure her. Coyote pretends to be an old, powerful, reluctant shaman, who knows about cases like this. At last he arrives, gets raucous birds outside the house to help him sing his curing song, goes in, and copulates with the girl. The parts unite. Although when the people find out what he has done, they kill his helpers, he himself escapes, intact, the girl cured. He and the audience have had the fun of embarrassing a chiefly family and have presumably learned that the balance of things has to do with what Martin Luther King would call a double victory. The last act is a few lines, undramatized, reporting that Coyote went on, made a fish trap (alluding to a story in which he makes it possible for people who have no fish to catch them), has children (this the one who ordinarily is always traveling and leaving children and wife behind).[17]

Like Coyote, Blue Jay can be the focus of humorous repetition and at the same time diverse viewpoint and exploration. West of the Cascades in Oregon and Washington, he is never clever, unlike Coyote, but may range from boastful and troublemaking to sympathetic and suffering, from comic insert to protagonist. There is a remarkable example in which the type-scene, or pair of scenes, is that of "Benevolent Host, Bungling Host." In one scene, someone comes to a host who has power to provide food by cutting his own body or killing a family member, either then being magically restored. In the second scene, he is invited in turn by his guest (reciprocity), who tries to emulate him and fails. Repeated versions of the type show it to have been a favorite among peoples of northwestern corner of Washington, and among the Quinault, remarkably, a series of nine such episodes opens a cycle integrated around Blue Jay (Farrand and Kahnweiler 1902:85–101). Interest is sustained by varying (exploring) possibilities of motivation and response, usually humorous, and on the visit by Blue Jay and his wife to the Shadows, there is only a first part. No emulation follows; unable to perceive the Shadows, the couple have to give up and come back. In these nine episodes, the attempt at emulation implicitly confirms the existence of the powers displayed in the first part. The set comes to a motivated end, when Blue Jay's child dies, unrevived, at the end of the ninth. He can no longer bear to stay there and sets out. The narrator then has him join with others in otherwise separate cycles, first of a pair traveling to name rivers and creeks, then of transformers traveling to set the world right. There follow other kinds of Blue Jay story, including a journey to the land of the dead. The matrix is in effect a treatise on the name and nature "Blue Jay." The emblematic name generates almost certainly some of the stories of the initial nine, together with an architecture that first establishes, with repetition and humor, a family man who wishes to be chiefly with magical power but fails, and because of the death of a child goes away to become part of the establishment of the world as companion to others.

If generation from emblematic names of comic repetition and exploration of character are features of literature, these stories are literature.

(2a) Riffaterre devotes his third chapter to commentary or gloss that presupposes the reality of the language in which the topics are broached and thus functions as if it presupposed the reality of what it glosses (metalanguage).

A verbal device of just this sort occurs often in Chinookan myths and in each of the first two scenes of the appended text (lines 2, 19).[18] The idiom is "definite indefinite." To say one does not know is to presuppose there was a time to be known, to indicate that the narrator would tell you that as well, if only she could. A touch of ignorance makes the rest true.

The end of the appended next is a telling instance. In the daughter's remonstrance to her mother, the third scene rehearses the events of the first and the second. As metanarrative, it presupposes them. At the same time, it treats what has happened as something that might not have: there was another possibility. As remonstrance, the daughter's speeches state two truths: the consequence of having acted as did the mother, and that there might have been another story.[19]

Conversely, when foreknowledge is fulfilled, the fulfillment confirms the prior language and event. There is a general circle here familiar in the culture. A myth, set in the world before the people have come, may end with a pronouncement of what will be when they do. The sisters, for example, will not hoard salmon for themselves but be frogs on the bank or swallows that come upriver when the salmon do. In the world in which the myth is told, frogs are on the bank, swallows do herald salmon. Experience confirms story, story explains experience. The circle obtains within stories. In each of two parts of the Clackamas myth "Gitskux and His Older Brother," Grizzly Woman comes while the brothers are hunting, kills the elder's wife, and dons her skin. The brothers know how to test her and what to do to overcome her, because each of the wives has foreseen it all and told them what to do.

Remonstrance, prediction and pronouncement, and post hoc explanation (recall Coyote's fecal advisors in section 1b) are frequent metalinguistic instruments of fictional truth in myths.

(2a) For Riffaterre, metalanguage is connected to symbolism. His dimensions do indeed intersect and mingle across chapters, and symbolism especially links the second and third dimensions of his argument (symbolism, subtext, intertext). There is a gap, he writes, between the metalinguistic structure that enters into referentiality, the sequential telling of the story, and the hierarchy of aesthetic values that makes the novel into an artifact: The gap is bridged, so it seems to him, by subtexts, texts that are neither subplots nor themes but concrete actualizations whose sole function is to be vehicles of symbolism. "They offer a rereading of the plot that points to its significance in a discourse closer to poetry than to narrative." The connection between the two types of discourse comes through verbal overdetermination, welding narrative text and symbolic subtext by either or both of two intermediaries, sustained metaphors, "as an imagistically motivated consecution," or phonetically motivated syllepses (words with two possible meanings) (1990:xvii). Let me identify this understanding as (2b).

Whether or not such relations hold for all myths, I doubt, but that some myths answer to what Riffaterre delineates, I feel certain. There might be syllepses and associated pieces of actualization, if emblematic names are taken to embody conflicting possibilities, natures realizable in more than one way. Sustained metaphors, imagistically motivated consecutions, do exist.

One example has been described with regard to the appended text. The public consequence, and moral, is to act as does Seal, first named in the title of the myth. Two ethical dimensions inform Chinookan stories: to maintain social norms and to respond to empirical realities (to be proper, to be smart). Heroes show both dimensions, numskulls neither. This myth has a tragic outcome because the mother does the first at the expense of the second. But in the story is an alternative account, of a daughter who responds to reality at the expense of norms. She is not named in the title, and she does not shape the outcome, but she shapes the words. The way of referring to the man as uncle, not brother, and the consecutive imagery of darkness to light, external to internal wetness, focus on her. I find it hard to deny to this aspect of the story terms such as *subtext* and *theme*, but to use Riffaterre's words, there is here "a discourse closer to poetry."

The "Sun's Myth," as told by Charles Cultee to Franz Boas, is a striking parallel (Boas 1901:26–33; cf. n. 6 of this chapter and Hymes 1975b:345–69). A great chief (he has five towns of relatives) rises each morning to see the sun, but it does not quite come out. He tells his wife he will go to find it; she asks ironically, "Is it nearby?" but he persists. After wearing out ten sets of moccasins, he finds a house, enters, and finds a girl. Questioning her, he learns that the wealth of the house will be given away when she matures (has a puberty rite and is ready to marry). He stays. For a few idyllic lines, they are together while the old woman goes out each morning to carry the sun across the world and comes back, always bringing gifts. But he cannot forget the shining thing that caught his eyes. When he becomes homesick and wants to return, he again and again rejects all other gifts and insists on the shining thing. "It is you who choose," the old woman says, as she hands him it and an ax. When he nears the first town of his relatives, the ax sings. He loses consciousness, he awakes to find the town and its people destroyed, he tries to get rid of the ax but cannot. This happens at each town, though he tries to hold back his feet at the last, his own town. Then the old woman appears, saying, "I tried to love you, and I do love you. It is you who chose. You took that 'blanket' of mine." She takes back what he had taken. He goes a little distance; there he builds a house, a small house.

The title indicates that the public meaning of the myth is the nature of the sun. It is in the nature of the powers of the world to enter into reciprocity with human beings, to provide them wealth. The old woman observes the norms of this relationship and responds to reality. As a relative, she cannot finally refuse to give the chief what he asks. Only there are powers too great for human beings. That the chief could not see the sun when he looked and had to close his eyes when he looked at the shining thing in the house of the sun was indication enough that he did not have knowledge of it and therefore could not control it. Sensory detail is concentrated on him. It is he who sees or does not see, who wears out moccasins, and who, in graphic, varied detail, tries five times to get rid of the ax, to throw it, to scrape it off in the crotch of a tree, to burn it, but always it would stick to his fingers. Successive images of not seeing and of taking what cannot be released and failure twice to heed the warning of a wife point to hubris in relation to the reality of the sun. She and her power remain. His people are destroyed, and he is released to live alone.

It would be going too far to use Riffaterre's words and speak of a rereading of the plot (1990:xvii). The narrative tells both stories at once; there is here, as with Seal, a dialogic, dialectic interrelation. But both the sensory detail and images of the secondary story can be said, as Riffaterre says is usually true of a subtext, to be "strung along the main narrative line in separate successive variants" (131). The detail and images would, I think, evoke identification, and in both myths remonstrance points to responsibility and the foregone possibility of another ending. That seems close to Riffaterre's next statement: "The story it tells and the objects it describes refer symbolically and metalinguistically to the 'novel' as a whole or to some aspect of its significance" (131).

It seems reasonable to generalize a bit and to take the essence of Riffaterre's notion to be the welding together of two trajectories, one primary and one secondary, what is secondary being dramatically foregrounded through sensory detail (what a body experiences) and imagery (of darkness and light in both).

(3) Riffaterre remarks on the unconscious of a text as represented by the symbolism of a subtext and by the intertext the symbolism mobilizes. He points to two kinds of clues, perception of constants in subtexts and of "ungrammaticalities," inappropriatenesses that derive from reference to an intertext that is not part of the temporal dimension of the text in question. They give a narrative the authority of the real paradoxically by eliminating or suspending its most basic feature, time.

Perhaps the cumulation of the sensory detail in the text at the end of this chapter and the Sun's myth can be taken as perception of constants, dimensions with symbolic significance. True "ungrammaticalities" are rare, but there is one that is striking in Louis Simpson's version of a benevolent host, bungling host myth involving Coyote and Deer (see chap. 8 of this volume). Deer has offered both meat and blood from his own body. Invited in return, he sees Coyote raise a knife to his wife and stops him, offering meat and blood again and repeating that they should come to him. In the course of the text, choice of verb forms and initiation of address associate Deer and Coyote's wife, but isolate Coyote. Strikingly, what Deer says is accompanied by transitive verbs of speaking, what Coyote says by intransitive verbs. When Coyote raises a knife to his wife, the word is without a relational prefix. All nouns of kinship and other relationships require such a "possessive" prefix—one does not say "son," but "his son," "her son," "my son," and the like. But here the word is not "his wife," but, ungrammatically, "wife." It is the culmination of verbal detail that isolates Coyote and begins the peripety of the story. Coyote does not fail in an attempt to be a host; he is not allowed to make the attempt. (Contrast stories in which Blue Jay makes such an attempt and his wife or child dies.)

The same text involves, not an ungrammaticality, but the unique promotion of the usual word for "and" into a marker of verse units. It marks just those units in which Deer offers blood. No other version of this kind of story in the region involves blood as well as meat, and this, together with the tone of Deer's words, suggests than the Methodism Louis Simpson had been taught has introduced the symbolism of the Eucharist. Not to a Christian purpose, for it is Deer who offers both, and not in sacrifice, but as participant in an order in which he can restore himself. Simpson here does two things: he reduces to its nadir his negative conception of Coyote, a conception reinforced in the remonstrance by the wife that concludes the text, telling Coyote no one would want to eat coyote (not to be useful to people being a punishment, and for the punishment to be applied to Coyote a double degradation); and he finds in his own tradition an equivalent to the appeal of the outstretched hands of the host of the Lord's table (see chap. 8 of this volume).

An element that suspends time is built into Chinookan myth. The second element of a text is commonly an evaluation of one of the actors, phrased, not in a narrative tense, but in the "future." Not he or she did something, but he or she will do something, that is, will always, characteristically do something. But this element does not point beyond the text to an intertext. Rather, it implies a constant. The outcome for the actor in question will fit the goodness or badness of the conduct described. (Recall discussion with regard to Alter (section i) of the outcome of "Seal Took Them to the Ocean.")

Certainly, inappropriateness can recur as a frame for myths, a frame independent of time. The coming of a woman to a headman as his wife is one. No relationship began that way in actual life. Again, the domestic group in Victoria Howard's telling of "Seal and Younger Brother Lived There" — a consanguineal trio of elder sister-mother : younger brother-uncle : niece-daughter — is not a normal one, yet it recurs in four of the myths we have from her, each distinct, each working out the relation in a different way. In each a different person in the trio dies (except in one story, in which none does). (Cf. chap. 8 of Hymes 1981b:286–91.)

But a search for "ungrammaticality," even for "inappropriateness," yields little in these myths. The spirit of Riffaterre's approach is better served by generalizing its concern with suspension of time. Suppressed or implicit meanings, connected with symbolism and associated with suspension of narrative time, do appear if one attends to what may be called *set pieces and inserts*.

In Louis Simpson's "The Deserted Boy," the extrapolated scene in which the boy celebrates success is in principle indeterminate in length. The boy sings, and the song can be repeated as often as desired (in the text we have, three times, but it could have been five). Nothing further happens. It is like an aria in opera. And the scene with the song is followed by a stanza whose first verse repeats that the boy had camped overnight five times, whose second describes him as waking to find a woman beside him, followed by a number of lines (for Chinookan narrative, a great many lines) describing her beauty in terms of adornment, house, and blanket, and a third verse with a number of lines enumerating the kinds of food she has brought. The third and concluding scene of the act has five verses describing the man and the woman together. Each is a line beginning with "now" and not "then." Simpson's verses usually begin with both ("now then"). Here the "now" of summation is repeated five times, and the "then" that moves to a succeeding point is suppressed. Time is suspended.

All this can readily be associated with the implicit model for Simpson's handling of the story, the model of a successful guardian spirit quest. In the first act, narrativity began by moving steadily to the abandonment, then circled round three times to the repeated final line of being entirely alone. In this second act, narrativity moves steadily, almost ploddingly to the moment of success and then virtually ceases. Two things are required of a guardian spirit quest: to go alone, to obtain signs of the pity of a power. (In the third act, the young man takes charge.)

In the appended text, again the first two scenes move steadily ahead, and the third presents a portrait as if the two women were to be frozen forever, one reproaching and weeping, one keening, one reproaching and weeping. The portrait etches the apartness of the daughter, come into knowledge of sexuality and blood unattended, only she knowing. It stands implicitly over against expectations of a girl's puberty rite, sponsored, managed, gifts given to make it remembered by others, within a family and a community. (See Spier and Sapir 1930:262.)

A subtler form of subtext and symbolic meaning emerges when a certain characteristic of the narrative action is linked to a tellingly placed suspension of narrativity itself. One such emerges in Cultee's Kathlamet telling of the myth of the Southwest Wind, if one considers that some portions of the ongoing action of a myth are presented with quoted speech on the part of the actors, while other parts are described without it. A group make their way into the sky to overcome five brothers who are repeatedly destroying their homes. The culminating conflict between the two parties is narrated vigorously but succinctly: this happens, this happens, this happens. The larger part of the text is devoted to the interaction of the party that goes to the sky, much of it incidental to the outcome, much of it displayed through what they say to one another. The speakers are small animals, not strong ones. And after the victory, when they return, a good many are left behind in the sky, and their names are retired, one after the other. The two things seem to go together: small animals talking, a litany of such creatures now in the sky as stars, to suggest something besides the principal outcome, the overcoming of all but one of the Southwest Winds. That, I think, is a sense of the domestication of the sky. Small creatures accomplish it; some of them are forever there now. In sum, suspension of action in a litany here is linked with one of the two modes of narrative progression, a mode (quoted speech) whose quality of focusing and dramatizing voices is like pausing for a set piece.[20]

Another myth links set pieces to a subtext and intertext having to do with the natures of women. In Victoria Howard's "Gitskux and His Older Brother," the latter part begins when Grizzly Woman has killed the older brother's first wife and all the community and taken the younger brother with her. The older brother, alone, comes to a house, enters, and sees what he takes to be a hunter entering the other end with a deer. Later, the same person reenters and lets down her hair: it is a woman. At night he lies down away from her bed, but step by step she causes him to be bitten by insects and, as the fifth step, to end beside her. Soon she tells him that he is to be the hunter.

This is done in ten lines of verbal exchange. Unlike every other part of the myth, the lines have no smaller groupings (three, five, three pairs, anything). Their internal shape is not one of parts, not quite one of linear progression, but in words used more as a circle within which places are exchanged: the two, she to him, he to her, the two (see Hymes 1983d:129–70; cf. 155–56).

Now the two stayed.
  She told him,
    "Now, you will be doing the hunting.
    You will have thought,
      'Perhaps there is some man.'
    Here I have lived alone,
    I would be the one hunting."
  "Indeed,"
    he told her.
Now that is what the two did.

Formally, the story is about the brothers of the title, the younger active and alert to what happens, the older passive and needing instruction. They belong to a matrix of younger and older brothers, one smaller, one larger, drawn from Panther, Fisher, Marten, Mink, and Wildcat, that is widespread in the region, but in character, they stand in contrast. The myth might also be said to be about Grizzly Woman, who initiates most of what happens. She comes to the unnamed older brother (actually, Panther) as a wife. In the event she kills the first wife and puts on her skin; but the wife had foreseen it (this is told out of temporal order, after the event), the brothers test her, and kill her. She returns, kills and eats all the people, and takes the younger brother off to be a slave on whom she will wipe her anus. After the scene quoted above, the second wife is able to tell the older brother what has happened to the younger and how to rescue him; after a poignant recognition scene, Grizzly Woman is again killed. The second wife, having cleansed Gitskux (evidently Fisher) five times, restores his long black hair, making it fall not only to the ground, but even a little longer than before. Here again there are ten units that stand apart. The first five verses form an arc, but the sequence does not stop, it barely pauses, a caesura as the combing continues to its ultimate result.

  These two ten-part displays cannot be said to suspend narrativity, time, entirely. A further point is reached. Yet they hold us within a frame that is formally apart, an extended formal unity not otherwise found. And they connect with a subtext brought out in doubling wives, their foreknowledge, and Grizzly Woman's donning the skin of each. Grizzly Woman wishes to be accepted as a human wife (but fails). Implicit in the contrast between her behavior and that of the true wives is the question of strength in women. Grizzly Woman tries to control what she does but cannot; she kills and degrades. The true wives defend and foresee, and the second knows what has to be done to kill Grizzly Woman forever (not only burn her, bur mash her bones and blow them away). She does not need a man to hunt, yet can have the older brother be the hunter; having directed the rescue of the younger brother, she can restore him and give him black hair longer than before. That, I submit, is strength, a womanhood so strong and secure that it not only chooses its partner but is a freely giving source of identity in men. In contemporary terms, aggression versus assertion.

This myth is one of four that form a cycle of intertextuality that I can only indicate briefly. Another myth also ends with Grizzly Woman destroyed for good by having her mashed bones blown away. The tendency in folklore in such cases has been to pardon native inconsistency. To do so mistakes the reason such myths exist. Queen Victoria can have died but once, but Grizzly Woman can die as often as there are motives to think through what she best enacts. Each of the myths in which she dies for good complements a myth that has ended with her alive. Each pair contrasts in the gender of her active opponents and in her motivational concern. In the pair in which the opposition is by male protagonists, her motives have to do with being a wife. In its first myth, sons revenge a mother; in the second, brothers restore a wife. In the pair in which the opposition is by female protagonists, her motives are revenge against women, first one, then all. In its first myth, a daughter overcomes a mother, in the second, a mother-in-law. In the first of each pair, a child or children are pursued and are aided by a bird; in the first of each pair, Grizzly Woman ends without kin, destroyed by others and herself. There are other connections as well. Although nothing is recorded to indicate that Victoria Howard thought of these four myths together (she did not tell them together), either she or the women from whom she heard them evidently had thought them through to the point of alignment in terms of common concerns and elements of frame.[21]

A striking suspension of narrativity through inserts occurs in Victoria Howard's "Seal Took Them to the Ocean." As discussed under section i in relation to Alter, the main narrative has to do with the men who go under the ocean and engage in dangerous contests. Between the contests and return come two scenes, not of action so much as of observation by Blue Jay, disclosing Sturgeon. After the return, Blue Jay fatally attempts to imitate Sturgeon, killing his wife to the dismay of others. The scenes with Sturgeon and Blue Jay interrupt the progress of the main action and are themselves disjunct. They connect with the opening account of the relation between two brothers, and the remark at the end that he, Seal Hunter, despite heroic success, remains poor with all his people, evidently having violated reciprocity at the outset. The inserted, disjunct sequence shows the principle as more than a relation between persons such as brothers, one of whom has ceased to share. It presents reciprocity in the fundamental terms of life (life-sustaining food) and death, as inherent in the being of the world. In his cleverness (and with advice), Blue Jay has helped his side defeat the people under the ocean in contest after contest with life at stake. Like the chief with regard to the shining of the sun, however, he overreaches. He interprets a providential gift as one more in a series within the control of beings like himself. The emulation destroys.

Greimas

A. J. Greimas has proposed a model of the elementary structure of signification to which the course of a narrative is held to correspond (Greimas and Courtes 1976: 433–47; Prince 1987:85–86). It is interesting to see that such a model, accepted as part of narratology, has application to a myth discussed in this essay, not only in terms of semantic units but also in terms of ethnopoetic form.

The model is that of a "semiotic square." A unit signifies in terms of relations with its contradictory, its contrary, and the contradictory of its contrary. For a concept such as "smart" or "proper" (s_1), the contradictories would be "not smart" or "not proper" ($-s_1$); the contraries, "dumb" or "improper" (s_2); the contradictories, "not dumb," "not improper" ($-s_2$). The course of a narrative can be said to correspond to a movement along the square, through operations or transformations from a given unit to its contrary or contradictory.

The model can be applied to the appended text. The four states would be the opening consanguineal situation in which the trio (older sister and mother, younger brother and uncle, niece and daughter) live together (s_1); the addition of the affinal "wife" (a man disguised) who comes to the brother (s_2); the girl's discovery of the murder of the uncle by the "wife," now gone ($-s_2$); the daughter's remonstrance and the mother's lament, as their relationship ends ($-s_1$). The movement is from opening moment to its contrary; from contrary to contradictory; and from contradictory to its contrary, which is contradictory of the initial state. The four states can be highlighted as follows:

s_1: consanguineal family ("they lived there")
s_2: augmentation by affine (daughter's warning, mother's reproach)

-s_2: loss (uncle murdered, "wife" gone)
-s_1: separation (mother : daughter)

These four states intersect the ethnopoetic, or rhetorical, form of the text. The text has three scenes, consisting of three stanzas, three stanzas, five verses, respectively. Each scene begins with specification of a relation between participants and location. The four states of the semiotic square overlap the formal demarcations. Each scene involves two states. In particular, the second and third scenes continue a preceding state (relation), and against that a new one begins.

The initial state (s_1) is expressed in the first verse, an introductory descriptive statement. It is a statement of a kind with which such myths commonly begin: so and so lived there. The second state (s_2) is introduced by the next verse. This state continues into the first part of the next scene. The third state (-s_2) is introduced in the second stanza of the second scene and continues through the third verse of the third scene. The fourth state (-s_1) is in the concluding two verses of the third scene.

The intersections of the subsequent states of the semiotic square coincide with markers of narrative time. As said, the first state is a conventionally continuing one. The second state is introduced with the first reference to a specific moment of time (a "definite indefinite" time, "I do not know when it was"), and the third state by the only other (the same expression of "definite indefinite" time). These are the only occurrences of the expression in the narrative. Each is salient against the background of what precedes it. In scene i, the opening "they lived there" indicates a stable continuing state. The next verse punctuates it with arrival of a woman. In scene ii, the opening lines about going to bed are not in a narrative tense, but in a future of characteristic activity, "they would," continuing the sense of the preceding stanza of "a long, long time . . . like that." The next verse punctuates it with something dropping onto the girl's face.

Finally, the fourth state coincides with a shift from the primary tense of narrative sequence to a tense that is associated with continuing states. The actions of the preceding scenes have been set in the remote past (marked by *ga-*). The third scene (continuing the third state) opens with *na-*, the first use of *na-* in the text, but the other tenses of the first verses and the first tense of the third verse (all within the third stare) are *ga-*. The last tense in the pivotal third verse is *na-*, as are all the tenses of the last two verses (the fourth state).[22]

That the fourth state contradicts the initial state is marked by lexical selection and framing on two counts. The myth shows the consequences of acting as does the mother, who insists on observing social norms at the expense of empirical evidence. There are actually two consequences, each enacted in a sequence of the three verses. To recognize this, one must recall that in Chinookan and other languages with three- and five-part patterning, a sequence of five can be organized around its third member as a pivot, completing one three-member series and initiating another.

The first three verses of the scene relate the girl's discovery of blood, then her discovery that her uncle is dead, and her remonstrance to her mother. This series discloses the first consequence of acting like Seal, the death of the man. (It uses the present tense for immediacy.)

The second series of three verses discloses the second consequence, the breaking of the relation between the girl and her mother. The girl remonstrates and weeps, her mother does not answer but formally laments, the girl again remonstrates and weeps.

A choice of verb forms coincides with the distinction among consequences, and, as described, so does the distribution of past tenses (granted a line of anticipation). The third verse (consequence 1) continues the use of the transitive, addressing verb "told." The concluding two verses have the intransitive, broadcast verb "said." And the selection of a marker of simple pastness, *na-*, in the last two verses brings the narrative round again to a continuing state, although one far different from that with which it began.

The two contradictory states thus are integrated within the movement of a single scene. The integration within five verses may have a further appropriateness to the second consequence, if one interprets this third scene against the expectations of the first and the second.

On the one hand, in the preceding scenes a verb of saying precedes each turn of talk by the daughter, but not the turns of the mother. Her words come in direct response, nothing intervening. In this third scene, all three turns at talk are enclosed on each side: "The girl told her . . . she wept"; "Seal said . . . she kept saying that"; "The girl wept, she said . . . the girl wept." The separation seems iconic.

On the other hand, the pattern of the preceding scenes is threefold: participants and (a change of) location, verbal exchange, verbal exchange. If the third scene is heard in terms of the same pattern, then the breaking of the relation between mother and daughter is expressed yet again. The first two sets of lines identify participants and a change of location: the girl moves to discover her uncle. The third and fourth verses give two turns at talk, but it is not truly an exchange. The daughter addresses the mother, but the mother speaks broadcast in lament. There is a further turn at talk by the daughter, but then there is no further talk at all. Formal expectations as to a sequence of verses have been fulfilled; the scene ends with a fifth. But ex-

pectations from the first two scenes of a second verbal exchange are denied.
That in itself may suggest an absence of completion, a silence that highlights
what has happened.[23]

In sum, both the primary and the secondary plots and consequences are
given in this final scene: the outcome for the man in its initial arc of three
stanzas, the outcome for the relation between mother and daughter in its
second.

That the relations proposed by Greimas find overt marking within a culturally specific narrative form suggests the scope of their relevance and its
standing as narrative.

An Inversion

Intricate, motivated form may be accepted as a sign of literary art. In the
story "Seal and Her Younger Brother Lived There," it is an outcome, not
only of art, but of change, of a transvaluation of dramatic values. Seal is a
woman's inversion of a myth told elsewhere to entirely different purpose.

Along the North Pacific Coast there are a number of recorded myths of a
man or men seeking revenge. A father or son has been captured and is near
death; a wife has been stolen; a sister has been killed by her husband. All
have in common a journey to an enemy village. There the avengers disguise
themselves as wives of the chief, or, in one type, a man dresses himself as his
sister, his identical twin. They are almost found out. This may happen several times, but the climactic moment is at night within the house, when the
imposter is going up a ladder to bed. A child (not hitherto mentioned) calls
out that it is not a woman, but a man; he has a knife, or a penis, beneath
his dress. An older person shushes the child, and the avengers succeed. They
kill the chief and, if the victim was father or son, rescue him.

In such a story, the child's crying out is a last, perhaps poignant, moment
of suspense. For Howard it is the focus of an exploration of relations between
mother and daughter. Dramatic motivation (suspense) has found motivation in experience of life.

Narrators as Creators

This section speaks to a kind of change not much noticed in regard to Native
American myths. For a long time narratives have been considered mostly
as properties of groups, narrators as witnesses to tradition. Today one still
sees stories identified by the name of a tribe or a culture, that is, identified
with a group, not a person. The man who skillfully and sensitively preserved

the Clackamas narratives of Victoria Howard published them as *Clackamas Chinook Texts* and discussed them as evidence of the Clackamas Indians in general, not of Victoria Howard, of a woman, who had been born into the remnant of a shattered group. In such a context change is taken as occurring from tradition to tradition, group to group.

There will always be much to learn from study of difference and change at such a level. One value of the work of Lévi-Strauss is that he discovers new collocations that give new perspectives.[24] It is what makes possible recognition of individual transformations of the sort found with Victoria Howard. One must read and reread, seeking to recreate in the mind something of the resources and alternatives a narrator might have had. Each story may bring into relationship details and stories otherwise not particularly noticed.[25] Those who interpret change and artistry must as much as possible have in mind what a narrator might have had in mind. No scholarly resource will suffice, for lists of motifs and tale types abstract from details and vantage points that may matter in the given case. Each tradition needs its own guide, and where traditions no longer live in the minds of narrators, they must come alive again in the minds of readers. The goal of such comparison, as envisaged here, is not reconstruction (of a past starting point), reduction (to a structure), or reflection (of a culture), but to identify resources and relations so as to interpret something emergent.

Much of the current study of oral narrative focuses on the event of narration itself, on narrators as performers. Focus on occasion brings attention to change as between one performance to another, one performer and another, and within a performance itself.

Such differences might best be called variation rather than change. There may not be a fixed (memorized) original, or if there is, it may not itself change. Think of narrators in command of resources of both content and form: content, in the sense of story frames, matrices of actors, sequences of incident, image, and event, and form in the sense of conventions for the ordering of relations between narrative units (lines, verses, stanzas, scenes). Think of audiences conversant with these things as well. One telling might differ from another simply in explicitness. "But the story [text] doesn't say that it was a feather," I said once to Hiram Smith, a Wasco friend of almost forty years. "Everyone knows it was a feather" was his reply. A pronominal prefix ("it") could be enough. (See Hymes 1981b:111–15.)

The mood, interests, and identity of the narrator, of the audience, the relation between the two, affect what and how much is said.[26] The cases to be taken up here are examples, and such variation is familiar in the conception of the oral-formulaic poet as one who draws upon a stock of precoded expressions, adapting length of performance to occasion.[27] Generative adaptation, whether of epic or other genres, is being carefully studied today in many parts of the world (cf. Blackburn 1988; Blackburn et al. 1989; Metcalf 1989; Mills 1991; Reynolds 1991; Sherzer 1990; and the general discussion in Bauman and Briggs 1990). On the Native North Pacific Coast, a striking instance of adaptation to occasion is when a story that validates privileges being ritually assumed by an heir is told in outline to a public assembled outside the place of investiture. To share the full story would give away something itself protected as hereditary right, but enough is told to show that the right is genuine (McIlwraith 1948).

Tellings to outsiders, especially in English, may be more elaborate, because they make explicit motives and details that a native audience would be expected to know. Sometimes a practiced source may even take on the role of collaborator, carefully interspersing ethnographic and linguistic explanation.[28]

Sequences within a myth and of myths may affect their components. One widely popular story has a trickster-transformer juggle his eyes, throwing them up to fall back in his sockets, only to have them stolen by a passing bird. Having made imitation eyes from a flower, he deceives someone else into thinking his eyes are superior and trading eyes with him. In a version told in Klamath by Patsy Ohles, the juggling is a major focus, as Coyote first admires the sound the eyes of Beaver make ("lolololok!") when Beaver juggles, then learns to do it himself. In a sequence told in Santiam Kalapuya by William Hartless, there is no juggling at all. The sun got warm, he became sleepy, he went to sleep, Blue Jay stole his eyes (cf. Hiram Smith, "The News about Coyote," chap. 12 of this volume). The loss of eyes is barely described, and the focus of the scene is on the sequel, one of a series of scenes in which Coyote trades body parts.[29]

Creative recombination of myths in sequences is so common that it can be grounds for suspicion of authenticity when sequences from related but different communities are too much alike (cf. Brightman 1989). Stories vary, then, by incorporation in larger sequences. So also genres other than story, such as songs, may vary when incorporated within one.

If one performance is the one recalled or best recalled by someone who later undertakes to tell it, variations may lead to versions. And sometimes variation and remaking go hand in hand for the narrator himself. Such seems the case with Charles Cultee's two tellings (1891, 1894) of the "Salmon's Myth," discussed earlier in this chapter (see note 22). In each a first part of acceptance by Salmon of insult is followed by a second in which Salmon reasserts authority. In the first telling, reassertion goes with abrupt, marked change of poetic form; in the second, the key to reassertion is a new ending in unmarked form.[30]

I have emphasized a kind of change that occurs between performances or perhaps without anticipation of performance at all. Change because of personal felt need to reflect, to interpret experience, with narrative as framework and resource. Change for which the narrator is not so much witness or performer as "remaker," interpreting fundamentals, deconstructing and reconstructing both.[31]

So, at least it seems, must have been the case for the late Linton Winishut of Warm Springs, Oregon. Some years ago, he told six hours of myth to Virginia Hymes, while others in the household watched television. He said he had had to memorize the stories as a child and also that he had never told the whole cycle before. If so, then between childhood and advanced age the cycle had become a vehicle for asserting foreknowledge, for weaving myths together around the figure of a Coyote who constantly predicted correctly what would occur. Another might say both how fine it was that Winishut was bringing out old words again and that the stories were not well told. What one has, I think, is an assertion of the validity of the tradition itself through the voice of its most salient protagonist. The satisfaction and confidence that gave might but for chance have remained a private matter.

So, I think, it was for Victoria Howard, living in Oregon City without other speakers of her language, and for Charles Cultee, living in Bay Center, Washington, with one or two others still knowing some Kathlamet, but neither with a community and an occasion for myth, so far as we know. With Victoria Howard we have again and again a fundamental reshaping of narratives known elsewhere from the perspective of male protagonists. Such is the case with "Seal Took Them to the Ocean," in which a myth told elsewhere as male adventure has a crucial woman advisor, an outcome in which adventure is explicitly not rewarded, and a subtext of reciprocity. Such is the case with her handling of the figure of Salmon. Such is the case with the first myth of the pair about Grizzly Woman that focuses on women protagonists. Cultee told Boas a myth (known elsewhere) in which five brothers seek in turn to rescue a sister who has been taken by a bear. The fifth succeeds, killing the bear. In Howard's narrative, we know nothing of any brothers until a revelation after the fourth has come and been killed, and no fifth comes. The niece-daughter and sister-mother take his place. Again and again, Howard's narratives think through narratives from the standpoint of the women in them. Again and again, these tellings seem to show the effect of growing up in a shattered culture, one in which caretakers are uncertain, unreliable, and in which women must muster what strength they can.

Cultee's Sun's myth uniquely reverses a type of frame known far and wide. In the Southwest, among the Navajos, Apaches, Acomas, and others, a woman is magically impregnated by the Sun. Her two children go to seek their father, who tests them severely. They endure, obtain his powers of lightning and the like, and go about the world eliminating dangerous beings. Among the Kwakwala (Kwakiutl) Indians of British Columbia, a woman similarly conceives, bearing Mink, who is teased by other children and seeks his father. Welcomed, he is allowed to carry the sun but goes too low (Phaeton). Elsewhere in the Northwest, myths of a man put through life-threatening tests by a prospective father-in-law are widespread (for example, the Tsimshian myth of Asdiwal, studied by Lévi-Strauss).

In all of these one can see something of the frame of the Kathlamet myth, except that all have to do with the world before the people have come. The Kathlamet myth does not tell of a world being begun, but of one being ended. Nothing has to be established, by going or by staying. The protagonist is not tested but welcomed. The destruction from carrying the sun is not what might be expected of a certain character (Mink), but the consequence of the act of a human who might have chosen otherwise. There are other myths of hubris in which characters must learn the limitations of their nature (Coyote seeking to trade body parts [Kalapuya], Coyote or Blue Jay seeking to emulate their hosts). Again, these stories are set before the people have come, when the world is being set right. In the Kathlamet myth, the world of people is already right, and an offer is made to make it more than right, but in the end it is destroyed. It is difficult not to see in this unique myth a reflection on the destruction of communities in western Oregon through introduced disease that began in isolated cases in the late eighteenth century and became widespread in the early nineteenth. Here history is absorbed and interpreted in terms of a fundamental tenet of the way of life, participant maintenance and reciprocity among the beings of the world, ineluctably conditioned by their respective natures. The theme of hubris, of overreaching one's nature, in stories of a bungling host is generalized to the fate of a people whose leader has only to receive. Perhaps there is also a resonance of accepting things not properly Indian from the new natures who had come, the whites.[32]

Myths are good to think, it seems, and those who have absorbed them may carry certain of them with them all their lives. Artistry is inseparable, one may think, first, from eliciting absorbed attention that makes the heard myth part of one's imagination, then from offering patterns and details that can give expression to new understandings. Depth of realization, interlocking form and detail, seem most present in just those narratives with depth of transformation, through depth of identification and reflection.

In part, such tellers of Native American myth are like users of Greek myth as described by Jameson: "The attitude of the user of myth may be compared to that of a historian who is convinced of the outlines of the history he is studying but feels free to rearrange, reject, and add to the incidents and persons reported by tradition in order to make sense of his subject. The analogy is cogent since, as we have seen, for the Greeks myth was in fact a kind of history. The originality of the Greek artist lay in the sense he made of his material" (Jameson 1961:234). And in part, they are like the medieval authors characterized by C. S. Lewis. The situation is different, in that there can be transforming imagination and penetrating imagination, and there may be efforts to heighten (characteristics he denies to these medieval authors). But whether engaged in change or not, it is true to say: "It is a realizing imagination . . . their matter and their confidence in it . . . possesses them wholly. Their eyes and ears are steadily fixed upon it, and so— perhaps hardly aware how much they are inventing—they see and hear what the event must have been like. . . . They sometimes profess to be deriving something from their *auctour* at the very moment when they are departing from him . . . like a historian who misrepresents the documents because he feels sure that things must have happened in a certain way" (Lewis 1967: 204-11). Remakers of myth have no *auctour* before their eyes, but voices and images in their minds, as may someone who knows much of the Bible, or Milton, or Shakespeare by heart. Perhaps the fact that it is the hearer of a myth who must supply the images involves a mingling of what was said and what was imagined from the outset. To have heard more than one performance, perhaps more than one performer, will have taught that rightness is not a question of always the same words. To have understood that myths have only partly to do with the past, that myths are a dialogue between past, present, and future, will allow them to "realize" (in two senses) what must have happened, from reflection on any of those three vantage points: received tradition, present circumstance, projected need.

Coyote pronounced that swallows would fly upriver in the spring when the salmon are about to come. How do we know that is true? Because we see that it happens. Why does it happen? Because Coyote said it would in the myth.

Circular, to be sure, but such circularity can be creative, a spiral. Caretakers insist on propriety, blinding themselves to danger in their own house. Why does it happen? It must have happened in a myth.

It is inherent in the dialectic of thinking myth, then, for myth to change. It must change, if it is to be coherent with experience. It must give pleasure of shape and detail, if it is to convince. And it must be abstract. Indeed, it is.

In discussing Riffaterre (section 1c), I mentioned that among the American Indian languages I know best, those that once prevailed along the Columbia River, from its Pacific mouth past the Cascades into the treeless plateau, a term for "myth," *k'ani,* means "nature." To refer to a myth of the hero Salmon as *I-gunat i-ya-k'ani* is to say "Salmon his-nature." Such a title indicates that the point is to show the consequences of having that nature, of acting as does Salmon in the story in question. An aged Wasco woman of Warm Springs, Annie Smith, once told me that people may hear and read the myths today but not understand them, not realize what they teach. I take her to have meant that it is not enough to know what a story says. One must know that it shows the consequences of having a certain nature and so acting in a certain way. Simple enough, one might think. But in the tradition, when a trickster such as Coyote acted with greed or lust, people might well laugh, but they would attend as well to the consequence of acting that way.[33]

Myths in effect are thought experiments (cf. Hymes 1965). Actors enter into a hypothetical experiment cast in narrative terms. The narrative exhibits the consequences, if a single motive were to have its course, embedded in an actual personality and not crosscut by circumstance. In this respect, the myths can be said to be abstract calculi of motives, providing by verbal means a symbolic "laboratory" for cognitive understanding.

It is possible for a story to be retold, much as it had been heard, without much active involvement. Again and again, however, it appears that those who most knew myths and best told them had experienced them, some of them at least, deeply. In part, they were agents of selection, finding in certain stories, rather than others, a fundamental or radical myth of personal meaning.[34] These might not be the myths most widely known, of which almost everyone could give an account, part of public conversation, when salmon came or one passed a place. Understanding of Native American myths as artistry and insight has to be in terms of the concerns, imagination, and resources of individual narrators. That does not imply only a very few. Those who stand at the end of traditions, such as Victoria Howard of Clackamas and Charles Cultee of Kathlamet, stand out alone against a context of loss, but were there access to their communities a century before, very likely there would have been many such.

Orality and Change

Little of what has been said has to do with the oral existence of myths as a cause of change. Some still may hold that oral myths change just because they are oral, without writing, without institutions that preserve texts and records. Others may expect such traditions to be preserved by memorization, almost from time immemorial. Some American Indian people themselves will hold this to be the case, and four impressive volumes of analysis of New World myths find in them a system that preserves, despite all change, an ancient knowledge (Lévi-Strauss 1964–1971). Neither view is wrong, but neither is right. Orality ensures neither. One cannot read off a mode of cultural life from this one physical means, just as one cannot ascribe the same mode of life to every group that gathers and hunts. Technological determinism is not accepted when technocrats and Marxists propose it; why then when classicists and media theorists do so? The common fact of oral tradition did not make American Indians and West Africans the same in interactive style or other modes of communication. The effect of orality, as of writing, depends on the practices of which it is part. In classical India remarkable analytic feats in grammar and other fields were orally created and orally preserved, through memorized sutras, for centuries (cf. Staal 1989). The Nootka Indians of British Columbia say that accounts of the origins of family crests and privileges are true, because they are transmitted in unbroken succession from the person to whom the originating experience happened.[35] When the Coos of the Oregon coast told myths in winter, those hearing repeated each sentence.[36] Such practices may support considerable stability, as may the meaningfulness of traditions to individuals. Some of the most valuable knowledge now preserved of Native American culture is attributable to remarkable individuals who remained in command of a language and narrative tradition for years with no one with whom to share them. At the same time, orality may permit divergent versions of events and narratives to continue side by side without prejudice, until the writing of one privileges it and disrupts.[37] In general, orality, like writing, is a means that may be shaped to a variety of ends.

Pleasure

Myths, then, change in response to personal desire. One may think them through out of existential need. There is satisfaction in this. There is also an element of sheer pleasure in the world and form of the myths and the situation of telling and listening. If one has the opportunity just to be with people for whom myths and their actors have been part of imaginative life, one learns this. One evening a Wasco friend brought her aunt to a workshop my wife and I were giving on the languages and afterward had me read to her aunt a story she knew I had written down from someone else. "That," she said, "is her reward"—to hear the language and the form and to chuckle.

The principal "bearers of tradition," as a phrase once had it—"re-creators of tradition" is more accurate—were such often because of pleasure. The last source of narrative in the Coos language of the Oregon coast, Annie Miner Peterson, survivor of many cities, occupations, and husbands, pointed out to her rapporteur, Melville Jacobs, that

> the reason she knew so many more stories than Mr. Drew (source for another linguistic anthropologist two decades before), and could tell them as well as she did, was because she enjoyed going out with the older people when they went root digging, berrying, camping out; she liked to accompany the older people in all their out of door activities. . . . There the people recounted and discussed folktales incessantly when they were drying salmon, camas digging, hunting, or camping out during travelling. Other and somewhat younger people at Yachats Reservation stayed at home more and seemed to have less attentiveness for the stories of the older people, which is why they learned fewer (of them). (Jacobs 1940:130)

The literature about myths mostly ascribes them to modes of rationalization of a natural world and social order: how a world came to be. Myths do serve ontology, social organization, ethics. A common cause of change is proliferation of a type of story for the sake of social identity. Just as mythographers in classical Greece connected a locality or town through narrative to someone mentioned in the Homeric poems, so the lineages of the Bella Coola, Bella Bella, Kwakiutl, and the like, of the North Pacific Coast, would proliferate legitimating accounts of their origin on a common model.[38] I have stressed that they not only rationalize but explore, and for individuals as well as for groups. Let me say now that there is here an evident element of desire and pleasure as well.

Probably the most familiar cause of myth is to explain something about an animal or the topography. Such are the stories perhaps most often retold for children and the principal stuff of a well-known Northwest anthology (Clark 1953). Myths do often enough end with explanations of why a chipmunk has stripes and bears no tail. Any location may have an account of its name. To think of explanation only in terms of such motifs, however, is to mistake passing clouds for the sky. Myths may *enact* explanation, without such motifs, as we have seen. And beyond motifs and calculi of motive, there is a general, constitutive openness to being, a cognitive eros of the sort experienced by Tillich (1955:72).

The world of myth is an open world. No one narrator has knowledge of all the myths, of all that might have happened. That is why Victoria Howard can end a Clackamas myth with "Now I know only that far." It is not that there is more to the myth; it is that there may be more to the world (see Hymes 1981b:322–27, 330–31). Nothing in the nature of the world need be in principle without a story. That is why one finds myths that seem hardly myths at all. Butterball Duck's wife sings that her husband is ugly, he sings that her clitoris is short, and that is all. But that gives something of the nature of such ducks. Notes Jacobs: "All the Coos knew this little thing. It is called a myth like any myth of greater length, because it narrates an occurrence of the myth age. When a Coos saw a butterball duck he would quote the lines, sing the song and laugh merrily" (1940:67). Cognitive eros: asking Hiram Smith the name in the language (Wasco) for, say, "otter," one gets not just a name, but where they are seen, how many, and the sliding that otters characteristically do. And so with other coinhabitants of the world. Myths inhabit a world closely observed and enjoyed in the observing.

Such enjoyment goes with the pervasive presence of a kind of story frame. The people of the myth world gather and come forward one by one. It may be for each to sing its guardian spirit song in winter, to decide who shall be elk when the human beings come, to compete for a chief's daughter. Whatever the reason, each has a moment of activity, perhaps only a song. Conversely, a traveling protagonist may encounter plants, plants and animals as foods, trees, one by one, identify each, pronounce about it.[39] Or encounter places and rivers and name each one. Scholarly indexes will distribute the stories that do this under different headings, according to principal actor and associated plot. But what unites and defines such framing myths cuts deeper: not a principal actor, but a category of being; not a plot, but a stage.

Repertoires may change to include more of the world. If someone tells an adventure one does not already know for a character one does know, or for a character one did not know had a story, if a pushy fieldworker simply asks, "Do you know a story about. . . ?" the response is, "I never heard that one," not that there is no such story.

A living tradition incorporates new elements, as when in the Navajo origin myth, the people, coming in four stages from below the earth, bring with them the horse, or when the late Linton Winishut of Warm Springs, Oregon, elaborating the role of the trickster-transformer Coyote as prophesier of what is to come, has Coyote at one point fly over the Pacific and compares a man who carries the sun to a jet plane. Perhaps every Indian group has a story in which some old person foresaw the coming of the whites.

A living tradition incorporates new stories. French-Canadians reached Oregon early in the nineteenth century, and at least one who married a Kalapuya woman left a fine set of stories of Petit Jean, told early in this century fluently in Mary's River Kalapuya.[40] Hiram Smith, a Wasco of Warm Springs,

Oregon, directed my attention to some fine Coyote stories he hadn't heard before that had been on public television.

A living tradition changes stories so as to keep them. Smith shared with me stories that he classified as "the kind of Coyote stories Tom Brown tells" (Tom Brown was a quite elderly Warm Springs Sahaptin). No myth world, but the same trickster-transformer, coming along, who bribes his way out of a trap with dollar bills that turn into excrement when the trapper gets home. A subsequent generation has the story, with Coyote bribing an anthropologist with money and a story, the money turning into fur and dirt, the story, when he plays his tape for other professors, turning into droppings (Toelken 1977:xi–xii).

But such change is not new, a result of the impact of Whites, nor has it been incidental.

And how can one explain that reflections that might never find an audience took and kept the form of stories, for Charles Cultee, Victoria Howard, and others, except to say that narrative is a way to think the world one knows, a way that even in inner enactment is satisfying in both content and form.

Altogether, the pleasures of imaginative life and satisfying form. Not a fixed corpus, memorized and recited, though there can be that, but a genre engaging the world. A resource for imagining what must have been and, therefore, what may be, in relation to what is; a way to give experience and speculation a shape that is flexible yet certain—open at point after point to elaboration, curtailment, an even tenor or intensification, full of voices, yet ineluctably the realization overall of a finite rhetoric, one that comes round and again comes round and can have rather a classical sound.[41] A mingling of forms and meanings that must be abstract, that must change, that must give pleasure.[42]

Appendix

Seal and Her Younger Brother Lived There

(i)

They lived there, Seal, her daughter, her younger brother.   (A)
I don't know how long, now a woman got to Seal's younger brother.
They lived there.   (B)
They would go outside in the evening.
The girl would say,   5
   she would tell her mother,
    "Mother! Something is different about my uncle's wife.

It sounds just like a man when she 'goes out.'"
"Shush! Your uncle's wife!"
A long, long time they lived there like that.   (C)   10
In the evening each would "go out."
Now she would tell her,
   "Mother! Something is different about my uncle's wife.
   When she 'goes out' it sounds just like a man."
"Shush!"   15

                                        (ii)

Her uncle, his wife, would lie down up above on the bed.   (A)
Pretty soon the other two would lie down close to the fire,
   they would lie down beside each other.
I don't know when at night, something comes onto her face.   (B)
She shook her mother,   20
   she told her:
"Mother! Something comes onto my face."
"Mmmm. Shush. Your uncle, they (two) are 'going.'"
Pretty soon now again, she heard something escaping,   (C)
She told her,   25
   "Mother! Something is going *t'úq t'úq* [dripping].
   I hear something."
"Shush. Your uncle, they are 'going.'"

                                       (iii)

The girl got up,   (A)
   she fixed the fire,   30
     she lit pitch,
       she looked where the two were:
         Ah! Ah! Blood!
She raised her light to it, so: (B)
   her uncle is on his bed,   35
     his neck cut,
       he is dead.
         She screamed.
She told her mother,   (C)
   "I told you,   40
    'Something is dripping.'
   You told me,
    'Shush, they are going.'
   I had told you,
    'Something is different about my uncle's wife.   45
    She would "go out,"

with a sound just like a man she would urinate'
You would tell me,
   'Shush!' "
She wept.   50
Seal said,   (D)
  "Younger brother! My younger brother!
  They (house-posts) are valuable standing there.
  My younger brother!"
    She kept saying that.   55
As for that girl, she wept.   (E)
She said:
  "In vain I tried to tell you,
   'Not like a woman,
   With a sound just like a *man* my uncle's wife would urinate.'   60
  You told me,
   'Shush!'
  Oh, oh, my uncle!
  Oh, my uncle!"
  She wept, that girl.   65

16

Robinson Jeffers's Artistry of Line

For almost a half-century it has been known that Jeffers did not write what is loosely called "free verse" but had a "metrical intention."[1] Since Herbert Klein's pioneering work, the nature of that metrical intention has not been much studied or well understood. William Everson rightly argues that recognition of Jeffers's true stature requires attention not only to Jeffers's ideas but also to his craft (1968:29). Close study will show that Jeffers was resourceful and inventive in technique. Indeed, when Everson writes that a critic who rejects Jeffers's metric in the name of aesthetic norms of "clarity and precision and vigor" has to be shown that there are other norms, whose "uses are vital to the life and well-being of language and hence of civilization," he concedes too much (1968:29–30). Such a critic can be shown that Jeffers himself achieves clarity and precision and vigor.

Line Relations in Jeffers

THE NEW MEASURE

Most critics agree that "Tamar" is the beginning not only of Jeffers's fame but also of his greatness as a poet. It marks a dramatic change in the creative vigor both of story and style from what he had published previously. The two changes go together. Robert Zaller observes of Jeffers earliest narratives: "The elements of the mature narratives—balladlike dramas of passion played out against the somber beauty of the California coast—were already present in these first works. But the characters remain curiously unrealized, figures of a pastoral idiom as stilted as the meters they are cast in" (1983:3–4, 5). What if "Tamar" had been written in the rhymed couplets of the "The Coast-Range Christ," a predecessor that accompanies it in the volume that made Jeffers's reputation?

Zaller has analyzed the development that led to "Tamar" in terms of Jeffers's self-understanding: "Not until Jeffers could see in human passion a worthy analogue of natural process was he able to transcend melodrama and create fully realized characters in a dialectically conceived relation to the external world. But that would not occur until he had come to terms with passion in himself and confronted the Oedipal sources of his art" (1983:5). To tell his truth "he could hope to do so only through a female protagonist. . . . What Jeffers found in search of his father's spirit was Tamar, who sought the father through the flesh. If Tamar herself could not resolve Jeffers's conflict, she would provide him with a way of objectifying it, of suggesting transcendence not through self-immolation but through carnality and violence. And if for her the end would still be a holocaust, it would not be until she had won through—and survived—the very limits of human experience" (1983: 14, 15). To my surprise I agree with Zaller. Freudian interpretations of literature usually had seemed to me misleading, missing the actuality of a story in a selective and arbitrary grasping at preestablished symbols. Not in Zaller. His readings of Jeffers's narratives make point-for-point sense of their unfolding. The Oedipal dialectic penetrates and clarifies.

The problem of tragic art, as posed by Nietzsche, is that great works require a balance between a Dionysian foundation and an Apollonian order imposed upon it. A summary of the argument of *The Birth of Tragedy* reads as if written with Jeffers in mind: "Its epitome is mastered energy, its poles are chaos and epic harmony. When the Dionysian element rules, ecstasy and inchoateness threaten: when the Apollonian predominates, the tragic feeling recedes" (Stern 1979:47). A feminine protagonist releases the energy in "Tamar," and a new measure masters it. Zaller explains the Dionysian pole: the Apollonian requires explanation as well.

In this essay I particularly want to extend investigation of Jeffers's new measure. Attention has gone mostly to the scansion of the lines themselves, to the bases and sources of their patterning as lines. Relations between lines have not, so far as I know, been much attended.[2] It is this aspect on which I concentrate.

NARRATIVE: AN ENDING AS BEGINNING

"The Coast-Range Christ," written about 1917 (1925:175–204), is the only major narrative between *Californians* and "Tamar" that Jeffers published. To Zaller, it is central to his development: "Perhaps more than any other single work . . . [it] reveals the mind and art of Jeffers in crisis" (1983:14, 6). Speaking of the dialectic of characters, however, Zaller comments, it "is a static, not to say stillborn, work, and in it Robinson Jeffers is still a poet stepping . . . on the throat of his own song" (1983:12). Frederic Carpenter observes: "The long and irregular but sometimes monotonously rhymed couplets illustrate the poet's transitional experiments with verse; they are interesting, but contrast sharply with the wholly original and skillfully modulated versification of "Tamar" . . . although the narrative remains somewhat pedestrian, the concluding strophes and antistrophes of choros and antichoros seem, by contrast, to take wings and soar" (1962:65). Soaring there is, but the narrative is not over. These final lines complete it within the perspective of God, dawn, and the breadth of the world, in a partial departure from rhyme and a thoroughgoing alternation of length of lines. Here is a sketch of the grouping and scansion of the lines. (Space indicates pairing of lines; numbers indicate beats.)

Choros	(1) 8 4 10 6 9 5 10 4	(unrhymed)
Antichoros	(2a) 10 5 10 6 9 5	(unrhymed)
	(1b) 8 7 8 7 8 8 8 7 7 7	(couplets)
Choros	(2) 10 6 12 6 12 4 9 5	(quatrains)
Antichoros	(2a) 10 5 10 4 10 6	(unrhymed)
	(2b) 7 8 7 8 7 9 8 9 7 7	(couplets)
Choros	(3) 9 7 12 5 12 6 11 6 9 10	(quatrains couplet)
Antichoros	(3a) (9)6 8 8 8(9) 8 9	(couplets)
	(3b) (8)7 7 7 6 8 7 7	(couplets)

The nine parts move from unrhymed (1, 2, 5) to rhymed couplets (3, 6, 8, 9, and the couplet ending choros 3) with rhymed quatrains (*abab*) intervening (4, 7). The one regularity is alternation of longer and shorter lines. This holds for the first and every subsequent choros and for the first part of each antichoros except the last. Length of line is not fixed, but alternation of long and short is constant. The second part of each antichoros and the first of part of the last as well keep close to an intermediate length, commonly eight or seven beats. Each antichoros appears to end with a pair of seven-beat lines.

The soaring at the end of "The Coast-Range Christ" thus goes together with a new relation among lines.

MATRIX FOR LYRIC

The shorter poems in the breakthrough volumes of 1924 and 1925 (*Tamar, Roan Stallion*) show the new relation in full flight. It is the pattern for most of them, a pattern for experiment.

"Mal Paso Bridge" (*Tamar*, 1925:171–74) is the poem with the often-quoted clause, "To shear the rhyme-tassels from verse," and the shearing goes with sheer exuberance of invention. There is no rhyme, but there are eight sections, no two alike: twenty-six lines all of five beats (section 1); ten lines

of alternating five and four (2); three tristichs, all of four beats (3); two unrhymed quatrains, both of the pattern 4-4-4-4 (if the last two syllables of
each last line can be taken as metrically unmarked) (4); seven distichs of
alternating five and three (5); six distichs of alternating six and four (6); two
unrhymed quatrains of the pattern 5-5-5-3 (7); four tristichs of the pattern
4-4-2 (8).

"Mal Paso Bridge" does not have the variety of foot and patterning of line
that the mature style will soon display, but the breakthrough is broached.
The shorter poems of *Tamar* and *Roan Stallion* show a development that
makes rhyme virtually impossible as a structural element, a marker of
equivalance.[3] Jeffers "masters energy" in three respects: with a variety of
types of feet within a line; with a variety of lengths of line; with lines
grouped in a variety of ways. In each respect, he invents novel relationships.
The relations within a line allow both a variety of unfamiliar feet, notably
the ionic and the paeon, and juxtapositions of feet whose metrical stresses
are adjacent. Lines have an unfamiliar variety of lengths and unfamiliar
length altogether. Lines are related to each other in novel, varied ways.

Patterns of Relation

The shorter poems of *Tamar* and *Roan Stallion* show Jeffers experimenting
with relations among lines. The experimentation involves three dimensions: patterns of grouping line lengths; variability in the length of lines
that correspond within a pattern; the range of difference between lines of
contrasting length.

Grouping

All the poems group lines. There are no poems with seriatim, ungrouped
lines. Line length may be constant; it is then long, or normatively so, and
such lines are grouped as distichs ("Point Joe" [1925:233–34; 1938:78], "Continent's End" [1925:252–53; 1938:87–88], "Shine, Perishing Republic" [1925:
95; 1938:168]). The common pattern is to have lines of two different lengths
alternate. The triadic pattern of "Divinely Superfluous Beauty" (1925:205;
1938:65) is a lovely extension. In later volumes one finds inventive larger
groupings of lines. "Be Angry at the Sun" (1941:152–53) has sets of four, in
which a variety of short lengths are brought round each time to a yet shorter
concluding line, three beats in the second stanza, two in all others. "The
Bloody Sire" (1941:151) has sets of five, in which three stanzas of the form
4-4-4-4-6 are completed by a summative 4-6 pair. "The Excesses of God"

(1941:104) is sonnetlike, with fourteen lines in which five alternations of 5-3 are concluded by four summative lines that alternate 6-3 6-3. Some more extended shorter poems, meditative in character, have different line lengths between one sequence and another: "Point Pinos and Point Lobos" (1925: 235–41); "Night" (1938:158–60).

Variability

In a given pattern of relationship, lines may be constant in their differences of length. Such is the case with "Natural Music" (1925:245; 1938:77), where the six distichs are uniformly 7-4 (seven beats, four beats), and "To the House" (1925:246; 1938:82), where six distichs are uniformly 4-5. As noted, "The Bloody Sire" has three regular pentatstichs: 4-4-4-4-6, followed by a final pair, 4-6, and "The Excesses of God" has five alternations of 5-3, followed by two of 6-3. (Of course, a poem whose lines are of constant length has constancy in the lack of difference.)

Where lines alternate, the odd-numbered are usually long, the even-numbered short. Sometimes, however, a poem begins with the shorter line. Such is the case with "To the House" and "To the Rock That Will Be at Cornerstone of the House" and also "Wise Men in Their Bad Hours" and "Science." The marked, concluding line of each stanza of "The Bloody Sire" has six beats, following four four-beat lines.

Corresponding line lengths within a pattern commonly vary around a norm. Sometimes the variation is quite localized, a single line or two. Such is the case with "Divinely Superfluous Beauty," whose four triplets are 6-3-3 7-4-3 6-3-3 6-3-3; "To the Rock That Will Be a Cornerstone of the House" (1925:247; 1938:83), whose two stanzas show 4-7 4-7 5-7 4-7 4-6 4-7 4 and 6-4 6-4 6-4 6-5 6-4 6, respectively, and "Joy" (1925:97; 1938:170), whose ten lines show 5-4 6-3 6-3 6-3 6-3.

In other cases variation is more frequent, but a norm is still evident. Such is the case with "Salmon-Fishing" (1925:245; 1938:81), whose lines alternate as 6-3 5-3 5-3 5-3 5-3 5-4 6-3 5-5-3 (the additional longer line at the end [5-5-3] may be another closing device); "To the Stone-Cutters" (1925:249; 1938:84), where the lines may be scanned as 6-4 7-3 6-4 7-4 6-4); "Wise Men in Their Bad Hours" (1925:251; 1928:86), where a rather steady alternation of four-beat lines is interrupted by a sequence of four with five beats, 4-6 4-5 4-5 4-6 4-6 4-6 4-6 5-5-5-5 4-6 4-5; "Birds" (1925:86; 1938:161), with 8-4 7-4 7-6 8-6 8-4 8-4 8-6 7-5; "Fog" (1925:87; 1938:162), with almost constant alternation of three-beat lines, 7-2 5-3 3-3 5-2 5-3 5-3 7-3 6-3 7-3; "Boats in a Fog" (1925: 88; 1938:163), which settles into alternating four-beat lines at the end, 7-3

8-3 7-4 6-3 6-4 7-3 6-4 6-4 7-4 7-4 6-4; "Granite and Cypress" (1925:89; 1938:
164), with clearly polarized lines of 9-2 10-3 9-3 9-3 10-2 9-2 9-3; "People and
Heron" (1925:92; 1038:166), with a constant eight-beat in odd-numbered
lines (8-3 8-4 8-4 8-5 8-4); "Science" (1925:101; 1938:173), with 4-9 5-9 4-9
4-9 4-8 5-8; "Post Mortem" (1938:179), with clearly polarized lines of 9-3
9-3 10-3 10-3 10-3 8-3 9-4 8-3 8-4 9-3 8-4 10-4; "Summer Holiday" (1938:
181), with 4-6 5-7 4-6 5-6 5-6, where the almost constant length of the even-
numbered lines seems defining, but where a different picture emerges when
one groups the lines into the two five-line verse paragraphs of the syntax:
4-6-5-7-4 6-5-6-5-6. Note also the clearly but contrastingly marked short /
long of "Ante Mortem" (1938:178), with 4-8 4-8 5-9 5-8 5-9 4-8; and the
long / short of "Post Mortem," with 9-3 9-3 10-3 10-4 10-3 8-4 9-4 8-3 8-4 9-3
8-4 10-4.

Range

The examples just given show that alternating lines, contrasting lines, differ
in the amount of variation that obtains between them. Let us call this a matter of range. There are three types, which can be dubbed *polar, double,* and
adjacent. (Obviously if lines have the same length their relation is constant.)
Mixing occurs, but one of the three types appears to frame a poem.

   "Granite and Cypress" and "Post Mortem" are examples of a polar relation. In both, the odd-numbered lines are in the upper range of a Jeffers line
(nine, ten, and some eight in "Post Mortem"), while the even-numbered
lines are in the lower range (two, three, some four in "Post Mortem"). The
interval of difference is great.

   Many poems are examples of a doubled relation. The beats of adjacent
lines may not be precisely in a two-to-one relationship, but fall within a
range close to that. The interval of difference is at least three beats. Such
are "Divinely Superfluous Beauty" (6-3), "Natural Music" (7-4), "Salmon-
Fishing" (taking the opening and closing 6-3 as norm); probably "To the
Rock That Will Be a Cornerstone of the House," which seems defined by 4-7;
"People and a Heron" (8-3 8-4); "Joy," almost entirely 6-3; "Science," with
4-9 5-9 4-8 5-8; "Ante Mortem" with 4-8, 5-9; "Cassandra," with almost entirely 6-3; "To the Stone-Cutters" (6-4, 7-3); "Boats in a Fog," with 7-3 (four
times), 7-4 (three times), 8-2, and 6-3 dominating 6-4 (four times).

   Sometimes lines alternate in the relations six to four and five to three.
Each is one step from six to three and can be considered akin to doubled
relations. "To the Rock That Will Be a Cornerstone of the House" seems to
belong here, 4-7 dominating the first stanza and 6-4 the second. "Fog" fits

here, although one should note its exceptional pair of three-beat lines early on, as does "Boats in a Fog" and also "The Excesses of God," which is almost entirely 5-3, ending as it does with 6-3-6-3.

In "Birds" there is a steady maintenance of a long odd-numbered line (eight or seven); half the even-numbered lines are four, but half of them six or five. Maintenance of an interval of at least two beats appears to constitute a pattern in such a case.

A few poems show an adjacent relation. Lines alternate in length, but the difference is entirely or preponderantly a single beat. Such are "To the House," which is 4-5 throughout, and "Wise Men in Their Bad Hours," predominantly 4-6 and 4-5.

LINE LENGTH AS DEVICE (1)

Study of any individual poem may show significance for any of these dimensions in relation to its thrust. Groups of poems may show one or more of these dimensions to have recurrent significance, and instances will be taken up later in this discussion. There is a great need for study of all of Jeffers's poems with attention to both his evident inventiveness of form and his recurrent, prosodic practices. There is more than the presence of a measure; there is its varied deployment.

It does seem likely that much of the variation in Jeffers's verse is ad hoc. A poem got started and began to take shape in a certain way, and a feeling for pattern carried it out. It seems likely that in the short poems of the initial breakthrough, it is the pervasive alternation of lines of different length itself that is meaningful. There is often little connection between a line of a given length and particular content. Sentences and clauses hardly coincide with lines. One ends, another begins, in the midst of a line. Syntactic units continue from a line of one length to a line of another like water escaping down a wheel (cf. "Divinely Superfluous Beauty" and "Natural Music").

Such alternation of lines allows a dialectic of movement on the page, a way of getting away from confining, a priori form, a way of keeping open the relation on the page between the movement of language and the movement of the world. If this statement seems one that might be made about William Carlos Williams, the parallel is intentional. Jeffers and Williams both achieved a pattern of freedom, a measure alert to the emerging thrust of a poem, open to continuing experimentation (on Williams, see Cushman 1985). The difference is that Williams is famous for doing so while Jeffers is not. Williams announced a program; Jeffers left it to the chance of another to discover his metrical intention and even then remained reticent. He did not wish to found a school, but perhaps over time others still will adopt and extend his discoveries as a distinctive tradition.

LINE LENGTH AS DEVICE (2)

Significant connotations for length of line do emerge within individual poems. Sometimes the position of a difference in length seems significant. At the end of the last sequence in "Point Pinos and Point Lobos," for example, the summative expression at the end (111) has six lines of ten beats, followed by a split line of eleven beats in all (eight and three, with space and indentation preceding the three) and two lines of twelve beats. The enhancement seems intended. One might call it simple augmentation, somewhat like a concluding alexandrine. Especially perhaps in later poems, the longer line of an alternating pair may be lengthened at the end. In "The Excesses of God" (1941:104), five regular distichs of five and three beats are completed by a pair of distichs that are 6-3, and in "Cassandra" (1948:117), five regular distichs (6-3) are completed by one whose lines are 7-5. Again, the augmentation seems a device (sonnetlike in the case of the fourteen lines of "The Excesses of God"). On the other hand, framing lines may be shorter. In "Be Angry at the Sun" (1941:152-53), it seems no accident that in each quatrain the first and last lines are shorter than the second and third, and the fourth line always shortest of all: 3-5-6-2 4-6-5-3 3-6-5-2 4-5-6-2 3-5-6-2.

It may be possible to discover that particular lengths of line and particular patterns of alternation have meaningful associations, at least in certain sets of poems. The long lines at the end of "Point Pinos and Point Lobos" and in the ten-line distichs of "Continents End" both reach toward the sublime. It seems striking that both "To the House" and "To the Rock That Will Be a Cornerstone of the House" have the less common pattern of shorter line first. Other cases will be discussed later. Only a comprehensive study can tell the full story.

Whether or not associations of meaning between lengths of line and patterns of alternation of line-length prove pervasive in the shorter poems, it can be shown that such connections may emerge in the course of a particular poem. Three short poems from *Solstice* provide a demonstration.

In "Rock and Hawk" (1935:133; 1938:563), the seven stanzas each have three lines, and the first two lines of a stanza have invariably three beats.[4] The third line has two beats, or so the first three stanzas establish. In the fourth stanza the third line may tempt one to hear a pair of amphimacers, "Not the cross, not the hive," but is easily taken as having just two beats (cross, hive). In the fifth stanza, the third line, "Disinterestedness," might be taken as two beats, with elision of the third vowel ("Disint(e)restedness"), but may read more easily as three: "Disinteréstednéss." In the sixth stanza, the third line is inescapably three beats: "Márried tó the mássive (/Mysticisms of stone)." The seventh, final stanza renews the predominant pattern: 3-3-2. One has then 3-3-2 3-3-2 3-3-2 3-3(-2) 3-3(-3) 3-3-3 3-3-2.

The possibility of added beats in the fourth, fifth, and sixth stanzas, increasing to certainty in the sixth, penultimate stanza, seems intentional. Otherwise the final lines of the stanzas could have been made to conform: "Not cross, not hive"; "Disinterést"; "Márried to mássive." The intention seems a formal one of arousing, suspending, and fulfilling an expectation. The two-beat line has a sense of ending in stanzas one and three: the return to it in the final stanza brings a sense of affirmative conclusion.

There is a similar effect in the modified sonnet "The Cruel Falcon" (1953: 93; 1938:562). The fourteen lines are grouped 4, 4, 2, 4 and rhymed (mostly with assonance) *abab cdcd ee ffff.* The first four explore and qualify the theme "Contemplation would make a good life," the second four a contrary assertion, "Pure action would make a good life," each with corresponding imagery as to how that life should be (strict, sharp). The third stanza states briefly, without imagery, something lacking the good of either.

In pleasant peace and security
How suddenly the soul in a man begins to die.

In the fourth stanza the inevitable consequence is stated, the need and necessity of intensity.

He shall lóok up abóve the stálled óxen
Envying the cruel fálcon,
And dig únder the straw for a stone
To brúise himself ón.[5]

For the most part, there is no regularity of line length within stanzas nor of corresponding lines across stanzas. (I scan the poem as follows: 6-5-3-4; 5-4-3-2; 4-6; 4-4-4-2). One stanza, the last, does have a sequence of lines of the same length (4-4-4), and the second and fourth stanzas both end with two-beat lines, the one bringing the octet to a conclusion, the other the poem as a whole. The intervening stanza, the third, seems a pivot and contrast, having only two lines and going as it does from four to six beats, thus reversing the movement of other stanzas, all of which end with a line shorter than that with which they began. In the context, six beats is expansive. Thus patterning of line length supports meaning; regularity following variation and the return of a two-beat end line after departure fit a sense of inevitable consequence in the final stanza.

"Life from the Lifeless" (1935:134; 1938:564) is in yet a different pattern of stanza and line length, yet also with an emergent connection between alternation of line length and meaning, and one that has analogy to the two others from *Solstice* just discussed. There are five stanzas, each of three lines. None are identical. (I scan the poem as follows: 4-2-4; 6-2-2; 7-3-3; 3-6-3; 4-4-4). The fifth and final stanza gathers the poem together, as it were, stating the outward-pointing moral in three lines, all of four beats. It is the only stanza to have all its lines of the same length. Moreover, in the stanzas that precede it, lines of two and four beats almost always coincide with positive meanings, lines of three and six beats with negative meanings.

Spirits ánd illúsions have died,
The náked mind lives
In the béauty óf inánimate thíngs.

Flówers wíther, gráss fádes, trées wilt,
The fórest is búrnt;
The róck is nót burnt.

The déer stárve, the winter birds
Díe on their twigs and lie
In the blúe dawns in the snów.

Mén suffer wánt and becóme
Cúriously ignóble; ás prospérity
Made them cúriously vile.

But lóok how nóble the world is,
The lónely-flówing wáters, the sécret-
Kéeping stónes, the flówing sky.

The connection between length of line and kind of meaning is not perfect: "The deer starve, the winter birds" is part of the negative imagery, but with four beats (following "grass fades, trees wilt," "deer starve" can only be taken in the same way). The positive assertion "[t]he rock is not burnt" might be read with three beats, although that seems less likely than two. Not everyone would find a fourth stress on "is" in the last stanza, although Jeffers's regular use of ionic feet and the weight of the word at this point convince me that it is to be taken so. But clearly the poem opens and closes with positive assertions and images in its first and fifth stanzas, set off against negative images in the three stanzas between; clearly the opening and closing stanzas are dominated by four-beat lines; clearly the negative imagery is introduced with a six-beat line ("Flowers wither"); clearly the negative descriptions are concentrated and accumulate in three- and six-beat lines just preceding the closing stanza.[6]

These three poems published in 1935 show a certain consistency, a use of two- and four-beat lines, as opposed to three and six, for a sense of conclusion and, sometimes, of positive statement. The poems themselves are of quite varied shape—four stanzas of four, four, two, four lines; seven stanzas of three lines each; five stanzas of three lines each—and show quite varied relation among line lengths within and across stanzas. There is always pattern and measure, yet they emerge individually in each case.

Again, the sense of form adapted to the emerging thrust of the poem in hand, of continuing experimentation with form, is parallel to the work of William Carlos Williams. That Williams and Jeffers were contemporaries is important to remember, despite the difference in the way each broke from the "tassels of rhyme."

LINE LENGTH AS DEVICE (3)

Given that pattern and measure emerge individually and that Jeffers continued to experiment with form throughout his career, it is not possible to say that the meanings of line length found in these three poems hold for other poems. Only a study of Jeffers's short poems as a whole could tell. But it is possible to suggest recurrent kinds of meaning for broad contrasts of line length in the sequences of his longer poems. There alternation of length occurs, not line to line, but section to section. Let me explore this with two meditations, "Point Pinos and Point Lobos" and "Night," and then take up "Tamar."

In his sensitive assessment of "Night" Brophy calls it "Jeffers's pivotal lyric . . . simply and effectively structured in classic meditation form—a natural scene is offered for contemplation, followed by the considerations arising from it" (Brophy 1976). Length of line enters into the structuring in a subtle way.[7] How it does so can usefully be assessed against the background of another early meditative poem, "Point Pinos and Point Lobos" (1925:235–41).

"Point Pinos and Point Lobos" anticipates the lovely second stanza of "Night" in its lines of invocation—

O shining of night, O eloquence of silence,
    the mother of the stars, the beauty beyond beauty,

The sea that the stars and the sea and the mountain bones
   of the earth and men's souls are the foam on, the opening
Of the womb of that ocean.

                        (1925:236)

and in lines that say of the Buddha:

and to meditate again under the sacred tree, and again
Vanquish desire will be no evil.

The form also remembers "Tamar": the Buddha, found here as well as in
Asia, smiles his immortal peace, commanding Point Lobos.

And the burnt place where that wild girl whose soul was
   fire died with her house.

                        (1925:240)

"Point Pinos and Point Lobos" has intrinsic interest as a sympathetic
meditation and address on and to Jesus and Gautama as complementary
teachers of men whose messages fall short. Part 1 addresses Jesus in relation to Point Pinos; part 2 addresses Gautama in relation to Point Lobos.
Before doing so, it opens with a panorama of the mountains of the world
that Jeffers's spirit has visited (reminiscent of the panoramic view within
which the action of "The Coast-Range Christ" concludes in choros and antichoros). It then says of the coastal point

        [T]here is no place
Taken like this . . .
Our race nor the great springs we draw from, . . .
 . . . .
has known this place nor its like nor suffered
The air of its religion.

This is to imply a third religion, native to the continent's end. Part 1 ends
depicting its nature in the case of Jesus, part 2 in regard to Gautama. Part 3
proclaims it generally. The two men whom "wisdom made Gods" tell nothing so wise or sweet as the eternal recurrences of nature. They foolishly re-
belled against the laws of the instinctive God, the essence and the end of
whose labor is beauty, for whom life and death, darkness and light, are one
beauty, one rhythm.

   Like "Night," "Point Pinos and Point Lobos" envisages acceptance, but of
recurrence and beauty, not, as in "Night," of personal death. It ends with
exultance, the other poem with tenderness.

   Like "Night," this meditation has sections associated with length of line.
Let me show the lengths, then briefly discuss them.[8]

1 A   88888 8888 (Point Pinos)
   B   66666 66666 66666 66666 66 4 (split line) (to Jesus)
   C   2 11 12 10 12 11 12 10 3 (split line) (to ocean and night)
   D   5 66666 68666 66666 666 4 (split line) (to Jesus)
   E   2 55655 55555 655 (to Jesus)
2 A   88878 86768 97989 98886 88988 88888 88888
        6 (split line) (mountains, Point Lobos, Buddha here also)
   B   2 88988 98888 8884 (split tine) (to Gautama)
   C   2 877888 (of Gautama and here)
3   10 10 10 10 10 10 8 (split line) (recurrence vs. Jesus, Gautama)
        3 12 12 (invocation of praise]

There are three typical lengths of line. Lines of eight beats are used for the opening description (1A), the catalog of mountains (2A), and the rest of the part concerned with Buddha (2B) and the character of the coast (2C). Lines of six or five beats are used for Jesus. Lines of invocation of the true nature of the world are lines of ten beats and more.

The differences in typical length of line go together with their content here and with their uses in other poems. The eight-beat line is one Jeffers uses in distichs (or another poem describing a point, "Point Joe," a poem that immediately precedes "Point Pinos and Point Lobos" in the volumes *Tamar* and *Roan Stallion, Tamar and Other Poems* [1925:233–34; 1938:78–79]). Evidently, Jeffers found the eight-beat line suitable for such odelike description and reflection. He uses distichs of ten-beat lines in the hymnlike invocations and adjurations of "Continent's End" and "Shine, Perishing Republic" just as he uses ten-beat lines in the early moment of invocation and the concluding evocation here. The use of shorter lines with regard to Jesus goes together with a more intense personal focus on Jesus. Jesus is personally and passionately addressed several times, Gautama barely once (and then as his smile).

Which tortured trunk will you choose, Lord, to be hewn to a cross?
I am not among the mockers Master, I am one of your lovers,
Ah weariest spirit in all the world, we all have rest
Being dead but you still strive . . .
. . . .
Unhappy brother
That high imagination mating mine
Has gazed deeper than graves: is it unendurable
To know that the huge season and wheel of things
Turns on itself forever.

                                                        (1925:235, 237)

In this poem, then, an intermediate level of length (dominantly eight beats) serves for accounts of nature and Buddha. It lies between two poles of line length used for heightening intensity. One (ten and more beats) invokes the sublime, the other (six and five) personal identification and pain.

Lines that are long and lines that are short, often lines of ten beats and lines of five, are prominent in Jeffers, but "Point Pinos and Point Lobos" shows that a simple dichotomy is unable to do justice to his virtuosity or to one indication of explicit intention. His notes for an early version of "Tamar," while they do not describe the final poem either as to plot or verse, do state a plan to distinguish three lengths of line, five, ten, and eight beats.[9]

There is a special significance to the patterning of line length in "Night." As in "Point Pinos and Point Lobos," there are degrees of length of line. These degrees function within a strict pattern.

As previously stated, length of line enters into the structuring of "Night" in a subtle way. First of all, it is stanzas that alternate, not lines except as part of stanzas. There are three contrasts among the stanzas as to length: (a) in number of lines, (b) in typical length of line, and (c) in form of ending. All are consistently maintained.

(a) The seven stanzas alternate as to number of lines: 7, 12, 7, 12, 7, 12, 7. Odd-numbered stanzas, including the first and the last, have fewer lines; even-numbered stanzas (ii, iv, vi) more.

(b) Shorter stanzas have a shorter range of lines in terms of length. Here is a scansion of them:

(i)	4 3 4 4 2	**4 2**	
(ii)	6 6 6 8 6	7 6 6 6 6	**7 7**
(iii)	3 3 3 4 3	**4 2**	
(iv)	6 7 6 6 7	7 7 7 7 7	**7 10**
(v)	3 3 3 3 3	**4 2**	
(vi)	6 6 6 6 6	6 6 6 7 6	**7 7**
(vii)	2 7 5 4 6	**7 2**	

(The last two lines of each stanza are given in boldface to call attention to the third relationship, form of ending.)

(c) Each of the shorter stanzas ends with a two-beat line, all but the last with the same pattern (4-2). In each of the shorter stanzas, the final cadence is a fall from the longest to the shortest of its lines: 4-2 in (i, iii, v), 7-2 in (vii). Two of the longer stanzas (ii, vi) end with 7-7, the other (iv) with 7-10. In each of the longer stanzas, the final cadence is a continuation or an augmentation of its dominant longest length of line. In (ii, vi), six-beat lines have dominated, and the ending is 7-7. In (iv) seven-beat lines have dominated, and the ending is 7-10.

Let me take up the connotations of differing lengths of line and then the significance of the form of ending.

Like "Point Pinos and Point Lobos," "Night" makes use of three typical lengths of line, but the quantities are scaled down. That is appropriate to the tone in which the subject is treated. In "Night" the longest lines are commonly of six and seven beats. It is these lines that are associated with the intensity of reaching toward the universe, the sublime. Their twelve-line stanzas (ii, iv, vi) invoke "Night" ("O soul worshipful of her," "O passionately at peace," "O passionately at peace"), while vividly depicting sources of light (the sun, human fires, stars, and planets). The one longer (longest) line, ten beats, is the last line of a stanza of six and seven beats, and in its position as last line of the middle stanza (iv) and in its content, linking cliff and tide, is a pivotal line:

To us the near-hand mountain
Be a measure of height, the tide-worn cliff at the sea-gate a measure of
    continuance.

It marks the point at which the poem turns to make explicit the respect in which it articulates the idea of the turning of the tide (see discussion of the final stanza).

The middle range has lines of four and three beats. Like the middle-range lines of eight beats in "Point Pinos and Point Lobos," these lines are associated with descriptive calm. The three short stanzas before the last, dominantly of four and three beats (i, iii, v) assert nothing but simply depict movements of return—to darkness, to water, to land—tide ebbing from rocks, sun setting, and a ship's light far out on the ocean (i); deer moving to a mountain stream (iii); the tide turning toward the land (v).[10]

The lowest range in "Night" is in the two-beat lines. Each seven-line stanza ends with one, as does the poem. But where in "Point Pinos and Point Lobos" the lower range is associated with intensity of personal feeling and pain, here the lower range is associated with quietness and, in the end, peace.

Initially the association is a formal one, a function of cadence that provides a sense of closure. In the initial stanza, after lines of 4-3-4 beats, the fourth line pictures light that is fading or faint:

[T]he slow west
Sombering its torch; a ship's light
Shows faintly, far out,
Over the weight of the prone ocean
On the low cloud.

With the image of a ship's light, the initial stanza moves twice to closure in the 4-2 4-2 cadence.

In the next short stanza (iii), after lines of 3-3-3 beats, there is an analogous movement of 4-3-4-2, with quietness in movement to the stream (no twigs crackling) and darkness (ferns) about the water.

In the third short verse (v), after lines of 3-3-3-3-3 beats, there is a single 4-2 cadence, and the ultimate quietness is addressed, anticipating the theme and prophecy of the last long stanza (vi) and the premise of the ending (vii).

[Y]ou Night will resume
The stars in your time.

The association of a two-beat line with quietness and peace is a function of overt statement in the final short stanza, framing the rest of the stanza with an opening question ("Have men's minds changed") and closing answer ("And death is no evil"), but also of form in the relation of these lines to the other lines of the stanza and to lines of other length in the poem as a whole.

The final stanza, itself renewing the pattern of shorter length of stanza and line, at the same time encompasses the longer line length of the longer stanzas. It begins and ends with two-beat lines and has a four-beat line at its center, yet incorporates lengths (7-6-7) found otherwise only in the long stanzas. In its own ending, it falls from seven, its own longest length and the longest normal length of line in the poem as a whole, to two, its shortest and the shortest in the poem.

These relationships indicate an opposition, or polarity, that is resolved in the final stanza in favor of that which such shorter stanzas and their shorter lines or final cadences express. In "Point Pinos and Point Lobos," the longest lines invoke and hail the discovery of eternal recurrence and return. In "Night," the shortest lines accept it. In the meditation on the two points, the discovery is developed by imagining Jesus and Gautama as ultimately subject to it (parts 1, 2) and then asserting the inadequacy of the two in comparison to it in a grand expansive tutti (part 3). In "Night," there is final assertion too, but as quiet recognition. All is natural process, and its description begins, mediates, and ends the passionate contemplation and reflection of the intervening longer stanzas. Recurrence is not a lesson learned, but implicit in the governing image of tide, now enlarged beyond the human world. It means not only "alternation of white sunlight and brown night" (1925:241), day and night, seasons and "fierce renewals," as in the meditations at the points, but also a world eventually again without sun ("he will die" ["Night" ii]) and human beings. The penultimate short stanza ends: "[Y]ou Night will resume / The stars in your time." To be sure, the deeper fountain, Night, immortal, is the grandest tide and might be imagined ultimately to recede and to be followed by another lighted world. But the poem itself ends with the acceptance of personal death and universal dark. Following the one ten-beat line at the end of the middle stanza, the tide turns to the land and Night will resume the stars (v). Life is said to remember quietness and to live ready for harbor (death) (vi). A rock hidden deep in the waters of the soul breaks the surface (vii). (The passage is framed as a question, but the preceding lines make clear the positive answer.) The tide rocks (i) and the grave depths of the poet's soul in which the splendor without rays dwells always (ii) are identified and generalized to humankind, for whom the darkness beyond the stars now is empty of harps and habitations and death is no evil.

The contraries of the longer stanzas—on the one hand, Night, on the other, human delight, effort, passion, and consciousness, recognizing, addressing, and invoking Night—are formally absorbed and framed within the shorter stanzas. Until the end of the third of the shorter stanzas (v), they assert nothing but simply describe. The natural processes of the short stanzas are identified with the human history of the long stanzas through the image of the tide rock.[11] And the pattern of return to quietness is enacted as a conclusion.

The final transcendence is formally prepared from the start. To accept the opening stanzas as description in the pattern given in each is to be prepared for accepting the end. Each of the preceding seven-line stanzas is associated with the description of natural process, and in each the length of line associated with such description falls to two beats, associating natural process with rest and peace. In its position, framing, and lengths of line, the final seven-line stanza connotes a natural process, but now one that occurs in men's minds ("Have men's minds changed") and encompasses in its long penultimate line their most passionate quest: "But now, dear is the truth. Life is grown sweeter and lonelier," and the recognition that "[d]eath is no evil" is of a piece with the low cloud, dark ferns, and Night resuming the stars.

The foregoing observations may be useful in regard to other of Jeffers's shorter poems. No single conclusion should be proposed on the basis of the few poems considered here. Quite possibly Jeffers's concern and practice varied over time, responsive to expressive concerns, an internal evolution, or the sheer desire to experiment with possibilities.

The shorter poems, however, are the lesser challenge. To show a further dimension of artistry may commend them to a wider readership. Still, they have never lacked for admirers. It is the long narratives, which are central to Jeffers's own purpose and effort, that have most suffered neglect.[12] The work of Brophy, Everson, Zaller, and others is doing much to restore their place. In a further study, I hope to show how the principle of relations among types of lines enters into the organization of the long narratives, adding a level of organization whose recognition enters into the interpretation of their form and foci of intensity.

Appendix 1

Index of Narrators and Narratives by Chapter

1. Survivors and Renewers

Cultee, Charles, Kathlamet, "Sun's Myth" (discussed)
Cultee, Charles, Kathlamet, "Salmon's Myth" (noted)
Howard, Victoria, Clackamas, "Coyote Made the Land Good" (noted)
Howard, Victoria, Clackamas, "Seal and Her Younger Brother" (discussed)

2. Franz Boas on the Threshold of Ethnopoetics

Cultee, Charles, Kathlamet, "Sun's Myth," act 3
Cultee, Charles, Kathlamet, "Swan's Myth" (noted)
Simpson, Louis, Wishram, "The Deserted Boy," act 2

3. Use All There Is to Use

Beynon, William, Tsimshian, Tricksters and bilingualism (discussed)
Cultee, Charles, Kathlamet, "Salmon's Myth" (discussed)
Howard, Victoria, Clackamas, "Tongue" (discussed passim)
Howard, Victoria, Clackamas, "Gitskux and His Older Brother" (discussed passim)
Howard, Victoria, Clackamas, "Grizzly Woman Began to Kill People" (discussed)
Hudson, John B., Santiam Kalapuya, "Coyote Releases Water Dammed Up by the Frogs" (discussed)
Hudson, John B., Santiam Kalapuya, Tricksters and bilingualism (discussed)
Kahclamat, Philip, Wishram, Tricksters and bilingualism (discussed)
Kaltaṗau M̃asemata, Nguna (Central Vanuatu), "The Heron" (discussed)
Pearson, Clara, Tillamook, "Split His Own Head" (discussed)
Peynetsa, Andrew, Zuni, "Coyote and Junco" (discussed)
Reuben, Nettie, Karok, "Coyote's Journey"
Rush Buffalo, John, Tonkawa, "Coyote and Eagle's Daughter" (discussed and text presented with profile)
Simpson, Louis, Wishram, "Coyote and Deer" (discussed)
Starrit, Julia, Karok, "Coyote's Journey"

Several Quileute narrators, Tricksters and bilingualism (discussed)
Unidentified narrator, Klamath, "Thunderbird," opening verses

4. Variation and Narrative Competence
Cultee, Charles, Kathlamet, "Sun's Myth" (discussed)
Davis, Marion, Upper Chehalis, "Crow, Her Son, Her Daughter" (discussed)
George, Larry, Sahaptin, "Celilo" (discussed)
Howard, Victoria, Clackamas, "Gitskux and His Older Brother" (discussed)
Hunt, Joe, Klikitat Sahaptin, "Sun and His Daughter" (noted)
Irish English (noted)
Johnson, Frances, Takelma, "Coyote and Frog" (discussed)
Maddux, Phoebe, Karok, "Spring Salmon Stays Single" (discussed)
Pearson, Clara, Tillamook, "Split-His-Own-Head" (discussed)
Rush Buffalo, John, Tonkawa, "Coyote and Eagle's Daughter" (discussed passim)
Young, Tom, Maidu, "Night-Hawk-Man" (discussed)

5. When Is Oral Narrative Poetry?
Aune, Halver O., Frontier Norwegian (two versions analyzed)
Blommaert, Jan, Belgium (work discussed)
Capps, Lisa, and Elinor Ochs, agoraphobia (work discussed)
Cultee, Charles, Kathlamet, "Sun's Myth," act 6, stanza A
Howard, Victoria, Clackamas, "Coyote Made the Land Good" (discussed)
Howard, Victoria, Clackamas, "Gitskux and His Older Brother," part 3, act 1,
    scene 3
Howard, Victoria, Clackamas, passage from "Tongue" ("They became people")
Howard, Victoria, Clackamas, "They Died of Hunger" (discussed)
John L., New York City, "Well, One Was with a Girl" (analyzed)
Johnson, Frances, Takelma, "Coyote and Frog" (noted)
Kahclamat, Philip, Wishram, "The Crier" (discussed)
McRae, Jill, Australia (work discussed)
Pearson, Clara, Tillamook, "Split-His-Own-Head" (discussed)
Simpson, Louis, Wishram, "The Deserted Boy," act 2 (discussed)
Urban, Greg, Shokleng (Brazil) (work discussed)

6. Language, Memory, and Selective Performance
Cultee, Charles, Kathlamet, 1891, 1894 tellings

7. A Discourse Contradiction in Clackamas Chinook
Howard, Victoria, Clackamas, early 1930 telling

8. Bungling Host, Benevolent Host

Howard, Victoria, Clackamas, "Seal Took Them to the Ocean"

Simpson, Louis, Wishram, 1905 telling

Table of four dimensions of narratives regarding the nature of oneself and others

9. Coyote, Polymorphous but Not Always Perverse

Deer in various North Pacific Coast narratives (noted)

Deer in North Pacific Coast myths (discussed)

Gould, Owen, Nez Perce, "Coyote and White-Tail Deer," (presented)

Simpson, Louis, Wishram, "Deer and Coyote" (discussed)

Simpson, Louis, Wishram, "Coyote and Fish Hawk" (noted)

Watters, Samuel M., Nez Perce, "Coyote and White-Tailed Buck" (presented)

10. Helen Sekaquaptewa's "Coyote and the Birds"

(Hopi text and translation presented)

Peynetsa, Andrew, Zuni, "Coyote and Old Lady Junco"

11. John Rush Buffalo's "Coyote, Rabbit, and Eagle's Daughter"

(Tonkawa text and translation presented)

12. Coyote, the Thinking (Wo)man's Trickster

Howard, Victoria, Clackamas, "News about Coyote" (presented)

Hudson, John B., Santiam Kalapuya, "The News Precedes Coyote" (presented)

Pichette, Louis, Colville-Okanagan (presented unanalyzed)

Savage, Stevens, Molale, "The News about Coyote" (presented)

Simpson, Louis, Wishram, "Coyote and Antelope" (finale)

Simpson, Louis, Wishram, "Coyote and Deer" (presented)

Simpson, Louis, Wishram, "The News about Coyote" (presented)

Smith, Hiram, Wasco, "Coyote and Fish Hawk" (presented)

Smith, Hiram, Wasco, "The News about Coyote" (presented)

13. Ethnopoetics, Oral-Formulaic Theory, and Editing Texts

Buchanan, Jim, Coos (unpublished lines presented)

Chapman, John W., Deg Hit'ana (Ingalik) (work discussed)

Cochiti Pueblo, "Coyote Imitates Crow" (discussed)

Cultee, Charles, Kathlamet, "Salmon's Myth" (what is skipped, what is restored)

Howard, Victoria, Clackamas (discussed with regard to order in which actually told)

Pearson, Clara, Tillamook, "Split-His-Own-Head" (scene presented and discussed with regard to the English of the translation)

St. Clair, H. H., Coos fieldwork (unpublished versions, unknown details)

Simpson, Louis, Wishram, "The Deserted Boy," scene 1, later discussion

Wolfson, Nessa, "She's a widow" (Philadelphia), scenes 3–4 (work discussed)

14. Anthologies and Narrators

Hartless, William, Mary's River Kalapuya, "Coyote Looks around the Country" (discussed)

Hartless, William, Mary's River Kalapuya, "Coyote Releases Water and Salmon Dammed by the Frogs" (presented)

Hudson, John B., Santiam Kalapuya, "Coyote Releases Water Dammed Up by the Frogs" (presented)

15. Notes toward (an Understanding of) Supreme Fictions

Alter, Robert, *The art of Biblical narrative* (discussed)

Brown, Tom, Sahaptin, modern Coyote stories (discussed)

Cultee, Charles, Kathlamet, "Salmon's Myth" (discussed)

Cultee, Charles, Kathlamet, "Southwest Wind" (discussed)

Cultee, Charles, Kathlamet, "Sun's Myth" (discussed passim)

Hartless, William, Mary's River Kalapuya, five Petit Jean stories (discussed)

Hartless, William, Mary's River Kalapuya, (see chap. 14) (discussed)

Howard, Victoria, Clackamas, "Coyote Made Everything Good" (discussed)

Howard, Victoria, Clackamas, "Gitskux and His Older Brother" (discussed)

Howard, Victoria, Clackamas, "Grizzly and Black Bear Ran Away with the Two Girls" (discussed)

Howard, Victoria, Clackamas, "Seal and Her Younger Brother Lived There" (discussed, analyzed in terms of semiotic square, presented)

Howard, Victoria, Clackamas, "Seal Took Them to the Ocean" (discussed)

Howard, Victoria, Clackamas, "Tongue" (discussed)

Hudson, John B., Kalapuya (see chap. 14) (discussed)

Johnson, Frances, Takelma, "The Otter Brothers Recover Their Father's Heart" (discussed)

Kwakwala (Kwakiutl) Mink myth (noted)

Lewis, C. S., *The Discarded Image* (discussed)

Peterson, Annie Miner, Miluk Coos, "Butterball Duck and His Wife" (discussed)

Peynetsa, Andrew, Zuni, "Coyote and Junco" (discussed)

Pope, Bob, Quinault, "The Adventures of Blue Jay" (discussed)

Riffaterre, Michael, *Fictional Truth* (discussed)

Simpson, Louis, Wishram, "Coyote and Deer" (discussed)

Simpson, "The Deserted Boy" (discussed)

Tsimshian, myth of Asdiwal (noted)

Winishut, Linton, Sahaptin, Coyote cycle (discussed)

16. Robinson Jeffers's Artistry of Line

The poems discussed or noted are:

"Ante Mortem"
"Be Angry at the Sun"
"Birds"
"The Bloody Sire"
"Boats in a Fog"
"Cassandra"
"The Coast-Range Christ"
"Continent's End"
"The Cruel Falcon"
"Divinely Superfluous Beauty"
"The Excesses of God"
"Fog"
"Granite and Cypress"
"Joy"
"Life from the Lifeless"
"Mal Paso Bridge"
"Natural Music"
"Night"
"People and Heron"
"Point Joe"
"Point Pinos and Point Lobos"
"Post Mortem"
"Rock and Hawk"
"Salmon-Fishing"
"Science"
"Shine, Perishing Republic"
"Summer Holiday"
"Tamar"
"To the House"
"To the Rock That Will Be a Cornerstone of the House"
"To the Stone-Cutters"
"Wise Men in Their Bad Hours"

Appendix 2

Verse Analyses in Native American Languages

Language	Analysts
Alsea	Dell Hymes, Eugene Buckley
Apachean (Athapaskan)	Keith Basso, Eleanor Nevins, Anthony Webster
Arikara	Dell Hymes, Douglas Parks
Bella Coola (Salish)	Dell Hymes
Chasta Costa (Athapaskan)	Dell Hymes
Chehalis & Cowlitz Salish	M. Dale Kinkade
Chinook Jargon	Henry Zenk, Robert Moore, Dell Hymes
Clackamas Chinook	Dell Hymes, Robert Moore
Cochiti (New Mexico)	Dell Hymes (English telling/translation)
Coeur d'Alene	Rodney Frey
Coos (Oregon)	Dell Hymes
Cree	Deborah Blincoe, H. C. Wolfart
Crow	Rodney Frey
Cuna	Joel Sherzer
Deg Hit'ana (Ingalik)	Dell Hymes
"Eskimo" Yupik	Anthony Woodbury, Dell Hymes
"Eskimo" Greenlandic	Arnaq Grove, Kirsten Thisted, Virginia & Dell Hymes
Eyak (Na-Dene)	Dell Hymes
Fox	Amy Dahlstrom
Haida	Elizabeth Bowman, Dell & Virginia Hymes, Robert Bringhurst
Hopi (Uto-Aztecan)	David Shaul, Dell Hymes
Hopi-Tewa (Arizona)	Paul Kroskrity, Dell Hymes
Hupa (Athapaskan)	Dell Hymes, Victor Golla
Isleta (New Mexico)	Dell Hymes (Lummis text in English)
Joshua (Oregon/Athapaskan)	Dell Hymes (text in English)
Kalapuya (Oregon)	Dell Hymes (Santiam, Mary's River), Robert Moore (Santiam)

Kalispel (Salish)	Paul Kroeber, Dell Hymes
Kamsá (Colombia)	John McDowell
Kathlamet Chinook	Dell Hymes
Kawaiisu (Uto-Aztecan)	Dell Hymes
Klamath	Dell Hymes, Noel Rude
Koasati (Alabama)	Geoffrey Kimball
Koyukon (Athapaskan)	Dell Hymes
Kootenai	Rodney Frey (English telling), Dell Hymes
Kutchin (Athapascan)	Dell Hymes
Kwakwala (Kwakiutl)	Judith Berman, Dell Hymes
Laguna (New Mexico)	Dell Hymes
Lakota (Siouan)	Richard Lungstrum
Lower Umpqua (& Siuslaw)	Dell Hymes
Lushootseed (Salish)	Crisca Bierwert, Toby Langdon
Maidu	Dell Hymes
Mattole (California Athapaskan)	Dell Hymes
Miwok (California)	Dell Hymes
Molale (Oregon)	Dell Hymes
Mono (California)	Chris Loether
Napa (Venezuela)	Maria Eugeneia Villalon
Nez Perce (Idaho)	Dell Hymes, Rodney Frey
Nootka	Dell Hymes
Ojibwe (Algonquian)	Ridie Ghezzi, John D. Nichols, J. R. Valentine
Okanagon English	Wendy Wickwire, Dell Hymes
Paiute	Dell Hymes (in English)
Penobscot	Jill McRae
Pomo (California)	Sally McLendon, Mary Catherine O'Connor
Puget Sound Salish	Dell Hymes (in English)
Quechua	Nancy Hornberger, Michael Uzendowski, Sabine Dedenbach-Salazar Sáenz, Lucy Therina Briggs
Quileute (Salish)	Dell Hymes, Jay Powell
Quinault (Salish)	Dell Hymes (in English)
Sahaptin (Warm Springs, Klikitat)	Virginia Hymes, Dell Hymes, Rodney Frey, Robert Bringhurst
Sanpoil (Salish)	Rodney Frey, Dell Hymes
Shoalwater (Chinook)	Dell Hymes
Takelma (Oregon)	Dell Hymes, Daythal Kendall
Tillamook (Salish)	Dell Hymes, Terry Thompson, Steve Egesdal
Tlingit (Na-Dene)	Richard Dauenhauer, Dell Hymes
Tonkawa (Texas)	Dell Hymes

Tsimshian	John Dunn, Ralph Maud
Ute	Dell Hymes (English telling)
Wasco/Wishram (Chinook)	Dell Hymes, Robert Moore, Rodney Frey
Winnebago	Karen Danker, Dell Hymes (English version)
Wintu (California)	Dell Hymes, Alice Shepherd
Wishram	(see Wasco)
Yana (California)	Herbert Luthin, Dell Hymes
Yuma (California)	Margaret Langdon, Dell Hymes
Zuni	Dennis Tedlock, Jane Young, Virginia Hymes, Dell Hymes

Appendix 3

Verse Analyses in Other Languages

Language	Analysts
Bulgarian	Liliana Perkowski
Egyptian (ancient)	John Foster
Egyptian Arabic	Dwight Reynolds
English (United States & Britain)	Dell Hymes, Virginia Hymes (Appalachian, Philadelphia, British), students in classes
Finnish	Thomas Du Bois
Greek (New Testament)	Dell Hymes (Letter of James)
Guyanese Creole	Hirokuni Masuda
Hawai'i Creole English	Hirokuni Masuda
Japanese	Konoko Shiokawa, Hirokuni Masuda
Kiriwina (Trobriands)	Dell Hymes
Koryak (Siberia)	Alexander King
Nguna (Vanuatu)	Ellen Facey, Dell Hymes
Norwegian (Frontier United States)	Dell Hymes (texts taken down by Einar Haugen)
Farsi (Persian)	Margaret Mills
Portuguese (Brazilian)	Dell Hymes
Pukhtun	Benedicte Johnson

Notes

Introduction

1. Some have put forward the view that oral narratives cannot have lines, because they are not written. That is like saying that speech cannot contain sentences.

2. Another point that perhaps needs to be made: a narrator may carry over into one language the traditional patterns of another (cf. V. Hymes forthcoming).

3. Some years ago I made a study of the Loon Woman myth as told by Wintu narrators (Hymes 2002) for a book edited by Herbert Luthin. My study includes discussion of interplay between Lévi-Strauss's use of the myth and this kind of interpretation.

4. I like to think it no accident that I began life at one end of the Lewis and Clark Trail and am ending it at the other. And that I graduated at one end from Reed College with a joint major in literature and anthropology and have retired at the other end as a professor of both anthropology and English.

5. A tradition of organization in terms of lines and sets of lines appears to have relevance for some work that exists as writing. See "Oral patterns as a resource in children's writing: Ethnopoetic notes," in Hymes 1996b. *The Epistle of James* appears to have some such organization (Hymes 1986). Chap. 16 of this book indicates relevance to Robinson Jeffers's metrics and use of contrasting lengths of line. Tim Hunt, editor of *The Collected Poetry of Robinson Jeffers* (Stanford University Press), is investigating oral narrators as indications of oral narrative lines as an influence on Jeffers's distinctive use of lines.

6. Niles 1999 is intended as a work of general scope but barely finds room in a footnote for work such as this. On p. 222, n.21 discusses "textualization": "I use the term to refer to the process by which a work of oral literature becomes more and more of a literary artifact through the process of recording, copying, and editing. The process, problem, and challenge of making texts out of words that are meant to be sounded out aloud is discussed from a folklore perspective by Tedlock 1987 and Hymes 1994, among others." Missing also is the important body of Finnish work by Lauri Honko and others (see Honko 1998, 2000b; Honko et al 1998a, b).

1. Survivors and Renewers

1. I broached some of the thoughts in this essay in a letter to Glassie (9 January 1996).

2. I give the rest of the myth in its poetic form, as lines and groups of lines, so as to be able to comment on form later.

3. In the 1970s the typographer and poet Charles Bigelow and I talked with Hiram Smith, one of the last fluent speakers of Wasco Chinook, about an account he told us of the demise of real Indian doctors (with spirit power). They had gathered at the coast and held a contest as to which was strongest, and the strongest killed off the others. Chuck mentioned such factors as white domination, missionaries, compulsory schooling, and the like. Hiram acknowledged them. But there was also an account in terms of Native forces alone.

4. Both Trafzer and Hines reproduce a story told on 7 June 1926 to Lucullus McWhorter by Owl Child, and likely learned by him from his wife. At least Owl Child said he didn't know the details of the ending and would ask her. (See notes in each book.) One does not have to accept every interpretation offered by Lévi-Strauss to realize that his principle of transformational relationships and his unparalleled scouring of the literature of New World mythology are lasting contributions.

5. Note that Chinookans on the eastern side of the Cascades did not suffer nearly as much from introduced disease as did those to the west.

6. I quote the New Revised Standard Version from *The HarperCollins Study Bible* (Meeks 1993); emphasis is mine. This anticipation of Jerusalem is an example of revision in terms of "what should be" (section b, *Should have been*).

7. In his valuable account of the dynamics of canonical interpretation (taking the Bible as a whole), Sanders distinguishes two basic hermeneutic axioms, constitutive and prophetic (1984:70). The first emphasizes God saving and comforting his people, the second God judging them. Certainly "Sun's Nature" is prophetic, warning and making possible (the axe) destruction. The final verses in which the Sun is shown as still continuing and in charge, seem constitutive, an image of an ultimate order not destroyed.

8. Let me note that Kroeber's book is valuable, and I am glad to find that he has included a study of my own. As to imagination as distinct from performance, let me quote the stage director Herbert Blau, in the course of a marvelously rich account of the difficulty of encompassing *King Lear:* "In the years I have spent in the theater (nearly forty) I directed a lot of plays, but have always had a tendency to believe that a staging in the mind (like that by Edgar on the cliffs of Dover) can exceed by far anything realizable on stage, which is why I tell my students— contrary to established pedagogy in dramatic literature—that, no, it is not necessary to go to the theatre to really see the play; that, in fact, seeing a performance there, even if it is brilliantly acted, especially if it is brilliantly acted (however you

determine that), often gets in the way of imagining it for yourself, though to do so with *Lear* . . . will if you see it cut to the brain" (1998:269).

2. Franz Boas on the Threshold of Ethnopoetics

1. I am grateful to Bruce Mannheim for calling my attention to Reichard's work.

2. The example for "Rhythmic Repetition of Contents and Form is Found Commonly in Primitive Narrative" has to do with repetition of incidents five times in Chinook tales. Relations of form within incidents or throughout a narrative are not mentioned.

3. For ease of printing, here and later, I adopt the conventions followed in Hymes 1981b of using *C* for alveolar affricate, *G* for velar *g*, *L* for voiceless lateral fricative, *S* for sibilant, and *X* for velar *x*.

4. Boas indeed analyzed the elements in the Chinook verb in terms of categories expressed and their order relative to one another, recognizing nouns as what would today be called adjuncts to the person-markers in the verb that mark relations of transitive subject, transitive object/intransitive subject, and indirect object, in successive positions. The first-person singular *n-* could occur in any of the three positions but not in the same word. A person acting on himself or herself would be indicated by an occurrence of the marker followed by a reflexive element. But all three positions may occur in one word.

5. Cultee's Kathlamet "Swan's Myth," the example from Boas noted by Stocking, also exemplifies nicely the dual aspect of ethnopoetic form, grounding in a recurrent kind of relation, on the one hand, here three and five and, on the other hand, change of actual rhythms from part to part.

Cultee's "Swan's Myth" is an inversion of his development of "Salmon's Myth" (Hymes 1985a; chap. 6 of this book). In the first, a woman guarantees winter food from the river, while banishing from the river creatures who have mocked her (swans). In the second, a man guarantees winter food from the river (flounder), while banishing those who have mocked him (Blue Jay, Crow).

3. Use All There Is to Use

1. I want to thank Brian Swann for encouraging me to contribute these reflections.

2. See the opening pages of the title essay in Burke 1941.

3. On the first four, see Hymes 1962, 1964, 1972, 1974a, and the chapters "What Is Ethnography" and "Educational Ethnology" in Hymes 1980a.

4. These relationships have been important to Bright in his work with Karok (1984).

5. See Bright's analysis: "Carefully re-listening to Mrs. Starritt's taped narration, along with analysis of the type proposed by Hymes, permits identification of the following features of structure: (a) *Verses* . . . are marked syntactically by the presence of 'sentence-initial particles' at the beginning, and phonologically

by a falling pitch and audible pause at the end. . . . Lines . . . are marked syntactically by the occurrence of predications. . . . Most lines are marked by a final falling pitch without audible pause. However, lines containing verbs of saying may
end in a final mid or high pitch, with or without pause before a following quotation. . . . Tedlock's and Hymes' approaches . . . coincide 90 percent of the time
in their identification of basic units—the verse (Tedlock's strophe) and the line.
Because of this, occasional ambiguities in the application of one approach can be
resolved by reference to the other" (1987:93–94). Regarding Kroskrity's study of
Arizona Tewa: "Lines of narrative speech are marked by both particle and pause,
whereas lines of quoted speech are distinguished solely on the basis of pause criteria" (1985:186).

6. See Tedlock (1999 [1972]:76–83), where the Zuni telling of "Coyote and
Junco" by Andrew Peynetsa is presented, and Wiget 1987, where a Hopi telling of
an analogue of "Coyote and Junco" by Helen Sekaquaptewa is given.

7. I hope to display the two comparisons in full in another place.

8. Presumably North American Indian myths do not describe the world at least
in important part because their hearers know what it looks like. It may be relevant how large a house is and how many fires it has, but not that it is made of
wood. When Coyote goes upriver, he goes up a river most hearers have traveled
many times. Even in imagined worlds, like that of the dead, what is said and done
declares the nature of the place. There is no scene painting for atmosphere. The
images are of action. Often one senses that a narrator is picturing a scene, and
hearers may indicate that they picture it as well. This then would authorize a freedom in interpretation in the very process of transmission. This is the story as I
heard it, yet the picture in my mind may be my own and affect the retelling.

9. We are fortunate to have Stern's texts and fortunate that Rude has been able
to do some work with them. The famous nineteenth-century Swiss linguist Albert
Gatschet collected almost no narratives. When M. A. R. Barker worked with the
language a generation ago, he did not obtain very many. Stern worked earlier
than Barker, and much of what can be known about Klamath tradition will depend on the eventual publication of his materials. I am grateful to Rude for sending me copies of his work.

10. For example, one would see and wonder about the lack of apparent consistency in the number of sections within major parts and of relations within major
sections of Muluku's "Saganafa" as analyzed in Basso 1985:41–54.

11. The page reference in the preceding part of the note is to page 52, not 48,
as the original edition and the reprinting both have it.

12. This account revises my published analysis, in which the coordinate status
of the scene involving the young man as intermediary was not recognized.

13. The myth is "Štank'íya," the name of a certain mythical Coyote.

14. I am grateful to Richard Dauenhauer for pointing out this pervasiveness in

his comments on my finding five-part patterning in one of the texts published by him and Nora Dauenhauer (see Hymes 1989b).

15. I have done this for a long time, and Virginia Hymes long ago pointed out to me the variety of relations that appear within sets of four in various languages. Some remarks about these variations appear in my paper "Some Subtleties of Measured Verse." Yet it is the work of Henri Meschonnic that has encouraged me to address the practice explicitly here in terms of the notion of rhythm. See his *Critique du rhythme* (1982). I am grateful to Professor Meschonnic and to the Commonwealth Center for Literary and Cultural Change for the opportunity to consult with him during the course of his seminar at the University of Virginia in the fall of 1989.

16. In "Tongue" lines 186-91 are another example, as are lines 204-14. In the former, the five markers all are "now"; in the latter, the markers are "now, now; all day, now; now."

17. This is one of the reasons I suspect that there was a two- and four-part tradition in Victoria Howard's background. She did, after all, have Molale relatives and know some Molale, and if the Molale texts recorded early in the twentieth century by Leo Frachtenberg are ever published and analyzed, they may shed light on her heritage of resources.

18. For a book-length discussion of such issues, addressing much that is not touched on here, see Fine 1984.

19. For his response to criticism of mine, see Lévi-Strauss 1987.

20. On the mocking of chiefs in Kalapuya Coyote myths, see the last section of Hymes 1987a.

4. Variation and Narrative Competence

1. Harrington 1932:22-24. Harrington has the title "Two Girls Apply for Marriage with Spring Salmon." "Spring Salmon Stays Single" is my suggestion. See Hymes 1997c for a full presentation of the story in Karok and English.

5. When Is Oral Narrative Poetry?

This paper was presented at the International Pragmatics Association in Rheims, France, July 1998.

1. Especially clear accounts of the identification of lines in spoken narratives are given by Virginia Hymes (1987) and Joel Sherzer and Anthony Woodbury (1987, chap. 4; 1990:17). On the vocal articulation of lines in ritual wailing in three South American cultures, see Urban 1991:110-11, 152-59.

2. Also in modern times in terms of variation and display of space on the page. Gary Snyder once asked me if familiarity with the poetry of William Carlos Williams and others did not play a part in my discovering what is discussed here. I was not conscious of that but could see that it must have done so. Not in first

intimations of the kind of organization involved—linguistic features prompted that—but in being comfortable in working with lines of varying length.

Fabb 1997 is a textbook informed by both contemporary linguistics and analyses of oral literatures (note, e.g., 203–6, 212–33, and chap. 9, "Performance," for attention to ethnopoetics).

3. I hope to record one or more Chinookan texts for the language program of the Grand Ronde community in western Oregon.

4. *Couplets.* Cf. Hymes 1994a (chap. 7 in this book) with Hymes 1981b, chap. 4. The earlier presentation was never satisfactory. It had inconsistencies and irregularities. Finally, I realized that each verse did not count separately in the expected patterning in terms of three or five. Certain pairs of lines, semantic couplets (e.g., "All died in the water / the people were drowned"), go together, count as one unit (see Hymes 1994a:346–47).

The Northwest Coast narratives I have examined agree with the concern of Kugel 1981 and Alter 1985 to recognize that in the poetry of the Hebrew Bible the second of two "parallel" lines goes beyond the first, adding to it or intensifying it. Cf. "died in the water" versus the specificity of "drowned" in the example just given. And cf. the pairs of lines at the end of the Sun's myth (given in this chapter).

5. Cf. discussion of the published English for a Tillamook narrative in Hymes 1994a:355–57.

6. "Seal . . ." is reprinted in Swann 1994:307–10; "Sun's Myth" is in Swann 1994: 273–78 and in Penn 1997:88–93.

7. The textual sources are Jacobs 1958, 1959a. He discusses each text in Jacobs 1959b, 1960, and several articles. See also Hymes 1984c for a short text recorded by Boas. My translation of "Tongue" has been published in Penn 1997.

8. For the other version known to us, see "The Skookum's Tongue" and "Skookum and the Wonderful Boy" in Ramsey 1997:94–95. Ramsey's source is Lyman 1900. In Lyman's account the young man revives the people by shooting an arrow. When the arrow hits the ground, they are revived and come back from downriver. Only then does the young man meet his father (for the first time). His father does not recognize him and hits him. The young man then turns himself into a fish. His travels determine which streams fish that climb the falls at Oregon City will enter. There is no speech such as that with which Howard ends.

The myth of Tongue thus was told in more than one way. Either ending is prophecy realized, as one expects from these myths, but the ending Lyman heard from Louis Labonte was of a kind Native American myths are likely to have—where a food would be found when the people came and why. Howard's ending gets Salmon into the water but not to particular streams. Instead, for their misbehavior the people themselves are forced to disperse. This anticipation of an ultimate historical fate makes me wonder if Howard, or her mother's mother or mother-in-law, from whom she heard the story, had absorbed an element of the

Hebrew Bible. That the myth mattered to her may be reflected in the fact that she told it to Jacobs in the first days of their work together (1959a:635 n.314).

9. For the considerable influence of Labov's work, see Bamberg 1997. The fact that none of the contributions in Bamberg's volume of 415 pages considers narratives in terms of the kind of relationships taken up here is one reason for taking up this story here. It is rich in form.

Such things may not seem a problem in stories for which one needs no translation. The point is that one may need a translation, an interpretation, not of words, but of form. The principle has been stated by Jakobson: "[P]oeticallness is not a supplementation of discourse with rhetorical adornment, but a total re-evaluation of the discourse and of all its components whatsoever" (1960:377). That statement may be too sweeping. Yet when someone has given motivated form and point to what they say, we should attend to it.

10. The interpretation of scene iii may be objected to on the ground that the pairing of verses in the first three stanzas ignores that the second line of A is a question to which the answer is the first line of B. There are three reasons not to couple those two lines.

First, since the start of scene ii the action proper has been in pairs, and the two verses following the part of scene iii that is in question are the most strongly marked pair in the story (So . . . , So . . .).

Second, the central theme is how the narrator deals with a moral and practical dilemma. That the third scene opens with him going to school is not incidental. It is based on an answer to one part of the dilemma, that is, a decision not to play hookies, because his mother will whup him if he does. The basis of that is played out in scene ii.

In scene iii the other part of the dilemma, the girl, is faced. The focus is on what he does. He goes to school (rather than play hookies), and the girl confronts him. He says that he has no candy; she says powww! *Notice that the narrator equates speech and action, using "say" for both.*

"I said, 'I don't have it.'
She says, powww!"

The parallel supports the pairing of the two verses.

Overall, there are two sequences before the final comment. Each begins with "So."

1. He goes, she demands; he answers, she responds with powww!
2. He reflects doubly (So, So), he proceeds with a powww! of his own in a triplet of action and outcome (I . . . , I . . . , I . . .).

A breakthrough in decisiveness and victory is matched with a formal flourish. All this agrees with Labov's report that John L. was admired as a storyteller. One could still insist that it cannot be so, that question and answer must always be bracketed together, that John L. is not (at least here) a remarkable narrator. To do so is to insist that a lower level of ordering must command all into which it enters. (As if syntax had to fit into phonology, as some linguists thought a generation or two ago. It is to fail to recognize that interpretation of meaning has a role in discovering what is to be explained, and the possibility that poetic principles may be more than coating, but play a part (cf. the quotation from Jakobson in note 9). And as noted, it is to prefer an interpretation that shows a story and its narrator in a poor light as against one that finds artistry.

11. I draw here on Hymes 1996b, chap. 9, p. 205, reprinted from Hymes 1995b. An earlier version of this account was part of my talk at the September 1996 Sociolinguistics Symposium in Cardiff.

12. Two and four relations are shown in a Zuni myth, "Coyote and Junco," told by Andrew Peynetsa to Dennis Tedlock. Three and five relations are shown in the Clackamas myth, "Seal and Her Younger Brother Lived There" already cited (n. 5). For two and four relations, see also Hymes 1995c.

13. For the phrasing, see Burke 1957:viii and 241. For major analyses, see "Psychology and Form" in Burke 1925 and "Antony in Behalf of the Play" in Burke 1957:279–90.

14. I am indebted to Lewis Feuer for discussion of the information about May Mandelbaum.

15. Cf. the printings of my analysis cited in note 7. The alignment of the final stanzas varies slightly.

16. In each couplet the second member adds something, may be more pointed. Cf. took it > lifted off what he had taken; left > went home; stayed > went a little distance; built a house > a small house. See the discussion of couplets in note 4.

17. For examples of alternation in underlying pattern as between narrators and across texts in the northern California language Karok, see Hymes 1985c. For an instance within a Karok text, see Hymes 1997c.

18. The related devices of rank shift, fading explicitness, and amplification are discussed and exemplified in Hymes 1985a:408–13.

19. Simpson repeated the verses three times for Sapir. Fifty years later I was told a narrator could sing them an indefinite number of times.

20. See esp. Hymes 1981b:82–89, 102–5, 118, 132. The use of initial markers by the narrators, Louis Simpson, Hiram Smith, and Philip Kahclamat (Wishram-Wasco speakers), and Victoria Howard (Clackamas) differs significantly, as is shown in chap. 6, written after I had discovered verse analysis.

21. The details are subtle and intriguing. They are discussed in Hymes 1986, included here as chap. 7. The fact that Howard falls into four-part relations in this myth no longer seems a puzzle but rather a formal signal of woman's control.

22. Haugen took down some ten hours of dictation from Aune. There may be much of value as to narrative form and meaning waiting to be found in this material.

23. The first text is published as no. 57, the second as no. 58, in Jacobs 1959a: 458–61, 459–62.

24. On performance as a dimension of texts, see chap. 9 of Hymes 1981b.

25. In the narratives discussed in Moore 1993, "now" is the initial particle used by Lucinda Smith when she does use one. Moore's article demonstrates nicely another kind of alternation, alternation between speakers and languages by a speaker in one kind of performance situation.

6. Language, Memory, and Selective Performance

The first version of this paper was presented at the Nineteenth International Conference on Salish and Neighboring Languages, University of Victoria, B. C., August 16, 1984, and distributed in a special issue of the *Working Papers of the Linguistics Committee*, 4, no. 2:162–228, June 1984. I thank Joel Sherzer and Greg Urban for comments on that version and David French for comments on the identification of plants. A few words have been given in Kathlamet. Stress is usually on the penultimate syllable. "L" is the symbol used by Boas for a voiceless lateral fricative as (as with Welsh "ll"). In recent times is written with *ł; t'* is a glottalized voiceless stop; *q* is a velar voiceless stop; *x* is a voiceless velar fricative.

1. Boas 1901:50–53 (1891 version) and 1901:54–57 (1894 version) for "Salmon's Myth"; 1901:182–84 (1891 version) and 1901:185–86 (1894 version) for "The War of the Ghosts."

2. Not, however, with regard to the myth discussed here. The Kathlamet tellings are not included in Boas's *Tsimshian Mythology* (1916); see the reference list to the Kathlamet texts included in this massive comparative study (1916:1015). Lévi-Strauss refers to the Kathlamet text in the following words: "[S]kunk-cabbage; this foul-smelling aracea, which is still closer to the category of the rotten, is the first plant to flower in the spring, even before the snow has finished melting. At that time of year, it was often the only food the Indians had to save them from famine, and the Kathlamet say in one of their myths (M794; Gunther 3, pp. 22–23) that before discovering salmon, humans lived almost entirely on skunk cabbage" (1981 [1971]:569). (M794 identifies the myth in the index of myths analyzed in the book [which is fourth in the series *Introduction to a Science of Mythology*]; Gunther is a reference to Gunther 1940.)

In point of fact, the myth has five plants that share the honor of being necessary to survival, although Skunk Cabbage has pride of place. In relying on Gunther as to the "pre-salmon" era, Lévi-Strauss is in effect relying on Haskin (1967:7), whom Gunther cites. All three are wrong in taking the word translated as "first" to mean first in history. *T'otsnix* in Kathlamet refers to "firstness" in a series, or recurrent context, as that of a season, or even the first moment in the birth of a child (Boas 1901:7). See also Sapir 1909b:183: "The first catch of the season" is meant with reference to the statement *q'atsEn aqigElgay(a) igunat walxiba* 'For the first time salmon is caught at the fishing post' (*q'atsEn* is the Wasco-Wishram equivalent of Kathlamet *T'otsnix;* the common root is *-tsn; t'o-* is "good, proper, normative"; *-ix* is locative or evidential of time and space). Salmon's myth is a myth of the annual cycle, not of evolutionary time. (I take this up in a discussion of what is new and what is assumed in the myth later in this chapter.)

Lévi-Strauss (1981 [1971]:726) gives M794 the title: "Kathlamet, 'Humanity's first food.'" By the end of this chapter it should be clear how misled someone would be who knew of the myth only by this substituted title and the summary of what it is supposed to say. My analysis makes use of insights Lévi-Strauss has developed as to the dialectics of opposition between myths (and parts of myths), but in a case of retitling and summary such as this, structuralism has abandoned text.

3. On personal meaning as something that evolves in relation to a story, see Krauss 1982. (These narratives appear to be organized in lines and groups of lines.) On the development of research in the region, see Maud 1982.

4. Boas's field notebooks were examined in the Rare Book Room of the Butler Library, Columbia University (1891) and at the Library of the American Philosophical Society (1894). Many thanks to both.

5. See Hymes 1981b:155–59 for a parallel instance in Louis Simpson's Wishram "The Deserted Boy."

6. Silverstein 1985 stresses the importance of verbs of saying. The statement "a narrative . . . does not have an internal organization based on any overall hierarchical pattern" (142), however, exhibits a surprising unawareness of the discoveries reported in some of the articles collected in Hymes 1981b as to the presence of such pattern.

7. Presumably this refers to the starry flounder (*Platichthys stellatus /Pallas/*):

Flounders are marine flatfish that have both eyes on the same side of the head and are white on the "blind" ventral side. . . . It usually does not venture far from the head of tidewater, but occasionally goes further upstream, and has been reported as far as 75 miles up the Columbia River. . . . The starry flounder can tolerate the full range of salinities from completely fresh water to sea water. . . . In shallow estuaries it moves onto flats during high tide and returns to the river channel as the tide recedes and exposes the flats. . . . Starry flounders may reach a length of 3 feet and a weight of 20 pounds. . . . Females generally are reported to grow faster than males and to be heavier at a given length. . . . The spawning season in California is from late November through February." (Wydoski and Whitney 1979)

7. A Discourse Contradiction in Clackamas Chinook

This chapter is slightly revised from a paper of the same title included in papers prepared for the Twenty-First International Congress of Salish and Neighboring Languages, Seattle, Washington, 14–16 August 1986, compiled by Nile Thompson and Dawn Bates, pp. 147–213. Seattle: University of Washington, Department of Anthropology.

1. This territory is evidently in Oregon on either side of where the Willamette flows into the Columbia, just above the present site of the city of Portland. Its westernmost point presumably is the upriver boundary of Kathlamet territory, at about Rainier, Oregon, or just above, for Salmon and his party are said to encounter the trio at what is now Saint Helens (just downriver from Portland). Its easternmost point presumably is the Cascades, which the trio claims to have reached in a day, some fifty-odd miles upriver from Portland. The Clackamas lived just south of what is now Portland with a hinterland perhaps extending eastward to the Cascades. The area is poorly known linguistically, but evidently its various communities spoke a variety of Chinookan generally intelligible with that of the Wasco and Wishram further upriver, though recognizably distinct. The Clackamas and the Wasco use the same term, Kikšt, to refer to their language. Kathlamet is quite distinct from Kikšt, e.g., in the development of tense-aspect in the verb and a good deal of vocabulary, so much so as to lead one to judge the two to have been different languages (cf. Silverstein 1974, 1990).

2. This is the only myth known to us in which Coyote has this name. Howard knew three other names for Coyote in myths: the Coyote who "went around the world" was Tánaq'iya (from which Štánk'iya may be derived); Sasáylax̣am, in one of the myths of Coyote and a grandson (who overcomes Mountain Cannibals); and It'álap'as, the name in other stories and ordinary life (shared with Sahaptin).

3. I draw on a transcript I made on 13 August 1986, from Jacobs Notebook 16, 1930. It was in the Jacobs Collection in the Archives of the University of Washington, as Archives Notebook 67 in Box 79 (formerly Box 53).

4. It now seems likely that four-part relations come to the fore as an expression of the very issue at stake between Howard's telling and those by Cultee. Cultee's second telling finds a way to reassert masculine control. Howard's telling shifts the context of identification of foods from a journey captained by a male to domestic pedagogy and also shifts much of the myth's dialogic core to four-part relations. Four-part relations can be seen as associated with female control, at least in western Native North America (see chap. 4 of this volume). (The work of Liliana Danilova Perkowski suggests that in Bulgarian folk narrative four-part organization is associated with masculine control.)

5. The preposed Kathlamet element, šč, is not otherwise attested. My phonesthematic hunch is that it is an intensifier.

6. Regarding the indication whether the speaker is a definite person, the one exception is the last. In (O) the last fish of the second series is introduced with two lines, instead of the usual one, marked by doubling of pronoun ("another," "he too"). The initial tense prefix changes from the remote past *ga-* to the generic past *a-*, and the person-marker prefix is not indefinite *ł-* but masculine singular *i-*. There follows the usual sequence of description with indefinite prefix plus "per-

son" and response by the announcer with number-gender prefix plus "person" (193–94). The unusual opening (two lines, generic past, definite pronoun) mark the climax and crux.

7. In the culminating announcement all of the edible plants (A–F) begin with a statement as to status as person. (I take the remark "she just says so" in D (line 56) to be a negation of "She speaks the truth" (cf. B, line 28 and thus a part of the person component). Five (A, B, C, E, F) have altogether the order person, name, use. Thus it may be structurally significant here that the one case in which the description of use precedes the name (E) is something not eaten. But it may also be that the position for a name is withheld in hopes of remembering it.

Notice that among the birds, two of the three (G, I) have the same order as the plants, while Female Grouse (H) again has the order person, use, name. This order, inverting that for name and use found with plants, is the constant order for all six fish (J–O), although a person element is missing (K, M) or not clearly present (J) in three of them.

8. Here not only is a gloss followed by a fuller account, but the fuller account is followed by another gloss. (I am indebted to Gail Jefferson for her pioneering work calling attention to glossing).

8. Bungling Host, Benevolent Host

1. This story of Fish Hawk (or Kingfisher) as the initial host may be the most widely told form of such a story. There is a Wasco Chinook version with Kingfisher in Curtin (1909:269–70); a version was told me by Hiram Smith in Wasco in 1954.

2. The comparison in Boas 1916 contains at least one slip: contrary to what is said on p. 695, the idea that an animal kills children who are transformed into food and then revived does occur on the North Pacific Coast in stories of a Bungling Host. The idea occurs in Boas's own collection of Chinook texts, as he himself notes on another page (698, where "Chin 181" is cited under this topic). The use of one's own wife is known now from Clackamas Chinook in the myth "Seal Took Them to the Ocean" (Jacobs 1958:222, 225–26).

3. The phonetic orthography used in these names and in the other Chinookan words in this discussion, including those in the text, is explained on pp. ooo.

4. The order, Coyote and Deer, seems appropriate. See the discussion of titles of Chinookan myths in the preceding section.

5. In English, "referential" (phonemic) contrast makes "pig" a different word than "big." Expressive, or stylistic, contrast makes a heavily aspirated "p^{h}ig" convey something different than a "pig" with normal aspiration: a clarification, perhaps ("I said 'pig'") or attitude ("He's such a *pig*").

6. Verses are indicated in the profile by lowercase letters (a, b, c, etc.). All verses in this text are marked by an initial particle or constituted by a turn at talk, except the initial frame, widely used in stories, "Coyote was going along."

Stanzas are groups of verses and are indicated by capital letters (A, B, C, etc.). Stanzas are not separately marked but are recognized in terms of Chinookan patterns for grouping elements of stories in threes and fives (and, occasionally, pairs). Some are of a common type, as in a travel triad, go, arrive, stay. Recurrences of the same or similar elements of the action often indicate that verses are to be grouped together as parts of a stanza. Thus, Deer's giving of his flesh and blood is taken to constitute a middle stanza in each of the scenes of the story. Change of participants may go together with a change of stanza and also of scene. Scenes, as the name implies, are major changes in the action. In this story it is evident that there are three scenes: Coyote comes to Deer, Coyote comes again to Deer, Deer comes to Coyote. Groupings at every level exhibit the patterning in threes, fives, and, occasionally, pairs. An audience would have readily recognized a coherence of organization that we must infer.

7. Ramsey (1983, chap. 4, 60-75) has an interesting discussion of a related Wasco story, recorded by Curtin, "The Hunter Who Had an Elk for a Guardian Spirit" (Curtin 1909:257-59). Ramsey unfortunately changes Curtin's reference to the guardian elk as female at certain points (see his note 7, p. 208), even though he shows awareness of the Chinook text recorded by Boas in which the guardian spirit of elk is clearly feminine (Boas 1894, "The Elk Hunter," pp. 234-37). Curtin's source no doubt was aware of such a tradition and reflected it at this point. Contrary to Ramsey, the use of "master" early in the story does not imply male but is a way of saying "guardian spirit." Later the power refers to the spirit claimed by the boy's father as male, to be sure, as indeed its own father. And the boy's own power is mentioned once in this later scene as "his." But earlier it has been twice named as feminine, "she" and "her." If the original was consistent, it is the later "his" that is to be taken as the slip. The great Elk power is about to talk about its father, a masculine context that the "his" could anticipate. But there is no apparent motivation at all for "she" and "her" in the preceding scene in which the boy's power leads him to the lake. The feminine pronouns are indeed surprising. Elk would never be so indicated unless prompted by a specific belief.

9. Coyote, Polymorphous but Not Always Perverse

This chapter is possible because of the years of dedication to the Nez Perce language of Haruo Aoki. I dedicate it to him, remembering as well the pleasure of having once been one of his teachers.

1. My early efforts are represented in Hymes 1981b. More recent understanding is represented in Hymes 1992a, 1992b, and 1994a, chap. 13.

2. These relations often constitute what Kenneth Burke called the essence of style, the arousing and satisfying of expectation.

3. It was Gould's elaboration of testing that made me realize that testing was present in Watters's text as well.

10. Helen Sekaquaptewa's "Coyote and the Birds"

I am grateful for the opportunity to contribute an essay in memory of Flo Voe-gelin. We began graduate work in anthropology at Indiana University a year apart (1950, 1951), when the department was young and American Indian languages were at its core. In later years much of her work concerned the Southwest, especially Hopi, and I offer as a tribute these observations on a Hopi text about the widespread inability of a trickster to master a song. (See discussion of a Zuni myth in what follows, and note, for example, Kroeber 1901:264–68: "After having succeeded in three consecutive imitations of his hosts, Coyote is fed in the house of the Puma with the instruction always to sing while eating. Thus his success in hunting deer will be certain. Coyote forgets the song several times and has to go back to Puma and request it. Once he makes nostrils for the deer and stops singing, neither he, nor the Puma, can catch any deer. "This is why in the end Puma and Coyote take revenge on each other.")

I am indebted to Andrew Wiget for sending me the transcript of the Hopi text that corresponds to the translation in his 1987 article. The transcript was produced by Emory Sekaquaptewa, Helen Sekaquaptewa's son, and Allison Lewis, one of her daughters, and provided to Wiget by Larry Evers, who directed the videotape of Sekaquaptewa telling the story. Wiget modified it at the level of lines and phrases "to bring it more in harmony with the Hopi-language transcript of the performance" (Wiget 1987:298). I infer that he meant more in harmony with lines and phrases to be heard on the videotape.

Virginia Hymes and I have each used the videotape in classes at the University of Virginia, and we are grateful to all who participated in its production but most of all to Helen Sekaquaptewa and her family.

1. Although Wiget (1987) cites the form as *puu*, the transcript he sent me has *pu'* (sometimes, presumably a slip, *pu* without the glottal stop); Albert and Shaul (1985:67) also have *pu'*, so I give this form.

2. The words of the winnowing song are not arbitrary. Wiget (1987:310) reports the translation by Larry Evers, Emory Sekaquaptewa, and Allison Lewis as

> Plaque, plaque, plaque
> Plaque, plaque, plaque
> that which is contained, that which is contained
> ph ph ph ph.

The third and fourth lines are the basis of the song sung by Old Lady Junco in the Zuni narrative published by Tedlock (1999 [1972]:76–84).

3. Wiget (1987:300) shows prompting by the audience at this point. In his English translation the prompt is given as "in a circle." The Hopi transcript does not give the prompting, but I infer that it is in Hopi. Wiget gives the interchange as Sekaquaptewa saying the equivalent of "tire" preceding the prompt "in a circle." The transcription has her speech as "round" and "around in a circle."

The repeated morpheme *qön* in fact has the meaning "round" in Albert and Shaul, which seems to me more natural in English.

4. A shallow saucerlike basket, made by women, and decorated.

11. John Rush Buffalo's "Coyote, Rabbit, and Eagle's Daughter"

1. Some of the stories John Rush Buffalo told Hoijer had been recorded much earlier by Albert S. Gatschet. John R. Swanton lent copies of them to Hoijer. Hoijer says: "[T]hese I read to JRB who, in most cases, recognized the tales and gave me his version of them" (Hoijer 1972:1; Gatschet 1884). Rush Buffalo also persuaded the two oldest Tonkawas to tell stories to him, which he then repeated to Hoijer. Again, field notebooks might show whether the two stories involving Eagle's daughter were among these and if they were in the same group. In any case, it seems likely that John Rush Buffalo told them for himself ("gave me his version of them").

12. Coyote, the Thinking (Wo)man's Trickster

1. See poems by William Stafford, Wendy Rose, Lance Henson, Joseph Bruchac, Barney Bush, myself, Jim Barnes, Louis Oliver, Joy Harjo, Carroll Arnett, and others in Koller 1982; see also Blue Cloud/Aroniawenrate 1989; and Ortiz 1992, especially "The Creation According to Coyote," 41; "The Boy and Coyote," 124–25; "Telling about Coyote," 157–60; and "How Much Coyote Remembered," 224; as well as poems by Gary Snyder, Jarold Ramsey, David Wagoner, and myself in Bright 1993.

2. More seriously, Ilana Pardes (1992:87–97) finds traits of polytheism and antipatriarchal bent (for Moses is saved by his wife) in a period of transition.

3. Instances from several Native American traditions are noted in my unpublished "Without a Song" (written in 1983), intended for a sequel to *Coyote's Journal* that was to have been called "Backward Dancer." For a rare exception, see my "A Coyote Who Can Sing" in Halper 1991:394–404.

4. Linton Winishut invited Virginia Hymes to record his Coyote cycle in 1975. She translated it in collaboration with the late Hazel Suppah. The Thompson Coyote cycle was obtained by James Teit (1898:20–41), "The Old Man and the Coyote" is on pages 48–49, second of three narratives about Old Man. The rich accounts by Jim Yoke and Lewy Costima were recorded and published by Melville Jacobs (1934:228–37, 239–46; these are the English translations in part 1). Louis Simpson's texts are in Edward Sapir 1909b, reprinted in Bright 1990. The quoted passage is in Sapir 1909b:75.

5. These presentations supersede earlier ones. The stories from Louis Simpson, Hiram Smith, and Victoria Howard have been discussed in some detail in Hymes 1981b:91–118, 211–42. The version by John B. Hudson was discussed in Hymes 1981a:144–50.

The text from Louis Simpson was published in Sapir 1909b:30–35; the version in my earlier study and here has been revised in light of Sapir's field notebooks (Hymes 1981b:134–38). The text from Hiram Smith was first published in my 1981 book; that from Victoria Howard was first published in Jacobs 1958:95–96; that from John B. Hudson was published in Jacobs 1945:91; that from Stevens Savage is from the notebooks of Frachtenberg MSS:52–58: Frachtenberg took down these stories in 1910, when Savage may have been fairly old, for he dictated texts to Albert Gatschet at Grand Ronde in December 1877. (Bureau of American Ethnology MS 2029, "Words, sentences and various texts collected at the Grande Ronde Agency, Northwestern Oregon, in November & Decb., 1877.") "Marriage Ceremonies" is identified as "given by Stephen Savage" at the head of page 37, and "SS did not know his name" appears on the bottom of the first page of a manuscript identified as "Story of a conflict between the Cayuse and Molala" (or "The Molale Tribe Raided by the Cayuse Indians," MS 998, the source cited by Rigsby 1969: 141 n.29). The intervening three pages of "Myth of the Coyote" (overcoming Bear on his way to set up the world) have no legible name but have the ring of the Savage of 1910. I am indebted to Donald Whereat, of the Confederated Tribes of Coos, Lower Umpqua, and Siuslaw Indians, for xeroxes of these materials. A handwritten copy of Frachtenberg's notebooks was made for Jacobs at the direction of Franz Boas and is in the archives of the University of Washington.

6. The stories here have been analyzed for their intrinsic form and are presented in terms of it. Oral narratives generally, here those of Native Americans, are poetry of a certain kind. They consist of lines organized in certain ways. The ways in which narrators shape their stories are part of what the stories say and mean. I try to show this by the visual relations among lines and groups of lines, indentation, and spacing and by providing for each story a profile that abstracts these relations. In such a profile, lowercase letters indicate verses, uppercase letters indicate stanzas, lowercase roman numerals indicate scenes, and uppercase roman numerals indicate acts.

On ethnopoetic analysis further, see Hymes 1992a:128–78; 1992b:83–124; and 1981b.

7. The English is largely from Hiram Smith. In translating, he partly retold the story as a story in English. In Wasco, line 8 is literally "Just not half"; line 10 has just what was said, as here. In translating, Smith clarified the line by putting before it "someone told him."

8. Louis Simpson's "Coyote and Deer" is in Sapir 1909b:145–47; compare the analysis in Hymes 1984a:171–98. Hiram Smith's story was told to me in Wasco in 1956 and has not been published.

9. Italics in English indicate words that show expressive contrast of stress or length of vowel in the original. Thus,

lines 2, 17, 36   *ná·wit*   'straightway'
lines 13, 22   *pá··ł*   'full'

line 16	wit'á·x̣	'again' (rather than wít'á·x̣)
lines 30, 55	náikaba	'to me' (rather than penultimate naikába as in line 26)
line 40	ágikal	(as discussed in text, no second-position 'possessive' [relational] prefix, stress not penultimate [agíkal]
line 45	gačiulxam	(where i- is direct object, first person rather than usual penultimate stress gačiúlxam)
line 60	iáge:wôk	'his meat' (rather than ìagéwôk)

10. The English is primarily from Hiram Smith. In translating, he would in effect retell the story, keeping closely to the Wasco but sentence for sentence rather than word for word. Expressions in brackets represent Wasco words that Smith did not translate. His expressions in parentheses elucidate the sense.

11. Note the parallel endings of each group of three lines: "they were starving." The next group of lines also contains a parallel, "he thought," which might be parallel endings but woven into three pairs of verses (a group of three pairs is a frequent pattern in Chinookan). Each of the three pairs begins with successive steps in Coyote's location: wandering, went toward, sat down. The next group illustrates the common Chinookan triad of three steps in change of location in minimal form: went, got there, went in. The final group of the act again has three pairs. The elaboration of the third and fifth groups fits the frequent role of third and fifth steps in a series as points of culmination.

12. The Wasco is literally 'These future your children'. In English, Hiram Smith explained, "Take this home to feed his children," before saying, "This your children will eat." In lines 49–50, the Wasco is literally 'Starting he-took-them Coyote'.

13. The Wasco text has simply two verbs in sequence without conjunction or other marker. Formally, they constitute a single verse: In line 60, Hiram Smith deployed the single word for "dead" with the intonation of a separate sentence.

14. Act III seems clearly to have three parts. Coyote is active alone in the first; Fish Hawk, in the second; Coyote again, in the third.

Scene i has three groups of three verses, fitting neatly into three stanzas. Scenes ii and iii each seem clearly to have five components, but in scene ii, the second and fourth components are themselves composed of components. The same is true of the second component of scene iii. In short, the first scene has two component levels, stanzas and verses, while the second and third scenes have three.

The odd components are the second and fourth of scene ii and the second component of scene iii. In this respect, they are equivalent to the stanzas of scene i in having verses as elements, but to consider them stanzas in scenes ii and iii would imply that the other units of these scenes are stanzas as well (lines 60, 64, 69, and lines 70, 75, 76–78, and 79). That seems silly.

The alternative is to consider the three-line components in scenes ii and iii as special cases of expressive elaboration, what I would call amplification within a frame of what are otherwise single verses. See Hymes 1985a:391–434. The special status of these components is indicated in the profile by capital letters (such as stanzas would have). Runs of three are a stylistic trait of narratives in the language.

15. See Jeremiah Curtin, "Wasco Tales and Myths," in Sapir 1909b:269–70, 287–88, where Fish Hawk is Coyote's son-in-law, of whom he is proud. The latter narrative has Eagle defeat them in diving. Where Coyote would nearly die, striking his head against natural ice, Fish Hawk here nearly dies, striking his head against ice that Eagle has caused (288).

16. No native title is certainly known for any of the five versions. Edward Sapir's "The Story about Coyote" might have been suggested by Louis Simpson, but there is no indication of that in the field notebook; Hiram Smith did not suggest an alternative. Victoria Howard's story is an unnamed part of the longer narrative of how the Coyote named Tənaq'ia went round the world. Melville Jacobs headed John B. Hudson's story with "The News Precedes Coyote"; the Stevens Savage story has no heading in its notebook. I use Jacobs's "news" and Sapir's "about." The story names "news" as its topic and evokes the delight that he and others would take in whatever news might come along. "Precedes" is accurate but too precise; "about" allows for all the rest of what happens.

17. Here is the story as excerpted from *Ethnogeography of the Franklin D. Roosevelt Lake Area,* an unpublished monograph by Randy Bouchard and Dorothy Kennedy (1979). I am grateful to them for it.

"Some people were gathering eggs at Npak (new Inchelium, not far from the Columbia River) and preparing a pit to cook them in. Once the eggs were being cooked, the people laid down to rest. Coyote came along, saw these people sleeping, and blew on them, causing them to sleep more deeply. Then he dug up their eggs, ate all of them, and piled the shells around each sleeping person. When they woke up, they noticed eggshells around them, even though they had not eaten anything. Also they noticed that Coyote had changed some of their features while they were sleeping—he put tufts on Lynx's ears and twisted Crossbill's beak.

"They knew it must have been Coyote, so they all followed his tracks to try to catch him. But one by one they tired, until only Lynx was left.

"Lynx knew what to do—he caused rain and sleet to fall. Coyote took shelter and Lynx caught up to him, as he knew where Coyote would go. Coyote was sitting under an overhanging rock cliff, amusing himself by swallowing his own penis. Lynx hit Coyote on the back of the head, causing Coyote's penis to stick in his own throat. Then Lynx ran away to tell everyone about Coyote, so that when Coyote reached the nearest camp, people were already laughing at him. He went to another camp, but they had also heard the news and were laughing at him. Coyote went to a third camp, but they were also laughing at him, so he passed judgment. 'News will travel fast, because it has no legs.' This has been true ever since."

18. Tillamook: the opening section of "Wild Woman," told by Clara Pearson to Elizabeth Jacobs, and published in her *Nehalem Tillamook Tales* (1990:61–62). Miluk Coos: "The Young Man Lived with His Grandmother," told by Annie Miner Peterson to Melville Jacobs, and published in his *Coos Myth Texts* (1940:172–73). Colville-Okanagon: Mourning Dove [Christine Quintasket] (1990:117–18).

19. Close brackets (]) at the end of lines 19, 22, 29 indicate the close of a pair of verses in a sequence of pairs.

20. "But" (line 36) and "could have been" (line 38) render a Kalapuya particle expressing wonder, *čú-nak*.

21. I am grateful to William C. Sturtevant of the Smithsonian Institution and to its Department of Anthropology and Archives for the opportunity to read the unpublished notebooks in which the narratives of Stevens Savage are preserved.

13. Ethnopoetics, Oral-Formulaic Theory, and Editing Texts

This paper was prepared for the spring 1993 meeting of the Society for Textual Studies. I want to thank John Foley for inviting me to take part. Since the meeting I have revised the analysis of the text, "The Deserted Boy," after recognizing the role of couplets in it, and have added comments on the recognition of lines in Anglo-Saxon studies. I want to thank Nick Doane and Joe Russo for their stimulating papers at the meetings and Hoyt Duggan for his encouragement.

1. Sung epic poetry is famous for oral formulae, which have been taken as enabling a narrator to meet the constraint of the metrical line in the midst of performing. (I realize that there is more to oral formulae than that.) The narratives with which I have worked, not having metrical lines, do not have the same performance constraint. One does sometimes find evidence of fulfilling the constraint of a patterned sequence in an ad hoc way. Among Native Americans in the Pacific Northwest, formulae seem to have two roles. Prayers and exhortations at ceremonies may be full of them, not to meet formal constraint, but to invoke tradition. Narratives employ them at major junctures, such as openings and closings, and there are classes of words to be expected as markers. All these could be said to be required by a genre. There are also words that are expected for characteristic actions in the course of a type of scene or story. The choice, position, and frequency of these words is particular to a given narrator and performance. They seem to give shape as much as to fulfill it.

A founder of oral-formulaic theory, A. B. Lord, has remarked several times on sets of lines as a feature of traditional epic (Lord 1995). Foley (1995:88–90) carefully discusses lines in my work, together with an example from the Tonkawa myth taken up in chap. 3 of this volume.

2. African American narratives collected in New York City by William Labov can be more accurately appreciated when seen to be poetry in this sense. Labov's

much-used analysis of stories in terms of a set of universal functions misses their shape. The stories are not a linear sequence of temporal events, intersected by nontemporal effects, but rather successive arcs of arousing and realizing expectation. See Hymes 1991c, 1995a, and chapter 4 in this book.

3. There is also "free verse," much of which actually has recurrences and relations of various kinds.

4. Rhyme and stanza forms are analogues, especially in a narrative poem. The difference is that larger units of oral narratives of the sort considered here do not have to be constant in number of lines or other parts. Narrators need not fill a fixed form. Rather, they match two sequences as they proceed, one of incident with one of formal options. The matching can differ from telling to telling. This (re-)generative competence needs to be taking into account in discussion of "entextualization" (Bauman and Briggs 1990).

5. Examples are given later in this chapter.

6. Stanza D is a brief form of what can be a full scene. It often occurs in versions of the story type "Bear and Deer." Bear has killed Deer while the two are away from home. Deer's children retaliate by killing Bear's children and flee before Bear returns. Bear, finding her children dead, pursues them but first asks a dog the direction they have gone. The dog has been instructed to bark in turn in directions other than the one in which the children actually have gone. Sapir did not record the myth from Louis Simpson (Sapir 1909b), but Victoria Howard dictated it in Clackamas to Melville Jacobs (the incident is in Jacobs 1958:149–50), with both women as bears, Grizzly and Black Bear. Charles Cultee told it to Franz Boas in Kathlamet (the incident is in Boas 1901:122), with neither woman a bear. I suspect that the doubling in Howard's version and the diminution in that from Cultee (to Robin [Thrush] and Salmonberry) reflects tension about the figure of a bear as a way of exploring the nature of women.

In Louis Simpson's "The Deserted Boy," presumably the reeds answer, first from one direction, then from another, so that the boy searches everywhere but in the direction the people have actually gone, to the river. We are to understand that they have taken the only canoe. The boy is left on a low, marshy bit of land (where reeds would grow), too far from either side of the river for him to get back. Simpson assumes an audience would understand this and subordinates explanation or elaboration to severity of form, in which the next stage, an analogue of a successful guardian spirit quest, is expeditiously reached.

7. This scene has several instances of the elementary three-step relation as well. The three spoken statements in (A) can be taken as three steps (onset, ongoing, outcome) of the initial plan. First, the boy is addressed (with the transitive verb-stem -*lxam*); then the people arc spoken to generally, broadcast (with the intransitive stem -*kim*); then some, not all, are addressed, as indicated by -*lxam* instead of -*kim,* presumably excluding the boy. After the first stanza, which has everyone in place, three stanzas each have changes of location with the onset, ongoing,

outcome pattern. The people cross, go on, arrive at the reeds (8, 9, 10); they run off, go straight home, none are left (17, 18–19, 20–21); the boy stares, follows, arrives running (28, 29, 30). Such a three-step change of location constitutes all of (C) and (E). Stanzas B and D overall have three-step sequences but not of movement as such. Reach the reeds, cut them, instruct them (B), boy calls to go home, reeds answer, boy searches in vain (D).

The entire translation is given as an appendix at the end of the chapter, because it will figure in other parts of this essay as well. This version replaces that in chap. 4 of Hymes 1981b.

8. Benedict herself remarks of the tales she recorded: "They give the literary style to which all the stories in Cochiti conform but which can never be completely reproduced without recording the text" (1981 [1931]:xiii). Her relative confidence about style probably was based on the fact that Franz Boas recorded a number of tales in the language itself and published a characterization of it (Boas 1928). The translations of the stories he recorded in text are included in her monograph.

9. The communities from which come the South Slavic epic poetry studied by Lord and Foley very likely also tell unsung stories that make use of ethnopoetic patterning; see Foley 1995. L. D. Perkowski (2002) has shown its presence in a series of recently collected Bulgarian narratives.

10. For the organization of lines in a Zuni text published by Tedlock, see Hymes 1980b, 1982. Tedlock's response (1987:56–61) seems not to allow for the possibility of relations not auditorily perceptible. For rhetorical relations among verses, stanzas, and scenes, disclosed by quotative particles in a Hopi performance, see Hymes 1992b. I have sketched the verses and stanzas of the first text in Parks 1991, Alfred Morsette's "How Summer Came to the North Country," and have prepared an account of the stanzas and scenes in Dewey Healing's "Bird Story" (Arizona Tewa) presented by Kroskrity 1985 (cf. Kroskrity 1993).

11. This example was intended to form section 5 of the original article (Hymes 1976b), but was omitted from both it and Hymes 1981b. Cf. 1981b:163, line 15. For the symbol G, see note 12 to this chapter.

12. In Wishram words C is used for voiceless affricate (English "ch"), E is used for schwa (like the vowel in English "but"), G is used for a voiced velar stop, L for a voiceless lateral fricative, S for a voiceless "shibilant" (English "sh"), x far a voiceless velar fricative such as in German *Ich*, X for a voiceless velar fricative such as in German *ach*. A consonant followed by ' is glottalized.

13. Lines 152–55 and 162–64. Line 153 is an English explanation that is not part of the narrative proper.

14. For all the features of the act, please see the appendix, which replaces the text presented in Hymes 1976b and 1981b, chap. 4.

15. See Hymes 1981b:159–64 for the earlier consideration. These pages and

others cited above are captioned "Structural philology (a)" and "Structural philology (b)".

16. It is possible to take the stanza as five interlocking verses, since the first three verses make sense as a three-step progression of onset, ongoing, outcome (with traditional reference to other versions in which how the news gets out is spelled out). The third step, becoming news, might in turn be the onset of another three-step progression (there is food at the boy's place, let us go, now snow). But that would ignore the lines of the couplet, which have no normal place in any of the five verses.

17. Lines 30–31, "he arrived running: / Now, no people," might seem a couplet from the standpoint of counting lines. To take it as a unit would give the stanza three elements. What we have here, however, is the conjunction of two other narrative patterns: the first three lines are an example of the common three-step pattern of action (onset, ongoing, outcome): he started home, he followed behind, he arrived running. The third and fourth lines are an example of an action coupled with an object of perception: he arrived running; now, no people. With regard to the second pair of lines, I cannot help remembering 2 Samuel 17:22ab (as translated in the *New American Bible*): "So David and all his people moved on and crossed the Jordan. By daybreak, there was no left who had not crossed." As if "all on that side / not a person on this side."

18. The relations given in Hymes 1985 (chap. 6 of this volume) should be revised as follows:

(i)   (Encounter) (A) 92, 93–94, 95
(ii)   (Colloquy)   (A) (abc) 95–99, 100–101, 102
                    (B) (abc) 103, 104, 105–9
                    (C) (abc) (110–11, 112–17, 118–23)
(iii) (Outcomes)   (A) (Twisted) (abc) 124–26, 127–29, 130–31
                    (B) (Pronouncement) (a) 132–34
                    (C) (Thrown) (abc) 135, 136–38, 139–43

19. These considerations are an instance of the general issue raised by McGann (1983), that of the need to locate editing and literary production in their particular social nexus. Cf. Gorman 1989:194.

20. Berman does not actually indicate the verses in the text, only the two parts to each stanza. Verses can be recognized in terms of the initial element *lál'ai* 'then' (1992:130, 131–32) and turns at talk. Stanza A has two verbs of saying in its first part, "Then" twice initially in its second part. Stanza B appears to be marked by having four framing verbs of speaking, the first of each pair with initial "Then" but then a third initial *lál'ai* and a fifth framing verb (of singing). These lines (14–17) are the peripety and the only song. Stanzas C and D resume even-numbered patterning. Stanza C has initial "Then" and a turn at talk with a verb of saying, while (D) has twice initial "Then."

Carrying through the verse analysis and showing it in translation, (as Berman does in other work) brings out the special status of stanza C. The peripety is marked in form against the background of the rest.

21. "Split-His-Own-Head" (Jacobs 1990:220–28) with an appendix for this story by myself; the analysis into verses is slightly revised here. Cf. Hymes 1993 and Seaburg 1992. I am indebted to Seaburg for the notebook original.

22. The order of the published *Wishram Texts* (Sapir 1909b) is not identical with the order of the notebooks. The Coyote cycle is interrupted by part of the Salmon Myth, and the moving observation printed at the end of the cycle does not appear there in the notebook. In Jacobs's *Clackamas Chinook Texts*, part 1, the last section of a myth important for its performance sequence (Hymes 1986) is taken from a separate comment on a different notebook page (cf. chap. 7 of this volume).

23. Sapir's field notebooks for Wishram Chinook contain an unpublished version from the same narrator, Louis Simpson, of the first myth published in 1909 ("The Origin of Fish in Columbia," pp. 3–7). The degree to which there is something like formulaic recurrence could be established.

24. Buchanan spoke in Coos and then provided a translation, written down by St. Clair word by word below the Coos. The last words of line 3 and line 8 are the same in Coos, "their land, earth, country, ground, place."

25. I hope soon to prepare a collection with such a title, "River Poets in Native Oregon."

26. A repeated vowel symbol shows prolongation.

27. The sound of the fire is phonetically a glottalized voiceless lateral affricate; that is, *t* plus voiceless *l* plus glottal stop.

28. *ats'E'pts'Ep* is the name of a delicacy, a mixture of dried salmon and mashed huckleberries, has *a* (feminine gender), *ts,* glottal stop, schwa (as in English "but"), and *p.*

29. A repeated vowel symbol shows prolongation.

30. The woman is the daughter of ICE'xian, the spirit power who lives beneath a whirlpool. His name has *i-* (masculine gender), *ch,* glottal stop, schwa, palatal voiceless fricative (as in German *Ich*), and *i,* a, *n.*

14. Anthologies and Narrators

This essay arose out of a review of Erdoes and Ortiz (1984) invited by *The Nation* (see Hymes 1985a). I would like to thank Elizabeth Pochoda for the invitation. Let me also thank Judith Berman for information in connection with the Kwakiutl myth mentioned in this chapter.

1. Since the original article was written, Ortiz died, a serious loss.

2. Hudson lived at Grand Ronde, Oregon. Henry Zenk, who has worked with speakers of Chinook jargon there, reports that his two daughters concur.

3. I have indicated the presence of these principles in the language in a re-

view of the Lopez anthology (Hymes 1979b) and in a comment on another paper (Hymes 1981a). The review simply shows the presence of parallelism and repetition in accord with a Kalapuya logic of organizing actions in groups of three and five for a passage of travel by Coyote that Lopez had omitted in his retelling of William Hartless's telling in Mary's River Kalapuya (a dialect related to Santiam) of "Coyote Gambles Playing the Hand Game" (Jacobs 1945:205–15; Lopez 1977: 165–68). The comment shows that John B. Hudson's Santiam version of the "News about Coyote" is the same in shape, despite difference in the language, as that told in Clackamas Chinook by Victoria Howard (see Hymes 1981b:235–37). This is the first full published account in ethnopoetic terms of a Kalapuya text.

4. A different repeated doubling can be imagined, adding an initial element of framing. That would give, not seven steps, but eight, paired. One can think of the four pairs in the progress of the action.

Frame (stanzas AB)
Need (CD)

Deception (E)
Trade (F)

Deception (GHa)
Detection (Hb)

Righting (Hcde)
Establishment (I)

The first three pairs of elements (AB, CD, EF) align well with formal parts of the narrative. Then with (H) there is an apparent playing off of theme against form. (H) encompasses three elements, the second Deception (a), the second Detection (Hb), and the Righting (Hcde). Such a failure to match neatly could be taken as evidence against the eight-part scheme. Or it could be taken as evidence of artistry, as if like a musical score in which bar measures continued, while a complex figuration played against them, becoming wholly coordinated just at the end (I).

5. "Coyote Looks around the Country" (my title). Jacobs (1945:222) has "Coyote Removes Dangerous Being from Streams; He Cuts People's Mouths."

6. Lévi-Strauss has indicated that in his view we are pursuing complementary goals (1987).

15. Notes toward (an Understanding of) Supreme Fictions

1. Foley 1988. The limitations of its extension to Anglo-Saxon poetry are commented upon by Opland 1980, chap. 1. Some of the recent New World work can be seen in Hymes 1981b; Tedlock 1987; and Swann and Krupat 1987.

2. A fact discussed forty-five years ago by the linguist and folklorist Melville Jacobs(1945:6–7). Cf. Hymes 1974a:192 n.4.

3. "Seal and Her Younger Brother Lived There." The text was told in 1930 in the Clackamas Chinook language of the Willamette Valley of Oregon by the last speaker of that language, Victoria Howard, to the anthropologist Melville Jacobs. It is discussed in chaps. 8 and 9 of Hymes 1981b. (Chap. 9 is revised from an article titled "Discovering Oral Performance and Measured Verse in American Indian Narrative," *New Literary History* 8 [1977]: 431–57.) I will refer to the text several times, and this presentation and discussion go beyond what has been previously published. The fact that continued reading does not exhaust the text may itself be an indication of a quality that is literary.

4. "Grizzly Bear and Black Bear Ran Away with the Two Girls," in Jacobs 1958.

5. "Panther and Owl," in Boas 1901. But in a Koyukon Athapaskan myth (Alaska), shared with me by Eliza Jones, the beaver asks a young woman who has fallen to the bottom of the river about each of four body parts only to be sure that she is all right.

6. "Sun's Myth," in Boas 1901:26–33. The scene is evidently inverse to a type in which young men ask their grandmother to whom salmon spears and other fishing gear belong and, when told they are hers, know she lies ("The Otter Brothers Recover Their Father's Heart," in Sapir 1909a).

7. See the discussion of Philip Kahclamat's telling of "Coyote's People Sing" in chap. 3 of Hymes 1981b.

8. Nor that it is absent. Chinookan speakers make good use of consonantal changes that express augmentative versus diminutive. When Coyote borrows the wrapped-around penis of an old man, he attaches the latter's *i-galxix* ('large') to his *i-k'alxix* ('small').

9. Philip Kahclamat, a Wishram Chinook speaker, told it to me in the Rainbow Cafe above the Deschutes one evening in the summer of 1956. See Hymes 1981b: 87–91, 203–8.

10. See chap. 8 of this volume for "Benevolent Host" as part of the name of a type that has been called simply "Bungling Host."

11. To be sure, I believe another myth is a sequel to this story, one in which another daughter overcomes the Grizzly Woman who comes to her father, a chief. See "Grizzly Woman Began to Kill Them;" in Hymes 1981b, chap. 10.

12. See chap. 4 of Hymes 1981b. I have since revised the account of acts 2 and 3.

13. See Hymes 1980b. The text was recorded by Dennis Tedlock (1999).

14. In the next stanza, to be sure, he sees a very little bit of flame, takes the flame, builds a fire. But he has seen the flame already; that is why he dries his tears.

15. See V. Hymes 1987:62–102, and for such patterns in English narrative, Hymes and Hymes 2002.

16. Regarding the role of form, see Burke 1925:34–46.

17. The sequence is analyzed in chap. 14 of this volume. Versions of the last episode are recorded from many narrators, but none say how the tip can still be Coyote's, once he has added the old man's penis to his own. The later recovery

of his own tip would seem to require adding the old man's instrument like extra lengths of hose behind a nozzle. Often enough the old man is said to feed his penis constantly with wood chips. Sometimes such a version has Coyote forced to trade back, simply because the voraciousness wears him out. Always, however, a tip inside the girl is simply stuck, not calling for food. Evidently, the point of the penis depends on the point of the story.

18. The idiomatic phrases "I don't know at what time" and "I don't know when at night" consist of the stem "to think," used as uninflected particle, and a compound adverb, "how / what—with reference to time," plus in one case a postposition for "when" and in the other the noun "night." See the discussion in this chapter on their use in the appended text with regard to Greimas's semiotic square.

19. I echo the language used by Riffaterre (1990:32–33) in analyzing a passage from Trollope's *Barchester Towers*. Victoria Howard does not speak in her own voice, as Trollope does in his, but the remonstrance, unique in all known versions of related myths, is hers.

20. Cf. Alter 1981:182: "As a rule, when a narrative event in the Bible seems important, the writer will render it mainly through dialogue, so the transitions from narration to dialogue provide in themselves some implicit measure of what is deemed essential." For this myth, see Hymes 1985d:953–76.

21. The myths concerned with revenge against women are (a) "Grizzly and Black Bear Ran Away with the Two Girls," then (b) "Grizzly Woman Killed People." The myths concerned with being a wife are (c) "Grizzly and Black Bear Ran Away with the Two Girls," then (d) "Gitskux and His Older Brother." The order of narration in her work with Jacobs was (c) (notebook 6), (d) (notebook 12), (a) (notebook 14–15), (b) (notebook 15). In other words, first the second of each pair, then the first of each pair. The four texts (a, b, c, d) are in Jacobs 1958, no. 17, pp. 156–66; 1959a, no. 34, pp. 315–21; 1958, no. 14, pp. 130–41; 1958, no. 16, pp. 143–56, respectively.

22. In strict chronological contrast, *na-* would indicate past of about a day ago but does not do so here. The tense prefixes within the girl's remonstrance show as much. In the third verse of the final scene, the girl says "I told you" twice with the tense prefix *i-*, indicating action earlier in the same diurnal period. She next says "I had told you" with the prefix *ni-* and the direction marker *t-*, indicating action over a period earlier than that, but (because of the *t-*) nearer rather than farther back. She then confirms the implication of a period of time by using the future, "You would tell me." Her second remonstrance has only the *i-* of the immediate past.

In sum, the quoted narration of what has happened makes precise reference on either side of "yesterday" the meaning of *na-* if taken as part of a chronological series. "Yesterday" makes no sense in relation to these motivated indications of relative time.

Evidently *na-* has another significance here. Its use in other texts and in elicited forms shows that it does have reference to the past, and here it at least indicates a lessening of the distance indicated by *ga-* (the most remote marker). In narratives *na-* is favored by intransitive verbs of personal state such as "weep" and "think" (a point investigated by Robert E. Moore [1980, 1982].) But it is not required by such or restricted to them. The key would appear to be that the shape *na-* is an old marker of location in the language family. There is reason to think that in the set of initial tense prefixes, it may retain a sense of aspect as well as of tense, of "where" as well as of "when." Its use here may have a sense simply of location in past time, perhaps with a sense of states that endure as well as occur: she will continue to be up (line 29), to weep (lines 50, 56, 65), to say (lines 51, 55, 57) (but not fix fire, light pitch, look, raise her light, scream).

23. Cf. Alter 1981:183: "When does the dialogue break off sharply, withholding from us the rejoinder we might have expected from one of the two speakers?"

24. Although in the last volume of *Mythologiques* (1964–1971), Lévi-Strauss sometimes takes details out of context and misrepresents them. See discussion at the end of chap. 14 and the beginning of chap. 6 of this volume.

25. Working with myths told by Philip Kahclamat in the spring of 1933, I thought at first that one, involving an alternation of languages, was unique. Then a Quileute myth came to my attention, then a Tsimshian in a new collection, then a Kalapuya. This last reminded me that everything must be used. It was not obtained in the Indian language, and it was obtained by a person scholars put down as a popularizer of limited understanding. But here was unique testimony, not recorded by the anthropologists who had worked with the very same narrator, helping to illuminate a newly recognized semantic field.

26. Among Indian people someone in the audience, perhaps the audience as a whole, would respond with a certain sound (*i* . . . among Sahaptin speakers in Oregon and Washington). A decline in that sound or its absence would let the narrator know the audience was losing interest, falling asleep. When George Forman, a Wishram living at Yakima, did not recall a story, he would not say he had not heard it, but that he had fallen asleep when it was told.

27. For recent surveys of the work begun by Milman Parry and Albert Lord, see Foley *1988*.

28. See the discussion of Philip Kahclamat's telling of "Coyote's People Sing" in chap. 3 of Hymes 1981b.

29. See "Coyote and Badger" in Barker 1963, and chap. 14 of this volume. Hartless, like other Kalapuya narrators, knew also a sequence in which Coyote loses his eyes by throwing them out of a tree in which he is trapped in winter. The sequel is that he finds the place where people are gambling with them and gets them back. The sunny setting of this scene may serve to contrast it and its sequel (imitation eyes) with the other.

30. Perhaps remembered between performances, perhaps constructed. Either

way, after telling the story in 1891, Cultee continued to think about it, although having no way of knowing he would be asked to tell it again. The case shows that interpretation should not separate narrative content from poetic form or, as so often the case with Native American narratives, neglect poetic form.

31. "Maker" is not an ideal term, but "author" will not do, for narrators did not think of themselves as authors in the sense of personal originators, and the verb that goes with "myth" in Chinookan is "make."

32. One early term for whites, because of their extraordinary nature, used the stem for "nature," -k'ani. On myth as interpretation of history, cf. Hill 1988; and Sullivan 1989.

33. Earlier, Whites found Coyote stories disgusting. Enlightened people now find them funny. Neither univocal response does justice to the moral complexity of the tradition and its enactments.

34. On continuation of myth as selection in history, see Blumenberg 1985.

35. Susan Golla, who is engaged in an extended analysis of such accounts, many of them recorded many years ago by Edward Sapir and still unpublished, made this point in a talk at the University of Virginia.

36. Jacobs: "It was expected that child auditors, if not older people, repeat in unison each phrase or sentence verbatim after the raconteur. 'They kept on telling it until the children got it right. They wanted them to have it right. They did not want them to get is mixed up and "lie" when they told it' (Annie Miner Peterson)" (1940:130). When told to adults only, just one auditor repeated each sentence verbatim. This is an aspect of conversational etiquette: the person spoken to usually if not always repeated verbatim what was said to him.

37. I owe this point to Dennis Demert.

38. Thus Franz Boas writes that "the desire for privilege and for the authorization of privilege is a source of the exuberant diversification of Kwakiutl mythology" (1932:viii). Cf. McIlwraith 1948.

39. Not that a narrator would wish to exploit the possibility to the limit. A frame widespread in the Pacific Northwest is one in which in the course of a myth a protagonist questions trees and shrubs one after the other. If the answer is favorable to the questioner, they are rewarded by a pronouncement as to how they will be useful to the human beings who are about to come; if the answer is unfavorable, they are not. Relating a Nehalem Tillamook myth of two Wild Women asking tree after tree how well they looked, Clara Pearson, after thirteen trees, concluded, "That is ended. That is enough. It is too tiresome. They asked too many things, grass, dirt, rocks, everything" (Jacobs 1990 [1959]:150.

40. By a superb narrator, William Hartless, recorded in 1914 by L. F. Frachtenberg, and edited by Melville Jacobs (1945:275–85).

41. With apologies to Wallace Stevens, "The Pleasures of Merely Circulating" 1952:168.

42. Reflecting on this essay, I realize that its concerns and the concerns of

those whose narratives it is about fit naturally with what Kenneth Burke thought and wrote about more than seventy years ago—vocabularies of motive, attitudes toward history, orientations, frames of acceptance (and rejection) caught up in history, actors acting in terms both of a sense of piety (what goes with what) and categories essentially poetic (comedy, plaint, burlesque, tragedy), and that it ought not to be a surprise, my having been his student for nearly forty years. (Cf. Kenneth Burke 1984a, 1984b).

16. Robinson Jeffers's Artistry of Line

This study is part of a larger one. In the larger study the conclusions reached as to Jeffers's use of types of line are used to explore the organization of "Tamar" in some detail, and the whole is framed by a concern to place Jeffers as a narrative poet of the West in relation to American Indian narrative poets who preceded him. On the one hand, it appears that both Jeffers and American Indian narrators have assigned meaning to contrast and alternation of types of line. The ways in which they do so are different, but the common principle points to what may be a universal basis of poetry. On the other hand, there are links between Indian myths and Jeffers in the handling of character as an abstract calculus of motives and in a sacramental sense of the relation between the world and those who live in it. Indeed, certain Indian myths express that relation in the light of experienced destruction and loss, analogous to Jeffers's response to the devastation of the lives and expectations of a generation in the First World War. There is in particular a myth of the sun, told by the last narrator of a people who lived on the coast at the mouth of the Columbia River, of which "Tamar" seems in many points a transformation—so much so that if "Tamar" had been found, couched in Indian style, in a text collection from northern California, someone practicing the structural approach of Claude Lévi-Strauss could hardly fail to count it and the Chinookan "Sun's Myth" as part of the same series. William Everson (1976: 71–74) has also pointed out a striking parallel between "Tamar" and a California-Oregon myth, "Loon Woman," in regard to sister-brother incest and death by fire. Cf. Lévi-Strauss, 1981, introduction, and Hymes 2002.

    1. Herbert Arthur Klein, "The Prosody of Robinson Jeffers," M.A. thesis, Occidental College, 1930, as reported in Powell 1940:118ff.

    2. Regrettably I have not seen the 1930 master's thesis by Klein. What I know of it through quotation and published letters (Ridgeway 1968) seems generally correct and sensible. I very much hope that the further inquiry he had undertaken before his death will become available. If what I say should duplicate any of his work, I hope it will be regarded as independent confirmation. In a fuller study, I want to offer my own sense of the scansion of Jeffers's lines and the bases of his practice with regard to stress, types of feet, and types of line.

    3. Not entirely impossible. The English poet Paul Muldoon is currently exploiting rhyme as a marker of equivalence within a great diversity of serious poems,

as did Ogden Nash in light verse. Edward Nickerson (1974:12–20) has discussed Jeffers's renewed experiments with rhyme and stanza form in later years as an indication of his lifelong experimental interest in craft.

4. Within each stanza, all the lines are adjacent on the page. I separate pairs of lines to make the patterning of length more perceptible.

5. In terms of types of feet, anapest anapest antispast / trochee trochee trochee trochee / iamb choriamb anapest / iamb anapest. The conjunction of iamb and choriamb in the third quoted line illustrates a common Jeffers practice: following a foot that ends with stress by a phrase that begins with "under," "over," or "out," and so requires initial stress.

6. I take "curiously" in the fourth stanza as having three syllables, with "ious" representing a single syllable. "Curiously" has metrical stress on its last syllable in the second line, followed by an unstressed syllable, but not in the third line, which is followed by a syllable that is stressed. Alternatively, "curiously" might be taken as having a second syllabification in its second occurrence and the line scanned as "Made them cúrióusly víle," but that seems quite unlikely, especially because it detracts from the intended contrast between "ignoble" and "vile."

All three lines of the stanza are taken as stressed on the initial syllable. "Men súffer" is unlikely; "Mén" takes stress because of its place in the series (flowers, grass, trees, deer, birds).

7. Not previously noted, so far as I know. I have not yet seen the dissertation by Kiley, which includes attention to prosody and a study of "Night" (*Robinson Jeffers Newsletter* 24 (1969): 6).

8. The separation into groups of five is entirely for convenience of perception. The lines represented by a line of numbers for a section (A B C D E) are continuous on the page.

9. In a letter to Donald Friede of 25 November 1925, Jeffers explains his inability to provide the typewritten manuscript of "Tamar" but does report finding a great sheet containing "1) The first germ of the Tamar story, dramatis personae (several of whom were lost or changed in the telling), incidents, metrical indications" (Ridgeway 1968:53). Section 1 of the note sheet is reproduced by Ridgeway (1968:53) and has at the bottom:

5 beats to the line
  doubled in a few passages to [?] 10s
  quickened to anapests, [?] anapestic
  ᵘᵘᵘ—lyrical passages, [?] to 8s

The markings are 3 breves and a raised line of equal length, perhaps intended to represent the fourth paeon, a foot of four syllables, with three unstressed syllables followed by a stressed fourth.

Notice that although subsequent writers often refer to Jeffers as having rejected meter, he himself uses the term here ("metrical indications"), five years later in writing to Klein ("metrical intention"), and eight years later writing to Keppel ("All my verses are metrical, or imagine themselves to be") (Ridgeway 1968:173, 206).

10. One so readily recognizes that stanza iii has to do with deer that it may come as a surprise to realize that deer are not named. Perhaps that assists a focus on natural inanimate process, making salient a quiet movement toward water.

11. Presumably the rock in the soul (vii, line 2) breaks the surface at a turning point. What has risen with the withdrawal of the tide in human life will be covered again, just as the tide rock whose streaming shoulders emerge from the slack at the outset of the poem will be covered with the incoming tide. (In stanza v, the coming of [general] Night is associated with the tide turning toward the land.)

12. There is a parallel to another reader of Nietszche's *Also Sprach Zarathustra,* the composer and contemporary of Jeffers, Frederick Delius, who is mostly known for his short orchestral pieces, while his major works in opera and for chorus and orchestra (*Appalachia, Sea-Drift, A Mass of Life, Requiem "To the memory of all young artists fallen in the war"*) are seldom performed.

References

Abrahams, Roger D., ed. 1995. *Fields of folklore: Essays in honor of Kenneth Goldstein.* Bloomington IN: Trickster Press.

Adamson, Thelma. 1934. *Folk-tales of the Coast Salish.* New York: American Folklore Society.

Albert, Roy, and David Leedom Shaul. 1985. *A concise Hopi and English lexicon.* Amsterdam: John Benjamins.

Alter, Robert. 1981. *The art of biblical narrative.* New York: Basic Books.

———. 1985. *The art of biblical poetry.* New York: Basic Books.

———. 1995. Imagining history in the Bible. In *History and histories with the human sciences,* edited by Ralph Cohen and Michael .S. Roth, 53–72. Charlottesville: University Press of Virginia.

Andrade, Manuel. 1931. *Quileute texts.* Columbia University Contributions to Anthropology 12. New York: Columbia University Press.

Aoki, Haruo. 1970. *Nez Perce grammar.* Publications in Linguistics, no. 62. Berkeley: University of California Press.

———. 1994. *Nez Perce dictionary.* Publications in Linguistics, no. 122. Berkeley: University of California Press.

Aoki, Haruo, and Deward E. Walker, Jr. 1989. *Nez Perce oral narratives.* Berkeley: University of California Press.

Bahr, Donald M. 1975. *Pima and Papago ritual oratory: A study of three texts.* San Francisco: Indian Historian.

Bahr, Donald, Juan Smith, William Smith Allison, and Julian Hayden. 1994. *The short swift time of gods on earth: The Hohokam chronicles.* Berkeley: University of California Press.

Ballard, Arthur C. 1929. *Mythology of southern Puget Sound.* University of Washington Publications in Anthropology, vol. 3, no. 2. Seattle: University of Washington Press.

Bamberg, Michael, ed. 1997. Oral versions of personal experience: Three decades of narrative analysis. *Journal of Narrative and Life History* 7, nos. 1–4. (The journal is now *Narrative Inquiry.*)

Barker, M. A. R. 1963. *Klamath texts.* University of California Publications in Linguistics 30. Berkeley: University of California Press.

Basso, Ellen B. 1985. *A musical view of the universe: Kalapalo myth and ritual performances.* Philadelphia: University of Pennsylvania Press.

Bauman, Richard, and Charles L. Briggs. 1990. Poetics and performance as critical perspectives on language and social life. *Annual Review of Anthropology* 19: 59–88.

Benedict, Ruth. 1981. *Tales of the Cochiti Indians.* Bureau of American Ethnology, Bulletin 98. Washington DC: GPO, 1931. Reprint, with introduction by Alfonso Ortiz, Albuquerque: University of New Mexico Press.

Berman, Judith. 1991. The seal's sleeping cave: The interpretation of Boas's Kwak'wala texts. Ph.D. diss., Department of Anthropology, University of Pennsylvania.

———. 1992. Oolachan-Woman's robe: Fish, blankets, masks, and meaning in Boas's Kwakw'ala texts. In *On the translation of Native American literatures,* edited by Brian Swann, 125–62. Washington DC: Smithsonian Institution.

Bernstein, Michael Andre. 1994. *Foregone conclusions: Against apocalyptic history.* Berkeley: University of California Press.

Blackburn, Stuart H. 1988. *Singing of birth and death: Texts in performance.* Philadelphia: University of Pennsylvania Press.

Blackburn, Stuart H., Peter J. Claus, Joyce B. Fleuskyer, and Susan S. Wadley. 1989. *Oral epics in India.* Berkeley: University of California Press.

Blau, Herbert. 1998. "Set me where you stand": Revising the abyss. *New Literary History* 29, no. 2:247–72.

Blommaert, Jan. 1997. *Workshopping: Notes on professional vision in discourse analysis.* Antwerp Papers in Linguistics, no. 91. Antwerp: Universitaire Instelling Antwerpen.

———. 1998. Narrative patterns in Dutch interview data. Notes. Department of African Languages and Cultures, University of Gent.

Blue Cloud, Peter/Aroniawenrate. 1989. *Elderberry flute song: Contemporary coyote tales.* Buffalo NY: White Pine.

Blumenberg, Hans. 1985. *Work on myth.* Cambridge MA: MIT Press. Originally published as *Arbeit am Mythos.* (Frankfurt am Main: Suhrkamp, 1979).

Boas, Franz. 1887a. Poetry and music of some North American tribes. *Science* 9: 383–85.

———. 1887b. A year among the Eskimo. *Bulletin of the American Geographical Society* 19:383–402. (Reprinted in Stocking 1974c, 44–55.)

———. 1894. *Chinook texts.* Bureau of American Ethnology, Bulletin 20. Washington DC: Smithsonian Institution.

———. 1901. *Kathlamet texts.* Bureau of American Ethnology, Bulletin 26. Washington DC: Smithsonian Institution.

———. 1911. Introduction to *Handbook of American Indian languages.* Bureau of American Ethnology, Bulletin 40, pt. 1. Washington DC: GPO.

———. 1914. Mythology and folk-tales of the North American Indians. *Journal of American Folklore* 27:374–410.

———. 1916. Tsimshian mythology, based on texts recorded by Henry W. Tate. *Bureau of American Ethnology Annual Report* (1909–1910). Washington DC: Bureau of American Ethnology.

———. 1917. Introduction to *International Journal of American Linguistics* 1:1–8.

———. 1925. Stylistic aspects of primitive literature. *Journal of American Folklore* 38:329–39.

———. 1927. *Primitive art.* Oslo: Instituttet for Sammenlignende Kulturforskning, H. Aschehoug.

———. 1928. Abstract characteristics of Keresan Folk-tales. *International Congress of Americanists* 20, no. 1:223–24.

———. 1932. *Bella Bella tales.* Memoirs of the American Folklore Society 25. New York: American Folklore Society.

———. 1940. *Race, language and culture.* New York: Macmillan.

———. 1974. Letter to W. H. Holmes of 24 July 1905. In Stocking 1974c, 122–23.

Borg, Marcus J., and N. T. Wright. 1998. *The meaning of Jesus: Two visions.* San Francisco: HarperSan Francisco. (Cf. review by William Brosend, Christian Century 116(11) (April 7, 1999):394–95).

Bowden, John. 1983. *Edward Schillebeeckx: In search of the kingdom of God.* New York: Crossroads.

Boyd, Robert. 1994. The Pacific Northwest measles epidemic of 1847–1848. *Oregon Historical Quarterly* 95:6–47.

Briggs, Charles, ed. 1997. Conflict and violence in pragmatic research. *Pragmatics* 7, no. 4.

Briggs, Charles L., and Julián Josué Vigil. 1990. *The lost gold mine of Juan Mondragon: A legend from New Mexico performed by Melaquias Romero.* Tucson: University of Arizona Press.

Bright, William. 1982. Poetic structure in oral narrative. In *Spoken and written language: Exploring orality and literacy,* edited by Deborah Tannen. Norwood NJ: Ablex.

———. 1984. *American Indian linguistics and literature.* Berlin: Mouton.

———, ed. 1990. *Wishram texts and ethnography.* Vol. 7 of *The collected works of Edward Sapir.* Berlin: Mouton.

———. 1993. *A coyote reader.* Berkeley: University of California Press.

Brightman, R. 1989. Tricksters and ethnopoetics. *International Journal of American Linguistics* 55 (1989): 179–203.

Bringhurst, Robert. 1998. *Native American oral literatures and the unity of the humanities.* 1998 Garnett Sedgewick Memorial Lecture. Vancouver: University of British Columbia.

———. 1999. *A story as sharp as a knife: The classical Haida mythtellers and their world.* Vancouver BC: Douglas & McIntyre.

Brisman, Leslie. 1998. Biblical revisionism. *New Literary History* 29, no. 2:247–72.

Brophy, Robert J. 1973. Night: A prayerful reconciliation. *Robinson Jeffers Newsletter* 37 (December): 6–7.

———. 1976. *Robinson Jeffers: Myth, ritual and symbol in his narrative poems.* Cleveland: Case Western Reserve University Press, 1973. Reprint, Hamden CT: Archon Books.

Burke, Kenneth. 1925. Psychology and form. *The Dial* 79, no. 1 (July): 34–46. (Reprinted in his *Counter-statement.*)

———. 1950. *A rhetoric of motives.* New York: Prentice-Hall. (Reissued Berkeley: University of California Press, 1984.)

———. 1957. *The philosophy of literary form.* Rev. ed. New York: Vintage Books.

———. 1968. *Counter-statement.* 3d ed. Berkeley: University of California Press.

———. 1984a. *Attitudes toward history.* New York: Editorial Publications, 1937. Reprint, Berkeley: University of California Press.

———. 1984b. *Permanence and change.* New York: New Republic Books, 1935. Reprint, Berkeley: University of California Press.

Camuto, Christopher. 1997. *Another country: Journeying toward the Cherokee Mountains.* New York: Henry Holt.

Capps, Lisa, and Elinor Ochs. 1995a. *Constructing panic: The discourse of agoraphobia.* Cambridge: Harvard University Press.

———. 1995b. Out of place: Narrative insights into agoraphobia. *Discourse Processes* 19:407–39.

Carpenter, Frederic I. 1962. *Robinson Jeffers.* New York: Twayne Books.

Chafe, Wallace. 1993. Seneca speaking styles and the location of authority. In *Responsibility and evidence in oral discourse,* edited by Jane H. Hill and Judith T. Irvine, 72–87. Cambridge: Cambridge University Press.

Chapman, John. 1914. *Ten'a texts and tales from Anvik, Alaska.* Edited by Pliny Earle Goddard. Publications of the American Ethnological Society, no. 6. Leiden: E. J. Brill.

Chappell, Warren, and Robert Bringhurst. 1999. *A short history of the printed word.* New York: Knopf, 1970. 2d ed., revised and updated. Point Roberts WA: Hartley & Marks.

Cheshire, Jenny, and Penelope Gardner-Chloros. 1998. Code-switching and the sociolinguistic gender pattern. *International Journal of the Sociology of Language* 129:5–34.

Chomsky, Noam. 1995. *The minimalist program.* Cambridge: MIT Press.

Clark, Ella E. 1953. *Indian legends of the Pacific Northwest.* Berkeley: University of California Press.

Cove, John J., and George F. MacDonald, eds. 1987. *Tricksters, shamans and heroes: Tsimshian narratives I.* Collected by Marius Barbeau and William Beynon. Canadian Museum of Civilization, Mercury Series, Directorate Paper No. 3. Ottawa: Canadian Museum of Civilization.

Curtin, Jeremiah. 1909. Wasco tales and myths. In Sapir 1909, 239-314.

Curtis, Edward S. 1911. The Chinookan tribes. *The North American Indian* 8:85-154.

Cushman, Stephen. 1985. *William Carlos Williams and the meanings of measure.* Yale Studies in English, no. 163. New Haven CT: Yale University Press.

Demetracopoulou, Dorothy. 1933. The loon-woman myth: A study in synthesis. *Journal of American Folklore* 46:101-28.

Demetracopoulou, Dorothy, and Cora Du Bois. 1932. A study of Wintu mythology. *Journal of American Folklore* 46:101-28.

Dixon, Roland B. 1912. *Maidu texts.* Publications of the American Ethnological Society 4. Leiden: E. J. Brill.

Dundes, Alan. 1964. *The morphology of North American Indian folktales.* Folklore Fellows Communications, vol. 81, no. 195. Helsinki: Academia Scientiarum Fennica.

Dyk, Walter, and D. H. Hymes. 1956. Stress accent in Wishram Chinook. *International Journal of American Linguistics* 22:238-41.

Edel, May M. 1944. Stability in Tillamook folklore. *Journal of American Folklore* 57:118-27.

Ellis, John M. 1983. *One fairy story too many: The brothers Grimm and their tales.* Chicago: University of Chicago Press.

Erdoes, Richard, and Alfonso Ortiz, eds. 1984. *American Indian myths and legends.* New York: Pantheon.

Evers, Larry, and Barre Toelken, with Helen Sekaquaptewa. n.d. *Iisaw: Hopi coyote stories.* New York: Clearwater.

Evers, Larry, and Barre Toelken, eds. 2001. *Native American oral traditions: Collaboration and interpretation.* Logan: Utah State University Press.

Everson, William (Brother Antoninus). 1968. *Robinson Jeffers: Fragments of an older fury.* Berkeley CA: Oyez.

———. 1976. *Archetype West: The Pacific Coast as a literary region.* Berkeley CA: Oyez.

Fabb, Nibel. 1997. *Linguistics and literature.* Oxford: Blackwell.

Faber, Mac Jean. 1970. *The tale of the bungling host: A historic-geographic analysis.* Master's thesis, San Francisco State College.

Facey, Ellen E. 1988. *Nguna voices: Text and culture from Central Vanuatu.* Calgary: University of Calgary Press.

Farrand, Livingston, and Bettina Kahnweiler. 1902. *Traditions of the Quinault Indians.* Memoirs of the American Museum of Natural History 4. New York: American Museum of Natural History.

Feintuch, Burt, ed. 1995. *Common ground: Keywords for the study of expressive culture,* a special issue of the *Journal of American Folklore* 108, no. 430.

Fine, Elizabeth C. 1984. *The folklore text: From performance to print.* Bloomington: Indiana University Press.

Fletcher, Alice. 1901. The Hako: A Pawnee ceremony. In *Bureau of American Ethnology Annual Report*, no. 22, 282–368. Washington: GPO.

Foley, John Miles. 1988. *The theory of oral composition: History and methodology.* Bloomington: Indiana University Press.

———. 1991. *Immanent art: From structure to meaning in traditional oral epic.* Bloomington: Indiana University Press.

———. 1992. "Word-power, performance, and tradition." *Journal of American Folklore* 105:275–301.

———. 1995. *The singer of tales in performance.* Bloomington: Indiana University Press.

Frachtenberg, Leo J. 1913. *Coos texts.* Columbia University Contributions to Anthropology, no. 1. New York: Columbia University Press; Leiden: E. J. Brill.

———. 1917. Myths of the Alsea Indians of northwestern Oregon. *International Journal of American Linguistics* 1:64–75.

———. 1920. *Alsea texts and myths.* Bureau of American Ethnology, Bulletin 67. Washington DC: GPO.

———. Manuscripts. Box 2517, NB 5, 52–58, Archives of the Department of Anthropology, Smithsonian Museum of Natural History.

Gammie, John. 1989. Alter vs. Kugel: Taking the heat in struggle over Biblical poetry. *Bible Review* 5, no. 1:30–33. (The issue includes an introduction to the background by Herschel Shanks, 26–9.)

Gatschet, Albert S. 1884. Tonkawa texts. MS 8001, Bureau of American Ethnology, Smithsonian Institution.

Gayton, A. H. 1935. The Orpheus myth in North America. *Journal of American Folklore* 48:263–93.

Gill, Sam D. 1981. *Sacred words: A study of Navajo religion and prayer.* Westport CT: Greenwood.

Glassie, Henry. 1994. On identity. *Journal of American Folklore* 107, no. 424:238–41.

———. 1995. Tradition. *Journal of American Folklore* 108:395–412.

Gorman, David. 1989. The worldly text: Writing as social action, reading as historical reconstruction. In *Literary theory's future(s)*, edited by Joseph Natoli, 181–220. Urbana: University of Illinois Press.

Graves, Robert, and Raphael Patai. 1966. *Hebrew myths: The book of Genesis.* New York: McGraw-Hill.

Greenberg, Joseph. 1954. A quantitative approach to the morphological typology of language. In *Methods and perspectives in anthropology*, edited by R. Spencer, 192–220. Minneapolis: University of Minnesota Press.

———. 1963. Some universals of grammar with particular reference to the order of meaningful elements. In *Universals of language*, edited by J. Greenberg, 58–90. Cambridge MA: MIT Press.

———. 1978. *Universals of human language.* Vol. 1, *Method and theory.* Stanford CA: Stanford University Press.

Greimas, A. J., and Joseph Courtes. 1976. The cognitive dimension of narrative discourse." *New Literary History* 7: 433–47.

Gunther, Erna. 1940. *Ethnobotany of western Washington.* University of Washington Publications in Anthropology, vol. 10, no. 1. Seattle: University of Washington.

Hallowell, A. I. 1960. Ojibwa ontology, behavior and world view. In *Culture in history,* edited by S. Diamond. New York: Columbia University Press.

Halper, Jon, ed. 1991. *Gary Snyder: Dimensions of a life.* San Francisco: Sierra Club.

Handler, Richard. 1984. Review of *One fairy story too many,* by John M. Ellis. *Journal of American Folklore* 97:485–87.

Harrington, John P. 1932. *Karuk Indian myths.* Bureau of American Ethnology, Bulletin 107. Washington DC: GPO.

Harris, Zellig. 1951. *Methods in structural linguistics.* Chicago: University of Chicago Press.

Haskin, Leslie L. 1967. *Wild flowers of the Pacific Coast.* Portland OR: Binsford & Mort.

Haugen, Einar. 1980. Frontier Norwegian in South Dakota. In *Languages in conflict: Linguistic acculturation on the Great Plains,* edited by Paul Schach. Lincoln: University of Nebraska Press.

Hill, Jane H., P. J. Mistry, and Lyle Campbell, eds. 1997. *The life of language: Papers in linguistics in honor of William Bright.* Berlin: Mouton de Gruyter.

Hill, Jonathan D., ed. 1988. *Rethinking history and myth: Indigenous South American perspectives on the past.* Urbana IL: University of Illinois Press.

Hines, Donald M. 1998. *Where the river roared: The Wishom tales.* Issaquah WA: Great Eagle.

Hockett, Charles F. 1955. *A manual of phonology.* International Journal of American Linguistics Memoir 11. Bloomington: Indiana University Publications in Anthropology and Linguistics.

Hoijer, Harry. 1933. Tonkawa, an Indian language of Texas. In *Handbook of American Indian languages,* part 3, edited by Franz Boas, 1–148. New York: Columbia University Press.

———. 1946. Tonkawa. In *Linguistic structures of Native America,* Viking Fund Publications in Anthropology, no. 6, edited by Cornelius Osgood, 289–311. New York: n.p.

———. 1949a. Tonkawa syntactic suffixes and anaphoric particles. *Southwestern Journal of Anthropology* 5, no. 1:1–74.

———. 1949b. *An analytical dictionary of the Tonkawa language.* University of California Publications in Linguistics vol.5, no. 1, 1–74.

———. 1972. *Tonkawa texts.* University of California Publications in Linguistics, no. 73. Berkeley: University of California Press

Honko, Lauri. 1998. *Textualizing the Siri epic.* FF Communications, no. 264. Helsinki: Academia Scientarium Fennica.

———, ed. 2000a. *Textualisation of oral epics*. Trends in Linguistics, Studies and Monographs, no. 128. Berlin: Mouton de Gruyter.

———. 2000b. *Thick corpus, organic variation and textuality in oral tradition*. Helsinki: Finnish Literature Society.

Honko, Lauri, with Chinnappa Gowda, Anneli Honko, and Viveka Rai. 1998a. *The Siri epic as performed by Gopala Naika*. Part 1. FF Communications, no. 265. Helsinki: Academia Scientiarum Fennica.

———. 1998b. *The Siri epic as performed by Gopala Naika*. Part 2. FF Communications, no. 266. Helsinki: Academia Scientiarum Fennica.

Hunk, Joe. The deer are made to be dangerous beings no longer. In Jacobs 1934, 124-16, and Jacobs 1937, 11-13.

———. Coyote kills his deer power, Tick, and his own wife. In Jacobs 1934, 57-59, and Jacobs 1937, 50-52.

———. Coyote kills his deer power, Tick, and his own wife (second version); Cloud tells news about him; he tries to shoot the moon. In Jacobs 1934, 59-62, and Jacobs 1937, 52-55.

———. Coyote tricks and eats his brother, Deer. In Jacobs 1934, 54-55, and Jacobs 1937, 50-52.

———. Mountain goats give mountain footwear to Deer. In Jacobs 1934, 19-20, and Jacobs 1937, 15-17.

Hymes, Dell. 1955. The language of the Kathlamet Chinook. Ph.D. diss., Linguistics Department, Indiana University.

———. Linguistic features peculiar to Chinook myths. *International Journal of American Linguistics* 24:253-57.

———. 1962. The ethnography of speaking. In *Anthropology and human behavior*, edited by Thomas Gladwin and William C. Sturtevant. Washington DC: Anthropological Society of Washington.

———, ed. 1964. *Language in culture and society*. New York: Harper & Row.

———. 1965. The methods and tasks of anthropological philology (illustrated with Clackamas Chinook). *Romance Philology* 19:325-40.

———. 1966. Two types of linguistic relativity. In *Sociolinguistics*, edited by William Bright. Berlin: Mouton.

———. 1967. Interpretation of a Tonkawa paradigm. In Hymes with Bittle 1967, 264-78.

———. 1968. The "wife" who goes out like a man: Reinterpretation of a Clackamas Chinook myth. *Social Science Information/Studies in Semiotics* 7, no. 3:173-99. (Cf. Hymes 1977. Both reprinted in 1981).

———, ed. 1972. *Reinventing anthropology*. New York: Pantheon.

———. 1974a. *Foundations in sociolinguistics*. Philadelphia: University of Pennsylvania Press.

———, ed. 1974b. *Studies in the history of linguistics: Traditions and paradigms*. Bloomington: Indiana University Press.

————. 1975a. Breakthrough into performance. In *Folklore: Performance and communication,* edited by Dan Ben-Amos and Kenneth S. Goldstein, 11-74. The Hague: Mouton. (Reprinted as chap. 3 in Hymes 1981b.)

————. 1975b. Folklore's nature and the sun's myth. *Journal of American Folklore* 88:345-69.

————. 1975c. From space to time in tenses in Kiksht. *International Journal of American Linguistics* 41, no. 4:313-29.

————. 1976a. The Americanist tradition in linguistics. In *American Indian languages and American Indian linguistics: Papers of the Second Golden Anniversary Symposium of the Linguistic Society of America,* edited by Wallace L. Chafe, 11-33. Lisse, Netherlands: Peter de Ridder Press. (Reprinted in Hymes 1983b.)

————. 1976b. Louis Simpson's "The deserted boy." *Poetics* 5, no. 2:119-55.

————. 1977. Discovering oral performance and measured verse in American Indian narrative. *New Literary History* 7:431-57. (Revised as chap. 9 in Hymes 1981b).

————. 1979a. The grounding of performance and text in a narrative view of life. *Alcheringa* 4, no. 1:137-40. (From a letter to the editor, Dennis Tedlock, in the summer of 1976.)

————. 1979b. Review of *Giving birth to thunder, sleeping with his daughter,* by Barry Holstun Lopez. *Western Humanities Review* 33, no. 1:91-94.

————. 1979c. Sapir, competence, voices. In *Individual differences in language ability language behavior,* edited by Charles J. Fillmore, Daniel Kempler, William S.-Y. Wang, 33-45. New York: Academic.

————. 1980a. *Language in education.* Washington DC: Center for Applied Linguistics.

————. 1980b. Particle, pause and pattern in American Indian narrative verse. *American Indian Culture and Research Journal* 4:7-51.

————. 1980c. Tonkawa poetics: John Rush Buffalo's "Coyote and Eagle's daughter." In *On linguistic anthropology: Essays in honor of Harry Hoijer 1979,* edited by Jacques Maquet, 33-87. Malibu CA: Undena Publications, for the UCLA Department of Anthropology.

————. 1981a. Comments. *Journal of the Folklore Institute* 18, nos. 2-3:144-50.

————. 1981b. *"In vain I tried to tell you": Essays in Native American ethnopoetics.* Philadelphia: University of Pennsylvania Press.

————. 1982. Narrative form as a "grammar" of experience: Native American and a glimpse of English. *Journal of Education* (Boston) 164, no. 2:121-42.

————. 1983a. Agnes Edgar's "Sun's child": Verse analysis of a Bella Coola text. In *Working papers for the Eighteenth International Conference of Salish and Neighboring Languages,* compiled by William Seaburg, 239-312. Seattle: Department of Anthropology, University of Washington.

————. 1983b. *Essays in the history of linguistic anthropology.* Amsterdam: John Benjamins.

———. 1983c. Poetic structure of a Chinook text. In *Essays in honor of Charles F. Hockett,* edited by Frederick B. Agard, Gerald Kelley, Adam Makkai, and Valerie Becker Makkai, 507-25. Leiden: E. J. Brill.

———. 1983d. Victoria Howard's "Gitskux and his older brother": A Clackamas Chinook myth. In Swann 1983, 129-70.

———. 1984a. Bungling host, benevolent host: Louis Simpson's "Deer and Coyote." *American Indian Quarterly* 8, no. 3:171-98.

———. 1984b. Cultee's Kathlamet "Salmon's myth" as twice-told to Boas: Language, memory, and selective performance. In *Working papers for the Nineteenth International Conference on Salish and Neighboring Languages,* edited by Thomas Hukari. Victoria BC: University of Victoria.

———. 1984c. The earliest Clackamas text. *International Journal of American Linguistics* 50:358-83.

———. 1984d. *Vers la compétence de communication.* Paris: Hatier-Crédif.

———. 1985a. Language, memory, and selective performance: Charles Cultee's "Salmon's myth" as twice-told to Boas. *Journal of American Folklore* 98:391-434.

———. 1985b. Review of *American Indian myths and legends,* by Richard Erdoes and Alfonso Ortiz. *The Nation* 240, no. 3 (January 26): 85-86.

———. 1985c. Some subtleties of measured verse. *Proceedings, Niagara Linguistic Society,* Fifteenth Spring Conference 1985, edited by June Hesch, 13-57. Buffalo NY: n.p.

———. 1985d. Verse analysis of a Kathlamet Chinook text preserved by Franz Boas: Charles Cultee's "Southwest wind." In *Aims and prospects of semiotics: In honor of Algirdas Julien Greimas,* edited by Herman Parret and H. G. Ruprecht. Amsterdam: John Benjamins.

———. 1986. A discourse contradiction in Clackamas Chinook: Victoria Howard's "Coyote made the land good." *Twenty-First International Conference of Salish and Neighboring Languages,* compiled by Eugene Hunn, 147-213. Seattle: University of Washington, Department of Anthropology.

———. 1987a. Anthologies and narrators. In Swann and Krupat, 41-84. (Reprinted as chap. 14 in this volume.)

———. 1987b. A theory of irony and a Chinookan pattern of verbal exchange. In *The pragmatic perspective,* edited by Jef Verschueren and Marcella Bertuccelli-Papi, 293-338. Pragmatics and Beyond Companion Series, no. 5. Amsterdam: John Benjamins.

———. 1987c. Tonkawa poetics: John Rush Buffalo's "Coyote and Eagle's daughter." In Sherzer and Woodbury 1987, 17-61. (See chap. 3 in this volume).

———. 1989a. Three Wishram texts, told by Philip Kahclamat to Walter Dyk. *Twenty-Fourth International Conference of Salish and Neighboring Languages,* compiled by Nile Thompson, 120-62. Steilacoom WA: Steilacoom Tribal Community Center.

———. 1989b. Tlingit poetics: A review essay. *Journal of Folklore Research* 26, no. 3: 236–48.

———. 1990a. Thomas Paul's "Sameti": Verse analysis of a (Saanich) Chinook Jargon text. *Journal of Pidgin and Creole Languages* 5, no. 1:71–106.

———. 1990b. Verse retranslation of "Split-His-Own-Head." In Elizabeth Jacobs, *Nehalem Tillamook tales,* 220–28. Northwest Reprints. Corvallis: Oregon State University Press.

———. 1991a. A coyote who can sing. In *Gary Snyder: Dimensions of a life,* edited by Jon Halper, 394–404. San Francisco: Sierra Club.

———. 1991b. Custer and linguistic anthropology. *Journal of Linguistic Anthropology* 1, no. 1:5–11. (In honor of Vine Deloria.)

———. 1991c. Ethnopoetics and sociolinguistics: Three stories by African-American children. In *Linguistics in the service of society,* edited by I. G. Malcolm, 155–70. Perth, Australia: Institute of Applied Language Studies, Edith Cowan University. (Reprinted as chap. 8 in Hymes 1996.)

———. 1991d. Is poetics original and functional? *Language & Communication* 11, no. 1/2: 49–51. (Issue of peer commentary on Newmeyer 1991.)

———. 1991e. Review of *California Indian nights,* compiled by E. W. Gifford and Gwendoline Harris Block. *Canadian Journal of Native Studies* 11, no. 1:171–75.

———. 1992a. Notes toward an (understanding of) supreme fictions. In *Studies in historical change,* edited by Ralph Cohere, 128–78. Charlottesville: University Press of Virginia.

———. 1992b. Use all there is to use. In *On the translation of Native American literatures,* edited by Brian Swann, 83–124. Washington DC: Smithsonian Institution Press. (Reprinted as chap. 3 in this volume.)

———. 1993. In need of a wife: Clara Pearson's "Split-His-(Own)-Head." In *American Indian linguistics and ethnography in honor of Laurence C. Thompson,* edited by A. Matting and T. Montler, 127–62. University of Montana Occasional Papers in Linguistics, no. 10. Missoula: University of Montana Occasional Papers in Linguistics.

———. 1994a. Ethnopoetics, oral formulaic theory, and editing texts. *Oral Tradition* 9, no. 2 (fall): 330–70.

———. 1994b. Sun's myth. In Swann 1994, 273–305. New York: Random House.

———. 1995a. Bernstein and ethnopoetics. In *Discourse and reproduction: Essays in honor of Basil Bernstein,* edited by P. Atkinson, B. Davies, and S. Delamont, 1–24. Cresskill NJ: Hampton Press. (Reprinted with slight revisions in Hymes 1996, chap. 9.)

———. 1995b. Coyote: Polymorphous but not always perverse. *Weber Journal* 12, no. 3:79–92.

———. 1995c. Reading Takelma texts: Frances Johnson's "Coyote and Frog." In *Fields of folklore: Essays in honor of Kenneth S. Goldstein,* edited by Roger D. Abraham, 90–159. Bloomington IN: Trickster Press.

————. 1996a. Coyote, the thinking (wo)man's trickster. In *Monsters, tricksters, and sacred cows: Animal tales and American identities,* edited by A. James Arnold, 108-37. Charlottesville: University of Virginia Press.

————. 1996b. *Ethnography, linguistics, narrative inequality.* London: Taylor & Francis.

————. 1997a. Coyote goes gambling, Part two from Coyote and Eagle's daughter (Tonkawa). In Penn 1997, 152-55.

————. 1997b. Frontier Norwegian in South Dakota: The situated poetics of Halvor O. Aune. In *Language and its ecology: Essays in memory of Einar Haugen,* edited by Stig Eliasson and Ernst Haakon Jahr, 161-77. Berlin: Mouton de Gruyter.

————. 1997c. A Karok narrative dictated by Phoebe Maddux to J. P. Harrington. In Hill, Mistry, and Campbell 1997, 281-97.

————. 1997d. Tongue (Clackamas [Chinook]). In Penn 1997, 145-49.

————. 1998a. *Reading Takelma texts.* Bloomington IN: Trickster. First published in Abrahams 1995, 90-159.

————. 1998b. When is oral narrative poetry? Generative form and its pragmatic conditions. *Pragmatics* 8, no. 4:475-500.

————. 2000a. Loon Woman. In *Surviving through the days: Translations of Native California stories and songs,* edited by Herbert Luthin, 192-218. Berkeley: University of California Press. (Wintu myth told and translated by Jo Bender, recorded by Dorothy Demetracopoulou [later Lee].)

————. 2000b. Sung epic and Native American ethnopoetics. In Honko 2000, 291-342. (Includes Wintu examples.)

————. 2002. Loon Woman. In *Surviving through the days: Translations of Native Californian stories and songs,* edited by Herbert Luthin, 192-218. Berkeley: University of California Press. (Wintu myth told and translated by Jo Bender, recorded by Dorothy Demetracopoulou [later Lee].)

————. MS a. Birds and Coyote's downfall among the Pueblos.

————. MS b. John Rush Buffalo's "Coyote, Jackrabbit, and Eagle's daughter."

————. MS c. A Shokleng example.

————. MS d. Tom Young's "Night-Hawk-Man": A Maidu myth.

Hymes, Dell, ed., with William Bittle. 1967. *Studies in Southwestern ethnolinguistics: Meaning and history in the languages of the American Southwest.* Studies in General Anthropology, no. 3. The Hague: Mouton.

Hymes, Dell, and John Fought. 1983. *American structuralism.* Janua Linguarum series maior 102. The Hague: Mouton. (Reprint, with table of contents, addendum, and index, of D. Hymes and J. Fought, American structuralism, in *Historiography of linguistics,* vol. 13 of *Current trends in linguistics,* edited by T. A. Sebeok, 903-1176. The Hague: Mouton, 1975.)

Hymes, Dell, and Virginia Hymes. 2002. Enlisting patterns, enlisting members. In *Discourses in search of members: In honor of Ron Scollon,* edited by David C. S. Li,

541–58. Lanham MD: University Press of America. ("Big Mama" text provided by L. Capps and E. Ochs, verse analysis by V. Hymes.)

Hymes, Virginia. 1987. Warm Springs Sahaptin narrative analysis. In Sherzer and Woodbury 1987.

———. Forthcoming. Larry George's "Celilo." In Swann forthcoming.

Jacobs, Elizabeth Derr. 1990. *Nehalem Tillamook Tales.* Edited by Melville Jacobs. Eugene: University of Oregon Press, 1959. Reprint, Northwest Reprints, Corvallis: Oregon State University Press.

Jacobs, Melville. 1934. *Northwest Sahaptin texts.* Part 1 (English). Columbia University Contributions to Anthropology, no. 19. New York: Columbia University Press.

———. 1937. *Northwest Sahaptin texts.* Part 2 (English). Columbia University Contributions to Anthropology, no. 19. New York: Columbia University Press.

———. 1939. *Coos narrative and ethnologic texts.* University of Washington Publications in Anthropology, vol. 8, no. 1. Seattle: University of Washington Press.

———. 1940. *Coos myth texts.* University of Washington Publications in Anthropology, vol. 8, no. 2. Seattle: University of Washington Press.

———. 1945. *Kalapuya texts.* University of Washington Publications in Anthropology, no. 11. Seattle: University of Washington Press.

———. 1955. A few observations on the world view of the Clackamas Chinook Indians. *Journal of American Folklore* 67:283–89. (Reprinted in Seaburg and Amoss 2000, chap. 2, 64–74.)

———. 1958. *Clackamas Chinook texts.* Part 1. Research Center in Anthropology, Folklore, and Linguistics, no. 8. Bloomington: Indiana University. *International Journal of American Linguistics* 24(2), Part 2.

———. 1959a. *Clackamas Chinook texts.* Part 2. Indiana University Research Center in Anthropology, Folklore, and Linguistics, no. 11. Bloomington: Indiana University. *International Journal of American Linguistics* 24(1), Part 2.

———. 1959b. *The content and style of an oral literature.* Viking Fund Publications in Anthropology, no. 26. New York: Wenner-Gren Foundation; Chicago: University of Chicago Press.

———. 1960. *The people are coming soon: Analyses of Clackamas Chinook myths and tales.* Seattle: University of Washington Press.

———. 1972. Areal spread of Indian oral genre features in the northwest states. *Journal of the Folklore Institute* 9, no. 1:10–17.

Jakobson, Roman. 1960. Closing statement: Linguistics and poetics. In *Style in language,* edited by Thomas A. Sebeok, 350–77. Cambridge MA: MIT Press.

Jameson, Michael H. 1961. Mythology of ancient Greece. In *Mythologies of the ancient world,* edited by Samuel Noah Kramer. Garden City NY: Doubleday.

Jeffers, Robinson. 1925. *Roan stallion, Tamar and other poems.* New York: Boni & Liveright, 1925.

———. 1935. *Solstice and other poems.* New York: Random House.

———. 1938. *The selected poetry of Robinson Jeffers.* New York: Random House.

———. 1941. *Be angry at the sun.* New York: Random House.

———. 1948. *The double axe and other poems.* New York: Random House.

Jonaitis, Aldona, ed. 1995. *A wealth of thought: Franz Boas on Native American art.* Seattle: University of Washington Press.

Kahclamat, Philip. 1933. Texts dictated to Walter Dyk at Yale University.

Kari, James. 1981. *Athabaskan stories from Anvik: Texts collected by John W. Chapman.* Fairbanks: Alaska Native Language Center, University of Alaska.

Kiley, George B. 1969. Abstract of Ph.D. dissertation, "R. J.: The short poems." *Robinson Jeffers Newsletter* 24 (1969): 6.

Kimball, Geoffrey. 1989. Peregrine falcon and great horned owl: Ego and shadow in a Koasati tale. *Southwest Journal of Linguistics* 9:45–74.

Kinkade, M. Dale. 1992. Translating Pentlatch. In *On the translation of Native American literatures,* edited by Brian Swann, 163–75. Washington DC: Smithsonian Institution.

Klein, H[erbert] Arthur. 1930. *The prosody of Robinson Jeffers.* Master's thesis, Occidental College. (So cited in Powell 1940; Ridgeway 1968:173 cites as "A Study of the Prosody of R. J."]

Koller, James, "Gogisgi" Carroll Arnett, Steve Nemirov, and Peter Blue Cloud, eds. 1982. *Coyote's journal.* Berkeley CA: Wingbow.

Kovacs, Maureen Gallery. 1989. *The epic of Gilgamesh.* Stanford CA: Stanford University Press.

Krauss, Michael E. 1982. *In honor of Eyak: The art of Anna Nelson Harry.* Fairbanks: Alaska Native Language Center, University of Alaska.

Kroeber, A. L. 1901. Ute tales. *Journal of American Folklore* 14:252–85.

———. 1908. Catch-words in American mythology. *Journal of American Folklore* 21:222–27.

Kroeber, Karl, ed. 1997. *Traditional literatures of the American Indian: Texts and interpretations.* 2d ed. Lincoln: University of Nebraska Press.

———. 1998. *Artistry in Native American myths.* Lincoln: University of Nebraska Press.

Kroskrity, Paul V. 1985. Growing with stories: Line, verse, and genre in an Arizona Tewa text. *Journal of Anthropological Research,* 41:183–99.

———. 1993. *Language, history, and identity: Ethnolinguistic studies of the Arizona Tewa.* Tucson: University of Arizona Press.

Krupat, Arnold. 1988. Anthropology in the ironic mode: The work of Franz Boas. *Social Text* 19/20:105–18. Revised and reprinted in *Modernist anthropology: From fieldwork to text,* edited by Marc Manganaro, Princeton: Princeton University Press, 1990; and in Krupat 1992, 81–100.

———. 1992. *Ethnocriticism: Ethnography, history, literature,* Berkeley: University of California Press.

Kugel, James L. 1981. *The idea of Biblical poetry: Parallelism and its history.* New Haven CT: Yale University Press.

———. 1997. *The Bible as it was.* Cambridge: Harvard University Press.

Kugel, James L., and Rowan A. Greer. 1986. *Early biblical interpretation.* Philadelphia: Westminster Press.

Labov, William A. 1972. *Language in the inner city: Studies in the black English vernacular.* Philadelphia: University of Pennsylvania Press.

Labov, William. 1997. Some further steps in narrative discourse. *Journal of Narrative and Life History* 7, nos. 1-4:395-414.

Lévi-Strauss, Claude. 1963. The structural study of myth. In his *Structural Anthropology,* 206-31. New York: Basic Books.

———. 1964-1971. *Mythologiques.* 4 vols. Paris: Plon. Translated under the title *Introduction to a science of mythology* (New York: Harper & Row, 1969-1981).

———. 1979. *La voie des masques.* Paris: Plon. Translated under the title *The way of the masks.* Seattle: University of Washington Press, 1982.

———. 1981. *The naked man.* Vol. 4 of *Introduction to a science of mythology.* Translated by John and Doreen Weightman. New York: Harper & Row. Originally published as *L'homme nu.* Vol. 4 of *Mythologiques.* (Paris: Plon, 1971).

———. 1987. De la fidelite au texte. *L'homme 101* 27, no. 1:117-40.

Lewis, C. S. 1947. On stories. In *Essays presented to Charles Williams,* edited by C. S. Lewis. Oxford: Oxford University Press.

———. 1961. *An experiment in criticism.* Cambridge: Cambridge University Press.

———. 1967. *The discarded image: An introduction to medieval and Renaissance literature.* London: Cambridge University Press.

Lopez, Barry Holstun. 1977. *Giving birth to Thunder, sleeping with his daughter: Coyote builds North America.* New York: Avon.

Lord, Albert Bates. 1995. *The singer resumes the tale.* Edited by Mary Louise Lord. Ithaca NY: Cornell University Press.

Lowie, R. H. 1908a. Catch-words for mythological motifs. *Journal of American Folklore* 21:24-27.

———. 1908b. The test theme in North American mythology. *Journal of American Folklore* 21:97-128.

———. 1909. Additional catch-words. *Journal of American Folklore* 22:332-33.

Luckert, Karl W. 1984. Coyote in Navajo and Hopi tales. Introductory essay in *Navajo Coyote tales: The Curly Tó Aheedliinii version,* by Father Berard Haile, edited by Karl W. Luckert, 3-19. Lincoln: University of Nebraska Press.

Lyman, Horace S. 1900. Reminiscences of Louis Labonte. *Oregon Historical Quarterly* 1:167-88.

———. 1903. *History of Oregon.* Vol. 1, *The growth of the American state.* New York: North Pacific Publishing Society.

Marcuse, Herbert. 1978. *The aesthetic dimension: Toward a critique of Marxist aesthetics.* Translated and revised by H. Marcuse and E. Sherover. Boston: Beacon

Press. Originally published as *Die Permanenz der Kunst: Wider eine bestimmte marxistische Aesthetik* (Munich: Hauser, 1970).

Mattina, Anthony, and Timothy Montler, eds. 1993. *American Indian linguistics and ethnography in honor of Laurence C. Thompson.* Missoula: University of Montana

Maud, Ralph. 1982. *A guide to B. C. Indian myth and legend: A short history of myth-collecting and a survey of published texts.* Vancouver BC: Talon Books.

McRae, Jill F. Kealey. 1995. The Fannie Hardy Eckstorm collection: An ethnopoetic analysis; Penobscot ways with story. Ed.D. diss., Graduate School of Education, Harvard University.

McIlwraith, T. F. 1948. *The Bella Coola Indians.* Toronto: University of Toronto Press.

McGann, Jerome J. 1983. *A critique of modern textual criticism.* Chicago: University of Chicago Press.

Meeks, Wayne A., general ed. 1993. *The HarperCollins study Bible.* London: Harper-Collins.

Meschonnic, Henri. 1982. *Critique du rythme: Anthropologie historique du langage.* Lagrasse: Editions Verdier.

———. 1988. Interview. *Diacritics* (fall): 93–111.

Metcalf, Peter. 1989. *Where are you, Spirits? Style and theme in Berawan prayer.* Washington DC: Smithsonian Institution Press.

Mills, Margaret. 1991. *Rhetorics and politics in Afghan traditional storytelling.* Philadelphia: University of Pennsylvania Press.

Moore, John H. 1998. Truth and tolerance in Native American epistemology. In Thornton 1998, 271–305.

Moore, Robert E. 1980. How Coyote thinks: Exploration of a narrative and linguistic option in Upper Chinookan." B.A. thesis, Reed College.

———. 1982. An optional form and its patterning in Kiksht narratives: Semantics, metapragmatics, poetics. Working Papers for the Seventeenth International Conference on Salish and Neighboring Languages, 9–11 August 1982, Portland State University.

———. 1993. Performance form and the voices of characters in five versions of the Wasco Coyote cycle. In *Reflexive language: Reported speech and metapragmatics,* edited by John A. Lucy, 213–240. Cambridge: Cambridge University Press.

Musil, Robert. 1995. *The man without qualities.* 2 vols. Translated by Sophie Wilkins and Burton Pike. New York: Knopf. Originally published as *Der Mann ohne Eigenschaften,* edited by Adolf Frisk (Reinbek bei Hamburg: Rowohlt, 1978). (Cf. *The Man Without Qualities,* trans. Eithne Wilkins and Ernst Kaiser. 3 vols. London: Secker & Warburg, 1966. The unfinished work was first published in three volumes in 1930, 1933, and 1943. Cf. Bernstein 1994:164 n.22.)

Newmeyer, F. J. 1991. Functional explanation in linguistics and the origins of language. *Language & Communication* 11, no. 1/2:3–28.

Nickerson, Edward. 1974. Return to rhyme. *Robinson Jeffers Newsletter* 39 (July): 12–20.

———. 1975. Robinson Jeffers and the paeon. *Western American Literature* 10 (November): 189–93.

Niles, John D. 1999. *Homo narrans: The poetics and anthropology of oral literature.* Philadelphia: University of Pennsylvania Press.

Ong, Walter. 1982. *Orality and literacy.* London: Methuen.

Opland, Jeff. 1980. *Anglo-Saxon oral poetry: A study of the traditions.* New Haven CT: Yale University Press.

Ortiz, Simon J. 1992. *Woven stone.* Tucson: University of Arizona Press.

Pardes, Ilana. 1992. *Countertraditions in the Bible: A feminist approach.* Cambridge: Harvard University Press.

Parker, Hershel. 1984. *Flawed texts and verbal icons: Literary authority in American fiction.* Evanston IL: Northwestern University Press.

Parks, Douglas R. 1991. *Traditional narratives of the Arikara Indians.* 4 vols. Lincoln: University of Nebraska Press.

Penn, W. S., ed. 1997: *The telling of the world: Native American stories and art.* New York: Stewart, Tabori & Chang. (See especially acts II and III)

Perkowski, Liliana D. 2002. Bulgarian folktales: A study of narrative form and content. Ph.D. diss., Department of Anthropology, University of Virginia.

Powell, Lawrence Clark. *Robinson Jeffers: The man and his work.* Pasadena CA: San Pasqual Press, 1940.

Prince, Gerald. 1987. *Dictionary of narratology.* Lincoln: University of Nebraska Press.

Quintasket, Christine/Mourning Dove. 1990. *Coyote stories.* Caldwell NE: Caxton, 1933. Reprint, Lincoln: University of Nebraska Press.

Ramsey, Jarold, ed. 1977. *Coyote was going there: Indian literature of the Oregon country.* Seattle: University of Washington Press.

———. 1983. *Reading the fire: Traditional Indian literatures of America.* Lincoln: University of Nebraska Press.

———. 1995. Generic and racial appropriation in Victoria Howard's "The honorable Milt." *Oral Tradition* 10, no. 2:263–81.

———. 1999. *Reading the fire: The traditional Indian literature of America.* Seattle: University of Washington Press.

Reagan, Albert B., and L. V. W. Walters. 1933. Tales from the Hoh and Quileute. *Journal of American Folklore* 46 (October 1933): 297–346.

Reichard, Gladys. 1921. Literary types and dissemination of myths. *Journal of American Folklore* 34:269–307.

———. 1922. The complexity of rhythm in decorative art. *American Anthropologist* 24:183–207.

———. 1930. The style of Coeur d'Alene mythology. *International Congress of Americanists* (Hamburg) 24:243–53.

———. 1944. *Prayer: The compulsive word.* Monographs of the American Ethnological Society, no. 7. New York: J. J. Augustin.

———. 1947. *An analysis of Coeur D'Alene Indian myths.* Philadelphia: American Folklore Society.

———. 1990. *Navaho religion: A study in symbolism.* Bollingen Series, no. 18. New York: Bollingen Foundation, 1950. Reprint, Princeton NJ: Princeton University Press.

Reynolds, Dwight. 1985. *Heroic poets, poetic heroes: The ethnography of performance in an Arabic oral epic tradition.* Ithaca: Cornell University Press.

———. 1991. The interplay of genres in oral epic performance: Differentially marked discourse in a northern Egyptian tradition. In *The ballad and oral literature,* edited by Joseph Harris, 292–317. Cambridge: Harvard University Press.

Ridgeway, Ann N., ed. 1968. *The selected letters of Robinson Jeffers, 1897–1962.* Baltimore: Johns Hopkins University Press.

Riffaterre, Michael. 1990. *Fictional truth.* Baltimore: Johns Hopkins University Press.

Rigsby, Bruce. 1969. The Waiilatpuan problem: More on Cayuse-Molala relatability. *Northwest Anthropological Research Notes* 3, no. 1:141 n.29.

Rubin, Rick. 1999. *Naked against the rain: The people of the lower Columbia River, 1770–1830.* Portland OR: Far Shore Press.

Rueckert, William H. 1982. *Kenneth Burke and the drama of human relations.* 2d ed. Berkeley: University of California Press.

Russo, Joseph. 1994. Homer's style: Non-formulaic features of an oral aesthetic. *Oral Tradition* 9, no. 2:371–89.

Sammons, Kay, and Joel Sherzer, eds. 2000. *Translating Native Latin American verbal art: Ethnopoetics and ethnography of speaking.* Washington DC: Smithsonian Institution Press.

Sandars, N. K. 1972. *The epic of Gilgamesh.* Rev. ed. Harmondsworth, England: Penguin Books.

Sanders, James A. 1984. *Canon and community: A guide to canonical criticism.* Philadelphia: Fortress Press.

Sapir, Edward. 1909a. *Takelma texts.* Philadelphia: University of Pennsylvania Press. Reprinted in *The collected works of Edward Sapir,* vol. 8, *Takelma texts and grammar,* edited by Victor Golla. (New York: Mouton de Gruyter, 1990).

———. 1909b. *Wishram texts, together with Wasco tales and Myths.* Collected by Jeremiah Curtin. Edited by Edward Sapir. Publications of the American Ethnological Society, no. 2. Leiden: E. J. Brill. Reprinted in *The collected works of Edward Sapir,* vol. 7, *Wishram texts and ethnography,* edited by William Bright (Berlin: Mouton de Gruyter, 1990).

Schaffer, Harwood D. 1989. BR article spawns new theory of Biblical poetry. *Bible Review* 5, no. 4:6–7.

Scott, Robert Ian. Robinson Jeffers as an anti-imagist. *Robinson Jeffers Newsletter* 63 (June 1983): 8–12.

Seaburg, William R. 1992. The Americanist text tradition and the fate of Native texts in English. Paper presented at the annual conference of the American Anthropological Association, 4 December 1992.

Seaburg, William R., and Pamela T. Amoss, eds. 2000. *Melville Jacobs on Northwest Indian myths and tales.* Corvallis: Oregon State University Press.

Sekaquaptewa, Helen. 1969. *Me and mine: The life story of Helen Sekaquaptewa, as told to Louise Udall.* Tucson: University of Arizona Press.

Senier, Siobhan. 2001. *Voices of American Indian assimilation and resistance: Helen Hunt Jackson, Sarah Winnemucca, and Victoria Howard.* Norman: University of Oklahoma Press.

Shanley, Kathryn W. 1998. "Writing Indian": American Indian literature and the future of Native American studies. In Thornton 1998, 130–51.

Sherzer, Joel. 1982. Poetic structuring of Kuna discourse: The line. *Language in Society* 11:371–90.

———. 1990. *Kuna ways of speaking.* Austin TX: University of Texas Press.

Sherzer, Joel R., and Anthony C. Woodbury, eds. 1987: *Native American discourse: Poetics and rhetorics.* New York: Cambridge University Press.

Silverstein, Michael. 1974. *Dialectal developments in Chinookan tense-aspect systems: An areal-historical analysis.* Indiana University Publications in Anthropology and Linguistics, Memoir 29. (Distributed with the *International Journal of American Linguistics* 40, no. 4, part 2, pp. S45-99.)

———. 1985. The culture of language in Chinookan narrative texts; or, On saying that . . . in Chinook. In *Grammar inside and outside the clause: Some approaches to theory from the field,* edited by Johanna Nichols and Anthony C. Woodbury, 132–71. London: Cambridge University Press.

———. 1990. Chinookans of the Lower Columbia. In *Handbook of North American Indians,* edited by William C. Sturtevant, vol. 7, *Northwest Coast,* edited by Wayne Suttles, 533–46. Washington: Smithsonian Institution.

———. 1996. Encountering language and languages of encounter in North American ethnohistory. *Journal of Linguistic Anthropology* 6, no. 2:126–44.

———. 1997. Commentary: Achieving adequacy and commitment in pragmatics. *Pragmatics* 7, no. 4:625–33.

Skeels, Dell. 1949. Style in the unwritten literature of the Nez Perce Indians. Ph.D. diss., University of Washington.

Spier, Leslie, and Edward Sapir. 1930. *Wishram ethnography.* Seattle: University of Washington Press.

St. Clair, H. H. 1905. MS in the Bureau of American Ethnology, now Department of Anthropology, Smithsonian Institution.

Staal, F. 1989. The independence of rationality from literacy. *European Journal of Sociology* 30:301–10.

Stern, J. P. 1979. *Friedrich Nietzsche.* Edited by Frank Kermode. New York: Penguin Books.

Stevens, Wallace. 1947. *Transport to summer.* New York: Alfred A. Knopf.

———. 1952. *The Man with the blue guitar.* New York: Alfred A. Knopf.

Stocking, George W., Jr. 1962. Matthew Arnold, E. B. Tylor, and the uses of invention, with an appendix on evolutionary ethnology and the growth of cultural relativism, 1871–1915: From culture to cultures. Prepared for Conference on the History of Anthropology, New York, Social Science Research Council, 12–14 April. (Cf. Stocking 1968:69–90).

———. 1968. *Race, culture and evolution: Essays in the history of anthropology.* New York: Free Press.

———. 1974a. The basic assumptions of Boasian anthropology. Prepared for The Nature and Function of Anthropological Traditions Conference, Wenner-Gren Foundation for Anthropological Research, New York, 17–21 April 1968. (Reprinted in Stocking 1974c, 1–20.)

———. 1974b. The Boas plan for the study of American Indian languages. Prepared for a conference on the history of linguistics at the Newberry Library, Chicago, 1968. (Reprinted in Hymes 1974b, 454–83.)

———, ed. 1974c. *The shaping of American anthropology, 1883–1911: A Franz Boas reader.* New York: Basic Books.

Sullivan, Paul R. 1989. *Unfinished conversations: Mayas and foreigners between two wars.* New York: Knopf.

Swann, Brian, ed. 1983. *Smoothing the ground: Essays on Native American oral literature.* Berkeley: University of California Press.

———, ed. 1994. *Coming to light: Contemporary translations of the Native literatures of North America.* New York: Random House.

———, ed. Forthcoming. *Voices from four directions.* Lincoln: University of Nebraska Press.

Swann, Brian, and Arnold Krupat, eds. 1987. *Recovering the word: Essays on Native American literature.* Berkeley: University of California Press.

Tedlock, Dennis. 1968. *The ethnography of tale-telling at Zuni.* Ann Arbor: University of Michigan Microfilms.

———. 1970. Notes to "Finding the middle of the earth." *Alcheringa* 1:6.

———. 1977. Toward an oral poetics. *New Literary History* 8:507–19.

———. 1978. Coyote and Junco. In *Coyote stories,* edited by William Bright, 171–77. International Journal of American Linguistics, Native American Texts Series, Monograph 1. Chicago: University of Chicago Press.

———. 1985. *Popol Vuh: The definitive edition of the Mayan book of the dawn of life and the glories of gods and kings.* New York: Simon & Schuster.

———. 1987. *The spoken word and the work of interpretation.* Philadelphia: University of Pennsylvania Press.

———. 1999. *Finding the center: Narrative poetry of the Zuni Indians.* New York: Dial Press, 1972. Reprint, 2d ed., Lincoln: University of Nebraska Press.

Teit, James. 1898. *Traditions of the Thompson River Indians of British Columbia.* Memoirs of the American Folk-Lore Society, no. 6. Boston: Houghton Mifflin for the American Folk-Lore Society.

Thompson, Stith. 1946. *The folktale.* New York: Dryden.

———. 1955–1958. *Motif-index of folk-literature.* 6 vols. 2d rev. ed. Bloomington: Indiana University Press.

———. 1961. *The types of the folktale.* 2d rev. Folklore Fellows Communications No. 184. Helsinki: Academia Scientarium Fennica.

———. 1966. *Tales of the North American Indians.* Cambridge: Harvard University Press, 1929. Reprint, Bloomington: Indiana University Press.

Thornton, Russell, ed. 1998. *Studying Native America: Problems and prospects.* Madison: University of Wisconsin Press. 978-0299160647

Tillich, Paul. 1955. *Biblical religion and the search for ultimate reality.* Chicago: University of Chicago Press.

Toelken, Barre. 1977. Foreword to *Giving birth to Thunder, sleeping with his daughter: Coyote builds North America,* by Barry H. Lopez. Kansas City KS: Sheed Andrews & McMeel.

Trafzer, Clifford E., ed. 1998. *Grandmother, Grandfather, and Old Wolf: Tamánwit Ku Súkat and traditional Native American narrative from the Columbia Plateau.* Lansing: Michigan State University Press.

Urban, Greg. 1991. *A discourse-centered approach to culture: Native South American myths and rituals.* Austin: University of Texas Press.

———. 1993. The represented functions of speech in Shokleng myth. In *Reflexive language: Reported speech and metapragmatics,* edited by John A. Lucy, 241–59. Cambridge: Cambridge University Press.

———. 1996. *Metaphysical community: The interplay of the senses and the intellect.* Austin: University of Texas Press.

Valentine, J. Rudolph. 1998. Linguistics and languages in Native American studies. In Thornton 1998, 152–81.

White, Richard. 1998. Using the past: History and Native American studies. In Thornton 1998, 217–43.

Wiget, Andrew. 1987. Telling the tale: A performance analysis of a Hopi coyote story. In Swann and Krupat, 297–336.

Wolfson, Nessa. 1982. *CHP: The conversational historical present in American English narrative.* Topics in Sociolinguistics, no. 1. Dordrecht, Netherlands: Foris.

———. 1989. The conversational historical present. In *Analyse grammaticale de corpus oraux,* 135–50. LINX, vol. 20, no. i. Paris: Université de Paris-X-Nanterre, Centre de Recherches Linguistiques.

Wycoco (Moore), Remedios. 1951. The types of North-American Indian tales. Ph.D. diss., University of Indiana.

Wydoski, Richard S., and Richard R. Whitney. 1979. Inland fishes of Washington. Seattle: University of Washington Press.

Zaller, Robert. 1983. *The cliffs of solitude: A reading of Robinson Jeffers.* New York: Cambridge University Press.

Zenk, Henry. 1984. Chinook jargon and Native cultural persistence in the Grand Ronde Indian community, 1856–1907: A special case of creolization. Ph.D. diss., University of Oregon.

Zolbrod, Paul. 1995. *Reading the voice: Native American oral poetry and the written page.* Salt Lake City: University of Utah Press.

Source Acknowledgments

CHAPTER 1. "Survivors and Renewers." *Folklore Forum* 31, no. 1 (2000): 3–16.

CHAPTER 2. "Boas on the Threshold of Ethnopoetics." In *Theorizing the Americanist Tradition,* ed. Lisa Valentine and Regna Darnell, 84–107. Toronto: University of Toronto Press, 1999.

CHAPTER 3. "Use All There Is to Use." Reprinted from *On the Translation of Native American Literatures,* edited by Brian Swann, 83–124.Washington DC: Smithsonian Institution Press, 1992. Copyright © 1992. Used by permission of the publisher.

CHAPTER 4. "Variation and Narrative Competence." In *Thick Corpus, Organic Variation and Textuality in Oral Tradition,* ed. Lauri Honko, 77–92. Helsinki: Finnish Literature Society, 2000.

CHAPTER 5. "When Is Oral Narrative Poetry? Generative Form and Its Pragmatic Conditions." *Pragmatics* 8, no. 4 (December 1998): 475–500.

CHAPTER 6. "Language, Memory, and Selective Performance: Cultee's 'Salmon's Myth' as Twice Told to Boas." *Journal of American Folklore* 98 (1985): 391–434.

CHAPTER 7. "A Discourse Contradiction in Clackamas Chinook: Victoria Howard's 'Coyote Made the Land Good.'" In *Proceedings of the Twenty-First International Conference of Salish and Neighboring Languages (August 14–16, 1986),* comp. Nile Thompson and Dawn Bates, 147–213. Seattle: University of Washington, Dept. of Anthropology, 1986.

CHAPTER 8. "Bungling Host, Benevolent Host: Louis Simpson's 'Deer and Coyote.'" Reprinted from *American Indian Quarterly* 8, no. 3 (1984) by permission of the University of Nebraska Press. Copyright © 1984.

CHAPTER 9. "Coyote: Polymorphous but Not Always Perverse." *Weber Studies,* Native American Special Issue 12, no. 3 (1995): 79–93.

CHAPTER 10. "Helen Sekaquaptewa's 'Coyote and the Birds': Rhetorical Analysis of a Hopi Coyote Story." *Anthropological Linguistics* 34, nos. 1–4 (1994): 45–72.

CHAPTER 12. "Coyote, the Thinking (Wo)man's Trickster." In *Monsters, Tricksters, and Sacred Cows: Animal Tales and American Identities,* New World Studies, edited by A. James Arnold, 108–37. Charlottesville: University Press of Virginia, 1996. Reprinted with permission of the University Press of Virginia.

CHAPTER 13. "Ethnopoetics, Oral-Formulaic Theory, and Editing Texts." *Oral Tradition* 9, no. 2 (1994): 330–70.

CHAPTER 14. "Anthologies and Narrators." In *Recovering the Word: Essays on Native American Literature,* ed. Brian Swann and Arnold Krupat, 41–84. Berkeley: University of California Press, 1987.

CHAPTER 15. "Notes toward (an Understanding of) Supreme Fictions." In *Studies in Historical Change,* ed. Ralph Cohen, 128–78. Charlottesville: University Press of Virginia, 1992. Reprinted with permission of the University Press of Virginia.

CHAPTER 16. "Jeffers' Artistry of Line." In *Centennial Essays for Robinson Jeffers,* ed. Robert Zaller, 226–47. Newark: University of Delaware Press, 1991.

Index

CPSIA information can be obtained at www.ICGtesting.com
Printed in the USA
LVOW11s0734180713

343229LV00009B/108/P